THE PSYCHOANALYTIC THEORY OF NEUROSIS

By Otto Fenichel, M.D.

THE COLLECTED PAPERS OF OTTO FENICHEL

IN TWO VOLUMES:

First Series

Second Series

THE
PSYCHOANALYTIC THEORY
OF NEUROSIS

By OTTO FENICHEL, M.D.

W · W · NORTON & COMPANY · INC · New York

ISBN 0 393 01019 8
PRINTED IN THE UNITED STATES OF AMERICA
FOR THE PUBLISHERS BY THE VAIL-BALLOU PRESS
3 4 5 6 7 8 9

PREFACE

NEARLY twenty years of teaching at different psychoanalytic institutes and training centers both in Europe and in America—as staff member in five cities and
as occasional guest lecturer in ten others—have convinced me of the need to summarize the psychoanalytic doctrines in a systematic and comprehensive manner,
and thus to provide teaching aids for psychoanalytic training.

Among the different disciplines a textbook of psychoanalysis should embrace,
the theory of neurosis interested me in particular. At European psychoanalytic
institutes the custom was to subdivide this field into a general part, treating the
mechanisms common to all neuroses, and a special part, treating the characteristic features of the individual neuroses. Because chance first brought me to the
special part, I published in 1932 *Spezielle Psychoanalytische Neurosenlehre* at
the Internationaler Psychoanalytischer Verlag in Vienna, Austria. This book
was translated by Dr. Bertram D. Lewin and Dr. Gregory Zilboorg, and published in 1934 in the *Psychoanalytic Quarterly* and, as a book, by W. W. Norton
and Company, New York, under the title *Outline of Clinical Psychoanalysis*
(424).

The lack of a "General Part" was the main drawback of this book. Therefore,
when I was asked to prepare a second edition, I preferred to write a new book,
which would not only treat the subject matter of the *Outline* in a more systematized and up-to-date form, but the questions of "general" theory as well.

Among the many acknowledgments I wish to make, I want to express my
gratitude first of all to the listeners of the various courses from which the following pages have been derived. Their suggestions and remarks during the discussion proved to be very helpful. For advice concerning the final English formulation, I am especially obliged to Drs. David Brunswick, Ralph Greenson, and
Norman Reider, and to Mmes. Dorothy Deinum and Ruth Lachenbruch.

OTTO FENICHEL

CONTENTS

· Hysterical Motor Disturbances · Hysterical Dream States and Disturbances of Consciousness · Hysterical Disturbances of the Special Senses · Hysterical Disturbances of Sensation · Somatic Compliance · Archaic Features in Conversion · General Significance of Conversion · Oedipus Complex, Masturbation, and Pregenitality in Conversion Symptoms · Course and Psychoanalytic Treatment of Conversion Hysteria

Restitutional Symptoms in Schizophrenia · The Break with Reality
· Borderline Cases · Question of Prognosis · Therapeutic Psychoanalysis in Schizophrenia

D. Psychoneuroses, the Secondary Elaborations of Symptoms

E. Combinations of Traumatic Neuroses and Psychoneuroses

F. Course and Therapy of Neuroses

PART I

PRELIMINARY CONSIDERATIONS

A. Introduction

Chapter I

INTRODUCTORY REMARKS ON PSYCHOANALYSIS AND THE THEORY OF NEUROSIS

CONCERNING the origin of the young science of psychoanalysis one often hears two diametrically opposed opinions. Some people say that Freud transferred the principles of the materialistic biology of his time to the field of mental phenomena, and sometimes they even add that Freud therefore, through being limited to biology, failed to see the cultural and social determinants of mental phenomena. Others state that at a period when the natural sciences were at their height, Freud's contribution consisted in turning against the spirit of the times and forcing the recognition of the irrational and the psychogenic in defiance of the prevalent overestimation of rationalism.

What should we think of this contradiction? Through gradual development, scientific thinking is winning out over magical thinking. The natural sciences, originating and evolving at definite periods in the development of human society (when they had become a technical necessity), have had to overcome the most violent and stubborn resistances in their attempt to describe and explain actual phenomena. This resistance affected different fields to a different degree. It increased in proportion to the approach of the subject matter of the science to the personal concern of man: physics and chemistry freed themselves earlier than biology, biology earlier than anatomy and physiology (not so long ago, the pathologist was forbidden to dissect the human body), anatomy and physiology earlier than psychology. The influence of magic is greater in medicine than in pure natural science, due to the tradition of medicine, which stems from the activities of the medicine men and priests. Within medicine, psychiatry is not only the youngest branch of this magic-imbued science but it is also the one most tainted with magic.

For centuries psychology was considered a special field of speculative philosophy, far removed from sober empiricism. If one considers the more or less metaphysical questions that used to be of paramount importance, it is easily recognized that the problems discussed continued to reflect the antithesis of "body and soul," "human and divine," "natural and supernatural." Everywhere valuations influenced, unfortunately, the examination of facts.

A glance at the history of science teaches that the process of overcoming magic has not been a continuous one. There have been advances and retreats which certainly cannot be explained merely in terms of a history of ideas. The fluctuations in this struggle are dependent on complicated historical conditions. They can be understood only through the study of the society in which the struggle takes place and of the conflicting interests of its various groups. That the history of medical psychology is no exception to this rule can be seen from the interesting book by Zilboorg and Henry (1636).

Psychoanalysis represents in this struggle a definite step toward the aim of scientific thinking in psychology—away from the magical. Recently Bernfeld again stressed the completely materialistic orientation of Freud's teachers and of Freud's own prepsychoanalytic thinking (140).

Certainly it must be admitted that Freud was not the first to consider the field of mental manifestations from a natural-scientific point of view. There were natural-scientific psychologies before him. But compared to the "philosophical" psychologies, these natural-scientific psychologies have always been in the minority, and they have only been able to treat disparate mental functions. An understanding of the multiplicity of everyday human mental life, based on natural science, really began only with psychoanalysis.

Now the question can be answered concerning the contradictory statements of Freud's place in the history of science. The golden days of materialistic biology and medicine simply did not regard the whole field of humanity as their universe of discourse. The neglect of the mental field indicates that the progress of scientific thinking was purchased at the price of allowing one entire realm of nature, the human mind, to remain a residue of religious and magical thinking; and the contradiction in the historic evaluation of Freud's work is solved by recognizing that actually he did both: by opposing the idea that "mind is brain" and by emphasizing strongly the existence of the mental sphere and the inadequacy of physical-scientific methods to deal with it, he won this terrain for science. In spite of assertions that Freud by giving the "subjective factor," the "irrational," its just due has turned against rationalism, his procedure clearly reveals the spirit of that broad cultural trend which proclaimed as its ideal the primacy of reason over magic and the unbiased investigation of reality. What had previously been considered sacred and untouchable, now had to be touched, because the validity of the taboos was denied. Freud investigated the mental world in the same scientific spirit as his teachers had investigated the physical world, which implied the same rebellion against the prejudices that had been taught up to that time. The subject matter, not the method of psychoanalysis, is irrational.

The objection may be raised that such a statement is a one-sided presentation of psychoanalysis. Does not this science include quite a lot of mystic tradition? Did it not develop out of hypnotism and the latter from "mesmerism"? Is it not a "mental healing," which means a sort of magic? Certainly psychoanalysis has developed directly out of magical therapeutic methods. But it has eliminated the magical background of its forerunners. Of course, in every mental development rudiments of earlier phases persist. Actually, it is not difficult to find many magical features in the theory and practice of psychoanalysis. (Probably this would not be difficult in other branches of medicine either.) Psychoanalysis as it is now constituted undoubtedly contains mystic elements, the rudiments of its past, as well as natural-scientific elements toward which it is striving. It cannot help retaining some mystic elements, at least in the same sense in which the activity of a police dog in police investigations is—as Reik has recognized (1295) —a survival of the animal oracle. However, the police dog has the ability to scent out the criminal. It is the aim of psychoanalysis to reduce its magical elements at least to the same level of insignificance as that to which modern criminal investigation tries to reduce the magical elements in its detective methods.

Scientific psychology explains mental phenomena as a result of the interplay of primitive physical needs—rooted in the biological structure of man and developed in the course of biological history (and therefore changeable in the course of further biological history)—and the influences of the environment on these needs. There is no place for any third factor.

That the mind is to be explained in terms of constitution and milieu is a very old conception. What is characteristic for psychoanalysis is *what* it regards as biological structure, *which* environmental influences it recognizes as formative, and *how* it relates structural and environmental influences to each other.

As to the biological structure, a scientific psychology first of all must posit itself within biology. Mental phenomena occur only in living organisms; mental phenomena are a special instance of life phenomena. The general laws that are valid for life phenomena are also valid for mental phenomena; special laws that are valid only for the level of mental phenomena must be added.

Thus a scientific psychology investigates, as does any science, general *laws*. It is not satisfied with a mere description of individual psychic processes. An exact description of historical processes is its means, not its goal. Its subject is not the individual X but the comprehension of general laws governing mental functions.

Besides, a scientific psychology is absolutely free of moral valuation. For it, there is no good or evil, no moral or immoral, and no what ought to be at all; for a scientific psychology, good and evil, moral and immoral, and what ought to be are products of human minds and have to be investigated as such.

As to the influences of the surroundings, these must be studied in detail in their practical reality. There is no "psychology of man" in a general sense, in a vacuum, as it were, but only a psychology of man in a certain concrete society and in a certain social place within this concrete society.

Concerning the relation between biological needs and the formative environmental influences, this book will demonstrate adequately how psychoanalysis approaches the problem. At this point, only the following needs to be said. In the endeavor to investigate the relationship between biological needs and external influences, one or the other of these two forces may be overestimated. The history of psychoanalysis has seen both types of deviation. Certain authors, in their biologistic thinking have entirely overlooked the role of outwardly determined frustrations in the genesis of neuroses and character traits, and are of the opinion that neuroses and character traits might be rooted in conflicts between contradictory biological needs in an entirely endogenous manner. Such a point of view is dangerous even in therapeutic analysis; but it becomes entirely fatal if it is assumed in applications of psychoanalysis to sociological questions. Attempts of this kind have sought to understand social institutions as the outcome of conflicts between contradictory instinctual impulses within the same individuals, instead of seeking to understand the instinctual structure of empirical human beings through the social institutions in which they grew up.

But there are also certain authors at the other extreme who reproach psychoanalysis as being too biologically oriented, and who are of the opinion that the high evaluation of the instinctual impulses means that cultural influences are denied or neglected. They are even of the erroneous opinion that the demonstration of the importance of cultural influences contradicts any instinct theory. Freud's own writings contain, essentially, descriptions of how instinctual attitudes, objects, and aims are changed under the influence of experiences. Thus it is absurd to be of the opinion that the proof of the existence of this influence contradicts Freud.

We agree with Zilboorg that it is not difficult to find in all such "culturistic" deviations a distorted return to magical thinking and to the contrast of body and soul (1637). At first glance it looks as if the stressing of cultural factors, because of their significance for mental development, expressly brought about an emphasis on reality; but actually this viewpoint denies reality by denying man's biological basis.

Certainly not only frustrations and reactions to frustrations are socially determined; what a human being desires is also determined by his cultural environment. However, the culturally determined desires are merely variations of a few biological basic needs; changing the primitive biological values of "gratifying" and "frustrating" into the highly complicated systems of values of modern man is just the thing that can be explained by psychoanalytic study of the history of the particular man and the influences of social forces to which he has been subjected. It is the task of sociology to study these social forces, their genesis, and their function.

The application of the general principles of natural science to the special field of psychology naturally presupposes the development of new *methods* of research that are adequate to its subject matter. Attempts to keep the mental realm outside of causal and quantitative thinking ("theory grays the many-colored pattern of life") thwart real insight, as does also a pseudo exactness which believes it necessary to transfer the biological methods of experiment and scientific protocol to a field where these methods are not suitable. (Astronomy also is unable to resort to experiments and nevertheless is a natural science.)

Against the statement that psychoanalysis aims at the full scientific research into mental phenomena, it might be objected that this formulation is either too narrow or too broad. Psychoanalysis maintains that there is an unconscious mental life, and that it studies this unconscious. Since under the term "the human mind" the conscious phenomena are usually understood, it would seem that psychoanalysis is concerned with more than just human mental life. On the other hand it may be asked: is not psychoanalysis above all a psychology of neuroses, or a psychology of instincts, or a psychology of the emotional components in mental life—whereas the more intellectual components and the individual functions, such as perception, the formation of conceptions, judgment, would have to be investigated by other psychologies?

These objections are not valid. The thesis that in investigating the unconscious, psychoanalysis is undertaking something that lies beyond psychic phenomena may be compared to an assertion that optics is investigating something other than the phenomena of light when it occupies itself with the wave lengths of light waves. The existence of the unconscious is an assumption that forced itself upon psychoanalytic research when it sought a scientific explanation and a comprehension of conscious phenomena. Without such an assumption the data of the conscious in their interrelationships remain incomprehensible; with such an assumption, that which characterizes the success of every science becomes possible: to predict the future and to exert systematic influence.

As to the argument that psychoanalysis is concerned with neuroses or with instinctual and emotional phenomena only, it must be admitted that these subjects are predominant in psychoanalytic research. This can be explained historically and practically. Psychoanalysis began as a therapeutic method and even today secures its research material principally because of the happy circumstance that its psychological research method and the medical therapeutic method coincide. What Freud observed during the treatment of his patients, however, he could apply later to an understanding of the mental phenomena of healthy persons. When psychoanalysis then went on to study the conscious phenomena and the various mental functions, it could do this in a way different from that of other psychologies, for it had previously studied the unconscious and the instincts. It conceives of all these "surface manifestations" as structures that have been formed out of deeper instinctual and emotional sources through the influence of the environment. Of course it should not be claimed that except for the Freudian findings there is no scientific psychological knowledge; but it should be asserted that all psychological knowledge gains new light when considered from the psychoanalytic point of view.

However, this book is *not* a textbook of psychoanalytic psychology; it limits itself to the theory of neurosis. It is true that neuroses, for the analyst, provide the most fruitful study in the realm of mental phenomena; after having studied the neuroses, it will be easier to study other mental phenomena. In this sense, this is perhaps a first volume of a textbook on psychoanalytic psychology.

The theory of neurosis has the same relation to psychoanalytic therapeutic practice as pathology has to internal medicine: inductively arrived at through practical experience, it furnishes the foundation for further practical work. It represents an attempt to ascertain that which is regular in the etiology, the manifestations, and the clinical course of neuroses, in order to furnish us with a causally directed method of therapy and prophylaxis.

Nothing should be demanded of such a theory that a medical man would not demand of pathology. The search for "regularity" permits a formulation only of that which is of general significance and so, in a sense, does violence to the uniqueness of the individual case. In compensation, however, it gives the practitioner a better orientation, even though it must be remembered that this orientation alone is not sufficient for the actual treatment of individual cases.

We shall endeavor to clarify the theory by clinical examples. But it will remain "theory," that is, abstraction. All the examples tend only to illustrate mechanisms; thus they are illustrations but not case histories. What may be reported in a few lines as a result of psychoanalytic research, sometimes required months of work.

Thus only the typical will be presented here. Actually the psychological facts represented by the terms Oedipus complex or castration complex are infinitely varied. This book presents the framework which, in clinical reality, is filled with thousands of specific facts. Clinical experience with practical cases (supervised work with patients and case-history seminars) cannot be supplanted by a book like this; neither can it substitute for training in psychoanalytic technique. It can, however, give an impression as to why special training in technique is necessary, and why a personal analysis is an irreplaceable part of this training.

Those who have not undergone a personal analysis will probably be able to understand intellectually what is presented in this book; but probably many things will seem to them even more incredible and "far-fetched" than psychoanalytic case reports. Persons who "do not believe in psychoanalysis" will not be convinced by reading this book. They can only inform themselves about what the teachings of psychoanalysis actually are.

> But even this seems very necessary. Many critics who "do not believe in psychoanalysis" do not know what psychoanalysis is about, and are in the habit of ascribing to Freud a great many things he never said or wrote.

However, the reading of case histories offers the best method for remedying deficiencies in personal experience, and is therefore the most important supplement to the reading of this book, just as attendance at clinical lectures or the reading of clinical case reports is the best supplement to the study of pathology.

It is in no way true that in discussing events of human life one has to choose between the vivid, intuitive description of an artist and the detached abstractness of a scientist thinking only quantitatively. It is not necessary and not permissible to lose feeling when feeling is investigated scientifically. Freud once stated that it was not his fault that his case histories gave the impression of a novel. To understand neuroses one would have to read such novel-like case histories as well as books like this; but it can also be promised that such case histories will be understood in quite another way after this book has been studied.

The admission that the practical art of analyzing cannot be acquired through reading this book is no cause to underestimate its value for the student of psychoanalysis. When objections, such as the claim that the essential therapeutic intuition and sensitivity cannot be taught, are hurled at a scientific pathology, it is a sign of magical thinking. Just as scientific pathology is no barrier to the intuitive medical art but an indispensable prerequisite for it, so it is with the theory of neurosis and the practice of psychoanalysis. It is true that not everything can be taught; but first one has to learn what *is* teachable.

We shall try to engage as little as possible in polemics, but concentrate, rather, on explaining that which already seems established. It is unavoidable that, in the choice of the material to be presented, in the decision as to which problems should be given more space and which less, and in the arrangement of the book, the personal beliefs of the author are reflected. However, since he hopes that his scientific convictions are well founded, he is of the opinion that this will not be a disadvantage.

In one respect, a theory of neurosis differs from a somatic pathology. A pathologist is in a position to assume that his audience knows physiology; he does not have to explain the "biological basic principles" before he demonstrates his real subject matter. Because of the newness of psychoanalytic psychology, we have to clarify first, at least in a sketchy way, the general system by which we shall orient ourselves.

These basic principles were uncovered by the laborious empirical method. It is important to emphasize this, because in what follows it cannot be shown how these insights were gradually built up from experience; they will be presented, rather, in a definite, somewhat dogmatic fashion, which might lead to a misunderstanding of their nature and appear to be purely speculative. Their form of presentation will be a deductive one; actually, knowledge of these principles has been gained inductively, and further inductive scientific research can and may change them.

Chapter II

THE DYNAMIC, THE ECONOMIC, AND THE STRUCTURAL POINTS OF VIEW

MENTAL DYNAMICS

MENTAL functions should be approached from the same angle as the functions of the nervous system in general. They are manifestations of the same basic function of the living organism—irritability. The basic pattern which is useful for the understanding of mental phenomena is the reflex arc. Stimuli from the outside world or from the body initiate a state of tension that seeks for motor or secretory discharge, bringing about relaxation. However, between stimulus and discharge, forces are at work opposing the discharge tendency. The study of these inhibiting forces, their origin and their effect on the discharge tendency, is the immediate subject of psychology. Without these counterforces there would be no psyche, only reflexes (495).

With such a starting point, it is apparent that psychoanalytic psychology attempts more than mere description. It explains mental phenomena as the result of the interaction and counteraction of forces, that is, in a *dynamic* way. A dynamic explanation is also a *genetic* one, since it examines not only a phenomenon as such but the forces that brought it about as well. It does not examine single acts; it examines the phenomena in terms of processes, of development, of progression or regression.

The idea of looking at mental phenomena as a result of interacting forces certainly was not derived merely by transferring the concept of energy from the other natural sciences to psychology. Originally it happened the other way around: the everyday assumption that one understands mental reactions when one understands their motives has been transferred to physics.

One special kind of mental phenomena, instinctual drives, is directly experienced as an "urging energy." Certain perceptions have a provocative character: they press for immediate action; one feels oneself impelled by forces of various intensities. In connecting this experience with the reflex pattern, it may be assumed that the instinctual impulses have the general tendency to lower the excitation level by the discharge of tensions that have been brought about by exciting stimuli. Counterforces, to be investigated later, oppose this, and the struggle so created constitutes the basis of the realm of mental phenomena.

This certainly does not mean that psychoanalytic psychology assumes all mental phenomena to be instinctual in nature. It only means that noninstinctual phenomena have to be explained as the effects of external stimuli on biological needs. The noninstinctual part of the human mind becomes understandable as a derivative of the struggle for and against discharge, created by the influence of the external world. Nor does the cell theory maintain that all living substance is made up only of cells; its position remains justified as long as it succeeds in proving that the noncellular components of living substance, like tendons, hair, or intercellular material, are parts or products of cells. The same holds true for psychoanalytic psychology as long as it can prove that the noninstinctual mental phenomena are derivatives of more primitive instinctual ones. Therefore Freud's short paper, "On Negation" (616), is of principal importance, for therein he shows how the seemingly very remote function of judgment is derived from instincts.

However, the expression *Trieb* which Freud uses does not signify exactly the same thing as the English expression *instinct,* as it is customarily translated. Inherent in the concept of instinct is the idea that it represents an inherited and unchangeable pattern; in the German concept of *Trieb* this unchangeability is by no means implied. On the contrary, the *Triebe* obviously are changed in aim and object under influences stemming from the environment, and Freud was even of the opinion that they originated under the same influence (588). This incorrect equating of *instinct* and *Trieb* has created serious misunderstandings (1105).

The assumption has been made in various forms by many biologists that there is a basic vital tendency to abolish tensions that have been brought about by external stimulation and to return to the energy state that was effective before the stimulation. The most fruitful conception in this respect is Cannon's formulation of the principle of "homeostatis" (241). "Organisms, composed of material which is characterized by the utmost inconstancy and unsteadiness, have somehow learned the methods of maintaining constancy and keeping steady in the presence of conditions which might reasonably be expected to prove profoundly disturbing." The word homeostasis "does not imply something set and immobile, a stagnation"; on the contrary, the living functions are extremely flexible and mobile, their equilibrium being disturbed uninterruptedly, but being re-established by the organism equally uninterruptedly.

It was the same basic principle Fechner had in mind when he spoke about the "principle of constancy" (605), and for which Freud, following Barbara Low, often used the expression "Nirvana principle" (613). It seems more appropriate to see the ultimate goal for all these equalization tendencies as the aim of maintaining a certain level of tension characteristic for the organism, of "preserving the level of excitation," as Freud put it very early (188), rather than the aim of the total abolition of all tension (517).

It can be seen everywhere that this principle of homeostasis does not remain unopposed. Some behavior seems to be directed not toward getting rid of tensions but rather toward creating new tensions, and the main task of psychology is to study and understand counterforces that tend to block or to postpone immediate discharge.

However, this understanding will never be arrived at if an attempt is made to differentiate a "homeostatic instinct" from other "nonhomeostatic instincts" (1211). Homeostasis is, as a principle, at the root of all instinctual behavior; the frequent "counterhomeostatic" behavior must be explained as a secondary complication, imposed upon the organism by external forces.

> Just as there is no homeostatic instinct but only a homeostatic principle at the basis of all instinctual behavior, there is likewise no "instinct to master," as distinguished from other instincts (766, 767, 768). Mastery means the ability to handle outer demands and inner drives, to postpone gratification when necessary, to assure satisfaction even against hindrances; it is a general aim of every organism but not of a specific instinct. However, there is no doubt that there is a "pleasure of enjoying one's abilities," that is, of enjoying the cessation of the tension of "not being able yet," the cessation of anxiety connected with insufficiency of motor control.

Thus the forces whose interaction is supposed to explain the actual mental phenomena have definite *directions*—toward motility or away from motility. The impulses toward discharge are representative of a primary biological tendency; the opposite impulses are brought into the organism by influences from the outside.

> Slips of the tongue, errors, symptomatic acts are the best examples of conflicts between strivings for discharge and opposing forces; some tendency that has been warded off, either definitely by "repression" or by a wish not to express it here and now, finds a distorted expression counter to the opposing conscious will (553).

When tendencies to discharge and tendencies to inhibit are equally strong, there is externally no evidence of activity; but energy is consumed in an internal hidden struggle. Clinically this is manifested by the fact that individuals subject to such conflicts show fatigue and exhaustion without doing perceptible work.

MENTAL ECONOMICS

With this example we find ourselves in the field that Freud has called psychoeconomics (588). The above-mentioned persons were tired because they were consuming energy in a struggle between inner forces. When a person suppresses an irritation and subsequently in another situation reacts violently to an insignificant provocation, it must be assumed that the first quantity of irritation, which was suppressed, was still at work in him as a readiness to discharge, later seizing the first possible opportunity. The energy of the forces behind the mental phenomena is displaceable. Strong impulses demanding discharge are more difficult to restrain than weak ones; however, they can be restrained if the counterforces are equally strong. What quantity of excitation can be borne without discharge is an economic problem. There is a "mental energy exchange," an economic distribution of the energy at hand between intake, consumption, and output. Another example of the usefulness of the economic concept is seen in the fact that neuroses frequently break out at puberty and at the climacterium. The person affected was able to withstand a certain amount of undischarged instinctual excitation; however, when physical changes increased the absolute quantity of this excitation, the countermeasures no longer sufficed. Countless other examples exist which bring home the importance of the economic point of view for the understanding of factually observed phenomena. The person who was tired after having done nothing represents but a special type of general inhibitions due to silent internal tasks. Those who have inner problems to solve must apply a great deal of their energy to them, and there remains little for other functions.

The concept of a "quantity" of mental energy is exactly as justifiable or unjustifiable as the introduction of other scientific working concepts that have proved practical. It is regrettable that this quantity cannot be measured directly; it may be measured indirectly by its physiological manifestations.

CONSCIOUS AND UNCONSCIOUS

In the exposition of the dynamics and economics of the mental organization, nothing has been stated as yet about the significance of whether a given phenomenon is conscious or unconscious. This is due to the fact that the differentiation is initially purely descriptive, not quantitative. Posthypnotic suggestion demonstrates the existence of a psychic unconscious before our very eyes. The forgetting of a name makes us feel it subjectively. One knows that one knows the name and still one does not know it.

When the dynamic and the economic points of view are applied, the problem of conscious or unconscious should be put in the following way: Under what circumstances and through what energies does the condition of consciousness arise? It is in these terms that all mental qualities should be examined. Too, the feelings of pleasure and pain as qualities are describable only; to "explain" them means to determine under what dynamic and economic conditions they are experienced.

This way of putting the problem would find a simple justification if a direct correlation could be found between fundamental quantities and the definite qualities that appeared only with them: for example, if Fechner's hypothesis—that every increase in mental tension is felt as displeasure and every decrease as pleasure—could be confirmed. Many facts are in accordance with such a viewpoint, but unfortunately there are contradictory facts, too (555, 613). There are pleasurable tensions, like sexual excitement, and painful lacks of tension, like boredom or feelings of emptiness. Nevertheless, Fechner's rule is valid in general. That sexual excitement and boredom are secondary complications can be demonstrated. The pleasure of sexual excitement, called forepleasure, turns immediately into displeasure if the hope of bringing about a discharge in subsequent end pleasure disappears; the pleasure character of the forepleasure is tied up with a mental anticipation of the end pleasure. The displeasure of boredom turns out, on closer inspection, not to correspond to a lack of tension but rather to an excitement whose aim is unconscious (422). A further discussion of the problem at this point would lead us too far astray (cf. 613). It was brought up in order to demonstrate that attempts to co-ordinate quantitative factors and qualitative phenomena are warranted.

Returning to the quality "conscious," the fact whether or not an impulse is conscious reveals nothing of its dynamic value. Conscious phenomena are not simply stronger than unconscious ones; nor is it true that everything unconscious is the "real motor" of the mind, and everything conscious merely a relatively unimportant side issue. The many memory traces that can be made conscious by a simple act of attention are "unimportant" though unconscious (they are called preconscious). Other unconscious phenomena, however, must be imagined as intense forces striving for discharge but kept in check by an equally strong force, which manifests itself as "resistance." Unconscious material under such high pressure has only one aim: discharge. Its freely floating energy is directed according to the "primary process"; that is, it is unburdened by the demands of reality, time, order, or logical considerations; it becomes condensed and displaced, following only the interests of increased possibilities of discharge. This mode of functioning of the archaic mind remains effective in the realm of the unconscious; in the more differentiated parts of the mind it gradually becomes supplanted by the organized "secondary process" (590).

THE MENTAL STRUCTURE

Mental phenomena are to be regarded as the result of the interplay of forces pressing respectively toward and away from motility. The organism is in contact with the outside world at the beginning and at the end of its reaction processes, which start with the perception of stimuli and end with motor or glandular discharge. Freud looks at the mental apparatus as modeled after an organism floating in water (608). Its surface takes up stimuli, conducts them to the interior, whence reactive impulses surge to the surface. The surface is differentiated gradually with respect to its functions of stimulus perception and discharge. The product of this differentiation becomes the "ego." The ego proceeds selectively in its reception of perceptions as well as in its allowing impulses to gain motility. It operates as an inhibiting apparatus which controls, by this inhibiting function, the position of the organism in the outside world. Alexander in his "vector analysis" regards all mental tendencies as combinations of intake, retention, and elimination (44). We add: living begins with intake; but with the initial intake the first urge to eliminate appears; retention, however, arises later under complicating influences.

The ego develops abilities with which it can observe, select, and organize stimuli and impulses: the functions of judgment and intelligence. It also develops methods of keeping the rejected impulses from motility by the use of energy quantities kept ready for this purpose; that is, it blocks the tendency toward discharge and changes the primary process into the secondary process (552, 590). All this takes place by means of a special organization which aims to fulfill its different tasks with a minimum of effort (principle of multiple function) (1551).

Underneath the organized periphery of the ego lies the core of a dynamic, driving chaos of forces, which strive for discharge and nothing else, but which constantly receive new stimulations from external as well as internal perceptions, influenced by somatic factors that determine how the perceptions are experienced (590, 608). The organization proceeds from the surface to the depth. The ego is to the id as the ectoderm is to the endoderm. The ego becomes the mediator between the organism and the outer world. As such it has to provide protection against hostile influences from the environment as well as enforcement of gratification even against a restricting outside world. There is no reason to assume that the ego, created for the purpose of ensuring the gratification of the organism's impulses, is in any way primarily hostile to the instincts.

What does the differentiation of ego and id have to do with the qualities of conscious and unconscious? It would be simple if ego and conscious, id and unconscious could be co-ordinated. But unfortunately things are more complicated. That which takes place in consciousness consists of (corresponding to "intake" and "discharge") perceptions and impulses. We may regard imagery as consisting of impulses with a weaker cathexis (774). However, not all impulses and perceptions are conscious. There are "below threshold" stimuli which can be proved to have been perceived without ever having been conscious (1228). Further, there are repressed perceptions, in hysterical blindness, for example, where the effectiveness of unconscious perceptions can be observed. There is also unconscious motility, as in somnambulism. Unconscious perceptions and movements have specific peculiarities which differentiate them from the conscious ones. All living organisms must maintain exchanges with the outside world through the basic functions of perception and motility—this is true even before there is any differentiation of an ego, and in the same way that nourishment and breathing must be performed by each living cell even before there is a differential development of a multicellular respiratory and metabolic apparatus. Before a systematic conception of reality can be developed there must of necessity exist a certain unsystematic perception.

Consciousness comes into being at some point in the process of systematization (*see* p. 34). This process depends on the ability to utilize memories. Memmory traces are remnants of perceptions; they apparently arise on a second level below that of the perceptions themselves (522, 615). The ego broadens out from the layer of these memory traces, called the preconscious. The differentiation of the ego is a gradual process. There are deeper layers of the ego which are unconscious. The transition from ego to id is a gradual one and is only sharp at those points where a conflict exists. However, where such conflict does arise, even highly differentiated forces of the ego become unconscious again.

The portion of the conscious that is best known is the "repressed"—that which is unconscious because strong, dynamic forces hinder its becoming conscious. The repressed pushes toward consciousness and motility; it consists of impulses seeking outlets. In this seeking activity it tends to produce "derivatives," that is, to displace its cathexes onto associatively connected ideas that are less objectionable to the conscious ego. In psychoanalysis, preconscious derivatives are encouraged and caught by the patient's attention; this is the way repressed content gradually becomes known. The repressed consists, first of all, of the ideas and conceptions connected with the aim of the warded-off impulses which, by being warded off, have lost their connection with verbal expression; by regaining verbalization, unconscious ideas become preconscious (590). But it is also meaningful to talk about unconscious sensations, feelings, or emotions. Certainly the qualities of feelings come into being only by being felt. But there are tensions in the organism which, were they not hindered in their discharge and development by blocking countercathexes, would result in specific sensations, feelings, or emotions. They are unconscious "dispositions" toward these qualities, unconscious "longings for affects," strivings toward development of affects that are held in check by opposing forces, while the individual does not know that he has such readiness toward rage or sexual excitement or anxiety or guilt feeling or whatever it may be (608). Of course, such "unconscious dispositions toward affects" are not theoretical constructions but may be observed clinically in the same way that unconscious ideas may be observed: they, too, develop derivatives, betray themselves in dreams, in symptoms, and in other substitute formations, or through the rigidity of the opposing behavior, or, finally, merely in general weariness.

The mental apparatus, however, does not consist only of an ego and an id. Its further development brings a further complication.

Previously it was stated that the question as to the nature of the forces blocking discharge was the basic one of all psychology. In the main, these forces were thrust upon the mind by the environment. It is the consideration of reality that keeps the ego from immediately complying with the discharge drive of the impulses. However, such inhibiting tendencies, which according to the definition are derived from the ego, are not in all respects the opposite of "instinctual drives." Often, for example in ascetics or moral masochists, the anti-instinctual behavior betrays all the characteristics of an instinct. This contradiction can be explained genetically. The energy with which the ego carries out its instinct-inhibiting activities is drawn from the instinctual reservoir of the id. A portion of the instinctual energy is changed into counterinstinctual energy. A certain part of the ego which inhibits instinctual activity develops on the one hand closer to the instincts and on the other hand is in conflict with other parts of the ego that are hungry for pleasure. This part, which has the function (among others) of deciding which impulses are acceptable and which are not, is called the super-ego. While the ego is also a representative of the outside world, here again we have a special representative of the outside world within the first representative (608).

INITIAL ESSAY AT A DEFINITION OF NEUROSIS

After bringing forth the dynamic, economic, and structural points of view, an initial attempt will be made to clarify what takes place in a neurosis. Is there any common denominator in the manifold neurotic phenomena that may be utilized for comprehending the essential nature of neuroses?

In all neurotic symptoms something happens which the patient experiences as strange and unintelligible. This something may be involuntary movements, other changes of bodily functions and various sensations, as in hysteria; or an overwhelming and unjustified emotion or mood, as in anxiety spells or depressions; or queer impulses or thoughts, as in compulsions and obsessions. All symptoms give the impression of a something that seems to break in upon the personality from an unknown source—a something that disturbs the continuity of the personality and that is outside the realm of the conscious will. But there are also neurotic phenomena of another kind. In "neurotic characters" the personality does not appear to be uniform or disturbed only by one or the other interrupting event, but openly so torn or deformed and often so involved in the illness that one cannot say at what point the "personality" ends and the "symptom" begins. But different as "symptom neuroses" and "character neuroses" seem to be, both have this in common: the normal and rational way of handling the demands of the external world as well as the impulses from within is substituted by some irrational phenomenon which seems strange and cannot be voluntarily controlled. Since the normal functioning of the mind is governed by a control apparatus that organizes, leads, and inhibits deeper archaic and more instinctual forces—in the same way that the cortex organizes, leads, and inhibits impulses of the deeper and more archaic levels of the brain—it can be stated that the common denominator of all neurotic phenomena is an insufficiency of the normal control apparatus.

The simplest way to "control" stimuli is to discharge by motor reactions the excitation they arouse. Later the immediate discharge is replaced by more complicated control mechanisms of counterforces. This control consists in a distribution of counterenergies in an adequate economic stability between incoming stimuli and outgoing discharges.

All neurotic phenomena are based on insufficiencies of the normal control apparatus. They can be understood as involuntary emergency discharges that supplant the normal ones. The insufficiency can be brought about in two ways. One way is through an increase in the influx of stimuli: too much excitation enters the mental apparatus in a given unit of time and cannot be mastered; such experiences are called traumatic. The other way is through a previous blocking or decrease of discharge which has produced a damming up of tensions within the organism so that normal excitations now operate relatively like traumatic ones. These two possible ways are not mutually exclusive. A trauma may initiate an ensuing blocking of discharge; and a primary blocking, by creating a state of being dammed up, may cause subsequent average stimuli to have a traumatic effect.

A model of the first type can be seen in irritations that everyone experiences after little traumata, like a sudden fright or some smaller accident. The person feels irritated for a certain time, cannot concentrate because inwardly he is still concerned about the event and has no energy free for attention in other directions. He repeats the event in his thoughts and feelings a few times—and after a short while his mental stability is re-established. Such a little traumatic neurosis can be explained as flooding of the organism by amounts of unmastered excitation and as attempts at a belated mastery. The severe traumatic neuroses must be looked at from the same angle (*see* pp. 117 ff.).

A model of the second type of neurosis, characterized by a previous blocking of discharge and called psychoneurosis, is represented by the artificial neuroses that have been inflicted upon animals by experimental psychologists (65, 286, 923, 1109). Some stimulus which had represented pleasant instinctual experiences or which had served as a signal that some action would now procure gratification is suddenly connected by the experimenter with frustrating or threatening experiences, or the experimenter decreases the difference between stimuli which the animal had been trained to associate with instinct gratification and threat respectively; the animal then gets into a state of irritation which is very similar to that of a traumatic neurosis. He feels contradictory impulses; the conflict makes it impossible for him to give in to the impulses in the accustomed way; the discharge is blocked, and this decrease in discharge works in the same way as an increase in influx: it brings the organism into a state of tension and calls for emergency discharges.

In psychoneuroses some impulses have been blocked; the consequence is a state of tension and eventually some "emergency discharges." These consist partly in unspecific restlessness and its elaborations and partly in much more specific phenomena which represent the distorted involuntary discharges of those very instinctual drives for which a normal discharge has been interdicted. Thus we have in psychoneuroses, first a defense of the ego against an instinct, then a conflict between the instinct striving for discharge and the defensive forces of the ego, then a state of damming up, and finally the neurotic symptoms which are distorted discharges as a consequence of the state of damming up—a compromise between the opposing forces. The symptom is the only step in this development that becomes manifest; the conflict, its history, and the significance of the symptoms are unconscious.

NEUROTIC SYMPTOMS AND AFFECTS

These considerations of the essence of the neuroses call forth an objection that should not be overlooked. Much of the given characterization of neurotic phenomena seems valid also for a category of very normal mental phenomena, namely, of affective or emotional spells.

Actually a search for a common denominator for all sudden outbursts of affect reveals a close relationship between outbursts of this kind and neurotic phenomena.

Affective spells consist of (a) movements and other physiological discharges, especially changes in the muscular and glandular functions, and (b) emotional feelings. Both the physical and the mental phenomena are specific for any given affect—and in particular the correlation of both phenomena is specific. Emotional spells occur without the consent or even against the will of the individual; persons who undergo emotional spells have "lost control." Apparently something of a more archaic nature is substituted for the normal ego—there is no doubt that children and infantile personalities are more unstable emotionally.

Such spells occur as a response to (a) extraordinarily intense stimuli, the quantity of which explains the temporary insufficiency of the normal control apparatus of the ego; in this case the emotional spells seem to be a kind of emergency control supplanting the normal ego control; or (b) to ordinary stimuli when certain conditions obtain in the organism. The simplest example is displaced rage. A slight precipitating factor evokes a fit of anger if there was a readiness for it in the organism rooted in a previous experience that afforded this tendency no means of expression. In general the organism tends toward emotional regressions if it is in a state of tension. This is why an unduly intense emotional reaction generally can be regarded as a "derivative" of something that was previously suppressed. In summary, emotional spells occur when the normal ego control has been rendered relatively insufficient by (a) too much influx of excitation, or (b) a previous blocking of the efflux (191, 440, 697, 1013, 1021).

This definition is identical with that given for neurotic symptoms. The neurotic symptoms, too, are discharge phenomena that occur without the consent of the ego; and if their precipitating factors, too, are analyzed, either an increased influx of excitation (traumatic neuroses) is found or defense activities of the ego that had previously blocked discharges and thus brought the organism into a state of tension (psychoneuroses). Thus the causation of emotional spells and of neurotic symptoms is essentially the same: a relative insufficiency of ego control because of either increased influx or blocking of discharge. Both emotional spells and neurotic symptoms are partial substitutes, of a more archaic nature, for the normal ego motility. Neurotic symptoms could be called a kind of "personally structured" affective spells. The difference lies in the nature of what is substituted. In neurosis the substitute is subjectively determined in the history of the individual. In affect the substitute is objectively determined; the syndrome is more or less the same in different individuals and is caused by chemically induced nervous reactions—just where it comes from, we do not know. The impression that there is a general similarity between neurotic and emotional spells impelled Freud, after having discovered the historical determination of the hysterical fit, to look for a historical determination of the anxiety syndrome also (618).

The similarity between neurotic symptoms and emotional spells seems less striking in the case of compulsive symptoms. However, the compulsive symptom is less primitive than other neurotic symptoms; it is not a simple breaking through of the repressed forces. Similarly, not all affects have the character of sudden spells; the compulsive symptoms may be compared to tension affects like grief. If a conversion symptom corresponds to an outburst of intractable sexual excitement or of rage, then the compulsive symptom is paralleled by the more gradual work of mourning. Both compulsion and mourning represent a secondary elaboration of the original tendency toward stormy discharge.

The psychoneuroses are essentially the result of a conflict between instinctual demands and defensive forces of the ego. This knowledge shows how best to organize a theory of neurosis. To be studied are (a) the defending ego and its development, (b) the instincts and their development, (c) the types of conflicts between the two, their motives, methods and manifestations, and (d) the consequences of the conflicts, the neuroses proper.

However, these four points cannot be strictly separated from each other; they are too closely interwoven. We shall have to deal with the same facts repeatedly, looking at them from different angles. The interrelationship between ego and id makes it necessary to subdivide the ego chapter; first the early stages of development of the ego will be taken up, next the development of the instincts, and only then the later development of the ego. A brief chapter about the psychoanalytic method of research precedes the discussion of mental development.

Chapter III

THE METHOD OF PSYCHOANALYSIS

INTRODUCTORY REMARKS

WHAT follows is neither a presentation of the technique of psychoanalysis nor an explanation of the therapeutic procedure. The former is beyond the scope of this book and the latter will be discussed later (Chapter Twenty-three). Only a few basic facts will be presented concerning the scientific method used in gathering the psychological and psychopathological findings that are to be discussed (cf. 748, 779).

Today the presentation of the principles of the psychoanalytic method is easy. Historically they were gradually developed out of the needs of psychotherapeutic practice (188). Every bit of newly acquired method brought forth new findings which again could be used in improving the method. Today it is possible to justify the method by explaining its theoretical background. Actually the theory did not precede the method; rather, it was established with the help of the method.

THE BASIC RULE

Dynamic psychology has the task of reconstructing, from certain given manifestations, the constellation of forces that produced the manifestations. Behind the changing manifest picture are its dynamic foundations, impulses striving for discharge and inhibiting counterforces. The initial efforts of the analyst are devoted to eliminating obstacles that prevent a more direct expression of these forces. He undertakes to achieve this by the so-called basic rule. The patient is requested to say everything that enters his mind, without selection.

To understand the meaning of this rule, we should recall how a person acts in everyday life who does not follow the rule. His impulses toward actions or words are determined by (a) external stimuli of any kind to which he reacts, (b) his physical state which gives him internal stimuli and determines the intensity and mode of the impressions by external stimuli, (c) certain conceptual goals, the thought of what he wants to do or say, which makes him suppress that which does not belong to the subject, and (d) the derivatives of all the warded-off impulses that try to find discharge.

The psychoanalyst wants to understand the last group of determinants and for this purpose tries to exclude the first three as much as possible, with the aim of making this last more recognizable. The external stimuli during the psychoanalytic hour are reduced to a minimum and remain relatively constant.

In his earlier days Freud even asked patients to close their eyes for the purpose of excluding distracting visual perceptions (543, 544). Later, however, it turned out that the danger of inducing the patient to isolate the analytic procedure from "open-eye reality" is usually greater than the possible gain.

An acute extraordinary physical state, such as pain, hunger, or an impending real danger, actually is a hindrance to the production of fruitful associations because it overshadows the production of derivatives.

A patient used to dream exclusively about food, and the analysis apparently made no progress. It turned out that he actually did not have enough to eat. After he succeeded in getting a job, the "oral" dreams disappeared and the analysis went on normally.

The elimination of the third disturbing factor, the conscious conceptual goals of the ego, is the main object of the basic rule. When the selective conceptual goals of the ego are excluded, what is expressed is determined rather by tensions and impulses within the individual awaiting the opportunity to gain expression. The analyst tries to make the patient learn to eliminate the conceptual goals and not to select the things he tells. In fact, the patient is not to be active at all; his one task is *not* to prevent the expression of impulses that rise within him.

"To tell everything" is much more difficult than one imagines. Even the individual who conscientiously tries to adhere to the basic rule fails to tell many things because he considers them too unimportant, too stupid, too indiscreet, and so on. There are many who never learn to apply the basic rule because their fear of losing control is too great, and before they can give expression to anything, they must examine it to see exactly what it is.

It is, therefore, not so simple for the unconscious to find expression simply by attempting to obey the basic rule. It is true that the regulation eliminates thousands of conceptual goals of everyday life, but it cannot eliminate all the counterforces of the ego. Even if it were possible to cut off all purposeful thinking and to concentrate only on what comes up spontaneously, still the pure drives striving for discharge would not be encountered. The very strongest and deepest resistances—that is, those that originated in childhood and that are directed against unconscious instinctual outbursts—cannot be swept out of existence by a stipulation to tell everything. Thus the utterances of a patient obeying the rule are not simply a reflection of the unconscious that now becomes conscious. The picture presented is, rather, one of a struggle between certain unconscious impulses (which reveal themselves relatively more clearly in analysis than in ordinary conversation) and certain resistances of the ego, which likewise are unconscious to the subject or become apparent to him in distorted form only. In the patient's expressions, minima and maxima of an approach to something "really meant" can be recognized.

INTERPRETATION

Now, what does the analyst do? (1) He helps the patient eliminate his re-sistances as far as possible. Though he may apply various means, fundamentally the analyst calls the attention of the patient, who is either completely unaware or insufficiently aware of his resistances, to the effects of his resistances. (2) Knowing that the utterances of the patient are really allusions to other things, the psychoanalyst tries to deduce what lies behind the allusions and to impart this information to the patient. When there is a minimum of distance between allusion and what is alluded to, the analyst gives the patient words to express feelings just rising to the surface and thereby facilitates their becoming conscious.

This procedure of deducing what the patient actually means and telling it to him is called interpretation. Since interpretation means helping something unconscious to become conscious by naming it at the moment it is striving to break through, effective interpretations can be given only at one specific point, namely, where the patient's immediate interest is momentarily centered. The actual shocking infantile instinctual impulses are so far removed from the possi-bility of being felt that, in the beginning, interpretation is of course not con-cerned with them but rather with their derivatives. Defensive attitudes are closer to the patient's capacity to understand and so are interpreted first.

It has been asked why the theoretical knowledge about content and mech-anisms of neuroses cannot be applied toward shortening the regrettably long time required by psychoanalysis. If it is known that the basis of a neurosis is the so-called Oedipus complex, why not tell the patient immediately that he loves his mother and wants to kill his father, and cure him by this information? There was once a comparatively large school of pseudo analysis which held that the patient should be "bombarded" with "deep interpretations" (1479); and even psychoanalytic literature contains statements to the effect that a speedy, "deep interpretation" can overcome the patient's anxiety (958). Efforts of this kind remain necessarily unsuccessful. The unprepared patient can in no way con-nect the words he hears from the analyst with his emotional experiences. Such an "interpretation" does not interpret at all.

Even the mere information that something within him is fighting his adher-ence to the basic rule tends to make the patient discover something in himself of which he was previously unaware. An interpretation that directs the patient's attention to something hitherto unnoticed serves the same purpose as does the histology teacher who tells his pupils what to look for in the microscope. Of course it is not mere lack of experience that prevents the analysand from noting his attitude. There are powerful motives that make him unwilling to know.

Actually resistances are attacked not only by interpretation; other means of influencing people to do something unpleasant are used as well. The analyst tries to convince the patient that the unpleasant task is necessary; his friendly feelings toward the analyst are utilized. However, wherever possible, interpretation is used. The concurrence of perceiving the interpreter's words and the preconscious presence of the derivative in statu nascendi changes the dynamic conflict between defense and warded-off impulses in favor of the latter and new, less distorted derivatives can be tolerated. The interpretation splits the ego into an observing and an experiencing part so that the former can judge the irrational character of the latter.

How can the analyst know what the words of the patient actually allude to? Resistances have twisted his utterances beyond recognition. It is the task of the analyst's interpretative work to undo and make retroactive the distortion caused by resistances. This work of reconstruction has often rightly been compared to the interpretation of archaeological findings. It can be more readily demonstrated with examples of errors, slips of the tongue, and dreams than with neuroses in toto (553).

DEVICES OF DISTORTION

There are many ways in which distortion is brought about. A few examples of the devices employed in distortion may be enumerated:

1. Links may be missing in the associations of the patient which, when examined, reveal themselves as being connected with affects, specific recollections, or, generally, specific attitudes that may be expected in certain situations. When the analyst observes such hiatuses, he knows that the censoring forces of the ego have been busy with their scissors.

2. Affects that have once been suppressed express themselves in some other connection. If a man must swallow his anger at his boss, he may easily become enraged at his wife. Therefore, when the analyst observes that an affect is incommensurate with a given situation—whether it be too strong or whether it be different in quality—he knows that he is dealing with a derivative of something else.

3. Not only affects may reveal themselves as "substitutes"; the distortion may also consist in replacing any idea with another one which is associatively connected. Whatever the patient expresses, not only in words but also in movements, attitudes, errors, may be allusions to something else. The associative connections are of various kinds. Allusions and what is alluded to may have common or similar characteristics. What is said and what is meant may represent different parts of one and the same whole. So long as the analyst does not know the whole, he cannot surmise what is meant. The more the analyst knows about the history of his patient, the better he can understand. Neurotic symptoms, especially, often become understandable only through their historical connections.

Since the unconscious continually strives for expression, the best way for the analyst to find out what is actually meant is to look for a common factor in the various utterances of the patient. Frequently it is the interplay or the contradiction between the patient's various statements or between his words and his gestures or between his words and his feelings that puts the analyst on the right trail. At times the very manner in which the patient relates something or experiences something must itself be interpreted as the expression of a specific unconscious thought. Also to be noted is the fact that everyone shares a common reservoir of expressions that serve to distort meaning—symbolism.

The interpretative work of the analyst does not, of course, consist in stopping to examine every utterance of the patient by saying to himself: "Did he omit something here? Is the patient's remark only a fragment of some complete train of thought? Perhaps I must find some historical connection in it. What is the connection between the patient's utterance and what he said five minutes ago, or yesterday? Is the patient's facial expression in harmony with or in contradiction to what he is saying? Is that which he just mentioned to be found in Freud's table of symbols? Is his affect commensurate with his utterance?" and so on. By the time the analyst considers all these points the patient will have gone on to something else. No, discovering what the patient really means does not involve the conscious analysis of all possible distortions but rather an intense empathy with the personality of the patient. In performing this part of his task the tool of the analyst is his own unconscious.

Does this admission deny the scientific character of the psychoanalytic method? How can the analyst, working with his intuition, actually know if that which he has surmised is really correct? The answer to this question may be postponed for the time being.

An interpretation, it has been stated, can only be effective if it is given at the moment when the distance between what is said and what is meant is at a minimum. How can the analyst know *when* to interpret? He must constantly have an awareness of the strength of the resistances operative at any given moment.

TYPES OF RESISTANCES

Resistances find expression in manifold ways. Everything that prevents the patient from producing material derived from the unconscious is resistance. It is impossible to tabulate the various ways in which resistance can be expressed. The patient may stop talking, or he may talk so much that a common factor cannot be deduced from his utterances. What he says appears to deviate further and further from what he actually means; it seems to be extensive rather than deep.

If we call the patient's attention to this, he may reply: "You asked me to say *everything* that comes to my mind. If my associations tend to spread out in all directions, should I therefore abandon the basic rule of analysis?" The answer is simple: The patient must follow the basic rule as closely as he can. If, however, no common factor develops, the analysis is confronted with an antecedent problem, which must be recognized before what is actually meant can be surmised: *Why* do the patient's associations extend in all directions? Both the analyst and the patient must co-operate to find out why the patient expresses his resistance in this specific form.

The patient may forget certain things, important events of the day before, or something that has already been discussed in the analysis. He may criticize every comment of the analyst; he may feel antagonistic or ill at ease.

It is the aim of analysis to demonstrate to the patient the disturbing residues of the past in his present feelings and reactions—to connect the present with the past. Thus a certain form of resistance consists in the patient's talking only about the present and refusing to see the past; in the converse form of resistance the patient talks only about childhood memories and refuses to see their representations in present reality.

It is the aim of analysis to confront the patient's reasonable ego with the irrational emotions effective within him. Thus a certain form of resistance consists in the patient's always being reasonable and refusing to have any understanding for the logic of emotions; in the opposite type of resistance the patient floats continuously in unclear emotional experiences without getting the necessary distance and freedom which would permit him to look at them reasonably.

All these are forms of resistance that are easily recognizable as such. Some resistances, however, operate far more secretively. A patient may, for example, appear to be doing good analytic work; he may make progress in understanding the forces working within him, sense connections, and dig up new childhood recollections—and yet there is no change in his neurosis. This may be due to the operation of various hidden resistances. A certain attitude of the patient, which itself has not been analyzed, may nullify the effect of the analysis. For instance, he may have a feeling of doubt: "That would all be very fine if it were true, but I don't know if it is true." Or the patient may have understood what his associations and the analyst's interpretations showed him and yet the knowledge remains entirely separated from his real life. It is as if he said to himself: "This is all valid only as long as I lie on the couch." Or a patient may accept everything the analyst tells him merely as a matter of courtesy; but it is just this courteous attitude which protects him from reliving to the full his instinctual conflicts, and which therefore must first be analyzed. There are intellectual resistances in which patients try to refute the theoretical validity of psychoanalysis instead of seeking to clarify their own mental life. But there are also intellectual resistances of the reverse type: some patients become enthusiastic supporters of psychoanalysis in order to avoid applying it to themselves.

An acute resistance, one that is directed against the discussion of some particular topic, is far easier to handle than "character resistances." These are attitudes which the patient had previously developed in order to maintain his repressions, and which he now exhibits toward the analyst. These attitudes must first be broken down before the repressions can be resolved.

TRANSFERENCE

The repetition of previously acquired attitudes toward the analyst is but one example of the most significant category of resistance, the handling of which is the core of analysis: the transference resistance. Understanding the contents of the patient's unconscious from his utterances is, relatively, the simplest part of the analyst's task. Handling the transference is the most difficult.

It seems very natural that in the course of an analytic treatment the patient should produce powerful affects. They may appear as anxiety or joy, as an increase in inner tension beyond the point of endurance, or as a happy feeling of complete relaxation. They may also take the form of specific feelings toward the analyst: an intense love, because the analyst is helping him, or bitter hatred, because the analyst forces him to undergo unpleasant experiences. But the problem becomes more complicated when a patient's affect is in contradiction to what is happening in the analysis, as, for example, when a patient hates the analyst for helping him, or loves him for imposing an unpleasant restriction. The problem is even more complicated when the patient obviously misconstrues the real situation and loves or hates the analyst for something which, in the judgment of the analyst, is nonexistent. Such misconstruing of the actual psychoanalytic situation is a regular occurrence in almost every analysis. Freud was at first surprised when he met with this phenomenon (577); today Freud's discoveries make it easy to understand it theoretically. The analytic situation induces the development of derivatives of the repressed, and at the same time a resistance is operative against it. The derivatives may make their appearance as highly concrete emotional needs directed toward the person who happens to be present. Resistance distorts the true connections. The patient misunderstands the present in terms of the past; and then instead of remembering the past, he strives, without recognizing the nature of his action, to relive the past and to live it more satisfactorily than he did in childhood. He "transfers" past attitudes to the present.

In analysis, transference has a twofold aspect. Fundamentally it must be considered as a form of resistance. The patient defends himself against remembering and discussing his infantile conflicts by reliving them. Transference actions (since the object is not the right one and the situation is not fitting) serve the purpose of distorting the original connections, and the discharge thus attained is necessarily insufficient. The analysand, seeking immediate satisfaction of derivatives instead of facing his original impulses, attempts to use a short-circuit substitute for his repressed drives. On the other hand, the transference offers the analyst a unique opportunity to observe directly the past of his patient and thereby to understand the development of his conflicts.

In everyday life, too, there are transference situations. It is a general human trait to interpret one's experiences in the light of the past. The more that repressed impulses seek expression in derivatives, the more hampered is the correct evaluation of the differences between the present and the past, and the greater is the transference component of a person's behavior. However, the psychoanalytic situation in particular promotes the production of transference in two ways: (1) The environment which is reacted to has a relatively uniform and constant character and therefore the transference component in the reactions becomes much more pronounced. (2) Whereas in other situations people react to a person's actions and words—thus provoking new reactions and creating new realities all of which obscures the transference character of the original action—the analyst, in contrast to this, provides no actual provocation to the patient and responds to his affective outbursts only by making the patient aware of his behavior. Thus the transference character of the patient's feelings becomes clearer. The analyst's reaction to transference is the same as to any other attitude of the patient: he interprets. He sees in the patient's attitude a derivative of unconscious impulses and tries to show this to the patient.

Practically, this task is far more difficult than any other type of interpretation. Were the analyst to behave as the patient's parents had previously done, he could not help him, for then what had occurred in the patient's childhood would merely be repeated. And were the analyst to behave in a contrary way, he would not be able to cure the patient either, for then he would only be fulfilling the patient's resistance wishes. The analyst, therefore, must do neither the one nor the other. If he were to feel flattered by the love of the patient and responded in kind, or if he were hurt by the patient's feeling of hate, in short, if he were to react to the affects of his patient with counteraffects, he could not successfully interpret; for the patient could respond to interpretations in some such way as: "No, I love you or hate you not because of unresolved love or hate tendencies of my past but because you have actually behaved in a lovable or hateful way."

There are several reasons why analytic institutes require that all analysts themselves first be analyzed. One of the reasons is that in psychoanalytic courses it is not possible to give clinical demonstrations, and consequently the future analyst can learn analytic technique only by personal experience. A second reason is that the analyst's own repressions would make him overlook certain things in his patient, or see others in an exaggerated way and therefore falsify their significance. Much more fundamental is a third reason. It is not easy to face the innumerable and various affects with which patients bombard the analyst without reacting with counteraffects, whether conscious or unconscious. The unconscious tendencies of the analyst to express his own unresolved love and hate tendencies by reacting to transference with countertransference must therefore be eliminated through a training analysis.

Systematic and consistent interpretative work, both within and without the framework of the transference, can be described as educating the patient to prooduce continually less distorted derivatives until his fundamental instinctual conflicts are recognizable. Of course, this is not a single operation resulting in a single act of abreaction; it is, rather, a chronic process of working through, which shows the patient again and again the same conflicts and his usual way of reacting to them, but from new angles and in new connections.

CRITERIA FOR THE CORRECTNESS OF INTERPRETATIONS

The problem of how the analyst knows his interpretations are correct has been postponed until now. A familiar objection made to psychoanalysis is that interpretations are arbitrary, that the analyst more or less projects his own fantasies onto the patient. He is said to make things easy for himself: if the patient says "yes" to an interpretation, that is taken as a proof of its validity; if he says "no," he thereby shows a resistance to the interpretation, proof positive of its validity. As for scientific certainty, there simply is no evidence of it.

What is the real situation? As a matter of fact, it is correct that a patient's yes usually is accepted as a confirmation and that, under certain circumstances, a no is not regarded as a refutation. Freud very rightly called attention to an analogous situation, that of the judge (596). The confession of an accused person is generally valid as proof of guilt, although in exceptional cases the confession may be false; but a denial on the part of the accused is by no means proof of innocence. The difference between the accused and a psychoanalytic patient is merely that the former consciously conceals the truth, the latter unconsciously.

Hence neither a yes nor a no in reply to an interpretation is a final criterion as to its validity. It is rather the manner in which the yes or no is expressed. Certainly there is a kind of no that merely represents a final attempt to maintain an attitude that has become insupportable. There are various signs by which such a patient betrays, immediately after uttering his no, that he has been inwardly affected by the interpretation and feels that what the analyst has called to his attention really exists within himself. But in general one can say that an interpretation to which the patient objects is wrong. That does not necessarily mean that it is wrong in content, that, for instance, the impulse which the analyst surmised and imparted to the patient had never been operative. The interpretation may be correct in content but incorrect dynamically or economically, that is, given at a moment when the patient could not grasp its validity or get any farther with it. Sometimes a yes may be simulated by the patient out of politeness or negligence or fear of the consequences of a contradiction or for some other reason, whereas his behavior may show that inwardly he is saying no.

To put it differently, it is not a matter of the words used by the patient in responding to an interpretation. In giving an interpretation, the analyst seeks to intervene in the dynamic interplay of forces, to change the balance in favor of the repressed in its striving for discharge. The degree to which this change actually occurs is the criterion for the validity of an interpretation. It is the patient's reactions in their *entirety* that give the answer, not his first yes or no. A valid interpretation brings about a dynamic change, manifested in the subsequent associations of the patient and in his entire behavior.

Freud once compared psychoanalysis to a jigsaw puzzle, in which the aim is to construct a complete picture out of its fragments (550). There is but one correct solution. So long as this is not discovered, one can perhaps recognize isolated bits, but there is no coherent whole. If the correct solution is found, there can be no doubt as to its validity, for each fragment fits into the general whole. A final solution reveals a unified coherence in which every hitherto incomprehensible detail has found its place. And, also before this happy point is reached, dynamic-economic changes in the state of the patient are decisive for determining whether or not the procedure of the analyst is adequate.[1]

[1] Many problems merely touched upon in this chapter are discussed at some length in (438).

B. The Mental Development

CHAPTERS IV-VI

Chapter IV

EARLY MENTAL DEVELOPMENT: THE ARCHAIC EGO

METHODOLOGICAL DIFFICULTIES IN THE INVESTIGATION OF THE EARLY PHASES OF DEVELOPMENT

IN CONTRAST to the affect storm or emotional spell, where the phenomena are determined by biological and phylogenetic factors, in the neuroses the phenomena are conditioned by the individual history. Since earlier levels of development are retained or returned to in neuroses, they cannot be understood without a thorough knowledge of these early stages. The following chapters, therefore, present a brief and schematic outline of mental development.

Conclusions concerning early mental life have been very slowly worked out from the material gained in the analysis of adult neurotics. Later these findings were confirmed through direct observation of children. The earliest years have necessarily remained most obscure. First, it is not always imperative to go back to the earliest period in order to analyze and cure a neurosis; second, it becomes increasingly difficult to grasp mental reactions the further one delves into periods in which there is as yet no language and in which many later separate functions are still undifferentiated from each other. Attempts to overcome these obstacles by the direct observation of infants are difficult before the development of speech; data gained in this way allow a variety of psychological interpretations. The temptation is great to apply concepts and ideas valid for higher stages of maturation to the behavior of young children. In fact it seems that this criticism applies to various psychoanalytic studies about the early phases of the ego. Few systematic observations of infants have as yet been undertaken from the standpoint of psychoanalysis (645, 671, 1300, 1301, 1302, 1303, 1596). Observations made by experimental psychologists have contributed much (134, 714); however, such research approaches the material chiefly in a way very different from that of psychoanalysis.

The analysis of psychotics with their regression to primitive ego phases greatly increases the knowledge of these earliest stages. Analysis of psychotics

does for the understanding of early mental development what analysis of neurotics with their return to infantile sexuality did for the understanding of the
infantile stages of sexuality. The psychoses are, of course, not the only states
where regressions of the ego are observable. In the healthy person, too, archaic
ego functions return under conditions of intoxication, exhaustion, and especially
in the states of falling alseep and awakening (726, 837, 1546).

THE EARLIEST STAGES

The mental functions represent a progressively more complicated apparatus
for the mastery of stimuli. Thus the earliest phases must be comprehended by
means of the expressions "excitation" and "relaxation," and only the later
phases can be characterized in more definite and differentiated terms.

The ego becomes differentiated under the influence of the external world.
Correspondingly, it can be said that the newborn infant has no ego. The human
infant is born more helpless than other mammals. He cannot live if he is not
cared for. Innumerable stimuli pour out upon him which he cannot master. He
is not in a position to move voluntarily and is not able to differentiate the en-
croaching stimuli. He knows no object world and has no ability yet to "bind"
tension. One can guess that he has no clear consciousness but has at most an undifferentiated sensitivity to pain and pleasure, to increase and decrease of tension.
Precisely the functions that later constitute the ego and consciousness are not yet
developed: the taking in of the external world (perception), the mastery of the
motor apparatus (motility), and the ability to bind tension by countercathexis.

Of course, even prior to the development of the ego there are reactions to
stimuli; the subsequent functions of the ego are carried out in an undifferentiated
manner by the organism as a whole.

The origin of the ego is not a homogeneous process. It begins with (or perhaps
even before) birth and is in a strict sense never completed. At birth, the organism
emerges out of a relatively quiet environment and enters an overwhelming state
of stimulation with a minimum of protection from stimuli. This flooding with
excitation without an adequate defense apparatus is, according to Freud, the
model for all later anxiety (618).

Probably this being flooded by excitation is highly unpleasant and evokes the
first mental tendency, namely, the tendency to get rid of the state of tension.
When the outside world succeeds in helping the infant cope with these stimuli
satisfactorily, he falls asleep. New stimuli, such as hunger, thirst, cold, awaken
him. The first traces of consciousness do not differentiate between ego and
nonego but rather between greater and lesser tension; at this time relaxation is
concomitant with loss of consciousness. If every need could be immediately taken
care of, a conception of reality would probably never develop.

THE FINDING OF OBJECTS AND THE CONSTITUTION OF THE EGO

The life of the infant alternates between hunger (cold and other disturbing stimuli) and sleep. Hunger (and disturbing stimuli) leads to a state of tension and thus to a tendency to get rid of the tension. It disappears with satiation, and sleep, a relative freedom from stimuli, sets in. The first signs of object representation must originate in the state of hunger. When more distinct beginnings of the later ego functions appear, the infant's grasping of the fact that something has to be done by the outside world in order to alleviate stimuli leads to the first longing toward objects. An object relationship of this primitive kind exists only as long as the object is absent. With its appearance, the longing disappears and sleep follows (425).

Before the establishment of this "first object" the infant is physically dependent on persons whose ministrations keep him alive. These persons, however, are not the infant's objects in a psychological sense, since he is not aware of the outside world but only of his own tension or relaxation. The first awareness of an object must come from a longing for something already familiar to the infant— something that has the ability to gratify needs but that is not present at the moment (507).

The first acceptance of reality is only an intermediary step on the road to getting rid of it. This is the point at which a contradiction of basic importance in human life arises, the contradiction between longing for complete relaxation and longing for objects (stimulus hunger). The striving for discharge and relaxation, the direct expression of the constancy principle, is necessarily the older mechanism. The fact that external objects brought about the desired state of relaxed satisfaction introduced the complication that objects became longed for; in the beginning, it is true, they were sought only as instruments which made themselves disappear again. The longing for objects thus began as a detour on the way to the goal of being rid of objects (of stimuli). This is probably meant when it is sometimes stated that hate is older than love. The truth is, however, that the first object relations are neither hate nor love but the still undifferentiated forerunner of both (79).

The origin of the ego and the origin of the sense of reality are but two aspects of one developmental step. This is inherent in the definition of the ego as that part of the mind which handles reality (295, 700). The concept of reality also creates the concept of ego. We are individuals inasmuch as we feel ourselves separate and distinct from others.

In the development of reality the conception of one's own body plays a very special role (608). At first there is only the perception of tension, that is, of an "inside something." Later, with the awareness that an object exists to quiet this tension, we have an "outside something." One's own body is both at the same time. Due to the simultaneous occurrence of both outer tactile and inner sensory data, one's own body becomes something apart from the rest of the world and thus the discerning of self from nonself is made possible. The sum of the mental representations of the body and its organs, the so-called body image, constitutes the idea of I and is of basic importance for the further formation of the ego (1372). The body image does not coincide with the objective body; for example, clothing or phantom extremities may be included within it (521, 1612).

> A compulsion neurotic patient was obsessively worried about his clothes which had to fit perfectly because otherwise he felt extremely distressed. He had a kind of hypochondriasis about clothes. It turned out that actually it was his physical well-being about which he was concerned. Something wrong with his clothes meant something wrong in his body. The clothes were included in his body image.

EARLY PERCEPTION AND PRIMARY IDENTIFICATION

The first state without any object representation is called primary narcissism (585). The first reactions to objects recognized as such contain much, integrated as a unit, which will later be further differentiated. These reactions are like reflexes; that is, every stimulus demands an immediate reaction, in accordance with the constancy principle. Stimulus intake and stimulus discharge, perception and motor reaction stand extraordinarily close together; they are inseparably interwoven. Primitive perception is precisely characterized by its closeness to motor reaction. One perceives by first changing one's body through the influence of the perceived object—and then taking cognizance of this bodily change. Many perceptions usually considered optic are really kinesthetic (379, 1456). Similarly, eidetic research has shown that primitive optic perceptions are bound up with motor reactions ready for discharge (83); the same is shown by the findings of the motor attitudes in hypnagogic and hypnopompic hallucinations (837).

The original connection between perception and motor action is also demonstrated by Freud in his paper, "A Note upon the Mystic Writing Pad" (615). He makes clear the activity in the function of perception. As long as intensive stimuli from the outside world flood the organism, the organism experiences this passively. The construction of a perception apparatus, coinciding with an apparatus protecting against too intense stimuli, brings about a change from passivity to activity. The perceptions take place rhythmically, obviously under the influence of centrifugal (motor) throbs of cathexes, which may be regarded as a first attempt at mastering the outside world. This is the basis for the differentiation of systems of perception and systems of memory (552), and the origin of a more differentiated consciousness. After the completion of this differentiation, the organism is in a position to protect itself against too much influx of stimuli by shutting off the function of perception (917). The newly formed ego can again sink back into the id. This ability can be observed in fainting and in the symptoms of traumatic neuroses. It is clearly the model for all later defense mechanisms and can be applied against internal pains as well as against displeasure of an external origin. Repression, too, may be looked upon as a specific blocking of the perception of particular instinctual demands. Another kind of return of the ego into the id takes place in sleep.

An important function of the ego is the phenomenon of fascination which Bernfeld described (130). A primitive attempt at the mastery of intense stimuli consists in the primitive ego's imitating that which is perceived. Apparently, perceiving and changing one's own body according to what is perceived were originally one and the same thing. Goldstein's patients with brain injury could compensate for their alexia by outlining the letters they saw with head movements, and then they could read by becoming aware of their kinesthetic sensations (704, 1476). This primitive imitation of that which is perceived is a kind of identification, the awareness of which brings perception.

Another primitive reaction to the first objects appears simpler and more comprehensible: the infant wants to put them into its mouth. It was hunger, repeatedly disturbing the peacefulness of sleep, which compelled the recognition of the outside world. The experience of satiation, which first banished this tension, then became the model for the mastery of external stimuli in general. The first reality is what one can swallow. Recognizing reality originally means to judge whether something helps to gain satisfaction or whether it raises tensions, whether one should swallow it or spit it out (616). Taking-into-the-mouth or spitting-out is the basis for all perception, and in conditions of regression one can observe that in the unconscious all sense organs are conceived as mouth-like (420, 430).

The primitive reactions of imitating what is perceived and the oral introjection of what is perceived belong close together. "Identification" in normal psychology and in psychopathology gives the impression, as Freud always emphasized (606, 608), of being a regression, a "secondary" identification, repeating an archaic "primary" one. The concept of a primary identification denotes that actually "putting into the mouth" and "imitation for perception's sake" are one and the same and represent the very first relation to objects. In this primary identification, instinctual behavior and ego behavior are not differentiated from each other. It is all one: the first (oral) object love, the first motor reaction to external stimuli, and the first perception (408). Identifications play a great part in the process of building up the subsequent ego, whose nature therefore depends on the personalities of the persons around the infant (cf. 101). The imitation of the external world by oral incorporation is also the basis for the primitive mode of thinking, called magic, to be discussed later.

This incorporation, which is the first reaction to objects in general and the precursor of the later sexual and destructive attitudes, in a psychological sense destroys the existence of the object. The attitude that the object exists only for the ego's satisfaction and may disappear once satisfaction is achieved can still be observed in some childish types of love. But the aim of the incorporation of objects does not necessarily reflect a subjective destructive tendency toward the object. This primary incorporation is the matrix of what later becomes love as well as destructive hate, but it is not yet either of these. An exaggerated desire to destroy, which actually appears in some children (and is not merely later projected back into childhood by manic-depressive patients), is not active in every infant sucking at the mother's breast. Certainly the existence of early infantile oral-destructive drives can be proved in pathological cases. The oral strivings of the normal infant do not contain such highly destructive aims and such correspondingly great fears of retaliation. Too, it must not be forgotten that incorporation is only secondarily destructive, its objectively destructive nature being used for subjective purposes; the first hostile strivings toward objects, which bring pain or hinder pleasure, is not to swallow them but to spit them out. It is also questionable whether the same object which once brought satisfaction and later refuses satisfaction is recognized as one and the same by the primitive ego; it is more likely that first there are different conceptions of a "good" object, which one wants to possess by swallowing, and a "bad" object, which one wants to spit out and only later wants to destroy by swallowing. It is a matter of definition whether primitive incorporation is designated "ambivalent" and the ambivalence of emotions thus described as "congenital." It is ambivalent in so far as elements of subsequent love and hate are contained in it; it is not ambivalent in so far as love and hate as opposites do not exist as yet (707). An urge to get satisfaction without consideration of the object (whereby the object may be destroyed) and an urge to destroy an object out of hate are not the same.

To return to the study of perception: The differences between the perceptions of infants and of adults have the consequence that they experience the world differently. Observations made on psychotics, who have regressed to primitive modes of perception, confirm the fact that they experience the world in a more vague and less differentiated way. Objects are not necessarily sharply distinguished from one another or from the ego or from parts of it. The first images are large in extent, all enveloping and inexact. They do not consist of elements that are later put together, but rather of units, wholes, which only later are recognized as containing different elements. Not only are perception and motility inseparable, but also the perceptions of many sense organs overlap. The more primitive senses, especially the kinesthetic sensations and the data of depth sensibility (proprioception) prevail.

Besides the form of infantile perception, the contents that are perceived are also different. Hermann called perceptions "which the small child possesses, but which later disappear for inner or external reasons," primal perceptions (778). The different nature of these primal perceptions is partly due to the biological characteristics of the child. The world appears to the child in quite another perspective due to his small size and to his different experience of space (134, 1147). To a greater part the characteristics of archaic perception result from its "unobjective" character, its emotional nature. The world is perceived according to the instincts as a possible source of satisfaction or as a possible threat; instinctual wishes and fears falsify reality. A more objective perception presupposes a certain psychological distance of the perceiving ego from the data of perception, a judgment about the sources of the experienced sensations and, more than that, a *correct* judgment, an ability for differential learning, whereas the primitive experiences are felt as still undifferentiated wholes which make their appearance repeatedly. The pleasure principle, that is, the need for immediate discharge, is incompatible with correct judgment, which is based on consideration and postponement of the reaction. The time and energy saved by this postponement are used in the function of judgment. In the early states the weak ego has not yet learned to postpone anything (575).

OMNIPOTENCE AND SELF-ESTEEM

The primitive ego, in contrast to the more differentiated ego, is considered weak, that is, powerless in relation to its own instincts as well as to the outside world. But since the psychological separation of the ego from the external world is still incomplete, through comprehending the outside world or parts of it within itself, the ego comes to feel itself omnipotent. Ferenczi spoke of a first unlimited omnipotence, which persists as long as no conception of objects exists. It becomes limited through the experiencing of excitation which cannot be mastered and which leads to un-co-ordinated discharge movements. When these are understood by the environment to be a signal calling for a change in the situation, the child may experience this train of events as an "omnipotence of movements" (457).

The separation of the ego from the external world is not a sudden but a gradual process.

It is, of course, also a heterogenous process, since ego-forming encounters with reality and with one's own body occur in connection with manifold needs. The subsequent ego, therefore, has manifold "nuclei" (694, 695). A final ego is formed by a synthetic integration of these nuclei, and in certain states of ego regression a split of the ego into its original nuclei becomes observable.

There always remain certain traces of the original objectless condition (878), or at least a longing for it ("oceanic feeling") (622). Introjection is an attempt to make parts of the external world flow into the ego. Projection, by putting unpleasant sensations into the external world, also attempts to reverse the separation of ego from nonego. There is a stage in development in which anything unpleasant is considered nonego, anything pleasant is considered ego, which Freud called the purified pleasure ego (588). The most primitive method of getting rid of pain was to "hallucinate it away," a method that quickly breaks down in the face of reality. Then the young organism tries to join pleasurable stimuli to the ego and unpleasurable ones to the nonego. In later life, traces of this phase are manifested in persons who without question acknowledge any pleasurable body sensations as "their own" but reproach aching organs as if they did not belong to them. Many other traces persist from the "transitivistic" world in general. An example of this is presented by the child who when playing hide-and-go-seek closes his eyes and believes he now cannot be seen. The archaic animistic conception of the world which is based on a confusion of ego and non-ego is thus illustrated; it is a kind of reverse identification. The outside world is perceived as having the ego's characteristics, just as in primary identification the ego is perceived as having the object's characteristics (265, 712, 802).

When the child is forced through experiences to renounce his belief in his omnipotence, he considers the adults who have now become independent objects to be omnipotent, and tries by introjection to share their omnipotence again. Certain narcissistic feelings of well-being are characterized by the fact that they are felt as a reunion with an omnipotent force in the external world, brought about either by incorporating parts of this world or by the fantasy of being incorporated by it ("secondary narcissism") (608). Religious ecstasy, patriotism, and similar feelings are characterized by the ego's participation in something unattainably high. Many social phenomena are rooted in the "omnipotents'" promise to the powerless of the desired passive participation on condition of their fulfillment of certain rules.

The individual's experiences connected with omnipotence lead to a most significant need of the human mind. The longing for the oceanic feeling of primary narcissism can be called the "narcissistic need." "Self-esteem" is the awareness of how close the individual is to the original omnipotence (1238).

The primitive methods of the regulation of self-esteem arise from the fact that the first longing for objects has the character of a longing for the removal of disturbing displeasure, and that the satisfaction by the object removes the object itself and revives the narcissistic state. The longing for the return of omnipotence and the longing for the removal of instinctual tension are not yet differentiated from each other. If one succeeds in getting rid of an unpleasant stimulus, one's self-esteem is again restored. The first supply of satisfaction from the external world, the supply of nourishment, is simultaneously the first regulator of self-esteem.

The tendency to participate in the adult's omnipotence after the renunciation of one's own differentiates itself from the desire for the satisfaction of hunger. Every token of love from the more powerful adult, then, has the same effect as the supply of milk had on the infant. The small child loses self-esteem when he loses love and attains it when he regains love. That is what makes children *educable*. They need supplies of affection so badly that they are ready to renounce other satisfactions if rewards of affection are promised or if withdrawal of affection is threatened. The promise of necessary narcissistic supplies of affection under the condition of obedience and the threat of withdrawal of these supplies if the conditions are not fulfilled are the weapons of any authority (427, 436).

Subsequently narcissistic and sexual needs become differentiated; sexual needs develop in the relationship to objects, narcissistic ones more in the relationship between ego and superego. Every feeling of guilt lowers self-esteem; every fulfillment of ideals raises it. But since, as in all mental development, the old and primitive remain underneath the new, so a part of the relationship to objects remains governed by the needs of self-esteem. This is best studied in persons who are fixated at this level. They need a narcissistic supply from the outside in order to maintain their self-esteem. Among such persons there are innumerable subtypes. There are aggressive types who want to procure by force the essentials that the wicked outside world withholds, and there are types who try to avoid force and instead seek the essential supplies by submissiveness and demonstration of suffering. Many persons try both methods simultaneously.

The fact that erotic and narcissistic needs compel the child to ask for affection, and the imperative character of this longing, allows us to speak of a passive object love in small children. The child wants to get something from the object without returning anything. The object is as yet no personality but an instrument for providing satisfaction (73).

The stage of primary narcissism, in which omnipotence was felt and "mastery" was no problem yet, is thus followed by a period of passive-receptive mastery in which difficulties are overcome by influencing powerful external objects to give what is needed. Whenever the subsequent active types of mastery fail or do not offer any hope of success, a temptation is at hand to fall back to the state of passive-receptive mastery.

THE DEVELOPMENT OF MOTILITY AND ACTIVE MASTERY

The development of active mastery is a long and complicated process. The mastery of the motor apparatus, too, is a task that the human infant only gradually learns in constant connection with the maturation of the sensory apparatus. It is, from a psychological point of view, a gradual substituting of actions for mere discharge reactions. This is achieved through the interposing of a time period between stimulus and reaction, by the acquisition of a certain tension tolerance, that is, of an ability to bind primitive reaction impulses by counter-cathexes (575). The prerequisite for an action is, besides mastery of the bodily apparatus, the development of the function of judgment. This means the ability to anticipate the future in the imagination by "testing" reality, by trying in an active manner and in a small dosage what might happen to one passively and in an unknown dosage. This type of functioning is in general characteristic of the ego.

Learning to walk, to be clean, and to speak are the main steps in the development of the mastery of physical motor functions. Walking and control of the sphincters form the foundation of the child's independence; these abilities help to develop the reality principle (575) and to overcome receptive dependence and the necessity for immediate discharge. The faculty of speech changes the anticipating functions of the ego; the establishment of name symbols for things consolidates consciousness and gives the possibility of anticipating events in the model world of words. The ability to judge reality and the ability to tolerate tensions are two aspects of one and the same faculty. To direct one's actions according to external necessity means to be able to foresee dangers and to fight or avoid them.

ANXIETY

The biological helplessness of the human infant brings him necessarily into states of painful high tension. States in which the organism is flooded by amounts of excitation beyond its capacity to master are called traumatic states (605). The pain of the unavoidable early traumatic states, still undifferentiated and therefore not yet identical with later definite affects, is the common root of different later affects, certainly also of anxiety. The sensations of this "primary anxiety" can be looked upon partly as the way in which the tension makes itself felt and partly as the perception of involuntary vegetative emergency discharges (690, 993). Freud suggested that the act of being born might be considered as an experience in which the syndrome of this primary anxiety is established. He had found that the apparently meaningless syndromes of hysterical attacks are historically determined—that is, that they had been purposeful in a certain situation in the past—and his hypothesis was based on the idea that normal affects might have a historical origin in an analogous way (596). Certainly this primary anxiety is in no way created actively by the ego; it is created by external and internal stimuli, still unmastered, and in so far as it is experienced as a conscious painful feeling, it is experienced passively, as something that occurs to the ego and has to be endured (431, 714).

In later life, experiences that are comparable to primary anxiety occur in persons who have to endure traumatic events. Uncontrollable spells of overwhelming anxiety, felt as something terrible that floods a helpless personality, form a typical symptom of traumatic neuroses. A similar type of anxiety is felt when sexual (and perhaps also aggressive) excitement is not permitted to take its normal course. Thus it becomes probable that traumatic anxiety or panic is dynamically the same thing as primary anxiety—the way in which an insufficiency of mastery, a state of being flooded with excitation, is passively and automatically felt.

When the child learns to control his motility, purposeful actions gradually take the place of mere discharge reactions; the child can now prolong the time between stimulus and reaction and achieve a certain tolerance of tension. The characteristic capacity for "trying out" that is thus acquired changes the ego's relation to its affects. Affects are originally archaic discharge syndromes that supplant voluntary actions under certain exciting conditions. Now the growing ego learns to "tame" affects and to use them for its own anticipating purposes (440). This holds true also for anxiety (618).

With anticipatory imagination and the resultant planning of suitable later actions, the idea of danger comes into being. The judging ego declares that a situation that is not yet traumatic might become so. This judgment obviously sets up conditions that are similar to those created by the traumatic situation itself, but much less intense. This, too, is experienced by the ego as anxiety. However, how different is this fear as compared with the original panic! Instead of an overwhelming spell of anxiety, a more or less moderate fear is experienced, which is utilized as a signal or protective measure. This anxiety is an anticipation of what might happen (618). The purposeful components which appear in anxiety in the face of danger are to be accredited to the judging ego; the unpurposeful components, like the possibility of paralysis, are due to the fact that the ego does not produce the anxiety but only uses it; it has no better means at its disposal (1485).

A complication that occurs in neurotic anxiety will be met with often in the following chapters. Sometimes the expectation of danger, instead of precipitating a purposeful fear that might be used to avoid a traumatic state, precipitates a traumatic state itself. The ego's judgment "danger ahead!" is followed by an overwhelming panic; the ego called forth something it cannot control. The attempt at taming anxiety has failed, and the original wild panic recurs and overwhelms the ego. This happens if the whole organism is in a state of tension which could be described as a latent readiness for the development of panic. The ego's judgment of danger then has the effect of a match in a powder barrel. The intention of lighting the match as a signal fails because it frees a vast power, incomparably mightier than the limited powers of the force that tried to use the match (see p. 133).

The content of the primitive ego's ideas of anxiety is determined in part directly by its biological nature and in part indirectly by its animistic ways of thinking, which make the ego believe that its environment has the same instinctual aims as it has itself (combined with much more power). In these animistic misunderstandings the primitive talion principle is at work, according to which any deed may be undone (or must be punished) by a similar deed inflicted on the original doer.

The most fundamental anxiety is apparently connected with the infant's physiological inability to satisfy his drives himself. The first fear is the (wordless) fear of the experience of further traumatic states. The idea that one's own instinctual demands might be dangerous (which is the ultimate basis of all psychoneuroses) is rooted in this fear.

> However, this does not mean that the ego is hostile to instinctual impulses from the very beginning or always in fear of being overrun by too intense inner strivings. Since the ego learns to master and actively to satisfy its impulses, it would not need to produce an anxiety of this kind after having achieved this ability, and normal adults actually do not fear their impulses. Certain neurotics who are still afraid of the experience of their own excitement, at least beyond a certain intensity of this excitement, are so not because of a primary "anxiety of the intensity of their own excitement" (541) but because other types of anxiety have caused them to block the natural course of their excitements, turning pleasure secondarily into an intense displeasure (431, 1522) (*see* pp. 543 f.).

This leads sooner or later to the fear that external means of satisfaction might possibly fail to arrive. It is the "fear over loss of love" or rather loss of help and protection. This fear is more intense than it would be if it represented only a rational judgment about real danger because the early self-esteem is regulated by means of external supplies so that a loss of help and protection means also a loss of self-esteem. An ego that is loved feels strong, a deserted one weak and exposed to danger. An ego that is loved fears the possibility of being deserted.

The animistic way of thinking and feeling complicates matters. If a child fantasies devouring his environment and then meets a rebuff, he fantasies that he might be eaten by the parents. In this way do fantastic anxieties of physical destruction originate. The most important representative of this group is castration anxiety, which eventually becomes the main motive for the defense activities of the ego (1417).

The ways by which the normal ego learns to overcome its early and still untamed anxieties is very characteristic. Whenever the organism is flooded with a very large quantity of excitation it attempts to get rid of it by subsequent active repetitions of the situation that induced the excessive excitation. This takes place in the early games of little children (605, 1552) and in their dreams as well (722). Between the original flood of excitation and these repetitions there is one fundamental difference: in the original experience the organism was passive; in the case of the repetitions, the organism is active and determines the time and degree of excitation. At first the passive experiences that aroused anxiety are reproduced actively by the child in his play in order to achieve a belated mastery. Later on, the child in his play not only dramatizes the exciting experiences of the past but he also anticipates what he expects to happen in the future. The use of fear as a signal is but one example of the purposeful use of this anticipation.

When the child discovers that he is now able to overcome without fear a situation that formerly would have overwhelmed him with anxiety, he experiences a certain kind of pleasure. This pleasure has the character of "I need not feel anxiety any more." It makes the child's play evolve from mere attempts at discharge to mastery of the external world by means of repeated practice. "Functional pleasure" is pleasure in the fact that the exercise of a function is now possible without anxiety (984), rather than the gratification of one specific type of instinct (766, 767, 768). It is the same pleasure that makes children enjoy the endless repetitions of the same game or of the same story, which has to be told in exactly the same words (1457).

Economically, this pleasure can be explained in the following way. An expenditure of energy is associated with the anxiety or the fearful expectation felt by a person who is uncertain whether he will be able to master an expected excitation. The sudden cessation of this expenditure brings its relieving discharge which is experienced by the successful ego as a "triumph" (436) and enjoyed as functional pleasure. Usually the pleasure originating from this source is condensed with an erogenous pleasure which again has become possible due to the overcoming of anxiety. When a child is tossed in the air by an adult and caught, he feels undoubtedly on the one hand erogenous pleasure in equilibrium (and cutaneous) sensations, and on the other hand pleasure due to an overcoming of the fear of falling. If he is certain that he will not be dropped, he can take pleasure in having thought he might have been dropped; he may shudder a little, but then he realizes that this fear was unnecessary. To make this pleasure possible, conditions of reassurance must be fulfilled. The child must have confidence in the adult who is playing with him and the height must not be too great. Thus in time real learning through practice occurs. When repeated experience has shown that the fear was groundless, the child becomes more courageous (423).

Both anxiety and functional pleasure disappear when the ego is sure of itself and no longer holds an anxious expectation in readiness. Adults no longer enjoy any special pleasure when they engage in long-familiar and automatic activities which made them very proud when first accomplished in their childhood (527, 530).

In neurotics, however, a pathogenic defense may perpetuate childhood fears. The anxieties remain effective, for the most part blocking the "dangerous" activities entirely; sometimes, however, the ways of fighting anxiety are repeated, too, and the ego may experience a "functional pleasure" of overcoming the fear by repetitions of the feared activity (435) (*see* pp. 480 ff.).

THINKING AND THE DEVELOPMENT OF THE SENSE OF REALITY

The ability to recognize, to love, and to fear reality is developed in general before the learning of speech. But it is the faculty of speech that initiates a further decisive step in the development of reality testing. Words allow for a more precise communication with objects, and also for making more precise the anticipation by trial actions. This anticipation of action now becomes thinking proper and consolidates consciousness finally (590). Of course there already had existed a consciousness without words, which can be observed later in regressive states as "preconscious fantasy thinking" (1426, 1545, 1546, 1547). But this is merely the undifferentiated predecessor of thinking, in which all characteristics of the primitive ego are still to be seen, such as wide scope of concepts, similarities taken as identities, parts as wholes, and in which the concepts are based on common motor reactions. Schilder has shown that every single thought before formulation, has gone through a prior wordless state (1363).

The acquisition of the faculty of speech, of the understanding that certain noises are used as symbols for things, and of the gradual capacity for rational use of this faculty and understanding (252, 1452, 1453; *cf. also* 1450) is a decisive step in the formation of the ego. The ways by which the ego proceeds from integrated to differentiated, from whole units to constituent elements, from large scope to narrow confines, can be investigated with the help of studies of the phenomena of aphasia.

Tying up words and ideas makes thinking proper possible. The ego has now a better weapon in handling the external world as well as its own excitations. This is the rational content of the ancient magical belief that one can master what one can name. The striving for mastery of instinctual drives in this way doubtless adds to intellectual development. A shift from emotional fantasy to sober reality takes place which serves the purpose of combating anxiety. A pathological distortion of this is the flight of the compulsive character from all emotion to the shadowy world of words and concepts (*see* p. 295). The lofty intellectual interests that make their appearance at puberty also serve to master the instinctual excitement of that period (541).

The achievement of the faculty of speech is experienced as the acquisition of a great power. It turns the "omnipotence of thought" into an "omnipotence of words" (457). The child's earliest speech is a charm directed toward forcing the external world and fate to do those things that have been conjured up in words.

Certain words retain their original magical power, for example obscene words (451), oaths, solemn formulae, or poetry (*see* p. 000).

Thinking itself is a further elaboration and differentiation of the more primitive types of judgment which distinguished between what can be swallowed and what is better spit out, and, subsequently, between harmless and dangerous things; reaction, again, is postponed, and this postponement occurs by means of trial acting; the movements necessary for the planned action are done on a small scale, by which what is planned and its consequences are "tasted." Muscular actions accompanying thinking have been demonstrated by experimental psychology (482, 776).

The working principle of the ego generally consists in a retardation of automatic id functions which provides the possibility of using these functions purposefully and in an organized way. In the same way that primary anxiety later is "tamed" and reduced to an "anxiety signal," so does the ego in the process of thinking tame two archaic automatic reactions: the drive to discharge tensions, which is slowed down, and the tendency to hallucinatory wish fulfillment, which is reduced to the imagination of the prospective events and subsequently of the abstract symbols of these events.

Just as the taming of anxiety may fail and the signal may start a recurrence of the primary panic, the tendencies to discharge at all costs and the hallucinatory wish fulfillment may come back in thinking. If persons are tired, asleep, intoxicated or psychotic, they think in another and more primitive way; and even in healthy, good thinkers who are wide-awake, every single thought runs through initial phases that have more similarity with dream thinking than with logic (1363). The characteristics of this prelogical emotional thinking have been investigated in detail by both analytic and nonanalytic psychologists (1545, 1546, 1547). It is less fitted for objective judgment as to what is going to happen because it is relatively unorganized, tolerates and condenses contradictions and is ruled by emotions and hence full of wishful or fearful misconceptions. This thinking according to the primary process seems to be directed only by the striving for discharge and is remote from any logic. But it is thinking nevertheless, because it consists of imaginations according to which later actions are performed, and it is done with reduced energy. It is carried out more through pictorial, concrete images, whereas the secondary process is based more on words. The retranslation of words into pictures in dreams and in fatigue is well known. Preconscious pictorial thinking is a magical type of thinking (916, 1047). The object and the idea of the object, the object and a picture or model of the object, the object and a part of the object are equated; similarities are not distinguished from identities; ego and nonego are not yet separated (1104). What happens to objects might (by identification) be experienced as happening to the ego, and what happens to the ego causes the same thing to happen to the object, a "transitivism" which makes the technique of "magical gestures" possible: by making a gesture someone forces another person to do the same thing.

> If a person feels ashamed, he looks away or covers his eyes with his hand; this means: "Nobody is to look at me." Children believe that they cannot be seen if they cannot see. One child had the idea that when the conductor closes his eyes, the train passes through a tunnel.

Another strange characteristic of archaic thinking is represented by symbolism. In adults a conscious idea may be used as a symbol for the purpose of hiding an objectionable unconscious idea; the idea of a penis may be represented by a snake, an ape, a hat, an airplane, if the idea of penis is objectionable. The symbol is conscious, the symbolized idea is unconscious. The distinct idea of a penis had been grasped but rejected. However, symbolic thinking is vague, directed by the primary process. It is not only a method of distortion; it is also a part of the primal prelogical thinking. Again, the censoring ego uses regressive methods. Again, when distorting through symbolism, the ego in its defensive activities makes use of mechanisms that previously operated automatically without any intent. The use of symbols is a falling back into an earlier primary stage of thinking, by means of which intended distortions are brought about. In dreams, symbols appear in both aspects, as a tool of the dream censorship and also as a characteristic of archaic pictorial thinking, as a part of visualizing abstract thoughts (552, 596).

The regressive nature of symbolic distortions explains two facts: (a) that the symbols, being a residual of an archaic way of perceiving the world, are common to all human beings, like affective syndromes; (b) that symbolic thinking occurs not only where distortions have to be made but also in states of fatigue, sleep, psychosis, and generally in early childhood, that is, in all states where archaic ego characteristics are in the foreground.

Silberer explained symbolism as an "apperceptive insufficiency of the ego" (1427, 1428, 1429, 1430). He certainly was right, although his superficial classification of symbols according to the cause of this insufficiency cannot be accepted. Jones is not convincing in his statement that retracing symbolism to insufficient apperception is like retracing slips of the tongue to fatigue (882). Slips of the tongue are not an essential part of the state of fatigue (they are only precipitated by this state), whereas it is an essential part of archaic thinking with insufficient apperception to experience the world in symbols. However, archaic symbolism as a part of prelogical thinking and distortion by means of representing a repressed idea through a conscious symbol are not the same. Whereas in distortion the idea of penis is avoided through disguising it by the idea of snake, in prelogical thinking penis and snake are one and the same; that is, they are perceived by a common conception: the sight of the snake provokes penis emotions; and this fact is later utilized when the conscious idea of snake replaces the unconscious one of penis.

Primitive symbolism is a part of the way in which conceptions are formed in prelogical thinking: comprehension of the world radiates from instinctual demands and fears, so that the first objects are possible means of gratification or possible threats; stimuli that provoke the same reactions are looked upon as identical; and the first ideas are not sums built up out of distinct elements but wholes comprehended in a still undifferentiated way, united by the emotional responses they have provoked.

These characteristics suffice to explain some of the common symbols, namely, the symbols based on similarity, on *pars pro toto* or on identity of the provoked responses, such as tools = penis, shell = vagina, but also departure = death, riding = sexual intercourse, king = father. In other cases the similarity of the provoked reactions is not obvious, but it can be found by an exact analysis of the child's emotional experiences (460). In this way the symbolic equation money = feces can be explained (*see* p. 281). However, in still other cases the connection between symbol and what is symbolized is not understood. The children who dream about spiders and mean cruel mothers (23) do not know anything about the spider's sexual characteristics. Ferenczi believed that the disgust reaction toward reptiles contains a kind of phylogenetic memory (497) and Freud was inclined toward similar speculations in this respect (632). This question must remain open.

The fact that the earliest thinking is not in accordance with reality but has all the archaic and magical features that have been described might be used as an objection to the statement that it, too, is "preparation" and an attempt to master reality. But the inadequacy of this type of thinking does not contradict the fact that it is relatively more adequate than immediate discharge and wish-fulfilling hallucinations.

However, this anticipation becomes incomparably more adequate through the development of words. The faculty of speech changes this prethinking into a logical, organized, and more adjusted thinking which follows the secondary process. Thus it is a decisive step toward the final differentiation of conscious and unconscious and toward the reality principle (575, 590).

Yet even after speech, logic, and the reality principle have been established we find that prelogical thinking is still in operation and even beyond the role it plays in states of ego regression or as a form of purposeful distortion. It no longer fulfills, it is true, the function of preparing for future actions but becomes, rather, a *substitute* for unpleasant reality.

The first ideas of objects came into being when a remembered gratification was missing. The first ideas about objects were both a substitute for the missing real object and attempts to master the real object magically. Primitive thinking attempted to control the object in a magical way (which, at that time, was believed to be real). The secondary type of thinking strives to control it in a real way. But when this real way fails, when reality is too unpleasant or one is unable to influence it, one regresses again to the magical method. In the older child and the adult, the two types of thinking have the two different functions of preparation for reality (anticipation of what is probable) and of substitution for reality (anticipation of what is desirable).

This co-ordination of types of thinking with different functions is valid in general only. Practically there are certain ways of returning from daydreaming to reality (art) as well as of using word thinking for withdrawal from reality (compulsive thinking).

As long as thinking is not followed by action it is called fantasy. There are two types of fantasy: creative fantasy, which prepares some later action, and daydreaming fantasy, the refuge for wishes that cannot be fulfilled. The former, rooted in the unconscious, certainly also starts in the primary process and imagination, but develops out of this sphere. The latter becomes a real substitute for action in the state of "introversion," when the "small" movements accompanying fantasy become intense enough to bring discharge. The problem has been discussed whether military games in boyhood increase or decrease belligerent tendencies. Does fantasy stimulate the wish so that the tendency to realize fantasied ideas increases, or does fantasy channelize the wish so that what has been satisfied in games no longer needs to be satisfied in earnest? The answer becomes obvious in the case of sexual fantasies. If a man merely anticipates in fantasy prospective sexual intercourse, his tension and his longing for fulfillment increase; but if his fantasies stimulate him to masturbation, the tension decreases or vanishes. A preparatory fantasy has regressed to the substitute type.

Neurotics are persons whose real actions are blocked. There are two ways of expressing this blocking which demonstrate very well the contrast between magical pictorial daydreaming and abstract preparatory thinking. The hysterical type regresses from action to unworded daydreaming; his conversion symptoms are substitutes for actions. The compulsive type regresses from action to the preparation for action through words; his thinking is a kind of eternal preparation for actions that never are performed.

It might perhaps be expected that one remains in direct contact with reality as long as one's thinking remains concrete, but that thinking ceases to serve as a preparation for real actions when it becomes too abstract, when it operates with sophistry and classification rather than with symbols for objects. This is true, but only to a certain degree. The pictorial nature of the elements of certain "concrete" thoughts may start daydreams instead of preparatory thinking.

Logical thinking presupposes a strong ego that is capable of postponements, tolerant of tensions, rich in countercathexes, and ready to judge reality according to its experience. If the ego is weak or tired or asleep or without confidence in its own ability and desirous of a receptive type of mastery, then the pictorial type of thinking becomes more attractive than objective intelligence. It is understandable that tired persons prefer the movies to Shakespeare and an illustrated magazine to difficult reading, that dissatisfied persons without any possibility of actively influencing their situation ask for more illustrations in newspapers or for comic strips rather than for difficult intellectual pursuits. Whenever reality becomes unpleasant, more pictorial daydream substitutes are sought.

DEFENSES AGAINST IMPULSES

Up to now the reality principle appeared as the ability to postpone the final reaction. But certain reactions not only have to be postponed but even curtailed more or less permanently. Simultaneously with the increasing mastery of motility—that is, with the change of mere discharge movements into actions—a nondischarge apparatus, a defense apparatus, also is developed. The ego learns to ward off impulses that are either dangerous or inappropriate. Mechanisms that first were used against painful external stimuli now become turned against inner drives.

The ego wants to be satisfied. It seems paradoxical that it frequently turns against its own instinctual demands. Causes that bring about such a paradox have already been mentioned. They are:

1. The biological fact that the infant is not able to control his motor apparatus and that he therefore requires external help to satisfy his instinctual demands leads to the consequence that he slips into traumatic situations, since the outside world cannot always immediately be at hand. The temporary disappearance of primary objects has in itself a traumatic effect because the child's tender longings become deprived of their possibility of discharge. The memory of painful experiences of this kind leads to the first impression that instinctual excitations may be a source of danger.

2. Threats and prohibitions from the external world create fear of instinctual acts and their consequences. Such external influences may be of two somewhat different types: (a) objective and natural ones—the fire will burn the child who instinctively grasps at it—or (b) the dangers may be artificially produced by educational measures. Voluntarily or involuntarily, adults give children the impression that instinctual behavior is to be decried and that abstinence is praiseworthy. The effectiveness of these impressions is due not only to the adult's real physical power but also to the dependency of the child's self-esteem upon getting affection.

3. The dangers feared may be entirely fantastic, in so far as the world is "projectively misunderstood" by the child. The violent force of his own repressed impulses is projected and makes him expect drastic punishments; the expected punishment is a retaliatory damage to the "sinful" parts of the body.

4. Later on a fourth factor comes into being through the ego's dependence on the superego, which is an intrapsychic representative of the objective, educational, and projectively misunderstood external world. This fourth factor turns anxiety into guilt feeling.

This systematic outline gives an answer to the problem of how forces that are hostile to the discharge of instinctual impulses originate.

FURTHER REMARKS ABOUT ADAPTATION AND REALITY SENSE

It is true that psychoanalysis has studied the defensive aspect of the ego more thoroughly than the development of its positive forces of adaptation (762). However, the ideas of defense and of adaptation are interwoven. Adaptation in a dynamic sense means finding common solutions for the tasks represented by inner impulses and outer (inhibiting and threatening) stimuli.

Hartmann, in a very interesting paper, tried to show that adaptation has been studied by psychoanalysts too much from the point of view of mental conflicts. He points out that there is also a "sphere without conflict," originating, it is true, in antitheses between organism and environment (750).

Because of the importance of these antitheses, the term sphere without conflict seems misleading, as tending toward an undynamic point of view. The ego's maturation is a result of the continuous interplay of the organism's needs and the environmental influences. Certainly the active types of mastery are rather complicated processes, many details of which still have to be investigated; but in the main it is understood how perception and motility are developed in connection with instinctual needs and with the functions of judgment and thinking (1176).

A field where the study of adaptation is especially fruitful is the psychology of will or desire. Biological needs are molded and modified through evaluations of the ego (or by influence of the superego); and just how these modifications occur, how subjective values are created by the influence of systems of values handed down by tradition, is one of the points clarified by individual psychoanalyses.

Constitutional factors as well as experience determine how far the development of the sense of reality succeeds, how far the primal, vague, magical, fear-ridden world based on projections and introjections becomes an objectively judged "real" world, responded to by the individual's alloplastic forces and uninfluenced by hopes and fears, and how far the old forms persist. It never succeeds entirely. Objective reality is differently experienced by different individuals. Laforgue had this in mind when talking about the relativity of reality (1003, 1004). In neurotics all the misjudgings of reality and all the inability to differential learning (which cause outer events to be experienced as repetitions of a few patterns only and which are characteristic for the archaic ego) make their appearance again.

Behind all active types of mastery of external and internal tasks, a readiness remains to fall back to passive-receptive types of mastery; this readiness has a very different intensity in various individuals as well as under various cultural conditions.

The sociological significance of the types of mastery that are encouraged or discouraged by various historically determined institutions was stressed by Kardiner in his promising earlier writings (918, 919, 920). Later, however, he felt that the social determination of the predominance of certain ego types in given cultures was incompatible with Freud's ideas about instincts (921).

The development of the ego and of the id does not occur separately but is interwoven, the one influencing the other. But before describing the development of the id, two concepts of fundamental importance to the psychology of the neuroses must be discussed: fixation and regression.

In mental development, earlier levels still persist along with or underneath higher levels. Constitutional or experiential factors may cause this to become more transparent. In ego fixations or ego regressions an earlier level of ego development persists or returns, which may mean various things. It may refer to isolated ego functions which retain or again take on certain features of a more primitive phase. In this sense the eidetic types may be designated as perception fixations. Thinking may have retained a more magical character than in normal persons, as in compulsion neurotics, where early overdeveloped intellect is to be seen simultaneously with superstition and with unconscious belief in omnipotence and in the law of retaliation. The relationships to objects may show primitive features. There may be fixations at the earlier love levels, with aims of incorporation, or at the types of self-esteem regulation characteristic of small children. Finally the ego fixation may limit itself to a repetitious use of specific types of defense (429) (*see* pp. 523 ff.).

Chapter V

EARLY MENTAL DEVELOPMENT (*CONTINUED*): DEVELOPMENT OF INSTINCTS, INFANTILE SEXUALITY

WHAT ARE INSTINCTS?

FREUD suggested that two kinds of excitation should be distinguished: one that is evoked by external, perceptual, discontinuous stimuli and another that arises from continuous instinctual stimuli within the organism (971).

This statement, however, deserves more detailed consideration. All perceptions, all sensory stimuli, whether they originate without or within the organism, have a "provocative character," provoke a certain urge to action. In the archaic types of perception this connection with motility, as has been pointed out, is more distinct than it is later. The intensity of the urge varies with the variable physical states of the body. Food has a variable meaning for the individual, depending on whether he is hungry or satiated; this also holds true for sexual stimuli. Only the physical conditions that determine the urge, the chemistry of the body, and not the sensory stimuli can rightly be called the sources of instincts. A certain impulse to action arises from every perception, whether it be internal or external. Under specific somatic conditions these impulses take on the character of urgent instinctual drives (1023, 1024).

At first glance one finds many contradictory presentations of the essence of the instincts both in Freud's writings and in psychoanalytic literature in general. First, instinct is explained as "the measure of the demand made upon the mind in consequence of its connection with the body" (588); an urgent state of tension, caused chemically and manifested through a sensory stimulus, is to be discharged. This concept is very illuminating since it is consonant with the reflex pattern as the basis for all mental functions, and it is clearly this concept of instincts that has enabled psychoanalysis to rest on a biological basis (555). In the same passage, Freud calls instinct "a borderline concept between the mental and the physical" (588); phenomena of instincts can be considered from the physical aspect by examining the source of instinct, or they can be considered from the mental aspect by examining the drive and the resultant psychological phenomena. At another place, instincts are called "mystical forces" whose mode of operation we investigate without knowing anything about their existence (628). That sounds strange since psychoanalysis tries to eliminate everything mystical. What is meant is that we are aware of the experience of instinctual impulses and actions but never of "the instinct." What constitutes the unity of "one instinct" is highly debatable. The definition will vary according to the classification applied, that is, according to whether aim, object, or source is made the main criterion. It is therefore necessary to define these concepts.

The *aim* of an instinct is its satisfaction or, more precisely, the very specific discharge action which dispels the physical condition of excitement and thus brings about satisfaction. The *object* of an instinct is that instrument by which or through which the instinct can attain its aim. The *source* of an instinct is the chemicophysical status which causes a sensory stimulus to bring about excitement (588). What instincts are to be distinguished and how many depends on whether the aim, the object, or the source is chosen as the basis of classification. In terms of aim or object an infinite number of instincts might be described. However, psychoanalysts know how readily interchangeable objects and aims can be. (This very fact makes it paradoxical to attribute to Freud the opinion that "instincts" represent entirely unchanging rigid patterns [1105].) Thus a classification according to source would be the preferable one. Unfortunately, physiology here disappoints us; the instinctual sources are a purely physiological problem, and in this field our knowledge is not yet sufficient. In spite of this deficiency two categories of instincts are definitely discernible.

The first category is represented by certain simple physical needs which, incidentally, present the best model for the course of an instinct: somatic changes cause certain urgent sensory experiences; the urge precipitates a specific action which eliminates the somatic change and relaxation is felt. The character of drive becomes especially apparent when the normal course is hindered. Examples are breathing, hunger, thirst, defecation, urination. Since the satisfaction of these urges is vital, the actions can be postponed for a short time only and their aims cannot be altered. Consequently there is hardly any variability in these needs and for psychology they are of relatively minor importance. The assumption that it is the lowering of the excitation level—relaxation—that is experienced by the ego as pleasure can be easily verified with these instincts.

Recognition of the second group as a cohesive unit was made possible only by psychoanalytic research (555). This is the group of the sexual instincts. In contradistinction to the imperative instincts discussed above, the sexual instincts, if they cannot find gratification in their original form, have the capacity to change, to alter their objects or aims, or to submit to repression by the ego and then to make themselves apparent again in various ways and in different disguises. The widely circulated reproach is still heard that Freud explains everything as sexual. This is far from correct, for Freud recognizes other instincts besides sexual ones. But it is true that Freud explains as sexual many phenomena which had previously not been recognized as having any connection with sexuality— in particular, the neuroses. He recognizes that human sexuality is by no means limited to the impulses and actions that lead more or less directly to sexual intercourse. He recognizes the field of *infantile sexuality* (550, 551, 552, 555).

It is generally known today that children exhibit numerous types of instinctual behavior which in content are identical with the drives which in perverse individuals replace normal sexuality. Indeed, it is difficult to observe children without seeing manifestations of this kind. Consequently, today it seems less appropriate to phrase the question: "Is there an infantile sexuality?" than to ask: "How was it possible that so obvious a phenomenon as infantile sexuality was not observed before Freud?" This striking oversight is one of the best examples of "repression."

Why does Freud call these infantile phenomena sexual? First, because they constitute the native soil from which the sexuality of the adult subsequently develops; second, because every adult who is in any way blocked in his sexuality falls back to infantile sexuality as a substitute; third, because the child experiences his sexuality with the same emotions the adult feels toward his; fourth, because the aims of these strivings are identical with the aims observable in adult perversions, and no one has ever doubted that the perversions are anything but sexual.

It is probable that the sexual instincts have a common chemistry as their basis. The study of the hormones has taught us some things about the sources of sexuality, but present knowledge is far from sufficient. Chemical changes in the body initiate sensory stimuli in the erogenous zones, bringing forth impulses of a particularly urgent character, demanding actions that lead to changes at the place of stimulation. The physiological basis of sexual impulses is comparable to the physiological occurrences that arouse sensations such as itching or tickling. Insect bites or internal physiological conditions produce chemical changes causing sensory stimuli in the skin which, in turn, create feelings of an especially urgent kind; the impulse to scratch is aroused and scratching finally leads to a change at the source.

> However, although scratching may be effective through changing the blood supply to the itching area, one gets the impression that scratching represents a remainder of a much deeper biological reflex which is also of basic importance for sexual discharges: the reflex to get rid of organs that create disturbing sensations. The autotomy of lizards' tails shows this biological tendency to its full extent. Later this reflex may degenerate to the idea to "scratch away" an itching area of skin, and probably also to the idea of the "detumescing" discharge in sexual tension (1242). An evaluation of the concept of autotomy shows the relativity of the contrast between satisfaction of an instinct and defense against an instinct; the autotomic reflex may be a common root for both the instinctive act and the defense against the instinctive act.

Subsequently sexual phenomena become much more complicated, but in the last analysis they remain within the same frame of operational mechanisms. During puberty, the various impulses of infantile sexuality fuse into a harmonious whole—the sexuality of the adult. But this development may undergo a variety of disturbances. Anxieties and other experiences of the child may cause single components to resist the fusion. In particular, the repressed components of infantile sexuality continue to exist in the unconscious, unchanged. When the adult person later experiences a sexual disappointment, he tends to fall back to infantile sexuality. The result is that the conflicts that raged about his sexuality in childhood likewise become mobilized again.

CLASSIFICATION OF INSTINCTS

The exceptional role that the displaceability of energy gives to the sexual instincts was the starting point for Freud's first classification of instincts. He found that neurotics fell ill because of their repression of certain experiences, and that these experiences were always representatives of sexual wishes. The forces fighting the sexual wishes were anxieties, guilt feelings, or ethical and esthetic ideals of the personality; these countersexual forces could be summarized as "ego instincts," since they serve the purpose of self-preservation. Thus the first classification of instincts, distinguishing "sexual instincts" from "ego instincts" (542, 548, 555, 585, 596), was supposed to represent the neurotic conflict, that is, the fact of repression. When Jung denied this dualism of instincts and wanted to call all ego instincts libidinal (907), his unification at that time would have obscured the newly discovered fact of repression (364).

Today repression is not conceived of as a conflict between two groups of instincts; the conflict is rather a structural one. The ego wards off certain demands of the id. And from the concept that the ego is a differentiated surface layer of the id, it is no longer tenable to expect the ego to harbor innately other instincts than are present in the id. Even if the instinctual energies in the ego are treated otherwise than in the id, it must be assumed that the ego derives its energy from the id and contains primarily no other kinds of instincts.

The criticism of the first classification of instincts originated in the discovery of narcissism, that is, of the libidinal character of some instinctual wishes, which until then had been attributed to the ego instincts. Part of the "egoism," of the high evaluation of one's own ego, turned out to be of the same nature as the sexual instincts with which objects are loved; this becomes manifest in the displaceability of the energy of the ego to objects and vice versa. The sum of interest turned toward one's ego and to outside objects is, for a given time, constant. He who loves himself more is less interested in outside objects and vice versa (585). Freud compared man in respect to libido with an amoeba that can stretch out pseudopodia, originally concentrated within its own body substance, toward the outside world, and then can draw them back again (585). Accordingly the designations ego libido and object libido are applied. However, there is no difference in quality between the two; by a mere displacement process, ego libido changes into object libido and vice versa. With these findings the former division of instincts into ego instincts and sexual instincts has become inadequate. The fact that this division reflected the facts of repression led at first to an attempt to preserve it. Freud undertook this on the assumption that the ego instincts were cathected with two different qualities of psychic energy: with "interest," corresponding to the energy of the ego instincts, and with libidinal elements, which constitute narcissism (585). Such a conception could not be maintained. After the recognition of displaceable libidinal elements, the view could no longer be accepted that in the repressing and in the repressed (or, in today's terminology, in the ego and in the id) there are two fundamentally different kinds of instincts at work. Both ego interests and libidinal drives, which later certainly are often in conflict with each other, have evolved from a common source.

Freud then proposed his new classification of instincts (605, 608). This new classification has two bases, one speculative and one clinical. The speculative basis is the conservative character of the instincts, as characterized by the constancy principle, namely, the fact that instincts tend toward getting rid of tensions. But there is also a phenomenon that seems to run contrary to the constancy principle, namely, a hunger for stimuli, seen most distinctly in the sexual instincts. Thus it seems as if the "Nirvana principle" characterizes some instincts and the hunger for stimuli others.

The clinical basis of the new Freudian theory is the existence of aggression. Aggressive tendencies of all kinds constitute a considerable proportion of all human drives. In part they manifest a reactive character; that is, they are the response to frustrations and have as their goal the overcoming of frustrations (335). In part they appear closely connected with certain sexual drives, especially with sexual drives that are prominent in pregenital levels of libido organization. Other agressions seem to arise quite apart from sexuality. Besides, there is the riddle of masochism, the fact that under certain circumstances our usual orientation in human behavior, the pleasure principle, seems to be put out of action, and self-destructive tendencies come to the fore. Further, clinically, masochism and sadism always are bound together: wherever masochism is found, analysis shows that a sadistic drive has undergone a "turning against the ego" (555, 601). The opposite also exists: an external sadistic type of behavior may veil an unconscious masochistic aim.

Freud combined the speculative and the clinical bases into a new instinct theory (605) which states that there are two qualities in the mind: a self-destructive one, the "death instinct" (which can be turned toward the outside world and thus become a "destructive instinct"), and an object-seeking quality, striving for higher units, the eros. The objection that in reality there is neither a pure self-destructive nor a pure object-seeking behavior is overcome by assuming that the real mental phenomena are composed of various "mixtures" of these qualities (138, 144, 890, 900, 1014).

CRITICISMS OF THE CONCEPT OF A DEATH INSTINCT

There are many possible objections to this new theory (425). Here the following may suffice. The instinctual aim of destruction is the opposite of the sexual search for an object to be loved; of this there is no doubt. Questionable, however, is the nature of this antithesis. Are we dealing with basically different instinctual qualities or is this contrast again a matter of differentiation of an originally common root? The latter seems more probable. One could group all the phenomena collected under the heading of death instinct not as a special type of instinct but as expressions of a *principle,* valid for all instincts; in the course of development this principle might have been modified for certain instincts by external influences. The concept of the constancy principle, as a starting point for all instincts, allows for a unified thesis not only for all mental processes but for all living processes in general as well. Just in that group of drives, the sexual instincts, where hunger for stimuli, search for objects, and striving for higher units becomes especially clear, it is most demonstrable that they strive for relaxation and for getting rid of tensions. Hence it is not possible that for one kind of instinct the constancy principle is valid and for another kind stimulus hunger is valid. On the contrary, stimulus hunger as a principle contradicting the constancy principle must be genetically a derivative of the constancy principle or a special elaboration of it. When the infant is awakened by somatically conditioned hunger, he follows his constancy principle and desires to quiet the hunger and to fall asleep again. When he later recognizes the external world as necessary for this achievement, he strives toward this necessity and asks for contact with this outside world. The goal of being stimulated by the external world is an intermediary one, a detour to the goal of not being stimulated (*see* p. 35).

Of course, the existence and importance of aggressive drives cannot be denied. However, there is no proof that they always and necessarily came into being by a turning outward of more primary self-destructive drives. It seems rather as if aggressiveness were originally no instinctual aim of its own, characterizing one category of instincts in contradistinction to others, but rather a mode in which instinctual aims sometimes are striven for, in response to frustrations or even spontaneously.

Aims are sought more readily in a destructive way the more primitive the maturation level of the organism—perhaps in connection with the insufficiently developed tolerance toward tensions. The archaic instinctual aim toward objects is incorporation, which is as much an attempt to achieve closeness as an attempt to destroy the object. It is the matrix of both. Freud describes this proneness to destructiveness on the archaic levels by saying that death instinct and eros are still "defused," while they fuse gradually during maturation, eros neutralizing death instinct (608). The facts are that in these early periods libidinal and aggressive tendencies are so interwoven that they never can be entirely separated from each other; it seems as if these stages represent an integrated state, from which, later, eros and aggression are differentiated; only later do love and hate develop as opposite qualities.

Likewise a death instinct would not be compatible with the approved biological concept of instinct as discussed above. The thesis of an instinct source that makes the organism react to stimuli with drives toward "instinct actions," which then change the source in an appropriate manner, cannot be applied to a death instinct. The dissimulation in the cells, an objective destruction, cannot be a "source" of a destructive instinct in the same way that the chemical sensitizing of the central nervous system in regard to stimulation of the erogenous zones is the source of the sexual instinct. According to the definition, the instinct attempts to remove the somatic changes at the source of the instinct. The death instinct does not attempt to remove the dissimulation.

It seems, therefore, as if the facts on which Freud based his concept of a death instinct in no way necessitate the assumption of two basically opposite kinds of instincts, the aim of one being relaxation and death, the aim of the other being a binding to higher units. In the chapters on masochism and depression an attempt will be made to show that the clinical facts of self-destruction likewise do not necessitate the assumption of a genuine self-destructive instinct and that all occurrences beyond the pleasure principle can be looked upon as created by external forces that disturbed the principles innate to the organism (*see* pp. 358 ff. and 387 ff.).

The idea that the concept of a death instinct is neither necessary nor useful does not refute possible speculations that life might be looked upon as a "process leading to death." The young organism embodies an abundance of prospective potentialities. Every moment of life that is lived through produces "structure" which limits the prospective potentialities, makes the organism more rigid, and brings it nearer to the inorganic. Whoever accepts this point of view may see in the mental functions once again a special case of the process of life in general.

We may summarize. Unquestionably there are often conflicts between the ego's interests and its sexual drives; there are quite as often conflicts between aggressiveness and sexual tendencies. However, both kinds of conflicts have a history; they came into being at a certain point of development and remain conflicts only as long as certain conditions prevail. There is no necessity to assume that either of these two pairs of opposites represents a genuine and unconditioned dichotomy, operative from the very beginning. For a better classification of instincts, we shall have to wait until physiology develops more valuable theses about instinctual sources.

INFANTILE SEXUALITY

If we turn now to the study of the development of sexuality we are able to leave speculation and return to an empirical basis.

The characteristics of the polymorphous perverse infantile sexuality are well known from Freud's *Three Contributions to the Theory of Sex* (555). Infantile sexuality differs from adult sexuality in several respects. The most impressive difference lies in the fact that the highest excitation is not necessarily located at the genitals, but that the genitals, rather, play the part of *primus inter pares* among many erogenous zones. The aims, too, are different; they do not necessarily lead toward sexual intercourse but linger at activities that later play a role in forepleasure. Infantile sexuality may be *autoerotic,* that is, take the child's own body or parts of it as its object. The components, which are directed toward objects, bear archaic features (incorporation aims and ambivalence). When a partial instinct is blocked, "collateral" partial instincts become correspondingly strengthened.

The small child is an instinctual creature full of polymorphous perverse sexual drives or, to put it more correctly, full of a still undifferentiated total sexuality which contains all the later "partial instincts" in one. Reality seems to be judged at first only as to whether it is compatible with instinct satisfaction. Reality, as conceived of by the primitive ego, is colored by the status of its sexual aims. Every kind of excitation in the child can become a source of sexual excitement: mechanical and muscular stimuli, affects, intellectual activity, and even pain. In infantile sexuality excitement and satisfaction are not sharply differentiated although there are already orgasmlike phenomena, that is, pleasureful sensations that bring relaxation and the end of sexual excitation. In time, however, the genitals begin to function as a special discharge apparatus, which concentrates all excitation upon itself and discharges it no matter in which erogenous zone it originated.

It is called genital primacy when this function of the genitals has become dominant over the extragenital erogenous zones, and all sexual excitations become finally genitally oriented and climactically discharged. The antithesis to genital primacy is the earlier pregenital period, when the genital apparatus has not yet assumed dominance, and as a result the relaxation achieved is never complete. The road from the early pregenital strivings to genital primacy can be described from two different points of view: from that of the change of the leading erogenous zones, and from that of the types of object relationships.

First of all it must be emphasized that the concept of developmental phases is a relative one, serving as a better means of orientation only. Practically, all phases gradually pass into one another and overlap.

When one attempts to organize the abundance of phenomena in infantile sexuality, one is struck by a period in which these phenomena are relatively few and the number and intensity of direct sexual manifestations are diminished. This is the so-called period of latency, extending from the sixth or seventh year of life until puberty. It is true that sexual manifestations never completely disappear; cultures have been described in which a period of latency seems to be lacking, and even in our culture there are many children who do not renounce their masturbation during these years; but even in these cases, sex is less in the foreground than it is earlier and later. Freud was of the opinion that the occurrence of the period of latency is a characteristic of the human species. The early blossoming of infantile sexuality is, as it were, "doomed to destruction" by nature, and this fact is a biological precondition for repression and thus for neuroses (618). Other authors have pointed out that since among some primitive tribes a latency period never appears, cultural restrictions must be responsible for the renunciation of sexual wishes (1102, 1278). However, there is no clear-cut contradiction between "biologically" and "socially" determined phenomena. Biological changes may be brought about by former external influences. It may be that the latency period is a result of external influences that have been in effect long enough to have left permanent traces; perhaps at this point we are watching external influences becoming biological. At any rate, during this period the forces operative against instinctive impulses, such as shame, disgust, and so forth, develop at the price of instinctual energies.

Thus preadult sexuality generally can be divided into three major periods: the infantile period, the latency period, and puberty. The beginning and the end of the infantile period are very well known today, whereas that which lies in between is still in need of much research. It is possible that in this in-between stage accidental variations are of greater import than they are in the beginning and end phases.

THE ORAL STAGE

The beginning is the oral (more correctly the intestinal) state of organization of the libido (13, 555). In discussing the development of the ego, factors were brought out as to how the knowledge of reality comes about in connection with experiences of hunger and satiation. Further, it was evident that the first perceptions were connected with a kind of oral incorporation, and that the first judging was the decision whether or not a substance was edible. These findings may now be supplemented by a discussion of the autoerotic phenomenon of thumbsucking. Thumbsucking is already evident in the newborn child and can, of course, be considered an innate reflex. That does not prevent us from noting that this reflex is concerned with a type of stimulation that usually is tied up with the function of nourishment but has become independent of it. Thumbsucking shows that the pleasure gained from breast or bottle is based not alone on the gratification of hunger but on the stimulation of the erogenous oral mucous membrane as well; otherwise the infant would disappointedly remove his thumb, since it produces no milk. There, sexual excitement has originally leaned upon the need for nourishment; in a similar way early sexual excitement has also leaned upon other physiological functions, upon breathing and cutaneous sensations and upon the sensations of defecation and urination.

It is not necessary to go into detail here about the many phenomena in which oral eroticism is still retained in the adult: kissing, perverse practices, drinking and smoking customs and many eating habits. One must not forget, however, that in drinking and smoking we are not dealing only with oral eroticism. Alcohol and nicotine are also toxins, which by chemical means produce wished-for changes in the balance of instinctual conflicts. These changes diminish inhibitions, heighten self-esteem, and ward off anxiety, at least for a short time and to a certain extent.

The aim of oral eroticism is first the pleasurable autoerotic stimulation of the erogenous zone and later the incorporation of objects. Animal crackers, loved by children, are significant remnants of early cannibalistic fantasies (165). The appearance of an especially intense greed, either manifest or, after its repression, in the form of derivatives, is always traceable to oral eroticism. Many peculiarities of persons fixated at this level can be explained by realizing that in this period objects are not looked upon as individuals but only as food or providers of food. By incorporating objects one becomes united with them. The "oral introjection" is simultaneously the executive of the "primary identification." The ideas of eating an object or of being eaten by an object remain the ways in which any re-union with objects is thought of unconsciously. The magical communion of "becoming the same substance," either by eating the same food or by mixing the respective bloods, and the magical belief that a person becomes similar to the object he has eaten are based on this fact. Abundant evidence of this is to be found in experiences ranging from religious rites to everyday habits. Hand-shaking means that union is sealed by letting one's body substance flow into the other person's. And a companion is still a "com-panion," a person whose bread is identical with ours.

Corresponding to the specific aims of oral eroticism and in accordance with the principle of animistic misunderstanding, we find specific oral fears, especially the fear of being eaten (414, 618).

Analytic experience shows that the fear of being eaten often serves as a cover for a more deeply hidden castration anxiety (566, 599). This is not to be taken as an objection to the archaic nature of this fear. The distortion, which aids in the defense against castration anxiety, may operate through regression.

Of course, the idea of being eaten is not only a source of fear but under certain circumstances may also be a source of oral pleasure. There is not only a longing to incorporate objects but also a longing to be incorporated by a larger object. Very often, the seemingly contradictory aims of eating and of being eaten appear condensed with each other. In the chapter on the ego the longing to be rejoined with an object to which one had yielded one's omnipotence was described. This rejoining, too, is unconsciously thought of as a kind of being eaten by a larger, more powerful object; it depends on individual circumstances whether this idea is met with positive longing or with anxiety (712).

Clinical experience shows that aims of oral incorporation often assume a sadistic character. This probably occurs under the influence of unknown constitutional factors or as a reaction to frustrations. Psychoanalysis of persons suffering from depressions or addictions shows that actually the sadistic character of the incorporation fantasies did not become added on later but was actually operative at the time of the oral phase. However, that is certainly no reason for assuming that every infant sucking at his mother's breast has the desire to kill and destroy her in a sadistic manner. The clinical material of British analysts who hold this point of view (958, 959, 1309) certainly should not be doubted. What is doubtful, however, is that the cases described are typical; they represent, rather, pathological cases with special oral-sadistic fixations (99, 429).

However, incorporation destroys the object objectively. This fact gives all the aims of incorporation a more or less "ambivalent" character. It has already been stated that this ambivalence does not exist from the very beginning. As long as there is no conception of objects, it is meaningless to talk about ambivalence. However, as soon as a conception of objects is developed, the objectively destructive character of the incorporation facilitates a connection of ideas of incorporation with sadism, especially if definite frustrations have been endured (26).

The oral-sadistic fantasies, reconstructed in the analysis of orally fixated patients (cf. 104) and sometimes manifest in orally oriented psychoses, are so fantastic that certain authors are even of the opinion that real experiences are not at all important for their formation (1312). Actually, however, these "fantasies" express the ways in which an undeveloped archaic ego perceives (and misunderstands) a frustrating reality.

Abraham differentiated two subphases of the oral stage: a preambivalent one in which subjectively no object exists and only pleasurable sucking is sought, and an ambivalent phase, appearing after the eruption of teeth, which has the aim of biting the object (26). Analysis of sadistic perverts often reveals that at the bottom of their symptoms there is a fixation on the oral sexual aim of biting (1205). This co-ordination of sucking and the phase before the establishment of objects, and of biting and oral-sadistic drives, does not entirely fit, however; often oral-sadistic sucking fantasies directed against objects can be observed (vampire).

Of the neuroses, the manic-depressive cycle and the addictions present manifestations of fixation on the oral level. However, since in mental development earlier developmental levels still persist behind the more mature ones, oral-erotic characteristics are also present in all other neuroses.

Because of their significance for the later development of neuroses, it is advisable to elaborate again upon the concepts of fixation and regression which were discussed in the chapter on the ego (see p. 53). It was stated that in mental development the progress to a higher level never takes place completely; instead characteristics of the earlier level persist alongside of or behind the new level to some extent. Disturbances of development may occur not only in the form of a total arresting of development but also in the form of retaining more characteristics of earlier stages than is normal. When a new development meets with difficulties, there may be backward movements in which the development recedes to earlier stages that were more successfully experienced. Fixation and regression are complementary to each other. Freud used the simile of an advancing army in enemy territory leaving occupation troops at all important points. The stronger the occupation troops left behind, the weaker is the army that marches on. If the latter meets a too powerful enemy force, it may retreat to those points where it had previously left the strongest occupation troops (596). The stronger a fixation, the more easily will a regression take place if difficulties arise.

What are the factors responsible for evoking fixations? Unquestionably there are hereditary tendencies that account for the various erogenous zones being charged with different amounts of cathexis or different degrees of ability for discharge. Little is known about such constitutional factors. Psychoanalysis did succeed, however, in studying the kinds of experience that favor the development of fixations.

1. The consequence of experiencing excessive satisfactions at a given level is that this level is renounced only with reluctance; if, later, misfortunes occur, there is always a yearning for the satisfaction formerly enjoyed.

2. A similar effect is wrought by excessive *frustrations* at a given level. One gets the impression that at developmental levels that do not afford enough satisfaction, the organism refuses to go further, demanding the withheld satisfactions. If the frustration has led to repression, the drives in question are thus cut off from the rest of the personality; they do not participate in further maturation and send up their disturbing derivatives from the unconscious into the conscious. The result is that these drives remain in the unconscious unchanged, constantly

demanding the same sort of satisfaction; thus they also constantly provoke the same defensive attitudes on the part of the defending ego. This is one source of neurotic "repetitions" (*see* p. 542).

3. One frequently finds that excessive satisfactions as well as excessive frustrations underlie a given fixation; previous overindulgence had made the person unable to bear later frustrations; little frustrations, which a less spoiled individual could tolerate, then have the same effect that a severe frustration ordinarily has.

4. It is understandable, therefore, that abrupt changes from excessive satisfactions to excessive frustrations have an especially fixating effect.

5. Most frequently, however, fixations are rooted in experiences of instinctual satisfaction which simultaneously gave reassurance in the face of some anxiety or aided in repressing some other feared impulse. Such simultaneous satisfaction of drive and of security is the most common cause of fixations.

THE ANAL-SADISTIC STAGE

The analysis of compulsion neuroses enabled Freud to insert between the oral and phallic periods another organizational level of the libido, namely, the anal-sadistic level (581). Anal pleasure certainly is present from the beginning of life. However, in the second year of life the anal-erogenous zone seems to become the chief executive of all excitation which now, no matter where it originates, tends to be discharged through defecation. The primary aim of anal eroticism is certainly the enjoyment of pleasurable sensations in excretion. Later experience teaches that stimulation of the rectal mucosa may be increased by holding back the fecal mass. Anal-retention tendencies are a good example of combinations of erogenous pleasure with security against anxiety. Fear of the originally pleasurable excretion may lead to retention and to the discovery of retention pleasure. The possibility of achieving a more intense stimulation of the mucous membrane, and with it a more intense sensation through the increased tension of retention, is responsible for the tension pleasure which is greater in anal eroticism than in any other eroticism. Persons who, in their pleasures, seek to prolong the forepleasure and to postpone the end pleasure are latently always anal erotics.

The origin and character of the connection between anal and sadistic drives, hinted at in the term for the organization level (anal sadism), is analogous to the discussed connection between orality and sadism. It is due partly to frustrating influences and partly to the character of the incorporation aims. However, two factors must be added. First, the fact that elimination objectively is as "destructive" as incorporation; the object of the first anal-sadistic action is the feces themselves, their "pinching off" being perceived as a kind of sadistic act; later on, persons are treated as the feces previously were treated. Second, the factor of "social power" involved in the mastery of the sphincters: in training for cleanliness, the child finds opportunity effectively to express opposition against grownups.

There are physiological reasons for the connection of anal eroticism to ambivalence and bisexuality. Anal eroticism makes the child treat an object, namely feces, in a contradictory manner: he expels the matter from the body and retains it as if it were a loved object; this is the physiological root of "anal ambivalence." On the other hand the rectum is an excretory hollow organ; as an excretory organ it can actively expel something; as a hollow organ it can be stimulated by an entering foreign body. Masculine tendencies are derived from the first faculty, feminine tendencies from the second; this is the physiological root of the connection between anal eroticism and bisexuality (846).

The first anal strivings are, of course, autoerotic. Pleasurable elimination as well as (later) pleasurable retention can be attained without any object. The fact that this pleasure is experienced at a time when the primary feelings of omnipotence are still operative can be seen in the magical narcissistic overvaluation of the power of the individual's bowel movements; this finds expression in many neurotic and superstitious remnants (19). Though the pleasure is attained by the stimulation of the rectal mucous membrane, the feces, as the instrument by which this pleasure is attained, also become a libidinal object. They represent a thing which first is one's own body but which is transformed into an external object, the model of anything that may be lost; and thus they especially represent "possession," that is, things that are external but nevertheless have ego quality. The impulse to coprophagia which certainly has an erogenous source (representing an attempt to stimulate the erogenous zone of the mouth with the same pleasurable substance that previously stimulated the erogenous zone of the rectum) simultaneously represents an attempt to re-establish the threatened narcissistic equilibrium; that which has been eliminated must be reintrojected. A similar attempt at cutaneous reintrojection is represented by the impulse to smear (1050). Thus the feces become an ambivalently loved object. They are loved and held back or reintrojected and played with, and they are hated and pinched off.

Certain anal pleasures are first perceived in the sensations accompanying the mother's care when diapers are changed. This care and, later on, conflicts aroused by the child's training toward cleanliness gradually turn the autoerotic anal strivings into object strivings. Then, objects may be treated exactly like feces. They may be retained or introjected (there are various types of anal incorporation) as well as eliminated and pinched off (21, 26). The training for cleanliness gives ample opportunity for sensual and hostile gratifications. The "narcissistic overvaluation" (19) expresses itself now in a feeling of power over the mother in giving or not giving the feces. Other anal tendencies directed at objects are the impulses to share anal activities with somebody else: to defecate together, to watch and exhibit anal activities, to smear together, to defecate on another person or to have another person defecate on oneself. All these anal object strivings are ambivalently oriented. They may express tenderness in an archaic way, as well as, after their condemnation, hostility and contempt ("to play a dirty trick on somebody") (463, 1074).

Abraham took this contradictory attitude of the anal erotic toward the object world as a starting point for his suggestion to subdivide the phase of anal organization of the libido into an earlier period having a sadistic aim in excretory pleasure without consideration for the object, and a later period characterized by a prevalent retention pleasure where the object is conserved (26). The consideration of the object's well-being, which constitutes love, probably starts in this second anal phase; its first manifestation is the readiness to sacrifice the feces for the object's sake.

Just as frustrations in the oral period through animistic misunderstanding lead to the formation of specific oral anxieties, so do frustrations in the anal period form specific anal anxieties. As a retaliation for anal-sadistic tendencies, fears develop that what one wished to perpetrate anally on others will now happen to oneself. Fears of physical injury of an anal nature develop, like the fear of some violent ripping out of feces or of body contents.

The other erogenous zones and partial drives are somewhat neglected in analytic literature since they do not become leading executive zones. Nevertheless, conflicts around them often play as decisive a role in the genesis of neuroses and in character formation as oral and anal eroticisms do.

URETHRAL EROTICISM

The appearance of infantile urethral eroticism is so closely interwoven with infantile genital eroticism that not much can be said about it before infantile genitality is discussed. Nevertheless, in later stages it often appears as a pregenital opponent to genuine genital sexuality. The urethral-erotic child necessarily becomes aware of the difference between the sexes with reference to urinating. Thus urethral eroticism often appears in combination with the castration complex.

Certainly the primary aim of urethral eroticism is pleasure in urination. However, there is also a secondary urethral-retention pleasure, analogous to the anal-retention pleasure, as well as conflicts revolving about it. This is more frequent in girls, probably for anatomical reasons. At any rate it does not seem justifiable to make retention pleasure synonymous with anal pleasure and excretory pleasure with urethral pleasure, as Ferenczi once tried to do (497).

The original aims of urethral eroticism certainly are autoerotic ones, just as are those of anal eroticism; later, urethral eroticism, too, may turn toward objects. The urethral apparatus then becomes the executive of sexually exciting fantasies about urinating at objects, being urinated on by objects, or of fantasies in which the connection with urination is more concealed (1337).

Children often actively wet their pants or bed for the sake of autoerotic pleasure. Later, enuresis may develop as an involuntary neurotic symptom having the nature of an unconscious equivalent of masturbation (see pp. 232 ff.). In general, the pleasure in urinating may have a double character: it may have, in both sexes, a phallic and even sadistic significance—urinating being the equivalent of active penetration with fantasies of damaging or destroying—or it may be felt as a "letting flow," as a passive giving oneself up and foregoing control. The aim of letting passively flow may be condensed with other passive aims in boys, like being fondled on the penis or being stimulated at the root of the penis or at the perineum (at the prostate) (1071). Whereas the active phallic part of urethral eroticism in boys is soon replaced by normal genitality, passive urethral-erotic aims may come in conflict with genitality, frequently condensed with anal aims; passive male urethral eroticism may, it is true, sometimes be combined with rather sadistic fantasies, as the analysis of cases of severe ejaculatio praecox shows (14). The idea of letting flow frequently is displaced from urine to tears. In women, later urethral-erotic difficulties most frequently express conflicts centered around penis envy.

Since the pleasure in the retention of urine is less outspoken than in the retention of feces, and in boys may even be entirely absent, the conflicts in the realm of urethral eroticism are less characterized by a struggle between drives to eliminate and drives to retain than by a temptation to enjoy primitive erogenous pleasure in excretion and narcissistic pride in controlling the sphincter of the bladder. This pride is due to the fact that failures in urethral cleanliness are usually punished by putting the child to shame—much more so than failures in rectal cleanliness. It is not easy to say whence the deep connection between urethral eroticism and shame comes; but it can be stated that just as the idea of being eaten is the specific oral fear and the idea of being robbed of the contents of the body the specific anal fear, so *shame* is the specific force directed against urethral-erotic temptations. *Ambition,* so often described as an outcome of urethral-erotic conflicts (794, 881), represents the fight against this shame (see p. 139).

OTHER EROGENOUS ZONES

The entire surface of the skin as well as all mucous membranes function as an erogenous zone. All skin stimulation, touch, as well as temperature and pain sensations are potential sources of erogenous stimulation which, if it meets internal contradiction, may result in conflicts. Temperature eroticism in particular is often combined with early oral eroticism and forms an essential part of primitive receptive sexuality. To have cutaneous contact with the partner and to feel the warmth of his body remains an essential component of all love relationships. In archaic forms of love, where objects serve rather as mere instruments for gaining satisfaction, this is especially marked. Intense pleasure in warmth, frequently manifested in neurotic bathing habits, is usually encountered in persons who simultaneously show other signs of a passive-receptive orientation, particularly in regard to the regulation of their self-esteem. For such persons, "to get affection" means "to get warmth." They are "frozen" personalities who "thaw" in a "warm" atmosphere, who can sit for hours in a warm bath or on a radiator.

Touch eroticism is comparable to scoptophilia, both representing the excitement brought about by specific sensory stimuli. After the achievement of genital primacy these sensory stimulations function as instigators of excitement and play a corresponding part in forepleasure. If they have been warded off during childhood they remain isolated, demanding full gratification on their own account and thus disturbing sexual integration. Touch eroticism is not necessarily connected with scoptophilia.

In the case of a sculptor with neurotic inhibitions, specific fears which had become connected with the goals of touch eroticism formed the basis of the neurosis.

It would be interesting to study the development of touch eroticism in blind persons (223). The sublimation of touch pleasure is of great importance to the ego in learning to master the external world (1405).

Pleasure aroused by painful stimuli of the skin is the erogenous basis of all types of masochism (*see* p. 359).

When the goals of skin eroticism are no longer autoerotic but have become directed toward objects, the archaic aim of incorporation is very distinct. "Introjection through the skin" plays a significant role in the magical thinking of all times as well as in the unconscious sexual fantasies of neurotics (1050).

Skin eroticism is not always to be distinguished from muscle eroticism or from the sexualization of the data of depth sensibility (1338). Muscle eroticism is manifested in many games, sports, and so on, and, pathologically, in many conversion symptoms or in inhibitions of certain (sexualized) muscle activities. Sexual pleasure gained from sensations of depth sensibility in neurotic phenomena is of far greater importance than is generally accepted (410, 444, 526, 837, 1384, 1386, 1391). The importance of pleasures and fears around kinesthetic sensations as well as around sensations of the senses of equilibrium and space have been mentioned in connection with the archaic levels of the ego. Since the excitement (and the conflicts) aroused by these sensations form an essential component of infantile sexuality, the sensations themselves may later become representatives of infantile sexuality in general. Kinesthetic sensations of the early ego levels are experienced by adults and older children while falling asleep, which may contribute to disturbances of sleep if these sensations, because of their latent sexual significance, have a frightening effect. The return of old and unclear equilibrium and space sensations is often the external sign for a remobilization of unconscious infantile excitement. They seem to be of special importance wherever sensations of excitement turn into sensations of anxiety (*see* p. 203).

The connection between anxiety and equilibrium sensations may have a deep physiological origin. Various authors have stressed the point that in the infant the fear of losing stability may form the pattern according to which, later on, other anxieties are built (72, 780, 1391).

PARTIAL INSTINCTS

Scoptophilia, the sexualization of the sensations of looking, is analogous to touch eroticism. Sensory stimuli which are normally initiators of excitement and executors of forepleasure may, if too strong or repressed, later resist subordination under the genital primacy. Wherever sensations of sense organs are sexualized all the features described as characteristic for primitive perception can be observed again: activity of the perceptual organs, motility inseparably connected with perception, "incorporation" of the perceived with a resultant change of the ego along the lines of what has been perceived. Observation of a child who is looking for libidinous purposes readily shows what the accompanying features or prerequisites of pleasurable looking are: he wants to look at an object in order to "feel along with him."

This is especially clear in the analysis of perverse voyeurs. Those who want to observe couples always identify themselves in fantasy with one of the two partners or even with both (*see* p. 348).

Very often sadistic impulses are tied up with scoptophilia: the individual wants to see something in order to destroy it (or to gain reassurance that the object is not yet destroyed). Often, looking itself is unconsciously thought of as a substitute for destroying ("I did not destroy it; I merely looked at it").

The typical obsessive idea in women that they must compulsively look at men's genitals often represents a distorted expression of the sadistic wish to destroy men's genitals.

In many scoptophilic fantasies, the fantasy of incorporating through the eye the object seen is particularly clear (430). Scoptophilia is the main component in children's sexual curiosity which often has the quality of an instinctual drive.

"Knowing sexual facts" may substitute for the observation of sexual facts and become a sexual aim of its own (249, 461, 1059). It may become displaced and give rise to the well-known continual asking of questions which can be so annoying to grownups. It may also become sublimated into a real interest in research, or its repression may block any intellectual interest, depending upon what experiences have become associated with this instinctive sexual curiosity (251, 561). "Primal scenes" (e.g. observing adults during sexual activities) or the birth of a younger sibling are the most common experiences that may stimulate or block curiosity.

Like other sexual components, scoptophilia may become the object of specific repressions (8). Freud once wrote a special paper about the various outcomes of these repressions (571). Extreme cases occasionally occur in shy, inhibited persons who actually do not dare to look at their environment. There are specific fears that are dreaded by inhibited voyeurs as a talion punishment. The "evil eye" and "being turned to stone" are examples (1430). Generally, shyness may be called the specific fear corresponding to the scoptophilic impulse (see pp. 177 f.).

The counterpart to scoptophilia is exhibitionism, which usually appears together with scoptophilia. Freud pointed out that this may be due to the fact that both have a common precursor in the sexual aim of looking at oneself (588). Due to this origin, exhibitionism remains more narcissistic than any other partial instinct. Its erogenous pleasure is always connected with an increase in self-esteem, anticipated or actually gained through the fact that others look at the subject. In the *perversion* of exhibitionism this gain is used as a reassurance against castration fears (see pp. 345 ff.). In a magical way exhibitionism which gives erogenous pleasure may simultaneously be used to influence the onlookers in various ways, either for apotropaic purposes (483, 634, 1249) or for showing them by magical gestures what they are supposed to do (555, 1296).

The relationship to the castration complex causes exhibitionism to have a different development in each sex. Since the man may quiet castration anxieties by exhibiting his genitals, masculine exhibitionism remains fixed to the genitals where it plays a role in sexual forepleasure. In women, since the idea of being castrated inhibits genital exhibitionism, there is a displacement of exhibitionism to the body as a whole. There is no feminine perversion of genital exhibitionism, but nongenital feminine exhibitionism plays a large role both inside and outside the sexual sphere (736) (see pp. 346 f.).

Just as there is a sexual impulse of touching and looking, so there are also sexual impulses of hearing, tasting, and smelling. About the connections between the so-called lower senses and sexuality, the same statements can be made as about the sexual connotations of kinesthetic sensations. The lower senses as well as the kinesthetic participate to a relatively great extent in the general orientation of the child; thus they are also highly cathected with infantile sexuality. Emotions (excitement as well as anxiety) which originally were connected with infantile sexuality may later be remobilized in a conflict situation around sensations of smelling, tasting, or hearing; again, where these sensations represent sexual impulses toward objects, the ideas of incorporation are in the foreground (11, 420, 838). In states of regression, scoptophilia often recedes into the background, whereas auditory and olfactory conflicts come to the fore again.

Actually phenomena of taste sexuality for the most part coincide with oral eroticism, and phenomena of smell sexuality with anal eroticism. Nevertheless their vicissitudes may be studied separately (838).

Sadism and masochism likewise certainly may be designated as normal partial instincts; they are present in all children. It may be that sadism initially develops from the instinctive greediness with which the incorporation aims of the pregenital impulses are prosecuted, representing a way of striving for instinctive aims rather than an original instinctual aim in itself. Another root of sadism is the negative instinctual aim of getting rid ("spitting away") of painful stimuli. Both greediness and hate become condensed when the destruction or the damage of an object turns into an instinctual aim of its own, the completion of which produces a kind of erogenous pleasure.

All pregenital impulses, in their aims of incorporation, seem to possess a certain destructive component. Unknown constitutional factors, and above all, experiences of frustration, greatly increase this destructive element. In addition to oral and anal sadism other erogenous zones may serve as sources of sadism. It is often the specific repression of this sadistic component of infantile sexuality that later leads to conflicts and thus to neuroses.

Masochism, the direction of the destructive component in sexuality against the individual's own ego, is the counterpart to sadism. It is of special theoretical importance since its manifest aim of self-destruction seems to contradict the pleasure principle. The problem is whether this is due to a genuine self-destructive instinct operative "beyond the pleasure principle" (605) or whether this contradiction is only an apparent one, the masochistic phenomena being reducible to changes in the direction of sadistic drives, necessitated by the environment (601, 1277, 1299). This will be discussed in connection with the perversion of masochism (see pp. 358 ff.). Concerning the partial instinct of masochism, it may suffice to say that its erogenous basis is represented by the component of skin (and muscle) eroticism, which is aroused by (not too intense) painful stimuli. Freud called this erogenous masochism (613). All further phenomena of masochism may be regarded as elaborations of this type of eroticism, provoked by certain experiences (see pp. 360 ff.). In principle, these elaborations can be understood in the following ways:

1. They may represent a turning of sadistic impulses against the ego.

2. They may represent a necessary evil in so far as experience has brought

the conviction that pleasure can only be attained by bearing a certain amount of pain; thus enduring this pain becomes an unfortunate but unavoidable intermediary aim. The masochistic act may represent a "lesser evil": by a self-destructive act one unconsciously pays a small price to avert a greater dreaded evil (1240). This is the psychology of "sacrifice." A greater hurt is averted by voluntarily submitting the ego to an earlier and lesser one.

3. The mechanism generally used to master traumatic experiences may complicate a person's sexuality: when something unpleasant is expected, it may be anticipated actively to a controllable degree and at a known time.

4. Experiences may inhibit activity and provoke a regression toward receptive behavior. Many masochistic phenomena appear in analysis as a strengthening of a passive-receptive giving oneself up for the sake of the pleasure of regaining participation in omnipotence. One's own smallness can be enjoyed if it serves as a way of feeling that one participates in somebody else's greatness (817, 819).

THE PHALLIC PHASE; CASTRATION ANXIETY IN BOYS

At the conclusion of infantile sexuality, the genital concentration of all sexual excitement is achieved. The interest in the genitals and in genital masturbation attains a dominant significance, and even a kind of genital orgasm makes its appearance. Freud called this phase the infantile genital organization or the phallic phase (609).

The fact that a general genital discharge of all kinds of sexual excitement comes into being around the fourth or fifth year of life certainly does not mean that the genitals did not previously function as an erogenous zone. As an organ of erogenous sensitivity the genitals are highly effective from birth on; genital masturbation can be observed in infants. Genital erogeneity is as primary as the anal- and urethral-erotic elements, and is not created by a displacement of these elements (497). However, the genital organs and the urinary organs coincide to a high degree. The first genital strivings are certainly closely interwoven with the urethral-erotic ones.

Displacements of pregenital cathexes onto genital impulses, however, do occur and increase the genital erogeneity. It is such displacement that is described in the formula: sexual excitement, wherever originated, becomes more and more concentrated at the genitals and eventually discharged in the genital way.

Whatever the physiology of erogeneity may be, from a psychological point of view it must be said: there is not a specific oral libido, anal libido, and genital libido; there is but one libido which may be displaced from one erogenous zone to another. But where certain fixations have developed, forces are at work that resist such a displacement, so that, for example, pregenital fixations in neurotics hinder the progressive genital concentration of excitement during the sexual act.

The displacements that govern the later vicissitudes of anal eroticism have been studied and described in detail by Freud and others (593, 832, 1634). Likewise a retrograde displacement of anal cathexes to oral functions may occur (1143, 1489) and does occur regularly in stammering (*see* pp. 311 ff.).

The infantile genital organization has common trends and differences as compared with adult sexuality. The similarities concern the genital concentration and the object relations. In general, the child at the phallic phase resembles the adult from a sexual standpoint more than is generally realized. Under our social conditions the main expression of the infantile genitality is masturbation, although acts resembling sexual intercourse occur, too.

This is perhaps the moment to insert a few general remarks about masturbation (*cf.* 455, 580, 1588). Masturbation, that is, the stimulation of one's own genitals for the sake of sexual pleasure, is normal in childhood; and under present cultural conditions is also normal in adolescence, and even in adulthood as a substitute when no sexual object is available. If a person whose sexual activities are blocked by external circumstances absolutely refuses to make use of this way out, analysis always reveals some unconscious fear or guilt feeling as the source of the inhibition (626). Patients who did not masturbate during adolescence likewise reveal that their sexual urges were overwhelmed to a high degree by fear and guilt feelings. This indicates a poor prognosis; it is usually due to an especially deep repression of infantile masturbation (1264, 1267).

The earliest masturbation of infants is a simple autoerotic stimulation of the genitals. Later the masturbatory activities become connected with fantasies concerning objects; in masturbation at the phallic phase, this is always the case (555).

An important function of normal masturbation in childhood can be retraced from data furnished by dreams and by unconscious thinking. There, masturbation is regularly equated with play. The play of children, as we know, at first has the function of achieving a belated mastery of intense impressions; later it anticipates possible events to a degree and at a time that suit the ego, preparing the child for future excitements (605, 1552). Similarly infantile masturbation may serve as a means of learning gradually the active mastery of the experience of sexual excitation.

The genital discharge of masturbation may be used as a discharge for sexual wishes of any kind. Its psychological valence varies accordingly. Fears or guilt feelings vary with this valence. Although it is understandable that children whose masturbation is prohibited by adults develop fears and guilt feelings about their activity as such, and even, according to the animistic misunderstanding, expect fantastic punishments like castration, analysis shows that fears and guilt feelings concern rather the accompanying fantasies. In the phallic phase, these fantasies, as a rule, express more or less directly the Oedipus complex (to be discussed later). In adolescence and later life, frequently not only fears and guilt feelings are still connected with masturbation but there is even a distinct resistance on the part of the patients against enlightenment about the harmless nature of masturbation. They seem to have some unconscious interest in believing that masturbation is a dreadful thing. Analysis, as a rule, shows that a guilt feeling arising from the tendencies of the Oedipus complex has been displaced toward the activity that serves as an outlet for these unconscious fantasies (the conscious masturbatory fantasies being a distorted derivative of the unconscious Oedipus fantasies); this displacement serves as a safeguard for the repression of the Oedipus complex. If the patients were to believe that masturbation as such is harmless they would not be rid of the guilt feeling; they would have to look for its source and might become aware of the repressed; thus they prefer to feel guilty "because they masturbate" (76, 789).

Masturbation is certainly pathological under two circumstances: (a) whenever it is preferred by adult persons to sexual intercourse, and (b) when it is done not occasionally for the purpose of relieving a sexual tension but at such frequent intervals that it reveals a dysfunction with respect to the capacity for sexual satisfaction.

A preference for masturbation instead of sexual object relationships shows either directly a neurotic shyness and inhibition due to deep fears or guilt feelings or there is a supposed "higher pleasure" achieved in masturbation, for the most part rooted in perverse fantasies which the patients do not dare to perform in reality or which actually could not be performed in reality; this, however, is due to unconscious fears connected with the idea of the sexual approach of real objects. Masturbation in this case is a kind of perverse symptom, a substitute for sexual activity when real activity is neurotically inhibited.

Overfrequent masturbation reveals its character as a neurotic symptom at first glance. It occurs when the capacity for satisfaction is disturbed. Problems regularly connected with this type of pathological masturbation are (a) conflicts centering around hostility and aggressiveness aimed at forcibly bringing about the lacking satisfaction, and (b) conflicts centering around the expectation of punishment for this aggressiveness. Unfavorable effects of the overfrequent masturbation may be perceived and even striven for as a well-deserved "castration" punishment. Masturbation of this type ceases if and when analysis succeeds in reestablishing the capacity for sexual satisfaction.

Thus it is clear that masturbation in adults under some circumstances operates as a *symptom* of a neurosis; but it does not *create* a neurosis. However, it may be a part of a vicious circle: if neurotic shyness induces a person to masturbate rather than to approach an object sexually, he never learns that an object actually is capable of giving a higher pleasure; the way to the masturbatory "substitute" is an easy one, and this *ease* may bring a kind of "spoiling," that is, make the subject more unwilling to sustain the difficulties of attaining an object, and thus increase the shyness that was the first cause of his masturbation.

Masturbation as such does not produce neuroses. It has been proven clinically, however, that *unsuccessful* masturbation, that is, masturbation that increases sexual tension but is not capable of discharging it adequately, results in actual-neurotic symptoms (76, 1268).

Since the genitals in the infant play only the part of *primus inter pares,* autoerotic activities of little children are by no means limited to genital masturbation. All erogenous zones may be stimulated autoerotically. If, however, an adult or an older child indulges predominantly in various kinds of anal, oral, urethral, muscular (etc.) masturbation equivalents, analysis regularly reveals that this represents a regressive substitute for genital masturbation after the latter had been repressed (733).

The relations of masturbation to neurasthenia, hypersexuality, and compulsion neurosis will be discussed in the respective chapters.

There are, of course, also characteristic differences between infantile genitality at the phallic phase and the full genitality of the adult. Particularly characteristic for a boy at this age is a manly *pride,* which is limited, of course, by thoughts that he isn't quite grown up, that his penis is smaller than his father's or that of other grown men. This fact is a severe narcissistic blow; the children resent being children and the idea of having too small a penis may become the expression of later neurotic inferiority feelings which actually are due to the impression of having been inferior to the father in the Oedipus rivalry (*cf.* 566).

The boy at the phallic phase has identified himself with his penis. The high narcissistic evaluation of this organ can be explained by the fact that just at this period it becomes so rich in sensations, and distinct tendencies actively to pierce with it come in the foreground.

Up to then, active phallic impulses have been coexistent with passive strivings to have the penis fondled (1071). Passive phallic strivings, subsequently often found at the basis of severe cases of ejaculatio praecox, are regularly condensed with urethral-erotic strivings and, as a rule, actually governed by "prostate sexuality" (*see* pp. 82 f.).

The fear that something might happen to this sensitive and prized organ is called castration anxiety. This fear, to which such a significant role for the total development of the boy is ascribed, represents a *result* and not a cause of this high narcissistic evaluation (423). Only the high narcissistic cathexis of the penis at this period explains the efficacy of castration anxiety; its forerunners in oral and anal anxieties over loss of breast or feces (36, 39, 1466) lack the dynamic force characteristic of phallic castration anxiety.

Castration anxiety in the boy in the phallic period can be compared to the fear of being eaten in the oral period, or the fear of being robbed of the body's contents in the anal period; it is the retaliatory fear of the phallic period; it represents the climax of the fantastic fears of body damage.

In the last analysis the idea of castration may be based upon traces of the ancient biological reflex of autotomy (1242); less deeply but more certainly it is based upon the archaic retaliatory idea of talion: the very organ that has sinned has to be punished.

However, children's surroundings meet their disposition toward such fantastic ideas of punishment more than halfway. Many adults, upon seeing a boy masturbate, still threaten him with "cutting it off." Usually the threat is less direct, but other punishments are suggested, either seriously or jokingly, which the child interprets as threats of castration (1051). But even experiences which objectively do not contain any threat may be misinterpreted in this sense by a boy with a guilty conscience; for example, the experience that there are really beings without a penis: the observation of female genitals. Sometimes an observation of this kind lends a serious character to a previous threat that had not been taken seriously (566). In other cases the achievement of the phallic phase alone may suffice to activate past threats which had not made too intense an impression during pregenital periods.

The castration anxiety of the little boy may be represented by manifold ideas, the special form of which becomes understandable through his individual history. There are infinite possibilities; a few of the more frequent ones will be mentioned.

After an operation the castration fear may be displaced to the operated area— for example, after a tonsillectomy. A child who has had to witness the decapitation of a fowl or has been impressed by stories about decapitation may substitute the idea of decapitation for that of castration. Conscious or unconscious fears of blindness or of injury to the eye, and also of being petrified, point to conflicts around scoptophilia. The localization of the fear at the thumb is indicative of thumbsucking.

The nature of the danger that is believed to be threatening the penis likewise varies. It might be believed that the penis is endangered by a masculine enemy, that is, by a penetrating, pointed tool, or by a feminine enemy, that is, by an encompassing instrument, depending upon whether the father or the mother appeared as the more threatening person, or depending upon what special fantasies the boy has had about sexual intercourse. Persons with oral fixations may fear that the penis will be bitten off, which results in confused ideas made up of both oral and genital elements.

Sometimes specific experiences shape rather grotesque forms of castration fear.

A boy who became sexually excited by equilibratory sensations aroused by turning himself around was later afraid his penis might fly away.

An orally oriented patient, in whom sexual gratification unconsciously was thought of as an eating process, and who had made his father his main sexual object, had heard about cancer and microbes. After having seen the female genitals as a young boy, he had developed the following fantastic idea: if I dare to eat my father's penis (or what comes out of my father's penis), the little bugs, which are the matrix of future children, will devour my penis from within.

Sometimes boys are less frightened by the idea that some harm may be done to their penis in the future than by the idea that their masturbatory activity may actually have injured their penis, that their penis is not a whole one any more, and that this may be found out some day. This might be called the feminine type of castration complex in boys. Circumcision or medical treatment in the genital region may facilitate its development, as may the sight of an adult's or older boy's bigger penis. Men with this type of castration complex frequently suffer from the conscious obsessive fear that their penis is too small. Their conviction is due to an impressive observation in childhood about the size of somebody else's penis when their penis actually was small. "Femininity" in boys does not always have the meaning: "I think I am already castrated." On the contrary, a turning to femininity (which is a turning away from an active use of the penis) often is attempted as a reassurance against a possible future castration: "If I act as if I had no penis any more they will not cut it off." Or even: "If castration cannot be avoided anyhow, I prefer to perform it actively in anticipation of what must come, and I shall at least have the advantage of ingratiating myself with the threatening person."

That adults so easily and eagerly threaten or joke about castration is, of course, an expression of their own castration complexes. Frightening others is an excellent method of quieting one's own fears. In this way castration complexes are passed on from generation to generation. We do not know how they came into being originally, but certainly they have a long history of development.

In many primitive (and civilized) societies, the adult generation places restrictions on the sexual freedom of the younger generation. The initiation rites that associate sexuality with painful experiences are an example of such conditions imposed upon the younger generation (1284). It may be that in certain cultures genital injury was actually perpetrated against those who rebelled.

The intensity of castration anxiety corresponds to the intense evaluation of this organ during the phallic phase. The same valuation makes the boy decide, when he faces the question of either giving up his genital functions or endangering his penis, in favor of renunciation of the function. An adult person might ask: "What good is an organ when I am forbidden to make use of it?" In the phallic period, however, the narcissistic factors outweigh the sexual, so that possession of the penis is the major objective (612).

Problems of this kind are due to another characteristic of the phallic stage. The boy at this age, according to Freud (609), does not yet take the possession of a penis as a matter of sex determination. He differentiates not in terms of male and female but in terms of with penis and castrated. When he is forced to accept the existence of persons without a penis, then he assumes that they once did have one but lost it. Analysts, who have confirmed such findings, have asked the question as to whether this way of thinking may not be a result of a previous repression. It may be that the boy has a more primary reason to fear the female genitals than castration fear (oral anxieties of a *vagina dentata* as a retaliatory fear for oral-sadistic impulses) and that he therefore tries to deny their existence. The idea that girls once had a penis but that it was cut off would represent an attempt at such a denial. True, it brings with it the anxiety "This could happen to me, too," but it has the advantage of denying the primary existence of the feared female genitals (898). However, one does not get the impression that boys find any consolation in knowing that creatures have had their penises cut off; this idea seems, rather, to be very frightening. Furthermore it seems natural for the boy to assume, as long as he is not taught otherwise, that everyone is built just as he is. Thus this assumption is not necessarily based on fear; rather, the insight that the assumption is incorrect arouses the fear.

THE PHALLIC PHASE IN GIRLS; PENIS ENVY

It is usual to refer to a phallic period in girls also (146, 609). What is meant by this? First, that the clitoris at that time is the part of the genital apparatus that is richest in sensations and that attracts and discharges all sexual excitation. It is the central point of masturbatory practices as well as of psychic interest. Second, it means that the girl, too, divides people into "phallic" and "castrated"; that is, the knowledge that there are creatures with a penis is typically reacted to not only by an attitude "I, too, would like to have that," but also by the idea "I once did have it but I lost it" (20, 555, 617, 626).

Objections have been raised to these findings of Freud; however, they do not seem convincing. Concerning clitoris sexuality, there is no doubt that it plays the most prominent role in the girl's sexual excitement. True, it is not the only infantile female genital sexuality. Several authors have shown that there is also an early vaginal sexuality (360, 1079). Others have gone so far as to state that clitoris erogeneity appears so strong because it is an overcompensating substitute for a repressed vaginal organization of the libido (744, 815, 1161). Certainly it has to be admitted that the genital excitability of girls is not limited to the clitoris. No one doubts the high erogenous sensitivity of the labia, the vulva, or the introitus. (However, as a rule, stimulation of these parts leads to discharge by the clitoris in this period.) It is difficult to judge whether the vagina beyond the introitus plays a regular role in this infantile stage. Clinical findings of foreign bodies in the vagina or even uterus apparently justify such an assumption (360). However, one has the impression that an infantile vaginal sexuality can hardly be separated from sensations at the vulva or labia. There is no evidence that it is present regularly or with great intensity, that it is then repressed, and that a reacting to such regular repression would be the cause for the intensity of clitoris sexuality in little girls (419, 421).

The objections to the regular occurrence of a primary envy reaction to the sight of a penis have been supported by the following argument. Analyses undergone by women with a strong penis envy show that these women have gone through a "flight from womanhood" (812), that they have developed some fear of their own femininity and have therefore built up a reactive penis envy. There is no doubt that such clinical findings are correct; but they do not contradict the existence of a primary penis envy. In the analysis of compulsion neurotics we find at first a host of repressed anal and sadistic drives, then later discover that deeper levels contain unconscious genital strivings, which have been warded off by a regression to anal-sadistic strivings. We, then, do not say that the reactive nature of anal-sadistic strivings contradicts the existence of an original anal-sadistic period in the child's libidinal development; we understand, rather, that the reactive strivings have used regressive paths. Similarly a woman who has made a flight from womanhood may develop a secondary penis envy by a reactive reinforcement of a primary penis envy. Often this can be proven clinically (421, 899, 1007, 1313).

Certainly the little girl, like the boy, as long as she is not taught otherwise, feels that everyone is built as she is. When she has to realize that this is not true, she feels this as a severe disadvantage. It has often been asked what determines this surprising reaction: is it actually only a psychological consequence of the anatomical distinction between the sexes (617), or is it rather a reaction to previous social experiences which gave the impression that girls are inferior (814, 1538)?

There is no doubt that every girl has the feeling that the possession of a penis provides direct erogenous advantages in masturbatory or urinary respects; the possession of a penis, in the girl's eyes, makes the possessor more independent and less subject to frustrations (811). This feeling is probably due to the concentration of all sexual feelings at the clitoris at this time, the clitoris being "inferior" as compared to the penis. The envy usually is condensed with the idea that the lack of a penis is a kind of punishment, whether deserved or unjust; in this respect the girl's idea of having lost a penis and the boy's idea that he may lose his penis are completely analogous. In the girl, too, the animistic misinterpretation of the world is effective as is the expectation of talion punishment. The fact that the girl thinks "I have been punished" whereas the boy is afraid "I may be punished" is responsible for remarkable differences in their respective later development (612, 617).

In older girls and in adult women, however, things become more complicated. In our culture, there are many reasons why women may envy men. Masculine strivings of any kind may be added to the primary penis envy, especially after unfortunate experiences, frustrations, and repressions in the feminine field. What is regarded as masculine and as feminine varies enormously in different cultures, and these cultural patterns and the conflicts around them complicate the "psychological consequences of the anatomical distinction" (617). In this respect Fromm's summary seems wholly accurate: "Certain biological differences result in characterological differences; such differences are blended with those which are directly produced by social factors; the latter are much stronger in their effect and can either increase, eliminate, or reverse biologically rooted differences" (655).

Evidence substantiates Freud's postulation of a phallic period in girls if it is kept in mind that this expression implies a physiological dominance of clitoris sexuality and a psychological conflict around penis envy. The postulation seems more problematic when it is assumed to imply that clitoris sexuality would always go hand in hand with outspoken masculine fantasies, and that clitoris sexuality would have as its aim the penetration of a hollow organ, as a rule of the mother, with the regular unconscious aim of procreating a child with her (1006). This would simply mean that the girl prior to the latency period is a kind of boy. Certainly it sometimes occurs that the preoedipal mother fixation is accompanied by masculine genital wishes (626, 628); but this is not always the case. Unquestionably, pure feminine fantasies can accompany clitoris masturbation. It is true that small girls regularly have impulses to enter into the mother; but as a rule this is not thought of as a clitoris activity but much more as an oral fantasy stemming from the earliest infantile period. Such fantasies are constructed in terms of penetrating into the mother's body with the teeth and of eating its contents (958). Some authors have been misled by such oral-sadistic fantasies in women to write of an early phallic phase, which is supposed to occur much earlier than Freud's phallic phase (761). The fantasy of having a child with the mother actually arises frequently in the unconscious of girls; but usually they fantasy the mother as the creator and themselves as the bearer of the child (421).

The significance of the phallic period for the female sex is associated with the fact that the feminine genitals have two leading erogenous zones: the clitoris and the vagina. In the infantile genital period the former and in the adult period the latter is in the foreground. The change from the clitoris as the leading zone to the vagina is a step that definitely occurs in or after puberty only, though it certainly is prepared and introduced by the push toward passivity which the girl experiences when shifting from her preponderant mother fixation and turning toward the father. It offers new opportunities for disturbances in development when either a strong fixation on clitoris sexuality or a repulsing fear of vaginal sexuality or both conditions work against the establishment of vaginal primacy. However, there is an analogy to this complication in the masculine sex. It is strange how little it is noted in analytic literature that the masculine genital apparatus, corresponding to its "bisexual" nature (216, 1243), likewise possesses two centers. If passive men, in whom passive anal and urethral tendencies are predominant over active phallic ones, are questioned as to where they feel the most intense sensations, they answer with about equal frequency: at the root of the penis, at the perineum, or in the rectum. What they actually refer to is a point that is not accessible from the outside and that is equidistant from the root of the penis, the perineum, and the rectum. This point lies in the prostatic part of the urethra and corresponds to the embryologically important seminal colliculus. Much of what is supposed to be anal and urethral sexuality in men is in reality collicular sexuality (798, 942). However, the seminal colliculus plays a lesser role in the life of men than the clitoris does in the life of women.

It has been stated that the boy's envy of the woman's ability to bear children is as intense as the girl's envy of the boy's penis (163). This argument, however, is not very convincing. It is true that children may have a passionate wish to give birth to babies, a wish that is doomed to frustration. But this disappointment affects girls as well as boys—little girls cannot have babies either. But little boys can actually get pleasure from their penis.

THE ARCHAIC TYPES OF OBJECT RELATIONSHIPS

The second point of view in the development of infantile sexuality is the alteration of the relationships to objects. Because the two aspects of sexual development are interwoven, this point has already been touched upon. In general, this development proceeds from an objectless state to aims of incorporation (first total, then partial), then to other ambivalent aims in which the object is merely an instrument for the sake of one's own pleasure, and finally to real love.

The state without objects is the primary narcissistic state, the sexual aims of which are entirely autoerotic. The very first types of object relationships have been discussed in connection with the ego development. What was called primary identification there is identical with what might be called oral incorporation from the point of view of the instincts. The first positive instinctual behavior toward a desired object consists in diminishing the distance between oneself and the object, and finally in swallowing it (later limited to taking it into the mouth). The first negative instinctual behavior toward a repulsive object consists in increasing the distance and in "spitting it out" (later condensed with eliminating it according to the pattern of defecation). The first incorporation is tied up with the objective destruction of the object, just as the object image disappears again when satisfaction is reached. This is the common root of hate and of love. Later the object is conserved at least for the purpose of having it available for the next time of need. There is no doubt that orality is the model for all incorporation; but similar aims are imagined in the realm of all other erogenous zones, too. Special mention has been made of the introjection through the skin (1050) and through the eye (430); respiratory (420) and auditory introjection (838) have been described. The personality of the object to be incorporated seems to be of very limited importance. As a subject it does not matter—it only has to be able to procure satisfaction and may disappear afterward. The image of mother has this potentiality whereas the image of stranger does not offer the hope of gratification but increases tension (73).

An object relationship may be called ambivalent, it has been stated, as soon as an impulse to destroy and an impulse to preserve the object coexist. The first aggressive reaction is represented by spitting away. Later, aggressive reactions may also be represented by introjection. Abraham showed how later conflicts of ambivalence may be solved by the aim of partial incorporation (26). A part of the object is made a permanent property by incorporation, while the remainder is preserved in the external world.

The early object relationships are complicated by the fact that direct erotic aims are as yet not clearly distinguished from the narcissistic aim of participating again in omnipotence. Consideration of the object begins to develop during the anal period (26). The earliest consideration, however, is still dominated by narcissistic aims and is ambivalent. The object is to be influenced by every means available to offer the necessary satisfaction. If this is achieved, the object fuses again with the ego. Some neurotic persons remain fixated to this phase, governed by passive aims, incapable of any active consideration of the loved object. Behavior of this kind is also called narcissistic, though it is entirely different from the objectless primary narcissism.

LOVE AND HATE

Before the egoistic attitude to the objects with all traces of the ambivalence associated therewith is overcome, children frequently are in love with themselves (secondary narcissism). They are capable of distinguishing objects and of loving objects as long as the objects procure satisfaction. If they do not, the child "identifies" with the object and loves himself instead of the object (608). This, however, is certainly not yet love. One can speak of love only when consideration of the object goes so far that one's own satisfaction is impossible without satisfying the object, too. This kind of feeling oneself in union with the object has surely something to do with identification. On the other hand we distinguish between object relationship and identification and we assume that understanding for the real object stops where identification becomes the means of the relationship. In love, it must be a kind of partial and temporary identification for empathic purposes which either exists alongside the object relationship or alternates with it in short intervals. We know nothing about the specific nature of this identification. We can only say that the experience of a full and highly integrated satisfaction facilitates it, and that genital primacy (ability to have an adequate orgasm) is the prerequisite for it (81, 1270, 1272).

Persons in whom the genital primacy is lacking, that is, orgastically impotent persons (1270), are also incapable of love. The full capacity for love not only changes the relations toward other persons but also the relation toward one's own ego. The contrast between object love and self-love again is a relative one: in primary narcissism there is self-love *instead* of object love; in secondary narcissism there is a need for self-love (self-esteem) which overshadows object love. With the capacity for object love another, higher, postnarcissistic type of self-respect becomes available (652).

It can be stated that at the height of full genital satisfaction identification comes back on a higher level; a feeling of flowing together, of losing one's individuality, of achieving a desired reunion of the ego with something larger which has been outside the boundaries of the ego, is an essential constituent of this satisfaction.

Consideration of the object as a condition of a full development of object relationships was called the erotic sense of reality by Ferenczi (505), who pointed out that a full appreciation of reality is lacking in persons who remain fixated at the precursive stages of love.

In the establishment of this consideration the development of tenderness plays a decisive part. But what is tenderness? Freud described it as an outcome of inhibition in the aim of sensual tendencies (555). Other authors have doubted this origin, stressing the fact that tender and sensual object relations do not exclude each other, and that a real love necessarily comprehends both tender and sensual strivings. If tenderness and sensuality so often are actually in conflict with each other, this is due to a secondarily defensive isolation rather than to the basic contradictory nature of these two conflicting forces. Schultz-Hencke tried to reduce them to different erogenous sources, suggesting that sensuality might be rooted in genital eroticism and tenderness in skin eroticism (1412); there is, however, a genital tenderness as well as a cutaneous sensuality. Thus it seems that the development of tenderness is not very likely to explain the type of "higher identification" which in love determines consideration of the object; it may rather be the other way round, that tenderness comes into being when object strivings (probably of an aim-inhibited nature) meet with the aforementioned kind of identification.

The fact that in this type of identification there is also a regressive element in love is clearer in women than in men. The passive aim of female sexuality is more closely related to the original aims of incorporation than is the active aim of male sexuality. Therefore, passive sexuality has more archaic features than active sexuality. The aim of being loved is more stressed in women than the aim of loving—the narcissistic need and the dependency on the object are greater (585).

The regressive element in love, however, is not limited to women. In the process of falling in love it comes to the fore with men, too. In this state it is obvious that an archaic type of self-regard (or even of omnipotence) comes back again in an oceanic feeling of losing one's ego boundaries (622). The ego accentuation is displaced from the ego to the partner: "I am nothing, the partner is everything"; and further: "I become everything again by being permitted to participate in the partner's greatness" (606). This idea may even falsify the "erotic sense of reality" (505): when a person in love estimates his partner's virtues he usually is not very realistic; by his projection of all his ideals onto the partner's personality, the reunion with him becomes the more enjoyable (850). This circumstance was characterized by Freud in the statement: the state of being in love represents a "group of two" (606). There is a gradual transition from the state of being in love to the perversion of extreme submissiveness (*see* pp. 351 ff.).

The nature of the identification on a higher level which constitutes love is still obscure; more is known about the time in which this decisive step normally is taken. According to Abraham (26) this takes place during the anal phase. It is established as soon as "retention pleasure" outweighs "elimination pleasure." A kind of tender feeling toward one's own feces (which once were ego but now are objects) usually forms as important a forerunner of tenderness as do feelings toward the mother's breast, the bottle, or the mother herself. All three of these were also once ego but now are objects.

Not only love but hate also presupposes a complete awareness of the object, which capacity is still lacking in the small child. Small children actually destroy objects and push around and hurt other children, and so on, probably not because they have a positive striving for destruction but rather because they do not care at all; their object interests are limited to potential sources of gratification and to potential threats, their "aggressive" goal is the end of uncomfortable situations, not a positive pleasure in destroying. The goal of positive destruction originates later, probably first as a means to enforce other goals (as a quality with which a goal is pursued in the case of difficulties or frustrations) and then, subsequently, as a goal in itself. It has already been explained why a pregenitally oriented organism is more inclined to include destructiveness with its erotic aims. In a normal genitally oriented person aggressiveness is a means of achieving his goals under certain adverse circumstances; the repression of these means may create as much a handicap in life as the repression of the ability to love.

SOCIAL FEELINGS

The object relationships of a mature person do not consist solely of love and hate. There are also: (1) Object feelings of less intensity, sympathy and antipathy of various degrees. They are not essentially different from love and hate; libido-economic changes may make them turn into love and hate, which proves that they are of a libidinal nature and originate through inhibition of aims. (2) In mental development the previous phases never disappear entirely; thus normal persons also have, to a certain degree, ambivalences and incorporation aims. The latter are responsible for the many object relationships that still are interwoven with identifications. (3) Among these identification relationships one type is of special importance: the use of objects as ideal models to be imitated or as bad examples to be avoided. (4) And this in turn forms a transition to the type of relations in which an object is not reacted to as such but is used as an instrument to relieve some inner conflict. Different types of such use will be discussed later (*see* pp. 496 ff. and 508 ff.).

All these types of object relationships which are not love or hate may have originated in childhood relationships to persons other than the parents, for example, to siblings. They are basic for what is called social feelings, that is, for the forces within individuals that favor group formation. Aim-inhibited strivings (under our cultural conditions especially of a homosexual nature), identifications (which are responsible for the blocking of intragroup aggressions, so essential for any group formation), and the choice of models and examples among objects are the mechanisms at the basis of group formation (606, 607, 624).

> Freud clarified the relation of "aim-inhibited strivings" and "identifications" on the one hand and "choice of models and examples" on the other in group formation by stating: if several persons have set the same object in the place of their superego (as their ideal model or as their meaning example), they identify, consequently, with each other and develop tender aim-inhibited feelings toward one another (606). Redl complemented this formula by stating: if several persons have used the same object as an instrument to relieve similar inner conflicts, they also tend to identify with each other and to feel tenderly toward one another (1258).
>
> It is perhaps worth while to add that social psychology is by no means limited to the study of what is going on in individual minds when groups are formed in this way or of how such groups operate; it must likewise face and solve problems of an entirely different nature, namely, not only that of subjective but also of objective groups, of the similar effects that similar external stimuli have on different individuals.

THE MOTHER AS THE FIRST OBJECT

The first object of every individual is the mother. This statement is not to be taken literally, for there are no grounds for assuming that the physical act of birth in any way binds the child psychologically to the mother. That person who performs the first care of the child is to be considered the mother. Groddeck maintained that children fed by a wet nurse may for the rest of their lives manifest conflicts or difficulties that originate from the situation of having had "two mothers" (720). Clinical experience does not confirm this idea which seems highly improbable. In the beginning there are no images of objects; the first object representations are diffuse and the process of forming images of objects takes place very gradually. The idea of mother is certainly not present at the beginning. Though it is very difficult to describe, we must assume that the first ideas concerning things which may bring satisfaction but which are momentarily absent include simultaneously the mother's breast (or the bottle), the person of the mother, and parts of the child's own body. The actual perception of a "person," which would make a distinction between mother and wet nurse possible, does not exist as yet. Later on, the child does learn to differentiate impressions; then the first differentiation is probably between "trusted" and "strange" impressions. "Strange" is felt as "dangerous"; narcissistic supplies are expected from the "trusted" sources. The "trusted" parts of the mother are "loved"; gradually the mother is recognized as a whole and "oral union with the mother" becomes the simultaneous aim of the undifferentiated erotic and narcissistic needs. In this way the mother attains a unique possibility for exerting influence.

The development of object relationships in the masculine sex is simpler because the boy in his later developmental states remains bound to his first object, the mother. The primitive object choice, developed from the care of the child, takes the same direction as that which arises from the attraction of the opposite sex. Of course the boy loves his father and other objects, too, and of course the boy suffers frustrations from his mother and may also hate her; but the boy's love for his mother remains the dominant striving during his infantile sexual phase. The contradictory strivings of love and hate, or of love for mother and love for father, and so on, seem temporarily to coexist without disturbing each other. It is characteristic of the primary process that contradictions may coexist without leading to disturbing conflicts. As the ego becomes stronger this gradually becomes impossible and conflicts do arise. The boy begins to realize that his love for the mother, his identification love for the father (based on the formula "I would like to be as big as he is and be allowed and able to do all that he does"), and his hatred of the father (based on the fact that the father has certain privileges) conflict with one another. "I love mother and hate father because he takes mother for himself" is an expression for the way in which the boy's impulses typically are condensed, under the conditions of family upbringing. This is called the positive Oedipus complex (552); it usually starts in the third year of life, occasionally earlier (93, 955), and reaches its climax in the fourth and fifth year. The high point of the Oedipus complex coincides with the phallic stage of libido development. We speak of a negative Oedipus complex in a boy when love for the father prevails and the mother is hated as a disturbing element in his love for the father (608). Certain traces of this negative Oedipus complex are normally present along with the positive. Constitutional factors and experience may augment this greatly.

A man patient with a very strong and ambivalent father complex had the following dream: "I got a long letter from my father. He wrote me that somebody had died. Finally, he asked me whether I would marry him."

In general, boys with a special development of the negative Oedipus complex have repressed phallic strivings toward the mother and mobilized pregenital passive aims toward the father instead. Sometimes, however, things are a little more complicated. Analysis of pregenitally oriented compulsive characters or of certain homosexuals sometimes shows that an infantile phallic period has not disappeared with the repression of an Oedipus complex directed at the mother, but that the repressed impulse connected with the penis had been directed toward the father. Love and competition are not mutually exclusive. The normal identification of a boy with his father, characterized by the formulae, "I should like to be like father," "I should like to have a penis like father's," "I should like to participate in father's penis," may, in certain cases, grow into a kind of love which may best be described as an apprentice complex, a temporary feminine submission to the father in order to prepare oneself for a later masculine competition with him. If this love meets a castration threat, this may result in an abandonment of the phallic position and make the boy turn to the mother again, but no longer in a phallic Oedipus striving but rather in a pregenital, passive, protection-seeking, identifying way.

It has been mentioned that in the phallic phase the narcissistic fear about the penis is stronger than the object relationship. Thus finally, castration anxiety leads to the renunciation of the boy's passionate Oedipus love for his mother, since its gratification could be attained only at the price of endangering the penis (612).

THE CHANGE OF OBJECT IN GIRLS

The object development in girls is somewhat more complicated. The girl undergoes one more step of development than the boy, namely, the transfer from the first object, the mother, to the opposite sex, the father. This transition takes place relatively late, between the ages of three and six; nevertheless it must be assumed that it is conditioned not only by experiences but is biologically founded as well. (Men's beards do not appear before puberty and still this phenomenon is not psychologically conditioned.) The biological foundation does not alter the fact that it is interesting to study the psychological connections under which this change of object takes place, especially since these mental factors not only influence the form the biologically determined process will pursue but also determine many complications and developmental disturbances that are important for the neuroses (626, 628, 1090).

The most important experiences that precipitate, facilitate, impede, or form the change of object are disappointments coming from the mother, which cause a turning away from her. Among these, weaning, training for cleanliness, and the birth of siblings have the most important repercussions. However, these disappointments are borne by boys without turning them away from the mother.

There is another disappointment, however, which is specific for the female sex. It was already mentioned that girls typically react to the discovery of the penis with a primary penis envy. Many girls, who for certain reasons have tendencies toward self-reproach, may react to this primary penis envy with strong guilt feelings, as though they themselves had injured their bodies. But *all* of them make the mother actually responsible: she deprived them of something, or she took something away from them (626). It is this specifically feminine disappointment that forms the main motive for the turning away from the mother. Remobilized anal- and oral-receptive elements prepare the ground for the subsequent femininity. The aim is now to get from the father the "supplies" that the mother had denied them. In the girl's fantasy, the idea "penis" is replaced by the idea "child," and the clitoris as a leading zone may again be regressively replaced by anal and especially oral—that is, receptive —demands (612, 617, 626). This revival of receptive longings has various consequences. Normally it prepares for the later vaginal sexuality, which often shows characteristics of an oral or anal origin of its cathexes (66), and of normal female receptivity. Actually pregnancy *is* a kind of incorporation. In pathological cases oral-sadistic strivings, too, may become remobilized and influence the woman's later sexuality in an unfortunate way. Certain character disorders are rooted in experiences connected with this step.

> The described turn toward passivity may, of course, in predisposed girls also mobilize the masochistic sexual components discussed above (*see* pp. 73 f.), and thus give rise to the development of a more or less pronounced masochistic perversion. In no way, however, does it seem warranted to identify the passive aims of normal female sexuality with masochism (322).

It is understandable that this development is open to many disturbances and that conflicts about the preoedipal love for the mother play an important role in the neuroses of women. In normal development, too, the relationship of women to their mothers is more frequently ambivalent than is that of most men to their fathers. Some remnants of the preoedipal mother fixation are always found in women. There are many women whose masculine love objects have more characteristics of their mother than of their father (626, 628).

The aims of the preoedipal mother fixation usually are first of all pregenital ones; but there are certainly also genital impulses directed toward the mother, and it is the genital disappointment that leads to the final renunciation. However, there is no reason to assume that the little girl originally is in every respect a little boy and that a negative Oedipus complex regularly would precede the positive (1006, 1007; *cf. also* 190, 421, 894, 899, 1313).

Once the attachment to the father is accomplished, the girl, under normal circumstances in our cultural milieu, develops an Oedipus complex analogous to that of the boy. The love for the father is combined with a guilt-laden jealousy hatred of the mother. Of course this jealousy hatred is condensed with old hate impulses from the preoedipal phases.

The general discrepancy in the development of object relationships for both sexes was expressed by Freud in the following formula: The masculine Oedipus complex is *resolved* by the castration complex; it is given up because of castration anxiety. The feminine Oedipus complex is *brought about* by the castration complex; out of disappointment over the lack of a penis, the girl's love turns toward the father (612).

THE OEDIPUS COMPLEX

In both sexes, the Oedipus complex can be called the climax of infantile sexuality; the erogenous development from oral eroticism via anal eroticism toward genitality, as well as the development of object relationships from incorporation via partial incorporation and ambivalence toward love and hate, culminate in the Oedipus strivings, which as a rule are expressed by guilt-laden genital masturbation. An overcoming of these strivings, to be replaced by adult sexuality, is the prerequisite for normality, whereas an unconscious clinging to the Oedipus tendencies characterizes the neurotic mind.

In individual cases, "love for the parent of the opposite sex" and "death wishes against the parent of the same sex" may mean various things, the special form of which depends again on constitution and experience. Investigating the formative experiences, we find a variability not easy to survey. Not only do the personalities of the parents make a lot of difference, but also the conceptions love and death vary from child to child. Love is built up of many components, and the relative accent on the different components may vary greatly; death may be thought of in many ways; a death wish may even be sadistically sexualized and thus simultaneously give expression to the negative Oedipus complex (418, 828).

There is no perception that does not immediately enter into emotional connections. Thus all experiences participate in determining the special form of the Oedipus complex, the experiences at the time of the phallic phase as well as the previous ones which may color the Oedipus complex pregenitally through fixations. Unique traumatic experiences are as important as chronic influences.

Traumatic experiences, especially stressed by psychoanalysis from its very inception, frequently are the decisive factors if the Oedipus complex has not been surmounted in a normal way. In talking about genital strivings, genital factors should be considered first. By seduction children's genitality may be aroused prematurely, and the intensity of the excitement which was stimulated by external factors may be beyond the child's power of control; this creates traumatic states which connect the realms of "genitality" and "threat" with each other. Anything that increases fears and thus increases sexual repressions causes disturbances in the subsequent overcoming of the Oedipus complex. In this way threats and all experiences that subjectively signify threats become effective, like accidents, injuries, deaths, and the sudden and unexpected sight of adult genitals. By means of displacement, pregenital experiences may have the same effects as genital ones, especially sudden oral and anal frustrations. Especially important for the forming of the Oedipus complex is everything the child learns or thinks about the parents' sexual life, the more so if it is experienced suddenly. Often combinations of real experiences and wrong interpretations are decisive. Here the realm of the sadistic perception of sexuality must be mentioned. A so-called primal scene (599), that is, the observation of sexual scenes between adults (between the parents) by the child, simultaneously creates a high degree of sexual excitement—the nature of which varies according to the child's age—and the impression that sexuality is dangerous. This impression is caused by the fact that the quantity of excitement is beyond the child's capacity to discharge and is therefore experienced as traumatically painful; the child may also sadistically misinterpret what he perceives, or the sight of adult genitals may give rise to a castration fear. The subjective content, the degree and time of the effect of a primal scene vary according to the details of the scene perceived. External circumstances and individual factors determine what the child actually becomes aware of, what he surmises and how he incorporates into previous mental experience what he has seen and surmised, and whether this incorporation and elaboration occur at the moment of viewing the scene or afterward (*cf.* 7, 1166).

Instead of a primal scene all kinds of primal-scene substitutes may have been experienced: observations of animals, of nude adults, and even of scenes that objectively are entirely nonsexual but that are subjectively experienced as sexual. The effectiveness of such scenes is greater if other objectively harmless experiences readily facilitate a transference of what had been witnessed to the parents. Arguments between the parents are often equated with sexual scenes by children, and thus create a sadistic idea of sexuality.

> Whether or not the sight of the genitals of adult persons creates morbid fear in children will depend on the whole previous history of the child, that is, on the psychic connections into which the new experience enters (1273).

Freud has called the infantile idea of observing the parents during intercourse a primal fantasy which, if not actually experienced, will in all probability be produced in fantasy, the child utilizing all the hints reality offers him (596). Certainly the effects of such a fantasy can never be the same as the effects of a real experience.

Another important typical traumatic event is the birth of a sibling. This may be experienced as a sudden disturbance of Oedipus gratifications because the mother's care must now be shared with somebody else; or perceptions and speculations about pregnancy and birth may increase sexual curiosity and sexual anxieties. Both may result in a tendency toward regression into babyhood.

Concerning chronic influences, a child's reactions and wishes toward the parents depend on their behavior and personalities. Unusual behavior will provoke unusual reactions. This is to be seen in the family anamnesis of the average neurotic. Neurotic parents bring up neurotic children, and the children's Oedipus complex reflects the parents' unsolved Oedipus complex. Very often the mother loves the son and the father loves the daughter. The parents' unconscious sexual love for their children is greater when their real sexual satisfaction, due to external circumstances or to their own neuroses, is insufficient. This love is felt by the children unconsciously as a sexual temptation, increasing their Oedipus complex; and sometimes it is even unconsciously felt by the parents, who then make up for it by sudden threats or frustrations, so that frequently the same children are excited and then frustrated by the same parents.

The ideal Oedipus complex reflects a triangle situation. Actually the Oedipus complex is most outspoken in only children (195, 637, 1116, 1339). Special forms of the Oedipus complex are created where more or less than three persons are present. Within the frame of the family, brothers and sisters represent persons who from the standpoint of the Oedipus strivings are superfluous. First of all, they are objects of jealousy (1039); individual circumstances determine whether their presence increases the unconscious hate toward the parent of the same sex or decreases it by means of diversion (827). But siblings may also serve as objects for the transference of love, especially older ones or those who are only a little younger, so that the world has never been experienced without them. If there are several older brothers or sisters, we may see "doubles of the Oedipus complex"; what is experienced with the parents is experienced with the older brother and sister a second time. This may have a relieving effect, but may also create new conflicts.

A patient with several older brothers had the following dream: "I return home with my mother after a walk and find that a gang of robbers has meanwhile taken possession of our home." The robbers stood for his brothers, with whom he had to share his mother again after returning from their walk.

Younger siblings, who usually are felt as competitors, may also be looked upon as one's own children, especially if the difference of age is great, and thus either stimulate the Oedipus complex (for example, in girls they may not only create the jealous idea "Father [or mother] will love the baby instead of me" but also the idea "Father gave mother the baby instead of me") or decrease the Oedipus wishes by a substitute fulfillment.

The counterpart, the Oedipus complex with too few participants, is developed in children who grow up either with only one parent or without any parents.

When one parent has died or left the family, the child's development will be decisively affected by whether or not the child has known this parent at all, whether or not there are stepparents, when and under what circumstances they entered the family, and by the behavior and the attitudes of the remaining parent (168, 355, 760).

Even children who have not known the missing parent are aware that such a parent once existed, that other children live with their father and mother. They therefore have a tendency to feel themselves exceptions, privileged to ask for certain compensations. In general the following can be stated. If the parent of the same sex has died, this is felt as a fulfillment of the Oedipus wish, and thus creates intense feelings of guilt. If the parent of the opposite sex has died, the frustrated Oedipus love most often creates a fantastic idealization of the deceased. The details depend on when and how the child became aware of the death. Three consequences seem especially important. First, an increased attachment to the remaining parent; the character of this attachment is determined by this parent's attachment to the child, and is usually of an ambivalent nature (355). Second, a frequent and intense unconscious connection between the ideas of sexuality and death, the two being connected by the conception of "secrets of the adults"; this may create an intense sexual fear, due to the idea that sexual fulfillment may bring death, or even a masochistic trend in which dying (reunion with the dead parent) may become a sexual goal. Third, a mourning person regresses to the oral phase; if this takes place at an early age, it implies permanent effects in the structure of the Oedipus complex and character; the Oedipus love as well as all later object relations are interwoven with identifications. The second and third points also hold true in connection with the early experience of the death of a sibling (1325).

A woman patient was afraid of marriage. Her mother had died when she was five years old. The patient had developed the fantasy that this death in some way had been due to childbirth or sexuality. As a punishment for the Oedipus gratification which she had felt at her mother's death, she now expected that she would have to endure the same fate if she married.

This is somewhat similar to a patient who as a boy reacted to his mother's death with anxiety and hypochondriasis. He had identified himself with the mother, and now was afraid that sexual satisfaction with the father might kill him as, in his fantasy, it had killed his mother. Here the condensation of the sexual secret with the secret of death was especially clear, because it colored the castration anxiety, shaping it into a fear that things might disappear.

A woman patient whose father had died when she was a baby later had a tendency to hate everybody: men because none of them were like her father who on account of his death had become idealized; women because her mother had taken the father for herself, letting him die before the daughter had had any opportunity to enjoy him.

In the case of the boy, if the father is missing (or "weak") this might create a predisposition toward femininity, because children identify more with the parent who is regarded as the source of the decisive frustrations.

Conflicts between the parents, divorce, and separation may have similar effects. If the children themselves are the subject of parental arguments, this circumstance easily creates an intensification of the complete Oedipus complex and a fixation on narcissism which makes them expect that everybody will feel the same exaggerated interest in them that the parents have shown, an expectation doomed to disappointment.

> The parents of a chronically depressed and generally inhibited woman patient had been divorced when she was only a year old. She had never seen her father. Her Oedipus complex became centered around the following fantasy: "Father did not like to live with mother; she was not worthy of him. I am different; one day he will come to take me with him." He did not come. This frustration aroused an intense hatred. The patient's depression represented a turning of this hatred against her own person. Her depressive loss of self-esteem meant: "I also am not worthy of being loved by my idealized father."

Unusual behavior on the part of the parents creates unusual Oedipus complexes on the part of the children. Unusual behavior again means unusual indulgence, unusual frustrations, or both. Unusual spoiling necessarily causes unusual frustrations, because spoiled children have not learned to take frustrations and therefore experience slight frustrations as severe ones. Planned educational measures are of less importance than the unintentional, natural, everyday behavior of the parents (1458). Two factors may be pointed out as especially significant. First, the mother's attitude toward the child's sex: some mothers wish for a son and make their daughters feel this. Second, the parents' attitudes toward each other, for these attitudes mold the child's ideas about sexuality.

Thus the family morals influence the form of the Oedipus complex of the children. To what extent a child feels his instinctual impulses to be permissible and to what extent naughty depends not only, for example, on whether and how his masturbation is prohibited but also, and even more, on the general attitude of the parents toward sex, which is constantly manifested by them, with or without their knowledge. This includes the reaction of the parents to the child's attitudes toward themselves, toward other children, toward masturbation, as well as their attitudes about weaning and training for cleanliness during the child's oral and anal development. Pregenital fixation gives the subsequent Oedipus complex an irrevocable pregenital cast. Especially worth mentioning are the passive-receptive forms of male Oedipus complexes created by maternal overprotection (1041). Certain types of authoritative fathers by their behavior block any possibility of the child's becoming independent.

A patient, forty years of age, with an intense ambivalent fixation upon his tyrannic father, having had a cold, received a wire from his father from a distant city: "Because of uncertain weather, do not leave house today."

There is still one very important factor which today creates different surroundings for different children and which may influence the special form of the Oedipus complex, namely, the parents' social position. Most children unconsciously equate "socially low" and "instinctual, uninhibited," and "socially high" and "sublimated, inhibited." If a person from a well-to-do home feels especially attracted to those of a lower social level, analysis frequently reveals not only a longing for reassurance against humiliation (castration) through intercourse with equally "humiliated" (castrated) persons but also a longing for the prohibited sensuality. This may be rationalized as an urge to help improve social conditions.

Many children, in their Oedipus daydreams, develop fantastic ideas of not really being the child of their parents; they dream of being some kind of foundling, an offspring of some family of very different social standing; this may be either a high and especially privileged family or a very poor and low one. Fantasies of this kind, called by Freud "family romance" (552), may serve various purposes: narcissistic pride, stubbornness, revenge on the parents, and hope for future gratifications.

However, unconscious fantasies about social differences do not tell much about the ways in which realities, due to social differences, influence the child's Oedipus complex. Actually they do so continually because sexual experiences as well as sexual frustrations vary according to social patterns. Freud has shown this in detail (596), and one needs only to recall, for example, the sexual, aggressive, and frustrating experiences of slum children to become aware of this. Experiences connected with the father's social position certainly shape the children's love or hate, awe or contempt, admiration or pity for him (496).

The impression nevertheless prevails that the objectively important factor of the social standing of the family finds less reflection in the form of the child's Oedipus complex than one might expect. This is rooted in the fact that the same set of morals (or even the same uncertainties in regard to morals) is effective in different social strata of one and the same society.

The idea has been suggested of investigating the advantages and disadvantages of family education (which creates Oedipus complexes) by comparing average children, ones who have been brought up in families, with children who have grown up outside of any family circle, for example, in institutions. However, even institutional children are not uninfluenced by the concept of family. They learn sooner or later that the institution of the family exists, that other children have fathers and mothers, and that in this respect they themselves are at a disadvantage. Thus they, too, have their Oedipus complex. They not only develop instinctual bindings of love, hate, jealousy, and so on, toward their educators, but in addition they develop fantasies about father and mother similar to the ideas of children reared within a family, only especially formed by their fantastic character. Their Oedipus complex is characterized by the discrepancy between fantasy and reality (250). What has been said about children who did not know one of their parents also holds true for institutional children, and in a double sense. If they do not grow up at one certain place but are subject to frequent changes of environment, this is not only reflected in typical disturbances of their character formation (see pp. 373 f. and 504 ff.), but they never get an opportunity to develop any lasting object relationships and their Oedipus complex remains pure fantasy. In any sort of permanent community there are always adults who serve as substitutes for the parents, but the fact that they were not the real parents will reflect itself in the special form of the Oedipus complex.

The special form of the individual Oedipus complex is shaped by experience. But what about the Oedipus complex itself? Is it a biological fact, inherent in the human species, or is it a product of the social institution of the family, subject to the same changes as this institution?

First it must be said that the difference between biologically determined and socially determined is a relative one. We stressed the point that Freud does not assume that instincts represent unchangeable patterns: they are rather residuals of older environmental influences (588). It was no innate mystical Oedipus complex that created the family as a place where it might be satisfied; it was the family that created the Oedipus complex. In the second place, the answer depends on the definition of Oedipus complex. The human infant is biologically more helpless than other mammalian children. He needs care and love. Therefore, he will always ask for love from the nursing and protecting adults around him, and develop hate and jealousy of persons who take this love away from him. If this is called Oedipus complex, the Oedipus complex is biologically founded.

However, Freud uses this term in a stricter sense: it signifies the combination of genital love for the parent of the opposite sex and jealous death wishes for the parent of the same sex, a highly integrated combination of emotional attitudes which is the climax of the long development of infantile sexuality. In this sense the Oedipus complex is undoubtedly a product of family influence. If the institution of the family were to change, the pattern of the Oedipus complex would necessarily change also. It has been shown that societies with family configurations different from our own actually have different Oedipus complexes (1101). Efforts to explain different family configurations as "repressions of the Oedipus complex" (891) seem to have failed.

The problem of the origin of the Oedipus complex is thus reduced to the problem of the origin of the family, an interesting and still unsolved chapter, which lies beyond the province of a theory of neurosis. Freud postulated a hypothesis about the phylogenetic origin of the Oedipus complex in some prehistoric period when mankind was organized in hordes, led by a chief who one day was killed and eaten by his sons, this incorporation inaugurating the first "remorse" and inhibition (579). This is not the place to discuss the fascinating hypothesis of *Totem and Taboo.* The hypothesis does not alter the fact that the sexual conflicts of children would be different if they did not live together with their parents and a few brothers and sisters, exposed to the typical family conflicts of sexual excitation and frustration. Different environments provoke different reactions.

Any child at the height of the Oedipus complex must experience disappointments and narcissistic injuries; the competitor is a grownup and this gives him advantages and privileges. These narcissistic injuries are reacted to in very different ways by different children, depending on their constitution, the concrete ways in which the injuries are experienced, and all earlier experiences. Every child longs to be adult and plays "adult."

However, being a child has advantages, too. Whenever a child is afraid of his own emotions and of the implacability of erotic and aggressive impulses, he may take refuge in the attitude: "All this is not too serious because I am still a child," and in the receptive longing for external help.

Both the longing to be adult (if contradicted by guilt feelings) and the feeling of being protected as long as one still is a child cause fixations and subsequently make many neurotics behave and feel as if they still were children at the phallic phase.

> A patient who was a successful doctor of many years' practice found out in his analysis that whenever a pharmacist filled a prescription he had written, he felt in amazement: "The pharmacist, a grown-up man, actually does this work for no other reason except that I, a child, have written a prescription!"

TYPES OF OBJECT CHOICE

It would be wrong to imagine that in childhood there are no other love objects than the parent of the opposite sex. Also siblings, uncles, aunts, grandparents (458, 877), friends and acquaintances of the parents may be of decisive influence. Many children experience love affairs of a sort with other children of the same or opposite sex or with adults. Probably more such affairs between children would occur if education did not aim at prohibiting them. Concerning the mechanisms of object choice, Freud distinguished between the anaclitic type of choice —in which an object is chosen because it provokes associations about another original object of the past, usually the parent of the opposite sex, sometimes the parent of the same sex, siblings, or other persons from the infantile environment—and the narcissistic type of choice, in which an object is chosen because it represents some characteristic of the person's own personality (585). Both types, the anaclitic and the narcissistic, may operate in (*a*) a positive way: the object chosen is similar to the past object or to one's own ego; in (*b*) a negative way: the object chosen is the opposite of the past object or of one's own ego; or in (*c*) the ideal way: the object chosen represents what one once wished the past object or one's own ego might be (585).

THE PROBLEM OF FEMALE CASTRATION FEAR

In boys, castration anxiety eventually makes the suppression of the Oedipus complex necessary. In girls, there seems to be no castration anxiety that could be considered a dynamic force. The idea of having lost an organ cannot condition the same restrictions of instinct as the idea that one might lose an organ by instinctual activity. True, many women, after their disappointment, have unconsciously built up the fantasy of possessing a penis (502). But an anxiety concerning a merely fantasied organ cannot have the same dynamic effect as a threat against a real organ.

It is not easy to answer the question about castration anxiety in women (1240). First, it can be asserted that the Oedipus complex in women actually is not combated to the same degree and with the same decisiveness as it is in men. There are many more women who all their life long remain bound to their father or to father figures, or in some way betray the relationship of their love object to their father, than there are men who have not overcome their mother fixation (1496). Second, analysis shows that other and older fears, above all the fear over loss of love, are stronger in women and in many ways take over the role that castration anxiety plays in men. Third, the fear that the state of being castrated, thought of as an outcome of a forbidden activity, might be found out often limits the girl's sexual expressions considerably; the idea of having destroyed one's own body is often encountered, as is that of having lost all possibility of bearing children, or at least of having healthy children, and other anxieties which anticipate that the disgrace is found out. Fourth, there are anxieties about anticipated retaliatory genital injuries which replace castration fear. Just as animistic misunderstandings determine unreal pregenital anxieties, so they also determine fantastic genital anxieties. Girls often do not know that they have a preformed hollow organ in their vagina, and this explains the fantastic fear that their genital longing to be penetrated by the father's organ may lead to bodily injury. Despite all this, the analysis of some women still reveals an unconscious fear that an organ will be cut off as a punishment for sexual practices.

An operation on the thumb had been undergone in childhood in the case of a woman in whom this anxiety was very marked. This real threat of amputation was then displaced to the fantasied penis.

Preanalytic authors (for example Wedekind) and more recently Fromm have emphasized the point that differences in the dominant anxieties of the sexes are partly due to the physiological differences in the performance of sexual intercourse (655). The man needs an erection to perform the act; the woman needs no corresponding change in her own body (she is capable of performing the act even without enjoyment) but is dependent on the man's erection. Thus the man's fear is a fear of impotence or failure; the woman's fear is a fear of being left alone or of loss of love.

No doubt this physiological difference contributes to the prevalent roles of castration fear or fear over loss of love in man and woman respectively. However, this cannot be more than a relatively late secondary contribution. The relative preponderance of the respective fears is established in childhood, long before the first experiences in sexual intercourse.

The change of object is one factor that complicates the development of women in comparison to men. A second factor is the double nature of female genital sexuality. There is no doubt that the "prostate sexuality" of men, which is so closely connected with anal and urethral eroticism, does not play as significant a role as does clitoris sexuality. However, it should not be forgotten that not only these physiological differences are responsible for a greater proclivity toward the development of neuroses in women; there are also—and this is of greater importance—cultural and social differences in the upbringing of the sexes as related to instincts.

SUMMARY

Abraham summarized the history of libido development by a diagrammatic table (26) which is presented here with slight modifications and an anticipatory additional column, Dominant Point of Fixation. The warnings Abraham expressed when publishing this table must also be repeated: "The table is comparable to the timetable of an express train, in which only a few of the most important stations are enumerated. What is situated between them necessarily remains disregarded. It must also be mentioned that the stages which in the main columns are recorded on the same level do not necessarily coincide."

Stages of Libidinal Organization	Stages in Development of Object Love	Dominant Point of Fixation in
1. Early oral (sucking) stage	Autoeroticism (no object, preambivalent)	Certain types of schizophrenia (stupor)
2. Late oral-sadistic (cannibalistic) stage	Narcissism: total incorporation of the object	Manic-depressive disorders (addiction, morbid impulses)
3. Early anal-sadistic stage	Partial love with incorporation	Paranoia, certain pregenital conversion neuroses
4. Late anal-sadistic stage	Partial love	Compulsion neurosis, other pregenital conversion neuroses
5. Early genital (phallic) stage	Object love, limited by the predominant castration complex	Hysteria
6. Final genital stage	Love (postambivalent)	Normality

Ambivalent

Chapter VI

LATER PHASES OF DEVELOPMENT: THE SUPEREGO

EARLY STAGES OF THE SUPEREGO

THE fear of punishment and the fear of losing the parents' affection are different from other anxieties motivating defense. While other dangers demand cessation of the dangerous activity unconditionally, in the case of these fears the activity may be continued in secret or the child may pretend he feels "bad" in situations where he actually feels "good." (Ferenczi once said in a lecture on this subject: "And out of this lie morality came into existence.")

An important step in further maturation is accomplished when prohibitions set up by the parents remain effective even in their absence. Now a constant watchman has been instituted in the mind, who signals the approach of possible situations or behavior that might result in the loss of the mother's affection, or the approach of an occasion to earn the reward of the mother's affection. This watchman fulfills the essential function of the ego: to anticipate the probable reactions of the external world to one's behavior. A portion of the ego has become an "inner mother," threatening a possible withdrawal of affection.

This internalization of the mother takes place through an act of introjection. Introjection is the first instinctual aim directed toward objects; subsequently it is also used as an expression of hostility because it is capable of bringing about the disappearance of objects; finally it may regressively replace more differentiated object relations. As an attempt at defense against objects, introjection frequently fails, for the fear of the external object may still continue as a fear of the introjected object.

The introjection of the parents' prohibitions brings about an adjusting alteration within the ego. Alterations of this kind are the forerunners of the superego, which Ferenczi has designated as sphincter morals (505).

> This term stresses the importance of training for cleanliness in the development of this "preconscience." When asked to evacuate the bowels under certain conditions only, the child experiences the conflict between "should" and "would like to." The intensity of the impulses to be suppressed and the feelings toward the adult who asks for this suppression determine the outcome.

Originally the child certainly had the wish to do the things the parents do; his aim was an identification with the parents' activities, not with their prohibitions. The standards and ideals of the parents are an essential part of their personality. If children want to identify themselves with the parents, they also want to identify with their standards and ideals. Prohibitions are accepted as a part of living up to these standards and ideals. The striving for the reward of feeling oneself to be similar to the parents facilitates the acceptance of prohibitions. The actual identification with the prohibitions becomes a displacement substitute for the intended identification with the parents' activities.

It is strange that the forces opposing instinctual impulses frequently have the stormy and irrational character of instincts themselves. This is most clearly discernible in the phenomenon of moral masochism; but the same thing can be observed in every normal guilt feeling, with its impulsive demand for a chance to make good, and in every analysis in the instinct-ridden character resistances. Freud, in his book *The Ego and the Id,* raised the question as to the instinctual characteristics of the anti-instinct forces and answered: the anti-instinct forces have an instinctual character because they are derivatives of instincts (608). The instinctual attitudes of the children toward their parents are turned into forces hostile to the instincts by an introjection of the parents. Thus through the influence of the external world instinctual impulses have been transformed into anti-instinctual impulses.

"Internalized parental prohibitions," the forerunners of the superego, are very strong in so far as they threaten the child with terrible punishment, the ideas of which are created by the aforementioned misapprehension; but they are weak in so far as they may be easily disobeyed or circumvented whenever no one is looking or when some other circumstance seems to permit something previously forbidden. The introjected objects can be easily warded off by a new projection, and the functions of the forerunners of the superego can be again shifted to persons in the external world (1266). Policemen or bogeymen represent these "externalized pre-superegos." The child fluctuates between giving in to his impulses and suppressing them; there is as yet no unified organized character in the prohibitions. At any rate, it is a situation where under the influence of the external world one portion of instinctual energy is utilized for suppressing other instinctual energies; and this change of direction is produced by an introjection.

THE ESTABLISHMENT OF THE SUPEREGO

Now the problem of how the Oedipus complex is normally resolved may be taken up again. The answer is: the object relationships of the Oedipus complex are regressively replaced by identifications (608). The introjection of the objects of the Oedipus complex furthers the development of the ego and complicates it in a decisive way. The frustration of the Oedipus complex causes a regression from more differentiated types of object relationships to introjection and orality, and the sexual longing for an object is replaced by an asexual alteration within the organization of the ego.

The identifications that resolve the Oedipus complex are, of course, not complete ones. They replace the sexual and hostile impulses toward the parents (at least the greater part of them); a tender object relationship with inhibited aims, however, continues along with the identification. That part of the ego that was altered by identification, "the introjected parents," cannot immediately fuse with the rest of the ego, for the objects introduced into the ego are too magnificent, and the distance between them and the ego feeling of the child is too great. The newly introjected objects become combined with the parental introjects already present in the form of the previously described forerunners of the superego. In describing this phase, Freud states: "The broad general outcome of the sexual phase governed by the Oedipus complex may, therefore, be taken to be the forming of a precipitate in the ego. . . . This modification of the ego retains its special position; it stands in contrast to the other constituents of the ego in the form of a superego" (608).

The ego "borrows" from its strong parents the strength that enables it to suppress the Oedipus complex. In this way the resolution of the Oedipus complex brings about the marked and decisive "step within the ego" (606), which is so important for subsequent ego development and which by its organization is differentiated from its forerunner—the superego.

The concept of the superego opens up a flood of problems that are often discussed but in no way entirely solved (cf. 37, 232, 348, 775, 781, 782, 835, 838, 843, 893, 895, 1175, 1179, 1196, 1287, 1289, 1333, 1379, 1567, 1602). Here it will suffice to sketch a few of these problems.

If the superego were simply an identification with the frustrating object of the Oedipus complex, then one would expect that the boy would develop a "motherly" superego and the girl a "fatherly" one. This is not the case. It is true that in accordance with the "completeness" of the Oedipus complex, everyone bears features of both parents in his superego. Under our cultural conditions, however, generally for both sexes the fatherly superego is decisive; in women, moreover, a motherly superego is effective as a positive ego ideal. Men who, contrary to the rule, have a pronounced motherly superego have regularly had a dominant mother (658, 1041, 1266). The outstanding identification takes place with that parent who was regarded as the source of the decisive frustrations, which in a patriarchal family is usually the father but which in exceptional cases may be the mother. Thus the substitution of an unattainable object relationship by an identification is not a simple matter. Apparently under normal circumstances biological reasons prohibit a boy from developing a too intense identification with a woman, or a girl with a man. The attempts at solving these problems have not yet advanced beyond Freud's formulation: "It would appear that in both sexes the relative strength of the masculine and feminine sexual dispositions is what determines whether the outcome of the Oedipus situation shall be an identification with the father or with the mother. This is one of the ways in which bisexuality takes a hand in the subsequent vicissitudes of the Oedipus complex" (608).

THE FUNCTIONS OF THE SUPEREGO

With the establishment of the superego various mental functions are altered. Anxiety changes in part into guilt feelings. It is no longer an external danger, loss of love or castration, which is feared, but an inner representative of this danger, which threatens from within. The "loss of the superego's protection" or "the inner punishment performed by the superego" is felt as an extremely painful decrease in self-esteem and in extreme cases as a feeling of annihilation. It has been stated repeatedly that small children need some kind of narcissistic supplies for maintaining their equilibrium. The privilege of granting or refusing these supplies is now taken over by the superego. The fear of being punished or abandoned by the superego is the fear of annihilation through lack of these supplies (*see* p. 136).

As long as this fear exists, the ego feels the need to abolish it just as urgently as it feels an instinctual drive. The origin of this drive is an example of how the origin of instincts may be understood in general: they come about through the incorporation of external demands (588).

The ego behaves toward the superego as it once behaved toward a threatening parent whose affection and forgiveness it needed. It develops a need for absolution. The need for punishment is a special form of the need for absolution: the pain of punishment is accepted or even provoked in the hope that after the punishment the greater pain of guilt feelings will cease. Thus the need for punishment can again be understood as the choice of a lesser evil. Instead of castration, a sacrifice is offered in order to obviate castration. The sacrifice is actively undertaken and is less unpleasant than the passive waiting for something to happen. However, sometimes things are more complicated. Just as "being beaten by the father" may become a sexual aim in masochists, so, too, may "being beaten by the superego" (613) (*see* pp. 364 and 501 f.).

After the superego is established, it decides which drives or needs will be permitted and which suppressed. The logical judgment of the ego as to whether an impulse might bring forth danger is now complicated by illogical guilt feelings. The ego now has to respect, besides reality, still another, often irrational, "representative of reality."

The superego is the heir of the parents not only as a source of threats and punishments but also as a source of protection and as a provider of reassuring love. Being on good or bad terms with one's superego becomes as important as being on good or bad terms with one's parents previously was. The change from parents to superego in this respect is a prerequisite of the individual's independence. Self-esteem is no longer regulated by approval or rejection by external objects, but rather by the feeling of having done or not having done the right thing. Complying with the superego's demands brings not only relief but also definite feelings of pleasure and security of the same type that children experience from external supplies of love. Refusing this compliance brings feelings of guilt and remorse which are similar to the child's feelings of being not loved any more.

The same mechanisms of defense which are used against discomfortable affects in general may also be brought into play against guilt feelings (*see* p. 136).

Guilt feelings that accompany the performance of a misdeed and the feelings of well-being that come with the fulfilling of an ideal are the normal models for the pathological phenomena of depression and mania.

The fact that self-esteem is dependent upon whether or not ideals are fulfilled makes the ways of regulating self-esteem as numerous as ideals are. Ideals are created in the child not only by real models to be imitated but also by stories, teachings, and dogma; they are transferred by tradition and are culturally and socially determined.

Sometimes attempts have been made to distinguish ego ideals, the patterns of what one would like to be, from the superego, which is characterized as a threatening, prohibiting, and punishing power. But it was Freud's insight into the origin of the superego that showed how closely interwoven these two aspects are (608). They are as intermingled as were the protecting and threatening powers of the parents. Even the ways in which these functions are tied up by "promises of protection on condition of obedience" are transferred from the parents to the superego.

Freud was criticized for not having differentiated between "real" ideals which are wholeheartedly accepted by the total personality and "ungenuine" ideals which one believes one has to follow because an external or introjected authority demands it (653). But even the most genuine ideals have been created by introjection. The difference lies in the commensurability or incommensurability of introject and subject, that is, in the previous history of the relationship to the objects whose introjections formed the ideal.

The relationship between superego and the external world is based on the fact that the superego is derived from the introjection of a piece of the external world; it is, therefore, the inner representative of a certain aspect of the external world. Since the same is true of the ego, in a certain sense the constitution of the superego is a duplicate of the constitution of the ego; a second ego, a "super" ego, is now formed which, it is true, is limited to the spheres of threat and promise, of punishment and reward. The incorporation of this piece of the external world occurs relatively late; thus the superego remains that part of the mental apparatus closest to the outside world. Many persons remain influenced in their behavior and self-esteem not only by what they consider correct themselves but also by the consideration of what others may think. Superego and objects that make demands are not always clearly distinguished. Superego functions may easily be reprojected, that is, displaced onto newly appearing authority figures. (This occurs especially when, for external or internal reasons, an active mastery of the external world becomes impossible.) A clinical confirmation of the existence of this close relationship between superego and outside world is found in delusions of reference. Superego functions (since they are, in a sense, half ego and half external world) are the ones that most readily appear when a patient, after experiencing a loss of the objective world, tries to regain it, without being fully able to do so (*see* pp. 431 f.).

The fact that the construction of the superego takes place on a higher level than the construction of the ego will become evident from the following discussion. The deepest layer of the ego is formed by sensations from one's own body; kinesthetic (and also olfactory) orientation in general are older than visual orientation. Visual orientation, however, also occurs very early and prevails in the preconscious fantasy type of thinking. The decisive step toward the consolidation of the conscious part of the ego is taken when the auditory conception of words is added to the more archaic orientations. In contradistinction, the sensations that form the basis of the superego begin with the auditory stimuli of words. Parental words of admonition, encouragement, or threat are incorporated by way of the ear. Thus the commands of the superego as a rule are verbalized (11, 608, 628). "The step within the ego" is felt by the child by "hearing the inner voice of conscience" (1289); accordingly, a person's relation to language is often predominantly governed by superego rules (838).

The superego is related to the id through its genesis. The most essential objects of the id, the objects of the Oedipus complex, live on in the superego. This genesis explains the urgent, instinctlike, irrational character of many superego strivings, which, in normal development, must be overcome by reasonable judgments of the ego (433). "The superego dips deeply into the id" (608).

On the one hand, the superego's strictness corresponds to the previous real strictness of the parents; on the other hand, due to the intimate relations between the superego and the id, it depends on the instinctual structure of the child (which in turn depends on constitution and previous experiences); a child who unconsciously hates the parents fears retaliation and may experience this retaliation from his superego. Thus the strictness of the superego may also express the original hostility of the child toward the parents.

THE "PASSING OF THE OEDIPUS COMPLEX"

The establishment of the superego brings to an end the strivings of the Oedipus complex and starts the period of latency. The superego, according to Freud, is the heir of the Oedipus complex (608, 612).

It is now understandable how it comes about that the Oedipus complex is the normal climax of infantile sexual development as well as the basis of all neuroses: the presence of Oedipus strivings is normal at a certain age but pathological at any other. The neurosis, based on an undue persistence of the Oedipus complex, is a retaining of a stage of development that normally should have been overcome (618).

However, we have evidence to indicate that the statement "a neurotic person has retained his Oedipus complex, whereas a normal person has not" oversimplifies matters. The analysis of dreams of normal persons (552) and also of works of artists (559, 568) shows that the Oedipus complex is still active in normal adults, too. The dreams, it is true, are not a full proof; in the state of sleep old childhood situations may be revived which during the day are perhaps not active at all. Nevertheless it must be admitted that the axiom given above is not absolutely correct; the normal adult, too, still has his Oedipus complex, but there is a quantitative difference between the normal and the neurotic individual. In any mental development, earlier stages persist to a certain extent behind the more recent ones and may be revived under special circumstances. The normal person has few "troops of occupation" remaining at the position "Oedipus complex," to use Freud's metaphor (596), the majority of his troops having marched on. However, under *great* duress they, too, may retreat, and thus a normal person may become neurotic. The person with a neurotic disposition has left nearly all his forces at the Oedipus complex; only a few have advanced, and at the slightest difficulty they have to go back and rejoin the main force at their first stand, the Oedipus complex. Thus the neurotic disposition is not characterized by the existence of an Oedipus complex but rather by a failure of the passing of the Oedipus complex.

The way in which this passing takes place (612) is necessarily reflected in the later personality. As a rule this occurs differently in each of the sexes. The boy gives up his sensual and hostile Oedipus wishes because of a castration fear, the intensity of which is due to the hypercathexis of the penis during the phallic phase. The complex, according to Freud, "is smashed to pieces by the shock of threatened castration" (612). In girls, however, it is given up because of fear over loss of love, because of disappointment, shame, and also fear over physical injury (*see* p. 99). All of these forces are of a lesser dynamic value than castration fear; thus the passing of the Oedipus complex in girls generally comes about in a more gradual and less complete way. Freud was of the opinion that this is the psychological basis for later character differences in the sexes (617; *cf. also* 843, 1164).

If the formation of the superego did not entirely succeed but was limited in its extent by a previous repression of the Oedipus strivings, the individual who thus retains a disposition for the development of neuroses feels a sense of failure over the frustration of his infantile sexuality. The narcissistic hurt aroused by this failure forms one of the sources of subsequent neurotic feelings of inferiority (585).

VICISSITUDES OF THE SUPEREGO

Identification with the objects of the Oedipus complex is but one example of many identifications that occur throughout life, first as a forerunner of any object relationship and later coupled with other object relationships and as regressive substitutes for them (408). These other identifications may influence the superego. Whereas early identifications constitute a great part of the ego's structure, some of them, which have been described as the pre-stages of the superego, stand out in contrast to the rest of the ego and assume the functions of observation, protection, criticism, and punishment. In identifications that occur in later life, it makes a considerable difference whether the introject is absorbed by the ego or takes the side of the superego. A person's ideals certainly are not unchangeable after he has entered the latency period. It is rather characteristic for normal development that ideals and values become more independent of the infantile models when the libidinal ties to the family are abandoned. Everybody experiences the dethronement of the parents; normal persons experience it more gradually, neurotic ones often more suddenly and with fear or triumph. Other persons who serve as models, or certain ideas, may become introjected into the superego and modify its content.

The adjustment of a newly acquired introject of this sort with the superego often gives rise to complications. If the new ideas bring but a new comment or a slight modification of old ideals, the situation is not difficult. Sometimes, however, internal or external circumstances may create "parasites of the superego" which usurp the functions of the superego for a varying length of time (603). This occurs, for example, under hypnosis (1235) or under the influence of mass suggestion (606). Extremely violent conflicts between an established superego and new introjects are found as the unconscious basis of depression (*see* pp. 393 ff.).

Reprojection of the superego onto external persons occurs frequently and in different forms. Certainly neither a belief in "ideal models" nor a certain degree of "social fear" (need for approval by others and fear of rejection) is necessarily pathological. If various persons take the same object as a representative of their superego, this circumstance makes them identify with one another, the basic mechanism of group formation (606). The belief in authority in general is always due to a projection of superego qualities (651). Other forms of reprojection of the superego are pathological—for example, projections that are carried out in the course of the ego's struggle against the superego in order to eradicate guilt feelings (*see* pp. 293 f. and 496 ff.).

To a certain degree the automatic and strict functioning of a rigid superego in normal persons is later replaced by a reasonable judgment of the real results of one's prospective actions.

THE LATENCY PERIOD

The influence of the superego first manifests itself typically after the passing of the Oedipus complex (612) as a cessation or as a decrease of masturbatory activities and of instinctual interests in general. Changes of partial instincts through inhibitions of their aims, sublimations of various kinds, and often reaction formations manifest themselves. The character of the person, that is, his habitual manner of handling external and internal demands, becomes consolidated during this period (63, 555, 800).

PUBERTY

The relative equilibrium of the latency period lasts until puberty. Then there is a biological intensification of sexual impulses. The ego, developed in the meanwhile, reacts differently than before, depending upon previous experience. All the mental phenomena characteristic of puberty may be regarded as attempts to re-establish the disturbed equilibrium. Normal maturation proceeds in such a way that upon the attainment of genital primacy the ego accepts sexuality as an important component of its personality and learns to adjust to it.

This is not simple in societies with our cultural conditions. The psychological task in puberty is the adaptation of the personality to new conditions which have been brought about by physical changes. However, this task of adaptation would be less difficult if the new conditions were really entirely new. Actually they are similar to the experiences of the period of infantile sexuality and of the Oedipus complex. Therefore, the conflicts of these times also reappear. However, in the interim they have become more complicated. The relatively pleasant equilibrium of the latency period has stabilized certain attitudes hostile to instincts, which may now increase anxiety and instability. During the latency period the instinctual demands themselves have not changed much; but the ego has. It has developed definite patterns of reaction toward external and internal demands. When in adolescence the ego comes into conflict with instinctual drives, the situation is different from what it was in childhood. Contradictory attitudes come to the fore. Side by side or following one another appear genital heterosexual impulses, all kinds of infantile sexual behavior, and attitudes of extreme asceticism, which not only try to suppress all sexuality but everything pleasant as well. The increased strength of the genital demands has a physiological basis. The return of infantile sexual impulses is partly due to the fact that genital primacy has not yet been completely established, and puberty brings with it an increase in *total* sexuality; in part, however, the return of infantile impulses is caused by the child's fear of the new forms of his drives, which makes him regress to the old and more familiar forms. The asceticism of puberty is a sign of fear of sexuality and is a defense against it. A similar set of contradictions in behavior is characteristic of the psychology of puberty also outside the strictly sexual realm. Egoism and altruism, pettiness and generosity, sociability and loneliness, cheerfulness and sadness, silly jocularity and overseriousness, intense loves and sudden abandonments of these loves, submission and rebellion, materialism and idealism, rudeness and tender consideration—all are typical. These contradictions can be traced back by analysis to conflicts between the newly strengthened drives and anxieties or defensive tendencies. The effectiveness of these defensive tendencies is not a sufficient basis for the assumption that the ego is primarily hostile to its instincts or basically afraid of them. It is true that up to a certain point every unexpected emotional experience, especially if it is intense, may have a frightening effect until the ego becomes familiar with the new phenomenon and learns to master it. This also holds true for the first pollution or the first menstruation. But for the most part the usual fears of new instinctual phenomena are much more intense than the fright over the initial incidents themselves would be. During the period of infantile sexuality and especially at the time of the suppression of the Oedipus complex, the child learned to consider sexual impulses as dangerous. In a society that treated infantile sexuality differently puberty, too, would assume a different course (1102).

As a matter of fact, in puberty sexual development seems to set in again just at the point at which it was abandoned at the time of the resolution of the Oedipus complex. Before the incestuous bindings are resolved, an intensifying of the strivings of the Oedipus complex regularly occurs. The fears and guilts connected with the Oedipus complex are primarily responsible for the fact that the ego in puberty is often very hostile to the instincts and very afraid of them. If it were possible finally to liquidate the Oedipus complex by satisfactory sexual experiences with nonincestuous objects, adjustment would be easier. The fact that this is difficult to achieve under present-day conditions leads to the intensification of the Oedipus complex and therefore to the intensification of sexual anxieties (1278). The prolonging of puberty, that is, the expenditure of so much time and work to restore the psychic equilibrium and to accept sexuality as a part of life, is definitely culturally conditioned (128). "Comparative pubertal research" under different cultural and social conditions is a sphere of study that has hardly begun.

These conflicts between drives and anxieties are felt consciously by present-day adolescents principally in the form of conflicts around masturbation. The heightened genital strivings sooner or later find expression in masturbatory activity. Only when the repression of infantile masturbation has been too intense is it not resumed at puberty. Fears and guilt feelings which originally were connected with the accompanying Oedipus fantasies are now displaced to the masturbatory activity. Adolescent personalities react differently to these fears and guilt feelings; they may take sides more with the drive and try to fight the anxiety (or the parents representing the prohibition); or they may, more frequently, side with the anxiety and the parents, and try to fight instinctual temptations as well as rebellious tendencies. Often they do both successively or even simultaneously. Some adolescents fight their consciences by proving to themselves that they are not worse than others; they congregate on a narcissistic basis for the purpose of swapping stories about sexuality, or even for common instinctual activity; others withdraw, hide their masturbation and their longings entirely and feel ostracized and lonesome, unable to participate in the "sexual" or "knowing" gatherings of the others. Fixations on the first type of reaction are represented subsequently by "impulsive characters," and fixations on the second subsequently by erythrophobics.

It is probably because of social factors that adolescents frequently prefer to meet in homosexual gatherings. In this way they avoid the exciting presence of the other sex and at the same time avoid being alone; thus they may find the reassurance they are looking for. However, what has been warded off returns, and the friendships that were founded in the hope of avoiding sexual object relationships assume a sexual character more or less obviously. Occasional homosexual experiences between adolescents should not be looked upon as pathological so long as they appear as temporary phenomena of adaptation and do not result in definite fixations.

The frequent preference for homosexual objects at this age may be due not only to shyness in regard to the other sex (and to cultural tradition) but also to the continued narcissistic orientation of the greater part of the object needs of that time.

Some types of modern pubertal reactions have been studied by Anna Freud (541). She described the ascetic type already mentioned who suppresses everything pleasant together with sexuality. Frequently periods of asceticism alternate with periods of wild instinctual activity. The increased intellectual, scientific, and philosophical interests of this period represent attempts at mastering the drives and the connected emotions. Anxiety often provokes partial regressions at puberty. This explains the contradictions in adolescent behavior toward objects. Many relations at this age represent identifications rather than genuine love; and in many ways objects are used as mere instruments to relieve inner tensions, as good or bad examples, as proofs of one's own abilities, or as reassurances. The "rudeness" sometimes shown by adolescent boys is often meant to intimidate others for the purpose of overcoming their own anxiety. Objects are easily abandoned if they lose their reassuring significance.

Puberty is overcome, that is, sexuality is worked into the personality, when the capacity for full orgasm is attained. Disturbances in this sphere, rooted in previous repressions, serve as the basis for neuroses. Persons afraid of the definiteness of adulthood, that is to say, the definiteness of their instinctual demands which they feel they must accept when growing up, resent growing up and prolong their puberty. Such prolongation is made easy for them by various cultural conditions (128). They may then, at least for a certain time, enjoy dependence and the advantages of youth in reality, whereas they anticipate future grandeur and independence in fantasy, while not daring to test the reality value of these fantasies in the slightest detail.

In psychoanalytic literature, there is less to be found about the normal course of puberty than about infantile sexuality (exceptions: 76, 128, 129, 139, 183, 226, 255, 256, 541, 555, 643, 678, 800, 836, 888, 1118, 1255, 1624, 1626, 1627). This is explicable by the fact that infantile sexuality was discovered by psychoanalysis, whereas puberty had been widely studied before. In no way is this period unimportant. It is true that puberty is a "repetition" of the infantile sexual period, and only rarely are conflicts encountered in puberty that have not had forerunners in infantile sexuality. Nevertheless, experiences in puberty may solve conflicts or shift conflicts into a final direction; moreover, they may give older and oscillating constellations a final and definitive form. Many neurotics give an impression of adolescence. They have not succeeded in getting on good terms with their sexuality. Therefore, they continue the behavior patterns of adolescent children, that is, of an age at which it is usually considered normal not to have achieved these good terms and to feel life as a provisional state, with "full reality" still waiting in an indefinite future.

PART II
PSYCHOANALYTIC THEORY OF NEUROSIS

A. Traumatic Neuroses

CHAPTER VII

Chapter VII

TRAUMATIC NEUROSES

THE CONCEPT OF TRAUMA

THE basic function of the mental apparatus is the re-establishment of stability after a disturbance by external stimuli. This is achieved first by discharge of the excitement aroused, later by its "binding" and by combinations of discharge and binding. Whenever the maintenance of a (relative) equilibrium fails, a state of emergency arises. Too high an influx of excitement within the given unit of time is the simplest type of such an emergency.

However, the expression "too high" is a relative one; it means beyond the capacity of mastery. This capacity depends on constitutional factors as well as on all of the individual's previous experiences. There are stimuli of such overwhelming intensity that they have a traumatic effect on anyone; other stimuli are harmless for most persons but traumatic for certain types with a readiness to become overwhelmed traumatically. Such "weakness" may have a constitutional root. It further depends on the mental economics of the person: for a child, the disappearance of a beloved person may be a trauma, because the libidinal strivings directed toward this person, having lost their aim, overwhelm the child; an adult is more subject to traumatic experiences when tired, exhausted, or sick. Another decisive difference is whether or not, at the time of the trauma, motor reactions are possible; the blocking of external motor activity increases the probability of a breakdown, and foxhole waiting is more dangerous than active warfare. The most important factor, however, is represented by previous repressions; those persons are "weak" whose binding capacity is fully taken up by the maintenance of earlier repressions. Thus trauma is a relative concept; factors of mental economy, dependent on constitution as well as on previous experiences and on the actual conditions before and during the trauma, determine what degree of excitation overtaxes the individual's capacity.

The ego may be regarded as having been developed for the purpose of avoiding traumatic states. Its sifting and organizing (discharging and binding) of incoming excitation are facilitated by its ability to anticipate in fantasy what might occur, and thus to prepare for the future. Economically, such preparation consists of making ready amounts of countercathexis for the purpose of binding the excitations to come. Events that have not been anticipated are experienced more forcefully than those prepared for. Therefore, an incident is likely to have a traumatic effect in direct relationship to the unexpectedness with which it occurs.

Unmastered quantities of excitement, built up by sudden overwhelming events as well as by chronic strain, create very painful sensations of tension, and set in motion pathological and archaic attempts to master what could not be mastered in the usual way. A kind of emergency regime of discharge is created (1292), partly as an automatic function against the will and without any participation on the part of the ego and partly by the remaining and restored forces of the ego.

The symptoms of traumatic neuroses are (a) blocking of or decrease in various ego functions, (b) spells of uncontrollable emotions, especially of anxiety and frequently of rage, occasionally even convulsive attacks, (c) sleeplessness or severe disturbances of sleep with typical dreams in which the trauma is experienced again and again; also mental repetitions, during the day, of the traumatic situation in whole or in part in the form of fantasies, thoughts, or feelings, (d) psychoneurotic secondary complications.

BLOCKING OF OR DECREASE IN EGO FUNCTIONS

The blocking of ego functions can be explained as a concentration of all mental energy available on one task, the building of counterenergies to master the intruding overwhelming excitation. The urgency of this task makes all the other ego functions relatively unimportant; these functions have to relinquish their energies in favor of the emergency task which completely governs the person.

The blocking of some of the functions, especially of the perceptive and apperceptive ones, acts simultaneously to prohibit the influx of further excitation. The excitation already at hand has to be mastered before new stimuli can be accepted. The organism develops different ways of protecting itself against too great a quantity of stimulation (*Reizschutz*) (605); refusing to accept new stimulation is a primitive means of re-establishing such protection after it had been broken down by the trauma.

Among the functions that might be weakened or blocked, because they have become relatively unimportant after the trauma, is sexuality. Generally the sexual interest of traumatic neurotics is diminished, and in male patients temporary impotence occurs very frequently (340, 1616). Although this symptom often may be due to psychoneurotic complications, it may also be an entirely unspecific symptom. The sexual energy, like other mental energies, is mobilized for the purpose of mastering the intruded excitation and is no more at the disposal of sexuality. Just as sexual interest generally decreases in sick persons because they become narcissistic, so may sexual energy lose its specific character after a trauma (340).

In traumatic neurotics regressive phenomena of all kinds in the realm of the instincts as well as of the ego have been described. They are to be looked upon as the result of a general loss of differentiation of the higher functions, again for the purpose of the overwhelming task, the "unspecific" mastery. Besides, this "primitivation" may serve another purpose as well: helpless persons usually tend to regress to the times of their childhood, because as children they actually were helped by "omnipotent" grownups. Traumatic neurotics sometimes develop a kind of demonstrative attitude of helplessness and passive dependence and show certain oral trends; this is a regression to the more primitive passive-receptive type of mastery of the outer world following their failure to succeed in an active way. This reaction will be stronger in persons who were inclined to this type of mastery even before the trauma: limited in their active abilities from the beginning, they will more quickly go into a traumatic state than persons with a more active ego.

Ego blocking, represented in fainting as a response to a trauma, is the most archaic and primitive "defense mechanism." In fainting, the organism, which has been overwhelmed with too intense stimuli, shuts out the influx of further stimuli. The complicated defense mechanisms of the psychoneuroses may be looked upon as partial faintings. In fainting, all perception is blocked; in repression, some selected perceptions are blocked (*see* p. 144).

EMOTIONAL SPELLS

The various emotional spells, too, represent more archaic and involuntary emergency discharges. To a certain extent, they are entirely unspecific; a person after suffering a trauma may be restless, hyperkinetic, may tend to cry and shout. In part, these reactions are specific and their nature can be explained either by the motor and sensory situation at the moment of the trauma or by the pre-traumatic history of the person. The fact that the emotional quality of such spells is most often felt as anxiety or rage is important and should be kept in mind. A study of the development of anxiety shows that all later spells of anxiety represent repetitions of early traumatic states. The objective state of being flooded with unmastered excitation is subjectively felt as being very painful, and the quality of this pain is very similar to anxiety. This is brought about partly by the unmastered inner tension itself and partly by involuntary vegetative "emergency discharges" (618). Later states of rage, too, are rooted in situations of frustrations, that is, in states where an urgent need is not fulfilled and the available discharges are not adequate. Thus anxiety and rage in traumatic neurotics represent discharges of excitations that were aroused in the traumatic situation but could not be discharged sufficiently. Their specific nature, however, often can be explained by the emotions felt (or aroused but not felt) during the trauma. In this sense the emotional spells belong in the category of "repetition symptoms" in traumatic neurotics, to be discussed later.

The archaic epileptic syndrome probably functions as an emergency outlet in certain constitutionally predisposed individuals (917).

SLEEP DISTURBANCES AND REPETITION SYMPTOMS

Sleep presupposes a state of relaxation. An organism flooded with excitation is unable to relax. It is understandable that the unmastered amounts of excitation in the traumatic neurotic makes sleeplessness one of his main symptoms.

The active repetition of the trauma in dreams, which is so torturing to the patient, is economically a relief for him nevertheless. The archaic ego, before it was able to anticipate the future, mastered the outer world by the active repetition of what had been experienced passively. The repetition dreams of the traumatic neurotic represent a regression to this primitive mode of mastery; by experiencing again and again what once had to be gone through in the trauma, the control may slowly be regained. It brings belated discharge and thus helps to get rid of tensions (605). Besides, these dreams make sleep possible in spite of the inner tension.

Repetitions of the trauma are not limited to dreams. They occur also in the waking state. In part they are conscious: the patient cannot free himself from thinking about the occurrence over and over again. In part they are unconscious: the patient experiences spells or makes certain ticlike movements which manifestly have no meaning whatsoever but which in analysis betray themselves as repetitions of movements performed in the traumatic situation, or as movements that would have been purposeful in the traumatic situation but were omitted. It may occur that the movements do not fit into the precipitating traumatic situation but into some still older and forgotten situation which had been newly remobilized by the trauma (1434).

Whereas an obsessive rumination about the trauma represents an attempt at the belated binding of the intruded excitation, the active repetition of what has been passively experienced, like the emotional spells and movements, represents attempts at belated discharge. If such active repetition is compared to the aforementioned mobilization of a passive-receptive attitude, it is seen that the same goal may be striven for by precisely opposite means.

A trauma is a situation in which a person's usual modes of adjustment have failed; he then has to find new and better ways of adaptation. This statement does not differ from what has already been said. Adaptation consists in nothing more than a complicated system of bindings and primitive discharges. One aspect, it is true, is stressed more when the term adaptation is used, that is, the active role of the ego. Actually, when the ego and its modes of adaptation fail, two things occur: (1) the ego is overwhelmed and symptoms beyond the ego occur, which are experienced passively; (2) the ego as soon as possible tries to re-establish its control even to the extent of applying more archaic principles of mastery—by regressing, if necessary (922).

Since the ego differentiated itself gradually from the id and there are deep archaic layers of the ego still very close to the id, it is not easy to state whether a given symptom of a traumatic neurosis occurs because the ego was overwhelmed or whether the ego makes an attempt at a new, archaic, and undifferentiated type of mastery. The word adaptation stresses the second point of view; actually, the concept of traumatic neurosis includes and justifies the first aspect: that not only the ego "adapts" itself, but also that something happened to which the organism was not "adapted."

PSYCHONEUROTIC COMPLICATIONS

It is not possible to describe the psychoneurotic complications that occur in traumatic neuroses before the psychoneuroses themselves have been studied in detail. After having discussed the psychoneuroses, a separate chapter will be devoted to neuroses that represent a combination of traumatic and psychogenic elements (*see* pp. 541 ff.). To complete the picture of the traumatic neuroses, however, it is necessary to characterize even at this point certain psychoneurotic trends that are never entirely missing in traumatic neuroses.

Every person has a certain amount of warded-off instinctual energies which are kept from being discharged by defensive forces and which try to break through nevertheless. As long as a certain stability prevails between the repressed impulses striving for discharge and the defensive forces preventing this discharge, the person may suffer from a certain impoverishment of his personality but otherwise remain relatively well. But any disturbance of this equilibrium brings the danger of a breaking through of the repressed impulses and the necessity to develop new and more effective means of defense—in other words, the danger of a neurosis (431). Experiences that precipitate neuroses always represent alterations in the earlier, relative equilibrium between warded-off impulses and warding-off forces (*see* pp. 454 ff.).

Freud has pointed out that in the etiology of neuroses the precipitating cause and the neurotic disposition (that is, constitution plus infantile experiences) are complementary. An individual who as the result of his constitution and infantile fixation has a neurotic predisposition will respond to even a minor difficulty with a reactivation of his infantile conflicts and therefore with a neurosis; an individual with less predisposition may also develop a neurosis, if his life experiences happen to be sufficiently severe. There is an etiological series of cases; at one end of the series are cases in which the actual precipitating cause is of no practical importance, and at the other, cases in which the specific precipitating cause plays a predominant role (596).

There is no doubt that a certain percentage of what is described as traumatic neuroses actually are psychoneuroses that were precipitated by some accident. This can be corroborated by the fact that sometimes there is a grotesque disproportion between the comparative insignificance of the "trauma" and the rather severe neurosis it is supposed to have precipitated. The more intense the previous repressions and the more unstable the equilibrium in the defense conflicts, the quicker an experience will have a traumatic character. Every individual has a "breaking point." However, in different persons the ease with which this point may be reached varies greatly.

In persons with a neurotic disposition there is not only a quantitative impoverishment of the ego which permits stimuli to provoke traumatic situations; there is also a qualitative sensitization at certain points of "complexes." Experiences in the realm of the complexes tend to have traumatic effects. (This will become clearer in the discussion of psychoneuroses.)

> It would be a paramount task for army induction psychiatry to screen out personalities for which the military situation as such is a "complex point." Ideas of "belonging to a great unit," as well as the provision of food and shelter, the limitation of personal responsibility, and an environment that almost excludes the other sex, have, of course, significance for everybody. The specific nature of this significance, however, varies enormously. Frequently the military situation involves a certain mental "infantilization," the army and the superiors representing the sheltering but also threatening parents. Some persons may accept this without much of a conflict and even be helped by it. Others, however, to whom the infantilization means a remobilization of repressed infantile conflicts, may become sensitized and weakened in their capacity for resistance. Still others may, according to their childhood experiences, be strengthened and weakened simultaneously or successively, or feel more protected under certain conditions, less protected under others; for instance, more protected as long as there is no combat, less in combat, or vice versa; or more protected in victory, less in defeat. Simmel explained the typical attitude of the soldier as an expectation of parental protection; this expectation may give place to a sudden and severe disappointment (1434).

Severe traumata that upset the entire economy of the mental energy also of necessity upset the equilibrium between the repressed impulses and the repressing forces. The first type of such a disturbance is a general and unspecific one. For the purpose of fulfilling the overwhelming task of a belated mastery of the intruding excitation, all differentiated mental functions, including sexuality, may be robbed of their specific cathexes; this also holds true for the cathexes that have been bound by conflicts of repression. The cathexis of the defending forces may be mobilized first; this is a general reason why repressed forces make a more or less open reappearance after traumata. The picture thus created is that of an unspecific disintegration of the personality, in which the abolition of differentiations and the regression toward childish dependence are predominant.

In a more specific way, latent neurotic dispositions may be mobilized by a trauma either (*a*) by an increase in the anxiety that motivates repression or (*b*) by an increase in the repressed instinctual forces.

If a person had developed a certain amount of castration anxiety or anxiety over loss of love, and subsequently has overcome this anxiety by certain inner reassurances ("It is not so bad after all, and probably there is no real castration, and I shall not be abandoned for good"), the experience of a trauma is apt to upset these reassurances and to remobilize the old anxieties. Persons who, for example, have hitherto denied their fears by partial regression to the security of primitive narcissism and omnipotence are forced by the trauma to admit that they are not omnipotent after all, and the old anxieties reappear. This is especially true in one type of anxiety over loss of love. Some persons have the capacity for hanging on to the belief that fate will protect them, just as their parents had protected them before in their childhood. Such persons experience a trauma as a betrayal by fate which refuses to protect them any longer. The frightening idea of having lost the protection of a powerful person with superego qualities varies in intensity according to the degree to which the subject had already submitted to a passive-receptive attitude before experiencing the trauma. This submission may have been acute, as in a soldier or sailor in combat, or chronic, as in persons whose self-esteem has remained dependent on constant reassurance of being protected or loved. The latter are not only inclined especially toward the development of traumatic neuroses but also traumatic neuroses in this personality type will be governed more by depressive clinical pictures (1244).

It was mentioned that chronic stress may have the same effect as a trauma. There is one particular kind of chronic stress that has a specific result: Extreme frustrations, which make a person feel that he is really abandoned and not cared for by anybody or anything, precipitate in adult persons states of apathy that are comparable to "primary depressions" in children (*see* p. 404) or even to the way in which hospitalized infants without mother's love remain somehow subdued.

The effect of castration anxiety is particularly clear in cases where the trauma has brought the intense danger of physical injury. (However, it is well known that traumatic neuroses occur more often in cases that have not suffered real injuries.) There are quite a number of postoperative traumatic neuroses, where, for instance, the patient had not been mentally prepared and the operation was then regarded as a castration. This actually occurs more frequently after genito-urinary operations than after operations involving other parts of the body (514).

> The fact that the castration fear created by an operation increases with the degree to which the operation has a traumatic effect necessitates a mental hygienic preparation of patients before surgical operations. Children especially have to be prepared by objective enlightenment about what is going to happen before they are operated upon, to avoid serious shocks.

The degree in which a trauma is experienced as a loss of the protection of fate or as castration is dependent, of course, upon the pretraumatic history of the patient. The intensity of the unconscious readiness to develop anxieties and the ways in which persons have learned to deal with anxieties are decisive.

What is most characteristic in the reaction to a trauma is that associative connections are immediately established between the trauma and the infantile conflicts that become activated. Old infantile threats and anxieties suddenly reappear and assume a serious character. The trauma may be experienced as a mere repetition of other older traumata of childhood. It has been mentioned that sometimes the symptoms of spells in traumatic neuroses may reveal themselves as determined not by the physical situation in the actual traumatic situation but by the physical situation in some forgotten childhood scene. The whole "trauma" may have a screening function (686).

> Staudacher studied a war neurosis precipitated by the explosion of a grenade in which the patient's reaction was determined in all its details by a childhood experience that took place at the age of three (1472).

Concerning an increase in the repressed impulses, it seems unlikely that a severe trauma should also be felt as a kind of temptation. It is true that in general a trauma is frightening and does not bring any instinctual satisfaction or temptation. But actually, there are persons whose sexual instinct has undergone a sado-masochistic distortion, and who have an immense (conscious or unconscious) interest in all dangerous, extraordinary, cruel, and "thrilling" events. The more an interest of this kind is repressed, the more likely it is that a trauma may unconsciously give the feeling: "Now, my sexual fantasies are becoming real at last." In this sense the trauma may be perceived as a sado-masochistic temptation. It is more probable, however, that it is perceived as a mixture of temptation and punishment: "What I have wished for is happening now; and it is happening in a terrible way, so that I shall be punished for having wished it." The trauma may signify the breakdown of a counterphobic attitude (*see* p. 549).

A third type of remobilization of latent conflicts by a trauma is the arousing of old conflicts between the ego and the superego. Even without having discussed the nature of these conflicts as yet, it will be conceivable that an ego when experiencing a trauma may not only feel "fate, the successor to my parents, is abandoning and castrating me" but also "And it serves me right, because I am guilty." This attitude, repeating on an internal level conflicts that originally existed between the external world and the ego, turns certain traumatic neuroses into a narcissistic affliction.

> All military psychiatrists know the depressive features in traumatic neuroses of soldiers whose "buddy" was killed while they themselves were saved. This does not necessarily presuppose that they have felt especially ambivalent toward the lost comrade. What they feel guilty about is rather that they had hoped that if "somebody's number is up," it may be another fellow and not they themselves.

In his discussion of war neuroses, Freud called attention to a fact that complicates the role played by the superego in traumatic neuroses (603): the intrapsychic representative of fate may consist not only of the genuine superego, which has been acquired in childhood, but also be made up of later and more superficial identifications with various other authorities. Such superficial and passing identifications may sometimes be very influential and come into conflict with the genuine superego. Freud spoke of these formations as "parasitic doubles of the superego," which for certain periods may usurp the power of the superego. Rado has demonstrated that the intrapsychic representation of a hypnotist may be considered as a parasitic superego. (It is even a "parasitic double of the ego") (1234). Freud stated that war conditions may create a "war superego" of this kind, which not only permits the expression of impulses otherwise forbidden but even makes demands that are tempting to the ego because its genuine superego never permitted such impulses to be brought into action. According to Freud, one finds in many war neuroses that a "peace ego" rises in defense against a "war superego" (603).

Whether or not a sudden influx of unexpected stimulation has a traumatic effect depends upon the personality experiencing the event. This concerns the actual situation at the moment of the trauma as well as the entire infantile history. As to the actual situation, first of all, the state of preparedness is decisive: the more preparation, the less likely a trauma. Traumatic neuroses are more intense when the trauma encounters an ego exhausted by a long endured stress (presupposing that the stress was not a kind of "expectation" of the event, in which case is would be a favorable circumstance) (1244).

As to the specific structure of the personality at the time of the trauma, Simmel and Rado showed that it is not only a "war superego" which in soldiers increases the dangers of a "neurotic breakdown"; the whole war situation is psychologically characterized by two contradictory features: it demands actions that represent instinctual outlets hitherto forbidden; but simultaneously it frees the personality from responsibility and causes a certain re-establishment of the old oral-receptive way of mastering the outer world. The commanding officer has the responsibility and the power; and he is believed to have the duty of and the capacity for giving protection. The disappointment is all the greater when this expectation fails (1244, 1434).

Not only are the commandments and prohibitions of the superego different in war from those that were valid in peace, but the "infantilization" in the military situation involves many of the superego's functions being reprojected onto the superiors. If the superiors fail in their role of protectors and rewarders, the worst has occurred, since the soldier is no longer in the habit of functioning as his own superego. The hatred thus mobilized against the nonprotecting father substitute may be condemned by the still existing superego and thus create guilt feelings and new severe conflicts.

The infantile history decides the degree of stability of the personality, that is, its amount of latent conflicts ready to be mobilized. In general: the more repressions, the less free energy is at hand to master newly arriving excitations, and the greater the readiness for traumatic effects. The fact that the development of a traumatic neurosis is contingent upon childhood history justifies the attempts to exclude from the armed forces potential victims of traumatic neuroses.

The fact that the pretraumatic personalities are reflected in traumatic neuroses betrays itself in the multiplicity of the clinical pictures, and also in the change of the clinical pictures in different cultures and times, analogous to the change of the clinical pictures of psychoneuroses in different cultures and times.

In World War II there are reported many more schizophrenic or schizoid episodes of short duration that ended spontaneously than in World War I. If reality becomes unbearable, the patient breaks with reality. But enough preconscious attention remains to re-establish the contact with reality as soon as it becomes bearable again. It may be that the recent prevalence of psychotic mechanisms in traumatic neuroses corresponds to the prevalence of "character disorders" among the psychoneuroses (*see* p. 447).

SECONDARY GAINS

In the traumatic neuroses, *secondary gains* play an even more important role than in the psychoneuroses; these are certain uses the patient can make of his illness which have nothing to do with the origin of the neurosis but which may attain the utmost practical importance. The symptoms may acquire secondarily the significance of a demonstration of one's own helplessness in order to secure external help such as was available in childhood. The question how to combat or to prevent secondary gains often becomes the main problem in treatment. In cases where a neurosis has been precipitated by a comparatively minor incident, the incident itself is often placed in the foreground by the patient, who in this way succeeds in again repressing the mental conflicts mobilized by it. Obtaining financial compensation or fighting for one creates a poor atmosphere for psychotherapy, the more so if the compensation brings not only rational advantages but has acquired the unconscious meaning of love and protecting security as well. Yet anyone who has a psychoanalytic understanding of the neurotic processes will not equate neurosis to simulation and will not repudiate compensation altogether. It may be that there is no fundamental solution of the question how compensations should be handled that would be equally valid for all cases. Perhaps the idea of giving one single compensation at the right time may be the best way out.

Since the course and the special nature of the symptomatology of traumatic neuroses are to a great extent dependent upon the "psychoneurotic complications" involved, many of their problems will be more easily approachable after the discussion of the psychoneuroses.

PSYCHOANALYSIS IN THE THERAPY OF TRAUMATIC NEUROSES

In traumatic neuroses, we see two sets of spontaneous attempts at recovery that seem to be actually contradictory: (*a*) attempts to get distance and rest, to collect energy, as it were, for the task of belated mastery: the stopping of or decrease in ego functions and the undoing of differentiations, a withdrawal toward a fresh start for the reconstruction of the collapsed equilibrium; (*b*) attempts at belated discharges: motor phenomena, emotional spells, repetition phenomena. The first set could be called the quieting-down method, the second the stormy method—both aimed at the same end of belated mastery.

Therapy can and should imitate both ways. On the one hand the therapist may give rest, reassurance, the satisfaction of wishes for passivity and dependency—"take-it-easy" suggestions. On the other hand he may give catharsis, the opportunity for stormy discharges and for the repeated re-experiencing of the trauma and a verbalization and clarification of the conflicts involved. The second method is, when applicable, a more direct help; the first one becomes necessary when the ego is too frightened, when a working through of the traumatic event is still unbearable and would still be too much of a repetition of the traumatic character of the experience. Apparently the therapeutic task in traumatic neurosis consists in finding out which blend of the two methods is necessary in a given case. To find the relatively correct amount of catharsis and reassurance is the main task of therapy, and it is of comparatively minor importance by which method catharsis as well as reassurance are achieved. While in general it will be better to encourage the patient to talk as much as possible about the trauma and to tell his experiences over and over again, some patients first need rest and greater distance from their experiences before they are capable of abreactions.

The more a traumatic neurosis has induced a secondary psychoneurosis, the more other measures will become necessary. Those are the cases that need psychoanalysis, the prognosis of which will depend on the nature of the induced psycho-neurosis. Cases in which the "traumatic" change represents a hysterical reaction are as amenable to psychoanalysis as hysterias are. Frequently, as has been mentioned, pronounced narcissistic admixtures are evident, which makes the prognosis of psychoanalysis more doubtful.

Kardiner described cases in which traumatic neuroses did not tend toward a spontaneous cure but rather toward the development of lasting defects of the personality (922). In these cases, the blocking of or decrease in ego functions, characteristic for every traumatic neurosis, created a lasting decrease in perception, judgment, and interest in the external world, a readiness to withdraw from any contact with reality, probably corresponding to a fear of repetition of the trauma. The resulting picture is that of a very restricted personality living a simple life on a low level, comparable to certain psychotics or to personalities that have overcome a psychosis with scars in their ego. Several cases of this irreparable type have been described (1149). Probably this unfavorable development is due to constitutional or psychoneurotic complications of a narcissistic nature. In such cases, therefore, psychoanalysis, too, may become difficult. Early treatment is indicated, before the alterations created by the trauma are imbedded too deeply into the personality.

The traumatic neuroses offer a unique opportunity to study the fact that the ego is an apparatus developed for the purpose of overcoming past traumata and for avoiding future traumata; traumatic neuroses represent an insufficiency of this basic function of the ego.

B. Psychoneuroses, the Neurotic Conflict
CHAPTERS VIII–X

Chapter VIII

THE MOTIVES OF DEFENSE

WHAT IS A NEUROTIC CONFLICT?

THE psychoneuroses are based on the neurotic conflict. The conflict results in the blocking of necessary discharges and in this way creates a state of being dammed up. This state gradually gives rise to a relative insufficiency of the ego's capacity to master excitation. The precipitating factors of psychoneuroses must be looked upon as relative traumata; stimuli which, were it not for the state of being dammed up, would have been mastered without difficulty, now create a relative insufficiency (*see* pp. 454 ff.).

The neurotic conflict, by definition, is one between a tendency striving for discharge and another tendency that tries to prevent this discharge. The intensity of the tendency toward discharge, it has been stated, depends not only upon the nature of the stimulus but, even more, upon the physicochemical state of the organism. In general it is permissible to equate the tendencies that strive for discharge with drives ("instinctual impulses"); the sieving of drives, that is, the decision as to whether or not their discharge should be permitted, has been defined as a function of the ego. Therefore, the general formulation would be: *the neurotic conflict takes place between drives, that is, the id and the ego* (608, 611).

ARE NEUROTIC CONFLICTS BETWEEN OPPOSING INSTINCTS POSSIBLE?

Is this formula valid for all neurotic conflicts? Or would it be conceivable for a neurotic conflict to take place between two instinctual demands with contradictory aims? Certain clinical facts seem to prove, for example, that homosexuality may repress heterosexual impulses or that sadism may repress masochism (42, 601).

However, if the history of conflicts of this type is investigated it is regularly found that the apparent conflict between instincts merely covers or represents another conflict between an undesirable instinct and some fear or guilt feeling that objects. This objecting force succeeded in increasing the intensity of some other drive—the aim of which was opposed to that of the original objectionable drive—because this increase helped strengthen the intended defense. An instinctual conflict at the basis of a neurosis is always a structural conflict as well; one of the conflicting instincts represents the ego, that is, is sustained by an ego defense, or strengthened for purposes of ego defense. Although itself an instinct, it acts as a defense against a more deeply repressed instinct. The concepts of "instinct" and "defense" are relative; the two are always interpenetrated; reaction formations especially make use of reinforcements of instincts with opposite aims. Instincts contradictory in aim, without such reinforcement by the defending ego, would not conflict with each other. Within the realm of the id there is no conception of contradiction, logical order is here nonexistent. Instincts contradictory in aim can be satisfied one after the other, sometimes even simultaneously, by one and the same derivative. Freud raised the question as to why certain persons experience contradictory instincts as conflicting and are troubled about them, whereas others do not feel them as conflicting at all (629). The answer is that this depends upon whether or not the contradiction between the instinctual aims involves a structural conflict as well (433, 438).

In the last analysis, anxiety and guilt feelings motivating structural conflicts also express instinctual demands, namely, demands of a self-preserving instinct, or of an instinct to preserve mother's love.

To summarize: The fact that there are conflicts between instincts does not necessitate any change in the formula: the neurotic conflict takes place between the id and the ego.

THE EXTERNAL WORLD IN NEUROTIC CONFLICTS

The motives of defense are rooted in external influences. However, the external world as such cannot repress. It can only compel the ego to develop repressing forces. Without an intrapsychic institution that represents and anticipates the external world, no defense and no neurosis could arise. An original conflict between the id and the external world must first have been transformed into a conflict between the id and the ego before a neurotic conflict can develop.

The external world cannot ward off impulses except through the ego. However, external perceptions perhaps may be warded off, and in this way participate in a neurotic conflict. In the discussion of traumatic neuroses, fainting and the blocking of further perceptions demonstrated that the external world (the perceptions) may be warded off. A similar phenomenon occurs in psychoneuroses: there are negative hallucinations, representing a warding off of some part of the external world; there is forgetting or the misinterpreting of outer events to achieve wish fulfillment; there are all kinds of mistakes in reality testing under the pressure of derivatives of unconscious wishes or fears. Whenever a stimulus gives rise to painful feelings, a tendency is developed not only to ward off these feelings but also to ward off the stimulus.

However, none of these neurotic falsifications of reality can be distinguished exactly from repressions that are directed against one's own impulses. The external world is warded off as a possible source of punishment or as a possible source of temptation to unconscious objectionable drives. Situations are avoided or forgotten because they represent an inner instinctual demand. Here, again, the conflict between the ego and the external world reflects a conflict between the ego and the id.

Sometimes a part of the external world is warded off not to avoid the mobilization of an instinct but to deny the idea that the instinctual act may be dangerous or cause pain; that is, the prohibitive character of the external world may be warded off. In general, this type of denial cannot be carried far in neuroses because the reality-testing function of the ego prevents a too obvious falsification (541).

Freud once expressed the opinion that herein may lie the basic difference between neurosis and psychosis. Both disturbances are based on a conflict between an instinctual impulse and a fear of the possible pain connected with it: the neurotic individual represses the instinct and thus obeys the threatening external world; the psychotic individual denies the external world and obeys his urgent instinct (611). This contrast, however, is only relatively valid (614). First of all, wish-fulfilling falsifications also occur in every neurosis. Freud studied them especially in fetishism (621); and he showed later that frequently persons who consciously know some fact very well indeed behave as if they had not noticed it or did not believe it. The ego of such persons is actually split into a conscious part that knows reality and an unconscious part that denies reality. Often such a split manifests itself in slips and errors (633, 635). Second, there is no doubt that psychotics who falsify reality do not always do so in terms of a simple wish fulfillment; very often they do so to escape an instinctual temptation, or to defend themselves against their instincts, exactly as neurotics do, only applying other mechanisms and deeper regressions (cf. 663) (see pp. 439 ff.).

To summarize: There are defensive attitudes against painful perceptions just as there are defenses against any pain. Nevertheless, in psychoneuroses based on the blocking of discharge, the defenses against instinctual impulses remain in the foreground; defenses against perceptions (and affects) seem to be performed first and foremost in the service of defenses against instincts. Again: the neurotic conflict takes place between the ego and the id.

THE SUPEREGO IN NEUROTIC CONFLICTS

The superego, of course, brings some complication into the picture. The conflict *ego vs. id* would in some neuroses more correctly be written *ego + superego vs. id,* and in others *ego vs. id + superego.*

After the superego has been established, it is responsible to a great extent for the decision as to which discharges are permitted and which are negated. The warding-off ego acts under the command of the superego, and wherever it is not simple anxiety but guilt feelings that motivate the defense, the formulation *ego + superego vs. id* is correct.

On the other hand, in many neuroses (especially in compulsion neuroses and, to an extreme degree, in depressions) the ego defends itself against guilt feelings. All the defense mechanisms usually employed in the fight against instincts may also become directed against the "anti-instincts" originating in the superego. In such cases, the ego develops a double countercathexis, one against the instincts and another one against the superego. And the warded-off guilt feelings may in turn break through against these defenses in a distorted form, in the same way as instincts do: *ego vs. id + superego* (*see* pp. 290 ff. and 397 ff.).

Again we may summarize: The superego may participate on either side in the neurotic conflict, but the formulation remains valid: the neurotic conflict takes place between the ego and the id.

ANXIETY AS MOTIVE FOR DEFENSE

Let us recapitulate what already has been stated about the motivations of neurotic conflicts (*see* pp. 51 f.). The infant, unable to attain satisfaction by his own efforts, necessarily often gets into traumatic situations, from which the first idea arises that instincts may be dangerous. Then more specific experiences show that instinctual acts may actually be dangerous; this impression may be warranted, or may be based on an animistic misinterpretation. The ego turns against instincts because it believes—correctly or incorrectly—them to be dangerous. Thus the problem of anxiety is the essence of any psychology of neurotic conflicts (618).

The primary anxiety, or the first experiences out of which later anxiety develops, is a manifestation of unmastered tension. It is an automatic occurrence that takes place whenever the organism is flooded with excitement; the symptoms of the traumatic neurosis show that it is not limited to infancy. This primary or traumatic anxiety occurs automatically, makes its appearance as panic, and is experienced by the ego passively; it can be understood partly as the way in which the unmastered tension makes itself felt and partly as an expression of vegetative emergency discharges.

Later on, the ego learns to use previously automatic archaic reactions for its purposes. The ego's judgment of impending danger brings the organism into a state similar to that of a trauma, but of lower intensity. The "tamed" anxiety, thus developed by the ego in the case of danger, may be called an anxiety signal, for it is used to indicate the necessity for starting defensive action (618). That component of anxiety appropriate to danger situations, preparation for defense, arises from the fact that it is the ego that uses anxiety; what is inappropriate, the fact that anxiety sometimes blocks the pertinent attitude, is due to the circumstance that the ego has no other material at hand than an archaic automatic mechanism.

Thus in the last analysis, all anxiety is a fear of experiencing a traumatic state, of the possibility that the organization of the ego may be overwhelmed by excitation. However, after the ego is developed enough to control instinctual actions and to bring about gratifications, the instinctual impulses ought not to be frightening anymore. If they still are, it is due to the fact that fears over loss of love or of castration have induced the ego to block the normal course of its excitements, thus creating an insufficiency of discharge (431).

Sometimes, as has been stated, the ego's capacity to tame anxiety fails. The judgment that was intended to avert a traumatic state may actually induce it. This happens in the anxiety spells of anxiety hysterias, but it also happens in normal persons when they react to danger with paralyzing panic. The ego's intention to give an anxiety signal fails when the person in whom the failure occurs is, as a result of previous repressions, in a dammed-up state; the slight anxiety added by the judgment of danger acts like a lighted match in a powder keg.

Among a group of persons subjected to the same real danger, those are more likely to react with panic who have no opportunity to master their tension in any other way. Such opportunity may be blocked by external circumstances; it is easier to master anxiety while some task is to be fulfilled or some motions can be made than if one is forced to wait quietly. Or the opportunity may be blocked by internal circumstances, by a state of "readiness for anxiety," due either to antecedent strain or to previous repressions. This also holds true for children, whose reaction, besides, is also dependent on that of the grownups around them (541).

This triple stratification of anxiety may be summarized in a short table:

ANXIETY

(1) Trauma	Anxiety automatic and unspecific
(2) Danger	Anxiety in the service of the ego, affect created by anticipation, controlled and used as a warning signal
(3) Panic	Ego control fails, affect becomes overwhelming, regression to state (1); anxiety spell in anxiety hysteria

The same triple stratification of anxiety will be found again in all other affects.

Should the anxiety signal be designated as a countercathexis? This seems warranted because it is initiated by the ego and based on an active anticipation of some future possibility. On the other hand it is the expression of an automatic occurrence in the depth of the organism as a consequence of the ego's reaction; it is not created by the ego; it is, rather, used by it. In this sense, the anxiety signal is a typical example of the dialectic nature of countercathexis in general. The forces the ego uses against the instincts are derivatives of the instincts themselves.

GUILT FEELINGS AS MOTIVE FOR DEFENSE

The neurotic conflict becomes more complicated when anxiety is replaced by guilt feelings. Guilt feelings represent a topically defined anxiety, the anxiety of the ego toward the superego.

Guilt feeling proper—that is, the feeling "I have done wrong," a painful judgment about some past occurrence which has the character of remorse—must be distinguished from feelings of conscience which do not judge the past but the future: "I should do this," or "I should not do that." This part of conscience has a *warning* function and directs future actions of the personality.

Having designated the ego's judgment "Do not do that, otherwise something terrible may happen" as the root of "danger anxiety," we now may assume that the warning conscience feeling is a special case of the same ego function: "Do not do this, otherwise some specific terrible thing may happen."

What is this specific thing? What does "punishment by the superego" or "loss of the superego's love" actually mean? Obviously, that type of pain is feared which is actually felt, to a greater or less degree, in guilt feeling proper. The warning function of conscience expresses the ego's tendency to avoid the pains of intense guilt feelings. These pains constitute a specific displeasure, the avoidance of which is the aim of the conscientious person. As long as a real punishment is feared, or hell is thought of as a threatening reality, there is no true conscience yet, for the tendency to avoid punishment and hell does not differ from tendencies developed by other anxiety signals. In "conscience" the fear is internalized, and the danger threatens *from within*. Fear is felt not only lest something terrible occur within the personality but also lest there be a loss of certain pleasurable feelings, such as well-being, protection, and security, which were hitherto present. This feared loss may be characterized as a loss of self-esteem, the most extreme degree of which is a feeling of annihilation.

To summarize, the warning conscience says: "Avoid this or that action, otherwise you will experience a feeling of annihilation." Guilt feeling proper is more or less a materialization of this threat, which in turn may be used to avoid future similar actions, which might even intensify the feeling of annihilation.

This feeling of annihilation must be characterized as a cessation of the narcissistic supplies which were initially derived from the affection of some external person and later from the superego.

The consideration that what the normal conscience tries to avoid has actually happened in melancholia makes the melancholic feeling of annihilation comparable with the paralyzing panic in the third type of anxiety. The table of triple stratification given for anxiety may also be applied to the problems of guilt feeling. Conscience and warning guilt feelings correspond to the second state (to the warning "danger anxiety"), the melancholic feeling of annihilation to the third state, panic. But what corresponds to the first state of "trauma"?

In anxiety, the first state was the unspecific painful experience which the infant had to undergo in a traumatic state. In the case of guilt feeling the situation must be similar, but more specific. The assumption that here the feeling of a "danger from within" is not so much based on a general "traumatic tension" but on specific feelings of hunger can be supported by many clinical experiences about the connection between guilt feelings and oral strivings, to be discussed more fully later (*see* p. 136). Thus a new triple stratification may be formulated for guilt feeling:

GUILT FEELING

(1) Trauma	Feeling of hunger or annihilation automatic
(2) Danger	"Annihilation" in the service of the ego, affect created by anticipation, controlled and used as a warning signal
(3) Panic	Ego control fails, affect becomes overwhelming, regression to state (1); "annihilation" spell in melancholia

Now an important complication must be added: the primary actual hunger is for milk. Later on, narcissistic supplies are missed in the same way in a kind of mental hunger.

Total lack of narcissistic supplies makes even grown-up people apathetic and pseudo depressed—in extreme cases they may even try to satisfy their hunger by a regression into a state of hallucinatory wish fulfillment. This apathy is the model of what subsequent guilt feelings tend to warn of.

When the ego is sufficiently developed to form a judgment that there is danger of a cessation of essential narcissistic supplies, the aim of its signal, "annihilation may occur," must be to influence objects to furnish these supplies. This state represents the anxiety over loss of love which plays so important a role as a motive for defense.

In persons whose self-esteem is regulated by the anxiety over loss of love, secondary anxieties and guilt feelings may be aroused if they try to enforce the necessary supplies by objectionable means. Particularly unfortunate are persons who need narcissistic supplies but who at the same time unconsciously are afraid of receiving them.

The anxiety over loss of love, or rather the anxiety arising out of loss of narcissistic supplies, turns into anxiety over loss of the superego's supplies, and the fear into guilt feeling. Thus the second stage of the table about guilt feeling must be divided into two substages: in the first, the loss of narcissistic supplies threatens from without, in the second from within. Now the parallelism between anxiety and guilt feelings may be completed with the table on page 137.

The change from state (2a) in the table to (2b) is initiated when the anticipating ego begins to guard against any action on its part that might result in a loss of the necessary parental love; the change is completed with the resolution of the Oedipus complex by the introjection of its objects. The state (2b) is an essential characteristic of mental normality. Everyone continually experiences slight "conscience signals" which regulate behavior and which are of far greater importance as constituents of the so-called mood than general anxiety signals are.

"Conscience" becomes pathological when it (a) functions in too rigid or too automatic a manner, so that realistic judgment about the actual outcome of intended actions is disturbed ("archaic superego") or (b) when the breakdown toward "panic" occurs and a greater or lesser sense of complete annihilation is experienced instead of a warning signal, which is the case in severe depressions. The causes of such failure of conscience will be investigated later (see pp. 388 f.). Here a few remarks are pertinent on certain features that are characteristic of guilt feelings in general.

Guilt feelings are connected intimately with oral sensations, or rather with intestinal sensations. The monograph by Nunberg about guilt feelings (1175, 1179; cf. also 849, 1178) supplies abundant evidence on this thesis. For example, remorse and compulsion symptoms with the significance of atonement as well as all attempts to "undo" something in order to satisfy conscience are regularly unconsciously thought of as a giving back of contents of the body (959). And this is the case not only if the deed itself has been regarded as an incorporation. It arises, also, from the circumstance that the superego is felt as an introject pressing from within.

The refusal of food by depressed persons generally expresses the idea that this pressure from internalized objects should not be increased by incorporating still other objects (see pp. 389 and 394).

	ANXIETY	GUILT FEELING (A SPECIFIC ANXIETY)
(1) Trauma	Anxiety automatic and unspecific	Feeling of annihilation automatic, caused by: (a) lack of food (b) lack of affection (of narcissistic supplies)
(2) Danger	Anxiety in the service of the ego, affect created by anticipation, controlled and used as a warning signal	"Annihilation" in the service of the ego, affect created by anticipation, controlled and used as a warning signal (a) Before establishment of the superego: anxiety over loss of love (over loss of narcissistic supplies) (b) After establishment of the superego: conscience (regulating inner narcissistic supplies)
(3) Panic	Ego control fails, affect becomes overwhelming, regression to state (1); anxiety spell in anxiety hysteria	Ego control fails, affect becomes overwhelming, regression to state (1); "annihilation" spell in melancholia

Guilt feeling not only has an oral character in general but an oral-sadistic character in particular. The term *qualms of conscience* expresses this as well as the German *Gewissensbisse,* both expressions being mere descriptions of the way in which the sensations are actually felt.

> However, guilt feelings are not manifested in bowel sensations alone. The genetic relation to anxiety is shown in the fact that a bad conscience may produce the same circulatory and respiratory sensations as anxiety. "My heart is heavy," or "I am not able to breathe freely" are expressions of bad conscience.

In the case of depression, a decisive pathogenic regression increases this sadistic nature of the superego.

> The idea has been expressed that anxiety may correspond to the repression of sexuality, whereas guilt feeling may correspond to the repression of aggressive drives (97, 624). This seems too gross a co-ordination.

The ego, wedged between instinctual demands and guilt feelings, has two possibilities: it may obey the superego and turn against the drives, or it may rebel against the superego. There are as many compromises possible between obedience to and rebellion against the superego as there are compromises between obedience to and rebellion against external authorities. A very frequent type of compromise is temporary ingratiation for the purpose of preparing a later rebellion.

A few words are relevant about the conception of a need for punishment. The pressure from the part of the superego to which the ego is exposed creates first of all a need for getting rid of this pressure, for regaining the lost self-esteem, and for reassurance against possible feelings of annihilation. This aim is best achieved by "forgiveness." After the experience that punishment may be a means of achieving forgiveness, a need for punishment actually may develop. The punishment longed for is a means of achieving forgiveness; the individuals in question certainly would prefer it if they could achieve forgiveness without first undergoing punishment. In "moral masochists," however, the situation may be more complicated: punishment may be asked for not as a means for forgiveness only but also as a kind of distorted substitute for sexual gratification (*see* pp. 364 and 501 f.).

DISGUST AND SHAME AS MOTIVES FOR DEFENSE

Less is known about other affective motives of defense, but it seems that their origin and development can likewise be clarified by applying the table of triple stratification.

Disgust as a motive of defense certainly is directed against oral demands, a fact that connects it with guilt feelings. Actually, certain feelings of disgust are very similar to certain types of guilt feelings, for example, disgust with oneself. The connection with anal eroticism is, of course, also obvious.

Applying the triple stratification table to disgust, we may say:

1. The forerunner of disgust is an archaic physiological defense syndrome which is automatically produced as soon as something repulsive reaches the digestive tract. The first negative judgment of the infant's pre-ego is "This is not edible," which means "I should spit this out."

2. The strengthened ego learns to use this reflex for its purposes and turns it into a defense—first into an expression of negation in general (616), later into a defense against certain sexual, especially oral and anal, drives. This, again, is a signal: "If you do not give up this demand, you will have to spit and vomit."

> In a normal child a part of his anal-erotic interest in feces may be turned directly into a readiness to develop reactions of disgust (555). Overly intense disgust reactions betray their character as a reaction formation by an occasional breaking through of the original coprophilia in dreams or in symptomatic acts. The disgust of hysterics as a response to sexual temptation may be looked upon as an extreme denial of unconscious receptive sexual strivings: "I not only do not want to take anything into my body; I even want to spit or vomit something out of my body."

3. There are neurotic "attacks of disgust," corresponding to "panic" in anxiety, in which the ego, because of previous blockings, is completely overwhelmed by the affect which was intended for defense purposes (440).

Shame as a motive for defense is mainly directed against exhibitionism and scoptophilia. It is not simply a specialized form of castration anxiety (fear of the castrating "evil eye") (430, 1420), but a more specific feeling, in the last analysis undoubtedly also rooted in a primitive physiological reflex pattern (470, 555, 636, 1177). Shame, too, in many respects is connected with guilt feelings—"shame of oneself" (588).

> "I feel ashamed" means "I do not want to be seen." Therefore, persons who feel ashamed hide themselves or at least avert their faces. However, they also close their eyes and refuse to look. This is a kind of magical gesture, arising from the magical belief that anyone who does not look cannot be looked at.
>
> It is an interesting fact but one not easy to explain that shame seems to be connected in a specific manner with the phenomena of urethral eroticism. That the specific shame punishment of pillorizing is customarily used against wetting only shows that the same connection between shame and urethral eroticism was already effective in the previous generation. The aim of ambition based on urethral eroticism is to prove that there is no need to be ashamed anymore.

Probably the following phases may again be differentiated: (1) Shame as an archaic physiological reaction pattern. Being looked at is automatically equated with being despised. (2) The ego uses this physiological pattern for defense purposes; signal: "If you do this or that, you may be looked at and despised."

(3) The signal fails to operate in dammed-up persons, so that an overwhelming paniclike shame is experienced.

As in guilt feelings, the ego may turn not only against instinctual impulses in obedience to disgust and shame but may also ward off the affects of disgust and shame themselves (440, 1486).

SUMMARY

In the neurotic conflict (between the ego and the id) an instinctual drive seeks discharge in a struggle against an opposing anxiety (guilt feeling, disgust, shame). The drive tends toward the world; the counterforces tend toward withdrawal from the world. The drive seems to be governed by its hunger for objects; the counterforces seem to be governed by a striving to avoid objects.

ARE THERE ANY INNATE PRIMARY ANTI-INSTINCT FORCES?

Do any innate tendencies exist to suppress or inhibit sexual or aggressive impulses, besides externally aroused feelings of anxiety, guilt, shame, and disgust, tendencies that might operate even without frustrating experiences? Perhaps the helplessness of the human infant, which necessarily brings about traumatic states, suffices to create a primary hostility of the ego to the instincts? Perhaps a taboo on incestuous love, which is so drastically expressed in many primitive societies, may be something innate, and a main cause for the forces effective against the Oedipus complex?

Ideas of this kind do not seem to be warranted. There is no evidence that hypotheses of this type are necessary for the purpose of explaining the facts of the neuroses. The effects of infantile helplessness would ordinarily be overcome when the child is no longer helpless; if they persist, it is due to experiences that convinced the child of the dangerous nature of his impulses. Whenever we analyze neurotics, whose incest taboo has made them repress their Oedipus complex, we find that experiences are responsible for the anxieties and guilt feelings, and that they are the motivating forces for their repression.

Chapter IX

THE MECHANISMS OF DEFENSE

CLASSIFICATION OF DEFENSES

Eco defenses may be divided into (*a*) successful defenses which bring about a cessation of that which is warded off, and (*b*) unsuccessful defenses which necessitate a repetition or perpetuation of the warding-off process to prevent the eruption of the warded-off impulses.

Pathogenic defenses, which are at the basis of neuroses, belong to the second category: when opposed impulses cannot find discharge, but remain in suspension in the unconscious and are still heightened by the continued functioning of their physical sources, a state of tension results and a break-through may occur.

Hence the successful defenses are of less importance in the psychology of neuroses; they are actually less understood (*cf.* 1032). However, the borderlines between the two categories are not always sharply defined, and sometimes it is not possible to distinguish between "a drive changed by the influence of the ego" and "a drive that breaks through in a distorted way against the will of the ego and unrecognized by it." The latter type of impulse will produce cramped attitudes, will repeat itself again and again, will never permit full relaxation, and will cause fatigue.

SUBLIMATION

The successful defenses may be placed under the heading sublimation. This term does not designate a specific mechanism; various mechanisms may be used in successful defenses, such as a change from passivity to activity, a turning round upon the subject, a reversal of aim into its opposite (588). The common factor is that under the influence of the ego, aim or object (or both) is changed without blocking an adequate discharge. (The factor of valuation usually included in the definition of sublimation had better be omitted [127, 137].) Sublimation is to be differentiated from defenses that use countercathexes; sublimated impulses find their outlet, though drained via an artificial route; whereas the others do not. In sublimation, the original impulse vanishes because its energy is withdrawn in favor of the cathexis of its substitute. In the other defenses the libido of the original impulse is held in check by a high countercathexis (555, 1499).

Sublimations require an unchecked stream of libido just as a mill wheel needs an unimpeded and channeled flow of water (773). For this reason, sublimations appear after a repression has been removed (596, 599). Metaphorically, the defensive forces of the ego do not oppose the original impulses head on, as in the case of a countercathexis, but impinge at an angle, producing a resultant, which unifies instinctual energy and defensive energy and is free to proceed. Sublimations are distinguished from neurotic substitute gratifications by their desexualization; that is, the gratification of the ego is no longer an obviously instinctual one.

What drives may experience such a vicissitude and what circumstances determine whether or not sublimation is possible?

If the pregenital impulses and the concomitant aggressive attitudes are not warded off by the development of a countercathexis (which would exclude them from the subsequent development of the personality), they are organized later under the genital primacy. The more or less complete achievement of this organization is the prerequisite for a successful sublimation of that part of pregenitality which is not used sexually in the forepleasure mechanisms. It is highly improbable that a sublimation of adult genital sexuality exists; the genitals represent an apparatus for the achievement of full—that is, unsublimated— orgastic discharge. Pregenital strivings are the object of sublimation. If, however, the pregenital strivings have been repressed, and remain in the unconscious, competing with genital primacy, they cannot be sublimated. The capacity for genital orgasm makes the sublimation (desexualization) of pregenital strivings possible (308).

What determines whether or not the ego will succeed in arriving at such a fortunate solution is not easy to say. Sublimation is characterized by (a) an inhibition of aim, (b) a desexualization, (c) a complete absorption of an instinct into its sequela, and (d) by an alteration within the ego. All these qualities can also be seen in the results of certain identifications, as, for example, in the process of formation of the superego. The empirical fact that sublimations, especially those that arise in childhood, depend upon the presence of models, upon incentives directly or indirectly supplied by the environment, corroborates Freud's assumption that sublimation may be intimately related to identification (608). Moreover, the cases of disturbances in the capacity to sublimate show that such an incapacity corresponds to difficulties in making identifications (173). Just as with certain identifications, sublimations, too, may more or less successfully combat and undo infantile destructive impulses (1422, 1424), but also and in a distorted fashion give way to these same destructive impulses; in a certain sense, every artistic fixation of a natural process is a "killing" of this process (1332). Forerunners of sublimations can be seen in certain children's games, in which sexual strivings are satisfied in a "desexualized" way after some distortion of aim or object; and identifications are also decisive in this type of game (541, 956).

The extent of the diversion of aim in sublimation varies greatly. In some cases the diversion is limited to an inhibition in aim; the person who has made the sublimation does exactly what his instinct urges him to do, but does so after the instinct has been desexualized and subordinated under the organization of the ego. In other types of sublimation, changes occur that are much more far reaching. It is even possible that an activity opposite in direction to the original instinct may really have replaced the original instinct. Certain disgust reactions —usual among civilized people—that show no trace of the infantile instinctual tendencies against which they were originally developed belong in this category (555). This is identical with what Freud has described as transformation into the opposite; after its completion the entire force of an instinct operates in the opposite direction (588).

PATHOGENIC DEFENSES

Conflicts between instinctual demands and fear or guilt feeling are not necessarily pathological. The way in which the conflicts are handled determines whether the further course is a normal or pathological one. As long as normal instinctual demands have their place within the total personality and can achieve periodic satisfaction, the remaining conflicts have a relatively minor intensity and can be solved without pathological results. The ability to discharge instinctual tensions by periodic gratification is the best guarantee for mental health and also a prerequisite for undisturbed sublimation. The parts of instincts which during childhood have clashed with defenses of the countercathexis type, however, are excluded from this possibility of periodic discharge. The countercathexes do not change the warded-off instincts into anything else; rather they suppress them. They simply attempt to block their discharge, thereby causing them to lose connection with the remainder of the personality and to remain unchanged in the unconscious. Herein lies the danger of the break-through, which is the basis of neuroses.

This development explains two facts of decisive importance: (1) The warded-off instincts exert a constant pressure in the direction toward motility. Deprived of their possibility for direct discharge, they use any opportunity for indirect discharge, displacing their energy to any other impulse that is associatively connected with them, increasing the intensity of this substitute impulse or even changing the quality of the affect connected with it. Such a substitute impulse is called a derivative (589, 590). Most neurotic symptoms are such derivatives. (2) All pathogenic defenses have their roots in childhood; and there is no psychoneurosis that is not rooted in childhood.

The isolating effect of childhood defenses explains why a patient whose infantile sexual impulses are freed from repressions by psychoanalysis does not simply strive to satisfy these infantile strivings that have now become conscious. After the infantile defenses have been canceled, the isolation is undone and the warded-off strivings are connected again with the total personality. They now participate in the maturity of the personality; infantile drives turn into adult ones, which can be discharged. Thereafter, remainders can be handled by sublimation or by other more effective types of suppression.

In discussing the traumatic neuroses, it was noted that the state of being flooded with excitation gave rise to the need for blocking acceptance of further stimulation; perception and other ego functions were blocked or diminished by forceful countercathexes. These types of "defenses," especially their climax— fainting—may be regarded as the pattern according to which all other pathogenic defenses are formed: fainting is a complete cessation of the functions of the ego; other defense mechanisms consist of a partial cessation of certain functions of the ego (410).

> In the last analysis fainting as a defense mechanism and as the blocking of endangered functions is an outgrowth of a deep-seated biological reflex which causes not only endangered functions but also endangered organs to be abandoned (autotomy). This reflex, with its aim to get rid of a tense organ for the sake of homeostasis, can be looked upon as the common root of both gratification of instincts and defense against instincts.

DENIAL

The tendency to deny painful sensations and facts is as old as the feeling of pain itself. In little children a wish-fulfilling denial of unpleasant realities is a very common thing, a simple expression of the effectiveness of the pleasure principle.

The ability to deny unpleasant parts of reality is the counterpart of the "hallucinatory wish fulfillment." Anna Freud has called this type of refusal to acknowledge displeasure in general "pre-stages of defense" (541). The gradual development of reality testing makes such wholesale falsification of reality impossible (575). However, these tendencies toward denial try to remain operative. They succeed best against certain single internal perceptions of a painful nature. Freud explained that the "negation" of such a perception may be a compromise between becoming conscious of the data given by the perception and the tendency to deny. The statement "I am glad that I have not had a headache for such a long time," made prior to the onset of a headache, means "I feel the headache coming, but for the time being I can still deny it." "I do not know whom this person in my dream represents, certainly not my mother," means "I feel that this person represents my mother, but I am still able to deny it" (616).

All attempts at denial in later phases of development have, of course, the ego's functions of perception and memory as their adversaries. Painful experiences and the memories of painful experiences, automatically reproduced whenever anything resembles the original painful experience, force the organism to abandon the methods of hallucinatory wish fulfillment and simple denial (507). The gradual development of the ego and of the reality principle strengthens experience and memory and slowly weakens the tendency to deny. As long as the ego is weak, the tendency toward denial may remain relatively superior; in later childhood, the characteristic solution is that the objectionable truth is denied effectively in play and fantasy, whereas simultaneously the reasonable part of the ego recognizes the truth and the playful or fantastic character of the denial (176, 541). Some of this "denial in fantasy" remains in the normal adult who, knowing an unpleasant truth, nevertheless (or, rather, therefore) may enjoy daydreams that deny this truth. However, in adults, daydreams of this kind have an "unimportant" character and merely represent a refuge that brings a short relief from the burdens of reality, whereas games and denials in childhood are of major importance. Only in the case of severe disturbances of the function of reality testing (psychoses) do serious and important denials remain victorious in adults. To a minor degree, a split of the ego into a superficial part that knows the truth and a deeper part that denies it may, as an outcome of "denial in fantasy," be observed in every neurotic. Though knowing the truth, he may act as if it did not exist (614, 633, 635). Freud described this first in the fetishist, who consciously knows the anatomy of the female genitals but who, in his neurotic symptoms, acts as if women had penises (621).

Sometimes the struggle between denial and memory can be directly observed. An unpleasant fact may alternately be acknowledged and denied. If in this situation a kind of substitute object can be offered to perception or memory— one which though related to the objectionable fact is harmless—the substitute will be accepted and the struggle will be decided in favor of repression. The repressing ego, while involved in such a struggle with perception and memory, is seeking a substitute idea or a substitute experience. It develops a "hunger for screen experiences" (409, 413, 686, 1437).

This explains the existence of retroactive "screen memories" (553). The ego searches its store of memories for images which it may offer to its consciousness as a substitute. But also actual perceptions that occur during the struggle are immediately scrutinized by the ego as to their suitability for forming substitute images. The ego has a "free quantivalence" for screen experiences, and is economically relieved upon finding them. This relief is often experienced by children in a characteristic way, which may be called the command to remember (413). During an experience which is more or less harmless, but which may form the basis of a later screen memory, the child senses a kind of inner command: "Attention: This scene you are to remember throughout life!" Sometimes this is felt not as a strict command but as a wish to test one's memory.

There is a significant connection between *command to remember* and *déjà vu*. The unconscious situation in both phenomena is very similar in that an actual experience is associated with a repressed one and serves as a substitute for it (582). Although the ideas "I have experienced this once before" and "I am going to remember this throughout life" differ greatly, the feelings that accompany the two types of experience are very similar; occasionally a *déjà vu* experience is actually connected with a command to remember. However, in *déjà vu* the repression has already been completed, the ego does not want to be reminded of something that has been repressed, and the feeling of *déjà vu* consists of its being reminded of it against its will. In the command to remember, repression is still in conflict with memory. The ego actively approves of the actual experience because with its help it can complete the repression.

At times some actual occurrence is experienced with a feeling similar to *déjà vu:* "So it is really true that . . ." This may mean either that the actual occurrence is reminiscent of something that was repressed, and this repression is now endangered by the occurrence (the repressed often being a guilt feeling), which is experienced as uncanny. Or it may mean that what is "really true after all" is a reality free from frightening unconscious conceptions that were anticipated in connection with it; that is: "I no longer need to be afraid of things I had mistakenly connected with reality." In that case the feeling similar to *déjà vu* is relieving and pleasurable (442, 631).

Sometimes certain types of behavior toward other persons can be explained as attempts to facilitate denials of unpleasant facts. For example, the obvious aim of lying is to make the other person believe something that is untrue or to disbelieve something that is true; the aim of habitual lying, however, may unconsciously be to produce the same effect in the liar himself. The attempt to convince someone of the reality of something that is unreal is made as a proof of the possibility that some data of memory may also be erroneous. The person who is deceived serves as a witness in the argument between one's memory and the tendency toward denial (437) (*see* pp. 528 f.).

PROJECTION

The first judgment of the ego distinguishes between edible and nonedible objects: the first acceptance is swallowing, the first rejection is spitting out (616). Projection is a derivative of the first negation; it has the content of "I want to spit it out" or, at least, of "I want to put distance between it and myself." Projection is essential in that early stage of development of the ego which Freud has called the purified pleasure ego (588) in which everything pleasurable is experienced as belonging to the ego ("something to be swallowed"), while everything painful is experienced as being nonego ("something to be spit out").

So long as the line of demarcation between ego and nonego is not yet sharp, which is true in the early years of childhood and again in psychoses, the mechanisms of the state of the purified pleasure ego may be used by the ego for defensive purposes. Emotions or excitations which the ego tries to ward off are "spit out" and then felt as being outside the ego. The offensive impulse is perceived in another person instead of in one's own ego. Thus in the defense mechanism of projection the same holds true as in anxiety and guilt feeling: archaic reactions which in the early phases of development occur automatically later are tamed by the ego and used for its defensive purposes. However, this primitive mechanism of defense can be used extensively only if the ego's function of reality testing is severely damaged by a narcissistic regression, thus blurring the boundaries between ego and nonego once more. The fact that projection is of utmost importance in archaic animistic cosmologies fits in with its essentially archaic nature (401, 810, 854, 886, 937, 967, 1484).

When the development of the libido leads to an overcathexis of the excretory functions, these functions, too, may be used as physical models for projection. To get rid of an objectionable object or impulse by removing it from the body in the way feces are eliminated is a very frequent fantasy (26). In paranoia, the disease in which projection reaches greatest height, this fantasy achieves its climax in persecutory delusions in which the persecutor outside the patient represents the sensations he feels in his bowels (1203, 1465) (*see* pp. 428 f.).

In general, the organism prefers to feel dangers as threats from without rather than from within because certain mechanisms of protection against overly intense stimuli can be set in motion against external stimuli only. Many projections give the impression that internal stimuli are misapprehended as external ones, with the intent of applying this protection to inner stimuli also (605).

> Whether every projection of certain tendencies or feeling attitudes necessarily always represents an expulsion of previously internalized objects—that is, in the last analysis, either a spitting out or a defecation—can hardly be decided clinically.

Usually, projections in general are not performed at random but are directed toward some point in reality where they are met halfway. The paranoid person is sensitized, as it were, to perceive the unconscious of others, wherever this perception can be utilized to rationalize his own tendency toward projection. He senses keenly the unconscious of others when this enables him to become oblivious of his own unconscious (607). Just as the "monsters" in the manifest content of a dream represent a "water animalcule" from daily life (1328), so the monster of paranoid delusion may be a distortion of a microbe of reality.

Animism is the most important general example of projection in normal ego development. Paranoid patients, whose function of reality testing is severely distorted, produce the most extreme projective misinterpretation of reality. Neurotic patients do the same thing to a lesser degree by misunderstanding the actual reality in the sense of their unconscious needs.

INTROJECTION

Originally, the idea of swallowing an object is an expression of affirmation (616). As such, it is the prototype of instinctual satisfaction, not of defense against instincts. At the stage of the purified pleasure ego, everything pleasant is introjected. In the last analysis all sexual aims are derivatives of incorporation aims. Simultaneously, introjection is the prototype of regaining the omnipotence previously projected onto adults. Incorporation, however, although an expression of "love," objectively destroys the objects as such—as independent things in the external world. Upon becoming aware of this fact, the ego learns to use introjection for hostile purposes as an executive of destructive impulses and also as a model for a definite defense mechanism (449, 454, 662, 886, 967, 1484).

Incorporation is the most archaic aim directed at an object. Identification, performed by means of introjection, is the most primitive type of relationship to objects. Therefore any later type of object relationship, upon meeting with difficulties, may regress to identification, and any later instinctual aim may regress to introjection. The use of introjection as a defense mechanism, again, provides an example of how primitive automatic mechanisms later are tamed and used by the ego for its purposes.

REPRESSION

Relatively less archaic is the mechanism of repression proper, certainly a derivative of the "denial" discussed above. It consists of an unconsciously purposeful forgetting or not becoming aware of internal impulses or external events which, as a rule, represent possible temptations or punishments for, or mere allusions to, objectionable instinctual demands. The purposeful exclusion of these data from consciousness is obviously intended to hinder their real effects as well as the pain on becoming aware of them. However, although the repressed is not felt consciously it remains effective. The ego can get rid of it entirely only in those instances which have been designated as sublimation and which sometimes are called successful repression. In repression proper, based on continual counter-cathexis, the repressed remains effective from the unconscious (159, 589, 999).

The pattern of repression is exemplified best in the case of the simple forgetting of a name or an intention. Analysis reveals that a name or an intention is forgotten if a suppressed motive resisted it, usually because it was associated with some objectionable instinctual demand. In the case of tendential forgetting, the fact that the repressed still persists in the unconscious is sensed directly in the subjective feeling that one ought to know what has been forgotten, or even that one does know it "somehow," "it is on the tip of the tongue," although actually one does not know it (553).

Sometimes certain facts are remembered as such, but their connections, their significance, their emotional value are repressed.

Conflicts arise when new experiences occur that are connected with what had previously been repressed. Then there is a tendency on the part of the repressed to use the new event as an opportunity for an outlet; it tends to displace its energies to it, to turn the new event into a "derivative." The tendency to use such a displacement as a means of gaining discharge sometimes succeeds. If neurotic exaggerations—namely, attitudes in which a relatively harmless thing is emotionally overevaluated—are analyzed, the results demonstrate that they are derivatives of something that had been repressed; the seemingly absurd emotional value becomes understandable as a product of displacement. At other times the attempt of the repressed to find an outlet in the form of derivatives fails: a tendency then develops to repress any event associatively connected with the originally repressed material, in short, a tendency to repress the derivatives just as previously the original demand was repressed. This is called secondary repression (*Nachdraengen*) (589). The impression arises that the repressed is like a magnetic force attracting everything that has any connection with it, so that it, too, becomes repressed; actually, it does not attract associatively connected material into the repressed, but tries to transform it into a derivative, whereupon the same forces that had originally repressed it repress the new material as well.

Sometimes derivatives of the repressed are alternately admitted to discharge and themselves repressed. Certain formations of this kind, such as daydreams, may be enjoyed in a highly emotional way up to a certain degree; but they are entirely and instantly forgotten when this degree is transgressed (590). The same holds true for dreams, where there is likewise but one step from highly emotional dreams, which obtrude obsessively upon consciousness, to dreams that are entirely forgotten.

Thus repressions may either betray themselves by voids—that is, by the fact that certain ideas, feelings, attitudes that would be expected as adequate reactions to reality are actually missing—or they may betray themselves by the obsessive character with which certain compensating ideas, feelings, and attitudes that represent derivatives are clung to (1532). The first is to be seen in secondary repression; the second in screen memories (553) and in obsessional ideas.

There are many connections between repression and projection as well as between repression and introjection. Sometimes repressed ideas are unconsciously felt as objects that have been removed from the ego; this brings repression near to projection. At other times repressed ideas are felt as if they had been swallowed, a similarity to introjection based on the fact that what has been swallowed has ceased to be visible but is nevertheless still effective from within (1436). Dreams occurring in the course of an analysis often show that the repressed material is unconsciously looked upon as swallowed food, or even as feces or vomitus.

Repression proper is the main mechanism of hysteria. It expresses an attitude in which the objectionable thing is treated simply as if it were nonexistent. Perhaps the fact that sexual impulses very often are repressed, whereas aggressive impulses are more often the subject of other defense mechanisms, is due to the circumstance that education frequently handles the subject of sex by simply not mentioning it, whereas the existence of aggressiveness is acknowledged but is designated as bad. The more consistently educators apply prohibitions by acting as if the objectionable things did not exist, the more repression proper is encouraged in children. The inconsistency of present-day education, uncertain as to which instinctual claims to permit and which to suppress, resulting in initial permission and in subsequent sudden, unexpected (and therefore frequently more cruel) deprivation, favors the use of defense mechanisms other than repression.

The motive of repression is unquestionably the tendency to withhold that which has been repressed from motility (552). Proof of this is the fact that repression becomes superfluous when the inactivation is guaranteed in some other way. Compulsion neurotics are able to think obsessively about murder because through the application of the mechanism of isolation they are sure that they will not actually commit the crime (*see* pp. 289 f.).

> Orgel described a manifest Oedipus dream that occurred after the patient had had some experience that made him actually hate his mother. Under other circumstances he certainly would have repressed his incestuous wishes. The hatred which assured him that he would not actually make love to his mother permitted the temporary lifting of the repression (1208; *cf. also* 1033).

Since the repressed continues to exist in the unconscious and develops derivatives, repression is never performed once and for all but requires a constant expenditure of energy to maintain the repression, while the repressed constantly tries to find an outlet (589). This expenditure may be observed in clinical phenomena: for example, in the general impoverishment of the neurotic person who consumes his energy in the performance of his repressions and who therefore does not have enough energy at his disposal for other purposes. This explains certain types of neurotic fatigue. Some of the typical neurotic feelings of inferiority correspond to awareness of this impoverishment (585); attitudes are developed to avoid situations in which a new mobilization of the repressed may occur (phobias); and attitudes even appear which, to ensure that the repressed remains repressed, are contrary to those of the original impulses.

> In describing repression, Freud first differentiated between the destiny of the repressed idea and the destiny of the quantity of emotional cathexis of the repressed idea (589). The idea, that is, the ideational content, is forgotten; the emotional cathexis, however, may make its appearance through displacement to another idea. It is certainly true that sometimes the displacement of the cathexis to a less objectionable derivative, which finds discharge or access to consciousness, facilitates the repression of the original idea, as in screen memories (354, 1532). However, it is not possible to separate the conceptions of "idea" and "cathexis of the idea" entirely. If the *whole* cathexis were displaced, the original idea would no longer exert any pressure toward motility, the defensive struggle would become superfluous, and the whole process would then be called sublimation rather than repression. Actually the typical "derivatives" contain only a *part* of the repressed

cathexis. Not mere "ideas" are repressed but "impulses," that is, cathected ideas of future actions, wishes for actions (of course not only primary id wishes but also their later elaborations and ego attitudes). The displacement of the emotional cathexis to a derivative already represents a kind of failure on the part of the repressing forces, which could not attain their aim of suppressing every expansion of the repressed impulse. However, this failure may facilitate the task of keeping the original idea unconscious.

REACTION FORMATION

There are many neurotic attitudes that are obvious attempts to deny or to repress some impulses, or to defend the person against some instinctual danger. They are cramped and rigid attitudes, hindering the expression of contrary impulses, which sometimes nevertheless break through in various ways. In such traits, psychoanalysis as an "unmasking" psychology can prove that the original opposite attitude still exists in the unconscious. These secondary opposite attitudes are called reaction formations (555).

Do reaction formations represent a separate and independent mechanism of defense? They seem rather to be a consequence and reassurance of an established repression. But at least they signify a certain type of repression, which can be distinguished from other repressions. It is a type of repression in which the countercathexis is manifest and which therefore succeeds in avoiding oft-repeated acts of secondary repression. The reaction formations avoid secondary repressions by making a "once-and-for-all," definitive change of the personality. The person who has built up reaction formations does not develop certain defense mechanisms for use when an instinctual danger threatens; he has changed his personality structure as if this danger were continually present, so that he may be ready whenever the danger occurs. Examples are the cleanliness or the sense of order of the compulsion neurotic who struggles, by means of those character traits, against his instinctual demands for dirt and disorder. The rigidity of such cleanliness or sense of order as well as the occasional breakings through of dirtiness and disorder betray the reactive quality of these character traits.

A break-through may occur in dreams as well as in the waking state. An occasional instinctual action may become possible again and the reaction formation may become insufficient under certain economic or qualitative conditions. Most pathological character traits correspond to the reaction formation type; that is, whereas normal character traits permit discharge, the majority of pathological traits primarily serve the purpose of keeping still existent opposite tendencies in the unconscious (*see* pp. 471 ff.).

Certain mechanisms of defense represent intermediate forms between simple repression and reaction formation. A hysterical mother who unconsciously hates her child may develop an apparently extreme affection for the child, for the purpose of making the repression of her hatred secure. Descriptively, this may be called a reaction formation. But it does not imply a change of the total personality in the direction of kindness or consideration in general. The kindness remains limited to the one object, and even there it has to be re-established whenever the occasion demands. In contradistinction, a compulsion neurotic who develops a true reaction formation against hatred turns once and for all into a rigidly and generally kind personality (618).

A reaction formation may make use of drives, the aims of which are opposite to the aims of the original drive. It may increase the strength of drives of this kind the better to hold the original drive in check, and in this way a conflict between an instinctual impulse and an anxiety or a guilt feeling may be masked as a conflict between conflicting instincts. For example, a man may be reactively pregenital for the purpose of warding off genitality; another person may be reactively (pseudo) genital to ward off pregenitality; or reactively heterosexual to ward off homosexuality or vice versa; reactively passive-receptive to ward off aggressiveness or vice versa (1279).

The fundamental difference between a reaction formation that suppresses an original impulse and a sublimation in which the original impulse finds discharge is not always clearly recognized in psychoanalytic literature. This is partly due to a contradictory terminology. The classification of attitudes according to whether the attitudes are superseded or suppressed does not necessarily coincide with the classification according to which the attitudes are subdivided into those that work in the same direction as the original impulse (or a slightly modified one) and those that are diametrically opposed. The following diagram may serve to clarify:

		Attitudes that work	
		A. in the same or modified direction as the original drive	B. in the opposite direction
Attitudes by which the instinct is	I. superseded	IA	IB
	II. suppressed	IIA	IIB

We call I (which includes IA and IB) sublimation and II (which includes IIA and IIB) reaction formation. The usual sublimation is represented by IA; but there is also the type of IB: for example, if in a normal person an original anal interest is replaced by a certain not too intense disgust for feces without an intense unconscious interest in feces remaining (555). The typical reaction formation would be represented by IIB; but there are also "counterphobic" attitudes of the category IIA in which doing the same thing one originally feared serves the purpose of holding the original intensive wish in check (435).

Sterba has advocated the contrary nomenclature. He wished to designate formations in which there is no trace of the original instinctual demand (IIB) as "true reaction formations," thus including the origin of the superego among the reaction formations (1493). Because in psychoanalytic terminology the term reaction formation has gained currency to designate formations due to countercathexis, we would prefer not to follow Sterba's suggestion.

To clarify the relation between reaction formation and sublimation let us compare (*a*) a child who learns to write well and enjoys it very much, (*b*) a child who has an inhibition for writing, (*c*) a child who writes very constrainedly and meticulously, and (*d*) a child who smears. All of them have displaced anal-erotic instinctual quantities to the function of writing. In the first child a sublimation has taken place; he no longer wishes to smear but to write. The other children have not succeeded in channelizing this impulse. They are forced to inhibit it through a countercathexis, or to "robot" through reaction formations, or even to retain the original impulse in an unchanged way.

Whereas the sublimation of any instinctual demand into an ego function increases the effectiveness of this function, a reaction formation against a "sexualized" function necessarily decreases it.

Sublimation is related to reaction formation in the same way that the successful construction of the superego is related to an immutable repression of the Oedipus complex.

It is sometimes stated that sublimation is necessarily a kind of repression; the painter who has sublimated his smearing impulse does not consciously know anything about his anal eroticism. This depends on the definition of repression. If the disappearance of the original aim from consciousness is called repression, every sublimation is a repression (a "successful" one: through the new type of discharge, the old one has become superfluous). If, however, the definition of repression includes the conception of a continuous countercathexis, repression and sublimation exclude each other. For the man who has repressed his smearing impulses by a countercathexis, the idea of painting would have to be repressed, too, because it is too similar to the original smearing. However, there are neurotic artists whose productions are mixtures of sublimations and neurotic symptoms.

UNDOING

There are no sharp lines of demarcation between the various forms of defense mechanisms. Reaction formation was related to repression, and undoing (618) is related to reaction formation. In reaction formation, an attitude is taken that contradicts the original one; in undoing, one more step is taken. Something positive is done which, actually or magically, is the opposite of something which, again actually or in imagination, was done before.

This mechanism can be most clearly observed in certain compulsive symptoms that are made up of two actions, the second of which is a direct reversion of the first (567). For example, a patient must first turn on the gas jet and then turn it off again. All symptoms that represent expiations belong in this category, for it is the nature of expiation to annul antecedent acts. The idea of expiation itself is nothing but an expression of belief in the possibility of a magical undoing.

Paradoxically, the undoing sometimes does not consist of a compulsion to do the opposite of what has been done previously but in a compulsion to repeat the very same act. Analysis shows that this is based on the following unconscious intention. The first act was done in connection with a certain unconscious instinctual attitude; it is undone when this same act can be repeated once more under other inner conditions. The aim of the compulsion to repeat is to carry out the very same act freed of its secret unconscious meaning, or with the opposite unconscious meaning. If, because of the continued effectiveness of the repressed, some part of the original impulse insinuates itself again into the repetition which was intended as an expiation, a third, fourth, or fifth repetition of the act may become necessary (*cf.* 88).

An irreligious patient who obsessively had to pray for the health of his sick mother had the further compulsion of slapping his mouth lightly after having said the prayer. This was an undoing of the warding-off symptom, a return of the warded-off death wish toward the mother which meant: "I am putting the words of prayer back into my mouth." The same mechanism is operative in children who think that a false oath is permissible if, while making the gesture of the oath with their right hand, they secretly make the opposite gesture with the left hand.

Another patient suddenly felt a compulsion to crane his neck upward. It turned out that, shortly before, he had been riding down in an elevator and had thought that the rapid downward movement might have injured his brain (a disguised castration anxiety, "displaced upward"). The symptom of craning the neck upward was an "undoing": the upward motion of the head was intended to throw the brain back to the place from which it slipped, and thus to annul the previous castration.

This symptom represents a special case of the frequent type of compulsive symptoms that are based on the magic of symmetry and that often have the unconscious meaning of undoing. If anything has been touched on the right side, a similar object has to be touched on the left side. The meaning is that the equilibrium between instinct and counterinstinct should not be disturbed. If it has been disturbed on one side of the scale, it has to be "undone" on the other. The "number magic" of compulsion neurotics makes them prefer even numbers because they do not disturb the equilibrium as odd ones do (*see* p. 288).

Often an intention to "undo" fails because what has been warded off returns in the very measure of warding off; "undoing" turns into "doing it again." This happens when the undoing consists in performing the very same act but with another attitude; instead it may be repeated with the same attitude. An example: A patient with scruples in regard to the unnecessary expenditure of money bought a newspaper for a nickel; unconsciously to him this was equivalent to a visit to a prostitute. He regretted it and, wishing to undo the act, decided to return to the newsstand. He was uncertain what to do because he would have been ashamed to return the paper to the boy and to ask for the money. Then it occurred to him that the purchase of a second paper might ease his mind. But the stand was already closed. Thereupon he took another nickel out of his pocket and threw it away.

Like reaction formation, the defense mechanism of undoing may be brought about by a reactive increase in the strength of a drive opposed to the original drive, thus condensing the defensive attitude with an instinctual attitude striving for erogenous pleasure. When a child experiences defecation as a loss of his narcissistic integrity and develops a tendency for compensating coprophagy (or, later, when the adult indulges in reading while on the toilet), this coprophagy represents both an undoing of the defecation and an oral-anal pleasure. When a person with castration anxiety regresses to the anal level and substitutes the idea of losing feces for the idea of losing the penis, the frequent repetition of defecation gives reassurance that the loss is not permanent; while the ego "is concerned in undoing the castration . . . the id by the same process is indulging in anal impulses" (1054). This possibility of simultaneous reassurance and pleasure is probably the explanation for the fact that the mechanism of undoing is so often applied in conflicts around anal eroticism.

A special significance is connected with actions and attitudes aimed at the undoing of imaginative destructions. Strivings for reparation may or may not be successful in holding sadistic drives in check. They may be the main motive for artistic or scientific sublimations (1422, 1424) as well as for painful compulsive rituals (895, 959).

A failing of the mechanism of undoing, due to the invasion of the defense by the warded-off impulses, explains several phenomena frequent in compulsion neurosis: (a) the increase in the number of necessary repetitions because no repetition gives complete reassurance that this time it is done without the instinctual intention, (b) some forms of counting compulsions, the unconscious meaning of which is to count the number of necessary repetitions, (c) the ever broadening scope of the ceremonial assurances, (d) obsessive doubts which sometimes are doubt as to whether the undoing has succeeded, and finally, in certain cases, (e) the futility of all these measures (see pp. 306 ff.).

ISOLATION

Another mechanism of defense prevalent in compulsion neuroses and of very general significance for psychopathology is *isolation* (618). Here the patient has not forgotten his pathogenic traumata, but has lost trace of their connections and their emotional significance. He shows the same resistance to a demonstration of the true connections that a hysteric shows to the reawakening of his repressed memories. Thus here again a countercathexis is operative; its operation consists in keeping apart that which actually belongs together (1000).

Sometimes the patient interpolates real spatial or temporal intervals between the two realms that are supposed to be kept separate. Spatial intervals are arranged so that certain things (representing ideas that are to be kept apart) cannot touch each other, or a certain order is assigned to them which maintains a distance between them. Temporal intervals are planned so that after an action there is an intermission keeping the act from impinging upon any other one. Measuring such temporal intervals is sometimes one of the determinants of a neurotic compulsion to count.

Of practical importance is the patient who hinders any therapeutic effect of his analysis by carrying on the whole analysis "in isolation." The analysis is accepted only as long as the patient lies on the couch, but remains isolated from the rest of his life. Sometimes such patients have to begin and end the analytic hour with certain rituals, which serve to isolate the analytic sessions from what occurs before and after (438).

The most important special case of this defense mechanism is the isolation of an idea from the emotional cathexis that originally was connected with it. In discussing the most exciting events, the patient remains calm but may then develop at quite another point an incomprehensible emotion, without being aware of the fact that the emotion has been displaced. Extremely objectionable ideational contents, like murder or incest wishes, may become conscious in the form of obsessions, because the obsessional neurotic is able to feel these ideas as mere thoughts, securely isolated from motility. The emptiness of affect, which is so characteristic for certain compulsion neurotics and which creates a serious difficulty in treating them, is based on an isolation of this type. Certain patients are even able to feel their emotions fully, but only as long as they can somehow pretend to be merely playing or to be making thought experiments or the like, that is, as long as the emotions remain isolated from "seriousness."

> Compulsive patients withdraw from the frightening experiences of emotional impulses into the "isolated" world of words and conceptions. In obsessive brooding, the repressed returns: involuted philosophical ideas, which were intended as a protection against instinctual impulses, become as highly important emotionally as instinctual impulses are for the normal person (*see* p. 297).

An isolation that occurs very frequently within our culture is that of the sensual and the tender components of sexuality (572). It is a consequence of the repression of the Oedipus complex that many men (and also quite a number of women) do not succeed in attaining full sexual satisfaction because sensuality can be enjoyed only with persons toward whom they have no tender feelings or, even, toward whom they have contemptuous feelings or none at all. "They cannot desire where they love, and they cannot love where they desire" (572). The institution of prostitution gives men of this type an opportunity to isolate their objectionable sensuality from the rest of their life, and thus relieves them of the necessity to repress it.

Many children try to solve conflicts by isolating certain spheres of their lives, from one another, such as school from home, or social life from the secrets of their loneliness; one of the two isolated spheres usually represents instinctual freedom and the other good behavior. They even split their personality and state that they are two children with different names, a good one and a bad one, and deny the good one's responsibility for the bad one's deeds.

Whether the famous cases of "dual personality" should be called isolations or repressions depends upon whether or not the person in one state knows about the existence of the other state. These cases show that isolation and repression are basically related to each other.

Also in the cases which Freud called "split of the ego" (621, 633, 635) an unpleasant knowledge is kept isolated from the rest of the personality.

Another type of isolation is represented by attempts to solve conflicts around ambivalence—that is, conflicts between love and hatred of the same person—by splitting the contradictory feelings so that one person is only loved, another one only hated, a countercathexis preventing the two feelings from having contact with each other. An example is the contrast of the good mother and the wicked stepmother in fairy tales (552).

Failure of an attempt at isolation can be seen in the frequent obsessive blasphemies. In order to isolate the awe-inspired positive attitude toward the father figure from all aggressive or sensual ideas, a religious attitude was intended; in the obsessive blasphemies, this intention fails.

Although isolation occurs in all cases of compulsion neurosis, there are some persons in whom this mechanism dominates the picture to such an extent that they offer excellent demonstration material of this mechanism. The following case (411) illustrates this point.

A young man of seventeen became neurotic as a result of his conflict about masturbation. For a time he masturbated without any guilt feeling and often also watched when his schoolmates indulged in mutual masturbation. He then heard his minister deliver a sermon, advising against association with anyone who masturbated. Since in childhood the patient's genitality had been inhibited by an excessive fear of castration, he took the minister's sermon to heart and decided to follow his advice and no longer speak to boys who masturbated. This had particular reference to a boy who, he knew, masturbated a great deal. For a while he succeeded in keeping his resolution. But then to avoid contact with the boy, he developed certain phobias and compulsive procedures to maintain the avoidance. First, whenever he met the boy, he had to spit; an obsessive decree about the number of times he had to spit was never clarified in analysis. The phobia spread; he refrained from any contact with the family and friends of "The Avoided One." (The patient gave the boy this title in order to avoid using his name.) Then, because the avoided one was the son of a barber, the patient kept away from barbershops. Later he even avoided contact with persons who let themselves be shaved by barbers, and found it imperative to stay away from the section of the city where the barbershop of the boy's father was situated.

And then the entire neurosis developed quickly into an "isolation neurosis." He made the compulsive stipulation that the members of his family, particularly the women, which meant his grandmother, mother, and sister, were not to go into the forbidden neighborhood. He suffered greatly because his relatives would not accept this restriction of their freedom. He himself followed his own prohibition implicitly; but the more stringently he limited his actions, the more intensely was he forced obsessively to *think* of the forbidden section of the city. It is easy to understand that this caused him pain. But he gave an unexpected explanation of the pain. It was painful, he said, because at home he saw his mother and grandmother, and therefore ought not to think of the forbidden localities or persons. Although he was aware of the relation between his illness and masturbation, he ignored the connection. His masturbation had been given up without much apparent difficulty. But in its stead, the neurotic effort to keep the idea of "member of the family" separated from "uncongenial persons and localities," to isolate them from each other, became more and more definite.

This isolation became the chief topic of the neurosis. The patient allowed himself to think of "uncongenial "things" but tried to avoid thinking of "congenial" persons at the same time. He thus demonstrated that the Oedipus complex was the content of his masturbation. The elaboration of this effort on the part of the ego to defend itself against the Oedipus complex by means of isolation led in a few months to a compulsion neurosis of the severest type.

The patient was like the man in Wedekind's play who was not supposed to think of a bear. Whenever the patient thought of the avoided one he immediately thought of his grandmother. This tormenting symptom he called connecting. He was able to use a defense to deal with it, namely, a so-called disconnecting, which is a good example for an "undoing" mechanism. After he had simultaneously thought of a forbidden locality and a congenial person, if he could form a mental picture of the uncongenial thing, completely isolated and freed from all congenial adjuncts, everything was set right again, and he was quieted. Before long, the patient was absorbed in making "disconnections" from morning till night.

Two other components which tend to increase the severity of a spreading compulsion neurosis then appeared: an immense extension of the field of symptomatology, and an invasion of the symptoms by the warded-off impulses.

The division of objects into congenial and uncongenial ones gradually embraced all persons and all localities. Thus "schoolmates" became "uncongenial," "relatives" became "congenial"; but also all other persons, through superficial associations, were placed in one category or the other and so were subject to connections and disconnections.

After having undergone a connection, he could not leave the place where he happened to be, nor could he interrupt the activity that engaged him at that moment, until he had completed disconnecting. This condition was most distressing to him. Thus it was always problematic whether he would be able to rise from the couch after his analytic hour, and he would be tortured throughout the hour by the fear that it might end just between a connection and a disconnection. Finally, the defense itself came to give expression to the rejected impulses. The compulsion to disconnect made it necessary for the patient to have a sufficient number of congenial persons, places, and things in constant readiness. The desire to put a quick end to the tormenting tension brought about a return of the repressed from the repression. The patient frequented uncongenial places and took careful notice of uncongenial persons, so that he might have them in readiness in case he needed them. However, he was not able to do this with all uncongenial objects. The avoided one, for example, remained avoided. In time he had a graduated series of differentiations. There were objects that were phobically avoided as completely uncongenial; then there were less uncongenial ones searched for which he had to have in readiness; then somewhat indifferent ones, slightly congenial ones, and completely congenial ones. He finally consciously exerted himself to think of uncongenial objects only, hoping that he would then more easily bring about the disconnection. Since the thought "uncongenial objects" stood for "masturbation," he now was unconsciously masturbating continually. And in point of fact, when his tension was greatest and he could not make a disconnection in spite of all his effort, he would occasionally, to his great astonishment, have an ejaculation.

Freud has drawn attention to a normal prototype of isolation and to a point relating to its origin (618).

The normal prototype is the process of logical thinking, which actually consists of the continued elimination of affective associations in the interest of objectivity. Compulsion neurotics, in their isolation activities, behave like caricatures of normal thinkers. This throws light on a factor of importance in analytic therapy. Free association appears to be essentially a suspension of the normal isolating countercathexes. The isolations that characterize normal thinking are supposed to be suspended by the injunction to express whatever comes to mind, so that the original unconscious connections may reappear. Since compulsion neurotics invest a considerable part of their countercathexes in the special mechanism of isolation, they find it difficult to associate freely. Indeed, some compulsion neurotics never learn to do so. They always desire order, routine, system. From the psychological point of view, this means that they do not wish to dispense with their isolations.

Genetically, the mechanism of isolation is related to the ancient taboo of touching. Threshold rituals and paving-stone compulsions express conflicts as to whether or not to obey this taboo (30, 390). The taboo of touching, as the prototype for the mechanism of isolation, may be directed against any instinctual impulse. There are no forbidden impulses, whether of a sensual, aggressive, or tender nature, the aim of which would not presuppose a touching of the object.

REGRESSION

The concept of regression was discussed previously (*see* pp. 53 and 65). Whenever a person meets a frustration, there is a tendency for him to long for earlier periods in his life when his experiences were more pleasant, and for earlier types of satisfaction that were more complete. The intensity of this tendency increases with two factors which are closely interrelated: the degree of hesitancy with which the individual accepts newer modes of satisfaction and the degree to which he is fixated to earlier types. Can regression, in this sense, be called a mechanism of defense?

The typical compulsion neurotic, experiencing a conflict between his phallic Oedipus wishes and his castration fear, substitutes anal-sadistic wishes for his Oedipus demands. Thus, actually, regression *is* a means of defense (618). What must be admitted, however, is that the part played by the ego in regression is different from the part it plays in all other defense mechanisms. Other defense mechanisms are set in motion by an activity of the ego (although in this activity the ego may use more archaic and automatic mechanisms); in regression the ego is much more passive. Regression happens to the ego; in general, regression seems to be set in motion by the instincts which, blocked from direct satisfaction, seek a substitute. The precondition for the use of regression as a mechanism of defense is, therefore, a peculiar weakness of the ego organization (*see* p. 305).

It has been mentioned that there is a complementary relation between fixation and regression; it is easy to give up something that is not very important. The more intense the pregenital fixations, the weaker the subsequent phallic organization. An individual fixed on the anal level will advance only with reluctance to the phallic phase, and he will always be prepared to relinquish his new acquisition upon slight disappointment or threat. However, very intense and sudden disappointments and dangers may provoke regressions even in individuals without strong fixations.

Two types of regression deserve special mention. The first is regression from adult forms of sexuality to infantile ones. This regression is the prerequisite of neuroses. Any disappointment in or threat to adult sexuality may influence a person to revert to those levels of his infantile sexuality to which he is unconsciously fixated; in other words, to levels that have been repressed and remained unchanged in the unconscious. However, a neurosis develops only if this mobilization of infantile sexuality in turn brings about a remobilization of the old conflicts which once in childhood raged around infantile sexuality. The regression to infantile sexuality may be limited to the leading erogenous zone, so that, for instance, a hysterical, orally fixated person may express his genital Oedipus wishes in fantasies of fellatio or in oral symptoms. Or there may be a full regression in which not only the consummation of genital wishes may be expressed in a pregenital way but also the whole complex of pregenitality, including such characteristics as ambivalence and bisexuality, replaces genitality. In this sense, the typical compulsion neurotic has given up his genitality and has become anal sadistic once more (*see* pp. 274 ff.).

The second special case of regression is the regression to primary narcissism, or to the stage of development before the final differentiation of ego and id. If this deepest regression occurs, it is a resumption of the very oldest type of defense—blocking of the ego.

What determines the choice of types of defense mechanisms will be discussed later (*see* pp. 523 ff.).

DEFENSES AGAINST AFFECTS

So far, discussion has been confined to the mechanisms of defenses against instinctual drives. Instinctual drives are warded off, however, because of anxiety or guilt feeling, that is, to avoid the pain of traumatic panic or of loss of self-esteem. Thus in the last analysis any defense is a defense against *affects*. "I do not want to feel any painful sensation" is the first and final motive of defense (589, 590). Although the more organized defenses against instinctual drives are of greater importance in the psychogenesis of neuroses, it should not be forgotten that archaic, less systematic defenses against affects are operative, too. Even the experience of anxiety or guilt feeling, which motivates defense against instinctual drives, is painful, and actually there are defenses that tend not to avoid instinctual actions or situations of temptations or punishment but that tend directly toward the avoidance of the very feeling of anxiety or guilt. This is especially marked in certain archaic character formations where large-scale defenses against anxiety may be observed (*see* pp. 479 ff.).

BLOCKING (REPRESSION) OF AFFECTS

It appears that the ego, having once been overwhelmed by affects, can regain its strength to such an extent that in similar recurring situations it may have adequate countercathexes on hand to ward off a new complete development of the affect. We may speak of unconscious affects as well as of unconscious sensations; in both instances there are certain states of tension which, were they not hindered in their development and discharged by countercathexis, would result in affects and sensations respectively, unconscious strivings toward the development of affects, which are held in check by opposing forces. "Unconscious sexual excitement" or "unconscious anxiety" can be observed clinically in the same way as unconscious material can be observed in general; the blocked unconscious dispositions toward affects develop derivatives, betray themselves in dreams, in symptoms, and in other substitute formations; they betray themselves merely in a general weakness which is caused by excessive consumption of energy (590, 608). "Emotional frigidity" (*see* pp. 477 ff.) and certain types of depersonalization (*see* pp. 419 f.) are examples of general emotional blocking. It has been said that a disproportion between the precipitating factor and the affect reaction is an index of the presence of repressions; it may be added that, through the development of derivatives, a general affective instability is the first consequence of affect defense through the blocking of discharge. The person may have learned to defend himself secondarily against this instability by strengthened counter-cathexes. If affective instability is the first result of affect defenses, general affective rigidity is the second.

The simplest derivatives are the delayed outbursts of affects. The temporal displacement, resulting simply in a later appearance of the affect reaction and in thus preventing the recognition of the motivating connection, is the most frequent special case of affect displacement. This type of defense is most frequently instituted against the affects of rage (or annoyance) and grief. Rage can obviously be endured without discharge for a short period, but for a short period only; then it must be released, no matter against whom. In the affect of grief, postponement seems to be an essential component. What happens in mourning is nothing other than a gradual "working through" of an affect which, if released in its full strength, would overwhelm the ego, that is, the quantity of cathexes released by the loss of the object. What today is called grief is obviously a postponed and apportioned neutralization of a wild and self-destructive kind of affect which can still be observed in a child's panic upon the disappearance of his mother or in the uninhibited mourning reactions of primitives (597, 1640) (see p. 394). Hence it is understandable that the mechanism of affect postponement has been studied with special reference to the phenomenon of grief. Freud's patient "wolf-man" did not show any reaction upon the death of his sister, but burst into tears at Pushkin's grave (599). Helene Deutsch has devoted a paper to this question (332).

Postponement of affect is, however, by no means limited to rage and grief. Pfister investigated the reaction of the ego to acute mortal danger and repeatedly found an absence of fear during the period of acute danger, but a subsequent appearance of intense fear when the danger was past (1225). Such postponement of fear may have a lifesaving effect because it makes possible purposeful action which otherwise might have been paralyzed by the fear. Similarly, the anxiety symptoms of traumatic neurotics represent in part such delayed fear. A "delayed fright" sounds like a contradiction, because fright is a sudden and immediate reaction. And yet there is such a thing. Frightful experiences may be calmly accepted by the person in question, who is, however, engulfed by fright some moments later. During these moments, the ego has been able to prepare itself, to protect itself from being completely overwhelmed.

The postponement of fright is so well known to movie writers that it is not only frequently used but also designated by a special term: double-take. It is illustrated by the anecdote according to which a man comes home after a strenuous day of work and finds a telegram about the death of a relative, reads it while going to bed and then exclaims: "Oh, what a terrible shock this will be in the morning!"

Not infrequently, postponed reactions of shame and disgust can be observed.

A patient had, in the course of his analysis, resumed the infantile habit of anal masturbation. In his analysis he explained that in so doing he had soiled his fingers. It was striking that he showed no disgust reaction, although his character would have led one to expect it. A few days later, he reacted to a relatively slight provocation with a disproportionately strong outburst of disgust.

The delay of reactions of fatigue while under stress, until the danger is over, apparently is based on the same mechanism.

Sometimes, after the endurance of great pain or of severe strain, a kind of apathy, of loss of sensitiveness to pain, and of frigidity toward feelings can be observed. This, too, must be due to a similar mechanism, protecting the ego against affects or sensations that would be overwhelming.

DISPLACEMENT OF AFFECTS

Postponement is but one special case among many types of displacement of affects (552). Another subtype is displacement in respect to the *object*. The affect, which was suppressed in relation to one object, bursts forth against another object. This type of displacement may be combined with postponement as in the case of the wolf-man's reaction at Pushkin's grave (599). The displacement of the feared object is known from animal phobias (566).

AFFECT EQUIVALENTS

The defense is more successful if the person can deceive himself as to the character of his own emotion. The typical discharge innervations may occur, wholly or partially, but their psychic significance remains unconscious. This is the way in which the so-called affect equivalents originate (*see* pp. 237 f.). Anxiety equivalents were described by Freud in his earliest work on anxiety neuroses (545, 547). Equivalents of mourning were collated by Landauer (1011). It cannot be doubted that all other affects can likewise be replaced in a similar way by equivalents of somatic sensations. It is characteristic of certain compulsive personalities that when analysis has successfully attacked their affect blocking, they begin to complain of certain changes in body sensations, without realizing their psychic significance. Before they can again experience the affects fully, they first find the road to affect equivalents. Schreber's somatic "basic language" (574) consists of affects reduced to body sensations.

REACTION FORMATIONS AGAINST AFFECTS

The denial of the true significance of an affect may be increased to a compulsive adherence to the opposite emotional attitude. Impudence may be developed as a defense against feelings of guilt, courage as a defense against fear.

We are accustomed to shame and disgust being used as sexual defenses. Thus we are prone to regard strikingly shameless behavior, or an ostentatious recourse to the disgusting, as an eruption of infantile sexual instincts rather than as a reaction formation against affects. But such an "eruption of instincts" is not necessarily simply constructed. Editha Sterba's analysis of a "shameless girl" showed that at least in this case there was not a definite lack of shame but a complicated reaction formation against a preceding period strongly characterized by intense shame (1486). The "counterphobic attitudes" (435) are reaction formations against anxiety (*see* pp. 480 ff.).

Change of Quality of Affects

It is also conceivable that the effect of defense mechanisms of the ego specifically changes the quality of affect experiences. Freud's old conception that under certain conditions sexual excitement is transformed into anxiety (551, 558) has not yet been refuted.

Isolation of Affects

Affects may be *isolated* from their entire psychic connections by a special expenditure of countercathexis. The analysis of affect disturbances consists largely in the re-establishment of connections that have been lost through distortions of this kind. Sometimes certain affect excitations are admitted only under certain conditions which unconsciously mean some reassurance against danger, but not under others, for instance, only so long as no real or serious character is ascribed to them.

Projection and Introjection of Affects

Affects may be projected, that is, perceived in someone else, to avoid perceiving them in oneself. The idea of an introjection of an affect seems to make no sense. However, the expression to swallow one's emotion should be taken into consideration. Undoubtedly there is an affect defense through introjection of the object against whom the affect was directed, as, for example, the mechanism of "identification with the aggressor" when an object is feared (541).

Like all defenses, defenses against affects may *fail*. Persons who deny their affects may, under some conditions, be completely overwhelmed by the return of their affects. Hence affect defenses frequently show a double-edged character; the absence of affect may be reversed into an attack of affect; an affective attitude of the nature of a reaction formation may be reversed into the original opposite affect.

Defenses against Guilt Feelings

There is a group of defenses against affect that deserve special attention because of their clinical importance: the defenses against guilt feelings. They are characteristic for certain types of neuroses in which the ego is compelled to establish a double countercathexis and to struggle against objectionable id wishes and superego demands simultaneously.

Guilt feelings may be *repressed*. Frequently rationalizations as to the necessity of committing a forbidden deed secure a repression of guilt feelings. Macbeth's belief in the witches' prophecy is an attempt to convince himself that the murder was necessary, and that he does not have to feel guilty about it. His realization that he has misunderstood the prophecy, when it is too late, represents the return of the repressed guilt feeling from the repression (442).

Frequent in occurrence are attempts at *projecting* guilt feelings. "Someone else has done it, not I" is the leitmotiv of many a neurotic character.

There are different types of quasi-projections of guilt feelings. Any guilt can be borne more easily if someone else has done the same thing. For the sake of the feeling of relief that can thus be attained, persons who either have done something about which they feel guilty or wish to do such a thing are searching for another person in the same situation; they feel greatly relieved if they succeed in finding anyone who does or has done the same deed. They may even provoke other persons to do things about which they feel guilty. The relieving function of sharing the guilt is one of the basic factors in the psychology of art. The artist relieves his guilt feeling by inducing the audience to participate in his deed in fantasy, and the spectator relieves his guilt feeling by becoming aware that the artist dares to express forbidden impulses (1332). Similarly the motive for telling a joke always consists of an attempt to get the approval of the audience for the underlying guilt in the offensive impulses concealed in the joke (556, 1294). Sharing the guilt is also of basic importance in group formation (1258).

Even if the guilt feeling is too intense to be overcome by sharing the guilt, a projection may still work in the form of a tendency to denounce tendencies in others which the person tries to deny in himself. This is the old story of the mote in the brother's eye.

At times the superego, which had its origin in the introjection of an external object, is reprojected onto external objects for the purpose of getting rid of guilt feelings. Compulsion neurotics often try to avoid a sense of guilt by appealing to others to forgive them.

> A compulsive patient used to relate his obsessive scruples at the beginning of the analytic hour and then would not associate to them. He eventually explained that his scruples had disappeared as soon as they were expressed. Since the analyst was not so infuriated or frightened as to fall out of his chair but listened, the patient felt free to assume that his scruples were trivial.

Similar phenomena are very frequent in ordinary social life. The individual needs confirmation by others or the applause of an audience as signs of forgiveness. An external pardon achieves the same end as the seduction of another person to share in the guilt.

> The patient mentioned above had an obsessive need to read the newspaper aloud. He felt indignation at the many examples of injustice in the world, but he needed the company of another person who would share his indignation. His reading aloud was intended to mitigate his internal sense of guilt, the agreement of his listener justifying his own aggressive tendencies.
>
> Many forms of exaggerated need to communicate with others or of compulsive loquacity are variations of the same tendency. They originate in a need to gain the approval of other persons for something inwardly felt as prohibited.

By provocation, seduction, ingratiation, and confession, the environment is drawn into the conflict between the ego and the superego, in the hope of obtaining some relief. Much of what is called object relationships are actually pseudo object relationships, in which the subject does not develop any feelings toward the object as a person but uses the object as an instrument for achieving relief in a conflict with his superego (see pp. 293 f., 496 ff., and 518 ff.).

Can there be any such thing as an introjection of a guilt feeling? At first glance this seems to be impossible. However, the "borrowed" guilt feeling (608, 1005), created by identification with another person who is likewise supposed to feel guilty, may be used in assuagement of one's own guilt feeling.

Certainly there are many *reaction formations* to guilt feelings. People may behave extremely and provocatively nonchalant and carefree, may even be proud of "having no conscience scruples," only to learn in analysis that their attitude needs a great amount of countercathexis to hold severe guilt feelings in check. Certain impulsive characters, by their unscrupulous behavior, protest against the intense pressure they feel from their very strict superego. In a less obvious manner, this may be the unconscious meaning of certain compulsive symptoms, the significance of which is a rebellion against the superego and the acquisition of proofs of innocence.

An *isolation* of guilt feeling is a frequent occurrence in compulsion neurotics; they do things without any guilt feeling, and experience an exaggerated feeling of guilt on some other occasion without being aware of the connection (567). Also, impulsive psychopaths, who often are considered to have no superego at all (1603), reveal in analysis that they have temporarily isolated the demands of their superego, so that these demands are not effective when the "psychopath" gives in to his impulses (1266) (see pp. 374 f.).

Regression as defense against guilt feelings may be observed in the case of moral masochism, where conscience, which has its origin in the Oedipus complex, is sexualized again and used as an occasion for distorted gratification of Oedipus wishes (613). A certain kind of regression is effective also in less extreme cases where the reaction to the superego is to resume, in some transference action, the type of behavior which had previously been shown toward the parents in order to achieve forgiveness or punishment.

Actually, defensive conflicts are more complicated than this description indicates. An isolated conflict between one particular drive and one particular opposing anxiety rarely occurs. More frequently there are complex and powerful interactions between many drives and many anxieties. A defensive struggle is rarely brought to a successful conclusion by one particular defensive activity. Defenses may be more or less successful; they may work under certain circumstances and be insufficient under others. All the minutiae of everyday life are perceived either as temptations for repressed impulses or as warnings of possible punishments, and may thus disturb the equilibrium anew. Certain experiences may evoke the return of what has been warded off in the defense, which may in turn necessitate defenses against the defenses. There are reaction formations against reaction formations. Conditions favorable and opposed to the objectionable impulses arise, so that many contradictory layers develop; however, the layers are not placed evenly one above the other but are full of rifts. Throughout the development of the individual, both progression and regression are operative. The actual picture is confusing until analysis succeeds in separating the layers historically. Here only a description has been given of the individual mechanisms by which the separate layers are constructed.

Chapter X

THE DIRECT CLINICAL SYMPTOMS OF THE NEUROTIC CONFLICT

CLASSIFICATION OF THE DIRECT CLINICAL SYMPTOMS OF THE NEUROTIC CONFLICT

THE neurotic conflict is not yet a neurosis. However, the effectiveness of the conflict manifests itself in certain pathological phenomena, which nevertheless are also frequently called neurotic.

The clinical symptoms of the neurotic conflicts are either direct expressions of the activities of the defensive forces, that is, manifestations of the counter-cathexis, or symptoms arising from the relative insufficiency of the ego in the state of being dammed up.

The activity of the defensive forces may manifest itself in various ways. First of all, the anxieties or guilt feelings motivating the defense may be conscious as such, though the person does not know what he feels afraid of or guilty about. Other manifestations of the countercathexis differ according to the mechanism of defense used. The results of denial and projection are manifest as such; intro-jection expresses itself in identification; repression shows itself in voids in the patient's thoughts, feelings, memories, behavior patterns or in the intensity with which substitute formations are preserved; reaction formations betray them-selves by their rigid character, which is nevertheless often broken through; un-doing and isolation form certain compulsive symptoms; regression changes the wishes and behavior of the personality. All the pathogenic defenses, however, build up *resistances* against attempts to interfere with their operation. Some of the manifestations of defenses are regularly expressions of the warded-off forces at the same time; therefore they will be discussed in the chapters on symptom formation that follow. A pure manifestation of countercathexis, however, is pre-sented by specific avoidances and inhibitions of functions arising from a defense against these functions.

The symptoms of the relative insufficiency of the ego created through the state of being dammed up are called actual-neurotic symptoms and are very similar to the symptoms in traumatic neuroses, since the decrease in discharge resulting from the defensive conflict creates the same condition as the height-ened influx of stimuli from a trauma. There are *negative* symptoms, consisting of general inhibitions of ego functions—in this case traceable to a decrease in available energy because of the energy consumed in the defensive struggle—and *positive* symptoms, consisting of painful feelings of tension, of emergency dis-charges representing attempts to get rid of the tension and including emotional spells of anxiety and rage, and producing sleep disturbances due to the impossibility of relaxation (*cf.* 41).

SPECIFIC AVOIDANCES AND INHIBITIONS

Persons with specific countercathexes frequently avoid certain situations or objects or activities or fields of interest or qualities of feeling, sometimes without being aware of the avoidance, sometimes with full consciousness of it. Or instead of a full avoidance, there may be a decrease in functions or a specific lack of interest.

Sometimes such persons feel consciously that they just "hate" the fields in which they are inhibited; sometimes they feel afraid of them or embarrassed if they have to face them; sometimes they assume that they have no objection to these fields but are merely "not interested" in them; sometimes they are not aware of the existence of any avoidances, but there are objective hiatuses in their mental continuity and analysis has to expose them and to make the persons face their antipathies; sometimes they may like to engage in the "inhibited" activities but experience the inhibition as an ego-dystonic disturbance occurring against their will. An intense dislike of formal parties, a shyness at such affairs, a lack of interest in or understanding of music, a feeling of fatigue and lack of power on occasions where others would feel rage, and a psychogenic sexual impotence are illustrations of these possibilities. It is not clear what determines the type of inhibition that is developed. It depends partly upon the person's constitution and history and partly on actual libido-economic circumstances.

Analysis always shows that the specifically avoided situations or the inhibited functions have unconsciously an instinctual (sexual or aggressive) significance. It is this instinctual significance against which the defense really is directed. What is avoided is an allusion either to a temptation for the warded-off drive or to a feared punishment or both.

IMPOTENCE AND FRIGIDITY

The instinctual significance of inhibited functions is, of course, manifest where the inhibition concerns sexuality. Sexual inhibitions constitute the most frequent symptoms occurring in every type of neurosis, and range from slight shyness in approaching the opposite sex to complete impotence or frigidity. The inhibition may be felt as an antipathy to sexual activities or as a lack of interest in them; it may be effective without any awareness by the individual (e.g., the individual may feel that it is mere chance that he has not found any partner, whereas actually he or she has actively prevented the possibility of finding a partner); or it may manifest itself as impotence or frigidity occurring when the individual consciously is longing for satisfaction. The inhibition may cover the whole field of sexuality or only certain aspects of it—for example, only sensuality or only tenderness or only the experience of orgasm or only certain types of partners or only certain accompanying features associatively connected with infantile experiences that aroused sexual fears. The inhibitions may be effective whenever the conditions arousing the infantile fears are present or only under certain special circumstances as, for example, in the absence of some specific reassurance.

It may happen that precisely the manifest inhibition offers an opportunity for some unconscious drive to find a distorted outlet. Persons who are unconsciously afraid of injuring their sexual partners may actually hurt them by their inhibited behavior; a feminine-receptive or masochistic attitude may find expression in a man's impotence, a sadistic one in a woman's frigidity. However, this is incidental. Essentially, impotence and frigidity are not returns of the repressed from the repression but clinical manifestations and bulwarks of the defense itself. Unconsciously the person believes that sexual activity is dangerous, and the defensive force that therefore demands avoidance of the sexual act is sustained and assured by physical interference with the physical reflexes. Impotence is a physical alteration arising from a defensive action by the ego which prevents the carrying out of an instinctual activity regarded as dangerous. The part of the ego that exerts this action certainly is an unconscious one; it is the part in which castration anxiety is operative and which has at its disposal pathways that are not subject to voluntary control (448, 1474).

The ego renounces sexual pleasure if this pleasure is believed to be connected with an intense danger. As a rule, the basic danger implied is castration, the unconscious idea being that the penis might be injured while in the vagina. Fear over loss of love plays a smaller part as a cause of impotence. Fear of one's own excitation, however, may complicate the castration anxiety. The reason these dangers are believed to be connected with sexual intercourse is obvious: the fear was once connected with infantile sexual aims; these infantile sexual aims were warded off and have thus been preserved in the unconscious; they come up again whenever sexual excitement is experienced. Since the preservation of infantile sexual aims is one of the characteristic traits of neurosis, disturbances of potency are found as accompanying manifestations of all neuroses.

The nuclear complex of infantile sexuality is the Oedipus complex. In the simplest and most typical cases, impotence is based on a persistence of an unconscious sensual attachment to the mother. Superficially no sexual attachment is completely attractive because the partner is never the mother; in a deeper layer, every sexual attachment has to be inhibited, because every partner represents the mother (555).

But this is not necessarily true of all cases. There is the "complete Oedipus complex" (608). The man with an unconscious feminine orientation may likewise avoid exercising his sexual functions because of anxiety, and "feminine identification" plays an important part in the psychogenesis of more stubborn cases of impotence (1475). That does not mean that "homosexuality represses heterosexuality" but rather that the same factors which made the man homosexual make him impotent toward women.

Undoubtedly the rejection of all other feared infantile sexual aims, that is, of pregenital fantasies, may also determine an impotence (111).

There are all degrees of impotence as well as innumerable variations of frequency. Many men are not constantly impotent, but experience only occasional failures or even only weakness of erection. Such relative impotence affords a special opportunity for analyzing the unconscious fears involved by analyzing the occasions on which the disturbance occurs. It invariably turns out that such occasions tend either to mobilize special infantile strivings or to increase special infantile anxieties.

Many men are impotent toward one woman or toward one type of woman and not toward others. Frequently, such men isolate sensuality from tenderness and are impotent toward women they love (572). Many men have subjective conditions of love, that is, conditions instrumental in soothing unconscious anxieties which oppose the sexual pleasure. These conditions may dictate, for example, the partner's body type or the behavior expected of the partner; the degree of the conditions may vary from being mere preferences to absolute necessities without which complete impotence occurs.

> The following case gives a typical example of conditions for potency with the significance of reassurance against infantile fears:
> A patient experienced his first sexual failure when he and his partner lay in bed covered by a blanket. He immediately blamed the blanket; and actually, later on, he was always potent when lying uncovered, impotent when covered by a blanket. This was a kind of claustrophobia. The patient had a sense of security as long as he had the feeling of being in control, and he had this feeling as long as he was able actually to see what was going on. Analysis brought out that as a boy he used to masturbate only when covered by a blanket because this condition was a guarantee of not being seen. Thus his present condition of potency could be translated: "What I am doing here is not masturbation, is not what I did as a child, and what I am still unconsciously afraid of."
> Of course, it may be added, this patient's sexuality was a mere narcissistic need to prove his potency. His intention was to show off: "You see how free I am!" He had many girl friends, but no deep or tender relationship with any of them. On a deeper level the idea of not being covered during intercourse meant having a way open for escape.

Paradoxically, sometimes conditions for potency seem to be less a reassurance against what had been feared in childhood than a stressing of the very facts that had once been frightening. The underlying idea is that potency is possible only if the man proves to himself that he can now face that which he once feared (counterphobic attitude) (435).

The form of impotence known as *ejaculatio praecox* represents a more severe disturbance than the inability to get an erection. In ejaculatio praecox the intensity and frequency of the symptom likewise vary greatly. A relatively short duration of the act may signify only a mild form of disturbance, whereas a chronic ejaculatio ante portas is a severe disorder. In typical cases, Abraham found three frequent and mutually supplementary determinants (14): (1) A leading feminine orientation, as in cases of severe disturbances of erection. This orientation is noticeable in the nature of the leading erogenous zone: the climax of excitement is felt at the root of the penis and the perineum (or, more precisely, at the "feminine" zone in the prostatic tract of the urethra) rather than at the glans and the shaft of the penis. This condition may indicate a constitutionally enhanced bisexuality; but it may also arise as a reaction to a psychogenic inhibition of active phallic sexuality. (2) A sadistic orientation, which is concealed under ostensible passivity, and which has as its aim to soil and to injure the woman (the mother). This sadism is typically pregenital, its execution a urethral-anal one; actually the passive prostatic sexuality of men never can be isolated from urethral and anal trends. We shall see later that cases of chronic neurasthenia are characterized by attempts to use the genital apparatus for pregenital aims (*see* p. 191); actually ejaculatio praecox is a frequent symptom in cases of this kind. (3) An intensified urethral eroticism which makes the individual unconsciously regard semen in the same way he regarded urine as a child. Also characteristic for cases of chronic ejaculatio praecox are strong feelings of guilt about masturbation, corresponding to the pregenital and sadistic aims of this masturbation. In the symptom, the patients try to inhibit the expression of these objectionable aims, which nevertheless find a distorted expression (1530).

Severe cases of ejaculatio praecox may also be rooted in conflicts of an oral-erotic nature. The patient may unconsciously be identified with a nursing mother; his original conflicts around being fed may have turned into conflicts around feeding, which find a distorted expression in the disturbance of ejaculation.

Certain mild forms of ejaculatio praecox are more related to hysteria, and the disturbance occurs only occasionally. The ejaculatio in these mild cases is not in the form of a flow but in the form of spasmodic spurts, and there are other signs that the genital development was completed. This genital form of ejaculatio praecox shows a displacement of the prohibition of masturbation onto the prohibition of touching, the symptom expressing the idea: "The penis should not be touched." In these genital cases the prognosis is much more favorable than in the pregenital cases related to chronic neurasthenia (1267, 1268).

The disturbance of *ejaculatio retardata* has, as a rule, more of the character of a true conversion symptom. It may express unconscious fears about dangers supposed to be connected with the ejaculation (castration, death), or strivings, anal (retaining) or oral (denial of giving [108, 110]) sadistic or masochistic in character.

Much has been written about female *frigidity*. Satisfactions that may be hidden in the symptom have been described, the role played by clitoris sexuality has been stressed, even anatomical causes for frigidity have been sought (171). But in general there is no doubt that frigidity is the expression of an inhibition of a complete sexual experience, rooted in anxiety about a danger which unconsciously is associated with the full attainment of the sexual aim—a condition completely analogous to male impotence (322, 796). The general cause for the frequency of cases exhibiting various degrees of frigidity is unquestionably ascribable to the education of girls which succeeds in creating the association between "sexuality" and "danger."

Here, too, it appears that the gratification of a persisting infantile sexual aim is perceived as a danger to be avoided, either as a danger of being injured or as a danger of losing love, both fears being frequently perceived as a fear of one's own excitement. As in impotence, the degree of severity of the disturbance varies greatly. There are women who occasionally fail to achieve a full vaginal orgasm, and those who never achieve such an orgasm but who do experience excitement and may achieve an orgasm at the clitoris. There are women who can be aroused but who never achieve any climax, and others who occasionally cannot be aroused at all. Finally, there are cases of total frigidity, whose genital erogeneity is entirely blocked. In these cases "not to feel anything" expresses the idea: "I do not want to have anything to do with it," which is a special case of the general type of defense of estranging oneself from one's own body. This estrangement is the same as in the sensory disturbances of hysteria (*see* p. 227).

The "dangerous" infantile sexual aims, which are connected with sexuality in cases of frigidity, vary more than the unconscious infantile sexual aims in impotent men, due to the fact that the sexual development of girls is more complicated than that of boys. Primary in significance, of course, is again the Oedipus complex; unconscious comparisons of the sexual partner with the father may disturb sexual enjoyment, just as thoughts of the mother may cause impotence in men. Then there is also the "masculine identification." However, masculine identification in women and feminine identification in men are not simply analogous. The facts of penis envy and of the long preoedipal attachment to the mother offer more opportunities for the development of fixations and disturbances. Since the aims of the preoedipal mother fixation are mostly pregenital ones, we see fears concerning pregenital aims very frequently as causes of frigidity (626, 628). Fear of losing control seems to be in the foreground. Very often one finds that the terrible thing that may happen when control is lost at the climax of excitement is unconsciously thought of as a loss of control of the sphincters and especially, in women with a penis envy and a heightened urethral eroticism, as involuntary wetting (421).

Masculine identification is connected with another point of great importance in frigidity. Many frigid women are frigid vaginally only; the clitoris has preserved its normal or more than normal excitability. Since the clitoris is the primary erogenous zone in feminine infantile genitality, such frigidity can be considered a form of arrested development. The refusal of the clitoris to turn over its primacy to the vaginal zone may be due to an anxiety related to the vaginal zone (which probably is the decisive factor); or it may be due to a special heightening of clitoris erogeneity, which may either be constitutional or be acquired during the phallic period. The actual state of affairs is further complicated by the aforementioned fact that clitoris masturbation, which is responsible for the excitability of the clitoris becoming fixated, serves as an outlet not only for autoerotic and masculine fantasies but also for definitely feminine sexual fantasies.

Like impotence, frigidity may secondarily give opportunity for a distorted expression of unconscious drives—of masochistic strivings or even of active sadistic impulses ("revenge on the man"), but certainly neither masochism nor hatred alone could determine frigidity; only the *anxiety* about what would happen if a striving for suffering or hatred were yielded to can be decisive. However, what has been warded off may return and penetrate the defensive measures.

Vaginismus is related to frigidity as reaction formation is to repression; not only is the sexual excitement inhibited, but something positive is done to ensure the maintenance of such an inhibition and to make intercourse physically impossible. The typical cases of vaginismus develop spasms which make the insertion of the penis impossible. Cases of *penis captivus* are the subject of many anecdotes but are rarely described in scientific literature. The anecdotes are probably based more on male castration fears and female active castration tendencies than on real occurrences. Vaginismus frequently is no pure inhibition but rather a positive conversion symptom; it then not only expresses the tendency to offer an obstacle to sexuality but also a distorted unconscious wish. This wish may be the idea to break off the penis and to keep it; in other words, vaginismus may be an expression of the revenge type of the female castration complex (20), or a spasm of the floor of the pelvis may be an expression of an anal conception of penis envy: the idea of pressing out and/or of retaining an anal penis (1136).

Whereas a man's impotence is obvious, a woman's frigidity can be hidden. Many women who feel their frigidity not as a virtue but as a being crippled lie about their condition. Various secondary complications and neurotic reaction patterns may develop out of such a denial of the symptom. Loss of erection in men cannot be hidden. There are, however, various ways in which a relative impotence may be disguised so that analogous secondary complications may occur in men, too. The most frequent complication of this type is an attempt to overcompensate the sexual inhibition. Women as well as men may behave especially "oversexed," to cover up an original inhibition. The narcissistic need to prove that one is not impotent or frigid is a frequent cause of pseudosexual behavior, that is, for sexual behavior which preponderantly is not produced directly out of a sexual need but out of a narcissistic need (*see* pp. 515 ff.).

Inhibitions of sexual intercourse are not necessarily the only genital inhibitions. Other genital functions, too, may be inhibited if they represent objectionable drives. A psychogenic resistance to pregnancy certainly can influence the course of pregnancy and childbirth in an unfortunate way, probably chiefly by influencing the muscular functions but also to some extent the circulatory and metabolic ones (27, 322, 359, 816, 902, 1128, 1139*a*, 1306). Whether there is a psychogenic inhibition of procreation, that is, a psychogenic sterility, is not certain. Some authors believe it, and cases in which women after years of sterility have become pregnant immediately after their decision to adopt a child (1210) increase such a suspicion.

INHIBITIONS OF PARTIAL INSTINCTS

Other specific inhibitions occur not directly in the sexual sphere but in those functions which in childhood had a sexual significance. In impotence and frigidity, the fears and guilt feelings that create the defense, and thus the inhibition, were so closely connected with the sensations of sexual excitement that they became shifted from infantile sexual functions to adult ones when the excitement was shifted in the same direction. In inhibitions that correspond to the repression of a particular component impulse, the infantile functions themselves remain inhibited (618).

If oral impulses have been subjected to specific repressions, a frequent result is in an inhibition of eating, or of eating certain kinds of food which are unconsciously reminiscent of the objects desired by the repressed oral-erotic strivings. Again, the inhibitions extend from hatred of such food or general lack of interest or enjoyment in food, to hysterical vomiting or spasms of the jaws (384, 1106, 1574). The oral inhibitions may be displaced onto other activities with a hidden oral significance, such as drinking and smoking, social activities, or reading (1512).

It is true that children who refuse to eat may do so to express some negative feelings toward their parents (or parental surrogates). However, the more such protests are concentrated on eating alone, the more probable it is that the basis of the protests is a specific oral conflict, and that the defense is not only directed against frustrating objects but against oral drives as well. Such defense is especially marked if the oral drives, after having been frustrated, have acquired a sadistic character.

Orality, as the oldest field of instinctual conflicts, can be used later on to express any other instinctual conflicts, especially if experiences in infancy have left an oral fixation that facilitates a displacement from subsequent frustrations (primal scenes, birth of siblings) to oral conflicts. Any conflict between activity and receptivity may result in eating disturbances. Since parents who have had difficulties in helping their children to make an adequate adjustment on an oral level usually have difficulties again in training their children for cleanliness, and since, among the anal frustrations, the prohibition of taking feces into the mouth is especially stressed, it is understandable that anal conflicts, too, may be expressed by children through oral inhibitions, through inhibitions in eating (1489), as well as through inhibitions in speech (291, 292, 708) (*see* pp. 311 ff.). If a refusal to eat has an especially stubborn character, expressing primarily the attitude "I will not let myself be controlled; I eat when and what I like," then anal components are mainly involved.

In the genital sphere, eating usually has the unconscious significance of "becoming pregnant," and this equation, too, may cause various inhibitions in eating. Since a high percentage of all oral pregnancy theories are based on the belief that the woman eats the man's penis, revenge types of feminine castration complexes (20), if inhibited, may also result in eating inhibitions.

Specifically disliked kinds of food unconsciously symbolize milk, breast, penis, or feces (126). However, a refusal of food does not necessarily represent a repression of eating cravings. A specific food may be rejected obstinately because it is not the desired one: "I do not want this food but that"; or "I do not want food but love (or a penis, or a child)." In this instance, it is not a drive that is refused but the acceptance of a substitute (24).

Specific eating taboos may secondarily become rationalized or idealized (*see* pp. 485 f.). It is cruel to eat animals, or dirty or unhygienic to eat this or that. Rationalizations of this kind are often suggested by modern food theories which tend to prohibit naïve sexual pleasure in food and to connect eating with the superego sphere. You are not supposed to eat what is good but rather "what is good for you" (1111).

If an eating taboo in later life is neither rationalized nor fixated in ego-dystonic conversions like vomiting or spasms of the jaws but becomes the core of a more or less ego-syntonic pathological behavior, this is called anorexia nervosa. Anorexia regularly can be traced back to eating disturbances in childhood which under certain libido-economic circumstances are subsequently taken up again (1324). Like the disturbances in childhood, later anorexias, too, may have a very different dynamic significance. It may be a simple hysterical symptom expressing the fear of an orally perceived pregnancy or of unconscious sadistic wishes. It may be a part of an ascetic reaction formation in a compulsion neurosis. It may be an affect equivalent in a depression, in which the symptom of refusal of food makes its appearance before other signs of the depression are developed. It may be a sign of the refusal of any contact with the objective world in an incipient schizophrenia.

However, two other types are chiefly thought of first if anorexia is mentioned. The one is an organ neurosis in which an interrelation of oral mental conflicts and hormonal metabolism is operative, the one influencing the other, resulting in a total loss of appetite and in loss of weight (1121, 1555) (*see* p. 260). The other type is a severe psychogenic developmental disturbance of the ego in which the anorexia in an orally fixated person is only one symptom of a general disturbance of all object relationships.

A patient of Eissler's (361) had not gone beyond an extremely archaic stage of ego development. The mother "remained the most important part of the patient's ego." The refusal of food represented the longing for the primary, still undifferentiated gratification by the mother and its sadistic distortion after frustration. The mother's total lack of tenderness and physical affection had created a severe disturbance in the patient's construction of her body image. A case of Lorand's was disturbed in a similar way (1082).

Since a repression may manifest itself either by an inhibition or by an exaggeration of a compensating opposite, the antithetic states of "anorexia" and "pathological craving for food" (bulimia) are related to each other, at least in the same sense as melancholia and mania are related to each other. As a rule, infantile eating inhibitions are found in the childhood history of subsequent food addicts (*see* p. 381).

Repressions of anal eroticism create specific anal inhibitions, either inhibitions in the physical functions like constipation (which simultaneously may bring a distorted discharge to anal-erotic strivings for retention) or an anal prudishness or a reactive cleanliness. Again, inhibitions of this kind may be combined with a substitutive obsessive interest in anal matters on some other level (21, 883, 1143).

How specific repressions of exhibitionism may create specific social inhibitions which occasionally are decisive for the individual's later life has been popularized by Moss Hart's *Lady in the Dark* (745).

If scoptophilia has been repressed, inhibitions of looking come to the fore (571). In extreme cases they may develop to such an extent that the person actually becomes unable to look at things and instead lives in abstractions only. In less extreme cases, the patient may turn away from seeing a special class of objects, for example, of things that remind him of facts that once aroused castration anxiety (8). Often frightening sights result directly in subsequent inhibitions of looking, and frightening sounds in subsequent inhibitions of hearing.

Fright, as is well known, paralyzes. Inhibitions in the realm of motility may mean "I am frightened"; very often they mean "I am paralyzed by a frightening sight," that is, by a sight that makes one face the possibility of castration or death.

Myths and fairy tales, dreams and neurotic symptoms portray petrification as the specific punishment for scoptophilic interests (296, 500). "Stone" means "immobility," and this punishment signifies the body feeling of motor inhibitions arising from fright. It may simultaneously be an anticipation of death or castration (430).

INHIBITIONS OF AGGRESSIVENESS

Whether aggressiveness is looked upon as a separate class of instinctual demands or as a way in which frustrated or pregenitally fixated persons try to approach their instinctual aims, there is no doubt that in either case there are various and frequent specific inhibitions of aggressiveness due to anxieties and guilt feelings in persons whose aggressive or sadistic (and masochistic) tendencies have been repressed. In this class belong the reactive kindness and politeness typical for compulsion neurotics. Frequently these persons avoid all arguments and react with "breakdowns" when certain conditions cease to be effective, which unconsciously mean reassurance that everything is peaceful. Many persons develop sexual inhibitions because for them sexual excitement and rage have become too closely interwoven. Such is the case when the frustrations of infantile sexuality have led to an intense longing for destructive revenge, the intrusion of which into any excitement is now rightly feared. Many an "occupational inhibition" turns out to be actually an inhibition of aggressiveness, since under our cultural conditions, aggressiveness is necessary for a healthy career. Characters of this type literally or emotionally withdraw from the world because for them it is a world filled with murder which they might either have to deal out or suffer. The passivity created in this manner in its turn may either become sexualized (passive homosexuality or oral receptivity being increased to hold a feared aggressiveness in check) or it may be overcompensated by a layer of cramped and false counterphobic aggressiveness.

An emotionally very cold patient, who monotonously discussed apparently indifferent matters for many analytic months, considered all aggression "unintelligent," neglected his technical profession because, as he said, all technical inventions are misused for warfare and he was not willing to further this purpose; he would, nevertheless, not associate for two minutes without subjecting conventional institutions or the behavior of other persons to intense criticism. Indeed, intellectual critique was the sole matter of his associations. In this manner, his warded-off impulses "forced themselves out through all pores," to use Freud's expression (553).

Another emotionally paralyzed patient, who usually turned all his aggressions against himself and could not harm a fly, aggravated his symptoms to the extent of yielding completely to every compulsion, even to the mildest. In self-justification he said: "I want to find out if the analyst can remove my symptoms if I do not want him to." Thus he distorted the analytic situation into a battle, the very thing he was supposedly trying to avoid.

Persons with a repressed intense hatred may perceive any activity as aggression; thus severe cases block all activity (469). "Specific inhibitions of aggressiveness," then, lose their specificity and turn rather into the generally inhibited types.

The contents of unconscious fears, too, may lead to definite inhibitions: a person governed by fear over loss of love will have to avoid anything that increases the danger of not being loved, and thus will develop definite social inhibitions corresponding to his social dependency. A person who is afraid of his own excitement will block all activities that might increase his excitement. And, last but not least, a man with a castration anxiety will develop specific inhibitions corresponding to the specific form of his castration anxiety. An individual, for example, who as a child was frightened by a tailor's scissors may become inhibited from going to the tailor's, and eventually become negligent in appearance.

INHIBITIONS OF SEXUALIZED FUNCTIONS

The same inhibitions that were applied to sexual functions in the cases discussed until now may also be applied to any function that has been sexualized through a previous displacement. In reference to this process, Freud stated: "We have gained insight into this situation, and understand that the ego function of an organ becomes affected whenever the erogeneity, that is, the sexual significance of this organ, increases. If I may be allowed a somewhat scurrilous comparison, I should say that the organ behaves like a cook who no longer wants to work in the kitchen because she and the master of the house are having a love affair. When the act of writing, which consists in letting a liquid out of a tube onto a piece of paper, acquires the significance of coitus, and when walking becomes the symbolic substitute of stamping on the body of Mother Earth, then both writing and walking have to be discontinued because it is as if the performance of these actions meant the carrying-out of the forbidden sexual acts. The ego thus gives up the functions in order to avoid the necessity of undertaking new repressions" (618).

On closer study, one sees that there actually is a dual origin to inhibitions of this type; practically, however, it is difficult to distinguish between them. The sexualization of a function leads to an inhibition, either because the ego is striving for or because it is blocking the sexualized pleasure. In some instances it may be very important to know whether the ego is functioning poorly because it is seeking sexual gratification, instead of performing its nonsexual task, or because it discontinues the sexualized function out of anxiety.

All the ego functions presuppose an overcoming of the phase of the pleasure principle in which they were used in the service of direct pleasure seeking. Thus a "sexualization" of an ego function is also a failure in "desexualization." Müller-Braunschweig developed the theory that the process in the young child of discovering his own organs and their functions is a process that closely resembles identification (1162, 1163). By mastering an excitation, the mastered function becomes a part of the ego and is thereby desexualized. Thus the ego function of the organ is established; any regression toward its autoerotic use impairs the function. The artist has sublimated his impulse to smear through a kind of identification with smearing activities; the pseudo artist who still (or again) seeks direct sexual pleasure in smearing impairs his ability.

Disturbances of functions that served the purpose of suppression of sexuality may gradually turn into hidden substitute gratifications; however, such cases are not to be considered as pure inhibited states any more but rather as conversions.

Just as any organ may serve as an erogenous zone, so may any function become the victim of an inhibition. It is impossible, therefore, to enumerate all possible types of inhibitions. A few types which are of clinical importance will be discussed.

Mention should be made, first of all, of social inhibitions consisting of a general shyness which may manifest itself in a fear of blushing or in the conversion symptom of blushing (erythrophobia). Severe cases may be inhibited to such an extent that they withdraw from any social contact; they anticipate possible criticisms to a degree that makes them hardly distinguishable from persons with paranoid trends. Less severe cases are unconsciously governed by the fear that (and the desire that) their masturbation may be found out or by sexual (scoptophilic) aggressive strivings (118, 356, 405) (see pp. 518 ff.).

Deserving special emphasis are certain body inhibitions both in the motor and sensory spheres. Motor inhibitions include not only such gross signs as hysterical abasia or physical clumsiness but also the more delicate awkwardnesses and purposeless motor actions and even the many local muscular spasms and rigidities of normal and neurotic persons. However, motor inhibitions are not necessarily manifested by hypertonic phenomena but may also appear as a limp and hypotonic muscular slackness which excludes the possibility of speedy and precise functioning (see p. 247). Among the sensory inhibitory disturbances are the sensations of physical estrangement and the whole field of inhibitions in respect to internal perceptions which are usually intimately associated with motor dysfunctions; the sensory inhibition (insufficient awareness of one's own body) causes secondary motor disturbances (410).

In addition to physical inhibitions, there are mental ones. Quite a percentage of so-called feeble-mindedness turns out to be pseudo debility, conditioned by inhibition (103, 173, 393, 842, 957, 1019, 1020, 1099, 1192, 1403). The existence of the mechanism of intellectual inhibition can be studied in every analytic hour marked by resistance. Every intellect begins to show weakness when affective motives are working against it. Analysts talk jokingly of "slight dementia by resistance."

People become stupid *ad hoc,* that is, when they do not *want* to understand, where understanding would cause (castration) anxiety or guilt feeling, or would endanger an existing neurotic equilibrium. Actually, psychoanalytic interpretations are nothing but attempts to give the patient insight or to show him connections when emotional resistances hinder his spontaneous understanding.

There are two main reasons why an ego may be induced to keep its intellect permanently in abeyance.

1. A repression of sexual curiosity may block the normal interest in knowing and thinking (561). Often the inhibited sexual curiosity corresponds to an intense unconscious scoptophilia (103) or stands in intimate relationship to sadistic impulses (1097, 1397); the consequent "stupidity" may represent simultaneously an obedience to and a rebellion against the parents from whom the patient had suffered frustrations of his curiosity (174, 519). Understanding the genetic relationship between the impulse to know and oral pleasure or, later, manual grasping pleasure and still later anal mastery (249, 461, 1059, 1405) makes it easier to understand why oral, manual, and anal repressions play such an important role in intellectual inhibitions, the latter appearing as "mental obstipation" (393, 1403). The stupidity that manifestly expresses the inhibition of curiosity may unconsciously be used in various ways to satisfy this very curiosity by gaining access to scenes that would be kept secret from a "less stupid" child (1099).

2. Exactly as in other inhibitions, the inhibited intellectual functions may have been sexualized in a much stricter sense. Actually, the function of thinking may be equated with the sexual functions in both men and women; its inhibition, then, has the meaning of castration (or of the avoidance of castration) (1192). The sexualization of the function of thinking always has special anal connotations (*see* pp. 299 f.).

Studies have been made of a number of specific disturbances of intelligence, such as the failure of children in certain subjects at school, or their inability or unwillingness to study certain things. The analytic study of such cases corroborates what has been said about inhibitions in general. The particular subject, or something associated with the first instruction in this subject, or the personality of the teacher and his way of teaching, or an accidental feature that essentially had nothing to do with the subject proper, like a particular number in mathematics or a particular letter in reading or writing, proved to be associated with fundamental conflicts around infantile sexuality (909, 1067, 1068, 1227, 1234, 1257, 1360, 1528, 1543, 1639, 1641, 1644, 1645, *et al.*).

Closely connected with the inhibition of thinking are the inhibitions of speech, ranging from hysterical mutism and stuttering to insecurity in the manner of expression or in the choice of words. Occasionally speech difficulties appear only in certain situations or in the presence of certain persons, situations or persons promoting the mobilization of old unconscious conflicts. Since thinking is intimately connected with speech, the conditions producing speech difficulties are quite similar to those producing inhibitions of thinking (*see* pp. 311 ff.).

Mental inhibitions are not limited to the sphere of intellect. There are also inhibitions in the spheres of emotions and will. Like psychogenically stupid persons, there are also persons who are psychogenically cold and affectless or indecisive and weak. Because their emotions are connected with instinctual conflicts, such persons inhibit their emotional life to avoid the conflicts; or they displace unconscious conflicts and therefore feel contradictory about any utterance of their will. They may overcompensate for emotional immaturity by an intense development of their intellectual life. There is also a real repression of the affective life, a sort of shutting out of all direct and warm relationships with persons and things, a general frigidity, so to speak. Such attempts to block all feelings may or may not be successful. Sometimes in such persons, explosive emotional outbreaks occur under certain exceptional circumstances or in dreams (*see* pp. 417 ff.). The alienation of one's own feelings, characteristic for compulsion neurotics, generally is a result of a long development. Sometimes, however, a general frigidity may originate in one specific traumatic scene so fraught with emotion that from then on the subject becomes afraid of emotions altogether. The phenomena of depersonalization, too, are to some extent related to these reactions; they are inhibitions of particular feelings or other internal perceptions, the countercathexis appearing as heightened self-observation (*see* pp. 418 ff.).

Inhibitions in the sphere of will are operative within persons who avoid independent decisions of any kind. This disturbance may be part of an obsessive tendency to doubt everything and to prepare for action instead of to act, which in severe cases may lead to a disastrous "paralysis of will" (109, 567). Or the disturbance may be due to a defect in the functions of the superego; the capacity of will is renounced and the making of decisions is left to others because of fear of aggression or of need for external approval (803) (*see* p. 520). Various kinds of conflicts with objects may also find expression in a neurotic indecisiveness (115).

It is very probable that a certain proportion of "lack of talent" is not due to an actual absence of ability (772), but to a special psychogenic inhibition. This seems to be true of a great many so-called unmusical people. In the course of analysis, a number of such individuals come to admit that music is not actually a matter of indifference to them, but that it is unpleasant. This feeling of unpleasantness then turns out to be connected with their repressed infantile sexuality (125, 845). The same point of view applies to persons with inhibitions in regard to painting, and even to some cases of color blindness and tone deafness (1505).

Other specific inhibitions have a still more complicated origin than the examples hitherto discussed. Certain persons with a particularly intense sense of guilt dating back to their infantile sexual conflicts labor under the constant necessity of paying off a debt to their conscience (618). The extreme representatives of this type are the personalities described by Freud under the headings "those wrecked by success" (592), the "criminal from a sense of guilt" (592), and the "moral masochists" (613). These individuals seem to feel that they must not utilize the talents or the advantages that are theirs by natural endowment and character; they inhibit those of their functions that might lead to success. Their inhibitions gratify the demands made by the superego on the ego.

Freud has repeatedly called attention to the fact that one of the most difficult tasks in psychoanalysis is that of conquering a severe unconscious sense of guilt (613, 629). There are, however, cases more amenable to treatment where the patient does not bow so completely to his superego that he fills his whole life with ruinous inhibitions, but instead inhibits one or two specific functions. To this group belong a considerable number of the so-called occupational neuroses, like writer's cramp or violinist's cramp (352, 867).

"Occupational inhibition" is not, of course, psychologically a unit. It occurs whenever a person's occupation requires the performance of actions that have become inhibited. Thus all types of inhibitions may form the basis of occupational inhibitions (952, 1318). However, four things are worth mentioning: (1) Work, under present-day conditions, is the way to independence and success. Thus all conflicts around dependence and independence (orality) and around ambition may present themselves in the form of inhibitions of working. This explains why occupational inhibitions often represent the superego type of inhibition. (2) Under present-day conditions children often become acquainted with the conception of work under the aspect of "duty," demanded by authorities, as the opposite of "pleasure." All conflicts around authorities, all struggles between rebellion and obedience, therefore, may be expressed in the attitudes toward work. (3) Modern ideologies make it possible for persons who try to repress any instinctual demands to do so by becoming relatively hard workers, robots so to speak, without any pleasure in work but compelled to do it uninterruptedly ("reactive type of work") (see p. 472). If the repressed impulses then rebel, the rebellion necessarily takes the form of a disturbance in working ability. (4) Often the conception of "occupational inhibition" is connected with "neurotic disturbances of attention and concentration." These disturbances are not specific but rather general symptoms of the state of being dammed up.

In other cases the inhibited spheres are still more circumscribed. Certain situations, like open streets or high places, are avoided because of their connection with instinctual conflicts. These phobias will be discussed in the chapter that follows.

Every forbidden instinctual drive, be it a sensual, hostile, or tender one, strives for expression in action in the establishment of a contact with objects. Therefore, any one of them may lead to a general inhibition of motor activity. Inhibitions of playing, which some children develop, represent an inhibition of sexual or hostile impulses that would have been expressed in the game. The rejection of certain entire fields of activity frequently turns out to be a generalized inhibition of masturbation; social inhibitions sometimes can be traced back to sexual fantasies built up by the child about adult social intercourse; inhibitions of intellectual grasp may represent inhibitions of sexual perceptions, for example, of recognizing the difference between the sexes (174). Some persons feel inhibited when they have to greet people or show any other social amenity. The root of this inhibition lies in unconscious ambivalence (594, 1290).

Everyone feels certain functions or situations as "unpleasant" in an irrational way, that is, has fields where he is slightly inhibited. Everyone, because of inhibitions, is deprived of one or another mode of experience that might normally be his. Many patients, upon completion of analysis, state that they have acquired a new sense of the fullness of life; this new feeling probably appears not only because they are relieved of the necessity of spending a great deal of energy on repressions and symptom formation but also because those experiential capacities that were inhibited have become accessible anew. However, the removal of an inhibition of this sort is by no means an easy task; the older and the more ingrained a given inhibition, the more difficult it is to remove. Psychoanalysis of children, in this respect, is in a better position than psychoanalysis of adults. It may succeed in preventing inhibitions from becoming deeply rooted in the personality, and thus may act as a prophylactic agent.

Some inhibitions fulfill their task; by avoiding or inhibiting the function in question, the remobilization of old feared conflicts is likewise avoided. Most inhibitions, however, due to the fact that the repressed tends to return and to develop derivatives, become structurally quite intricate. Inhibitions may widen to neighboring fields as well as inaugurate a highly cathected "substitute" by displacement of their energy. The person then gives the impression of being somewhat exaggerated in one respect or another; and the analysis reveals that the exaggerated field is a substitute for something that is lacking.

In still other cases, complicated secondary adaptations of the personality to the inhibition are inaugurated, denials and reaction formations against them as well as overcompensations of them (*see* Chapter Twenty).

In summary, the relation between the conception of "inhibition" and the conceptions of "repression" or "pathogenic defense" may be stated as follows. The inhibited states are clinical symptoms of the effectiveness of repression or other pathogenic defenses.

ACTUAL NEUROSES, SYMPTOMS OF UNSPECIFIC INHIBITIONS

Any defensive mechanism using a countercathexis necessarily creates a certain impoverishment of the personality. The patient must engage in unfruitful defense measures, and thus is impoverished in the rational activities of life. The results are manifold inhibitions of ego functions and a chronic fatigue, or at least a readiness to get tired.

This chronic fatigue doubtlessly is physical in character and probably due to the fact that the muscular attitudes of persons undergoing mental stress are altered (1523). It is very interesting that physiological research has shown that the degree of fatigue is not in direct proportion to the degree of obvious muscular stress but is rather dependent on the mental state in which the muscular task was fulfilled. Persons in conflict tend to become tired more quickly than persons with a free mind. However, the problem remains as to how the conflicts create the chemical alteration basic to fatigue (increase of lactic acid in the muscles and lowering of blood sugar); probably they do so by changing the person's muscular behavior.

The awareness of this chronic impoverishment and fatigue constitutes a portion of the neurotic inferiority feelings (585). Energies that are needed for the defensive struggles are deflected from other functions.

The patients become generally disinterested and moody. Some of them feel simultaneously the paralyzing fatigue due to impoverishment and the tension and restlessness originating in the warded-off impulses that demand discharge. They feel the necessity for an outlet and nevertheless a lack of enthusiasm and interest in anything that might be used as an outlet. They want to be told what to do (because the real aims are unconscious) and they reject all suggestions (because they want no substitute) (422).

Neurasthenic disturbances of the ability to concentrate, which form the main complaint of so many neurotics, are of the same nature. The first reason such patients cannot concentrate on a conscious task lies in their unconscious preoccupation with a more important internal task, their defensive struggle. In severe cases, archaic and integrated activities replace the more recently acquired and differentiated ones; a resistance is developed against differentiated tasks and even against the acceptance of new stimuli, the reaction to which would need new amounts of energy. Another cause of the disturbance of concentration is the fatigue originating in the consumptive defensive struggle. Actual neurotics are hypersensitive and irritable because their state of relative insufficiency of ego control makes them react to slight stimuli as if they were intense ones.

The feeling of being bored probably is generally, at least in its neurotic exaggeration, a state of excitement in which the aim is repressed; anything the person can think about doing is felt as not adequate to release the inner tension. Bored persons are looking for distraction, but usually they cannot be distracted because they are fixated to their unconscious aim (422).

The inner tension expresses itself often as an external muscular rigidity; other persons are more hypotonic and lax; still others are characterized by alternations of hyper- and hypotonic states (410). The "irritable weakness" of neurasthenia is an expression of this simultaneity of fatigue and tension.

The general neurotic inhibition due to quantitative impoverishment is an accompanying feature of all types of neuroses. Any repression may manifest itself objectively as an inhibition. However, there are pathological states in which the general inhibition dominates the clinical picture, sometimes in an acute, sometimes in a chronic form. The acute form sets in when some actual situation demands an immediate and sharp defensive measure; it disappears when the task is fulfilled or the situation is changed. The chronic form appears as a life-long attempt to keep down some "dangerous" impulse, at the expense of the development of the total personality. Such persons seem to live less intensely than others; they are conspicuous for their apathy, indifference, and lack of initiative. In unconscious content, the chronic forms, as a rule, represent defenses against aggressive and sadistic impulses.

Freud described a patient who would fall into a state of apathy under conditions which in a normal person would provoke an attack of rage (618). Analysis of chronically apathetic individuals reveals that they were originally extremely aggressive, but because of castration anxiety inhibited their aggression and sometimes turned it against their own ego.

A patient with a passive personality, the "model-boy" type, had been quite spoiled in the first years of his life, which he spent with his mother and grandmother. He sustained sudden and severe frustrations at the hands of his father soon after they met for the first time. It was about that time that a brother was born. In the process of defending himself against onsets of severe rage and hatred, he became afraid of action and withdrew into a kind of vita contemplativa. In consequence, he was always kind and polite, but cold, without any real contacts, longing to receive love and attain success without, however, any activity on his part. He withdrew from acting to talking, and in his daydreams he became a great orator who, merely by making speeches, won more admiration than others by their deeds.

Theoretically, the difference between these reactions and hebephrenia may readily be defined. In the inhibited states, the object relationships are impoverished because the unconscious relationship to childhood objects must be held in check; in hebephrenia, the cathexis is actually withdrawn from the objects, not merely from external behavior. In clinical practice, however, it is not always easy to make this differentiation. Even in hebephrenia the narcissistic regression may be a gradual one, and incipient hebephrenics, too, present a picture of extremely apathetic individuals with deep underlying conflicts over their hostility to objects (see p. 423).

ANXIETY NEUROSIS

The dammed-up state creates a relative insufficiency of normal ego control. Actually, the first clinical symptoms of actual neuroses are very similar to those of traumatic neuroses. The neurotic, being engaged in an acute inner defense struggle, becomes restless, agitated, upset, and feels that he needs some change but does not know what it should be. He, too, then develops symptoms in the form of "emergency discharges," such as apparently unmotivated emotional attacks, chiefly anxiety spells, and disturbances of physical functions which are in part inhibitions and in part equivalents of anxiety.

As a matter of fact, even in actual neuroses, these general symptoms often appear in a more "specific" form, which is determined by the history of the personality.

Such patients feel tense and do not know what to do to make relaxation possible again. Very often they refuse to go to bed at night because they cannot achieve the relaxation necessary for sleep, and those with yearnings for the earlier oral-receptive type of mastery cannot rid themselves of the idea that somebody must come to "liberate" them. Their not-going-to-bed becomes a kind of magical procedure to enforce this liberation. Frequently, vicious circles come into being when the patients become afraid of the violence of their own attempts to enforce magical help; they get fears of retaliation and therefore with still greater intensity refuse to go to bed, that is, to abandon control.

The fact that attempts to increase the countercathexis in order to bind the excessive amounts of excitation alternate with involuntary emergency discharges explains the aforementioned succession (or simultaneity) of hypomotility, with general lack of interest and with loss of elasticity, and hyperemotional restlessness. The clinical picture is similar to that of a person whose sexual excitement is stopped before gaining its natural discharge. Actually the condition in both cases is the same. The difference consists only in the circumstance that the interruption in the course of excitement is due to internal defenses, whereas in the case of interruption of sexual intercourse the disturbance is an external one (789). Actually, Freud's advice is still valid: if a person suddenly becomes irritable and moody and develops spells of anxiety or a general readiness for anxiety, one should first ask about his sexual life. Sometimes stopping the practice of coitus interruptus is sufficient to effect a cure (545, 547, 551).

The anxiety in these states, like the anxiety in traumatic neuroses, is a direct and automatic expression of the state of being dammed up, representing, in part, simply the way the flooding by uncontrolled amounts of excitement makes itself felt and, in part, involuntary vegetative emergency discharges (1117, 1371).

Reich pointed out that during sexual excitement typical autonomic nervous reactions occur. In normal sexual intercourse these autonomic cathexes become gradually transformed into genital ones, and find a genital outlet in orgasm. If the orgastic function is disturbed, this change does not take place. The autonomic system remains overcharged, and this fact produces anxiety (1270).

POSITIVE NEURASTHENIC SYMPTOMS

If the actual-neurotic state is characterized not so much by anxiety as by other emergency discharges, combined with the various symptoms described above, it is usual to speak of neurasthenia. This condition is psychoanalytically not precisely defined; probably a more exact definition would be the task of further physiological research about the chemical transformations in excitement, satisfaction, frustration, and being dammed up.

The positive actual-neurotic symptoms as vegetative discharges—nevertheless discharges, after other ways of discharging have been blocked—present a challenge to physiology. A normal instinctual satisfaction means a physical (chemical) alteration at the source of the instinct. If an instinctual need is not adequately satisfied, the chemical alteration connected with the gratification of the drive is missing, and disturbances in the chemistry of the organism result. Undischarged excitement and affects mean an abnormal quantity and quality of hormones, and thus alterations in physiological functions (see p. 238).

Freud once inclined to the belief that neurasthenic symptoms might be an outcome of exaggerated masturbation (558, 580). Probably a more correct formulation would be: Neurasthenia is an outcome of insufficient orgasm; it occurs if masturbation has become insufficient, that is, if anxieties and guilt feelings disturb the satisfactory character of the masturbation (1268).

The physical symptoms of neurasthenia vary greatly, depending upon the constitution and the history of the personality. In the foreground of the picture are either retentive spastic symptoms as expressions of the attempts to block discharges, such as muscular and vasomotor spasms, constipation, and various types of headache, or explosive involuntary "emergency" discharges, such as diarrhea, sweating, tremor, and restlessness (201, 1010, 1381).

There is a gradual transition from neurasthenic symptoms to real organ neuroses in which retention and discharge symptoms are much more specific and in which intermediary factors are interpolated between defensive struggle and physical expression (see p. 238).

DISTURBANCES OF SLEEP

If a person spends a night in an uncomfortable situation, such as an uncomfortable sitting position, his sleep is more or less disturbed; he either does not succeed in falling asleep or, having fallen asleep, he feels exhausted rather than rested the following morning. To achieve the complete fulfillment of the function of sleep, tensions must be excluded from the organism, a prerequisite, impossible in this case because of the uncomfortable position of the body.

Neurotic disturbances of sleep are based on a similar impossibility of relaxation. In the case of the uncomfortable position of the body this impossibility was externally determined, whereas in neurotic disturbances it is due to internal causes. Clinging to certain cathexes, despite the wish to sleep, has the same effect as has continued tension in certain muscles: either the state of sleep is not attained or, if it is, the function of sleep is disturbed and the effect on the organism is enervating rather than refreshing. After continued monotonous physical movements, falling asleep is usually very difficult because the muscular areas involved still tend to continue the movements. (It is interesting to note that if a person nevertheless does succeed in falling asleep, he dreams that he is still keeping up the movements; the unconscious meaning of such dreams is: "My sleep need not be disturbed by impulses to keep on skiing, riding, etc., for they correspond to my actions: I am actually skiing, riding, etc.")

The same condition, occasioned by an uncomfortable position or unconscious motor impulses, is even more frequently brought about by unconscious stimuli that resist the wish to sleep and still retain their cathexes. As is well known, the function of dreaming in general serves the purpose of making sleep possible even under the adverse condition of the continuance of unconscious cathexes (552). A quantitative increase in such dream-forming cathexes may endanger the possibility of maintaining the sleeping state through dreams. In a state of being dammed up, this inability to master the cathexes that resist sleep through dreams usually first becomes apparent in the frequent occurrence of dreams that fail, that is, in recurrent nightmares (876); and eventually sleep may become almost completely impossible (358, 441, 1113).

Furthermore, it is not only the cathexes of repressed wishes that may make sleep impossible. Acute worries or affect-laden expectations, whether agreeable or disagreeable, particularly sexual excitement without gratification, make for sleeplessness. In the case of neurotic disturbances of sleep, the unconscious factors of course outweigh the others.

The idea that the autonomy of the cathexes of the repressed, acting in opposition to the wish to sleep, either makes sleeping impossible or impairs its refreshing effect is so plausible that one wonders how restful sleep is possible at all, since everybody has repressions. With particular reference to neurotics, one would expect that all of them would suffer from disturbed sleep.

Actually the impairment of the function of sleep is one of the most common neurotic manifestations and is encountered in almost every neurosis (1152); however, sometimes it is possible to explain why such a disturbance is relatively slight. Some neurotics have learned to render harmless the sleep-disturbing stimuli coming from the repression by applying secondary measures, by channelizing them; however, it must be admitted that this does not sufficiently solve the problem. The fact that sometimes intense repressed cathexes seem not to interfere with the relaxation necessary for sleep obviously depends upon still other (constitutional?) factors. It is certain that the sleep-disturbing effect of the repressed is greater for all those involved in *acute* defensive conflicts than for those who have learned to avoid acute secondary repression struggles through rigid ego attitudes.

Some neurotic sleep disturbances are not of the general actual-neurotic type hitherto described. The ego opposing the warded-off impulses knows that these impulses push forward with greater force in the state of sleep or while falling asleep than during the wakeful state. Therefore, the ego fears the state of sleep or of falling asleep. This is the most general explanation of *sleep phobias;* fear of sleep means fear of the unconscious wishes that may arise in sleep (638, 1201). Frequently such a fear arises after the experience of a nightmare of traumatic effect. Fear of sleep then is a fear of dreaming, that is, of a failure of repression.

There are very definite instinctual temptations which more frequently than others are associated with the idea of sleeping. Inasmuch as the voluntary control of motility is lost during sleep, it is first and foremost the fear of forbidden instinctual *actions* which can assume the form of fear of sleep (175). It is understandable that children who are bedwetters, or adults who as children used to wet their beds, want to avoid sleep in order to avoid any opportunity for bedwetting. That which is valid in childhood for the executives of urethral (or anal) functions is later valid for the executive of the genitals. We know that young men with conflicts of conscience about masturbation undertake to substitute nocturnal pollutions for masturbation because they then feel less responsible. But the superego does not always accept this excuse. The fear of sleep or of falling asleep is very often a fear of the temptation to masturbate. Further, the state of falling asleep is accompanied by a reactivation of archaic levels of ego consciousness, and archaic forms of ego experience have in turn frequently become representatives of excitations experienced in the earliest period of development. Persons who have oral-erotic and skin-erotic repressions try to avoid everything that reminds them of the original period of their oral-erotic and skin-erotic excitations; and the ego states which they must experience when falling asleep arouse such recollections. These are, therefore, felt as prohibited temptations, which can become a motive for entirely avoiding the state of sleep or of falling asleep (1594). The main neurosis of orality, melancholia, goes hand in hand with the most serious disturbance of sleep. A further specific instinctual temptation that may be suggested by the state of sleep is the remembrance of a primal scene, which took place at night when the child was supposed to be asleep.

The unconscious association that disturbs sleep may also be a specific and unique one, explicable only by the life history of the individual (309).

Frequently, the state of sleep does not signify a temptation but rather some punishment or catastrophe, associatively connected with certain drives. The fact that the state of sleep precludes the free use of motility makes some persons fear sleep as an obstacle to their fleeing from supposed dangers or punishments. Not only may the unconscious thought arise that one may be castrated during sleep but the very loss of consciousness in sleep may itself have the meaning of castration.

This is not the place to analyze the neurotic fear of death in detail; it is regularly due to unconscious conceptions associated with the ideas of dying or being dead and to a turning away from active impulses to kill (*see* pp. 208 f.). If such a fear once has been established, it can easily lead to disturbances of sleep by equating sleep and death with each other.

Most frequently, however, disturbances of sleep unconsciously represent temptation and punishment simultaneously. The curtailment of ego functions occurring in the state of sleep is at the same time feared as the loss of the ego's censorship over the instincts, that is, as an opportunity to do anything one pleases, and as a minor death, as a castration, as a terrible consequence of pursuing instinctual activities.

The conflicts around disturbances of sleep may have a further development. The ego undertakes various measures in order to regain the lost control, sometimes with greater success, sometimes with less. An interesting example of such attempts may be observed in the sleep rituals of compulsion neurotics. Sleep is possible only as long as certain measures are carried out, which are intended to exclude the danger that is unconsciously associatively connected with the state of sleep (441).

The pavor nocturnus of children, as well as the occurrence of frequent nightmares, is a failure of such measures; the repressed, and thereby the fear of it, returns and disturbs sleep (123, 1098, 1232, 1341, 1343, 1407, 1548).

The manifold possibilities of sleep phobias should not mislead one into underestimating the more important actual-neurotic side of neurotic disturbances of sleep. In general, sleep presupposes a total relaxation; and a state of inner tension is therefore connected with the disturbance of sleep.

GENERAL REMARKS ABOUT CHRONIC NEURASTHENIA

If an actual neurosis is not due to a mere external disturbance of libidinal economy but rather to a defensive struggle, the state of being dammed up, after a certain time, is usually further elaborated. However, there are certain forms that remain on the level of neurasthenia. It is not easy to state what causes such a development (201, 1381). What can be stated with certainty is that the excitement, which cannot find any outlet, in such cases is exclusively pregenital in nature; in chronically neurasthenic individuals, even the genitals appear unconsciously to serve pregenital aims (1268). This circumstance may, for example, find expression in the symptom of ejaculatio praecox (14; *cf. also* 477). Sometimes analysis of the form of the masturbation suffices for the recognition of its pregenital latent content (1262). Since the attempted satisfaction never can be achieved, the patients try masturbation again and again, and this explains why compulsive masturbators and their extreme types, masturbation addicts (*see* p. 384), are frequently chronic neurasthenics. Masturbation may become the uniform response to any kind of stimulus.

A disturbance of the economy of the instinctual demands is the more likely to produce lasting effects, the less able the person is to treat difficulties actively, that is, the more he inclines toward passive-receptive longings. Actually chronic neurasthenics are always persons with a heightened narcissistic need. The types that will later be described as impulsive personalities, addicts and persons disposed to depressions, are often at the same time chronic neurasthenics.

It is understandable that some of the actual-neurotic symptoms, especially the physical ones, are very painful. Since a medical examination in such cases cannot find any cause for the pains, the complaints of the patients often are called hypochondriacal. And actually, there is not always a sharp borderline between neurasthenia and hypochondriasis (*see* p. 262).

THERAPEUTIC PSYCHOANALYSIS IN ACTUAL NEUROSES

With regard to therapy, those types of actual neuroses that are due to an unfortunate sexual regimen do not need any other therapy than a change of this regimen. Likewise, acute states of "nervousness" due to some specific experience, which upset the equilibrium between defensive forces and warded-off instincts, are frequently only temporary and end spontaneously when a new equilibrium is found. Cases in which an acute neurosis can be caught in statu nascendi, as long as actual-neurotic symptoms still are more in the foreground than psychoneurotic symptoms, often are readily accessible to psychoanalysis; and for states of anxiety that can be caught before the anxiety is finally fixated on a certain object, an especially good prognosis can be given. In contrast, the prognosis is poor in cases of chronic neurasthenia and hypochondriasis. It will become clear later why the lack of genital primacy and narcissistic orientation greatly hamper the therapeutic possibilities of psychoanalysis.

Actual-neurotic symptoms become further elaborated in different ways. Sometimes the symptoms themselves impress the patient in a traumatic way; he then may develop a kind of secondary traumatic neurosis (*see* p. 457). The sensations may unconsciously be interpreted as castration or as the loss of protection by the superego, which may be met by an intensification of the defending forces, and thus create a vicious circle. In cases with narcissistic fixations, actual-neurotic symptoms may induce increased self-observation and form the core of a hypochondriasis. And, last but not least, actual-neurotic symptoms may be transformed into psychoneurotic symptoms by a further and more specific elaboration.

Actual-neurotic symptoms form the nucleus of all psychoneuroses. Unspecific anxiety and general irritability and moodiness are present at the start of any psychoneurosis (392, 447). Actual-neurotic symptoms may also reappear at the conclusion of a psychoneurosis: if psychoanalysis succeeds in freeing a patient's repressed sexual energies, but the external situation prevents him from finding an opportunity for achieving the satisfaction of which he is now capable, psychoneurotic symptoms may again be replaced by actual-neurotic ones.

C. Psychoneuroses. Mechanisms of Symptom Formation, and Special Neuroses

CHAPTERS XI–XVIII

Chapter XI

ANXIETY AS NEUROTIC SYMPTOM: ANXIETY HYSTERIA

THE NATURE OF THE PSYCHONEUROTIC SYMPTOM

A CHANGE in a state of being dammed up, caused by a neurotic conflict, seems possible only through a break-through of the original impulse or through an intensification of the defense. Actually, however, there is a third possibility which at first glance seems paradoxical: both may occur simultaneously. Compromises are found in which the objectionable impulse finds some substitute outlet, but the substitute outlet may help to ward off the remainders of the original impulse. A part of the dammed-up energy is discharged, but in such a way as to intensify the defense against the rest. The typical neurotic symptom expresses drive and defense simultaneously. Slips, errors, and symptomatic acts constitute comparatively simple examples wherein the formation of compromises of this sort can be studied in relative isolation (553).

The great reservoir for substitute formations is constituted of daydreams. Wish-fulfilling fantasies which are developed as playful refuge and as a substitute for unpleasant reality (*see* pp. 49 f.) can easily be used as derivatives by warded-off impulses. Such fantasies, being intensified by the displacement of the cathexis of warded-off impulses, may offer a substitute discharge; but if they increase excessively or come too close to the repressed content, they in turn may be warded off. Neurotic symptoms, then, are not always direct expressions of the repressed impulses, but rather indirect ones determined in their specific form by derivative daydreams that are interpolated between the original impulse and the final symptom (590).

The simplest example for a derivative that may or may not find an outlet is given in an exaggerated or qualitatively changed affect. If a person reacts to an event in an exaggerated way or with a type of affect that seems inadequate, this is a sign of displacement; the affect actually belongs to some other situation which had been warded off.

The production of derivatives and the struggle of these derivatives for admission to motility are regulated by special mechanisms of symptom formation. The prevailing mechanisms of symptom formation determine the symptomatology and clinical course of a neurosis. Consequently the following chapters which deal with the mechanisms of symptom formation will at the same time examine the characteristics of the specific psychoneuroses.

It must be stressed, however, that practically all cases of neurosis exhibit various mechanisms of symptom formation concurrently. Freud stated definitely that in every compulsion neurosis there is a nucleus of conversion hysteria (599) and that behind every neurosis in general there is an infantile anxiety hysteria (618). Present-day character disorders, in which the ego itself is drawn into the illness, are multiform in regard to their underlying mechanisms. It is more exact, therefore, to diagnose mechanisms than to diagnose neuroses.

However, in any branch of medicine, diagnosis and special pathology are of relative value only. No single clinical case ever presents a disease entity as it is described in the textbook. Nevertheless everyone recognizes the theoretical and practical importance of diagnosis and special pathology. Certain features may differ from the typical, but by and large typical features prevail and only an understanding of the typical gives a foundation for an understanding of the atypical. In psychoanalytic investigation the customary method of procedure is to attain understanding of the usual complicated phenomena by a preliminary study of more unusual but more transparent examples. In the study of the neuroses, the typical mechanisms of symptom formation represent just such more readily understood instances. They represent typical components, atypical combinations of which constitute the majority of actual individual neuroses. In this sense we shall proceed from the simpler to the more complex. The descriptions of mechanisms that follow do not imply that the mechanisms always or even very frequently occur in these isolated forms. The chief value of the classification is a heuristic one.

ANXIETY IN ANXIETY HYSTERIA

The simplest compromise between drive and defense consists of the anxiety that was the motive for the defense becoming manifest, whereas the reason for the anxiety is repressed.

In anxiety neurosis, a general inner tension manifests itself as a constant, freely floating anxiety or readiness for anxiety. In anxiety hysteria, however, the anxiety is specifically connected with a special situation, which represents the neurotic conflict.

If the ego that appraises the danger—"This instinctual action or situation may bring castration or loss of love"—intends to "warn" in the same sense as a normal ego warns of a real danger, in anxiety hysteria this intention entirely fails. What was intended to prevent a traumatic state actually induces one. This state of affairs was mentioned in connection with the triple stratification of anxiety, where it was stated that in such cases the warning anxiety regresses to panic anxiety (*see* p. 133). This failure of the warning function of the ego finds its explanation in the fact that a heightened inner tension (the state of being dammed up) had previously created a general readiness for anxiety, a powder keg in which the danger signal of the ego acts like a match.

A tense person reacts to a danger situation differently from a normal person. The normal person develops a certain fear which may be used by the ego. The tense person develops a latent readiness for explosion which, through an additional influx of fear from the perception of danger, causes him to become paralyzed. In the same way that a "nervous" person reacts to a real danger with a panic instead of feeling fear and reacting accordingly, he also reacts to an imaginary danger with panic.

Most often a diffuse readiness to develop anxiety of the nature of an anxiety neurosis has existed for a certain period. Then something occurs which unconsciously mobilizes the basic pathogenic conflict. The ego intends to warn, the warning fails, and the first spell of the anxiety hysteria occurs. From then on the readiness to develop anxiety is bound to the specific situation that aroused this first anxiety spell. The limitation and specification of the feared situation can be described as a kind of secondary binding of the primary diffuse anxiety to the specific content (392, 873, 875). The continual explosive readiness in anxiety neurosis is now controlled as long as no matches of allusion to the specific situation are lighted. However, if these specific situations are touched upon, the anxiety becomes manifest. Secondarily the ego develops measures that attempt to fight off this anxiety, too. Anxiety hysteria, in which the fear that motivated the defense is still manifest, is the simplest kind of psychoneurosis. Thus the first neurotic reactions in children have, as a rule, the character of anxiety hysterias. All the other neuroses have elaborated the anxiety further.

THE DISPLACEMENT IN ANXIETY HYSTERIA

What determines the choice of the specific content? What situations or persons are believed to be dangerous?

In certain cases there is not much displacement; anxiety is simply felt in situations where an uninhibited person would experience either sexual excitement or rage. In discussing inhibited states, it has been mentioned that an inhibition sometimes manifests itself in a certain fear that is developed whenever the inhibited field is touched upon. Besides impotence and frigidity, there is also a sex phobia; that is, some persons, especially women, become frightened in the face of sexual temptations and try to avoid them. There are general eating phobias, and more specialized phobias about special kinds of food that have become connected with unconscious conflicts, either through historical associations or through their symbolic significance. There are anal phobias which try to avoid anal excitations at any cost. There are fighting phobias, seen in persons who become frightened whenever aggressive behavior would be indicated. For such cases, a formula is valid which would be an oversimplification in more complicated cases: what a person fears, he unconsciously wishes for.

In other and still simple phobias, the feared situation does not represent a feared temptation; rather, it is the threat that causes the temptation to be feared: castration or loss of love. There are knife and scissor phobias, the implication of which is that the touch or even the sight of these instruments awakens the feared thought of a possible castration (and, it is true, in most cases also an unconscious temptation for a repressed hostility). Certain persons are afraid of seeing cripples or of witnessing accidents, which means: "I do not want to be reminded of what might happen to me" (and, again, the fear may also arise from such sights being a temptation for unconscious hostile wishes). Small children are afraid of being left alone, which for them means not being loved any more.

> The fear of being turned into stone through a forbidden sight does not only mean death (and castration) but also expresses fear of the sensations of anxiety themselves. The idea of being stone represents the idea of being paralyzed by fear.

All these cases are characterized by their lack of displacement. More frequent, however, are cases of anxiety hysteria in which the defensive forces have achieved more than a mere development of anxiety and subsequent phobic attitudes. The connection between the feared situation and the original instinctual conflict has become more concealed. It is not sexual situations that are feared any more but rather *sexualized* situations. Regularly the feared situation or persons have a specific unconscious significance for the patient. In a more distorted way, they again symbolize either a temptation for a warded-off impulse or a punishment for an unconscious impulse or a combination of both.

This also holds true for all neurotic misapprehensions of actual events in terms of the past, even if not accompanied by patent anxiety: the warded-off impulses seek opportunities for satisfaction, but their reactivation likewise mobilizes the old anxieties; the neurotic repetitions consist in misunderstanding actuality in the sense either of unconscious temptations or of unconscious punishments or in both senses.

> *Examples of anxiety situations that represent unconscious temptations:* The idea of open streets in agoraphobias is, as a rule, unconsciously conceived as an opportunity for sexual adventures. The idea of being alone is perceived of as temptation to masturbate.
>
> *Examples of the punishment character of anxiety situations:* The feared street is thought of as a place where one might be seen and caught; being alone means

being unprotected against the punishing powers of the bogeyman. What anxiety hysterics fear often represents substitutes of the idea of castration. In little Hans, the unconscious meaning of the fear of being bitten by a horse was a regressive oral expression of the idea of being castrated (566). Another patient, who was afraid of being bitten by a dog, was astonished when analysis revealed that this fear, judging by the accompanying physical sensations, actually referred to his genitals.

Many hypochondriacal fears mean either "I may become castrated" or "It may turn out that I am already castrated." There are sickness phobias in persons during whose childhood castration fear was displaced to the idea of being sick. Frequently, in such cases "being sick" means "having fever," the sensations of the feverish state representing the feared infantile sexual excitement.

An example of the simultaneity of temptation and punishment is given in the case of the wolf-man (599). He had developed a passive-feminine attitude toward his father, and was afraid that the satisfaction of these feminine wishes might carry with it the dreaded castration. His fear of being eaten by the wolf was simultaneously a regressive oral expression of the wish to submit to his father and of the threat of being castrated.

Fears of being run over or of falling from a high place are typical expressions of feminine masochistic wishes and, at the same time, of the connected castration fear (884). Falling from a high place, connoting the danger of being killed, certainly represents punishment, probably most often punishment for wishes of killing; however, the sensation of falling itself simultaneously represents the sensations of sexual excitement which, having been blocked in their natural course, have acquired a painful and frightening character. The fear of being confined in a narrow space or a fear of narrow streets signifies the fear of the very sensations of anxiety which are experienced as a constriction and augmented through the painful vegetative sensations that replace blocked sexual excitement. Fear of high places later may be replaced by the conversion symptom of getting dizzy spells when looking down from high places. This symptom is physical expression of a mental anticipation of actual falling.

A simultaneity of punishment and temptation is, as a rule, also the basis of the frequent fear of "going crazy." With regard to this fear, it should be kept in mind that it may be justified. The rule that a person who is afraid of insanity does not become insane is not true; many incipient schizophrenics are aware of their increasing estrangement. However, more frequently this fear is not a warranted judgment but is rather a phobia. Even as a phobia the fear has an objective basis: what the patient senses in his fear of becoming crazy is the interaction of his unconscious strivings, especially the instinctual (sexual or aggressive) impulses operative within him (871). In this sense, the fear of going crazy is but a special case of the general fear of one's own excitement. Since the feared excitement of infantile sexuality is most often experienced in connection with masturbation, the warnings of adults that "masturbation drives people crazy" may easily be accepted by children as a substitute for the idea of castration.

Sometimes the idea of insanity has, unconsciously, a more specific significance. Experience may have established the equation *head = penis,* and therefore *insanity = castration.* A child may, depending upon various experiences, connect various ideas with insanity. The idea of being an idiot is sometimes connected with the idea of having a big head (hydrocephalus) which, as a representation by the opposite, again may mean castration. Babies have big heads; older siblings often hate babies and are, therefore, afraid of hurting them. "I might become an idiot like the baby" or "I might get a big head like the baby" may represent both the feared envy of the baby and the anticipated punishment for this envy.

Fears of being ugly or dirty may have the same significance as fears of being sick or insane; ugliness or a repelling appearance means being sexually excited (or being in a rage) or being castrated (or pregnant) or both. Phobias of this kind may form a transitional state toward delusions.

Still another example for a simultaneity of temptation and punishment is given by the states which Ferenczi has described as Sunday neuroses (484). On Sundays, some persons regularly suffer from anxiety (or from depressions). Sundays generally are looked upon as days when sexual activities are more likely to occur than on other days; but Sundays are also the days on which children are more under the supervision of their fathers.

What, now, is the relation between the manifest anxiety situation and its unconscious instinctual significance?

The fact that there is a displacement at all certainly is traceable to the defense, which makes the original ideas unconscious and thus necessitates the development of substitutes. The substitute, as Freud formulates it, "on the one hand has certain associative connections with an idea which was rejected; while on the other hand, because of the remoteness of that idea, it escapes repression" (590).

The displacement shows that in anxiety hysteria the defense is not limited to the development of anxiety or to avoidance of situations in which the anxiety would occur. The development of substitutes proves that repression and other defense mechanisms are used as well. The anxiety in anxiety hysteria initiates a powerful repressive activity.

Due to repression, phobias frequently have an indefinite, nebulous content, comparable in their lack of clarity to the manifest content of dreams; it often takes a great deal of analytic work to ascertain precisely what the patient is afraid of. In some cases the content of the fear had at one time been clear and definite, but later in the course of the neurosis it became vague and indefinite. The forces of repression continue to wage war on the symptom as an offshoot of the repressed. Thus an understanding of a complicated or vague symptom of long standing may frequently be attained by determining the circumstances of its first appearance.

The advantage offered by the displacement is that the original offensive idea does not become conscious. To be afraid of a horse instead of the father, as in the case of little Hans (566), has certain other advantages, too. Those who threaten are hated. If an individual no longer feels threatened by his father but by a horse, he can avoid hating his father; here the distortion was a way out of the conflict of ambivalence. The father, who had been hated and loved simultaneously, is loved only, and the hatred is displaced onto the bad horse (618). Freud also brings to our attention the fact that a boy is forced to associate with his father every day, whereas the threatening horse can be avoided simply by not going outdoors. To fear the wolf instead of the father (599) has still further advantages: horses were frequent in city streets in Hans's time, whereas wolves are to be seen only in picture books which one does not need to open, or at the zoo where one does not have to go very often (618). If a person has become afraid of going out, it is possible to avoid this feared situation, whereas one's own body and its sensations cannot be avoided; an advantageous projection from an internal instinctual danger to an external perceptional danger has taken place.

A projection of this kind, that is, the attempt to escape from an internal dangerous impulse by avoiding a specific external condition which represents this impulse, is the most frequent type of displacement in anxiety hysteria. It is true that the original danger, in the last analysis, also was an external one, for it is not the instinctual expression that is feared but its external consequences (castration, loss of love). But although the phobic individual primarily flees from his threatening parents, he nevertheless is in flight from his own impulses; for the external danger of castration is determined by his behavior.

The projection is more clearly evident in cases in which anxiety over an external object has supplanted a guilt feeling; an object in the external world is now feared instead of one's own conscience.

In certain animal phobias, the projection of one's own feared impulses is still more pronounced than it was in little Hans. A case described by Helene Deutsch had the following simple construction. An unconsciously passive-feminine young man was afraid of hens because they reminded him of his libidinous wishes and of the danger of being castrated, with which these wishes were associatively connected. He merely projected his internal instinctual conflict onto an avoidable external object (327).

Often not only the goal of an impulse is projected onto an external object but one's own sensations of excitement as well.

A projection seems to be lacking, however, in children's neuroses, when the feared external object "animal" simply replaces another feared external object "father."

The paths selected by the displacement are determined by various factors. To a considerable extent they are determined by the history of the individual. The significance of phobias cannot, therefore, be understood without taking into consideration the patient's history. In part the paths of displacement depend on the nature of the drives that are warded off. Anxiety over being eaten, for example, may correspond to oral-sadistic longings, anxiety over being murdered to death wishes.

It has been mentioned that anxiety over being eaten or over being bitten may be a disguise for castration anxiety. In such a case the castration fear has become distorted in a regressive way, that is, by choosing as a substitute an archaic autonomous fear. The regression may be a partial one, and frequently we see manifestations of anxiety that contain elements of both being eaten and being castrated. Among manifestations of this kind are the fantasies of the vagina dentata, and that of intrauterine castration (414).

Phobias about infection and touching often express the tendency to avoid dirt, and show that the patient has to defend himself against anal-erotic temptations.

Again it is possible that genital Oedipus wishes have been regressively replaced by anal impulses, and that in this way castration anxiety has regressively been supplanted by anal fears. The frequent bathroom and toilet phobias which are observed in children and in compulsion neurotics, such as a fear of falling into the toilet, of being eaten up by some monster coming from it, or the rationalized fear of being infected, as a rule show signs of a condensation of ideas of dirt with castration ideas.

Fear of open streets is often a defense against exhibitionism or scoptophilia. The role of these two partial instincts is even more prominent in phobias connected with appearing in public, whether this appearance involves special conditions such as being looked at (stage fright) or is merely a fear of being in a crowd.

The anxiety attacks of a female patient with agoraphobia and crowd phobia had the unconscious definite purpose of making her appear weak and helpless to all passers-by. Analysis showed that the unconscious motive of her exhibitionism was a deep hostility, originally directed toward her mother, then deflected onto herself. "Everybody, look!" her anxiety seemed to proclaim, "my mother let me come into the world in this helpless condition, without a penis." Originally the attack represented an attempt to exhibit a fantasied penis; the knowledge that this object was fictitious produced the transformation from perversion to anxiety hysteria.

The aforementioned fears of being ugly or otherwise repulsive (e.g., of exuding a bad odor) reveal themselves as fears of one's own exhibitionism. Persons with such fears are unconsciously striving to show their sexual excitement and are afraid of being rejected or punished for it. Further, this exhibitionism often has an aggressive, mandatory meaning. The patients may feel entitled to compensation and try to force by magical means the persons looking at them to give this compensation. The fear is that this intention may fail. The ugliness may represent pregnancy or the state of being castrated; making a demonstration of it may signify a magical gesture, as exhibitionism often is intimately connected with an equally strong scoptophilia. If the fear of being ugly or "stinky" is replaced by the conviction that this is the case, this is a transitional state toward delusion, as erythrophobics in general are prone to develop paranoid trends. The basic underlying feeling is one of guilt. In women the conviction of being repulsive (or ugly or physically disabled or unable to bear healthy children) is based on an awareness of their lack of a penis, an idea that is connected with masturbatory and incestuous guilt feelings; likewise in boys, an anxiety of this kind usually means that the terrible consequences of masturbatory activities may be found out.

In a case of perfume addiction, this symptom could be traced back to a previous fear of exuding a bad odor. The patient was fixated on an anal concept of sexuality. She was not only afraid that an early anal masturbation might be found out but also that she might give expression to her sexual longings, which were colored by a sadistic, castrating attitude toward boys and which she perceived in the special form of exuding an odor in their direction.

Stage fright and erythrophobia, however, are most often not simple expressions of the warding off of heightened exhibitionism and scoptophilia. The fact that the exhibitionism has been heightened is, as a rule, the result of other previous instinctual conflicts, the exhibition not only being aimed at producing sexual pleasure but also at producing or enforcing reassurance against anxieties, guilt, and inferiority feelings. The anxiety hysterias in question represent the failure of such strivings for reassurance. The idea is by magical gestures to force spectators to prove that no castration has occurred, or to give the approbation needed to contradict a guilt feeling; if the spectators do not fulfill these demands immediately and adequately, violent (oral) sadistic tendencies may be developed against them. Thus the unconscious content of erythrophobic and stage-fright types of fear (and shame) is not only the idea that exhibitionistic actions may provoke castration or loss of love, but more specifically the idea that what is done to protect the person's self-esteem against danger may result in the opposite, in his complete annihilation. And this again might be comprehended in different ways. Either the patient believes unconsciously that he is castrated and fears that his attempts to deny it might fail and that everything that was intended to make people like and feed him might result in their disliking him and withdrawing all support or he may be afraid of his own charming power: the sight of him might hurt and castrate the spectators and they will not be able to give anything any more; he is afraid of his own violent aggressiveness, often reduced to "aggressive looking" (96, 118, 356, 405, 446, 501, 522, 1085, 1568).

A fear of examinations is closely related to erythrophobia and stage fright. However, some of the above-mentioned features are here still more outspoken: an authority, an external representative of the superego, is about to decide whether one is accepted and permitted to participate in certain privileges, that is, to obtain the narcissistic supplies, or whether one is rejected and sentenced to isolation and narcissistic hunger. The relationship between modern examinations and primitive initiation rites has rightly been stressed (523, 1481). How a person reacts to this situation depends both on his sexual feeling relationship to authorities (to the father) and on his narcissistic needs. An anxiety hysteria will result whenever the person sexualizes the examination situation in the hope of thereby overcoming his inferiority feelings and castration fear, and then has to face the possibility of his efforts having the opposite result. Usually, conflicts around passive-feminine longings complicate the situation in examination phobias (105, 158, 405, 866, 1256, 1344, 1520).

Other typical phobias are directed against other partial instincts. Anxieties of high places frequently are connected with unconscious ideas concerning erection. Claustrophobias and fears of suffocation are often specially directed against fantasies of being in the mother's womb (1056). Fears of falling, of heights, car and railway phobias, show at first glance that they are developed in an attempt to fight pleasurable sensations connected with equilibrium stimulation.

This last factor, the struggle against sexual excitation as perceived in the pleasurable sensations of equilibrium, plays a special part in many anxiety hysterias.

Abraham has shown that it is not only exhibitionism and scoptophilia that are warded off in agoraphobia; in cases of fear of going out onto the street, the function of walking itself has acquired a definite sexual meaning, which presupposes an intensified equilibrium eroticism, possibly due to a fixation at the time of learning to walk (6, 9; cf. also 1282, 1402).

> A patient's agoraphobic fears were accompanied by the feeling that his legs were being pulled, or that they were running away of their own accord. Analysis showed that the prohibition of his masturbation coincided in time with his learning to walk. As a little boy, he took much pleasure and narcissistic pride in walking. His legs and their functions had usurped the place of the thwarted functions of his penis. A subsequent intensification of old conflicts permitted the fear of castration to become manifest, in the new field, as a fear of losing his legs (410).

Once this has attracted attention, it can be realized that many phobic fears directly concern sensations of equilibrium.

Sensations of equilibrium play an important part as a source of sexual excitement in children as well as in adults. Since sensations of the same sense generally are also an essential component of the experience of anxiety, connections between sexual excitement and anxiety are closer in the case of equilibrium eroticism than in any other partial instinct. Conflicts around erogenous sensations of equilibrium give rise to equilibrium phobias; but also the development of phobias in general, that is, the establishment of a close connection between sensations of anxiety and of sexual excitement, mobilizes infantile equilibrium eroticism. Often sensations of equilibrium have become the representatives of infantile sexuality in general. Many persons who have no conscious memory of having masturbated as children do remember various games and fantasies involving the situation of their body in space, about changes in the size of their body or of certain parts of their body, of ideas of their beds being turned around, or of still vaguer sensations:

"Something is rotating." Other persons do not remember any pleasure connected with sensations of this kind but do remember anxieties about them, alienations of the body or of certain organs, or fears about space sensations, all of which are the result of the repression of an older pleasure. Anxieties of this kind very often form the core of anxiety hysterias (444).

PROJECTION OF ONE'S OWN EXCITEMENT IN ANXIETY HYSTERIA

These facts must now be connected with the role played by projection in anxiety hysteria. In many phobias the physical state of sexual or aggressive excitement (frequently expressed in sensations of equilibrium and space) is projected and represented by a feared external situation (526, 1384, 1386, 1391). Persons who are afraid of falling asleep or of being anesthetized or of having fever are chiefly afraid of being overwhelmed by painful sensations of equilibrium and space. Often patients are afraid of monotonous noises, such as the ticking of a clock or other rhythmic occurrences; actually they are afraid of their own heart beat (or genital sensations) which are represented to them by what they notice in the external world.

In claustrophobias, the idea of being confined is not experienced so pressingly if there is any possibility of escape. The anxiety increases to the utmost when the idea arises that one might want to leave the room and be unable to do so. Mostly the feeling is that sudden suffocation might occur and that in this event there must be a way of escape. Persons who are afraid of trains, boats, and airplanes state that the worst fear is the impossibility of getting out if they should so desire, and that when on a train they hold their breath from one station to the next. That means that the excitement is projected onto the vehicle that precipitated the excitement, and the need for a sudden escape from the room in which one is confined is a need for escape from one's own feared excitement as soon as it has reached a certain intensity (431, 1522).

Phobias of vehicles, rooted in the warding off of erogenous sensations of equilibrium and space, have definite relations to the somatic disease of seasickness. The vegetative excitements aroused by equilibrium sensations in a purely physical way have a distinct similarity to sensations of anxiety, and these excitements may have become associatively connected with "too much sexual excitation" in childhood. Neurosis and seasickness, then, may influence each other. Persons with claustrophobia and similar neuroses probably tend more toward the development of seasickness; and an occasional seasickness in a hitherto nonneurotic person may mobilize infantile anxieties and have the effect of a trauma reactivating the memory of a primal scene. There are also conversion hysterias which are an elaboration of vehicle phobias in the sense that vomiting or dizziness, as a physical anticipation of feared equilibrium sensations, may have supplanted the anxiety.

There are also "claustrophobias in time" rather than in space. Some patients experience a fear of having no time, of always being "cooped up" by their duties, which is as oppressive to them as the space sensations are to the claustrophobic, and which also has the same psychological significance. Other persons are afraid of "broadness" in time; they hasten from one activity to the next one because empty time has for them the same significance as empty spaces for some agoraphobics.

Clinical experience shows that certain types of neurotic indecision are based on the same fear. Any definite decision means the exclusion of the possibility of escape and is therefore avoided. Certain forms of stubbornness represent a highly emotional rejection of commands, which are sensed as closing the ways of escape.

What is feared in an inordinate excitement is obviously a kind of breaking down of the organization of the ego.

A patient felt anxiety in a car only when somebody else, not when he himself, was driving. "Why should I be afraid," he said, "if I can stop the car at any time?"

It is the loss of voluntary decision that is feared, frequently represented in the unconscious by the idea of loss of control of bladder and rectum (557); and this loss of control is represented by the vehicle's moving uninfluenced by the wish of the passenger, by the room that cannot be left of one's own volition, and originally by the increasing sexual excitement approaching orgasm.

In Reich's analysis of the normal and pathological course of sexual excitement, he has explained that a phase of voluntary movements is followed by one of involuntary convulsions of the muscles on the floor of the pelvis; in this second phase the act can no longer be interrupted voluntarily without intense displeasure; the full development of this phase is the condition for an economically sufficient discharge in orgasm (1270). This loss of the ego at the climax of sexual excitement is normally also the climax of the pleasure. Certain egos, the "orgastically impotent ones," according to Reich (1270), do not experience this pleasure. For them, it turns into anxiety, loss of ego control and painful sensations of narrowness, suffocation or bursting.

The train or the room represents one's own body, or at least its sensations, which one tries to get rid of by projection.

What has been said about claustrophobia in general is certainly true about the special "mother's womb" type of claustrophobia, the fear of being buried alive (406). The two interpretations, "The feared room represents mother's womb" and "The feared room represents one's own body sensations," may be connected with each other by a third: "The feared room represents the interior of one's own body."

It is well known but not much discussed that the majority of agoraphobics show specific conditions of their symptom related to the width of the feared street. Sensations of narrowness are also a basic element of the experience of anxiety. Persons whose excitement turns into anxiety feel a stricture in breathing, as if *the chest* had suddenly narrowed. (The opposite feeling of expansion, of being "broad" again, is physiologically connected with overcoming anxiety and is pleasurable; but representing a sudden change in the sphere of "broadness," it may also serve, through "representation by the opposite," as a symbol for getting frightened.) It is an attempt to protect oneself against painful sensations of narrowness (or broadness) if one feels the "street" and not the body as "narrow" or "broad," and this circumstance may explain projection in agoraphobia. Some patients are afraid of narrow streets only, others fear broad places, still others are paradoxically afraid of both; and most of them fear a sudden change in the width of the street through which they are passing. Many agoraphobics also show the condition whose significance has been discussed in claustrophobia: they have to make sure of the possibility of escape, which represents the wish for an escape from their own sensations.

ANXIETY HYSTERIA AND ANIMISM

When a phobic person passes through a narrow street, he gets frightened because he feels as "narrow" as the street; he "introjects" the street's narrowness. If his fear is intense, he may even feel a relatively broad street as narrow; he projects his own narrowness. For him, because of the way he experiences his anxiety, the conceptions of narrowness and fear are identical. The same feelings are aroused in him by a narrow street and by another frightened person. He even behaves as if the street itself were afraid.

The primitive misapprehension of the world that assumes that processes we feel in ourselves also take place in the objects around us is called animism. The phobic mechanisms described make use of the animism still effective in the unconscious.

One common type of animistic misapprehension of the world is very similar to the way in which the agoraphobics connect their feelings of fear with the narrowness of a street. Sachs described the role played by narcissistic projection in the feelings with which we react to nature (1329). "Consciousness of nature" does not consist in becoming aware of the real physical and geographical elements in nature, but in becoming aware of feelings within ourselves, which we believe are connected with those physical or geographical elements (*cf.* 380).

It is true that not all projections of feelings into nature connote nature's becoming a representative of our own feelings. Nature may also represent another person, and feelings connected with it may have originated in feelings toward that person. A mountain, for example, may represent the father's penis, the endless ocean or desert may represent the mother's womb. But even in emotions aroused by mountains or oceans in this way, the narcissistic element is not entirely lacking. A person sensing himself in a landscape does not simply feel love or hatred for the natural objects, but generally experiences a kind of identification with the landscape, the *unio mystica* with "father's penis" or "mother's womb." In general it may be assumed that in "consciousness of nature" a projection of the kind described is at work. The esthetic categories used to describe landscapes are proof of that. We talk about "sublime" or "lovely" landscapes because we feel sublime or lovely when seeing a landscape of this kind. It is true that the same landscapes vary in effect according to the mood of the observer; and it is likewise true that certain landscapes create, or at least mobilize, the same or similar feelings in different persons: the endlessness of flat prairies makes man melancholic, mountains make man more active and impulsive; this effect is achieved by the reflection of projections back onto the ego.

There are numerous phobias (or preferences up to a certain intensity, and phobias beyond it) about landscapes, moods of the weather, light and shadow effects, times of the day, and so on. If these were collected and described in detail, they would teach much, not only about the projections in question but also about the historical connections between infantile sexual excitation and the feelings that later are projected. Probably many phobias of darkness or twilight contain memories of primal scenes.

The same holds true for fears of surroundings that imply the loss of the usual means of orientation, fears of eternity, of uniform noises, of the cessation of customary routines or sequences. Some anxieties about death are anxieties over the loss of temporal orientation, that is, the loss of forces that protect against the dangerous world of unmastered infantile excitement (338).

REGRESSION AND AGGRESSIVENESS IN ANXIETY HYSTERIA

A common factor in all phobias is the *regression to childhood*. In childhood, dangers could be overcome by finding protection at the hands of more or less omnipotent objects in the external world. The phobic, who fears his impulses or the subsequent punishment, tries to regain that favorable situation where external protection was available. In this sense, all phobics behave like children, whose anxieties are soothed if the mother sits by the bedside and holds their hand. Such a demand for reassuring measures on the part of parent substitutes is especially evident in those agoraphobics who feel protected in the presence of a companion. Since not all agoraphobics make this condition, the libidinal conflicts around the person who is used as a companion cannot represent the basis of agoraphobia in general. However, in many cases the findings of Helene Deutsch (325) can be confirmed. She stated that in phobias in which the companion is essential, the relationship to this companion is of basic importance.

The companion not only represents the protecting parent but also the unconsciously hated parent; his presence serves the purpose of diverting the patient's mind from unconscious fantasies to reality, that is, of reassuring him that he has not killed this person who is walking safely at his side. In such cases, the fear that something may happen to the patient is often preceded by a fear for the safety of the same person who, later on in the agoraphobia, is used as a companion.

A morbid fear for the well-being of one or several specific persons represents a frequent form of anxiety hysteria of its own. Analysis shows that the person who has to be protected represents an unconsciously hated person, who, therefore, actually needs protection not from external dangers but rather from inner death wishes (792, 1283). Often what has been repressed returns from the repression, and continuous caretaking or reassuring affection may become objectively a torture. Especially frequently, parents show a behavior of this kind toward their children (618); however, sometimes children also show it toward their parents.

The transformation of the earlier fear that the other person may be harmed into the phobic anxiety concerning oneself is due to a self-punitive identification with the unconsciously hated object. Many obsessive symptoms, which try to protect an unconsciously hated object in a more or less torturing and more or less magical way, represent this pre-stage of anxiety hysteria. These cases are clearly a transition to compulsion neuroses.

On a superficial level the companion protects the patient from temptation. A man cannot approach strange women and a woman cannot be approached if both are in the company of their respective spouses. The youth or the girl cannot have adventures if accompanied by their parents. The idea that the companion watches brings relief from the necessity to watch one's own impulses.

Freud has pointed out that the same procedure may give expression to numerous instinctual wishes. When a girl demands that her mother be with her constantly, she succeeds in fulfilling her unconscious desire to separate her mother from her father (618). The compulsion exerted upon the companion may gratify any hostile impulses in regard to this person.

The fact that the regression to childhood in phobias is a search for protection against an instinctual danger is not always seen very clearly.

Alexander writes about agoraphobia (53): "Such a patient is afraid in a situation which entails no danger for him. The symptom becomes intelligible only when one realizes that the patient has regressed to an early emotional attitude of childhood. As a child he felt safe only near his home and was afraid to go far from it. At that time, of course, his anxiety might have been quite rational because as a child he had not the capacity of sufficient orientation. The question in such a case is: why does the patient regress to such an unpleasant experience of his past? The analytic study then shows that this patient uses the symptom to barter a lesser evil for a greater. What he is really afraid of is not being far away from home, but of loneliness and lack of human contact. He does not have the confidence that he can solve this problem in his actual life situation; his symptom, fear when on the street, helps him to deceive himself about this seemingly insoluble issue. He persuades himself that he is afraid of the street, and thus saves himself the painful realization of how alone and isolated he is in his life. He also saves himself from the effort to build up a human relationship for which he feels inadequate and unwilling. This symptom has an additional determination. The patient craves to be back in the past as a child when his dependent feelings were satisfied; however, putting himself back into childhood in fantasy he must also face the unpleasant side of childhood: childish insecurity and fear."

However, the patient is not seeking the unpleasant experiences of his childhood as a lesser evil, but rather the relative security of that time, which came from the protecting adults. The actual anxiety of the neurotic which makes him long for the greater security of his past is not "loneliness and lack of human contact" but a remobilization of his infantile instinctual conflicts.

The regression in anxiety hysteria in general, as in all hysterias, is a limited one; the main temptation which has to be warded off is represented by the wishes of the genital Oedipus complex. Phallic wishes and castration fears may be disguised in a pregenital form. However, there are also cases in which a pregenital basis is more in the foreground. In some cases, the defense against *aggressive* temptations plays the decisive part (282, 325, 797, 935). Sometimes the fear of one's own excitement is based on the fact that this excitement actually contains self-destructive components which originate in a sadistic impulse, turned away from the object against the ego, so that a fear of death might appear under circumstances which, in normal persons, would lead to an attack of rage. This is true particularly in cases where there is a combination of anxiety hysteria with compulsion neurosis, in which cases a relatively intense participation of destructive tendencies can be recognized, frequently by virtue of the associative bridge of the unconscious equation *looking = eating* (430). The above-mentioned cases of street phobia in which a certain person is chosen as a protecting companion belong in this category. Their ambivalent conflict stands out sharply (325).

Even ambivalent persons without any agoraphobia often need a kind of companion, that is, an object supplying affection, interest, confirmation, protection, a kind of magical helper (653). The dependence on external supplies for the maintenance of self-esteem is a sign of an early, usually oral, fixation. The relationship to magical helpers is necessarily an ambivalent one: the helpers are hated not only as representatives of the hated Oedipus object but also because of the inadequacy of their protective power.

Aggression, of course, also plays a very considerable part in cases of anxiety hysteria centered around a *morbid fear of death* (206, 207, 254, 1638). It is questionable whether there is any such thing as a normal fear of death; actually the idea of one's own death is subjectively inconceivable (591), and therefore probably every fear of death covers other unconscious ideas. Certainly this is the case in intense and pathological death phobias. To understand them, one has to find out what ideas unconsciously are connected with the concept of death. Sometimes these ideas are libidinal in nature and become understandable through the history of the patient (284, 641, 1153, 1330, 1632). (For example, "to be dead" may mean a reunion with a dead person.) More frequently certain childhood experiences have turned a fear of castration or loneliness (loss of love) into a fear of death. Two connections are most often encountered: (1) The idea of death may be a fear of punishment for death wishes against other persons; it has been mentioned that certain persons react with fear of death to situations where others would feel rage; this is obviously a turning of destructive impulses against one's own person. (2) A fear of death may represent a "fear of one's own excitement." "Dying" has become an expression for the sensations of an overwhelming panic, that is, for the distorted conception which these patients have formed of orgasm. Every type of excitement tends toward ultimate relaxation. In cases in which the achievement of such relaxation is regarded as the terrible sensation of loss of one's ego, it may be identified with "death," and on occasions when other persons would hope for sexual excitement, death may be feared (1280).

Another example of a phobia in which unconscious sadistic strivings are predominant and which is, for the most part, combined with compulsion neurosis is the frequent fear of infection. The fear of being infected is, first of all, a rationalized fear of castration. Venereal infection as a real danger connected with sexual activity may serve as a rationalization of unreal dangers unconsciously believed in (1614). On a deeper level, the fear of infection represents a defense against feminine wishes, infection standing for impregnation. And on a still deeper level this fear is an expression of pregenital fantasies of incorporation, bacilli being the equivalent of introjected objects with a destructive (and destructible) character (1459). The interrelationship of sadism and masochism can easily be reflected in ideas of infection because it is equally possible to be infected by other persons and to infect them.

The idea of infection also lends itself to a rationalization of feelings connected with the archaic taboo of touching. In magical thinking, the characteristics of any object are thought of as material substances which may be communicated by touch in the same way as dirt or germs are communicated. The archaic fear of touching may vary in instinctual content. Freud called attention to the fact that there is no impulse whose goal would not involve the touching of an object, whether this drive aims at a hostile, a sensual, or a tender approach to another person, or at an autoerotic touching of one's own body (618), and all these impulses may be phobically feared. Frequently the objects that must not be touched show at first glance their character as genital symbols. These persons interpreted the prohibition of infantile masturbation, which frequently takes the form of "don't touch," as if it were literally merely a prohibition of touching, or they interpreted it in this way in "spiteful obedience." They may develop types of masturbation in which they avoid the touching of their genitals with their hands (1262). Not infrequently a wish to masturbate that has been warded off has been altered by regression, so that the phobia appears to be a protection against anal-erotic wishes to be dirty or to soil. Occasionally this is immediately apparent: things that are believed to be dirty, such as doorknobs, or things that come in contact with the water closet must not be touched; or the prohibition may concern things that are used for cleaning the body (*see* pp. 288 f.).

Cases in which the anxiety changes from a fear of impending infection to the idea of having been infected may represent transitional stages, in which a phobic idea is in process of becoming a delusion. Ideas of this sort may be hypochondria-cal in nature, such as notions of being devoured by bacteria or cancer cells, or of being poisoned (948). However, apprehensions of this sort are also met with in pure anxiety hysterias, where they correspond to unconscious conflicts over castration or impregnation.

FURTHER DEVELOPMENT OF ANXIETY HYSTERIAS

Most often the outbreak of an anxiety hysteria is followed by the development of a phobia, that is, of an avoidance of the situation or of the perceptions that produce the anxiety. Sometimes the anxiety can in fact be avoided by the development of an appropriate phobia, at the cost of a certain limitation of the ego's freedom. The illness can be brought to a standstill, the instinctual danger has been completely and successfully turned into a perceptual danger.

However, in other cases the development is not favorable. In the first stages, the neurosis may be complicated by a secondary traumatic neurosis, induced by the first anxiety spell which is experienced as a trauma (1569). Many anxiety hysterias develop, out of such an experience, a *fear of anxiety,* and simultaneously a readiness to become frightened very easily, which may create a vicious circle. Some phobias do not succeed in their attempts at projection and develop progressively; the projection becomes inadequate and the phobic conditions increase in scope. For example, a patient may at first not be able to walk across a certain square, later on he cannot go out of doors, and finally, perhaps, not even out of his room. The elimination of external situations has not diminished the effectiveness of the drives that were stirred up by the avoided situation. The impulses continue to operate. The fact that they do not find an outlet makes them still more intense, and this necessitates the extension of the phobia (590). Whether or not the projection succeeds depends on the economic equilibrium between impulses and opposing anxiety; and that means on the whole previous history of the personality (*see* pp. 551 ff.).

The projection of one's own excitement may sometimes succeed in the sense that a patient gets rid of certain anxieties, restlessness, and kinesthetic sensations if certain conditions are fulfilled which represent a projection of these features. If a patient can feel some external anxiety, restlessness, noise, confusion around him, he may get rid of the anxiety, restlessness, noise, and confusion within. There are not only persons who have a thunderstorm phobia (which means those who have projected their sensations onto the thunderstorm, and who thus have externalized but not overcome their anxiety), but there are also persons who enjoy thunderstorms, because becoming aware of the external noise enables them to achieve the aim of their projection: the actual noise outside makes them feel that there is no noise inside any more, and that therefore they no longer need to be afraid.

Certain persons state that they need "stimulation" or "distraction" to work at their best. They have neurotic disturbances of concentration. Their work is disturbed by inner tensions which make themselves felt as restlessness. However, they can overcome the disturbing feelings by seeking surroundings that provide external restlessness.

> The sociological role of the so-called *Caféhaus* in certain parts of Europe (or of the club in other countries) is certainly complicated and cannot be explained by a simple psychological formula. The following case history may be significant in this respect.
>
> A patient was an excellent worker in the *Caféhaus*—and he preferred the noisy ones, with music playing and many people around—but was unable to work in his study at home, where he was alone and everything was quiet. It is true this man found certain instinctual satisfactions in the café (especially scoptophilic and homosexual ones); but that was not particularly important. The fact that he felt he had to run away when it was quiet, but was able to become relaxed and quiet when people were making noise around him, was of greater importance (444).

It would be worth while to study which types of personality, when neurotically disturbed in their concentration, need absolute quiet around them and which types require the opposite. Probably it will turn out again that there are not two opposite types but that the need for external quiet or noise has again a double-edged character. What is comfortable and relaxing up to a certain degree of intensity may suddenly become unpleasant and frightening beyond this intensity. That persons can get rid of their anxieties by reassuring themselves that they are able to frighten others is simple enough (541, 784, 895, 971, 1298). But sometimes this simple mechanism is complicated by a successful projection of the kind under discussion here: persons with anxieties create an atmosphere of anxiety around them, and feel better if this anxiety is outside themselves. This also may have a double-edged character: if they succeed too well, and discover that everyone around them is really frightened, they may feel that they have destroyed their potential protection, are endangered by retaliation, and suddenly become extremely frightened themselves.

If often happens that individuals with phobias cannot succeed in avoiding the feared situations. Again and again they are forced to experience the very things they are afraid of. Often the conclusion is unavoidable that this is due to an unconscious arrangement of theirs. It seems that unconsciously they are striving for the very thing of which they are consciously afraid. This is understandable because the feared situations originally were instinctual aims. It is a kind of "return of the repressed out of the repression." The urge of the original drives, which are still effective, is also the basis for all attempts to overcompensate phobias by counterphobic attitudes (435), by a preference for situations originally feared (*see* p. 480).

Phobias, that is, the avoidance of situations that create anxiety, are not the only means by which the ego tries to cope with anxiety. Other methods of defense against anxiety, like the sexualization of anxiety, intimidation of others, identification with the frightening objects, collection of external reassurances are also used in anxiety hysteria (*see* pp. 479 ff.).

THE REPRESSING FORCES AND THE REPRESSED IN THE SYMPTOMS OF ANXIETY HYSTERIA

Any psychoneurotic elaboration of the consequences of the state of being dammed up results in a compromise between the conflicting forces. As a rule, this compromise consists of a substitutive and therefore painful discharge of a derivative to which a part of the cathexis of the repressed had been displaced; but the discharge of the derivative facilitates (or at least does not impede) the warding off of the remaining original impulse. At first glance, an anxiety spell seems, like a state of inhibition, a pure manifestation of the defending forces which give their danger signal when temptation or punishment approaches. However, the anxiety spells have the character of an emergency discharge also. The displacements in anxiety hysteria doubtlessly created substitutes for the impulse originally warded off, thereby facilitating the original defense. Thus anxiety in anxiety hysteria actually is more than a manifestation of the defending forces. It is a psychoneurotic symptom, although the unconscious anxiety motivating the defense still finds its expression as such.

If other psychoneurotic symptoms not connected with manifest anxiety are artificially suppressed, manifest anxiety, as a rule, makes its appearance. This shows that anxiety hysteria is relatively more primitive than other psychoneuroses. The neurotic symptoms without anxiety are more complicated elaborations in which the person has learned to avoid or to bind anxiety (618).

ANXIETY HYSTERIA IN SMALL CHILDREN

The primitive character of anxiety hysteria is also expressed in the fact that anxiety hysteria is the typical neurosis of childhood (*cf.* 175). To some extent, symptoms of anxiety hysteria seem to be regular incidents in the normal development of any child, at least under present cultural conditions. There is hardly a child who has not at some time been afraid of being alone or of the dark or of animals. Fear of the dark may be reduced to the fear of being alone. Freud quotes a child who was afraid of the dark as saying: "If someone talks, it gets lighter" (596).

To be left alone is an objective danger for the helpless child. However, the child actually is not afraid of objective dangers, which he is not able to judge. (Many worries connected with child rearing would become superfluous if children were able to judge real dangers adequately.) What the child fears is much more the possibility of a "traumatic situation," of being overwhelmed by excitation. It is not the objective helplessness of the child that creates his anxieties but his helplessness in the face of his drives which he is unable to discharge without the help of other persons. Besides, the disappearance of a loved person also prevents any expression of his love, and thus creates a state of being dammed up. It appears, as Freud said, as if the child were not yet able to manage the longing for absent beloved ones in any better way than by letting it be transformed into anxiety (596).

The relationship of anxiety to the instinctual conflicts is more obvious in the animal phobias. The child is not as arrogant as the adult person, who tries to believe in a fundamental difference between human beings and animals. A child can easily imagine human beings in the form of animals (579), and the animals feared in the phobias are as a rule distorted representations of human beings, usually of the father. The representation of the father as an animal signifies the sexually excited father. It expresses the perception of the father as animal-like, that is, as a passionate, sexual, or aggressive being. This frightening aspect of the father may sometimes express his punishing (castrating) force, as in the case of little Hans (566), and at other times the frightening aspects of the sexual demands directed toward him, as in the case of the wolf-man (599).

The case described by Helene Deutsch, which was mentioned before (327), shows that not all animal phobias are constructed in that way. The animal does not necessarily represent the feared parent. It may be a direct projection of one's own drives.

Likewise small animals such as insects, spiders, flies, and so on, which are often feared in phobias, do not represent the father. A spider may sometimes mean "the cruel mother" (23), but more frequently creatures of this kind are either symbols of genitals or feces, or of little children (brothers and sisters) (552), depending upon the unconscious equation *child = feces* (593). A patient whose conflicts centered around her hatred for her younger brother was afraid of all insects and believed, in her retaliation fear, that all insects are poisonous.

Some of the early anxiety hysterias find a spontaneous cure after a certain time. It is as if the children simply grow out of them. (Others do not have this favorable outcome; they form the basis of later neuroses in adult life.) This is made possible by two circumstances: (1) The ego of the child is still developing; the early anxieties are due to the incapacity to achieve active discharges; when the ego becomes stronger it becomes able to master its excitation with the help of its increased mastery of motility. (2) Where fear over loss of love was the reason for warding off certain impulses, increased experience and confidence may convince the child that such a danger does not exist, and the warding off becomes superfluous (*see* pp. 547 f.).

THE PRIMAL SCENE

It is not possible to discuss anxiety in children without mentioning anew the so-called primal scene, that is, the observation of sexual scenes between adults, especially between the parents (599).

Such an event creates a state of great excitement in a child. This excitement, not being produced spontaneously by the child but brought to it by external stimuli, goes beyond the capacity for mastery as yet developed. The scene, therefore, is likely to produce a "traumatic state" by flooding the organism with an inappropriate excitation. Thus such an experience is likely to connect the ideas of sexual excitation and danger. This connection may be further increased by misinterpretations of what is perceived (misinterpretations which, in turn, may be due partly to the fact that the child is in a "traumatic state"—but also, partly, simply to ignorance and animism). The most frequent types of misinterpretation are the interpretation of sexual intercourse as a cruel, destructive act, and the interpretation of the female genitals as a result of castration.

The psychic content of the aroused excitement and its intensity vary according to the child's age and previous history. Individual factors will determine what the child perceives, how he interprets his perceptions, what mental connections are established, and whether interpretations and the mental connections are made immediately or later: for example, identification with the parent of the same sex or with the other parent, fixation on the state of libido organization that prevails at the time, or special coloring of the Oedipus complex. But what is always present is the linking together of the conceptions "sexual satisfaction" and "danger," which creates a disposition for subsequent neurosis.

It has been mentioned that certain uncanny experiences of sensations of equilibrium and space may be the remnants of infantile sexuality. In psychoanalytic practice, we have the habit of stating, when sensations of this kind come up, such as unclear rotating objects, rhythmically approaching and receding objects, sensations of crescendo and decrescendo, that "primal-scene material is approaching." Practically, that is true. But of course sensations of this kind are not specific for "becoming aware of sexual scenes in the surroundings." They are, rather, specific for being overwhelmed by excitation.

It is well known that while falling asleep the inhibiting forces decrease before the drives do, and that, therefore, in this state the temptation to masturbate is most intense. In falling asleep, also, archaic types of ego feelings are regressively experienced before consciousness is lost and a high percentage of these "archaic ego feelings" are felt as sensations of equilibrium and space. A normal person is not bothered much by these sensations. He may even not be aware of them, unless he expressly directs his attention to them (837). This is different in persons whose infantile masturbation is represented by these sensations, and these again are mainly persons who have had primal-scene experiences. A minority of these persons may still enjoy such sensations as a kind of masturbation equivalent. The majority, after repression, are afraid of them, and in extreme cases such fears may become the cause of severe sleep disturbances.

Thus it is understandable that a marked tendency toward anxiety dreams and pavor nocturnus frequently follows a primal scene or an "equivalent" of a primal scene (7, 1166).

THERAPEUTIC PSYCHOANALYSIS IN ANXIETY HYSTERIA

In general, anxiety hysteria presents a definite indication for psychoanalysis, and only in the presence of some special contraindication should one advise against analysis. The capacity for transference is excellent. However, cases exhibiting compulsive symptoms and based more on pregenital and aggressive conflicts are less favorable. Freud has called attention to a modification in technique necessary in analyzing typical phobias. After the framework of the neurosis has been loosened enough by the analysis, the analyst must actively intervene in order to induce the patient to make his first effort to overcome the phobia; he must induce the patient to expose himself to the feared experiences for the purpose of bringing the full force of the neurotic conflict into the open (600).

Chapter XII

CONVERSION

WHAT IS CONVERSION?

IN CONVERSION, symptomatic changes of physical functions occur which, unconsciously and in a distorted form, give expression to instinctual impulses that previously had been repressed.

Any neurotic symptom is a substitute for an instinctual satisfaction; since excitement and satisfaction are phenomena that express themselves in a physical way, the leap into the physical sphere, characteristic for conversion, is in principle not so strange. However, conversion symptoms are not simply somatic expressions of affects but very specific representations of thoughts which can be retranslated from their "somatic language" into the original word language (543, 550).

The problem of conversion symptoms can be approached by a comparison with spells of affect. These, as was previously stated, occur when an intense stimulus (or a normal stimulus when a state of being dammed up exists) temporarily overthrows the ego's mastery of motility, and an archaic discharge syndrome replaces purposeful actions (and such syndromes subsequently may be tamed and used by the re-established ego). Conversion symptoms, too, are characterized by a sudden overwhelming of the ego's mastery of motility and by involuntary physical discharge syndromes. The difference, however, is that in normal affects the syndromes that supplant action are similar in every human being; we do not know where they originated, and revert to phylogenetic speculations for an explanation. The syndromes of conversion symptoms are unique in every individual, and analysis shows where they originate: they are historically determined by repressed experiences in the individual's past. They represent a distorted expression of repressed instinctual demands, the specific type of the distortion being determined by the historical events that created the repression.

PREREQUISITES FOR THE DEVELOPMENT OF CONVERSIONS

There are two prerequisites for the development of conversions, one of a physical, the other one of a psychological nature. The physical prerequisite is the general erogeneity of the human body, which makes it possible for every organ and every function to express sexual excitement. The psychological prerequisite is a prior turning from reality to fantasy, a replacement of real sexual objects by fantasy representatives of infantile objects; this process is called introversion.

It will be recalled that after the establishment of thinking as a testing action two types of thinking can be distinguished, one that prepares for action and one that substitutes for action. The first one is logical and verbalized, and functions according to the reality principle; the second is archaic, pictorial, magical, and functions according to the pleasure principle. Daydreams represent the second type of thinking; they are a pleasant substitute for a painful reality. Very often, daydreams find connections to repressed demands, become overcathected by displacement from the repressed and in this way become derivatives of the repressed (564).

In their introversion, hysterics have regressed from a disappointing reality to the magical thinking of daydreaming. This may be conscious as long as the daydreams remain far enough from the repressed contents, especially from the objectionable Oedipus complex, but if they come too close, they, too, will be repressed (*see* p. 193). They then return from the repression, distorted as conversion symptoms.

Due to the introversion, hysterical individuals appear to be turned inward. Their symptoms, instead of presenting actions directed outward (alloplastic activities), are mere internal innervations (autoplastic activities). In other words, the fantasies of hysterical individuals, after having been repressed, find plastic expression in alterations of physical functions. In this connection Ferenczi spoke of "hysterical materialization" of the fantasies (486, 489). Hysterics, when "materializing," only exaggerate something that likewise appears in normal fantasy, indeed in all thinking. Thinking, replacing action, is still a bit of action; the innervations of the actions that are thought of take place during the thinking, only to a lesser degree (482). It is this "bit of action" that is especially marked in introverted hysterics and that forms the basis of the innervations constituting the conversion symptoms.

HYSTERICAL SPELLS

The aforementioned possibility of retranslating conversion symptoms from their somatic language into the original word language is best demonstrable in major hysterical spells, which have become rare nowadays. These spells are pantomimic expressions of sometimes rather complicated fantasy stories (565, 1620). They can be analyzed in every detail, in the same way as dreams, and they use the same distortion mechanisms as dreams.

It is worth while to recall what these distortion mechanisms consist of: condensation, displacement, representation by the opposite, exaggeration of details that represent the whole, reversal of the sequence of events, multiple identification, symbolism, and suitability for plastic representation (552).

If the "latent seizure thoughts" are analyzed (as "latent dream thoughts" are analyzed from a manifest dream) it turns out that they represent a mixture of elements of forgotten events and of fantastic dream stories constructed around the events (550, 1620). They represent distorted expressions of the Oedipus complex and of derivatives of the Oedipus complex. Sometimes the spells clearly betray that they stand for a sexual gratification and they may terminate in states resembling orgasm. Freud compared the loss of consciousness at the height of the attack to the momentary loss of consciousness at the height of orgasm (565). In other cases the spell does not connote fantasies directly concerning intercourse or seduction; instead the daydreams are focused rather around some aspect of pregnancy or childbirth. The classical example is seen in the well-known cases of hysterical pseudo pregnancy (150, 804); but many a hysterical vomiting is also of this nature. The seizure may likewise express sexual sensations characteristic for a person of the opposite sex with whom the patient has identified (562).

> At the height of her fits, a woman patient used to have jerking convulsions in her arms. Analysis revealed that they portrayed the spasmodic contractions of the penis during ejaculation. A similar significance became evident in the sneezing spells of a hysterical woman patient; her nose represented her fantasied penis.

The seizure may also express pregenital actions which have become substitutes for the original Oedipus ideas.

Not all hysterical spells occur in the form of specific pantomimic actions or movements which give the analyst direct hints as to the past situation or daydream of which they form a part. Sometimes the manifestations of a spell are much less specific and occur either in the form of convulsions (*see* "motor disturbances," pp. 223 ff.), of exaggerated or apparently entirely unmotivated emotions or "moods," or as screaming, crying, or laughing spells (1464).

> Spells of this kind, too, are the emotional climaxes of complicated unconscious fantasies. The screaming, crying, laughing, then, are comparable to emotions felt on awakening from a dream, although the dream itself has been forgotten. The manifest emotion permits a few general conclusions about the emotional nature of the latent thoughts but nothing more can be said about it unless the latent thoughts are analyzed. Hysterical screaming, for example, may be the expression of very different emotions. Sometimes the type of screaming alone gives a hint. It may be an infantile screaming for help (1419), it may be an expression of the helplessness (and the joy) of a woman sexually attacked, it may belong to dreams about childbirth, or it may be an expression of rage; it may also mean an enunciation of "masculinity." The laughing in laughing spells frequently expresses triumph because of the fantastic fulfillment of hostile wishes (436), especially of revenge ideas arising from the revenge type of the female castration complex (20); however, the laughing may also simply be a *pars-pro-toto* distortion of sexual excitement, in the way in which children often express any type of excitement by obsessive and exaggerated laughing. Hysterical crying frequently corresponds to a "displacement upward" of conflicts around sexualized urination (428, 1055).

Related to seizures are those conversion symptoms that consist in a pathological appearance or disappearance of normal physical needs, like attacks of
hunger or thirst, a need to defecate or urinate (759), or a sudden lack of appetite
or thirst, constipation or oliguresis (1577), or difficulties in breathing. All these
conversion symptoms are rooted in periods of infantile sexuality when other
physical functions were still in the service of pleasure seeking, which permits the
physical symptoms to lend themselves to the expression of sexual fantasies. Hunger, thirst, and excretory needs may supplant sexual longing; anorexia—a denial
of sexual longing; constipation, or oliguresis may express retentive tendencies
connected with pregnancy wishes or incorporation fantasies (frequently occurring in accordance with the equation *child = penis = feces*) (593, 832); vomiting
and diarrhea may express resistance to both pregnancy wishes and incorporation
fantasies.

MONOSYMPTOMATIC CONVERSIONS

The historical basis of conversion symptoms is often very clear in monosymptomatic conversion symptoms. Instead of a memory, an innervation occurs,
which had actually taken place in the forgotten situation. Breuer's first patient,
Anna O, had a paralysis of her arm whenever she was unconsciously reminded
of her feelings toward her father. At the time her father died, she had been sitting at his bedside with her arm pressed against the chair at the side of the bed
(188).

It is misleading to call monosymptomatic hysterias organ neuroses, because
this expression should be reserved for another type of neurosis (*see* pp. 236 ff.); but
nevertheless it is frequently done. For example, so-called cardiac neuroses are
often really monosymptomatic conversion hysterias, the cardiac symptoms expressing sexual excitement, anxiety, or both, connected with specific unconscious daydreams.

The monosymptomatic hysterias frequently demonstrate Ferenczi's conceptions of hysterical "materialization" and "genitalization" (489). Repressed
thoughts find their substitute expression in a material change of physical functions, and the afflicted organ unconsciously is used as a substitute for the genitals. This "genitalization" may consist of objective changes within the tissues,
for example, hyperemia and swelling, representing erection; or it may be limited
to abnormal sensations imitating genital sensations. The so-called stigmata belong to this category (487, 1167).

A patient suffering from a cardiac neurosis related that the continual palpitation of his heart was accompanied by the feeling that his heart was getting larger
and larger, that his whole chest was becoming more and more tense, up to a
certain almost unbearable point, and that then the whole process would stop, the

palpitation would cease, and his heart would "shrink" again. These sensations represented an increasing erection, finally ending with orgasm.

A few days after this interpretation was given, the patient reported that a new symptom had set in. He now felt as if his heart were breaking open in order to take something in. Thus the "genitalization" of the heart in this case had a bisexual significance: it represented the masculine as well as the feminine genitals.

HYSTERICAL PAINS AND HYSTERICAL IDENTIFICATION

Conversion symptoms are intermittent or continuous discharge processes that appear in place of inhibited infantile sexual impulses with which they are connected by unconscious associations. A first type of hysterical pain, Freud states, "was really present in the situation when the repression took place" (618). In cases in which the original physical pain was experienced by the patient himself, the repetition of the pain in the conversion symptom is a substitute for a desired pleasant excitement which had somehow become connected with it; the pain is now simultaneously a warning signal not to yield to those pleasant sensations.

> A patient suffered from pain in the lower abdomen. The pain repeated sensations she had felt as a child during an attack of appendicitis. At that time she had been treated with unusual tenderness by her father. The abdominal pain expressed simultaneously a longing for the father's tenderness and a fear that an even more painful operation might follow a fulfillment of this longing.

Childhood diseases are often very impressive episodes in the development of instinctual conflicts in a child, sometimes in the nature of satisfactions (gaining more love or other types of love from the parents, or experiencing the body in a new way), oftener in the nature of threats (the disease may be perceived as castration or, generally, as a punitive consequence for previous masturbation or other instinctual behavior). Sensations experienced in fever are very apt to signify the sensations of a feared instinctual excitement, pleasurable up to a certain degree, painful and frightening beyond it. Subsequent conversion symptoms, in repeating pains of childhood diseases, mean the repetition of the instinctual conflicts developed or mobilized by these diseases. In other cases the associative connection between the instinctual conflict and the disease that is initiated may be a more superficial one. The special form of a conversion symptom that imitates a past sickness may be a mere time signal showing that a symptom alludes to an impulse from the time of this sickness.

In general, the formulation holds: whenever a functional disturbance has become associated with an emotional conflict in childhood and this conflict has been repressed, any subsequent allusion either to the functional disturbance or to the emotional conflict is apt to mobilize both components of the whole syndrome, the functional disturbance becoming the conscious manifestation, the emotional conflict the unconscious driving force of conversion symptoms (313, 316).

In a second type of hysterical pain, the original feelings that are imitated in the conversion symptom may, however, have been experienced not by the patient but by another person whom the patient imitates by producing his symptom. Hysteria, as is well known, may imitate any and every disease, a circumstance that makes the clinical picture of conversion hysteria so very multiform. This "hysterical identification" which expresses the wish to be in the place of another person needs further comment.

Identification is the very first type of reaction to an object. All later object relationships may under certain circumstances regress to identification. The *hysterical* identification is characterized by the fact that it does not involve the full amount of cathexis available (408). There are several variations of identifications of this kind.

1. The simplest case is the "hysterical identification with the fortunate rival," that is, with a person whom the patient envies and whose place he had wished to occupy from the beginning. Freud's patient Dora developed a cough like that of Mrs. K, whom she unconsciously perceived as a rival. Dora envied Mrs. K's sexual experiences; because of her guilt feelings about this rivalry she could not put herself in Mrs. K's position, in the place she would have liked, but had to select Mrs. K's affliction as the point of identification (557). This identification by way of her sense of guilt replaced the intended identification in instinctual experiences. It is as with King Midas, who was so greedy for gold. His wish was granted, but in such a way that he was destroyed by his gold.

> The mechanism of Midas' punishment can frequently be observed in all types of neuroses, in compulsion neuroses perhaps still more frequently than in hysterias. Obsessions may express the idea: "You shall get what you wished for, but in a way, to a degree, or at a time where it shall destroy you." In symptoms of this kind there are various layers of drive and defense condensed with one another, and it is not easy to distinguish between the instinctive impulse returning from repression and the tendency of the superego which caricatures the instinctive impulse for punitive purposes.

2. It sometimes happens that a woman whose hysteria is due to her Oedipus complex makes an identification not with her rival, her mother, but with her beloved father. This is a more complicated situation. Whenever a person is forced to relinquish an object, he may develop a tendency to compensate for the loss by identifying himself with the object (608). When a hysterical woman takes over her father's illness, she shows that she is vainly attempting to free herself from him.

A patient's hysteria imitated tuberculosis. Her father, as a young man, had been affected by this illness. She had furthermore taken up the same profession as her father, and was very close to manifest homosexuality.

An identification of this sort at the same time furnishes an opportunity for the gratification of the negative Oedipus complex (562).

3. The most frequent form of hysterical identification takes place with an object toward whom the patient has no genuine object relationship. It is formed "on the basis of identical etiological needs." Freud used a hysterical epidemic in a girls' school as an example. A girl reacts with a fainting spell to a love letter, and then the other girls also get fainting spells. The unconscious meaning is: "We should like to get love letters, too" (606). The object of the identification has no other significance than that she got a gratification for which the subject had likewise longed. Again, the fact that painful experiences are produced is an expression of the repressing forces, a kind of Midas wish fulfillment: "You wanted to be as happy as X? Well, just for that, here is the punishment she got!"

Identification on the basis of identical etiological needs, being temporary in character and performed with an object toward whom there is no other relationship, affords an opportunity to discuss the relationship between identification and imitation. This mechanism looks like a simple imitation; it is, however, unconscious. Any imitation, whether conscious or unconscious, presupposes a kind of identification, that is, an alteration of one's own ego which follows the pattern of an object model. However, the identification at the basis of imitation, as contrasted to other types of identification, is a superficial, limited, capricious one, employed for one definite purpose only. This purpose may or may not be conscious. Unconsciously, anyone may be imitated who as a prototype seems to promise some libido-economic advantage, some possibility of finding relief from internal conflicts. Related to this is the phenomenon of the infectiousness of slips and errors (1285, 1524).

4. There are also "multiple identifications," especially in seizures. A hysterical patient may simultaneously or serially play the part of various persons with whom she has identified herself, according to any of the described types. The seizures of such patients very often represent the enactment of a whole drama.

The classical example for this is Freud's patient who tried to take her clothes off with her right hand while making an effort to keep them on by grasping them with her left. She was identifying herself simultaneously with a man raping and a woman being attacked (562; cf. also 471).

A climax of multiple identifications is shown by the famous case of "multiple personality" (1065, 1586).

Hysterical identifications may even take place with a pain actually never experienced by the model for identification, but only in the fantasy of the hysteric.

One day a patient felt an intense pain in her finger. She stated that she felt as if she had cut her finger with a knife. She was in love with a cousin, a medical student, who did not live in the same city. She fantasied that perhaps, just at the moment she felt the pain, he might have cut himself while dissecting. This fantasy, giving the pleasure of a magical connection with the loved one, was a conscious daydream. The unconscious continuation of this daydream was the symbolic equation *knife = penis* and *cutting = coitus*. The analysis also revealed very clearly that the cousin was a substitute for the father, while her identification with a corpse led to specific infantile sexual theories.

In a certain sense it is even possible to speak of "hysterical identifications with oneself," namely, with a past ego state (387). Many conversion symptoms have the significance of a regression into that period of childhood when the repression occurred, the maintenance of which is now endangered.

In some hysterical pains the repetition of past actual (or imagined) pains is less impressive than an anticipation of desired events or of a prospective punishment for them. The pains may be a part of unconscious sexual fantasies. They may express the idea of being raped; some abdominal pains and even some headaches express the idea of being pregnant. Such painful illustrations of daydreams, however, are not necessarily opposed to the hysterical pains hitherto described. They illustrate the feared and hoped-for future by means of remobilizing related actual experiences of the past.

HYSTERICAL HALLUCINATIONS

Hysterical hallucinations "were perceptions at the time of the repression" (618).

A patient suffered from the torturing hallucination of a metallic taste in her mouth. It turned out that as a child she had been accustomed to drink by putting her mouth directly to the faucet. At that time what was now being hallucinated had been an actual perception. The childhood practice was a cover for unconscious wishes to perform fellatio.

Olfactory hallucinations, too, sometimes can be reduced to definite real perceptions of the past which had some instinctual significance. This certainly does not contradict the fact that hallucinations of this kind simultaneously may express a phobia concerning body odor. There are also transitional states between hysterical and psychotic hallucinations (just as between hysterical fears and delusions) (*see* p. 444).

HYSTERICAL MOTOR DISTURBANCES

"Motor paralysis is a defense against action" (618), namely, against an objectionable infantile sexual action.

Hysterical paralysis is usually accompanied by an increase in tonus; this represents both an insurance against the objectionable sexual action and a distorted substitute for it. Hysterical "masturbatory equivalents" often assume this guise. Historical circumstances and somatic compliance (*see* pp. 227 f.) determine which particular part of the musculature is affected by the paralysis. Symptoms of this kind are said to appear more frequently on the left side of the body than on the right; this may be explained, as suggested by Ferenczi, by the idea that the left side of the body is in general more accessible to unconscious influences than the right, because right-handed persons have less conscious interest in it (489). In addition the symbolic significance of right and left must be taken into account, *right* meaning *correct* and *left* meaning *wrong* (1479), sometimes, especially, *right* meaning *heterosexual* and *left* meaning *homosexual* (1463).

> Hysterical mutism is a special case of hysterical paralysis. It may express a hostility or an anxiety (a feared sexual temptation) toward the persons in whose presence the symptom develops, a general lack of interest in the persons with whom talking would be possible (Dora became mutistic in the absence of the man she loved [557]), or it may mean death or castration.

A spasm is a means of securing suppression of action, and simultaneously a tonic substitute for action.

> A spasm, limited to a certain part of the body, may represent erection; however, that is not necessarily the case. The muscular spasm may simply be the physical expression of repression. Hypertonus may be the representative of the general attitude "I have something to suppress."
>
> In a woman patient who experienced a severe spasm of the pelvic floor during sexual intercourse this symptom was, first of all, a generalized vaginismus, ensuring her resistance to sexual experiences; it also represented hostile impulses toward her sexual partner and tendencies to protrude a fantasied hidden penis. Ferenczi has shown how a general "suppression spasm" may be created by a displacement of the function of the anal sphincters (a part of the pelvic floor) to the muscular system in general (505).
>
> Some hysterical spasms have the function of an assurance of a specific inhibition. They occur if an activity is intended that is prohibited by the superego, either because of its hidden sexual meaning or because, in the case of moral masochists, a forbidden success might be achieved by it. Of this type are writer's and violinist's cramp (867).

The famous *arc de cercle* which has become rare nowadays represents, according to Freud, the innervations antagonistic to coitus, a representation by the opposite, expressing simultaneously the repressed desire and the repressing forces (565). Other writers have added that the symptom also gives expression to a masculine striving, an attempt to protrude a concealed penis (1564), as well as to a feminine one, the idea of childbirth (1025).

Contracture is a displacing substitute for an intended but inhibited muscular innervation. It usually represents the tonic rigidity which is the result of a struggle between opposing impulses.

Convulsions, too, represent affect equivalents or are a pantomimic expression of a sexual, an aggressive, or a sexual-aggressive daydream. Sometimes hysterical convulsions imitate organic convulsions that the patient had witnessed. The so-called hystero-epilepsy will be discussed later (*see* p. 267).

HYSTERICAL DREAM STATES AND DISTURBANCES OF CONSCIOUSNESS

Hysterical dream states are closely related to seizures. As in seizures, the day-dreams, which represent derivatives of the repressed, involuntarily take posses-sion of the personality, but here the pantomimic discharge is lacking. The day-dream, an outgrowth of Oedipus fantasies, breaks through as such, removing the patient from reality (3, 196). Sometimes the sexual meaning of this absence is directly apparent in a voluptuous pleasure the patient obtains from it. More often the affect, too, is repressed, and the new wave of repression against the mobilized derivatives keeps them so remote from awareness that the patient himself is unable to give any account of what he has experienced and is aware only of a gap in his consciousness (1015).

A kind of mixture of hysterical spells and hysterical dream states is repre-sented by the conversion symptom of *sleepwalking*. The "dream state," here, is a physiological one; sleepwalking occurs during normal night sleep; but a "pan-tomimic discharge" is achieved. This discharge sometimes only expresses the restlessness due to internal tension in an unspecific way. More frequently the discharge is a highly specific one. The movements of the sleepwalker are in re-sponse either to his manifest dream or to the latent conflicts at the basis of the dream. Sometimes running away from bed, which is felt as a place of tempta-tion, is in the foreground; more frequently the sleepwalking has a positive goal toward which the patient is striving: either a place of potential gratification of unconscious impulses or a place of effective reassurance against them or both simultaneously (711, 717, 1286, 1341, 1343).

> The typical aim of infantile sleepwalking is the wish to participate in the adults' night life. The typical goal is the parents' bedroom, signifying either a place where sexual secrets may be witnessed or disturbed or a place where protection against nightmares and temptations is to be found, but usually both. If sleepwalk-ing is combined with loss of bladder control, this is not necessarily a proof of organic petit mal but may be a sign of the child's unconscious sexual excitement. Sometimes sleepwalking expresses a tendency to run away from home. The old superstition of a connection between sleepwalking and moonlight is due partly to the emotional value of moonlight, which is simultaneously "light" and "dark-ness" and therefore suited to express unclear infantile conceptions of sexuality and sexual observations, and partly to the symbolic significance of the moon, *moon = mother* (430, 1322, 1579).

It is not known what physical or mental circumstances make it possible to use the motor system during sleep, in contradiction to the general rule that, nor-mally, in the process of falling asleep the motor system is paralyzed first (595), but in accordance with the fact that in hypnotic sleep the motility is freely accessible to hypnotic commands.

Disturbances in consciousness generally correspond to the repression of a current derivative of infantile sexuality (1015, 1336). The transitory elimination of all consciousness is, so to speak, a generalized repression, probably the archaic pattern of all repression (410). The ideational content of the impulses entering dream states or causing disturbances of consciousness is as varied as the fantasies that produce hysterical symptoms in general. In the dream state, the transitory clouding of consciousness may not only express repression but may have an unconscious significance of its own. It may (a) represent orgasm, (b) have the significance of death, which again may mean either death wishes against some other person turned against one's own ego or have some unconscious libidinal meaning, or (c) serve as a blocking (and distorted expression) of hostile impulses of all kinds. This is especially true for hysterical spells of hypotonus and sudden fatigue, which may sometimes form transitional states toward organic narcolepsy. Disturbances of consciousness, because of their effect on the environment, afford an opportunity for all sorts of secondary gains. In all hysterical dream states and disturbances of consciousness, the differential diagnosis of epileptic equivalents must be taken into consideration.

HYSTERICAL DISTURBANCES OF THE SPECIAL SENSES

Hysterical disturbances of special sensory perceptions represent elective "hysterical disturbances of consciousness," and what has been said about disturbances of consciousness in general holds true here, too. The disturbances of sensory perceptions represent the rejection of upsetting sexual perceptions. Inhibitions of this kind may extend from blindness or deafness, via negative hallucinations, to restricted limitations in the use of the senses, mentioned in the discussion of inhibitions (see p. 177). Symptoms of this kind sometimes start after a trauma as a posttraumatic ego inhibition (917), but soon get a hysterical "meaning" and are retained as conversion symptoms.

The restrictions of sensual perceptions are also a symptom of hysterical introversion, that is, of a lack of interest in external events; this lack of interest increases the possibility of substituting fantasies for realities.

Hysterical disturbances of vision were the subject of a very enlightening article by Freud (571). A hysterical "I cannot see" means "I do not want to see." It indicates a repressed impulse to look (and to exhibit). From a punitive standpoint it says: "Because you wish to see something forbidden, you shall not see at all" (367). A constriction of the visual field has often been described as characteristic for hysterics. Ferenczi explained it by the fact that peripheral vision has less significance for the ego, and is therefore more readily sexualized (489).

The sexualization of vision is not always due to simple scoptophilia or to the unconscious "genitalization" of the eye. The eye may also represent pregenital erogenous zones symbolically. As a sense organ it may express oral-incorporative and oral-sadistic longings in particular (430). Neurotic difficulties in reading usually are due to oral-sadistic conflicts (1512).

A defense against oral-sadistic strivings is also the usual cause of another conversion symptom of vision: micropsia, that is, the phenomenon that objects appear as if seen through a reversed opera glass. Hallucinations and illusions of the sense of space seem generally to repeat experiences from the earliest oral times (410), but in micropsia, this is especially evident. A patient of Inman's experienced this symptom whenever her intense and frustrated oral longing was mobilized (831). A patient of Bartemeier's had very early displaced an intense food envy onto her eyes; her micropsia expressed a tendency to push objects into the distance; this was an attempt to defend herself against the idea of killing objects by means of her eyes and a distorted return of this warded-off impulse (89).

HYSTERICAL DISTURBANCES OF SENSATION

Disturbances of sensation, in the same way as paralyses and sensual inhibitions, at first glance impress one more as a defense rather than as a return of the repressed. The elimination of sensation facilitates the suppression of memories that appertain to the body areas affected. However, they also serve the repressed impulses, for because of this very anesthesia, the anesthetic field may be used more by unconscious fantasies. Hysterical disturbances of sensation in general are repressions of internal perceptions in the same way that sensory disturbances are repressions of external ones (489).

Hysterical hypalgia is a kind of localized fainting; certain sensations that would be painful are not accepted. The basic mechanism probably is related to the archaic defense of "delay of affects" (see pp. 162 f.).

SOMATIC COMPLIANCE

In all these symptoms the entire cathexis of the objectionable impulses seems to be condensed into a definite physical function. The choice of the afflicted region is determined by the following:

1. By the unconscious sexual fantasies and the corresponding erogeneity of the afflicted part. A person with oral fixations will develop oral symptoms, a person with anal fixations anal ones; and fixations, for their part, depend on constitutional factors as well as on past experiences. However, the regression to fixation points in conversion symptoms is limited to the choice of the organ. What are expressed in a pregenital zone are genital fantasies; that is, nongenital organs are "genitalized" (489). It has been stated that chronic neurasthenics use

their genitals in a pregenital way (*see* p. 191); now it must be added that conversion hysterics use their pregenital zones in a genital way (565, 571).

2. By purely physical facts. It is apparent that a symptom will more readily utilize an organ that presents a locus minoris resistentiae. Such a locus, again, may have been created by a constitutional weakness or by an acquired disease. An individual of strong vasomotor lability will be more subject to vasomotor symptoms; an organically myopic individual is more likely to produce eye symptoms.

This type of "somatic compliance" is certainly at work in the cases that are called "hysteric superstructure of organic diseases" (285, 1028, 1508). Organically determined symptoms may simultaneously afford opportunity for the rise of a distorted expression of repressed impulses; that is, they may acquire a secondary conversion meaning. They are not produced by conversion but they are used by conversion, and hence they may continue on a psychological basis after the organic cause that created them has ceased to exist.

3. The choice of the organ may depend on the *situation* in which the decisive repression occurred. Those organs are likely to become the seat of disturbances that were most active or under the highest tension at the moment the decisive repression occurred (316, 532).

4. Sometimes the choice of the afflicted organ seems rather to be determined by the ability of the function of the organ to express symbolically the unconscious drive in question. Incorporative tendencies can be better expressed by the mouth, the respiratory organs, and the skin, eliminatory tendencies by the intestinal tract and also by the respiratory system. Convex organs like hand, foot, nose, breasts may symbolize the penis and represent masculine wishes; concave organs like mouth, anus, nostrils, flexing sides of extremities may symbolize the vagina and represent feminine wishes.

ARCHAIC FEATURES IN CONVERSION

Conversion symptoms are not limited to the voluntary muscular system but occur in the realm of the vegetative system as well. The urge to express unconscious sexual wishes in a distorted physical way has at its disposal a far more extensive area than has conscious will. As is well known, hypnotic commands have an influence over many more physical functions than normal conscious will; a concentrated training of constitutionally predisposed personalities may make these functions accessible to autosuggestive measures also (1410). The same functions are also made use of by conversion. Generally, the "archaic" ego controls more of the body functions than our adult ego does. The hysterical "hyperfunctions" represent a regression to the archaic conditions that still ob-

tain in early childhood. Actually, the described characteristics of archaic motility and perceptions (*see* pp. 36 ff. and 41 ff.) can be observed again in conversion
hysterics.

> The insight into this regressive nature of the phenomenon of conversion may
> be taken as a starting point for speculations about the archaic origin of the capac-
> ity for autoplastic conversion. Lamarck's theory of the evolution of species may
> be recalled, according to which evolution took place through the autoplastic
> adaptation of the body to the demands of the environment. A hysterical conver-
> sion may be a sort of last vestige of this primitive capacity of animals for auto-
> plastic adaptation.

During normal development to adulthood certain capacities of the body are
lost which become available again to the hysterical individual. Ferenczi once
remarked that education is not only the acquisition of new faculties but also the
forgetting of others, which, if not forgotten, would be called supernormal (489).
This implies that the repression of autoeroticism also forces into repression some
of the functions by means of which autoeroticism was effective.

The "hysterical hyperfunctions," as a return of the repressed, demonstrate the
fact that hysterics by repressing their infantile sexuality repressed too much of
their body functions. In hysterics the body is more or less "alien" to the conscious
ego; they failed to identify their ego with their body. In the state of the "purified
pleasure ego" (588) everything that was painful was regarded as nonego; those
persons regarded their body as painful, and accordingly perceived it as nonego.
They are inhibited both in respect to motility and sensibility. Persons who look
upon their bodies as alien, when developing conversion symptoms with apparent
"supernormal" physical capacities, are more readily able to repudiate the psychogenic nature of their symptoms.

Although there is no full regression of the personality to pregenitality in conversion hysteria, nevertheless there is, especially in women, often a regression to
the instinctual aims of incorporation. This is shown not only in the predominant
role played by identification in conversion hysteria but also in more direct
signs. The fellatio idea is extraordinarily common in the unconscious fantasies of hysterical women (globus hystericus). Analysis shows that this idea
is a distorted expression for the wish to bite off and incorporate the penis.
This fantasy is abundantly overdetermined. In individual cases the following meanings seem to be of different relative importance. It may mean (*a*) a
displacement upward of genital wishes, (*b*) the idea of impregnation, (*c*) a revenge on the man who possesses the envied organ, that is, an expression of active
castrating tendencies, and (*d*) an incorporation of the castrated penis and an
identification with the man (398, 407, 499).

By this fantasy the sexual partner is deprived of his penis. For the hysterical
woman the fantasy of genital union is so closely bound up with the Oedipus wish

that she becomes incapable of real love. She can love, to quote Abraham, only if the genitals are excluded, because the genitals represent the objectionable part of love. The hysterical woman seeks to set up this condition when, in fantasy, she excludes the genitals by biting them off (26).

An organ afflicted with a conversion symptom may also represent an object that has been introjected. However, in spite of such an incorporation the object still remains in the external world, too; hysterical introjection is a *partial* rather than a *total* regression from an object relationship to identification.

GENERAL SIGNIFICANCE OF CONVERSION

Conversion hysteria is the classical subject matter of psychoanalysis. As a matter of fact the psychoanalytic method was discovered, tested, and perfected through the study of hysterical patients (187, 188, 542, 543, 544, 548); the technique of psychoanalysis still remains most easily applicable to cases of hysteria, and it is psychoanalytic treatment of hysteria that continues to yield the best therapeutic results.

The compromise character of the symptoms, which express the repressed forces as well as the repressing ones, and the dynamic relationship between instincts and counterinstinctual forces are especially demonstrable in conversion.

> Some people blush at the slightest reference to a sexual subject. This is, first of all, certainly an expression of defense; simultaneously, however, it also betrays sexual excitement, the fact that the blushing individual responds to the sexual hint. The conversion symptom of habitual blushing as a rule expresses conflicts around exhibitionism (and around struggles for narcissistic supplies, sought by means of exhibitionism).
>
> In social gatherings which unconsciously represent sexual temptation, a patient regularly was seized with a need to defecate, which forced her to leave the room. She thus extricated herself from the disagreeable situation; but on the other hand, by her symptomatic act, she also showed, by regressing to an infantile expression of sexual excitement, that she had been stimulated.

From the standpoint of the repressed impulse, the conversion symptom is the distorted substitute for sexual gratification on the part of the hysterical person who is incapable of genuine sexual gratification. The fact that the "substitute gratification" of the symptom is not felt consciously as pleasurable but is usually rather a severe suffering is due to the effectiveness of the repressing forces. Sometimes this suffering can be regarded as a punishment inflicted upon oneself in order to undo guilt feelings (37). However, there are also symptoms that represent instinctual gratification exclusively and have no punitive significance; symptoms of which the patient himself is unaware certainly cannot serve as a punishment.

In conversion symptoms the countercathexis may manifest itself in various ways. It may also be secondarily intruded upon by the returning original impulses in various ways. In cases of motor and sensory disturbances as well as in disturbances of consciousness, the inhibition of function is due to the countercathexis, but it also gives opportunity for the use of the inhibited function to express unconscious fantasies. In the case of hysterical pain, the attention directed to the protection of the painful organ, as a manifestation of the countercathexis, has replaced the original attention directed toward avoiding the tempting or threatening situation (618). The striving to rationalize all symptoms as "physical," too, is a manifestation of the countercathexis. A kind of hysterical reaction formation is at work when an unconscious hatred is overcompensated in the form of an exaggerated consideration (618).

OEDIPUS COMPLEX, MASTURBATION, AND PREGENITALITY IN CONVERSION SYMPTOMS

Freud's statement that the Oedipus complex is the nuclear complex of the neuroses is particularly valid in hysteria, which remains on the level of the phallic phase of sexual development. Hysterical individuals have either never overcome their early object choice or else were so fixated on it that after a disappointment in later life they again returned to it. Because all sexuality thereby comes to represent to them the infantile incestuous love, the urge to repress the Oedipus complex represses all sexuality.

That hysteria occurs more frequently in women than in men is due to the fact that the sexual development of women is more complicated. The process of giving up the clitoris for the vagina may fail of completion. But not only Oedipus complex and "heterosexual identification" are characteristic for the structure of hysteria; inseparably connected with it are other characteristics, such as the particular means by which the Oedipus complex is suppressed. Frequently, children who have been allowed to become too intensely fixated on their parents are subsequently prohibited by those same parents in some particular manner from gratifying their Oedipus wishes. Among hysterical individuals, the type known as mother's boy is frequently to be found, or women who seem to have no need of men, but inordinately admire their father.

However, it would be erroneous to think that the ultimate content of the hysterical symptoms, the Oedipus complex, becomes immediately apparent under analysis. Between the Oedipus fantasies and the symptoms of the adult, the intermediate formations of daydreams are interpolated. And between the original Oedipus fantasies and the later daydreams there are inserted infantile masturbatory fantasies, whose Oedipus character is sometimes rather distorted. The conflicts which were originally connected with the Oedipus complex frequently are displaced onto the act of masturbation. That is why so frequently the struggle against masturbation is found as the unconscious content of hysterical symptoms. Spasms, rhythmical muscular contractions, and sensory disturbances often proved to be simultaneous defenses against and substitutes for masturbatory activities (357, 550, 733).

> Daydreaming, which consciously may be designed to suppress masturbation, is mainly unconsciously an elaboration of the original masturbatory fantasies. Sometimes this secret relationship becomes manifest again under certain circumstances in an unexpected manner (537). If the person succeeds in repressing the connections between the fantasies and the masturbation, the unrepressed fantasies, as unconscious equivalents of masturbation, sometimes develop into some exaggerated obsessive interests in certain fields. These interests are occasionally felt by the persons themselves as antimasturbatory measures, but betray themselves in analysis as offshoots of masturbatory fantasies connected with the Oedipus complex. The same holds true for certain habitual autoerotic games and symptomatic acts which give discharge to fantasies, in the main without the person being aware of them or at least of their importance for his mental equilibrium.

The fantasies that intervene between the Oedipus complex and the hysterical symptom sometimes themselves are of a genital nature, for example, ideas of pregnancy and childbirth. But this is by no means necessarily so. As intermediary links between the Oedipus wish and the apparently innocuous daydream, ideas are found originating in any erogenous zone and in any partial instinct. Although they are intermediary links only, they are certainly not unimportant from a practical point of view. Their discovery and working out may demand more time and attention in analysis than does the basic Oedipus complex, and the form the Oedipus complex itself has acquired as a result of the individual's past infantile experiences can be elicited only through the careful analysis of these intermediary constructions (418).

> An example of intermediary oral fantasies: A patient complained of vomiting and nausea. In associating, she became aware that the symptom occurred whenever she had eaten fish. Following this insight, she revealed several ideas dealing with the cruelty of eating animals. To eat fish seemed to her especially cruel, because fish had "souls" (the gut of a herring in German is called *Seele*, i.e., "soul"). The patient's father was dead. The idea of eating his soul to make it part of her own body was a screen for the unconscious fantasy of sexual union with him.

An example of a pregenital expression of predominantly genital wishes in a conversion symptom is presented by bedwetting, the most frequent masturbatory equivalent in children (91, 227, 263, 557, 667, 769, 793, 934, 1044, 1595).

> Infantile (nocturnal or diurnal) enuresis is a sexual discharge. Urinary excretion originally served as an autoerotic activity which gave the child urethral-erotic (and cutaneous) satisfaction. Memories of these autoerotic sensations are some-

times revived by patients under analysis—for example, in cases of ejaculatio prae-cox, where semen and urine are unconsciously equated. If, however, an already trained older child returns to this form of infantile satisfaction, it is no longer autoerotic; it is connected with fantasies concerning objects. If it is no longer per-formed actively and with conscious sexual pleasure but happens against the in-dividual's will, it certainly may be called a conversion symptom. Between the in-fantile autoerotic wetting and the later symptom of enuresis there was a time of masturbation; and the enuresis represents a substitute and equivalent of sup-pressed masturbation. In some cases it is actually possible to demonstrate that a prohibition of masturbation served as a stimulant in the direction of the develop-ment of enuresis as a substitute behavior. Like masturbation, enuresis may fulfill the role of an efferent function for various sexual wishes. At the height of the development of the Oedipus complex it is first and foremost a discharge instru-ment of the Oedipus impulses. But just as in the case of other conversion symp-toms, various intermediary wishes are interpolated between the deeply repressed Oedipus complex and the final urethral- and skin-erotic symptoms. It is inter-esting to note that bedwetting is very often an expression of sexual fantasies proper to the opposite sex. Girls in whom urethral eroticism is well marked are almost always dominated by an intense envy of the penis. Their symptom gives expression to the wish to urinate like a boy. In boys the incontinence usu-ally has the meaning of a female trait; such boys hope to obtain female kinds of pleasure by "urinating passively." Further, the passive way of urinating may express a regression to the early passive-receptive ways of pleasure, a yearning for the freedoms of babyhood. Actually, enuresis frequently represents a wish to have the privileges of a baby again. The symptom is often precipitated by the birth of a sibling. Sometimes the bedwetting in such cases has a pronouncedly aggressive, spiteful significance aimed at hurting the parents' feelings: "I will take the privileges of a baby, which you deny me." The aggressive and spiteful significance of the symptom may give an opportunity to express simultaneously other pregenitally (orally) determined ideas of revenge; this frequently occurs in those cases of enuresis that form the basis for a subsequent ejaculatio praecox.

The symptom of enuresis may have various consequences in the further devel-opment of the child. The tendency to suppress the symptom may, in a twofold way, influence character development. (1) It may turn the unspecific fear of "one's own dangerous impulses" into the specific fear of "losing control." And it is not infrequent that in analyzing patients' difficulties in giving in to free association in the analytic cure, a fear of wetting is found as the basis. (However, the fear of being overwhelmed by one's own excitement may also have other ori-gins.) This is more frequently found in girls, where frigidity is often character-ized by the unconscious idea that a full yielding to the climax of excitement would bring the disgrace of losing bladder control. The fact that this fear is more fre-quent in women probably is due to the circumstance that the retention of urine for the purpose of preventing enuresis is more apt to evoke a secondary erogenous retention pleasure (analogous to the anal retention pleasure) in girls than in boys. (2) The general fear of one's own dangerous instincts might acquire the special quality of *shame*. The specific connection between shame and urethral eroticism has already been mentioned (*see* p. 69). Whereas rectal incontinence in children is usually directly and actively punished, enuretic children are made to feel ashamed. Pillorizing is the most frequent punishment. Ambition as a urethral-erotic character trait is the striving to avoid this kind of shame (*see* pp. 492 f.).

Fecal incontinence is a much rarer occurrence in older children than urinary incontinence. It, too, has to be looked upon as a conversion symptom, expressing an unconscious tendency for anal discharge of instinctual conflicts. If it only happens occasionally, it probably represents an equivalent of anxiety. If it happens habitually, however, it represents a retention of anal sexual execution or a regression to it as an equivalent or substitute for masturbation. This certainly is a sign of a marked anal-erotic orientation. Actually, a history of anal incontinence is found more frequently in persons who subsequently develop compulsion neuroses than in those who develop hysterias.

It seems like a contradiction of the general thesis about hysterics' repressing their sexuality that hysterics so often are described as persons who are constantly preoccupied with sexuality, and who tend to "sexualize" any human relationship. But this contradiction is only an apparent one. Just because these persons block their sexuality, their sexuality is dammed up inside them, and therefore comes out in unsuitable places and at inconvenient times. Hysterical erotomania is a pseudo hypersexuality caused by lack of satisfaction (*see* pp. 242 ff.).

Sometimes patients with conversion symptoms are entirely free from anxiety; sometimes conversion and anxiety symptoms are developed alongside each other. The binding of the energy which has been dammed up through the neurotic conflict in alterations of somatic functions provides a certain capacity for discharge or at least for a more permanent binding of the cathexes, and as such is a means of getting rid of anxiety or of avoiding the open outbreak of it. In the cases in which anxiety is developed alongside conversion symptoms, this secondary elaboration of the anxiety has failed or was not sufficient.

COURSE AND PSYCHOANALYTIC TREATMENT OF CONVERSION HYSTERIA

Certain reactions of the patient's ego to conversion symptoms are so characteristic for hysteria that a few words about them may be said here in anticipation. On the one hand the ego attempts to continue the effort to repress the symptoms as a derivative of infantile sexuality, just as it previously repressed infantile sexuality itself. By so doing, the ego strives to separate the symptoms from the rest of the personality, to ignore them; when the tendency to deny the symptoms succeeds, the patient's attitude toward his symptoms is what Charcot, as reported by Freud, called *la belle indifférence des hysteriques* (589). On the other hand since they are unavoidable, the ego endeavors to utilize the symptoms for its own purposes. If it must suffer, it wishes to get as much out of it as it can. In this way, secondary gains from the illness are established, which are to be differentiated from the primary one, namely, the avoidance of facing the Oedipus complex. To say that a wish for a pension can cause a hysteria has been justly compared by Freud to the idea that a soldier in battle had his leg shot off in order to get a pension (618).

The prognosis of psychoanalysis in cases of conversion neuroses is favorable. In typical cases, the course of the treatment is especially satisfactory, in so far as the patients react immediately to interpretations with alterations in transference and symptomatology and thus offer an unfailing criterion of the progress of the analysis. Psychoanalytic therapy is most clearly indicated except in cases where individual complications originating in external circumstances or in the character structure of the patient (481) unpleasantly complicate the situation. Only those factors which, apart from the diagnosis, generally are barriers to psychoanalytic therapy (*see* pp. 575 ff.) are contraindications here, too. Wherever immediate help is mandatory, or where the complicated apparatus of analysis seems unnecessary because simpler measures will suffice, or in those rare cases where hysteria seems to be the best way out of an intolerable real conflict, or where there is an exceptionally great secondary gain, or advanced age, it is, of course, necessary to give careful consideration to the question whether or not to start psychoanalytic treatment.

Chapter XIII

ORGAN NEUROSES

WHAT IS AN ORGAN-NEUROTIC SYMPTOM?

NOT all somatic changes of a psychogenic nature should be called conversions because not all are translations of specific fantasies into a "body language." Unconscious instinctual attitudes may influence organic functions in a physiological way, also without the changes having any definite psychic *meaning*. This difference, though very simple, is not always recognized. It was defined long ago by Freud in his paper on the psychogenic disturbances of vision (571). He says:

"Psychoanalysis is fully prepared to grant, indeed to postulate, that not every functional visual disturbance is necessarily psychogenic. . . . When an organ which serves two purposes overplays its erotogenic part, it is in general to be expected that this will not occur without alterations in its response to stimulation and in innervation, which will be manifested as disturbances of the organ in its function as servant of the ego. And indeed, when we observe an organ which ordinarily serves the purpose of sensorial perception presenting as a result of the exaggeration of its erotogenic role precisely the behavior of a genital, we shall even expect that there are toxic modifications as well in that organ. For both kinds of functional disturbances . . . we are obliged to retain, for want of a better, the time-honored, inapposite name of neurotic disturbances. Neurotic disturbances of vision are related to psychogenic as, in general, are the actual neuroses to the psychoneuroses; psychogenic visual disturbances can hardly occur without neurotic disturbances, though the latter surely can without the former. Unfortunately, these neurotic symptoms are as yet little appreciated and understood, for they are not directly accessible to psychoanalysis."

The sentences quoted are of basic importance, although the terminology is rather confusing. There are two categories of functional disturbances. One of them is physical in nature and consists of physiological changes caused by the inappropriate use of the function in question. The other one has a specific unconscious meaning, is an expression of a fantasy in a "body language" and is directly accessible to psychoanalysis in the same way as a dream. Freud calls both categories neurotic and does not suggest any special term for the first category, whereas the second category is called psychogenic. This is rather confusing, because any misuse of an organ is psychogenic, too. It would be preferable to call the first category of symptoms organ neurotic, whereas for the second category the term conversion should be reserved.

Whereas the concept of conversion is very strictly defined, the first category needs further clarification.

Between the realm of organic disorders from mechanical, physical, and chemical causes and the field of conversion, there stretches a large field of functional and even anatomical alterations, which the term organ neurotic is meant to embrace. The modern term "psychosomatic" disturbances has the disadvantage of suggesting a dualism that does not exist. Every disease is "psychosomatic"; for no "somatic" disease is entirely free from "psychic" influence—an accident may have occurred for psychogenic reasons, and not only the resistance against infections but all vital functions are continually influenced by the emotional state of the organism—and even the most "psychic" conversion may be based on a purely "somatic" compliance.

The quotation from Freud contains the key for a classification of the organ-neurotic or psychosomatic phenomena. These sentences actually allude to two different things. Functional changes due to "toxic" influences, that is, to changes of the chemistry of the unsatisfied and dammed-up person, are not necessarily identical with changes caused by an unconscious use of these functions for instinctual purposes. Moreover, a third and simpler possibility must be considered first—the already mentioned affect equivalents. Thus four classes of organ-neurotic symptoms have to be distinguished: (1) affect equivalents; (2) results of changes in the chemistry of the unsatisfied and dammed-up person (expressions of "unconscious affects"); (3) physical results of unconscious attitudes or unconsciously determined behavior patterns; (4) all kinds of combinations of these three possibilities.

AFFECT EQUIVALENTS

All affects (archaic discharge syndromes that replace voluntary actions) are carried out by motor or secretory means. The specific physical expressions of any given affect may occur without the corresponding specific mental experiences, that is, without the person's being aware of their affective significance. Sexual excitement as well as anxiety may be supplanted by sensations in the intestinal, respiratory, or circulatory apparatus (545). A certain percentage of what are called organ neuroses actually are affect equivalents. Especially the so-called cardiac neuroses, which sometimes are conversion hysterias, seem frequently to be anxiety equivalents. The same holds true for those vegetative neuroses that occur when a compulsion neurotic or a reactive neurotic character gets disturbed in its relative rigidity. There are also "subjective affect equivalents." Once an emotion in childhood has become associated with a certain physical attitude, this attitude may be used in later life as a (distorting) expression of the emotion in question (316).

The fact that affect equivalents have a diminished discharge value as compared with fully experienced affects may result in the affective attitude becoming chronic (Breuer and Freud called it strangulated affects) (188). Symptoms created by chronic affective attitudes without adequate discharge may cease to be pure affect equivalents and belong rather in the next category.

THE DISTURBED CHEMISTRY OF THE UNSATISFIED PERSON

In the discussion of the nature of actual-neurotic symptoms (*see* pp. 185 ff.) the physical orientation of expressions like source of an instinct, satisfaction, frustration, state of being dammed up, became clear. These expressions refer to chemical as well as to nervous alterations. It is the hormonal state of the organism that forms the *source* of the instincts. The way in which external stimuli are perceived and reacted to depends upon it, and the instinctual action that brings about the cessation of the drive does so by altering the disturbing chemical condition. The omission of such action, whether determined by external circumstances or, as in the psychoneuroses, by internal inhibitions, necessarily interferes with the natural chemistry of the processes of excitation and gratification.

The normal interrelationship of hormonal physiology and instinctual phenomena has been the subject of a study by Benedek and Rubenstein, who tried to correlate psychoanalytic findings in women patients with their ovarian cycle (102). Although some of their conclusions may be open to criticism and require thorough checking, it can be stated that they have shown that instinctual impulses are actually dependent upon the hormonal state, and that psychodynamic changes secondarily influence the ovarian function.

Whereas actual-neurotic symptoms proved to be general and unspecific expressions of the state of being dammed up (*see* p. 188), symptoms due to the changed chemistry of a person with a disturbed instinctual economy may also be of a more specific nature; furthermore, other intermediary factors may be interpolated between the original drive and the final symptoms. In especial, those unconscious readinesses to develop specific affects that are the result of repressions certainly change the physical functions of the individual, and eventually the tissues themselves (41, 43, 48, 313, 315, 317, 1350, 1607). They have been called unconscious affects (608). In affect equivalents the mental content of the affect has been warded off, whereas the physical concomitants of the affect do take place. Now we are talking about states in which even the physical discharge is really warded off (*see* p. 188). Everybody knows what a latent rage or a latent anxiety is: a state in which neither rage nor anxiety is felt but where there is a readiness to react with exaggerated rage or exaggerated anxiety to stimuli that would normally provoke a slight rage or a slight anxiety. Certainly the qualities of feelings come into being only by their being felt, but there are states of tension which, were they not hindered in their development and discharge, would result in specific emotions. These are unconscious dispositions toward these qualities, unconscious "readiness for affects," strivings for their development, which are held in check by opposing forces, even while the individual is unaware of such readiness. "Unconscious" anxiety (1629) and "unconscious" sexual excitement in this sense are paramount in the psychology of the neuroses.

In considering the relationship between actual neuroses and psychoneuroses we may add that, theoretically, all psychoneuroses could be described as a subcategory of symptoms due to the disturbed chemistry of the dammed-up individual. Freud always stressed the fact that all neuroses will turn out, in the last analysis, to be organic diseases. However, this organic basis of the average psychoneurosis is entirely hypothetical, whereas certain physical symptoms of "unconscious" or "strangulated" affects are now accessible to research. Unconscious affects probably cause quantitatively and qualitatively different pourings out of hormones, and in this way influence the vegetative nervous system and the physical functions (343). Alexander is of the opinion that the difference in the hormonal state in conscious and in unconscious affects is only due to the chronicity of the so-called unconscious affective attitudes (56). It is more probable, however, that the physical concomitants of unconscious affects are also qualitatively different from those of conscious ones. It is even possible that these pourings out may be as specific as the physical syndromes of conscious affects, but this has been insufficiently investigated as yet.

PHYSICAL RESULTS OF UNCONSCIOUS ATTITUDES

The behavior of a person is continually influenced by his conscious and unconscious instinctual needs. Whereas the oscillations of conscious drives are regulated automatically through instinctual actions, warded-off impulses, which cannot find an adequate outlet but over and over seek to find discharge and to produce derivatives, have less obvious and more lasting effects. Attempts at substitute outlets are continued or repeated, and this may eventually produce physical alterations.

A simple example: A habitual forced clearing of the throat, kept up over weeks and months, has a drying effect upon the throat and may eventually result in a pharyngitis. Or the habit of sleeping with the mouth open also dries the throat and may cause a pharyngitis. Both habits at times may have organic causes; at other times they certainly are an expression of unconscious wishes (532). There are many kinds of behavior that provoke common colds (1125, 1352). Various authors have illustrated occurrences of this kind in detail (43, 56, 311, 317, 342, 343, 532, 1356, 1592) and have written papers about special "psychosomatic" conditions, to be quoted later.

To summarize: An unusual attitude, which is rooted in unconscious instinctual conflicts, causes a certain behavior. This behavior in turn causes somatic changes in the tissues. The changes are not directly psychogenic; but the person's behavior, which initiated the changes, was psychogenic; the attitude was intended to relieve the internal pressure; the somatic symptom, which was the consequence of the attitude, was not sought by the person, either consciously or unconsciously.

HORMONAL AND VEGETATIVE DYSFUNCTIONS

The three categories of organ-neurotic symptoms, affect equivalents, physical expressions of a disturbed chemistry, and physical expressions of unconscious attitudes, appear usually in a combined form. Often the symptoms remain limited to a given organ or system of organs, the choice depending primarily on physical and constitutional factors but also on all the other factors that likewise determine the "somatic compliance" in conversion symptoms (*see* pp. 227 f.). The hormonal-vegetative system, however, cannot be simply classified as one of the various organ systems, such as the intestinal, respiratory, or circulatory system. Rather, the greater part of the functional disturbances in these systems is created through hormonal-vegetative pathways, the symptoms "due to the distorted chemistry of the unsatisfied person" being exclusively determined in this way. Thus when introducing the heading "Hormonal and Vegetative Dysfunctions" before discussing the various organ systems, we only intend to discuss the influence of unconscious attitudes on hormones and to clarify a few points that occasionally are confused.

Attitudes caused by unconscious instinctual conflicts may, of course, influence the hormonal functions and thus produce secondary somatic symptoms not intended as such. The same kind of influence that an unconscious desire has on the production of the gastric juice in cases of peptic ulcer (*see* p. 245), other desires have on the production of hormones regulating metabolism (*cf.* 189), for instance a psychogenic identification with the opposite sex.

There is no doubt that in menstrual or premenstrual mental disorders in women, a somatic factor always plays a part, namely, the physical alterations at the source of the instinctual drives. But on the other hand the unconscious significance of the idea of menstruation and the mental reaction to this significance may likewise alter the hormonal events. In cases of disturbances, the premenstrual body feeling represents tension, retention (sometimes pregnancy), dirt, pregenitality, hatred; the menstrual flow may bring relaxation, and is felt as evacuation (sometimes birth), cleanliness, genitality, love; but it may also represent loss of anal and urethral control, Oedipus guilt, castration, the frustration of wishes for a child, and humiliation.

Every pregenital fixation necessarily changes the hormonal status. However, not all orally fixated patients become either obese or extremely thin. Probably this happens if an oral fixation coincides with a certain hormonal constitution. Many cases of obesity and extreme thinness belong in this category.

Hilde Bruch who has had a great and extraordinary experience with obese children (209, 211), states that the majority of cases do not seem to be primarily hormonal in nature but rather psychogenic, that is, brought about by an incorrect economics of energy, by too much food supply and too little motor discharge. Psychoanalytically, this mistake in economy is due to primary psychogenic conflicts or developmental disturbances. "Obesity in childhood represents a disturbance in personality in which excessive bodily size becomes the expressive organ of a conflict" (210).

Wulff has described a psychoneurosis, not infrequent in women, which is related to hysteria, cyclothymia and addiction (1619). This neurosis is characterized by the person's fight against her sexuality which, through previous repression, has become especially greedy and insatiable. This sexuality is pregenitally oriented, and sexual satisfaction is perceived of as a "dirty meal." Periods of depression in which the patients stuff themselves (or drink) and feel themselves "fat," "bloated," "dirty," "untidy," or "pregnant" and leave their surroundings untidy, too, alternate with "good" periods in which they behave ascetically, feel slim, and conduct themselves either normally or with some elation. The body feeling in the "fat" periods turns out to be a repetition of the way the girl felt at puberty before her first menstruation, and the spells often actually coincide with the premenstrual period. The menstrual flow then usually brings a feeling of relief: "The fat-making dirt is pouring out; now I am slim again, and will be a good girl and not eat too much." The alternating feelings of ugliness and beauty connected with these periods show that exhibitionistic conflicts also are of basic importance in this syndrome. Psychoanalysis discloses that the unconscious content of this syndrome is a preoedipal mother conflict, which may be covered by an oral-sadistic Oedipus complex. The patients have an intense unconscious hatred against their mothers and against femininity. To them being fat means getting breasts, being uncontrolled, incontinent or even pregnant. The urge to eat has the unconscious aim of incorporating something that may relax the disagreeable inner "feminine" tension, eating meaning reincorporation of an object, whose loss has caused the patient to feel hungry, constipated, castrated, feminine, fat; that is, the food means milk, penis, child, and narcissistic supplies which soothe anxieties. The exhibitionistic behavior signifies a tendency to compel the receipt of these supplies and the fear of not getting them because of repulsive ugliness. The depression signifies the recurrent failure of the tendency to regain the lost stability, a failure that occurs because of the forbidden oral-sadistic means by which this re-establishment is attempted. The ascetic periods, by pacifying the superego, achieve a greater degree of relaxation.

In some cases this neurosis is nothing but a kind of food addiction, and should rather be discussed in the chapter on addictions (*see* p. 381). In other cases, however, not only body feelings but actual body changes dominate the picture. Certain cases of obesity, especially of cyclical obesity, accord in structure with Wulff's description.

> In a patient who actually lost a great deal of weight with every menstruation, which brought a sudden relief from an unbearable premenstrual tension, the changes in weight were mainly due to cyclical alterations of her water metabolism. When the patient felt disorderly inwardly, her metabolism actually behaved in a disorderly manner. Water played a leading role in the unconscious fantasies of this patient. The deep pregenital mother binding as well as the early penis envy were urethroerotically determined; "castration," because of certain childhood experiences, was thought of as "developing a hydrocephalus."

> In another case the periodic changes of weight were due to actual spells of stuffing. The craving for food was a craving to get rid of the dangers of femininity; but on the other hand it created a severe guilt feeling because of its hidden sadistic meaning. The patient felt well and "masculine" when, after menstruation, she succeeded in being ascetic. Both cases had irregularity of the menses, described by their doctors as "probably due to psychogenic factors."

DIGRESSION ON HYPER- AND HYPOSEXUALITY

Before discussing special organ systems with reference to organ neuroses, a digression should be made into the psychology of hypo- and hypersexuality, although their connection with alterations in the hormonal functions is problematic or even doubtful. Theoretically, of course, such cases may be purely organic in nature, the result of a somatic endocrine disorder. Not much is known about neurotic reactions in such cases.

Much more frequently the hypo- or hypersexuality is apparent only and is due to psychogenic factors.

The diagnosis of "hyposexuality" is frequently due to a gross mix-up in the concepts of genitality and sexuality. Ostensibly deficient in sexual desire are those persons whose libido runs along other than genital channels. In the final analysis, all neurotic persons suffer from a disturbance of their sexuality, which, in their unconscious, has an infantile significance. The amount of libido bound in their symptoms or deprived by repression from adequate discharge is lacking in their actual sexual behavior. The neurotic's constant struggle with his repressed sexuality diminishes his disposable sexual energy. In certain cases the amount lacking may be sufficiently small to let the patient's sexual life superficially appear undisturbed, and to let him feel subjectively as if his sexuality were satisfactory. However, the great majority of neurotics have gross and manifest sexual disturbances. These disturbances may express themselves in a diminution of conscious sexual interest. (They may, however, also be expressed in the very opposite way: sexuality, deprived of its natural outlet, may "sexualize" everything.) A psychogenic decrease in sexuality thus is no separate clinical entity but rather a phenomenon that may occur in all neuroses, and that is to be included among the states of "inhibitions" (*see* p. 169).

The impression of hypersexuality may be created by the same factors that produce hyposexuality. Deprived of real satisfaction, many neurotic persons strive time and again (and always in vain) to discharge through genital activity the sexuality they are unable to satisfy. They thus produce the impression of being very vigorous genitally (555). If neurotics boast of the number of times in succession they can perform the sexual act, it takes no very profound analysis to perceive that the apparent *plus* conceals a real *minus*. A normal person loses his desire when satisfied. The neurotic suffers from an incapacity for satisfaction; he is "orgastically impotent" (1270). Hence he may attempt to achieve satisfaction by persistent repetitions of the sexual act. The inability to achieve satisfying relaxation also explains why most "hypersexual" persons are chronic neurasthenics as well; the amount of libido that finds no outlet in their genital activity produces restlessness, disturbance of the capacity for work, and so on.

The inability to attain genuine end pleasure induces many neurotics to lay more stress on the forepleasure mechanisms. This can hardly be ascribed to a greedy need of perpetual pleasure (1220); rather the cause is to be sought in the insufficiency of their orgastic function. (Usually an exaggerated insistence on forepleasure is determined by an anal-erotic fixation, for pleasure due to tension is experienced most acutely in anal retention.)

What has been said until now is correct for all neurotics. There must be an additional factor determining the nature of those cases in which the "hypersexuality" is so marked as to dominate the clinical picture.

Don Juan's behavior (1251) is no doubt due to his Oedipus complex. He seeks his mother in all women and cannot find her (572). But the analysis of Don Juan types shows that their Oedipus complex is of a particular kind. It is dominated by the pregenital aim of incorporation, pervaded by narcissistic needs and tinged with sadistic impulses. In other words, the striving for sexual satisfaction is still condensed with the striving for getting narcissistic supplies in order to maintain self-esteem. There is a readiness to develop sadistic reactions if this need is not immediately satisfied.

It is due to the archaic nature of the typical Don Juan's Oedipus complex that he is so little interested in the personality of his objects. He has not passed the archaic pre-stages of love. His sexual activities are primarily designed to contradict an inner feeling of inferiority by proof of erotic "successes." After having "made" a woman, he is no longer interested in her, first because she, too, has failed to bring about the longed-for relaxation, and second because his narcissistic need requires proof of his ability to excite women; after he knows that he is able to excite a specific woman, his doubts arise concerning other women whom he has not yet tried. Perverse inclinations of any kind may give rise to similar clinical pictures. An unconsciously homosexual man, for example, may be aroused by sexual contact with women but not satisfied; he then vainly seeks satisfaction in more and more sexual activity.

Pollution dreams following sexual intercourse betray the fact that the intercourse has been exciting but not satisfactory; they demonstrate an orgastic impotence; analysis of dreams of this kind leads to an understanding of the above-mentioned factors.

In general, exaggerated sexual activity is an "obsession" like any other exaggerated activity; that is, it is a derivative, an unsuccessful attempt to use the genital apparatus for discharging some nongenital, warded-off, and dammed-up need.

Actually an apparent sexual behavior sometimes covers a striving for power or prestige (see pp. 515 ff.). However, the exaggerated striving for power and prestige has, in such persons, a history that leads back again to infantile sexuality. Power and prestige are needed as defenses against an anxiety that has become connected with infantile sexual strivings.

Nymphomania, which is feminine pseudo hypersexuality, is based on the analogous psychological structure. A superficial anamnesis often shows that nymphomanic women are either totally frigid or at least do not have orgasms regularly or readily. The fact that intercourse may excite them but cannot satisfy them creates the desire to force the unattainable satisfaction by renewed and increased attempts, or by trials with different men or under different circumstances. And as in the male Don Juans, analysis shows that the condition depends on a marked narcissistic attitude, on a dependency on narcissistic supplies, on an intense fear over loss of love, and a corresponding pregenital and sadistic coloration of the total sexuality. The attitude toward the object is typically ambivalent because, consciously or unconsciously, he is believed to be responsible for the failure to attain satisfaction. The sadistic attitude is manifest in the attempt to coerce the partner by violence into "giving" complete sexual satisfaction and therewith a re-establishment of self-esteem. This may be combined with the revenge type of the female castration complex (20). What is so intensely desired is associatively intimately bound up with the envy of the penis, and thus nymphomanic passion often aims to fulfill the wish fantasy of depriving the man of his penis. The manner in which this penis is incorporated in fantasy indicates that the ostensibly incessant genital desire is pseudo genital and, basically, of an oral nature. Analysis uncovers early infantile experiences in the realm of the pre-oedipal mother relationship which from the beginning gave the subsequent Oedipus complex an oral, demanding imprint (421). Normally with the transposition of the sexual excitability from the clitoris to the vagina, the previous oral orientation is mobilized again. Nymphomanic women are excessively affected by this process, so that their vagina unconsciously signifies a mouth. Again, as in the case of male hypersexuality, similar symptoms may appear as a result of other unconscious perverse inclinations.

Not all hypersexual men and women have the capacity for alloplastic action. If persons of this type are more inhibited, excessive masturbation takes the place of excessive sexual intercourse. Excessive masturbation represents an attempt to find a genital discharge for nongenital tensions, which cannot succeed (*see* p. 384).

GASTROINTESTINAL TRACT

A good example of an organ neurosis psychoanalytically understood as a physical result of an unconscious attitude is peptic ulcer as seen by the research work of the Chicago Psychoanalytic Institute (43, 758, 1031).

Persons with a chronically frustrated oral-receptive demanding attitude, who have repressed this attitude and often manifest very active behavior of the reaction-formation type, are, unconsciously, permanently "hungry for love." It would be even more exact to state that they are "hungry for necessary narcissistic supplies," and the word hungry in this connection has to be taken literally. This permanent hunger makes them act like an actually hungry person does. The mucous membrane of the stomach begins to secrete, just as does that of a person who anticipates food, this secretion having no other, specific psychic meaning. This chronic hypersecretion is the immediate cause of the ulcer. The ulcer is the incidental physiological consequence of a psychogenic attitude; it is not a distorted satisfaction of a repressed instinct.

It may be questioned whether this etiology is valid for all cases of ulcer. It is possible that the functional changes which, in some cases, are brought about by repressed oral eroticism may be determined in other cases by purely somatic causes.

It is easily understandable that a colitis may be brought about by unconscious anal impulses that are continuously effective, similar to the way by which the secretions of the gastric juices are produced by unconscious oral demands. Such a colitis is the result of the organism's being chronically under eliminative and retentive pressure, as an ulcer may be the result of a chronic receptive pressure. The conflict between eliminative and retentive tendencies itself may be determined in different ways. It may represent a simple conflict between (anal) sexual excitement and fear; or the feces may represent introjected objects which the person wishes to preserve as well as to get rid of (67, 305, 306, 1034, 1165, 1589).

Children who like to postpone defecation (either for the sake of retention pleasure or because of fear) later often develop obstipation; the retention, which was voluntary in the beginning, has become an organ-neurotic symptom (555). The prolonged continuance of an obstipation must influence the smooth muscles of the intestinal tract. A spastic colon, that is, a readiness to react to various stimuli either with constipation or with diarrhea or with both, is either an anxiety equivalent or a sign of the patient's fixation on the anal phase of his libidinal development. No matter what stimulus started the excitation, the execution is an intestinal one. It may also be a symptom of a continuous and repressed aggressiveness, sometimes as a revenge for oral frustrations (104, 110, 302). In a deeper layer, then, diarrhea may express generosity or a readiness to sacrifice. Or it may reflect fantasies concerning internalized objects.

In neurasthenia, constipation is one of the characteristic symptoms. This is due to the fact that "retention" generally characterizes the state of being dammed up, which is the basis of neurasthenia (1268, 1381). Also among organ-neurotic symptoms in general, retention symptoms are frequent. However, organ-neurotic symptoms are also "emergency discharges." Some symptoms are compromises between retention and elimination. Some cases of spastic colitis have obstipation and diarrhea alternately. Certain types of pathological defecation betray a castration anxiety, displaced to the anal sphere.

Alexander took the relation between ulcer and colitis as a starting point for the idea that neuroses in general and organ neuroses in particular could be understood in their specific nature by measuring the relative participation of the three basic directions in which an organism's tendencies toward the external world may be effective: reception, elimination, and retention. He called the investigation of the relative participation of these three factors in a given phenomenon vector analysis (44). This point of view certainly is useful—for example, in the study of the differential etiology of ulcer and colitis. It also has drawbacks which will be discussed later (*see* p. 526).

MUSCULAR SYSTEM

The physical effects of the state of being dammed up emotionally are readily reflected in the muscular system. Pathogenic defenses generally aim at barring the warded-off impulses from motility (the barring from consciousness is only a means of achieving this); thus pathogenic defense always means the blocking of certain movements. This inhibition of movements means a partial weakening of the voluntary mastery of motility. Thus the struggle of the defense reflects itself in functional disturbances of the voluntary muscular system. The existence of these disturbances contradicts Alexander's idea that all disturbances in the muscular functions are conversions, whereas disturbances in the vegetative functions are organ neuroses (48, 56). When persons with localized or general muscular spasms that hinder their motility try to relax their spastic muscles, they are either totally unable to do so or they may fall into emotional states, as patients in a psychocathartic treatment do if their thoughts approach their complexes. This shows that the spasm was a means of keeping the repressed in repression. The observation of a patient during an *acute* struggle over repression likewise demonstrates this. A patient in psychoanalysis who can no longer avoid seeing that an interpretation is correct, but nevertheless tries to, frequently shows a cramping of his entire muscular system or of certain parts of it. It is as if he wanted to counterpoise an external muscular pressure to the internal pressure of the repressed impulses seeking an outlet in motility.

A patient whose speech was impeded was at first entirely unable to talk in analysis. She became visibly spastic whenever she tried to talk, tensing her muscles and clenching her fists. She experienced her inability to speak physically; she felt cramped, especially in the chest and limbs; she could "let nothing out" of her; after an hour of silence, she was as exhausted as after violent physical exertion. When she again became able to speak, it was like a sudden release. "I can't tell you how *physical* that is," she would say. Characteristically, the patient described her spasms as localized beneath the lower ribs (spasm of the diaphragm).

Ferenczi noted that many patients, particularly while showing resistance, display "an exaggerated stiffness in all limbs . . . which can turn into catatonic rigidity while exchanging greetings or taking leave, which need not necessarily imply schizophrenia. With the progress of the analysis, the physical tensions may disappear along with the solution of the mental ones" (505).

The muscular expression of an instinctual conflict is not always a hypertonic one. Hypotonic lax ("flappy") muscular attitudes, too, block or hinder muscular readiness. Hyper- and hypotonic states may alternate; thus the whole field is better designated as psychogenic "dystonia" (410).

Dystonia and intensity of repression are not necessarily proportionate to each other. Not only the question whether and to what extent mental conflicts find expression in alterations of muscular function but also the type and location of these alterations are very different in individual cases. Whether the dystonia concerns more the skeletal or the smooth muscles or both is different in different persons, probably due to both constitutional and early environmental influences; and this difference is decisive for the subsequent "psychosomatic" history. The location of the symptoms depends on physiological as well as on psychological factors. One of these factors is easily recognizable; it is the specificity of the defense mechanism used. In the case of compulsion neurotics the mechanism of displacement of spasms of the sphincters will play a more important part; in hysterics, the blocking of inner perceptions will be more predominant. Investigation will have to show in what cases and under what circumstances defense and muscular dysfunctions run parallel and where they diverge considerably.

Spasms paralyzing skeletal muscles are one of the physical signs of anxiety; they may appear as an anxiety equivalent.

A patient reported that her calisthenics teacher used to call her attention to the extremely cramped, tense condition of the muscles in her neck. Her attempts to relax only increased the tension, and a feeling of nausea would follow. Analysis revealed that as a child the patient had seen a pigeon having its neck wrung and had then watched the headless pigeon flapping about for a while. This experience had given lasting form to her castration complex; she had an unconscious fear of being beheaded, which also manifested itself in other symptoms, modes of behavior, and directions of interest.

In some persons a dystonic behavior is an expression of an anal retentive tendency (505). Not only fear but also other affects, especially *spite* and suppressed *rage,* may be physically expressed as a muscular spasm.

That sexual drives are at the basis of a dystonia is frequently substantiated by the fact that the most severe spasm is that of the pelvic muscles. The original autoerotic libidinization of the muscular system may be regressively revived. Just as repression represents a dynamic struggle between impulse and countercathexis, so does the dystonia represent a struggle between motor impulse and a tendency to block the intended movement.

Psychogenic dystonia seems to be decisive in certain organ-neurotic gynecological conditions, in which a hypotonus of the pelvic muscles may have unfavorable consequences that were not necessarily unconsciously intended as such (27, 359, 902, 1128, 1139a, 1144, 1306). Psychogenic dystonia may also be the decisive etiological factor in conditions like torticollis (268, 270, 1576).

It is very interesting that these disturbances of muscular functions are mainly co-ordinated with disturbances of inner sensitivity and of body feeling. The muscular functions become normal again if it is possible to re-establish awareness of the warded-off body sensations. Actually, dystonic phenomena accompany hysterical disturbances of sensitivity and general frigidity (410).

> A patient with strong exhibitionistic leanings, overcompensated by excessive modesty, had to undergo an examination by a gynecologist. She struggled against it for a long time, fearing that she could not survive such an ordeal. Just as it was finally to take place, something strange happened. She suddenly lost all feeling of her own body. The lower part of her body was "alien," did not belong to her any more, and she could now let herself be examined.
>
> Another patient demonstrated the connection between spasm and alienation. At a time when her castration anxiety, connected with infantile masturbation, had been mobilized in her analysis, she had to undergo an operation necessitating an anesthetic. She awoke from it feeling a "stiffness" in her arms and simultaneously having the sensation that her arms did not belong to her. This condition repeated itself on several occasions in analysis when her associations touched on the subject of infantile masturbation.

Thus organ-neurotic dysfunctions of the muscles are closely interwoven with corresponding dysfunctions in muscular sensations (1311).

The existence of a psychogenic dystonia has been taken as a starting point for various forms of "relaxation" therapies of neuroses (334, 839, 1280, 1410). However, usually the relaxation is not attainable as long as the defensive conflicts prevent it; sometimes a lax hypotonus is mistaken for relaxation; or a split between the mental state and its physical expression is achieved, so that a change of the muscular attitude may occur without a corresponding change in the mental dynamics. But apparently there are cases in which a genuine mobilization of the mental conflicts reflected in the muscular state may be evoked by the therapist through a kind of "seduction" to relaxation; this possibility may warrant the use of relaxation exercises as a method or as an auxiliary of cathartic treatment (*see* p. 555).

A continuous misuse of the muscles for "neurotic" spasms has necessarily a tiring effect. Actually the fatigue characteristic for all actual-neurotic states is probably due to the "dystonic" innervation of muscles. This fatigue is most outspoken in cases of inhibited aggressiveness; often it can be directly called an equivalent of depression.

Not much study has been done concerning psychogenic pains in muscles. Sometimes such pains are fully developed conversion symptoms. At other times, however, pains seem to be the result of dystonia. This probably holds true for certain types of lower backache.

Rheumatic diseases, the symptoms of which of course are not limited to the muscular system, apparently may also be influenced by psychogenic components, or at least by psychogenic predispositions. Dunbar distinguishes between two types, one of which is more "extraverted" and traumatophilic, tending toward afflictions of the joints, the other more "introverted," ambivalent, vacillating between activity and passivity, and inclined toward heart afflictions (343).

Not much is known about the part played by psychogenic factors in the etiology of some types of *arthritis* (1087, 1214, 1534). There are indications that in somatically predisposed personalities a continuous unconscious tendency to suppress movements may result not only in muscular spasms but also in unspecific alterations of the tissues of the joints.

A case of arthritis of the Bechterew type was characterized by the extremely important role played by pleasure in movements (and exhibitionism) during childhood. The girl had intended to become a dancer who would charm audiences by her beauty. Her father's criticisms broke up these fantasies and made her believe that she was rejected because of her lack of a penis. Thereafter she felt that she was not permitted to dance. She developed an intense reactive aggressiveness of which she was afraid and for which she tried to overcompensate. To the patient, her arthritis, which began many years later, meant punishment for and final prohibition of her dancing ambition, her exhibitionism and her reactive castration tendencies. The significance of these factors in the *etiology* of the arthritis was not disclosed.

RESPIRATORY SYSTEM

Breathing, like other muscular functions, has its characteristic dystonia. Variations of respiratory rhythm, especially transitory cessations of breathing, and variable and irregular participation of individual parts of the thorax in the act of breathing are the ways in which continuous, small psychological alterations exert an influence on the process of respiration (50, 54, 515). These phenomena become particularly evident when a new action or motion is initiated and in every change of direction of attention (807, 1519, 1539). The intimate connection between anxiety and respiration makes it probable that these constant variations in the respiratory function express slight degrees of anxiety. The "normal" respiratory dystonia may be considered as an anxiety signal of low intensity. It is as if the ego were cautiously testing the path, whenever a new thing is perceived, a new action undertaken, or the attention redirected—wondering, so to speak, whether or not it should be afraid.

"Signal anxiety" is a lower degree of "traumatic anxiety." Certainly crass alterations of the respiratory function also play an essential part in intense anxiety spells, and may later be used as anxiety equivalents. The awareness of the role played by respiratory sensations in anxiety in general explains the fact that every anxiety, to a certain extent, is felt as a kind of suffocation (741). Therefore, neurotic anxiety manifesting itself in respiratory symptoms is not necessarily a sign that the warded-off impulses concern respiratory eroticism. The reverse, rather, may be true: respiration may acquire an erotic quality only after and because anxiety has become connected with sexual excitement.

> Sometimes a manifest fear of suffocation covers a repressed idea of castration. A patient imagined that the analyst might cut off his supply of air with scissors. He fantasied that his supply of air was arranged like that of a diver's and was being cut off by his analyst, thus choking him. This fantasy was a cover for the anxiety lest the scissors cut off his penis. The connection between the ideas of castration and suffocation was the fear that he might suffocate during sleep under the blanket, a fear that had been prominent during his latency period. While under the blanket, he used to indulge in masturbatory fantasies.

However, the respiratory function may also have become "sexualized." In infancy, smelling and sniffling are not only connected with sucking (1184) but are in themselves a source of erogenous pleasure; this pleasure and infantile conflicts around it may be remobilized in a subsequent neurosis. Intake and outlet of air may symbolize "incorporation" and "projection of what had been incorporated." In primitive thinking, the respiratory apparatus becomes the site of incorporated objects, in the same way as does the intestinal apparatus. Primitive people, psychotics, and children sense that, by breathing, they are taking in some substance from the outer world and returning some substance to it. The incorporated substance is invisible and therefore suitable for conveying magical ideas, which is reflected in the equations of life and soul with breathing (1320). Breathing further lends itself to magical use because of the fact that it is the one vegetative function that can be regulated and influenced voluntarily. Inhaling the same air as another person means to be united with him, while exhaling means separation. "Respiratory introjection" is closely tied up with the "taking in of odors," that is, with anal eroticism on the one hand and with the idea of identification with dead persons ("inhaling the soul") on the other (420).

In bronchial asthma, it is particularly a passive-receptive longing for the mother which is expressed in pathological changes of the breathing function (531, 535, 1190, 1563, 1615). The asthmatic seizure is, first of all, an anxiety equivalent. It is a cry for help, directed toward the mother, whom the patient tries to introject by respiration in order to be permanently protected. This intended incorporation as well as the instinctual danger against which it is directed are characteristically of a pregenital, especially anal, nature; in fact, the whole character of the typical asthmatic patient shows pregenital features; the Oedipus complex of patients suffering from asthma has a typically pregenital character. Often the introjection is fantasied as already accomplished, and there are conflicts between the ego of the patient and his respiratory apparatus, representing an introjected object. It must be added that in asthma, purely somatic factors (of an allergic nature) (1355, 1509) likewise play a role, as well as full conversions (of a pregenital nature) (see pp. 321 ff.).

French and Alexander, who made a detailed psychoanalytic study of bronchial asthma (535), summarize their results in the following way which fully accords with the previous description: ". . . first that the asthmatic attack is a reaction to the danger of separation from the mother; second, that the attack is a sort of equivalent of an inhibited and repressed cry of anxiety or rage; third, that the sources of danger of losing the mother are due to some temptations to which the patient is exposed." The task of "mastering the fear of being left alone governs the patient's whole life" (318).

It has been mentioned that common colds are frequently an unintentional result of various neurotic behavior patterns (1125, 1352, 1590). It can be easily explained why the very persons who are afraid of colds tend to catch them frequently. Their fear expresses insight into their tendency to catch colds, and through the returning of the repressed, their attempts to avoid colds paradoxically direct them into situations that make them susceptible to colds.

The various kinds of "nervous coughing" may be classified as follows (443): (1) Coughing of an organic origin may produce disturbances of the mental economy; the patient's adjustment to the symptom may fail in the sense of a "pathoneurosis." (2) A cough of organic origin may be used secondarily for the purpose of giving discharge to repressed impulses, especially for expressing conflicts around incorporation. (3) Nervous coughing may be a conversion symptom, either a hysterical identification with a coughing person (557) or it may, through memories of organic childhood coughs, express some instinctual conflicts of childhood (1591). (4) Some nervous coughing is of the nature of a tic, being a substitute for and an equivalent of embarrassment or hostility. (5) Nervous coughing may be an organ-neurotic symptom, caused by a cold induced by some psychogenic behavior.

HEART AND CIRCULATORY SYSTEM

Rage and sexual excitation as well as anxiety manifest themselves physiologically in functional circulatory alterations. The heart is considered the organ of love, the heart beats fast in rage and fear, the heart is heavy if one feels sad. Vago- and sympathicotonic reactions are the very essence of the physical components of affect syndromes. These components may always serve as affect equivalents if a person wards off awareness of his emotions. Any kind of "unconscious emotion" may express itself in acceleration of the pulse.

However, certain personalities seem to be especially predisposed to develop just this type of expression. These personalities are by no means identical with those who have somatically impaired hearts. The "nervous heart" often has objectively the strongest power of resistance. The "somatic compliance" of the nervous heart, it seems, lies not in the heart but rather in the vegetative nervous system and its chemical and central control systems (71).

However, the contents of the leading conflicts also seem to be characteristic for these personalities. Whereas sexual excitement certainly may occasionally disguise itself also as palpitation, a chronic irritability of heart and circulatory system is more typically due to unconscious aggressiveness and retaliation fear of aggressiveness. Characteristically, such patients suffer from an inhibited hate toward the parent of the same sex, and simultaneously from a fear of losing his or her love or affection, if this hate were openly expressed. The fear of being abandoned, carried over from infantile experiences, takes the form of a fear of death. Very often an identification with a cardiac sufferer in the patient's environment is in the foreground (especially if the patient has wished for the death of this person and now fears retaliation). Attacks are frequently precipitated if circumstances necessitate competition with the parent of the same sex; the patient then tries unconsciously to escape into a passive-dependent attitude (344, 1129, 1150, 1608). These are apparently the typical unconscious conflicts in cases called effort syndrome (342, 1572).

A patient with heart symptoms had not only generally identified himself with his father, a cardiac sufferer, but unconsciously had introjected his father and then equated his heart and his father (*see* pp. 219 f.).

It has been demonstrated that extrasystoles are sometimes immediate reactions to events that stimulate repressed conflicts (728). However, certainly not all extrasystoles have such a tangible mental precipitator.

Deutsch and Kauf (312) have studied the physiological pathways of nervous system and chemical control by which psychogenic factors may influence the circulatory functions.

There seems to be a correspondence between the fact that persons who block the external discharge of their emotions entirely are more disposed toward reaction within the circulatory system and the physiological fact that the circulatory system, as contrasted with the digestive and respiratory tracts, is closed and not capable of intake or discharge.

General vasomotor reactions such as blushing, turning pale, fainting, and dizzy spells are very common in neuroses. This is due to the fact that vasomotor expressions are in the foreground of the physical manifestations of all affects and that vasomotor reactions are ready channels for emergency discharge whenever muscular discharge is blocked.

Vasomotor alterations, probably in combination with certain dystonic muscular phenomena, are also the cause of the majority of nervous headaches. The physiology of nervous headaches still presents many unsolved problems; psychologically it can be stated that actual-neurotic headaches, expressing a state of inner tension, organ-neurotic headaches, due to a more specific behavior caused by an unconscious conflict (e.g., specific muscular tensions during sleep), and conversion headaches (e.g., expressing pregnancy fantasies) should be distinguished from one another.

> Investigation of the personalities of patients suffering from migraine show that they must regularly be classified as "neurotic characters" of marked emotional instability (1544). They are easily frightened or depressed, are always ready to accept blame, have sexual inhibitions, and frequently an intense attachment to their parents. The authors stress that the patients give the impression of constantly fighting an unconscious hostility (972). Fromm-Reichmann (656) is of the opinion that the symptom is produced when an unconscious hostile tendency is directed in particular at the destruction of an object's intelligence ("mental castration") and guilt feelings turn this tendency instead against one's own head.

The severe "vegetative neuroses," like Quinke's edema or Raynaud's disease, have not yet been psychoanalytically investigated as to their possible psychogenic components.

BLOOD PRESSURE

Even in cases where the exact physiological pathways by which an organ-neurotic symptom is actually brought about are not yet known, it is possible to see what the underlying psychogenic attitude is. An example for this is *essential hypertension* which just recently has been made the subject of psychoanalytic research (51, 52, 783, 1134, 1353, 1413, 1571, 1572). Cases of essential hypertension are characterized by an extreme, unconscious instinctual tension, a general readiness for aggressiveness as well as a passive-receptive longing to get rid of the aggressiveness. Both tendencies are unconscious and are effective in persons who superficially seem to be very calm and permit themselves no outlets for their impulses. This unrealized inner tension seems to be at least one of the etiological components of essential hypertension; it becomes effective through hormonal influences due to unconscious conflicts via vasomotor responses and the kidneys; further physiological research will have to show exactly in which ways. The increase in essential hypertension in modern man is probably connected with the mental situation of individuals who, having learned that aggressiveness is bad, have to live in a world where an enormous amount of aggressiveness is asked for.

SKIN

For physiological reasons, manifestations on the skin often express irritations in the endocrine-vegetative system, and it is this connection that explains the tendency for the skin to become the site of emergency discharges in states of nervous tension. The simple symptom of nervous sweating and the symptom of dermography are examples for the general vegetative irritability of the skin in response to (conscious and unconscious) emotional stimuli. These symptoms may be chronic as a sign of the patient's state of inner tension or they may appear as temporary symptoms during actual neuroses; or they may appear in the form of "spells," whenever an event touches upon unconscious conflicts; or they may have become elaborated into conversion symptoms (676, 1151, 1199, 1387, 1507, 1510). There is no doubt that cutaneous irritability reflects vasomotor instability. A dermatologist who specialized in the study of the psychology of dermatoses, Barinbaum, put the problem as follows: "One would like to know how the excitation of a disturbed libido economy influences the vessels of the skin, since function and state of the skin depend on its vessels to the highest degree" (86).

The tendency of the skin to be influenced by vasomotor reactions, which in turn are evoked by unconscious impulses, has to be understood from the point of view of the general physiological functions of the skin. Four characteristics of the skin as the external cover of the organism, representing the boundary between it and the external world, are of general importance.

1. The skin as the covering layer has, first of all, a general protecting function. It examines incoming stimuli and, if necessary, blunts them or even wards them off. For the purpose of applying the same protective measures against internal stimuli, the organism has a general tendency to treat disturbing internal stimuli

as if they were external ones (605). This tendency also holds true for repressed impulses seeking discharge. In the same way that muscles become rigid unspecifically in the struggle against repressed impulses, so vasomotor functions of the skin, too, are used as an "armor." Physiology will have to explain how these vasomotor changes result in the outbreak of a dermatosis.

2. The skin is an important erogenous zone; if the drive to use it as such is repressed, the recurrent tendencies for and against cutaneous stimulation find somatic expression in cutaneous alterations.

The erogeneity of the skin is not limited to touching stimuli. Sensations of temperature are the source of an erogenous pleasure which is an important component of infantile sexuality. The displeasure of feeling cold and the pleasure of being warm again are as old as the displeasure of being hungry and the pleasure of being fed again. Actually oral and temperature eroticism regularly make their appearance together. Therefore, the narcissistic supplies, wanted urgently by persons with oral fixations, are thought of not only as food but also as warmth.

In addition to the stimuli of touching and temperature, pain, too, may be a source of erogenous cutaneous pleasure. In cases where the sexual aim of being *beaten* is paramount, this pleasure has become the representation of the individual's total sexuality (*see* pp. 359 f.). Actually, sado-masochistic conflicts are often found as the unconscious basis of dermatoses.

It has been suggested that outbreaks of psoriasis in particular may represent sadistic impulses turned against one's own ego (381, 1240). However, it does not seem probable that psoriasis has the nature of a conversion symptom. Psychogenic forces may be rather one determining factor among others, and it may be that certain sadistic strivings, if not discharged, influence the skin via chemical and nervous alterations.

3. The skin as the surface of the organism is the part that is externally visible; this makes it a site for the expression of conflicts around exhibitionism. These conflicts in their turn concern not only a sexual component instinct and opposing fear or shame but also various narcissistic needs for reassurance. Hence the same unconscious conflicts found in phobias around beauty and ugliness (*see* p. 201), in cases of perverse exhibitionism (*see* pp. 345 ff.), or in cases of social fear and stage fright (*see* pp. 518 ff.), may also be found as the basis of dermatoses.

4. Anxiety equivalents, too, may be localized as reactions of the skin. Anxiety is physiologically a sympathicotonic state, and sympathicotonic reactions of vessels in the skin may represent anxiety.

As to special affections of the skin, the torturing symptoms of pruritus probably are an organ-neurotic result of repressed sexuality in predisposed individuals (341). In men with pruritus ani and perinei, there seems to be a more specific connection with congestion due to undischarged anal-erotic (homosexual) trends (1351). It can sometimes be observed that the symptom becomes worse whenever latent homosexuality is mobilized. However, the impression persists that the pruritus has no specific "meaning" that could be retranslated into words. Probably the unconscious anal longings change the vascular responses of the whole region in such a way as to influence its chemistry. The corresponding comment can be made about pruritus vulvae in women who do not dare to masturbate and dam up their genital excitement.

Urticaria, as is well known, may have a varied etiology. It may be an allergic reaction without mental connotations. It may be an organ-neurotic "dermatosis." Saul and Bernstein are of the opinion that attacks of urticaria occur in states of an intense frustrated longing that cannot find any other discharge (1357; *see also* 1194). It may be that "emotional urticaria" is the expression of an allergic reaction to certain hormones mobilized by the emotion.

Perhaps further research will make it possible to subdivide the dermatoses into damming-up types and discharge types.

EYE

It has been mentioned that the mechanisms of organ-neurotic symptoms were first described by Freud in the example of eye symptoms (571; *see also* 823).

There has been some discussion in psychoanalytic literature about psychogenic myopia. In taking psychogenic myopia as a kind of conversion symptom, the question was asked: What does the patient gain by not being able to see distant objects or by hiding his face behind a pair of spectacles (720, 860)?

Put in this way, the question seems unwarranted. If there is a psychic factor in the genesis of myopia, it must be an organ-neurotic one. From the point of view of research, it is probably more useful to discover what somatic changes in the eye have resulted from its being used for libidinous purposes than to regard the incapacity to see at a distance as a symbol of castration.

Myopia is caused by an elongation of the axis of the eyeball. This elongation is attributed partly to the external muscles of the eye and partly to alterations in the lens and to general vegetative changes that alter the contour of the eyeball itself. It would seem, then, that an incapacity to see distant objects has no psychic significance but is the involuntary, mechanical sequel to sympathico-parasympathetic processes which affect either the external optic muscles or the sympathico-parasympathetic tonus within the eyeball. But what causes these processes? In any event the vegetative nervous system is, of course, dependent on the unconscious affective status of a person. Constant use of the eye for libidinous gratification of scoptophilic impulses may cause it actively to strain in the direction of objects in order psychically to incorporate them. It is conceivable that this may finally result in a stretching of the eyeball (430).

This, of course, is putting the problem very crudely. Exact knowledge of the mechanisms of such stretching would be necessary to explain why many persons with particularly strong scoptophilic impulses are not at all shortsighted. There is no difficulty about the converse fact, namely, that many shortsighted persons show no sign of a marked unconscious scoptophilic tendency. There is no reason to suppose that every case of myopia is psychogenically determined. While the stretching of the eyeball may sometimes be due to the attempt to incorporate objects at the bidding of scoptophilic impulses, in other cases the origin of the disability is undoubtedly purely somatic.

Patients with psychosomatic disorders of a more severe type and those who are chronically inclined to respond to any strain with physical symptoms usually show a rather clear-cut narcissistic orientation. This is a remarkable difference between them and conversion hysterics. Sometimes the organ neurosis gives the impression of being a protective defense against (and an equivalent of) a psychosis (1120, 1442). It can be assumed that the increase in cathexis of organ representatives, characteristic for all narcissistic states, facilitates the development of organ-neurotic symptoms.

PROBLEMS OF THE PSYCHOGENESIS OF ORGANIC DISEASES AND OF PATHONEUROSES

Not every organic symptom wherein analysis can demonstrate a correlation between it and mental connotations is necessarily of an organ-neurotic nature. Nothing happens in the organism without being drawn secondarily into the mental conflicts of the individual. The existence of such a connection alone does not prove anything about the genesis.

The coexistence in a patient of a tumor and of unconscious ideas of pregnancy or even the analytic proof of a coincidence of the development of a tumor and an intensification of the wish for pregnancy must not lead to unwarranted etiological conclusions. Even if the patient at a time preceding the diagnosis of the tumor dreams of being pregnant, though this would perhaps show that unconsciously he was aware of the tumor before he knew of it consciously, it does not indicate that the wish to be pregnant may have caused the development of the tumor.

A further complication in the relation between an organic symptom and mental conflicts is brought about by the fact that somatically determined conditions may secondarily change the psychic attitudes of the individual. The adaptation to pain or to changes of body functions is not always easy. The ways in which this adaptation is attempted, and whether or not it succeeds, depend, of course, on the total structure of the personality, its history, and its latent defense struggles. First of all, the somatic process in the organ requires much of the libido and the mental attention of the person; again, his other interests and object relationships are relatively impoverished, which explains why in general being sick makes a person narcissistic (585). Besides, the disease or physical change may unconsciously represent something to the patient which disturbs the existing equilibrium between repressed and repressing forces; a disease may, like a trauma, be taken as a castration or as an abandonment by fate, or at least as a threat of castration or abandonment; it may also be perceived as a masochistic temptation, or mobilize some other latent infantile longing and in this way provoke a neurosis.

The narcissistic withdrawal of the sick person as well as his unconscious misinterpretations of the disease in terms of instinctual conflicts are at the basis of the fact that neuroses sometimes develop as a consequence rather than as a cause of somatic diseases. Ferenczi called neuroses that are consequences of somatic diseases pathoneuroses (478).

Freud's statement that the sick person withdraws his libido from objects and becomes narcissistic (585) has been doubted because, according to Freud himself, this is what occurs in psychoses (574). Is it conceivable that the same process may be operative under such different conditions as the feelings of a mentally normal, physically sick person and a schizophrenic? The difference between the physically and the psychotically ill person is, to be sure, considerable. But there are also certain characteristic similarities, namely, the loss of externally directed interests and the increase in self-observation and self-interest. The physically ill individual has relegated a small part of his libido, and for a short time only, to the same fate as the psychotic individual has imposed on almost the sum total of his libido.

A confirmation of this point of view is to be found in the fact that pathoneuroses often show reactions that are psychotic in character. This led Meng to speak of pathopsychoses (1120). It is also true that individuals with a tendency toward narcissistic regression are predisposed to the development of pathoneuroses, and that pathoneuroses are most likely to develop as a result of an affliction of those organs that are most highly cathected narcissistically, such as the genital organs and the brain. Pathoneuroses also express the difficulties of the task of adapting oneself to the real (or imaginary) limitations set by a disease. Extreme cases try to deny or to overcompensate real consequences entirely; the majority of acute postoperative psychoses belong to this group (62, 1368, 1628). Ferenczi and Hollos have proved that much of the symptomatology of general paresis is not a direct consequence of the degenerative processes in the brain, but an indirect pathoneurotic reaction on the part of the patient to his becoming aware of the cerebral impairment (484; *see also* 1376). The aim of some psychoses after mutilating operations is very evidently a denial of the unpleasant reality; the clinical picture then is dominated by the struggle between the data of perception and the tendency to deny them.

In other organic brain diseases, too, the reaction of the mental personality to the disease—the struggle between attempts to adapt oneself to or even to make use of the organically determined symptoms and attempts to deny them—comprises part of the clinical picture (281, 723, 864, 1028, 1206, 1373, 1379, 1382,

1480, 1593). The conflicts are very illustrative, even contributing to the understanding of the adaptive functions of the normal ego during its development. Likewise Jelliffe's attempts to "psychoanalyze" encephalitic symptoms (861, 862, 865; *cf. also* 801) should be understood as a study of the ways in which the personality reacts to or makes use of the symptoms rather than as a belief in the "psychogenesis" of encephalitis.

Sometimes the acute narcissism provoked by an organic disease operates as a precipitating factor for the outbreak of an ordinary psychosis.

A special category of pathoneuroses, appearing mostly in combination with disturbances "due to changed chemistry," are the hormonal pathoneuroses.

A quantitative or qualitative change at the source of the instincts must necessarily also influence the intensity and nature of the instinctual conflicts and their mental outcome. The authors who have worked in this field stress especially the *interrelation* of hormonal and mental data, that is, the fact that neurotic symptoms or attitudes in hormonally sick persons also influence the hormonal state. A psychogenic identification with a member of the opposite sex, for instance, may change the hormonal equilibrium; but also certain changes of the hormonal equilibrium may facilitate this type of identification.

Therese Benedek analyzed patients with hyperthyroidism and was able to show that the somatically increased anxiety and restlessness stimulated mental reactions that differed in accordance with the different pre-morbid personality structure of the patients (98). The anxiety was regularly connected with aggressive strivings, sometimes expressed by an increased strictness of the superego, and was antagonistic to heterosexual libido (*cf.* 1061).

A case of eunuchoidism, psychoanalytically treated by Carmichael (244), showed a similar kind of interrelationship.

> The childhood history of this patient showed nothing that would have transgressed the realm of normality. The organic disturbance manifested itself at puberty, and mental difficulties started when the patient became aware of it. He unconsciously interpreted his disease as "castration." He developed into a "model boy," whose anal and compulsive character became more and more pronounced. His character showed many traits that represented attempts at a denial or overcompensation of his "inferiority." He even tried to deny the existence of any sexual feeling, and produced a complete amnesia for all his infantile sexual memories. Likewise, he denied and overcompensated his intense aggressive impulses which were based on his feeling of "being different."

Kasanin had the opportunity to study analytically two patients with tumors of hormonal glands (928).

> One patient had a tumor of the adrenal gland, the other a teratoma of the pineal body. Their mental pathological behavior seemed partly to be determined by an attempt to fight off or deny the somatic symptoms; partly, however, it seemed

that the anxiety and depression experienced by the patients were not genuine emotions but rather the physiological syndrome of the emotions without the accompanying mental experience of the specific feelings. This might have been due to defense; however, it might also have been due to the fact that the hormonal alterations produced only the peripheral physiological signs of affect and not the centrally determined full experience.

Daniels published a detailed report of a patient with *diabetes mellitus* (303, 304).

The patient was an intensely oral character with a mental structure of the addict type. Changes in the insulin requirements and in the urine sugar level were directly related to alterations of the emotional conflicts. The patient experienced much anxiety, which certainly was partly of a physiological origin, and developed various methods to ward off this anxiety by means of its sexualization.

According to Dunbar (343) inconsistency and indecisiveness are characteristic traits of diabetic personalities. Diabetics have an increased tendency toward homosexuality, or at least a bisexual or pregenital orientation. They show signs of social anxiety and of a weak ego. They show similarities to the compulsive character (*see* pp. 530 ff.) and even tendencies toward psychotic reactions of a cyclothymic as well as of a paranoid type. During the illness, frequently a progredient disintegration of the total personality can be observed; hence diabetes has been called the psychosomatic psychosis.

It seems that there are cases of "emotional glycosuria," due to the disturbed chemistry of the unsatisfied person. They have a good prognosis; their exact physiological pathways are not known.

Meng and Grote psychoanalytically investigated cases of pathological thinness (1121). They did not find anything very specific but were able to show that mental factors play a definite role in the ups and downs of the disease, that is, that they influenced the hormonal state.

Severe cases of anorexia show definite hormonal pathology; probably in some cases these alterations are primary ones. In others a primary disturbance of mental development, fixating the ego at the oral phase, may induce secondary hormonal changes (361, 1082, 1555). The mental significance of this fixation may vary; sometimes an anorexia represents an equivalent of a depression (*see* pp. 176 f.).

The same holds true for obesity. There are severe glandular disturbances (Fröhlich's disease, *status adiposogenitalis*) which influence the psychosexual development in the sense of retardation, oral fixation, and weakness of genitality. And there are other cases of "genuine obesity" that represent organ neuroses, starting with psychogenic developmental disturbances and resulting in hormonal abnormalities (209, 210, 211, 1327).

The opposite of a pathoneurosis would be a "patho-cure" of a neurosis that disappears with the outbreak of an organic disease. This happens in moral masochists whose neuroses represent first of all a suffering by which they pacify their superego. Neuroses of this type become superfluous when replaced by another kind of suffering (*see* p. 550).

Whenever a connection between an organic symptom and a mental conflict is encountered the first question must be: has the conflict produced the symptom or the symptom the conflict? No doubt there is sometimes a vicious circle, symptom and conflict perpetuating each other (182, 242, 317, 343, 858, 1137, 1233, 1414, 1442, 1511, 1573).

HYPOCHONDRIASIS

Hypochondriasis is an organ neurosis whose physiological factor is still unknown. It may be assumed that certain psychogenic factors, namely, a state of being dammed up and a narcissistic withdrawal, or rather a readiness to react to a state of being dammed up with narcissistic withdrawal, create organic changes which then in turn give rise to hypochondriacal sensations.

Theoretically, two situations have to be distinguished, though actually they are closely interwoven: (1) Organic processes due to the lack of adequate discharge heighten the tension in certain organs; this heightening makes itself felt as painful sensations. (2) A withdrawal of object cathexes changes the mental economics so that amounts of libido that were normally connected with the ideas of objects now intensify all ideas concerning one's own organs (585, 1374).

The term object cathexis means that the sum total of the ideas and feelings a person has in regard to another person constitutes an "intrapsychic object representation" (408), and that this representation is cathected with a special amount of mental energy. In an analogous way, an individual's own body and its organs are represented intrapsychically by means of a sum of memories of sensations and their interrelations. The "body image" (1372) thus created has great significance for the constitution of the ego. It is not simply identical with the real body. Clothes, amputated members, or even one's automobile may be included in the body image, whereas "alienated" organs are excluded from it. Hence there are also "intrapsychic organ representations." "Narcissistic withdrawal" means a transfer of libido from object representations to organ representations.

> That clothes unconsciously may be treated as parts of the body was demonstrated by a patient whose obsessive worries about his clothes turned out to be, descriptively as well as structurally and genetically, a "clothes hypochondriasis."

The chemical and nervous reactions to the state of being dammed up may sometimes precipitate an intrapsychic overcathexis of the organ representations. In other cases the processes may occur in the opposite order: a regression to narcissism may change secondarily the physical functions of the organs. This is the case in the hypochondriacal sensations at the beginning of schizophrenic processes.

The relation between cathexes of organ representations and physical processes in the organs manifests itself also in the previously discussed narcissism of sick persons. Apparently, in order to bring about the healing of a diseased organ and to raise the organ's resistance to the illness, an increase in the cathexis of the organ representation is needed, or is at least beneficial. Thus the "body libido" has a general vital function. There is not only a morbid *plus* of organ cathexes in hypochondriasis; a morbid *minus* is conceivable as well. It can be assumed that self-sustenance depends upon the infusion of a certain amount of cathexis to the organ representations. Tausk spoke of a "libidinal tonus" of all organs (1531). In hypochondriasis as well as in psychoses, the results of a pathological libidinal hypertonus of the organs are manifested. In persons who are afraid of their body sensations and ward them off, there may also be a pathological libidinal hypotonus of the organs.

> Not every alienation of an organ and not every removal of parts of the body or of sensations from the conscious body image can be interpreted as a pathological diminution of the cathexis of the organ representation. The organs or sensations may be really repressed, that is, invested with cathexis, and yet at the same time counteracted and prevented from becoming manifest by an equally intense countercathexis (410).

Hypochondriasis rarely appears as an isolated neurosis (1488). It appears more frequently as a factor complicating the picture of some other psychopathological condition. It is often combined with acute anxiety neurosis or neurasthenia. To a slight degree it is a complicating factor in some compulsion neuroses. To a higher degree it is an important complication in all psychoses, especially in their initial stages. Hypochondriasis may be brought about by a primary hypercathexis of the organ representations (in psychoses), or by primary unknown organic manifestations of the state of being dammed up (in actual neuroses).

Among the impulses that are withdrawn from object to organ representations in hypochondriasis, the hostile and sadistic impulses appear to play a particularly pronounced role. The orginal hostile attitude toward an object is turned against the ego, and hypochondriasis may serve as a gratification of guilt feelings.

Hypochondriacal sensations ("hypochondriacal delusions") should be differentiated from hypochondriacal anxiety, although frequently these two conditions are encountered together. In cases in which anxiety prevails, there seems to be rather an isolated hypercathexis of the organ representations, and in cases where sensations prevail, actual organic alterations.

It sometimes happens that psychoanalysis uncovers in a surprisingly clear and definite way the unconscious significance of a given hypochondriacal anxiety. As a rule it represents, in a distorted manner, castration anxiety.

As an example, the continuation of the analysis of the wolf-man by Ruth Mack Brunswick should be quoted. The wolf-man's outspoken hypochondriacal delusions bore definite earmarks of castration anxiety (1088).

Not infrequently psychoanalysis can also clarify the infantile history of the displacement of castration anxiety to hypochondriasis. Certain experiences may have transformed castration anxiety into fears of becoming ill or physically altered. The results are often clear-cut "sickness phobias." In such cases, as a rule, the mechanism of introjection has acquired outstanding importance. When hostile impulses become turned away from an object onto one's own organs, this process unconsciously is perceived as an introjection, usually an oral one, occasionally an anal, epidermal, or respiratory one. Hence the hypochondriacally affected organ represents not only the endangered penis but simultaneously the object which, along with its ambivalent cathexis, was introjected from the external world into one's own body.

The hypochondriasis of one patient had on the higher levels the significance of castration as a punishment; on a deeper level it meant a passive sexual gratification (pregnancy); on a still deeper level the organ affected was equated with the introjected object. The patient's nose, which played the chief role in his illness, stood not only for the endangered penis and the nostrils for a kind of anal feminine sex organ; the nose also stood for his dead mother, whom he had incorporated via the respiratory system (420).

Simmel has stressed especially the unconscious equation of the hypochondriacally affected organ and the introjected object. He writes: "The introjected parental substitute becomes the morbid material which must be eliminated if the patient is to recover," and further states that an organ may represent this morbid material (1436, 1438).

Painful sensations and the fear of physical illness also appear in conversion and anxiety hysteria respectively, and there are cases in which it is practically a matter of choice whether they should be considered hysterical or hypochondriacal. As a rule, however, it is not difficult to differentiate the hypochondriacal from the hysterical individual on the basis of personality traits that are due to differences in their libidinal situation. The typical hypochondriac is a conspicuously narcissistic, seclusive, monomaniacal creature (1380). Hypochrondriasis is thus a transitional state between reactions of a hysterical character and those of a delusional, clearly psychotic one.

A patient with a severe vasomotor neurosis suffered from attacks of pseudo angina pectoris. The attacks appeared for the first time when the patient, soon after the death of his mother, learned that his father, too, had become seriously ill. The patient, an infantile-narcissistic individual who was fixated to his parents and had hitherto been unable to live without them, thus found himself suddenly confronted with the danger of having to face life alone. The pseudo angina had for him, first of all, the obvious meaning of an identification with his father, who was ill with heart disease. The patient lost interest in his parents as well as in other objects and devoted himself to his attacks and his fear of dying. He was afraid that his heart would abandon him, just as in reality he faced the danger of being deserted by his father. Although he obviously surrendered himself in a passive, rather masochistic manner to his illness, he also constantly cursed his own heart, thus showing that he had transferred the ambivalence he once felt toward his father onto his heart. In particular the patient's dreams showed that his attitude toward his illness and his infantile attitude toward his father coincided. The validity of the unconscious equation *heart = introjected father* does not necessarily mean that an "introjection of the father into the heart" created the attacks. The attacks were organ neurotic in nature; that is, they were brought about by certain vasomotor responses of the patient which in turn were due to his repressed emotions.

Mention should be made here that not only may hypochondriasis in adult persons be an outcome of castration anxiety in childhood but sometimes, also, analysis reveals that some patients with a severe castration anxiety, who were frightened as little boys, then went through a period of a more or less severe hypochondriasis about their penis which later became limited to a simple fear.

PSYCHOANALYTIC THERAPY IN ORGAN NEUROSES

The great variety of phenomena designated organ neurotic makes impossible any general statement about their psychoanalytic treatment. There are states that have become "organic" to such an extent that immediate physical treatment is necessary. But whenever the symptoms are the outcome of chronic unconscious attitudes, psychoanalysis is indicated for the purpose of making this attitude conscious and thus overcoming it.

Freud stated that the organ-neurotic symptoms are not "directly accessible" to psychoanalysis. Indirectly they are. If the anxiety or other obstacles hindering the adequate discharge of a person's impulses are removed by analysis, the indirect symptoms disappear without having been made a specific object of psychoanalysis. The change of the function cannot be "analyzed" because it has no unconscious meaning; however, the attitude that produced it can be analyzed, and if the attitude is given up or the state of being dammed up is overcome, the involuntary consequences likewise disappear (41, 1350, 1592).

It is clear that the attitude or the blocking of discharge and not the symptom itself is the object of analysis. A trial analysis will first have to estimate the relative etiological importance of the unconscious factors and establish a dynamic diagnosis. A hysteria with the symptomatology limited to one single organ is, of course, not more difficult to analyze than any other hysteria; but the closer an organ neurosis is to a psychosis, the more doubtful is the prognosis.

As to the treatment of pathoneuroses, a number of them, as should be expected from the nature of the disturbance, run an acute course and recover spontaneously, when the basic somatic disease disappears. If the disease served as a precipitating factor of a genuine neurosis or psychosis, the treatment depends on the nature of the neurosis or psychosis provoked.

Regarding hypochondriasis, again the rule is valid: the more hysteriform the picture (hypochondriasis simply representing castration anxiety), the better the prognosis; the more narcissism predominates, the more doubtful and uncertain. In regard to the ability to develop transference, severe hypochondriacal neuroses differ but little from psychoses.

The ease or difficulty of eliminating the disturbances of an individual libido economy depends on the extent to which the individual has become psychologically ready for the establishment of genital primacy; a person who has failed completely or almost completely to reach the level of infantile genitality, upon which a therapy subsequently has to rely, is badly off (1267). The decision whether or not to apply psychoanalytic therapy to such cases depends upon the capacity for the development of a transference and the status of the infantile genitality. These factors can be ascertained by trial analysis only. Yet one may say that in doubtful cases the indications are nevertheless in favor of psychoanalysis: many individuals of this type cannot be helped by any other therapeutic method, and psychoanalysis offers at least some hope.

APPENDIX: EPILEPSY

Much has been written about the "psychosomatic" relationship in epilepsy This uncanny complex of symptoms is certainly prearranged organically; nevertheless the appearance of the syndrome sometimes seems to be dependent on mental factors, and in some cases even to be aroused by mental factors. How would psychoanalysis classify such a disease (3, 90, 267, 269, 271, 272, 276, 280, 339, 623, 714a, 765, 857, 863, 997, 1030, 1092, 1123, 1276, 1478, et al.)?

The epileptic seizure is best compared to a spell of affect. A traumatic stimulus, or a normal stimulus occurring when the organism is dammed up, precipitates a prearranged discharge syndrome, which breaks through the normal ego dominance over motility. This definition is equally valid for an affect attack and an epileptic seizure. The epileptic seizure can be looked upon as a kind of special affect attack, which occurs only in certain organically predisposed personalities. The predisposition consists in the patient's readiness to react to certain stimuli, or to the pressure of certain dammed-up states, with the production of this archaic syndrome of explosive convulsive discharge.

It is this predisposition that is caught in the characteristic changes of the electroencephalogram.

The stimuli that provoke the archaic reaction are of various kinds. Attacks of the "symptomatic" (Jackson) type occur as reflexive responses to purely physical stimuli; an organic injury of the brain results in higher levels of brain organization being inhibited and an archaic type of reaction being again produced. In genuine epilepsy, probably a more subtle brain defect of a still unknown type has the same effect; but the nature of the provoking stimuli and of the antecedent tension may become more specific. In some cases it becomes clear that specific mental impulses, instead of being reacted to on a higher level, provoke the seizure in a short circuit, as it were. Such a disease cannot be called an "organ neurosis of the brain" in the sense that a psychogenic attitude might have changed the reaction patterns of the central apparatus; however, it can be called so in the sense that the pressure of the repressed toward motility precipitates an archaic physiological syndrome, given a certain somatic disposition. It is, says Freud, "as if the mechanism of the abnormal impulsive discharge were organically prepared in advance, to be called upon in quite different conditions, both during disturbances of the cerebral activity due to serious histolytic and toxic affections, and also in case of inadequate control of the psychic energy" (623).

Clinical experience indicates that epileptic personalities are (a) generally very narcissistically oriented, showing the described features of an archaic ego and always ready to substitute identifications for object relationships, and (b) show very intense destructive and sadistic drives which have been repressed for a long time and which find an explosive discharge in the seizure. The repression of the destructive drives is due to an intense fear of retaliation, which often is very conspicuous in the clinical picture. As is well known, the aura is that part of the epileptic seizure that varies the most. It can therefore be expected that the aura, which precedes the more uniform "archaic discharge syndrome," will reveal more about the specific nature of the precipitating mental stimuli. This expectation is fulfilled. Hendrick, by psychoanalyzing the contents of the aurae of several cases, found that before the seizure a tendency toward the development of anxiety had been mobilized; then the incipient anxiety spell had been blocked, and the epileptic seizure occurred as a kind of substitute for the anxiety that was not experienced. "Discharge through the central nervous system replaced the discharge of autonomic tensions" (765). Experiences that provoke the spell turn out, in analysis, to be either allusions to repressed drives that were once experienced with anxiety or projective representations of the sensations of anxiety itself. The blocked anxiety probably is always a fear of the possibility that an intense and dammed-up destructiveness may be turned against one's own ego. The ability to supplant anxiety by the specific central convulsive phenomena would represent a purely physiological problem.

Bartemeier drew attention to the fact that in neurotic and normal persons, certain archaic explosive discharges occur which may be looked upon as normal prototypes of epileptic seizures, such as twitchings while falling asleep, grinding of the teeth and clenching of the jaw during sleep, unintentional biting of the tongue, and certain momentary disturbances of attention (90). All these phenomena are facilitated in states of fatigue and ego regression and in situations of latent rage.

Epileptic phenomena, outside the realm of seizure and aura, have not been investigated psychoanalytically as yet. However, a general speculative remark may be permitted about the final deterioration of certain cases. If the assumption is correct that the mental apparatus fulfills the functions of elaborating and finally discharging incoming stimuli, it is conceivable that a decisive change in the methods of discharge, through the establishment of a simple explosive and undifferentiated method, may result in a simplification and undifferentiation of the total mental apparatus.

There is a gradual transition between genuine epilepsy and conversion hysterias, in which epileptiform seizures express a definite idea and show all the characteristics of hysterical motor symptoms (hystero-epilepsy) (368, 647, 714a, 770, 1259, 1335, 1611).

Chapter XIV

OBSESSION AND COMPULSION

THE PHENOMENON OF COMPULSION

IN ALL psychoneuroses the control of the ego has become relatively insufficient. In conversion symptoms, the ego is simply overthrown; actions occur that are not intended by the ego. In compulsions and obsessions, the fact that the ego governs motility is not changed, but the ego does not feel free in using this governing power. It has to use it according to a strange command of a more powerful agency, contradicting its judgment. It is compelled to do or to think, or to omit certain things; otherwise it feels menaced by terrible threats.

Derivatives of warded-off impulses betray their nature as derivatives by their exaggerated character, that is, by the disproportion of the accompanying emotions or by the rigidity with which they are adhered to. *Obsessional* ideas are, first of all, derivatives. Sometimes they have preserved their character as impulses; sometimes they have lost it, and consist only of intense ideas that have to be thought about; their persistence represents the energy of some other associatively connected impulsive idea that had been warded off.

Sometimes the transition of a phobia into an obsession can be observed directly. First, certain situations are avoided; then constant attention is exerted to ensure the necessary avoidance. Still later, this attention assumes an obsessive character, or another positive obsessive attitude is developed, so irreconcilable with the situation originally feared that the avoidance is assured. Touching rituals replace taboos; washing compulsions, fears of dirt; social rituals, social fears; sleeping ceremonials, fears of falling asleep; rituals about the manner of walking, inhibitions of walking; compulsive ways of dealing with animals or cripples, the corresponding phobias.

> Some phobic ideas gain an obsessive character by their mere intensity, for example, ideas of being ugly or of having a bad odor. They are obsessive ideas as long as the patient feels: "I am compelled to feel as if this or that were the case"; they are delusions if the patient is convinced of their basis in fact.

In other cases an obsession does not provide the avoidance of what was originally feared but compels the person to do just that which he originally was afraid of. Obsessions of this type are not caused by a need for maintaining a phobia but rather by a fight of the original impulse or of the personality against the phobia.

> Such obsessions are but one category of counterphobic attitudes (435) (*see* pp. 480 ff.). An example is presented by a patient who had an obsessive interest in sailing and water sports which was an outcome of an infantile fear of flushing the

toilet. Fear of high places may be supplanted by the obsessive impulse to jump down.

Compulsions are obsessions that are still felt as impulses; they, too, are derivatives; their intensity, too, expresses the intensity of warded-off drives.

There are cases in which the distortion of the original instinctive impulse consists only in the fact that the "instinctive" urge has been changed into a "compulsive" urge. Obsessive thoughts about incestuous or murderous acts are not uncommon. They appear stripped of their character as instinctual wishes and of their appropriate emotional equality. Patients who try to express the fact that the horrible ideas are not felt as wishes often say that compulsive ideas of this kind "leave them cold." Actually, since compulsions are tormenting, they do not leave them cold at all (618). The defensive forces did not succeed in making the patients unaware of what is going on within them; they did succeed, however, in transforming the original drive into a compulsive form; the nature of this transformation is the problem of the mechanism of symptom formation in compulsion neurosis.

> A patient who suffered from the fear that he might give the impression of being a homosexual had the following obsessive thought whenever he became acquainted with a man whom he had not met before: "With this man I could have homosexual intercourse." He did not feel any sexual excitement or impulse, and was entirely unaware of the fact that the obsessive idea expressed a wish.

Other obsessions and compulsions do not seem to express a distorted instinctual urge but, as has been mentioned, an assurance of the defending forces. Compulsion can be described as a command from within. The idea of "being commanded" certainly is rooted in the child's experiences with grownups who used to "command" him, especially, in our culture, in experiences with the father. In compulsions this father commands from within; and an "inner father representative" is called superego. Thus in the formation of compulsive symptoms the superego plays a part different from that in conversion.

Now, it seems, we have arrived at contradictory statements. First it was stated that the phenomenon of compulsion is a distortion of the phenomenon of instinctual urges; now it seems as if it were a derivative of commands once given by the father to suppress instinctual demands.

INSTINCT AND DEFENSE IN COMPULSION SYMPTOMS

Actually, the phenomenon of compulsion is a condensation of both instinctual and anti-instinctual forces. The manifest clinical picture reveals the first aspect more in some cases, in others the second. The first holds true for obsessive incestuous or murderous ideas. More frequently the symptoms obviously express distorted commands of the superego; the defensive or penitential significance is emphasized much more than in conversion symptoms. The danger from which the person tries to protect himself is less in the nature of external loss of love or castration; it is rather a threat from within. What is mainly feared is a kind of loss of self-respect or even a feeling of "annihilation"; in other words, guilt feelings have a more decisive significance as the motive for the pathogenic defense. This is consonant with the fact that compulsion neuroses in children start later than hysterias, usually in the latency period.

In certain cases it is obvious that compulsions stand for superego commands. A patient with a washing compulsion, feeling the command "Go and wash yourself," simply repeats what he once heard as a child. It is of no importance that actually the parents gave this command for the sake of physical cleanliness, whereas the compulsion neurotic uses it as a defense against "dirty thoughts"; for as a child the patient felt that if the parents knew about his dirty thoughts, they would tell him to wash.

The same holds true of compulsions that are not felt as positive commands but rather as threats. The patient has obsessive ideas about what would happen if he yielded to the temptation. For example: "If you do this or omit that, you will die"; or: "If you do this or omit that, you will have to do this or that penance"; or: "If you do this or omit that, your father will die." In analysis, it turns out that the actions that have to be counteracted or avoided have an objectionable instinctual significance; as a rule they represent the tendencies of the Oedipus complex, distorted, it is true, in a very characteristic way. The threatening punishments mean either the danger that once was believed to be connected with the forbidden instinct (castration or loss of love) or some active self-punishment that should ward off (and substitute for) castration or loss of love. The threat "Or your father will die," which does not fit this interpretation, can be explained as a sudden awareness of the "anxiety signal." It means: "What you are intending to do is not a harmless thing; the truth is that you want to kill your father; if you give in to the temptation at hand, the murder of your father might be the outcome."

Whereas some compulsive symptoms are distorted modes of perceiving instinctual demands and others express the anti-instinctual threats of the superego, still other symptoms obviously show the struggle between the two. Most of the symptoms of obsessive doubt can be covered by the formula: "May I be naughty, or must I be good?" Sometimes a symptom consists of two phases, one representing an objectionable impulse, the other the defense against it. Freud's "rat-man," for instance, felt compelled to remove a stone from the road because it might hurt somebody, and then felt compelled to put it back again (567). In discussing the mechanisms of "undoing," occurrences of this kind were mentioned (*see* pp. 153 ff.).

Sometimes it can be observed how, in the course of a compulsion neurosis, a symptom may change its significance. A symptom that first expressed the defense may become more and more an expression of the returning original impulse.

A patient was able to dispel an anxiety which appeared after masturbation by tightening the muscles of his legs. This tension was later replaced by a rhythmic pounding on the legs, and still later by another masturbatory act. Another patient felt remorseful after taking gymnastic exercises. Analysis showed that the exercises represented masturbation. Then this remorse, with which he had come to terms in an obsessional manner, finally made him think: "Now masturbate, and ruin yourself completely!" and he was compelled to masturbate several times in succession without any pleasure.

Patients who have to reassure themselves that they have turned off the gas jet are often compelled to touch the jet again, so that the act which was intended to ward off the danger actually might precipitate it. A patient again and again had to rearrange the objects on top of a bookcase to keep them from falling on someone's head, thus giving them a real chance to fall. To protect their dear ones from their hostile impulses, many compulsion neurotics guard them against imaginary dangers so devotedly that in reality they torment them, expressing the hostility in spite of themselves.

The climax of a "returning of the warded off" is represented by a woman patient observed by Waterman. She suffered from so extreme a phobia against dirt that she remained in bed all day when she had the feeling that her clothing or the room in general was dirty. Her fear of dirt, on these days, would prevent her from leaving her bed at all, with the result that eventually she arrived at the point where she actually did soil the bed.

Thoughts like "Now you have ruined yourself by exercise, thus it serves you right if you ruin yourself entirely by masturbation" indicate how to explain the paradox that an instinctual content may be experienced as if it were a superego command. Symptoms of this kind represent a compromise between the warded-off drive and the threatening superego; the drive expresses itself by the ideational content, the superego by the commanding form into which the original impulse has been distorted. Pleasureless compulsive masturbation represents the peak of this kind of condensation. An apparent sexual act is performed not for the sake of sexual pleasure but for the purpose of punishment and the suppression of sexuality. This is frequently the end result of a long development; a compulsion, which was a defense against masturbation, is replaced, through a return of the repressed, by another masturbation which now has a compulsive and punitive character. The "Midas" punishment through spiteful pseudo wish fulfillment (see p. 221) is characteristic for many compulsion neurotics. Occasionally, compulsion neurotics will put an end to a state of doubt and hairsplitting by masturbating.

A similar development is frequent in regard to "masturbatory equivalents."

Compulsions such as knocking or ceremonial muscular movements, or rituals prescribing the mode in which things must or must not be touched, were first directed against masturbation, but may have turned into equivalents of masturbation. Sometimes the patient, in some vague way, is aware of this connection, and has in turn to punish himself for his "naughty" compulsive behavior. At other times, the patient has no inkling of the meaning of his symptom (357, 467, 733).

Compulsive rituals generally represent a caricature of masturbation (503). Sometimes a symptom which apparently has no connection with masturbation reveals such a connection when analyzed. A patient was forced to count up to five or six whenever she turned on a faucet or even passed a faucet. She was completely dominated by penis envy, so it could be expected that a symptom related to a water faucet would have some connection with her penis envy. Actually, she remembered that once, when her finger was infected, her mother had frightened her by telling her that the finger would have to be cut off. Thus the ritual was to be interpreted as follows. The sight of the faucet (of a penis) forced the patient to convince herself that she had not four but five or even six fingers. Later in analysis, it turned out that the ritual had a closer connection with masturbation; she used to masturbate by holding her finger in front of her genitals and letting the urine flow along it as if the finger were a penis.

The Oedipus complex often can be seen as the center of the warded-off impulses, sometimes even on cursory examination, which, in hysteria, repression would render entirely impossible.

A patient, unfortunately not analyzed, complained of two types of obsessive impulses. Whenever he saw a woman he was compelled to think: "I could kill that woman"; and whenever he saw knives or scissors he would think: "I might cut off my penis." The first of these two impulses originally had been expressed in the form "I could kill my mother"; its extension to other women was already a distortion by means of generalization. The patient lived a lonely life, and his only sexual outlet consisted in wet dreams in which he saw himself strangling women or killing them by some other method. Thus his impulse to murder women was a distorted expression of his incestuous desire. Eliminating this distortion, it can be stated that the patient suffered from two impulses: to attack his mother sexually and to chop off his penis. Now his impulses can be understood as a biphasic symptom: the first half represents the gratification of the Oedipus wish, the second half the punishment the patient dreaded. .

Unintelligible symptoms become intelligible when their history is studied. The original form in which they first appeared is closer to the unconscious meaning. A symptom may be an allusion to some event in the patient's past; this allusion cannot be understood so long as the whole context is not known.

Before going to bed, a patient was compelled to spend a long time repeatedly opening and closing the window. That symptom first appeared when, as an adolescent, he and his roommate would fight as to whether the window should be opened or closed. Thus the later compulsion meant: "Which of us will win? Which of us is the stronger?" With this formula as a starting point, it eventually became clear that the patient's problem was mobilized by the homosexual temptation involved in sharing the same room with his friend. The real question was whether he should compete with men as a man or resign himself to complying with their wishes in a passive, submissive, feminine way. This proved to be the conflict in which his compulsion neurosis was rooted.

REGRESSION IN COMPULSION NEUROSIS

The example given above of the open expression of the Oedipus wishes, in which the patient felt the two impulses of killing women and cutting off his penis, is typical of the manner in which incestuous wishes are distorted in compulsion neuroses. The patient talks about "killing" his mother, when he actually means having sexual intercourse with her. The patient's sexual dreams were evidently sadistic in nature. Thus not only was an infantile attachment to the mother operative, but specifically a sadistic distortion of this attachment.

Overt or concealed tendencies toward cruelty, or reaction formations against them, are constant findings in compulsion neuroses. With equal constancy anal-erotic impulses and defenses against them are found in the most varied forms. This constant association of traits of cruelty and of anal eroticism in compulsion neuroses, to which Jones first drew attention (879), was what convinced Freud of the close relationship of these two types of phenomena, and of the existence of an "anal-sadistic" stage of libido organization (581).

In hysteria, the repressed ideas remain unaltered in the unconscious and continue to exert their influence from there. In so far as the Oedipus complex is the basis of compulsive symptoms, too, this also holds true for compulsion neurosis; but here, in addition to the Oedipus complex, very strong anal and sadistic impulses, which originated in the preceding period, regularly are operative and combated. The anal-sadistic instinctual orientation of the compulsion neurotic can, as a rule, be easily recognized in the clinical picture, once attention has been directed to this point. Compulsion neurotics are generally and obviously concerned about conflicts between aggressiveness and submissiveness, cruelty and gentleness, dirtiness and cleanliness, disorder and order. These conflicts may be expressed in the external appearance and the manifest behavior, whereas questions concerning sexual life are characteristically answered: "So far as that goes, everything is in order." The physiological functions seem to be in order because they are isolated from their psychological content; the physiological discharge in the patients' sexual activities is not an adequate discharge for the sexual tension which is really expressed in their ideas about cruelty or dirt. Sometimes the anal-sadistic orientation reveals itself in the form of reaction formations only, like overcompensatory kindness, an exaggerated sense of justice or cleanliness, an incapacity for any aggression, punctiliousness in all matters relating to money. Mixtures of reaction formations and direct anal or sadistic outbreaks may make the patient's behavior appear contradictory. The patients are simultaneously orderly yet disorderly, neat yet dirty, kind yet cruel.

A patient, who was not analyzed, complained in the first interview that he suffered from the compulsion to look backward constantly, from fear that he might have overlooked something important behind him. These ideas were predominant: he might overlook a coin lying on the ground; he might have injured an insect by stepping on it; or an insect might have fallen on its back and need his help. The patient was also afraid of touching anything, and whenever he had touched an object he had to convince himself that he had not destroyed it. He had no vocation because the severe compulsions disturbed all his working activity; however, he had one passion: housecleaning. He liked to visit his neighbors and clean their houses, just for fun. Another symptom was described by the patient as his "clothes consciousness"; he was constantly preoccupied with the question whether or not his suit fitted. He, too, stated that sexuality did not play an important part in his life. He had sexual intercourse two or three times a year only, and exclusively with girls in whom he had no personal interest. Later on, he mentioned another symptom. As a child, he had felt his mother to be disgusting and had been terribly afraid of touching her. There was no real reason whatsoever for such a disgust, for the mother had been a nice and popular person.

This clinical picture shows that the patient's sex life was oriented anal-sadistically, and that incestuous fear was the basis for this distortion.

In analysis, the anal-sadistic orientation of compulsion neurotics becomes, of course, still much clearer. All compulsion neurotics, Freud stated, have "secret scatologic rituals" (555) which are partly anal-erotic games, partly reaction formations against such games, and partly both at once. W. C. Menninger has collated the most typical and frequent types of scatologic rituals (1143). The patients are always on guard against unconscious anal tendencies mixed with hostilities—for instance, against a drive to play "dirty tricks" on their fellow men.

Thus Freud stated that the instinctual organization of the compulsion neurotic resembled that of the child in the anal-sadistic phase of development. This seems to contradict the typical observation that the compulsion neurotics are engaged in a defensive struggle against the Oedipus complex, the climax of which is not supposed to be reached before the phallic period. Another apparent contradiction lies in the fact that in spite of the anal sadism, many compulsions are closely related to genital masturbation.

The explanation of these apparent contradictions is to be found in the concept of *regression*. One gets the impression that the anal-sadistic impulses grew at the expense of the original phallic Oedipus impulses; the genital Oedipus impulses decreased in strength as the anal-sadistic impulses increased. The patient, in attempting to ward off his Oedipus complex, regressed, in part, to the anal-sadistic level (567, 581, 596, 618).

However, the compulsion neurotic is no coprophiliac. Since his anal-sadistic impulses, too, are intolerable, or because in regressing to them the offensive element of the Oedipus complex was not entirely eliminated, the patient has to continue his defensive fight against the anal-sadistic impulses. The interpolation of regression complicates the picture of compulsion neurosis as compared with hysteria.

Freud's theory that regression to the anal-sadistic level forms the cornerstone in the construction of compulsion neurosis can explain many facts that otherwise would be contradictory.

That the warded-off impulses in compulsion neurosis are composed of phallic Oedipus tendencies and genital masturbatory impulses on the one hand and nevertheless are anal-sadistic in nature on the other is now comprehensible. The defense was first directed against the phallic Oedipus complex and supplanted it with anal sadism; then the defense continued against the anal impulses.

Occasionally analysis can show the actual process of regression and can prove that the compulsion neurosis came into being after it.

A girl suffered from the obsessive fear that a snake might emerge from the toilet and crawl into her anus. In analysis it turned out that this fear had had a forerunner: the first anxiety had been that the snake might be in her bed. To protect her from the phallic anxiety, a regression had taken place; the location of the fear was changed from the bed to the toilet, from genitals to anus.

A boy, still in the period of latency, was seized by an overpowering anxiety whenever he had an erection. He stated that he was afraid that he might injure his penis. He developed the habit of masturbating whenever he had an erection in order to get rid of it. This, however, created new anxieties. Later on, he developed the urge to urinate and to defecate very frequently. After this, he developed an extensive compulsion neurosis. It is evident that the genital impulses at first incessantly asserted themselves in spite of the menacing fear of castration, that they were then replaced by pregenital strivings, and that only after the regression to anal eroticism did the compulsion neurosis make its appearance.

A more indirect but almost experimental proof for the anal-sadistic regression in the etiology of compulsion neurosis is furnished by the rare cases in which a hysteria after a relinquishment of genitality is replaced by a compulsion neurosis. Freud observed this process in a woman who, owing to external circumstances, ceased to place any value on her genital sexual life (581). Something similar frequently can be observed after the climacterium, when organic factors have provoked a regression.

The operation of regression can also be proven by cases in which it fails in its defensive purpose. Though shifting his interest to the anal field, the patient, in such cases, does not succeed in avoiding castration fear. Instead he develops what might be called an anal castration fear. An otherwise compulsive patient may become incapable of defecating except in small or unformed masses, thus trying to avoid the danger of "losing an organ." The material treated by Freud under the heading of the symbolic equation *feces = penis* (563, 593) owes its origin in part to this regression.

Some of the typical fears relating to the toilet in children and in compulsion neurotics, such as fear of falling into the toilet bowl or of being eaten up by some monster coming from it or the rationalized fear of being infected there, prove in analysis to refer to castration anxiety. They are regressive distortions of the fear of castration. A child whose various fears could be traced back to a terror of seeing that his feces had disappeared expressed the fear that his penis might disappear in the same manner.

As in oral fears, the fact that anal fears cover castration anxieties does not contradict the autonomous nature of pregenital fears. This distortion of castration anxiety is a *regressive* one, formed by the remobilization of the old pregenital anxiety over the loss of feces. It is often very difficult to determine which fraction of an anal anxiety represents a vestige of original pregenital anxiety, perhaps contributing a certain quality to the castration fear right from the beginning (the pregenital experiences of parting with the breast and with the fecal masses are archaic forerunners of the idea of castration) (36, 1466), and which fraction is regressively distorted castration anxiety.

It is an ever recurrent source of surprise to find that, after analysis has uncovered a whole anal-sadistic world dating back to very early years of childhood, completely repressed memories appear of a still earlier period, purely phallic in orientation, which had been shattered by castration anxiety. It is important not to be misled into thinking that newly appearing memories with reference to anal-sadistic impulses are memories from the time of the original anal-sadistic organization. Very often they are not original but regressive in nature; they came after the phallic Oedipus complex; and the original pregenital organization must be dated still earlier.

Clinical material in which ideas and modes of behavior appropriate to the genital level are found intermingled with anal-sadistic material is abundant. Certain compulsion neurotics, for example, perceive sexuality in anal terms only, as if it were a bathroom affair; others regard sex as a financial matter—which may be expressed, for example, by prostitution fantasies—or as a matter of property. A man may lay much stress on retaining his semen in intercourse as long as possible, sometimes with the idea of increasing the forepleasure, sometimes with the idea of "preserving" the semen, sometimes rationalized as consideration of the woman's feelings; analysis shows that he does with his semen what he previously had done with his feces. In still other cases, the sadistic distortion of the entire sexual life is more in the foreground than the anal one. For certain compulsion neurotics sexual intercourse unconsciously means a fight in which a victor castrates a victim. Men patients of this kind may have no other interest in sex than to get the reassuring proof that they are not the victim (it seems that they never can achieve a full reassurance); women patients may develop longings to look at male genitals or to touch them, in which concealed expressions of destructive wishes are manifested.

The immediate effect of regression is twofold: the enhanced sadism combines with the Oedipus hostility felt for the parent of the same sex and imposes new defensive tasks on the ego; and the emergent anal eroticism changes the sexual aims and, in this way, the behavior of the person. Anal eroticism, it has been stated, is always bisexual in nature, the anus being simultaneously an active expelling organ and a hollow organ which may be stimulated by some object entering it (see p. 67). Vacillation between the original masculine attitude, now reinforced and exaggerated by the active-sadistic component of anal eroticism, and the feminine attitude represented by the passive component of anal eroticism (163) forms the most typical conflict in the unconscious of the male compulsion neurotic. The phallic Oedipus attitude is inhibited by the idea that gratification means the loss of the penis. The regression imposes a feminine attitude, yet does not entirely destroy the original masculine one.

The simultaneous emphasis on the opposite ideals of independence and submission in modern education increases the conflict between active-masculine and passive-feminine strivings in compulsion neurotics. This conflict may assume various forms. Superficial activity may be stressed as a reaction formation against deeper passivity and vice versa. In many ways an actual passivity may become rationalized as an activity. A normal compromise of this kind is the identification love of the boy for his father; by being temporarily feminine toward him he gets a promise of future participation in his masculinity. This "psychology of the pupil," passive toward the master for the purpose of later becoming master himself, is open to several pathological distortions (see p. 89).

The aim of the feminine wishes of male compulsion neurotics is not, of course, to be castrated; it is rather the wish for something to be inserted or retained in the body. The idea that this wish, too, is not a reliable protection against castration, that castration may even be a prerequisite for its gratification, causes the most intense anxiety, which in turn furnishes the motive for further defense. This was the state of affairs in the wolf-man, who repressed his inverted Oedipus complex because of castration anxiety. His fear of being eaten by the wolf expressed both his feminine wishes toward his father and his castration anxiety connected with them (599).

In this way, all sexual gratification may become so cemented with fearful ideas of castration that finally the one becomes inconceivable without the other. Often the patient behaves as if he unconsciously sought castration, but what he actually is searching for is something that will bring an end to the anxiety that prohibits his pleasure. The "castration" actually sought is either a castration symbol only, a lesser evil which the patient is ready to suffer in order to avoid full castration, or it is an active anticipation of what he otherwise would have to endure passively. Frequently, after the patient has carried out some activity that symbolizes castration, he goes through a ritual that stands for its "undoing."

Like bisexuality, ambivalence is a characteristic of increased anal eroticism. A marked ambivalence of the object relationships is typical of the pregenital stages of libidinal development; it reappears when the genital organization is given up again. In so far as an anal fixation is a precondition of the anal regression, the two qualities associated with it, bisexuality and ambivalence, can be looked upon as a precondition of the regression. But in so far as the regression intensifies and makes persistent the anal-sadistic orientation, bisexuality and ambivalence, being attributes of this orientation, are results of the regression.

In conversion hysteria with intestinal symptoms, the anal regression is limited to the choice of the afflicted organ that is used for expressing genital fantasies. This is different in compulsion neurosis. Here a full regression to the world of anal-erotic wishes and attitudes takes place and changes the total behavior. Frequently even the olfactory orientation characteristic of anal-erotic children and lost in normal adults comes back in compulsion neurotics (202). Often the regression also brings more or less narcissistic features to the fore, the increased bisexuality giving opportunity for fantasies about intercourse with oneself. There are transitional states between compulsion neuroses and manic-depressive psychoses or schizophrenias.

DIGRESSION ABOUT THE ANAL CHARACTER

Freud discovered that certain character traits are preponderant in persons whose instinctual life is anally oriented (563). These traits are partly reaction formations against anal-erotic activities and partly sublimations of them. The main traits of this kind are orderliness, frugality, and obstinacy. Actually, persons falling ill with compulsion neurosis regularly show an intensification of these trends. Therefore it is necessary to discuss them at this point.

The training for cleanliness in infancy is of great importance for the development of the relation between the child's ego and his instinctual drives. This training is the first situation in which the child may or may not learn to postpone or renounce a direct instinctual gratification out of consideration for the environment. On this occasion, the child acquires the active mastery of decisive instinctual demands; but simultaneously the hitherto "omnipotent" adult becomes dependent, to a certain degree, on the will of the child (*see* pp. 67 and 487 f.).

The anal character traits formed in the conflicts around this training have in part qualities of resistance offered by the instinct to the demands of the environment, in part qualities of obedience to them, and in large part form compromises between these two trends (21, 194, 883, 1143).

Frugality is a continuation of the anal habit of retention, sometimes motivated more by the fear of losing, sometimes more by erogenous pleasure. Orderliness and obstinacy are more complicated. Orderliness is an elaboration of the obedience to, obstinacy of the rebellion against the environmental requirements covering the regulation of excretory functions. Under certain (constitutional and environmental) circumstances, obstinacy may become so extreme that the person in question is compelled always to do the exact opposite of what is required of him.

> A compulsion neurotic patient used to sleep during the day and remain awake all night because "he could not see the point" of doing the customary thing. This obstinacy, however, was rather a kind of "rationalization" of a neurotic difficulty due to the dammed-up state of this patient's libido.

The word obstinacy (*ob-stinare*) itself expresses the idea "to hold one's position in spite of somebody." Originally, stubbornness meant only resistance, to pit one's will against somebody else's; later, it meant pitting one's own will against superior inimical forces; still later (because the inimical forces are superior), getting one's way indirectly, not through force but through guile, in a mode wherein the weak one may be unexpectedly strong. Stubbornness is a passive type of aggressiveness, developed where activity is impossible. This occurs for the first time in a child's life when he is able to spite the grownups' efforts by tightening his sphincters. Still later, the "power of the powerless" may be not of a real but only of a magical nature; and then a kind of "moral" superiority may replace the "magical" superiority. The entrance of the moral factor into the picture shows that the superego plays a decisive part in the later development of stubbornness. The same means a child applies to resist the superior forces of his educators he may apply later in his fight against his own superego. What is usually called stubbornness in the behavior of adult persons is an attempt to use other persons as instruments in the struggle with the superego. By provoking people to be unjust, they strive for a feeling of moral superiority which is needed to increase their self-esteem as a counterbalance against the pressure of the superego (1202).

The moral superiority may be experienced either through the feeling of being unfairly treated itself or through making the "unfair" adult sorry afterward, which should enforce affection from him.

In other words, stubbornness, initially the combative method of the weak, later becomes the habitual combative method in the struggle for the maintenance or the restoration of self-esteem. Stubborn persons are filled with narcissistic needs, whose gratification is required to contradict some anxiety or guilt feeling. Hence it must be concluded that stubbornness has an oral basis, too. However, it is decisively anchored in the anal stage and developed through experiences gained during the period of training for cleanliness. Persons who are afraid of being trapped, misused, and cheated of their narcissistic supplies are understandably more inclined to become stubborn. Frequently a tendency to keep open a line of escape determines stubborn behavior (444).

The objection has been raised that stubbornness may be acquired in social conflicts between the child and his environment during the training for cleanliness but that this does not necessarily mean that obstinacy is anal in nature (921, 1022). This argument does not take into account the findings of psychoanalysis, which show that the counterforces against the instincts are built up by the energies of the instinctual forces themselves which, under the influence of the environment, have changed their direction. The psychoanalysis of stubborn persons provides abundant proof that stubbornness is connected with anal sensations and gives an anal-erogenous pleasure (17, 21, 555, 563, 567, 593, 878, 1202, 1634).

The character trait of orderliness represents the elaboration of obedience. Tidiness, punctuality, meticulosity, propriety, all signify a displacement of the compliance with the environmental requirements in regard to defecation. In compulsion neurotics, the anal character traits, representing obedience, reveal themselves as reaction formations. The basic opposite mode of behavior breaks through or permeates them only too readily. It is the paragon of punctuality who in many instances is surprisingly unpunctual, the cleanest person who is in some curious respect astonishingly dirty. Abraham reported a number of such points of anchorage in the character of a perpetual struggle with the counter-cathexis: for example, persons who are scrupulously neat in regard to their top clothing and as much untidy in regard to their underclothes; others who keep their belongings in a very disorderly fashion but who from time to time must clear everything up, a practice that corresponds to the autoerotic habit of retaining feces for a long while and then "settling everything at once" (21).

Certain anal traits of character represent a diversion of the instinct by the ego, either to a new aim or to a new object. If this succeeds it may be called a sublimation. In compulsion neurotics it does not succeed, and the "displaced" activities become the scene of the same defensive struggle around frugality, stubbornness, and orderliness as were the original anal impulses. There are displacements of interest from the product, and others from the process of defecation.

Concerning the first ones, Freud has shown that the substitutes have a very complex relationship to the original (593). The connections of the concept of feces with the more genital ideas of penis and child are of less importance for the psychology of compulsion neurotics than are those with the ideas of gift, money, and time.

To understand the relation between feces and money, operative in every compulsion neurotic, it is first necessary to have an understanding of the psychological significance of the concept of possession (21). The child learns to differentiate between ego and nonego, but this is a long and complicated process. In its course, the child passes the stage that Freud has called the purified pleasure ego (588): everything that gives pleasure is perceived as ego, everything that brings pain as nonego. The original basis of this classification is the idea: "Everything that is pleasurable I should like to put into my mouth and swallow; everything that is painful I should like to spit out" (616). But there are pleasurable things that cannot be taken into the mouth. Those things are, sooner or later, called "mine," and that means: "I should like to take them into my mouth, but I cannot do so; I declare them as 'symbolically-put-into-my-mouth.'" When the child realizes that he loses his feces, which represent to him a very precious substance, a part of his own body, he feels: "This is something that ought to be in my body; but it is outside now, and I cannot put it back." Again, he calls it "mine," which means: "I should like to have it inside my body, but that is impossible; so I declare it 'symbolically-put-into-my-body.'" Thus "possession" means "things that do not actually belong to the ego, but that ought to; things that are actually outside but symbolically inside." Though they are in the external world, they are cathected with "ego quality." Possessions, as a rule, are provided with attributes for the purpose of identifying them: "The blue one belongs to me." This, however, is not easily done with feces, which look the same in all human beings. Later on, the child learns that "money" exists, something which grownups esteem as a possession but which is not "blue" but always looks alike, no matter in whose possession. What money and feces have in common is the fact that they are deindividualized possessions; and deindividualized means necessarily losable. Thus money, in the same way as was feces previously, is estimated and watched over as a possession which is in constant danger of losing its ego quality. Both substances, in spite of their high evaluation, are regarded with contempt because of their deindividualized, monotonous, unspecific nature. Actually analerotic persons who love money, love money that is *not* deindividualized; they love gold and shining coins or new bills, money that has still a "blue," individualized character. Ferenczi, in studying the paths of displacement that lead from feces to money, showed that shining things and stones are liked earlier than uncolored sand, and eventually money is accepted as a substitute (466). When this path of "sublimation" is disturbed because the old instinctual wishes referring to feces still determine the attitude toward money, the attitudes toward money become irrational. Money then becomes an object for pleasure (or for punishment), that is, a substitute for feces rather than an objectively useful thing. It may be irrationally retained or irrationally thrown away (15) or these two contrasting behaviors may be combined in various ways (480).

Anal personalities are as disturbed in their attitude toward time as they are in their attitude toward money: in respect to time, too, they may be stingy or prodigal or both alternately; they may be punctual or unpunctual; they may sometimes be accurate to the fraction of a minute, and at other times grossly unreliable.

> Abraham's statement that "patients often save time in small amounts and squander it in large ones" (21) was clearly exemplified in a case observed by Garma. The patient was a man who had no occupation but spent his time in neurotic activities and hour-long daydreams. Whenever he wished to leave home, he would open a window to watch for the suburban train to the city. When he heard the train, he would call his maid, who would then open the door, holding his coat in readiness for him. The patient would seize the coat, rush down the steps to the station across the way, and catch the train just as it was pulling out. The whole procedure was a simple repetition of his childhood habit of waiting till the last moment before going to the bathroom.

In compulsion neuroses the regression has turned the patient's relation to time, like his relation to money, into an arena wherein his instinctual conflicts are fought out. Sometimes one may follow a false lead in looking for object-libidinal conflicts in irrational, compulsive behavior toward time. To a large extent this behavior may represent a form of autoeroticism. Some compulsion neurotics are tardy not because they want to irritate the person who is expecting them but because the suspension of activity gives them the same autoerotic tension and pleasure which, as children, they enjoyed while retaining their feces.

The reconstruction of the genetic relation between time and feces is not as easy as that between money and feces. Harnik has collated a good deal of anthropological data which show that the awareness of the flow of time, especially the ability to measure time, unconsciously is deeply rooted in anal eroticism (738). How often defecation has to take place, at what intervals it has to be done, how long the process itself should take, how long it may be successfully postponed, and so on, are the situations in which the child acquires the ideas of order and disorder regarding time, and of measurement of time in general.

> These remarks are not intended to mean that the concept of time is gained in anal-erotic experiences exclusively. A much more basic role in this respect is played by kinesthetic sensations which convey internal biological rhythms within the body (breathing, pulse) (172, 1455). Anal experiences are of more importance for the measurement of time and for the development of schedules as a means of mastering reality (738, 1193). Neurotic disturbances in the subjective experience of the course of time actually occur more often in cases with unconscious conflicts around the eroticism of depth sensibility and equilibrium, whereas

neurotic disturbances in the practical use of time and time systems as protections against unforeseen events are more characteristic for typical compulsion neuroses with unconscious anal-sadistic conflicts (338, 1385).

The childhood attitude toward feces is often found transplanted into the later attitude toward the individual's personal achievements. A person may have a self-satisfied admiration for what he has done, or he may be discontented with all his achievements, or he may vacillate undecidedly between these two extremes, according to the outcome of his anal-instinctual conflicts.

A patient's tendency toward ruthless self-criticism was traced back to her third year of life, when she was afflicted by an intestinal illness that made her incontinent after she had already been trained in toilet habits. From this time on, she was convinced that she could produce nothing properly. Another patient, an author, dreamed of the galley proofs of her book being squeezed out of a small opening.

The anal retention, which always contains the two components, fear of loss and enjoyment of a new erogenous pleasure, may also be displaced to another object. Cupidity and collecting mania, as well as prodigality, have their correlating determinants in the infantile attitude toward feces.

As sublimations concerning the product of defecation may fail if anal eroticism is retained, sublimations concerning the function may fail, too. If reaction formations are at work instead of sublimations, painting, for instance, may have retained the unconscious meaning of anal smearing, which leads either to the failure of the person as an artist or, if the ego, recognizing the forbidden impulse, enters a protest, to an inhibition of the ability to paint. The displacement of cathexes from defecation to speech and to thinking activities is sometimes betrayed by irrational modes of retaining or expelling words or thoughts; it can be seen in inhibitions of these functions as well as in their irrational hypercathexis.

In addition, the behavior of anal personalities is pervaded by manifestations of the sadism that is always simultaneously present or of reaction formations against sadism. The fact that the child in retention finds narcissistic satisfaction in his ability to control the sphincters also forms a point of departure for sublimations or reaction formations. A strong desire for power may be derived from the sense of power that accompanies the control of the sphincters. The power desired may be obtained through self-control or through the control of other persons, and the longing for this power in general is determined by the fear of losing self-esteem.

Many other conflicts, once connected with anal eroticism, may be reactivated in compulsion neurotics. The renunciation of pleasure in consideration of objects, whether through love or fear of them, is the main achievement of the training for cleanliness. The individual learns to give, whereas during the oral period his interest was mainly in receiving. Disturbances during this period, therefore, occasion subsequent disturbances in relation to objects, so that no equilibrium can be reached between giving and taking.

Abraham's classic description (21) also attributed a number of less fundamental traits to conflicts around anal eroticism: the tendency, for example, to look at everything "from the rear" (which is the basis of many compulsive symptoms); the fear of "starting" which causes the beginning of all new activities to be postponed as long as possible, although once started, an interruption is difficult; the tendency to have others do everything for one, if enemas figured in the history of infantile anality, and the tendency to decide everything for oneself, if demands for anal regularity had been met with protest in childhood; the tendency to do many things all at the same time for the purpose of "saving time," which depends on autoerotic games played while defecating, often continued as a compulsion to read while sitting on the toilet, which means to regain material while other material is lost.

This description of anal character traits extends beyond the field of compulsion neurosis, and we shall have to come back to it when discussing character anomalies (*see* pp. 487 f.). However, these traits are characteristic for the typical compulsion neurotic. No compulsion neurotic can handle money and time rationally, though the difficulties manifested may vary greatly in nature and intensity.

COMPULSIVE SYSTEMS

"Orderliness," which has been used as a protective measure against dangerous instinctual demands in the original anal-erotic period, regains this protective function in a subsequent compulsion neurosis. The compulsion neurotic who is threatened by a rebellion of his (regressively distorted) sensual and hostile demands feels protected as long as he behaves in an "orderly" manner, especially concerning money and time. The unconscious anal-sadistic drives, however, usually sabotage orderliness and clinging to a "system." They reappear in the form of disorder or events that disturb the system, or they may permeate even the orderly syndrome itself.

Lucille Dooley, in an interesting paper, collated material concerning orderliness and systems in regard to time, clung to by compulsion neurotics for whom any disturbance of "routine" unconsciously means murder and incest (338). Many compulsion neurotics have an exaggerated interest in all kinds of timetables. They may even regulate their entire life according to systematized timetables. As long as the timetable functions as the regulator of their activities, they are sure that they are not committing the sins they are unconsciously afraid of; and as long as they know beforehand what they will do afterward, they are able to overcome their fear that their own excitement may induce them to do things they are afraid of.

"Orientation in time" is a typical reassuring measure. Many a fear of death means a fear of a state where the usual conceptions of time are invalid. States in which the orientation in time becomes more difficult—dusk or long evenings in winter or even long days in summer—are feared by many compulsion neurotics. However, fears of this kind may also be rooted simply in the fact that frightening events in childhood took place at that time of day that is feared later on (599).

Compulsion as such is used as a similar protection; it ensures against the menace of dangerous spontaneity. Everything that is done in a compulsive way is done as routine, according to a prearranged plan, from which the objectionable impulses are supposed to be excluded. As long as the rules are followed, nothing can go wrong. However, the compulsion neurotic is aware that he has instincts nevertheless. He never can achieve the satisfying feeling that he is actually following the rules, that enough rules are provided to govern all possibilities, and that he knows all the rules sufficiently.

Things become more complicated when other persons are needed as "witnesses" as to the validity of the compulsive demands of orderliness and system. The patient does not only feel compelled to keep systematic order himself but also requires others to accept the same system. The others as a rule refuse to submit to his system. This increases his hostility and makes him try various means to compel those around him to do as he wishes; he becomes afraid of the hostility expressed in these attempts and this fear in turn increases his systematic needs, starting a vicious circle. Things become still more complicated if the systems of different compulsion neurotics clash in such a way. And since compulsion neurosis is based on increased anal eroticism, which again is partly determined by constitution, several cases of compulsion neurosis occur frequently in the same family. Severe family troubles may be created in this way.

There is a compulsion neurotic counterpart to hysterical pseudologia (437). Some patients find certain gross falsifications of facts compatible with their obsessive conscientiousness and exactness, and even with an obsessive fanaticism for truth. Consonant with the compulsive tendency toward "displacement onto a little detail," the falsifications frequently concern unimportant details only. The actual small modifications of truth represent more important intended ones; and these more important modifications serve the purpose of forcing the world into a definite system. The facts are supposed to be not as they are but rather as the obsessive system demands them to be. The falsification expresses also the tendency to press the same system upon others: "You are not supposed to see things with your own eyes but in the way I am showing them to you." A violence of this kind, used against his fellow men, may satisfy the compulsion neurotic's sadism and anal obstinacy. The main aim of such behavior, however, is a more specific one. Freud once compared the spontaneous memories of early childhood with the creation of myths in which historical facts are falsified according to wishes (596). In compulsive attempts to force "witnesses" to accept obsessive systems, the creation of such myths frequently can be observed directly.

The patients' adherence to their systems does not at all mean that they are able to maintain them. Once more, what has been warded off enters into the methods of warding off. More and more the patients may feel that the systems into which they would like to force the world have been violated. They may react with attempts to increase the rigidity of the systems; but they are never assured that the demands of the system are entirely fulfilled. Usually these demands ask for an isolation of things that represent unconscious trends originally belonging together. The patients, therefore, often see a strict "either-or" cleavage where actually an "as-well-as" relation is in effect.

> A compulsion neurotic who played chess occupied himself for hours with the obsessive problem whether to use more "strategy" or more "tactics"; he thought of this only in the abstract, not in any way in a concrete situation in a concrete game. His either-or idea made him actually lose every game. The doubt was based on the unconscious doubt as to whether he should defeat his opponent or let his opponent defeat him, which meant whether he should assume a masculine or a feminine attitude.

Related is the phenomenon which Graber has designated "neurotic typing" (710). Compulsion neurotics have the tendency to make false generalizations, to classify hastily all ideas into certain mutually exclusive categories, and then to get into a state of doubt concerning the nature and evaluation of the categories. "I know already in which category a given phenomenon belongs" generally means "I do not need to be afraid of it as of a possible temptation or punishment." The more surprising an event, the more dangerous it is. The "typing" tries to exclude the possibility of surprises and to falsify new events into "already known" things.

> To order the unknown according to known categories is the task of science. Compulsive systematizing, performed not for the purpose of mastering reality but rather in order to deny certain aspects of it, falsifying reality, is a caricature of science (618).

The compulsion neurotic is ambivalent. He is so even toward his own systems and rules. When he takes side against his dangerous instinctual impulses, he needs systems and rules as protection. When he turns against his superego, he also turns against systems and rules imposed by the superego. He may openly rebel against them or he may ridicule them by tracing them ad absurdum (567).

OTHER DEFENSE MECHANISMS IN COMPULSION NEUROSIS

The alteration of character, typical of compulsion neurosis, is not always directly due to regression. It is also caused by the use of other defense mechanisms after the regression, namely, of reaction formation, isolation, and undoing. The use of these mechanisms, it is true, also depends on the pathognomonic regression, because reaction formation, isolation, and undoing are applied much more against pregenital strivings, while repression proper is related more to genitality.

Reaction formations become deeply imbedded into every compulsion neurotic's personality. In fighting unconscious hostilities, the compulsion neurotic tends to be a gentle person in all his relationships and in a general way. This may bring great narcissistic satisfaction, which creates an unfortunate difficulty for psychoanalytic treatment.

However, even the fixed reaction formations are rarely successful; the mind of the compulsive patient remains occupied with a perpetual struggle between reaction formation and the still-effective original impulse.

As for isolation and undoing, their appearance in compulsive symptoms was described previously (see pp. 153–159).

A few more examples of typical isolation may be added. A patient with obsessive doubts found it very difficult to comply with the analytic procedure, protesting strongly against the basic rule of free association. It turned out that he did so because he attempted to keep secret the existence of a certain girl friend—not because he did not wish to speak of this matter at all, nor yet because he did not wish to expose the particular person, but because in his analysis he had spoken of masturbation, and he wished to keep her image isolated from everything that had to do with masturbation. He felt that he would be able to speak about her if he were only sure that he would not think of masturbation during the same session. Later in analysis it became clear how unsuccessful this isolation was; a compulsive symptom which the patient regarded most anxiously and took the most pains to conceal was that whenever he saw the girl in question or heard her name, he obsessively had to think "Little whore." This symptom stood for the incestuous instinctual demand, against which the ego was defending itself. It offers an example of an unsuccessful attempt to isolate tenderness from sensuality.

It was interesting to observe how the patient, who had a certain tendency toward paranoid reactions, combined in his defense against instinct the mechanisms of isolation and projection. Once, in order to demonstrate the absurdity of psychoanalysis, he stated that free association was nonsense because people had only those ideas they wanted to have. He was told that this was not true, for he had the idea "little whore" without wanting to have it. A few days later he threw up to the analyst the analyst's sensuality and vulgarity in calling his friend a little whore and in misusing his confessions to accuse him of low behavior (411).

Sometimes compulsive patients effect a remarkable isolation by means of marriage. They resolve that their connubial life should have no connection with their infantile sexuality. "Now I am married; thus I do not need to worry about sexuality any more." Marriages on this basis cannot be happy. The patients erect severe compulsions and obsessions at points where infantile sexual strivings might enter the marriage despite the isolation.

It has been mentioned that the most important special case of isolation consists in the isolation of ideational content from its emotional cathexis. Typical compulsion neurotics appear to be cold, abstract, and emotionless; actually their emotions may be finding expression in some incongruous way.

An example of how "isolated" such expressions may be is represented by a patient who made a note that he should not "forget that he was angry."

The difficulty compulsion neurotics have in associating freely in analysis is due to their isolating propensities. They cannot associate freely because they are always on guard to prevent those things that originally belonged together from again making contact. They cannot let themselves be surprised either by feelings or by perceptions that have not as yet been put into categories. Thinking in compulsive categories represents a caricature of logical thinking: logical thinking, too, is based on a kind of isolation. But the logical isolation serves the purpose of objectivity, the compulsive isolation that of defense (618).

Isolation, it has been mentioned, is related to the ancient taboo of touching (618) (see p. 159). Numerous compulsive symptoms regulate the modes in which objects should be or must not be touched. The objects represent genitals or dirt. "Clean" things must not communicate with "dirty" ones (989). An application of the taboo of touching to the magical fear of changing a present situation and starting a new one (see p. 284) is presented in the frequent threshold rituals (30, 390).

Isolation frequently separates constituents of a whole from one another, where the noncompulsive person would only be aware of the whole and not of the constituents. Compulsion neurotics, therefore, frequently experience sums instead of unities, and many compulsive character traits are best designated as "inhibition in the experiencing of gestalten."

"Repetition" as a form of "undoing" has been mentioned (see pp. 153 f.). The idea is that for the purpose of undoing, an activity has to be repeated with a different intention. What once was done with an instinctual intention must be repeated with a superego attitude. The warded-off instinct, however, tends to enter the repetition also; thus the repetition has to be repeated. Usually, the number of necessary repetitions quickly increases. "Favorite numbers," the choice of which may have their separate unconscious meaning, are set up and determine the number of necessary repetitions; eventually, the repetitions may be replaced by counting.

The favorite numbers as a rule are even ones. Only even numbers give the guarantee that neither instincts nor superego will overbalance. Most "symmetry" compulsions have the same meaning (479).

It would be wrong, however, to believe that all compulsive counting is motivated in this way. Counting may have various other meanings. Frequently it represents a counting of seconds, that is, a measuring of time. The need for measuring time may have various determinants. Sometimes it is simply a means of making an isolation certain. It may be forbidden to start some activity immediately after another one, and the counting is to ensure the necessary time interval. The basic connections between time measuring and anal eroticism have been mentioned. The time measuring, being originally a measurement of the interval between two occasions of being placed on the toilet, may then be used as a defense against the temptation toward anal masturbation, and may eventually become a substitute for anal masturbation (737).

Compulsive counting can also be a defense against wishes to kill, for counting things is a reassurance that none of them is missing. But the defense may be invaded by the impulse, and counting unconsciously comes to stand for killing; then it, too, must be warded off (88). This is facilitated by the circumstance that counting in itself has the meaning of taking possession, of mastering; "counting" may mean "counting one's possessions."

A very simple example of the mechanism of undoing is the frequent washing compulsion. Washing becomes necessary as a means of undoing a preceding "dirtying" action (real or imaginary) (703, 989).

This dirtying action is, as a rule, masturbation or, later, the idea of a remote possibility of masturbation (503). The anal regression is responsible for the dirt conception of sexuality (485). Anal masturbation in childhood was actually betrayed by soiled or odorous hands, and this possibility of betrayal could be avoided by washing. Occasionally, patients with a compulsion neurosis can make all their scruples disappear by bathing or changing their clothes, "bad feelings" being conceived of as dirt that can be washed away. Ritual bathing as a means of washing away sins is also a manifestation of undoing. It is probably for this reason that neurotic ceremonials during the latency period so frequently are related to washing. Obstinate children, who refuse to wash, are really refusing to give up their pleasurable instinctual impulses. It is true, however, that rituals around undressing and going to bed are also prevalent for another reason: these occasions present a temptation to masturbate.

Many typical compulsive symptoms strive at undoing aggressive actions, usually imaginary. This intention is sometimes manifest, as in the compulsive closing of gas jets or the taking away of stones from the street; sometimes the intention is revealed in analysis only, as in the various symptoms with the unconscious meaning of penance. There is no sharp borderline between penance symptoms and creative sublimations performed as counteractions against infantile sadistic strivings (1422, 1424).

The use of regression, reaction formation, isolation, and undoing makes superfluous the employment of the defense mechanism of repression proper. This answers the question as to how it is possible, in compulsion neuroses, for offensive impulses to come to consciousness. The conscious impulse to kill, for example, is, through isolation, so far removed from any possible motor expression that there is no chance for the impulse to be materialized, and thus it may safely become conscious. Hence when the idea becomes conscious, it is "stripped of emotion"

(1054). The result of the disruption of the original connection is that a spontaneous consciousness of the pathogenic childhood events cannot be directly used by the analyst. Since the corresponding emotions are lacking, the analyst knows as little as the patient which of the childhood memories are important and in what their importance consists; even were he aware of it, he could not tell the patient before having overcome his resistance against seeing the true connection.

The lack of repression proper in compulsion neurosis, however, is but a relative one. The compulsions and obsessions themselves may undergo a secondary repressive process. Sometimes the patients are not able to tell what their compulsions consist of; the compulsions have a colorless, vague, dreamlike quality, and it takes a good deal of analytic work to remove the repressions sufficiently for the text of the compulsions to become legible.

Sometimes compulsive symptoms are secondarily repressed because the patient feels that his compulsions do not fit into his system; that is, they represent not only defensive forces but also the warded-off instinct intruding again. Trying to fit his compulsions into his system, he falsifies and obscures their original content. His own compulsions, like the whole world, have to be adapted to the system which is his only guarantee of security.

The displacement in compulsion neurosis often is a "displacement onto a small detail." Many compulsion neurotics have to worry very much about small and apparently insignificant things. In analysis, these small things turn out to be substitutes for important ones. The best known example is the "thinking compulsion" (Gruebelzwang) in which the patient is compelled to spend hours brooding about very abstract matters. This symptom is based on an attempt to avoid objectionable emotions by escaping from the world of emotions into that of intellectual concepts and words. This escape fails; intellectual problems, to which the patient tries to flee from his emotions, acquire, by the return of the repressed, the highest emotional value.

THE DOUBLE FRONT OF THE EGO IN COMPULSION NEUROSIS

Not only are the specific defensive mechanisms characteristic of compulsion neurosis but so also is the direction in which they are used. The relative preponderance of the ego's dependency on the superego in this neurosis makes it comprehensible that the ego is obliged not only to obey the superego in warding off instinctual demands but also to try to rebel against it. It may use the same defensive measures against the superego that it usually employs against the id impulses. This activity, too, needs a continuous expenditure of energy. It has been mentioned that the compulsive idea, "If you do this or that, your father will die," is an awareness of the superego's warning, "If you do this or that, you may be tempted to murder your father." The ego may react to such a threat with a counterthreat. When the rat-man had his first sexual experience, he had the obsessive idea, "This is glorious! One might murder one's father for this!" (567). Actually the ego behaves toward the superego as it did previously toward its educators: obediently, rebelliously, or obediently and rebelliously simultaneously. The ambivalence of the ego toward the superego is the basis of the frequent preponderance of religious symptoms in compulsion neurosis (560).

The ambivalent conflict in regard to the superego can be best observed when it produces a biphasic behavior. The patient behaves alternately as though he were a naughty child and a strict punitive disciplinarian.

> For obsessive reasons a patient was not able to brush his teeth. After not brushing his teeth for a while, he would slap and scold himself. Another patient always carried a notebook, in which he would make check marks according to his conduct to indicate praise or blame.

In dreams, absurdity signifies a mocking and malicious intention of the dreamer (552). Similarly, the crass absurdity of many of the pseudo problems which are the subjects of obsessive thoughts indicates a malicious and mocking attitude on the part of the patients toward their superego, often, during analysis, represented by the analyst. Thus the patient's absurdities are a continuation of the child's ridicule of the father (567).

> A patient, in his first consultation, asked the analyst whether analysis would relieve him of his excessive masturbation. The analyst assured him that if the analysis were successful at all, it would help in this respect, too. Many months later the patient reported that at this moment he had thought: "I wonder how it will be possible for analysis to make me stop masturbating if I do not stop it myself"; and he made the resolution not to stop, just to see how the analyst could perform the task of making his masturbation stop without effort on his part.

The regression to anal sadism has not only modified the ego, whose sadism and ambivalence are then directed against the superego as well as against external objects; it also has modified the superego itself, so that it becomes more sadistic and presents automatic and archaic features, such as working according to the talion principle and obeying the rules of word magic. The sadism of the superego, resulting from the regression, increases the more the ego refrains from externally directed aggression. One might suppose that a person strict with himself and outwardly unaggressive may be refraining from aggression because of his strictness; actually the blocking of the aggression is primary and the strictness of the superego secondary; the sadism, no longer directed against objects, is turned inward as the superego's aggression against the ego (613).

The morality demanded by the archaic superego of the compulsion neurotic is an automatized pseudo morality, characterized by Alexander as the corruptibility of the superego (37). If the ego makes a concession to an instinctual urge, it must comply with demands for atonement; when it has atoned, it may use the act of atonement as a license to engage in other transgressions; the result is an alteration of "instinctual" and "punitive" acts. The need for a relative stability between the two attitudes may be expressed in magical symmetry compulsions.

Symmetry compulsions have very manifold forms. They all consist of avoiding "disturbances of equilibrium." Whatever happens to the right has to happen to the left; whatever is done upward has to be done downward; no counting may stop at an odd number, and so on. All this may have special significance in individual cases. It always has the general purpose of preventing the *mental* equilibrium from being disturbed by the warded-off impulses; any "instinctual" movement is "undone" by the symmetrical countermovement (479).

Schilder collated forms of compulsions around symmetry that are based on conflicts around equilibrium eroticism (1384, 1386) and forms that manifest themselves in abstract drawings (1395).

To understand the "corruptibility" of the superego, one should consider the economic relation that has been discussed by Rado as idealization (1237). By fulfilling the demands of the superego, the ego gains a narcissistic pleasure which may bring with it such an exhilaration that it temporarily suspends or weakens its function of objectively judging reality and impulses.

The ideas that any suffering entitles one to the privilege of a compensating pleasure and that a threatening superego may be placated and forced to renew its withdrawn protective powers by means of voluntary suffering are very archaic ones. The same ideas are expressed in the attitudes of sacrifice and prayer. In both practices, the sympathy of God is bought, and more intense punishments are avoided by means of the active and voluntary acceptance of an unpleasantness as "prophylactic punishment." The extremes of this attitude are those actions that can be called prophylactic autocastrations. Buying God's sympathy may turn into blackmail. In impulsive and depressive neurotics we find many variations of such blackmail. Ultimately the circle, deed—punishment—new deed, can be traced back to the circle, hunger—satiation—new hunger (*see* p. 411).

The vacillation between deed and punishment is frequently expressed in obsessive doubts, which really mean: "Shall I follow the demands of the id, or those of the superego?" Severe compulsion neuroses may terminate in states in which the conscious ego, having become a football for the contradictory impulses of the id and the superego, is eliminated completely as an effective agent (109, 1292).

In defending itself against the demands of the sadistic superego, the ego may use a countersadistic rebellion as well as submission (ingratiation), or both attitudes simultaneously or successively. Sometimes the ego seems willing to take upon itself punishments, acts of expiation, and even torture to an astonishing degree. This "moral masochism" appears to be a complement to the "sadism of the superego," and this submission may be performed in the hope of using it as a license for later instinctual freedom. The ego's "need for punishment" is, in general, subordinated to a "need for forgiveness," punishment being accepted as a necessary means for getting rid of the pressure of the superego. Such a need for punishment on the part of a compulsive ego, however, may become condensed with masochistic sexual wishes. Then, in the words of Freud, morality, which arose from the Oedipus complex, has regressed and has become Oedipus complex once again (613) (*see* p. 364).

In general, a need for punishment is but a symptom of a more general need for absolution; this is clearly seen in the attempt to avoid punishment by attaining absolution without it, through using external objects as "witnesses" in the fight against the superego (1288, 1289, 1599).

> A patient invented a method for dispensing with scruples and hypochondriacal fears. After having masturbated, he would go to a physician who would make a physical examination and assure him that he was in good condition. Analysis showed that the assurance of the physician represented the renunciation by a "castrator" of his right to castrate; the declaration of health represented the needed absolution. This absolution ended the patient's bad conscience and made any other means of doing so unnecessary; in particular, the patient no longer needed to punish himself.

A reliance on the assurances of others to maintain his self-esteem often determines a compulsive patient's social behavior. The patient feels relieved when he finds that other persons do not regard his guilt as gravely as he does himself. It is as if he told his superego: "It cannot be so bad after all, since so-and-so does not condemn me." By this process, the fear of the superego is changed back into a social fear. This reprojection of the superego is found to a greater extent among persons with paranoid trends; but the analysis of simple compulsion neurotics, too, frequently shows that their social anxiety is a fear that their attempt to ease a severe sense of guilt may fail. The feeling that they are nevertheless guilty may be turned into a chronic social fear. And naturally a person who unconsciously is very aggressive toward the external world has every reason to fear that the world will not like him (*see* p. 519).

Although the conflicts of the compulsion neurotic are more internalized than are those of a hysteric, compulsion neurotics try to use external objects for the solution or relief of their inner conflicts. Hysterics who are afraid of being castrated or of not being loved any longer may try to influence the people around them directly, in order to dissuade them from doing the things they fear. The compulsion neurotic, more fearful of losing the protection of his own superego, of being compelled to despise himself, needs other people as an indirect means of gaining relief. Whatever the objects do or say is looked upon as either forgiveness or accusation. Various attempts, real and magical, are made to influence the testimony of these "witnesses." Sometimes the patient tries to induce objects simply to give signs of sympathy. Sometimes the objects are expected to do what the patients themselves do not dare to do. Sometimes they are expected *not* to do what the patients themselves do not dare to do because this would create a too intense temptation.

According to Freud the unconscious basis of the concept of justice is the idea: "What I am not permitted to do, no one else should be permitted, either" (606). The urge for justice is rooted in the tendency to maintain a prohibition by insisting that everyone else be subject to it, too (40). There is a relationship between "justice" and "symmetry." Some longings for justice mean simply: "It is fair that what happened to the right must happen to the left." And sometimes the longing for symmetry means: "Symmetry is achieved if what happened to one child happens to the other brothers and sisters as well."

Freud stated that persons who have put the same object in the place of their superego identify themselves with one another (606). Following Redl (1258) we may add: so, too, are persons who use the same "witness" united by mutual identification.

In extreme cases, eventually the patient's behavior may become entirely ungenuine. Whatever he does, he does for the purpose of impressing a fantasied audience or rather a jury.

An ambivalent dependence on a sadistic superego and the necessity to get rid of an unbearable guilt tension at any cost are the most frequent causes of suicide. Thus the question arises: If it is true that these factors play so prominent a role in compulsion neurosis, why is suicide so rare among compulsive patients? Freud gave the following answer. In compulsion neurosis, in contrast to depression, the libido of the individual is not totally involved in the conflict between the ego and the superego; a large part of the patient's object relationships is preserved, and this circumstance protects him from ruin; it may even be that the regressive distortion of these remaining object relationships, that is, their sadistic nature, contributes to this favorable effect: because the compulsion neurotic succeeds in actually expressing so much aggression against objects, he does not need to turn so much aggression against himself (608).

Guilt feelings nevertheless cause compulsion neurotics to suffer a great deal. The patients enter an ever growing cycle: remorse, penitence, new transgressions, new remorse. The compulsion neurotic tends to develop more and more displacements, to extend the range of his symptoms (analogous to the "phobic façade") and to increase the instinctual significance of the symptoms at the expense of their punitive significance.

The prevalent need to use objects for finding relief in inner conflicts, overshadowing all direct feelings toward objects, is not the only factor that generally distorts the object relationships of compulsion neurotics. A second one is the simple fact that the anal-sadistic regression prohibits the development of mature object relationships. It produces an unreliable, ambivalent attitude toward objects, conflicts of bisexuality and retention of the aims of incorporation. A third circumstance that disturbs object relationships is the isolation of emotions so that the object relationships lack genuineness and warmth. The cathexes, which are attached to symptoms and autoerotic substitutes, are absent when the patients have to deal with objects (*see* pp. 242, 508, and 515).

THINKING IN COMPULSION NEUROSIS

The regression toward anal sadism and the continuous conflict with the superego influence the thinking processes of the compulsion neurotic in a characteristic way: they become permeated or replaced by their archaic forerunners.

In contrast to the visual daydreams of the hysteric, the fantasies of the compulsion neurotic are verbalized and bring back the archaic attitudes that accompanied the first use of words.

The ego's function of judgment by anticipation is immensely facilitated by the acquisition of *words*. The creation of this replica of the real world makes it possible to calculate and act out in advance in this "model world" before real action is taken (*see* pp. 46 ff.). Words and worded concepts are shadows of things, constructed for the purpose of bringing order through trial acting into the chaos of real things. The macrocosm of real things outside is reflected in the microcosm of thing representatives inside. The thing representatives have the characteristics of the things, but lack the character of "seriousness" which the things have; and they are "possessions"; that is, they are mastered by the ego; they are an attempt to endow the things with "ego quality" for the purpose of achieving mastery over them. He who knows a word for a thing, masters the thing. This is the core of the "magic of names," which plays such an important part in magic in general (916). It is represented in the old fairy tale of Rumpelstilzchen, in which the demon loses his power once his name is known.

> A patient knew several hundred names of birds; as a child he had been afraid of the stork, as the demon of birth and death. A child knew all railway stations by heart; his analysis showed that he had had a phobia concerning railways several years before. Another child had an extraordinary memory for persons' names; it was a way in which he mastered an original social anxiety.

The compulsion neurotic, being afraid of his emotions, is afraid of the things that arouse emotions. He flees from the macrocosm of things to the microcosm of words. Being afraid of the world, he tries to repeat the process by which, as an infant, he learned to master the frightening aspects of the world. This time, however, under the pressure of warded-off impulses, the attempt fails. When he tries to flee from the emotion-arousing things to the sober words, what has been warded off comes back and the sober words do not remain "sober" but become emotionally overcathected; they acquire that emotional value which things have for other persons.

The first words acquired in infancy are magical and "omnipotent" because the microcosm is not yet differentiated enough from the macrocosm but still has its emotional value (457). Blessing and cursing are expressions of the still effective macrocosmic quality of words. In the further development of the faculties of thought and speech, the gay world is made drab in order to facilitate its management. Only certain irrational thoughts and words remain gay, like daydreams or obscene words (451). In compulsion neurosis, thinking and talking have become substitutes for the emotions connected with reality; they regain their original qualities, become "sexualized" and lose their value for practical use. Words once more become powerful blessings or curses (1154).

Words again can kill and resurrect. They can perform miracles and turn time back. By a mere verbal statement, the compulsion neurotic, unconsciously, believes that he can coerce reality into pursuing the course he desires. Because words and thoughts are believed to have such real effects, they are also dangerous. A careless word might make effective the sadistic impulses that have been warded off with so much care. Words and thoughts have to be handled cautiously and, if necessary, warded off and undone. Their misuse calls for the same punishment as a misdeed. They become the regressive substitutes for deeds (567).

> Because the omnipotence of words (457) is especially preserved in obscene words, which have kept their magical power, causing the speaker and hearer to experience the things mentioned as if actually perceived (451), they are often the subject of compulsive symptoms. An embarrassed reticence that prevents the utterance of obscene words (often disturbed by a sacrilegious compulsion to utter just these words in the most embarrassing connections) is a defense against a specific impulse to say them. This impulse, which may appear as a perversion (see pp. 350 f.), is more frequently felt as a compulsion. It has the goal of magically compelling the hearer to have a sexual experience. This, however, is usually not a simple sexual wish. It serves, rather, the purpose of combating some anxiety that is unconsciously connected with sexual ideas. The sadistic factor in this urge is obvious, as is the fact that anal words bring anal pleasure and sexual speaking itself is an oral-libidinous gain. Coprolalia is a matter of "regressed libido" and therefore plays a great part in the symptomatology of compulsion neurosis.

The fear of the omnipotence of his thoughts (457, 567) makes the compulsion neurotic dependent on his thinking. Instead of mastering the world by means of thinking, his (compulsive) thinking, replacing his uncontrolled sexuality, masters him.

The tendency to use "omnipotent" words as a defense against danger explains the fact that secondary defensive measures against compulsive symptoms often have the compulsive form of worded magical formulae. The relation of compulsive formulae to the magical formulae of primitives has often been discussed (579).

A patient who worried obsessively that the analyst might die during one of his sessions was, in consequence, compelled to turn and look at the analyst, and to reassure himself by uttering the formula: "The living doctor is sitting behind me at a distance." "At a distance" reassured him that he did not violate a taboo of touching.

Freud showed that the belief in the omnipotence of thought corresponds to a real fact. Thoughts, to be sure, have no such external efficacy as the compulsion neurotic imagines; but within himself, thoughts are really much more powerful than in normal persons. Compulsive thoughts are really compelling, and this quality is their power (567). This power is partly a derivative of the biological force of instincts and partly a derivative of the power of the father's demands. Compulsion neurotics, although dependent on their compulsions, actually are not aware of this connection. They really underestimate the internal power of thought as much as they overestimate their external force.

The retreat from feeling to thinking succeeds, as a rule, in one respect: compulsive thinking is *abstract* thinking, isolated from the real world of concrete things.

Compulsive thinking is not only abstract, it is also *general,* directed toward systematization and categorization; it is theoretical instead of real. The patients are interested in maps and illustrations rather than in countries and things.

But in another respect the retreat, as a rule, fails. The cleavages and contradictions that permeate the emotional life of compulsion neurotics are displaced to the sexualized intellectual problems, resulting in obsessive brooding and doubt. Doubt is the instinctual conflict displaced to the intellectual field.

A patient, looking at a door, was compelled to spend much time brooding about the problem: What is the main thing, the empty space, filled out by the door, or the substantial door, filling out the empty space? This "philosophical" problem covered the other doubt: What is the main thing in sexuality, woman or man? And this again meant: What is the main thing in me, femininity or masculinity?

The unconscious content of obsessive doubts may be manifold; yet the manifold conflicts are but special editions of a few general questions. They are conflicts of masculinity versus femininity (bisexuality), of love versus hate (ambivalence), and especially of id (instinctual demands) versus superego (demands of conscience).

The last formula is the decisive one. Bisexuality and ambivalence do not form conflicts in themselves; they do so only if they represent a structural conflict between an instinctual demand and an opposing force as well.

Certain obsessive doubts are of a somewhat simpler nature. Some doubts as to the validity of one's own perceptions or judgments represent the wish that what is doubted should not be true. The doubted facts may stand for primal scenes or for the anatomical sex difference. The relatively frequent symptom of obsessively doubting the news of a death is, first of all, a fear of the omnipotence of one's own thoughts: the patient tries to deny the news because he wants to ward off the idea that it might be his own fault. If the doubt becomes so torturing that the patient says "Thank heavens!" in relief at the very confirmation of the news, the psychological connection is the following. If the doubt were justified and the idea of the death had originated in a misapprehension, the fact that the patient had been thinking such bad thoughts would become obvious. Therefore the confirmation of the news is felt as a relief which nullifies the suspicion that one might have thought maliciously about a person's death.

An insight into the nature of obsessive brooding and doubting furnishes a simple technical rule: never to discuss with compulsion neurotics their obsessive problems. By doing so the analyst would confirm the patient's isolation mechanisms. As long as the patient's thoughts are isolated from his emotions, only this isolation should be the subject of analysis and not the content of what has been isolated.

Connected with the shift of emphasis from acting to thinking is the following idea. Thinking is preparation for action. Persons who are afraid of actions increase the preparations. In the same way as compulsion neurotics think rather than act, they also prepare constantly for the future and never experience the present. Many compulsive symptoms have the nature of preparations for a future that never becomes present. The patients behave like Tyll Eulenspiegel, rejoicing in the walk uphill because he thought of the future downhill trip, sad when going downhill because a later uphill trip was coming.

The main cause for exaggerated preparation is certainly the fear of the "real thing." Simultaneously, the tendency to prepare expresses an anal forepleasure, the infantile postponement of defecation, which in itself also had a double nature: striving for the avoidance of a sudden loss of control and for the achievement of an erogenous pleasure. The "trifling" parts toward which the compulsion neurotic displaces the emphasis from the important whole represent the "preparations" instead of the "real thing."

The compulsion neurotic, busy with preparations, acts according to the rule: the status quo is better than anything a change might bring. The status quo is a lesser evil.

The fear of any change from the known present condition to a possibly dangerous new state makes patients cling even to their symptoms. The neurosis, uncomfortable as it is, is well known and a "lesser evil," as compared with the possibilities any change might bring. Such an attitude often forms a latent resistance which limits the otherwise good progress of an analysis. To the patient, then, the neurosis is an old acquaintance. Some forms of "negative therapeutic reaction" to the analytic cure (608) express such fear of any change (818, 1315).

The fear of change may be replaced or accompanied by its opposite, a tendency to change continuously. Actually the world does not obey any patient's compulsive system. Hence some compulsion neurotics have the tendency to change everything everywhere, trying to bring the world into accord with their system.

Good examples of the belief in the omnipotence of thought, of guilt feelings due to this belief and an attempted defense against the guilt feelings by orderliness are shown by the following case:

In the days before the outbreak of the war, a patient was hanging up his coat in the closet. He suddenly felt the compulsive command: "You have to hang the coat especially neatly." He answered with a resistance: "I am too lazy." He felt the compulsive threat: "If you do not hang the coat neatly, war will break out." He did not care.

A few days later war broke out. The patient remembered immediately the episode with the coat. He knew, of course, that it was not his carelessness that had caused the war, but he felt as if this were the case. He had, earlier, been convinced that he would die in a war; now he felt it a just punishment for his carelessness in hanging the coat.

The patient's interest in war had a long history. As a child he was very much afraid of his tyrannical father, and warded off his anxiety by frightening his little brother. He behaved rather sadistically toward this little brother, especially when playing war. When the patient was adolescent, the brother died of an illness. The patient reacted with the obsessive idea that he, the patient, would die in a war. This obsessive thought expressed the unconscious idea: "I killed my brother while playing war; therefore I have to expect the talion punishment of death in war."

The patient's father stressed orderliness very much. Hanging up the coat correctly meant obedience to his father. Arguments like "You have to hang up the coat," "I am too lazy" had taken place frequently between the father and the patient. Later on, orderliness, meaning obedience to the father, acquired the unconscious meaning of an assurance that he would not kill the father. "Carelessness" meant "taking the risk of killing and of being killed." On the day when the incident with the coat occurred, the patient had experienced a professional frustration and was especially angry.

The connection of the "microcosm" of words with the idea of "mastering possessions" makes it comprehensible that wherever a sexualization of thinking occurs, the sexuality attached to the thinking has an anal quality. During analysis, compulsion neurotics frequently equate, consciously or unconsciously, the production or nonproduction of associations with the production or nonproduction of feces.

A woman patient, who often had to speak in public, showed the obvious equation of her words not with feces but with urine. When speaking, she often used to "lose control" of her words, which gushed from her mouth. Sometimes they suddenly stopped, and she experienced a kind of stage fright, not knowing what to say and feeling that she had run out of material. But she invented a simple trick for overcoming this inhibition: she had to have a bottle of water on her desk, and after having "filled herself up" with water, she would let the words run out again.

Analysis can also demonstrate that details in the manner of speaking or thinking of a much more delicate nature frequently are repetitions of corresponding details in infantile toilet habits. The fantasies of omnipotence that are connected with thoughts and words turn out to be repetitions of the infantile narcissistic overestimation of the excretory functions (19).

In accordance with the anal sexualization of thoughts and words is the fact that neurotic manifestations in head and vocal organs are often found in analysis to be dependent on anal eroticism.

This finding is not inconsistent with the fact that thought and speech are often used as symbols for the penis, and the ability to think or speak is thought of as a sign of potency (215, 520). The concurrence of anal and phallic significance in obsessions and compulsions is due to the regression.

It may be that the physiological relation between the blood volume of the head and that of the abdominal organs helps to establish this unconscious connection of "thoughts" and "feces."

An obsessive patient, who suffered from chronic headaches, referred to this symptom by saying: "My nerves are hurting me." "Nerves" he imagined as white or pinkish threadlike structures, an idea he had acquired at the dentist's, where he saw a "nerve" of a tooth. Once he dreamed of his "vagus nerve," that is, of the nerve that "wanders." He referred to a white thread that might have pushed its way into his head from below and now might walk around within his head and in this way cause his headache. This idea was connected with a definite childhood experience: he had had threadworms. Unconsciously he supposed these worms now to produce as many head symptoms as they had produced anal symptoms when he was a child.

MAGIC AND SUPERSTITION IN COMPULSION NEUROSIS

The overvaluation of intellect often makes compulsion neurotics develop their intellect very highly. However, this high intelligence shows archaic features and is full of magic and superstition. Their ego shows a cleavage, one part being logical, another magical. The defensive mechanism of isolation makes the maintenance of such a cleavage possible.

The superstition of the compulsion neurotic was the subject on which Freud first demonstrated "similarities in the mental life of savages and neurotics" (579). It is based on an augmented narcissism, connected with the regressive re-establishment of the more or less original infantile omnipotence (457). Obsessive games around this omnipotence are aimed at contradicting feelings of dependence and unconsciously are equivalents of "killing the father."

A patient derived much pleasure from playing with a little paper bouquet which changed its form when shaken, somewhat like a kaleidoscope. Analysis showed that he was "playing God," magically creating new worlds. Another patient, performing ceremonials with his bedcover, used to fantasy as a child that he was God creating the world. Analysis showed that "creating the world" meant "creating children," and that unconsciously he played the part of his father, having intercourse with his mother. This world-creating intercourse, however, was perceived as an anal act, and the pretended omnipotence was an outcome of the infantile narcissistic overestimation of the excretory functions (19). Another patient, whose analysis had sharpened his faculty for self-observation, found himself thinking how queer it was that he had to open a door in order to pass through it. He actually expected that his wish would be sufficient to make the door open by itself. The rejection of this idea by the upper levels of the ego differentiates such a belief from a delusion of grandeur.

The complement of creating worlds by magic is the "wishing away" of an undesired piece of the world, the strange ability to deny reality at the point where it opposes the patient's wishes. A true loss of capacity for testing reality is a characteristic feature of psychoses (611). In neuroses, the typical "turning away from reality" is "introversion," a turning away from real objects toward the images of infantile objects. In this respect, the compulsion neurotic, because of his "omnipotence," stands a step nearer to psychosis than does the hysteric. An unconscious part of the ego may repudiate parts of reality, while the conscious personality at the same time really knows what is true and what is false.

Because of his obsession for neatness, a patient with geographical obsessions was troubled by the artificial boundaries between countries. It was his wish that there should only be countries that are geographical units. Therefore, he referred to the entire Iberian peninsula as "Spain," ignoring the existence of Portugal. One day he was introduced to a foreigner. The patient asked him what his nationality was. The man said "Portuguese." The patient described the reaction he had to this statement in the following words: "I said to myself, 'I suppose he is Spanish. He calls it Portuguese!' " This example shows the relationship of "denial in fantasy" and "splitting of the ego" (see p. 145).

Children who, convinced by reality, have to give up their belief in their omnipotence believe instead that the grownups around them are omnipotent. Also, traces of the idea of the omnipotence of grownups persist in compulsion neurotics.

During the latency period a patient was still convinced that adults were omnipotent because they had the power to find out when she was resisting an impulse to defecate.

Later, the quality of omnipotence is displaced from the adults to God, and this omnipotent figure is the focus of severe ambivalent conflicts in compulsion neuroses. There is hardly a single compulsion neurosis without religious features: for example, obsessive conflicts between faith and impulses to blaspheme, which may occur in convinced atheists as well as in consciously pious persons (468, 560, 599).

A patient suffered very much from the impulse to yell during the church service. Once, in childhood, his father was sick, and the patient was told to be quiet. It was on this occasion that the compulsion to disrupt a "holy" silence by a blasphemous noise first appeared. Subsequently, God stood for the father, and the impulse to yell for the wish to kill him. Further analysis showed that the disturbing noise originally had not been thought of as yelling but as passing wind. The aggression against the father was an anal one and at a deeper level simultaneously expressed an archaic kind of love.

Since most patriarchal religions also veer between submission to a paternal figure and rebellion (both submission and rebellion being sexualized), and every god, like a compulsive superego, promises protection on condition of submission, there are many similarities in the manifest picture of compulsive ceremonials and religious rituals, due to the similarity of the underlying conflicts. Freud, therefore, has called a compulsion neurosis a private religion (560); likewise, the ceremonials of compulsion neurotics have been called rituals because of their similarity to religious rites. However, there are also basic differences between a compulsion and a religious rite, the discussion of which lies beyond the scope of this book.

The symptomatology of compulsion neuroses is full of magical superstitions, such as compulsive oracles or sacrifices. Patients consult oracles, make bets with God, fear the magical effect of the words of others, act as if they believe in ghosts, demons, and especially in a very malicious fate, and yet otherwise are intelligent persons, completely aware of the absurdity of these ideas.

Consulting an oracle, in principle, means either forcing permission or forgiveness for something ordinarily prohibited or an attempt to shift the responsibility for the things about which one feels guilty onto God. The oracle is asked for a divine permission, which may act as a counterweight against conscience.

A patient remembered that he habitually performed an oracular ritual to decide whether or not he should give in to the temptation to masturbate, that is, whether masturbation might be permitted just once more. If luck was with him, he gave way to the urge, hoping that he might displace the guilt onto the gods. If luck was against him, he invented an excuse in order to repeat the oracular process until he obtained the desired permission. Of course the displacement of guilt was unsuccessful; he did not escape his pangs of conscience and felt the absurdity of thinking that the same gods who had first forbidden masturbation should permit it on this occasion. An oracle of this kind is a device to accomplish the impossible: that the parents who forbid certain activities should be made to permit and even to encourage them.

Another patient's superstition was clearly aimed at getting forgiveness for masturbation. He used to differentiate all activities into those that bring "good luck" and those that bring "bad luck." Whether an activity belonged in the first or in the second category was not decided by his behavior but by fate; he could merely guess what brings good luck and what brings bad. In analysis it turned out that this superstition had first appeared in adolescence with the idea:

"Putting my hands into my pockets brings bad luck." This obviously meant: "Masturbation will be followed by punishment." The charm, then, was displaced from "pockets" to "clothes." Certain suits were lucky, others unlucky, according to whether the patient had worn them on lucky or unlucky occasions. The patient greatly enjoyed being well dressed; he wanted to be handsome and was constantly afraid he might be homely. "Handsome" meant "masculine," "homely" meant "castrated." By being well dressed he was provoking spectators to assure him that he was not castrated. In the superstition, "fate" was supposed to give him the same reassurance by telling him which suits would bring good luck.

The ambiguous meaning of oracular predictions corresponds to the contradictory demands of the ambivalent oracle seeker, who wants permission to gratify his instinctual needs and expects a refusal. He tries to interpret a prognostication of double meaning as a permission, but is unable to rid himself of the feeling that he should have interpreted it as a prohibition and a warning of punishment. Kris called attention to the connection between the interpretation of ambiguous prophecies and the solution of riddles. An individual who tries to repress his guilt and the significance of his acts is unable to solve a riddle, just as he is unable to understand a prophecy correctly. And the hero who solves every riddle must have been wise not so much because of his intelligence but because his emotional freedom, unhindered by repression, enabled him to recognize the hidden truth.

The motive of the *misapprehended oracle* also expresses a conflict of this kind. It consists in interpreting a warning utterance of an oracle as a reassurance, and thus is an attempt to repress guilt feelings. The frightening way in which the real meaning of the oracle becomes clear at last represents the return of the repressed guilt feeling out of the repression (442).

Besides enforcing permission or forgiveness the oracle is also a means of shifting the responsibility; this also is doomed to fail.

The projection of guilt-laden impulses onto fantastic "doubles" of the ego in an attempt to escape responsibility is frequent. Children often give themselves other names when they are naughty: "I am not the one who did that, but X." Remnants of such a primitive attempt to escape conscience are typical of certain character disorders (*see* p. 500).

Superstition may be used in still other ways in the fight against conscience. Many persons try to combat their guilt feelings by making various charms, with the aim of undoing the act they feel guilty about or of denying its guilty character or the danger of punishment. In some cases fantasy not only substitutes for an unpleasant reality but even denies reality (magically perceived) altogether.

For one patient, thinking was a charm to keep what had been thought from coming true. She said to herself it was very improbable that anything would happen just the way she had thought about it beforehand; so she imagined what she did not want to have happen. She constantly imagined: "Because I thought it, it is not true." Eventually she doubted reality altogether. During analysis she found out that she was under a chronic tension, constantly waiting for a curtain to fall so that at last the play would end and real life begin. With a kind of depersonalization she sometimes felt amazed that people eat or go to the bathroom, as if she had believed that instinctual things are only thought about but never actually done. She used to daydream horror stories about lunatics; her first great anxiety spell occurred when she suddenly witnessed a real temper tantrum of a psychotic.

The well-known phenomenon of "dream in dream" (552) may serve a similar purpose. It attempts to deny the reality of instinctual pleasure in order to render possible the enjoyment that is "only dreamed of," in spite of a fear of punishment. This attempt also may fail.

A patient remembered that, as an adolescent, he used to experience in dreams tempting situations which he did not dare to enjoy, doubting whether this was dream or actuality. He tried to escape from this dilemma by making the following mental note in the daytime: "Whenever I feel a doubt whether something is reality or dream, I may be sure that it is dream; when actually awake, I do not feel such doubts." It was of no avail; he doubted again in the next sexual dream.

THE PHYSICAL ATTITUDE OF COMPULSION NEUROTICS

That the morbid process in compulsion neurosis is more internalized than in hysteria does not mean that no physical symptoms occur. Most characteristic is the isolation of all the overemphasized thinking processes from the corresponding emotions, and therefore from physical expression. The tendency toward the separation of the body executive from the thinking is usually reflected in a general physical rigidity, manifested either by a muscular spasm, general or local, or by a general slack hypotonus. Certain physical attitudes of patients serve the purpose of "not letting the body be influenced by what is going on within the mind." They have been described by Reich as the "physical armor" which those patients have donned and which has to be broken through if an analysis is to be successful (1271, 1279). The whole physical state of the compulsion neurotic is typically a rigid one, characterized by retention and by an unreadiness for flexible reaction. Corresponding to the preponderance of anal eroticism, the patients are usually constipated or else have trained themselves to a rigid regularity in bowel matters.

THE PROBLEM OF DIFFERENTIAL ETIOLOGY

The basic conflict in compulsion neurosis is the same as in hysteria: the defense against the objectionable tendencies of the Oedipus complex. Nor does the prevalence of anxiety among the motives for the defense in hysteria and of guilt feelings in compulsion neurosis make a difference in principle, since guilt feelings appear also in hysteria and anxiety in compulsion neurosis.

Pathognomonic for the symptom formation in compulsion neurosis, as compared to hysteria, is the anal-sadistic regression. This regression must depend on one of three factors or on a combination of them—namely, on the nature of (1) the residuals of the anal-sadistic phase of libido development, (2) the phallic organization, and (3) the defending ego (396).

1. The outcome of the original anal-sadistic phase is probably the crucial factor. In general, regression occurs the more easily, the greater the fixation. Under the influence of castration anxiety, those persons will regress to the anal-sadistic state of organization who have the strongest anal-sadistic fixations. And fixations may be caused by (*see* pp. 65 f.) (*a*) constitutional factors; heredity in compulsion neurosis shows that a constitutional heightening of anal erogeneity is of importance (549, 1630); (*b*) unusual gratifications; (*c*) unusual frustrations; (*d*) an alternation of unusual gratifications and unusual frustrations (the greater the previous gratifications, the more apt are later frustrations to be experienced as traumatic); (*e*) a concurrence of instinctual gratifications with security gratifications, that is, with some denial of or reassurance against specific anxieties.

> The anal-erotic drives meet in infancy with the training for cleanliness, and the way in which this training is carried out determines whether or not anal fixations result. The training may be too early, too late, too strict, too libidinous. If it is done too early, the typical result is a repression of anal eroticism, characterized by a superficial fear and obedience and a deep tendency toward rebellion; if it is done too late, rebellion and stubbornness are to be expected; strictness causes fixations because of the frustration involved; a libidinous behavior on the part of the mother causes fixation because of gratification; however, such gratification is often a limited one, because the mother excites the child but prohibits gratification of the excitement. Laxatives are apt to increase tendencies toward dependency; enemas create enormous excitation and anxiety at the same time (626).

2. Concerning the phallic organization, its weakness might promote regression; it is easy to give up something that is not very important. But what is a "weakness" of the phallic organization? Clinically, this condition probably coincides with the previous one, for the more intense the pregenital fixations, the weaker the subsequent phallic organization. Regression appears to be facilitated also if the threat of castration comes upon children in a traumatic fashion, that is, if the phallic position is weakened suddenly.

3. The ego that is especially apt to resort to the use of regression for defense is "strong" in one respect and "weak" in another. The critical function of the ego and the need for preparatory thinking must have developed especially early, certainly in the phase when the thinking functions were still magically oriented; but this very necessity for the defensive ego to start functioning so early causes the methods used to be archaic and immature ones. The ego of compulsion neurotics must be strong enough to enforce its protests against the instincts at a very early date, yet it must be too weak to fight out this conflict by more mature methods. In contrast, many persons who are inclined toward introverted day-

dreaming and who later develop conversion symptoms show a relative inhibition of their intellectual functions.

The question may be asked whether all compulsion neuroses are actually based on a regression. Is it not possible that disturbances of the development during the anal-sadistic stage might have entirely prevented the development of a full phallic Oedipus complex (618)?

Cases of this kind do occur. However, they do not represent the typical compulsion neurosis. The great importance of the Oedipus complex, of castration anxiety, and of masturbation in the typical compulsion neurosis is well established. The disturbances of development during the anal-sadistic phase produce, rather, personalities without pronounced compulsive symptoms but with a character similar to that of compulsion neurotics, mixed with general infantile traits (*see* p. 531).

COURSE AND SUMMARY

Compulsion neuroses in adults fall into two groups: the rare acute forms and the more common chronic forms. The acute cases are precipitated by external circumstances. These precipitating circumstances are not different from those that might precipitate any other neurosis; they are remobilizations of repressed infantile sexual conflicts, disturbances of a hitherto effective equilibrium between repressing and repressed forces, increases, either absolute or relative, in the strength of the warded-off instincts or in the opposing anxieties (*see* pp. 454 ff.). To bring about a compulsion neurosis, the precipitation must affect a person who has had an appropriate predisposition since childhood, that is, a person who had carried out an anal-sadistic regression in childhood. This regression, it is true, may have embraced only a small part of the libido, so that genitality might be sufficiently preserved to allow puberty to develop without insuperable difficulties; nevertheless, the infantile defense must at one time have chosen the path of regression, else it would not be possible for a disappointment in later life—with a renewed flaring up of the Oedipus complex—to create a regression to the anal-sadistic level.

The chronic type is much more frequent. Compulsion neuroses of this kind usually continue more or less without interruption from adolescence, though particular external circumstances may precipitate exacerbations from time to time. Succeeding slight compulsive symptoms at the time of the Oedipus complex, compulsive rituals appear more definitely during the latency period when the intellectual faculties develop. The sexuality that emerges at puberty takes a course analogous to that pursued by the sexuality of early childhood, and another regression to the anal-sadistic level takes place. The superego, with whose protests the new wave of anal-sadistic sexual wishes now comes into conflict, is itself unable to escape the effects of the regression. It has become more sadistic and rages against the anal and sadistic instinctual demands not less than previously against the genital ones. It rages equally relentlessly against the offshoots of the phallic Oedipus wishes proper, which have persisted along with the anal-sadistic drives. "Thus the conflict in the compulsion neurosis is made more acute for two reasons: the defense has become more intolerant, the matter to be defended against more unbearable, both through the influence of the one factor, the regression of libido" (Freud, 618).

The continuous struggle on two fronts and the adjustments the ego makes to the symptoms (secondary defensive conflicts, countercompulsions against compulsive symptoms, further reaction formations, the tendency of the symptoms to evolve from defense to gratification) complicate the subsequent development. Reaction formations may give rise to secondary narcissistic gains, for example, to pride in being exceptionally good, noble, or intelligent, frequently forming resistances most difficult to overcome in the analysis of compulsion neurotics.

As among phobias, there are among compulsion neuroses stationary cases, in which the defenses are relatively successful, as well as progressive ones. In the latter, either "breakdowns" of relative, compulsive equilibriums occur, with the open production of anxiety and depressions (which may be favorable for analysis), or there is a continuous increase of the compulsive symptoms toward the feared final states of full paralysis of the conscious will.

> A simple example of the increase in symptomatology: A patient had the compulsion to avoid the number three because that meant to him sexuality and thoughts of castration. He used to do everything four times, to make sure that the three was avoided. A little later, he got the feeling that four is too near to three; for security's sake he began to prefer five. But five is odd and therefore bad. It was substituted by six. Six was twice three, seven was odd—so it became eight. And eight remained the patient's favorite number for years.

It is not easy to say what determines whether the course of the illness comes to a standstill or turns out to be progressive (*see* pp. 551 ff.).

A complication that may occur even in milder cases is represented by the aforementioned breakdown of a relative equilibrium which hitherto has been maintained by means of expiatory symptoms or other compulsive limitations of the ego.

> Upsetting events, unforeseen by the patient's systems, may break through a compulsive rigidity. The opposite of a "traumatic neurosis" is a "traumatic cure" of a compulsive character.

Such an occurrence demonstrates the connections between the compulsive symptom and the original actual-neurotic state and anxiety: the anxiety is "bound" secondarily by the development of the obsessive and compulsive symptoms. Compulsive rituals that replace previous phobias demonstrate this binding of anxiety most clearly. It is true, however, that this anxiety is always more or less tinctured with guilt feeling.

> Anxiety and guilt feelings that have been covered by compulsive symptoms make their appearance again when these symptoms are analyzed. Frequently, because the patients are in the habit of warding off their affects and of not recognizing them, they appear in the form of physical and actual-neurotic anxiety equivalents.

In summary, it is the concept of regression to the anal-sadistic level of libidinal organization that explains the differences between the symptom formation in compulsion neurosis and in hysteria. The seeming inconsistency that the warded-off impulses in compulsion neuroses are comprised of phallic tendencies associated with the Oedipus complex and at the same time are anal-sadistic in nature can be explained by recognizing that the defense is first directed against the phallic Oedipus complex, replacing it by anal sadism, and then continued against the anal-sadistic impulses. Many differences in the clinical picture are due to the fact that in hysteria, repression alone is used as a defense mechanism, whereas in compulsion neuroses, reaction formation, undoing, isolation, and overcathexis of the world of concepts and words (a special case of isolation) play their part; the use of these particular defense mechanisms is due to the fact that not genital but anal-sadistic wishes have to be warded off. The use of different defense mechanisms explains also the difference in the scope of consciousness in the two kinds of neuroses. Correlated with the factor of regression is the relatively later onset of compulsion neurosis. The introjection of the parents, meanwhile, into the superego in turn explains the differences in internalization, in the predominance of the superego, and in the relative predominance of punitive and expiatory symptoms over gratification symptoms. Furthermore, the regression is also responsible for the peculiar severity of the superego, since the superego cannot escape the regressive pull toward sadism. The fact that aside from the production of symptoms the illness affects the total personality of the patient to an extent much greater than in hysteria must also be related to the fundamental phenomenon of regression.

THERAPEUTIC PSYCHOANALYSIS IN COMPULSION NEUROSIS

As to the analytic therapy, compulsion neurosis is regarded as the second type of "transference neurosis" and as the second great field in which psychoanalysis is indicated. Nevertheless, consideration of the implied mechanisms shows how much more difficult analysis is in compulsion neurosis than in hysteria. As a matter of fact the difficulties are so great that, in severe cases with a history of many years' duration, one should be very cautious in making promises of cure. Often one must be satisfied with a greater or lesser degree of improvement.

What is the nature of the implied difficulties?

1. The particular type of countercathexis characteristic for compulsion neurosis makes compliance with the basic rule very difficult or totally impossible. This is due to a continuous censorial attention which does not forsake the patient for one moment and which compels him to flee continuously from unsystematic free association into programmatic substantial ideas that conform to reason. It is as though the patient, instead of giving voice to his subjective experiences, presented the analyst with a conscientious but incomplete table of contents, or of the names of his experiences. Attempts to instruct the patient in what is really required of him frequently serve as food for hairsplitting obsessions. Overconscientious through compensation, the patient wishes to do all that is required of him, but he applies his industry in the wrong direction, thus revealing that unconsciously he wishes the opposite of what he consciously intends. To find a way for the patient to learn what it feels like to associate freely, and at the same time to avoid holding theoretical discussions and furnishing him with new material for brooding, is perhaps the main technical task in the analysis of a compulsion neurotic.

2. The internalization of the conflict and the role played by the superego make the task of analysis much more difficult. Hysterics regard their symptoms as something alien to their ego; the ego forms an alliance with the analyst in the combat against the neurosis. This ideal working atmosphere is never present in the case of compulsion neurotics. The ego is split. The analyst can confidently depend on one part of the ego only. The remainder of the ego thinks magically, not logically, and practically takes sides with the resistance. The conscious part of the personality may be very co-operative, but to the degree in which this part is isolated from the unconscious magical part, the best-comprehended interpretations remain inefficacious, unless this isolation is broken up.

3. The regression implies that the analysis actually has to penetrate one more level than in the case of hysteria.

4. The regression also means that the nature of the patient's object relationships has changed; they are governed by anal-sadistic trends, especially by ambivalence and stubbornness, which are manifest in the transference, too. The mixed feelings of compulsion neurotics are exhibited in rebellious tendencies against the analyst and in simultaneous efforts to submit to him. Every impulse is accompanied in some way by its direct antithesis.

5. The isolation of ideational content from the corresponding emotions forms a special difficulty. There is always a danger that the analysis might be experienced by the patient as an intellectual understanding only; this kind of experience remains useless, of course, as long as it is not analytically worked through as a resistance against emotional experience.

6. The thinking and talking of compulsion neurotics are sexualized. Thought

and speech, however, are the instruments of psychoanalysis. The situation, therefore, in the case of compulsion neurotics is that they must be healed with the aid of functions that are themselves affected by the illness.

A patient made a comparison that fits the case. He said it was as if he had fallen into the water with a towel in his hand, and someone were trying to dry him with the towel which had become wet along with his body.

Apparently, there is no solution for this dilemma. However, practically, in so far as the conscious personality of the patient can form a judgment about the irrationality of his behavior, this piece of intact ego can be utilized to carry out the first bit of analysis, in the hope that the process will resuscitate another bit of usable ego.

7. Secondary gains are certainly effective in hysteria, too, but are never so integrally bound up in the personality as is the narcissistic gain from the reaction formations in the character in compulsion neurotics. Many analyses have failed because the analyst could not succeed in persuading the "good" compulsion neurotic that it would be to his advantage to be somewhat "corrupted" by analysis. The analyst does not only represent the patient's superego; he may also represent the seducer, the agent of the dreaded id, against whom the patient fights as a matter of course.

8. It also must be mentioned that the appearance of anxiety, and of physical vegetative symptoms representing anxiety, in the course of the treatment may create severe complications in persons who are not accustomed to affects and whose symptoms used to be limited to the mental sphere only.

All of these difficulties are not insuperable; but they must also not be underestimated. Because of them every analysis of a compulsion neurosis is a difficult and time-consuming undertaking. There are, to be sure, acute compulsion neuroses that clear up relatively quickly. But the analyst is more accustomed to see the severe cases of long standing, persons who have had their compulsion neuroses uninterruptedly since their latency period. These are the cases that need the notorious "long" analyses. Yet it is fair to say that these long analyses and the great energy expended are often worth while, and that a cure has often been attained even in cases of very long duration.

In each particular case, only the course of a trial analysis can convey an impression as to the degree of the difficulties outlined above, and thus permit an evaluation of the prognosis. Cases of short standing are the most amenable to analysis; "terminal states," transitions to schizophrenia, and developmental disturbances that never did reach the phallic phase, are least amenable. However, since other types of therapy are fruitless in such cases, it is pertinent to advise that any compulsion neurotic should at least try psychoanalysis, whenever external circumstances permit.

Chapter XV

PREGENITAL CONVERSIONS

GENERAL REMARKS ABOUT PREGENITAL CONVERSIONS

IN THE symptoms of conversion hysteria, genital wishes from the realm of the Oedipus complex find a distorted expression in alterations of physical functions; in compulsion neurosis these wishes have been changed by regression, and conflicts around the regressively distorted tendencies are expressed in the symptoms. There is a third type of neurosis whose symptoms are doubtless conversions, but the unconscious impulses expressed in the symptoms are pregenital: while the symptomatology is of the nature of conversion, the patient's mental structure corresponds to that of a compulsion neurotic. The pregenital orientation has changed the patient's behavior just as it did that of the compulsion neurotic; again, the increased ambivalence and bisexuality, the sexualization of the processes of thinking and talking, and the partial regression to the magical type of thinking make their appearance. Since the external clinical picture of such neuroses is that of a hysteria, only psychoanalysis was in a position to discover that their inner structure is different.

Theoretically it might be expected that a pregenital psychological content would be more frequently found in conversion symptoms that are directly related to the pregenital erogenous zones—for instance, anal-erotic material in cases with intestinal symptoms. This expectation actually is fulfilled to some extent. In the childhood of many subsequently compulsive individuals an account of psychogenic intestinal disturbances is found; these disturbances may be reactivated in the course of an analysis and appear again in the form of transitory conversion symptoms (599). Residues of these infantile disturbances, such as constipation and diarrhea, also occur as spontaneous symptoms in some compulsion neuroses. Yet not all intestinal conversion symptoms are of this nature. The role played by the pregenital fixation may be limited to the selection of the organ that becomes the seat of the symptoms.

STUTTERING

Those functional disorders of speech that are more than simple inhibitions are typical examples of the group of pregenital conversion neuroses.

The symptom of stuttering reveals more readily than other conversion symptoms that it is the result of a conflict between antagonistic tendencies; the patient shows that he wishes to say something and yet does not wish to. Since he consciously intends to speak, he must have some unconscious reason for not wanting to speak. This is necessarily due to some unconscious significance of speaking, either of the particular thing that is to be spoken or of the activity of speaking in general.

If a person makes a slip of the tongue, it is due to the fact that unconsciously he is somehow resisting what he consciously intended to say (553). The analysis of a slip discloses what tendency has disturbed the original intention to speak. If a person instead of making a slip of the tongue merely begins to stammer a little, it is obvious that some unconscious motive has disturbed his intention, but we cannot guess what the motive is (596). If such an occasional stuttering occurs regularly as a response to a specific stimulus, knowledge of the stimulus can be used as a starting point for an analysis of the disturbing factor. If, however, a person stammers not only as a reaction to certain stimuli but does so more or less whenever he talks, the disturbing factor must be rooted in the fact that the very intention to speak has an objectionable significance. Thus some types of occasional stammering may be due to the unconscious instinctual significance of the thing the person is going to say; whereas in severe cases of stuttering the function of speech itself represents an objectionable instinctual impulse.

In the discussion of compulsion neurosis, it became clear that certain factors and conditions led to a sexualization of speech, that such a sexualization is regularly of an anal nature and that this has specific consequences (*see* pp. 295 ff., esp. 299). All this holds true for stuttering.

Psychoanalysis of stutterers reveals the anal-sadistic universe of wishes as the basis of the symptom. For them, the function of speech regularly has an anal-sadistic significance. Speaking means, first, the utterance of obscene, especially anal, words and, second, an aggressive act directed against the listener.

The anal-erotic nature of speech is seen best when, in analysis, a specific situation, which either provokes or accentuates stuttering, proves to be an anal temptation. Unconsciously, speech in general or in certain situations is thought of as a sexualized defecation. The same motives which in childhood were directed against pleasurable playing with feces make their appearance again in the form of inhibitions or prohibitions of the pleasure of playing with words. The expulsion and retention of words means the expulsion and retention of feces, and actually the retention of words, just as previously the retention of feces, may be either a reassurance against possible loss or a pleasurable autoerotic activity. One may speak, in stuttering, of a displacement upward of the functions of the anal sphincters (708, 1406, 1461).

Two conditions frequently encountered which provoke or increase stuttering are correlated with its sadistic significance. Quite often a patient begins to stutter when he is particularly eager to prove a point. Behind his apparent zeal he has concealed a hostile or sadistic tendency to destroy his opponent by means of words, and the stuttering is both the blocking of and the punishment for this tendency. Still more often stuttering is exacerbated in the presence of prominent or authoritative persons, that is, of paternal figures against whom the unconscious hostility is most intense.

> Garma once observed a patient who, in addition to severe stuttering, suffered from a fear of injuring someone; the girl believed, in particular, that in sexual intercourse the woman might injure the man; in addition she had various day-dreams in which, by a look, she could destroy the whole world and kill all men.

In dreams, to speak is the symbol of life, and to be mute the symbol of death (552). The same symbolism holds true in stuttering. When the stutterer is unable to talk, his hesitation often expresses his desire to kill which has been turned against his ego.

For the same reasons as in compulsion neurosis, an anal-sadistic sexualization of the function of speech also means a remobilization of the infantile stage when words were omnipotent (457). "Words can kill," and stutterers are persons who unconsciously think it necessary to use so dangerous a weapon with care.

The circumstance that obscene words and curse words have retained more of their original magical significance than other words (451, 1154) (*see* pp. 296 and 350 f.) is important in the psychoanalysis of stutterers. For many of them, any talking is an unconscious temptation to use obscene or profane words, intended to attack the listener, violently or sexually.

The anal-sadistic significance of the symptom is also in keeping with the typically anal-sadistic personality make-up of the stutterer, which is identical with the personality make-up of the compulsion neurotic.

The anal-sadistic regression which is interpolated between the original Oedipus fantasies and the symptom sometimes can be directly observed.

> Alfhild Tamm reported a case of a young man who first had a period of conflict over genital masturbation; subsequently he replaced this practice by anal masturbation; and only following the suppression of these anal practices did he begin to stutter (1527).

That anal-sadistic wishes play the most prominent role in stuttering does not mean that other eroticisms or component impulses take no part in it. As in other symptoms, any kind of infantile component instinct may participate accessorily, along with the dominant sexual component. Three component impulses usually play a characteristic part in the symptom of stuttering: the phallic, the oral, and the exhibitionistic.

1. *Phallic impulses:* The function of speech is frequently connected unconsciously with the genital function, particularly with the male genital function. To speak means to be potent; inability to speak means castration (214, 215, 220, 520, 892). Boys frequently reveal that their eagerness to talk well has developed as a substitute for phallic competition ("Can I talk as well as my father?") (473).

Girls with a similar ambition have the unconscious wish to function genitally like men. Thus all conflicts involving the ideas of potency or castration can find expression in the symptom of stuttering, though in a regressively distorted form. The theme of having the tongue cut out is frequently met with in myths, fairy tales, dreams, and neurotic fantasies as a symbol for castration; the tongue, as the organ of speech, appears as a phallic symbol.

> A patient whose public speaking had an exquisite urethral (potency) significance has been mentioned (*see* p. 299). When she "ran out of words" she had to drink water, after which she was able to function again.
>
> Another woman patient was convinced that a surgeon who had removed her tonsils when she was a child had, in error, taken out her uvula. Only after analysis of her castration complex was she able to convince herself that her uvula was normal.

The appearance of phallic tendencies in stuttering is a proof that the anal orientation of the patient was brought about by a regression. Cases in which these phallic elements are missing may occasionally also be based on an arrest of development at pregenital stages.

2. *Oral impulses:* Speech is, in the broader sense, an oral-respiratory function. Erogenous pleasure in speech is in itself oral-respiratory eroticism; and actually the fate of the oral-respiratory libido is a significant element in the development of speech disorders. The regression in stuttering frequently has not ceased at the anal-sadistic level; oral eroticism, too, comes to the fore, with conflicts around wishes for the incorporation of objects as well as around autoerotic oral desires. The severity of a case depends upon the relative importance of the oral component.

Occasionally the words that should and should not be uttered have, on the deepest level, the significance of introjected objects. Conflicts that originally took place between the patient and an object are now expressed through a conflict between the ego and its speech products (signifying feces).

> The stutterer may not only unconsciously attempt to kill by means of words; at the level now being discussed his symptom also expresses the tendency to kill his words, as representing introjected objects.

Coriat, who studied many cases of stuttering (291, 292, 293), was impressed more by the participation of oral autoeroticism than by conflicts around introjection. Instead of using the function of speech for purposes of communication, he states, the stutterer uses it for attaining pleasurable sensations in the speech organs. Coriat even denies the conversion nature of the symptom, stating that nothing has been "converted," since the person simply yields to the tendency to play around in order to achieve pleasurable oral sensations (291). However, all stutterers probably would agree that the symptom is embarrassing and painful and in no way pleasurable, and that they are as completely unaware of the anal- and oral-sadistic fantasies that are expressed by the symptom as of their Oedipus and castration ideas. Thus although stutterers seek oral-erogenous pleasure, stuttering remains basically a pregenital conversion neurosis.

Intense oral erogeneity is frequently also expressed in a highly developed ambition in the field of speech. Sometimes this ambition develops after the symptom and constitutes an overcompensatory reaction to it. Demosthenes was not the only man who became a great orator because he had stuttered.

> A patient's pronounced interest in foreign languages and philological problems, combined with a high and specific ambition in respect to them, could be explained by analysis as an overcompensation of inferiority feelings due to a forgotten period in childhood when he had stammered and had been teased about it.

In other cases the ambition developed first and the symptom of stuttering followed, after the ambition had become the representative of forbidden sexual or aggressive tendencies. In some cases of stuttering, this oral ambition is not limited to speech, and its origin is even older than the ability to talk. Infantile narcissistic desires to be able to make more (oral or anal) noise than adults may reappear in rather grotesque forms (120, 463). Sometimes the original meaning of such wishes lies in the idea of being able to eat as much as adults do; this may be a defense, by means of "identification with the aggressor" (541), against a fear of being eaten.

> At times oral ambitions of this kind stand out definitely not only in the function of expressing words but also in that of "taking in" words, by hearing or reading, both unconsciously meaning "eating" (124, 1512).

Before speech became a practical means of communication, the activities of the organs of speech had a purely libidinal and discharging function. The development goes from the level of autoerotic babbling or screaming (1419), through the levels of magically influencing the environment by means of the vocal apparatus (457), to the gradual acquisition of the understanding of words (249, 251, 252), to the final attainment of the level at which speech is used as a purposive means of communication; this development is a highly complex process, subject to disturbances at various points. Unfortunately, this developmental process has not yet been studied in detail psychoanalytically. Severe cases of stuttering offer opportunity to study this developmental process through understanding the nature of its disturbances.

Speaking is a means of communication. In less severe cases of stammering, communication with objects has been sexualized, entirely or in specific associations, and therefore speaking has become disturbed. In more severe cases of stuttering the function of communication has been given up entirely; the organs of speech are again intended to be used autoerotically.

3. *Exhibitionistic impulses:* That exhibitionism plays a decisive part in stuttering has already been indicated by stressing the connections between stuttering and ambition. In cases where only public speaking evokes the symptom, obviously an inhibition of an exhibitionistic tendency is at work. Stuttering only when speaking in public resembles other neuroses built on the basis of inhibited exhibitionistic impulses, like erythrophobia, stage fright, and social fears. An actor, struck by stage fright, might not only forget his lines but actually begin to stammer (501, 522).

Exhibitionistic stuttering is based on the notion of magically influencing an audience by means of omnipotent words. When this intention becomes forbidden, the inhibition of speech is necessary. The unconscious aims of the objectionable exhibitionism are not only direct erogenous ones; as in perverse exhibitionism, the reaction of the audience is needed for a reassurance against castration anxiety or as a satisfaction of some narcissistic need; and the means by which this reaction is demanded may unconsciously be very sadistic. Because of the unacceptable sadistic way in which the reassurance is sought, the castration fear, against which reassurance was needed, is still further intensified; this makes an inhibition of the exhibitionism necessary and the stuttering is the result. In men, this type of stuttering means: "The exhibitionistic charm by which I sought reassurance against castration may actually bring about my castration." In women, the exhibitionism, displaced from the genitals, attempts to bring reassurance against a feeling of inferiority because of the lack of a penis. This type of stuttering means: "It will turn out that I actually have no penis" (*see* pp. 346 f.).

> Speaking means charming. The aim of the orator is to get the applause which he needs for fighting his fears. If there is danger that he may not succeed, the sadistic orator may feel that he must force the audience by violence to give him what he needs; he may feel that he even has to castrate or to kill them. Or he may try to achieve his ends in another way: to ensure influence over an audience, he must show that he has power over the audience. Stammering, under such circumstances, means: "Stop talking before you have actually killed or castrated your audience" or "Stop talking before it turns out that the truth is not that they are dependent on you but that you are dependent on them" (446).

The ego of the stutterer, like the ego of the compulsion neurotic, has to develop a double front: against his objectionable impulses, and also against his superego, now sadistic and archaic through regression. Many stutterers produce their symptom only when it puts them into a disadvantageous position. The impression arises that they use their symptom to gratify the demands of an oversevere superego. If the symptom appears only in the presence of persons of authority, this is not only because the patient is especially aggressive toward them but also because he may anticipate serious consequences from the failure.

Numerous secondary gains may be connected with stuttering. Two types are particularly characteristic: (1) Superficially, the stutterer, it is true, may appear funny; nevertheless he arouses pity which he may utilize. (2) On a deeper level, stuttering offers an opportunity for the gratification of a feeling of spite, increased by the pathogenic regression; the stutterer may obtain a bit of real gratification of the aggression latent in the symptom.

In less severe cases the symptom may be confined to definite letters or to definite word combinations. In such cases, analysis shows an associative relation between those letters or words and the infantile sexual conflicts, just as in inhibitions of reading or writing (*see* p. 181).

Concerning psychoanalytic therapy for stutterers, the main difficulty is that the function of speech is disturbed, and talking is the very instrument of psychoanalysis. But this is not the only difficulty that has to be overcome. Having gone through a pathogenic regression to the anal-sadistic level, stutterers in general present the same difficulties in analysis as do compulsion neurotics. The prognosis for such analyses, therefore, is in general the same as in compulsion neuroses. When stammering represents a rather simple "inhibited state" the prognosis is much more favorable, and quick cures have been reported (154, 155, 213, 292, 346, 1406, 1527). The deeply pregenital types of stuttering are as difficult to influence as are other pregenital neuroses. However, it is a favorable fact that the symptom of stuttering itself can often be eliminated before the underlying pregenital elements are thoroughly worked through in analysis. In general, psychoanalytic treatment should be advised, and a trial analysis undertaken with the same caution as in a compulsion neurosis (*cf.* 212, 1026, 1027, 1115, 1119, 1415).

PSYCHOGENIC TIC

The symptom of psychogenic tic owes its origin to the mechanism of conversion. Just as in the case of cramp, paralysis, contracture or major attacks in hysteria, here, too, the voluntary musculature of the body refuses to serve the ego and functions independently of the will. Yet even the external clinical picture shows tic to be different from hysteria. Long before psychoanalysis existed, clinical observers differentiated tic from hysteria. The stereotyped nature of the tic is unusual in simple hysterical symptoms and seems to give the tic a character nearer to catatonic manifestations. Actually, the tic patient shows all the archaic features of a "regressed" personality. He not only has a compulsive character, but as a rule shows a narcissistic orientation as well. Probably the term psychogenic tic covers a continuous series of links from conversion hysteria to catatonia. Some forms of tic even seem to have more connection with compulsions. The typical tic, it is true, has a different mode of manifestation. Compulsive individuals carry out their motor patterns voluntarily (obeying, of course, an ego-

alien command), whereas the tic occurs independently of volition and is an automatic action; nevertheless, compulsive motor patterns of long standing may
gradually become automatic tic movements (1018).

Tics may occur in any part of the voluntary musculature. They are comparable to the specific motor symptoms in traumatic neuroses which, as was pointed
out (see pp. 119 f. and 124), are movements originating in past situations, either
expressed or arrested at the moment of expression. In traumatic neuroses the overwhelming quantity of excitement determined the subsequent involuntary motor
expressions. In tics, the whole action, of which the movement forms a part, has
been repressed, and the repressed motor impulses return against the will of the ego.

The repressed situations, whose motor intentions return in tic, are highly
emotional ones representing again either instinctual temptations or punishments
for warded-off impulses. In tics, a movement that was once the concomitant sign
of an affect (sexual excitement, rage, anxiety, grief, triumph, embarrassment)
has become an equivalent of this affect, and appears instead of the warded-off
affect.

This may occur in different ways: (1) The tic represents a part of the original
affective syndrome, whose mental significance remains unconscious. (2) The
tic represents a movement whose unconscious meaning is a defense against the
intended affect. (3) The tic does not directly represent affect or defense against
affect but, rather, other movements or motor impulses that once occurred during
a repressed emotional excitement, either in the patient or in another person with
whom the patient has made a hysterical identification (492, 493).

These connections are clearest in those cases that resemble in their structure
hysterical spells. Genital masturbation, after repression, may be displaced from
below and make its appearance as a tic (357, 467, 733, 1265). Other tics represent
movements of rage or movements used to ward off hostile impulses or movements of a person with whom the patient has unconsciously identified himself.

> A patient's tic, consisting in a jerking movement of the jaws, which on a more
> superficial layer had the significance of a reassurance against the fear that the
> jaws might be paralyzed, turned out to represent an imitation of the yawning of
> the patient's father. This yawning had been perceived as a sexual threat and had
> been answered by an identification with the aggressor.

Many tics are not only involuntary motor equivalents of emotional activity in
general but rather disturbances of one particular emotional function, not yet investigated sufficiently by psychoanalysis: the mimetic expression of feelings and
emotions (986). The archaic discharge syndromes of affects consist, in part, of
innervations of the mimetic musculature. This fact turns mimetic expressions
into an archaic means of communication between persons. For infants, before the
ability to speak is achieved, it is the only means. Among adults, it still governs
many of their relations with one another (525, 998, 1517); even when full emo-

tional spells have become rare, the facial expression signifies an involuntary equivalent of affects which, by means of empathy, informs spectators of the nature of the subject's feelings (*see* pp. 424 and 438).

The involuntary play of the facial musculature can be looked upon as a normal model for tics. In some types of tic an affect representative of mimetic expression has made itself independent.

A patient with a tic and who was close to hysteria had been trained "never to show emotions." The tic represented the mimetic expression of a suppressed crying of which he was not aware. It occurred whenever something came up that might have provoked crying or that reminded him: "You should not express your emotions." Actually, he had a tendency to cry easily, and during a certain period of his analysis, after the tic as a suppression of crying had been analyzed but the unconscious meaning of the crying itself had not, he actually cried a great deal. The tendency to cry had a urethral meaning, and the conflicts around "not expressing emotions" meant conflicts around bedwetting.

In another case a facial tic turned out to be the representative of an intended, but forbidden, triumphant laughter directed against the patient's father and later against his own superego.

What has been said about the exhibitionistic component in stuttering holds true for tic as well. The exhibition is directed toward gaining narcissistic reassurance; this intention may fail and end in a new narcissistic hurt.

There is a definite relation between tic and children's (and actors') play with their facial expressions. "Making faces" is a game liked by all children, and "Don't make such an ugly face, it might freeze that way" is the customary threat against it. Some tics look as if they were fulfillments of this threat.

What is the unconscious meaning of the game of making faces? (1) The active play of being ugly is enjoyed as a proof that the person controls beauty and ugliness, that is, that one is not castrated for good, since one can bring about and undo castration at will. (2) Being ugly means being able to frighten others, that is, being powerful, which is felt as a reassurance. (3) To play the part of the ugly (castrated) one is an archaic means of misleading the powers that want to make one ugly (to castrate) (296, 483, 500, 634). (4) To play being ugly (castrated) serves as a magical gesture, an attack on the spectator: "I show you how ugly (how castrated) you ought to be."

The uncanny feeling that the facial muscles no longer obey and act independently means that these techniques have failed, that one does not control the castrating powers, and that the punishment of permanent ugliness (permanent castration) is at hand.

The independence of the emotional motor impulses from the organized ego thus is the main problem of tic. It has been stated before that certain simpler types of tic seem to differ little from hysterical seizures. A previously repressed impulse makes its appearance out of repression in a disguised form. The more characteristic cases, however, seem to be disturbed in a much deeper sense. The ability for ego control of motor disturbances seems lacking or insufficient. Instead of acting as a means for voluntary and directed action, the musculature has become again, to a greater or lesser degree, an instrument for immediate discharge (1012, 1100). A lack in ego organization is present. Individual impulses or affects are not integrated into a whole. This lack of integration determines the difference between a typical tic and a conversion hysteria. It may have an organic basis, at least in certain cases. Psychologically it is always connected with a deep pregenital regression (or a pregenital arrest of development) which has become interpolated between Oedipus complex and symptom.

A study of the personality of tic patients shows that their mental life is clearly pregenital in orientation. The tic, again, represents a "pregenital conversion." As a matter of fact, this designation was introduced by Abraham for the purpose of describing the nature of tics (22).

The two important factors observed in the mental life of tic patients, according to clinical writers on the subject (22, 321, 492, 493, 954, 976, 996, 1049), are, first, their well-defined anal character and, second, their marked narcissistic make-up. In severe multiple tics (*maladie des tics*) all these characteristics are still more outspoken than in patients with isolated and individualized tic movements. The anal orientation of patients with maladie des tics reveals itself frequently at first glance by the coughing, spitting, twitching, swearing, and coprolalia which are a part of their syndrome (492, 1100). The use of the musculature for immediate discharge rather than for directed action is here a symptom of an intolerance for tension and waiting, comparable to the corresponding intolerance in other infantile personalities (*see* pp. 367 ff.).

The anal character has the same origin as in compulsion neurotics and in stutterers. It mainly represents an anal-sadistic regression from the Oedipus complex. In a minority of cases it may represent an arrested development at the pregenital level. In the same way that the anal-erotic increment intensified the oral-respiratory eroticism of speech in stuttering, it augments an intensified muscular eroticism in tic. This muscular eroticism is manifest in cases in which the tic represents a simple equivalent of masturbation (357, 733, 1265).

The narcissistic orientation appears in cases of tic in various degrees and measures. In some cases one finds, at least in unconscious fantasies, as much capacity for relationships with objects as in the average compulsion neurotic. Other cases seem to have secluded themselves from the world of objects much more thoroughly. The muscles which behave like personalities independent of the ego may really represent introjected objects, and the involuntarily moving muscles may be feared and hated by the patient on a narcissistic level in the same way that threatening objects have been feared and hated previously. The relation between the ego and the rebellious muscles supplants, in narcissistic personalities, object relationships that have been lost. Object cathexes, by a narcissistic regression, have been replaced by cathexes of organ representations; the muscles try to discharge the cathexis of their "representations" which is accumulated as in hypochondriasis. Ferenczi referred to "muscular memory traces" which are "abreacted" in the tic. Whereas in hysteria the memory of repressed experiences in the form of object-libidinal fantasies breaks through against the will of the ego, in the narcissistic tic the corresponding organ-libidinal narcissistic memory traces break through (492).

Since belated motor discharges of exciting impressions are a typical symptom of traumatic neuroses, it is understandable that tics frequently occur in neuroses that are a mixture of traumatic neuroses and psychoneuroses (see pp. 541 ff.), for example, in neuroses developed under the influence of a frightening primal scene.

A very interesting case of tic, reported by Kulovesi, proved to be determined by a primal-scene experience in early infancy (996). In the excitement attending this experience, the frightened little boy suppressed certain motor impulses, particularly impulses to scream and weep. The motions he curbed at that time then occurred subsequently throughout life in the form of a tic. He remained fixated on the primal scene, and regressed to it whenever he suffered a disappointment in later life. Melanie Klein's contention, that in cases of tic the primal-scene experience has unfailingly been apprehended through hearing, does not seem convincing (954). It is more probable that the specific muscle-erotic orientation, with which patients of this type probably experience the primal scene, is connected with exciting sensations of depth sensibility and equilibrium. Generally, psychogenic dysfunctions of the muscular system are closely interwoven with defenses against body feelings and kinesthetic sensations (410). It is not rare that a memory of a primal scene is displaced and represented by a memory trace of the semicircular canals (526).

As to the prognosis for psychoanalysis of tic patients, first of all, cases of an organic origin have to be excluded. In other cases the outcome will depend on the specific mental structure. Hysterical and compulsive forms of tic will respond to treatment just as hysterias and compulsion neuroses do; catatonic forms will prove as refractory as catatonias. In view of the fact that it is characteristic for the more typical severe cases of tic to be narcissistically oriented, psychoanalytic treatment will be difficult. This certainly holds true for the severe ego disturbances in maladie de tic. However, in cases where there was an adequate capacity for transference, prolonged analysis has achieved therapeutic success.

BRONCHIAL ASTHMA

Bronchial asthma has already been discussed as an organ neurosis of the respiratory tract (see pp. 251 f.). It was mentioned that in practically all cases conversion symptoms are involved as well. Now it must be added that these conversion symptoms are pregenital in nature. In the discussion of the organneurotic basis of bronchial asthma, it became clear what physical conditions make conversions of this type possible. The unconscious content of the conversions is regularly seated in deep oral-respiratory conflicts around the mother or a mother substitute. In general, psychogenic disturbances of breathing are, primarily, anxiety equivalents. Whenever these equivalents are expressed primarily in the respiratory system, the anxiety, whether originally over loss of love or over castration, is perceived as a fear of suffocation (735, 741). In the asthmatic attack, the expression of such a fear is combined with a cry for help directed toward a mother figure, thought of as omnipotent and still perceived on a pregenital level, protection and sexual satisfaction remaining undifferentiated from each other. As a rule, this "protective sexual satisfaction" is unconsciously perceived as the aim of a respiratory introjection (420).

It is in accordance with the pregenital character of the basic conversion that patients with asthma mainly present a compulsive character, with all the features of an increased anal-sadistic orientation (ambivalence, bisexuality, personality deviations through reaction formations, sexualization of thought and speech). The anal orientation of the patients, as a rule, has developed from an interest in smelling to an interest in breathing.

The physiological model for "respiratory introjection" actually is smelling (202, 1184, 1190). In the act of smelling, a particle of the external world is actually taken into the body. The lower senses generally show a closer relation to pregenital eroticisms than do the higher ones (777). The repression to which pregenitality as a whole is subject makes the sense of smell in the average man much duller than it was in his childhood (624). It appears that the olfactory eroticism which has undergone repression becomes revived whenever there is a regression toward anal and respiratory eroticism.

As in the case of tic, the anal orientation in asthma is also closely related to tendencies rooted in still earlier phases of development. Asthmatic patients turn out to be passively-receptively directed, orally and temperature-erotically dependent, possessed by a very great narcissistic need to regain their lost omnipotence. Sometimes incorporation aims are in the foreground to such an extent that conflicts between the patient and his respiratory apparatus may represent conflicts that originally existed between the child and external objects. The asthmatic attack signifies, in the final analysis, a reaction to the separation from the mother, a cry of appeal to the mother (675, 1340, 1615). In a case described by Weiss (1563) the illness actually set in as a reaction to the loss of the mother and to a subsequent narcissistic identification with her. The research done by French and Alexander (531, 535) came to exactly the same conclusions.

As to psychoanalytic therapy for asthma, in view of the similarity of its unconscious structure to that of other pregenital conversion neuroses, the indications are about the same. The organ-neurotic and organic (allergic) features, however, complicate the prognosis. In asthma, it is more difficult to achieve a symptomatic cure than it is in stuttering; the analyst's task is the complete analytic treatment of the pregenital structure that underlies the symptom.

In discussing the problems of differential etiology, the conditions for regressions have been studied as the differentiating factor between hysteria and compulsion neurosis. In this respect, the pregenital conversion neuroses certainly fulfill the conditions of the compulsion neuroses. They, too, are based on regression. What, then, determines whether a compulsion neurosis or a pregenital conversion neurosis develops? Actually, the pregenital conversion symptoms very often are combined with compulsion-neurotic trends. Concerning their differentiation, it has to be admitted that no definite answer can yet be given. It may be assumed that in the pregenital conversion neuroses the same factor that brought about the regression in compulsion neurosis must be combined with a somatic compliance in the affected organs, either of a constitutional or of an acquired nature.

Chapter XVI

PERVERSIONS AND IMPULSE NEUROSES

GENERAL REMARKS

Perverse activities and the impulses of "psychopaths" (such as the drive to run away, cleptomania, or drug addiction) sometimes are designated as compulsion symptoms because the patients feel "compelled" to carry out their pathological action. But the way in which they experience their impulses is so characteristically different from compulsive experiences that it can be immediately assumed that there must be specific structural differences corresponding to the manifest difference. This manifest difference, however, is not adequately defined by the statement that, in general, perversions and morbid impulses are pleasurable or, at least, are performed in the hope of achieving pleasure, whereas compulsive acts are painful and performed in the hope of getting rid of pain; this rule has exceptions: guilt feelings may disturb a perverse action to such a degree that it actually is felt as painful; certain compulsive games may assume a pleasurable character. More characteristic is the difference in the way the urge is felt. The compulsion neurotic feels forced to do something that he does not *like* to do, that is, compelled to use his volition against his own desires; the pervert feels forced to "like" something, even against his will. Guilt feelings may oppose his impulses; nevertheless at the moment of his excitement he feels the impulse as ego syntonic, as a something he wants to do in the hope of achieving positive pleasure. The impulses in question have, in contrast to compulsive impulses, an "instinctual" character; they are felt in the same way that normal instinctual impulses are felt by normal persons. Because of this difference, perverts and impulse neurotics are sometimes not called neurotics at all but psychopaths.

PERVERSIONS IN GENERAL

Perversions manifestly are *sexual* in character. When the pathological impulses are given in to, orgasm is achieved.

A starting point for the investigation of perversions was initiated by Freud when he discovered infantile sexuality and disclosed that the sexual aims of perverts are identical with those of children (555). In the perversions sexuality is replaced by one component of infantile sexuality; the cause and the nature of this substitution constitute the problem.

Even before psychoanalysis, some observers had pointed out that perverse acts are a one-sided and exaggerated distortion of acts which in a less exclusive and less definite form also occur in the sexual behavior of normal persons, especially in introductory activities before intercourse. The condemnation of perversions as "constitutional inferiorities" is one expression of the universal tendency toward the repression of infantile sexuality. Actually, perversions are something universally human. Perversions have been practiced in all ages and among all races, and at certain periods some of them were generally tolerated or even highly esteemed. Freud added the observation that perverse tendencies or occasional perverse acts, or at least fantasies, occur in the life of every single individual, in the normal as well as in the neurotic, whose symptoms are revealed by psychoanalysis to be disguised perverse acts. Freud stated: "If it is correct that real obstacles to sexual satisfaction, or privation in regard to it, bring to the surface perverse tendencies in people who would otherwise have shown none, we must conclude that something in these people is ready to embrace the perversions; or, if you prefer it, that the tendencies must have been present in them in a latent form" (596). Since the aims of perverse sexuality are identical with those of infantile sexuality, the possibility for every human being to become perverse under certain circumstances is rooted in the fact that he was once a child.

Perverts are persons with infantile instead of adult sexuality. This may be due either to an arrested development or to a regression. The fact that perversions frequently are developed as a reaction to sexual disappointments points to the effectiveness of regression. The simple formula presents itself: persons who react to sexual frustrations with a regression to infantile sexuality are perverts; persons who react with other defenses or who employ other defenses after the regression are neurotics. This was the formula still applied by Freud in his *Introductory Lectures* (596).

Actually, things are not quite so simple. It is true there are pathological states that represent nothing but "regressions to infantile sexuality." But they are not the typical perversions. The perverse acts of such persons are polymorphous; the main emphasis of their sexual life is displaced onto the forepleasure, and it is not easy to say where stimulation ends and where gratification begins. Patients of this type are infantile in nonsexual respects also (701, 904).

The typical pervert has one way only of gaining sexual pleasure. All his sexual energies are concentrated on one particular partial instinct, the hypertrophy of which competes with his genital primacy. Nevertheless, if the perverse act is completed, the person achieves a genital orgasm, so that again it would be too simple a formula to state that these patients lack genital primacy. The capacity for genital orgasm is blocked by some obstacle that is more or less overcome by the perverse act. Thus perverse sexuality is not simply unorganized, as is the sexuality of "polymorphously perverse" children and of infantile personalities; it is, rather, organized under the guidance of some component instinct whose satisfaction makes genital orgasm possible again.

Analysis shows that perverts, like neurotics, have repressions; moreover, they, too, have specific pathogenic repressions. They have an unconscious Oedipus complex and an unconscious castration anxiety. Thus the overemphasis of one component of infantile sexuality does not exclude the possibility that other parts of their infantile sexuality are warded off. In fact, the pervert symptom, like the neurotic symptom, gives discharge to a part of the cathexis of impulses that originally had been warded off, and thus facilitates the warding off of the rest (58, 601, 1252). The difference between neuroses and perversions lies in the fact that the symptom is "desexualized" in the neuroses, but is a component of infantile sexuality in the perversions, and that its discharge is painful in the neuroses, but brings genital orgasm in the perversions.

The main problems can now be put in the following way: (1) What determines the disturbance of genital primacy? (2) Why does the gratification of a special partial instinct undo the disturbance of genital primacy?

1. The factor that primarily disturbs genital primacy is identical with the factor that has the same effect in neurotics: anxiety and guilt feelings, directed against the Oedipus complex. However, among the neurotic anxieties that motivate the defense, anxiety over loss of love is less important in perversions, nor can anxiety over one's own excitement be of much importance, since the attainment of orgasm becomes eventually possible. Thus *castration anxiety* (and guilt feelings, which are derivatives of castration anxiety) must be the decisive factor.

> In perversions, adult sexuality is supplanted by infantile sexuality. Something must be repulsive in adult sexuality, and something especially attractive in infantile sexuality. While the latter factor is variable, the former is constant; it is always the castration complex that interferes with the capacity for enjoying full genital sexuality. Actually the differences in the male and in the female castration complex directly correspond to the differences between male and female perversions.

2. After genital enjoyment has become impossible because of castration fear, the person will try to regress to that part of his infantile sexuality to which he is fixated. However, it is not merely that some infantile component that has not been feared is substituted for the feared genital sexuality. Explicit, decisive parts of this infantile sexuality are *repressed,* and apparently the hypertrophy of one sexual infantile component is used for the purpose of strengthening this repression.

The stressing of the fact that fixation determines the choice of the infantile component that is overcathected in the perversion (245) means, first of all, that there is a grain of truth in the old assumption that perversions are "constitutionally" determined. It is, however, surely not so simple as some writers who facilely employ Latin neologisms would have us imagine. Merely to allot to each component impulse a specific hormone, an exceptional amount of which is supposed to be present in the case of the corresponding perversion, is not convincing.

Besides, the fact that normal persons may under certain conditions become pervert definitely restricts the importance assumed for constitutional factors.

That perversions have to do with fixations on childhood experiences was known before psychoanalysis. However, the childhood experiences that were quoted by preanalytic authors were not the cause but rather the first manifestation of the perversion. To state that the first sexual excitement was experienced simultaneously with certain attendant "accidental" circumstances, and that thereafter the individual's sexual reaction remained bound to such circumstances, is an evasion of the question: what caused the sexual excitement to occur just at that time? Such events of childhood prove, in analysis, to be not merely fixating experiences but screen memories which serve as a disguise for the real causes of the fixation. This is further revealed by the fact that incidents of this kind are easily consciously remembered, and that the individual seems only too ready to ascribe to them the origin of the perversion.

> A patient recalled that when once, during his adolescence, he saw a girl with bare legs, he felt the "command to remember": "You must remember this throughout life—that girls, too, have legs." Later the patient developed foot-fetishistic interests. At the time of the incident the patient, out of castration fear, was unconsciously longing for some experience that might enable him to believe that girls have penises. Thus the perversion did not arise because "accidentally" the boy was sexually excited by the sight of girls' legs, but rather he became excited because the sight of girls' legs allayed his castration fear, which would otherwise have disturbed his sexual excitement (423).

Among fixating experiences at the basis of perversions, one type is prominent: experiences of sexual satisfactions which simultaneously gave a feeling of security by denying or contradicting some fear. The pervert, when disturbed in his genital sexuality by castration fear, regresses to that component of his infantile sexuality which once in childhood had given him a feeling of security or at least of reassurance against fear, and whose gratification was experienced with special intensity because of this denial or reassurance. To put it schematically, the pervert is a person whose sexual pleasure is blocked by the idea of castration. Through the perversion he tries to prove that there is no castration. In so far as this proof is believed, sexual pleasure and orgasm become possible again.

The hypertrophy of the reassuring infantile partial instinct simultaneously serves as a safeguard to maintain the repression of the Oedipus complex and of other warded-off remainders of infantile sexuality. This is achieved by a "partial repression" of infantile sexuality, whereas other parts of it are exaggerated (601).

In discussing the defense mechanism of denial, the psychology of screen memories became clear: a person who tries to repress a memory is seeking associatively connected substitute scenes which he may offer his memory (409, 553). This phenomenon finds a parallel in the symptom formation in perversion.

Whereas under other conditions everything that is related to the repressed also becomes the object of repression, in perversions, as in screen memories, the work of repression is apparently facilitated through something associatively connected with the repressed being consciously stressed. The fact that certain impulses, usually forbidden, remain in consciousness guarantees the repression of the Oedipus and castration complexes (1331).

> Some people think that perverts are enjoying some kind of more intense sexual pleasure than normal people. This is not true. Their discharge has become possible after hindrances and through distortions only and is therefore necessarily incomplete. They are, as Freud states, poor devils who have to pay a high price for their limited pleasure (601). The opposite opinion is probably rooted in the fact that the perverts, although experiencing less pleasure than normal people, in a certain sense experience more pleasure than neurotic people, whose repressed infantile sexual longings are not gratified. Neurotics, who have repressed perverse longings, may envy the perverts who express the perverse longings openly.

The following examination of the conditions obtaining in specific perversions will test this theory.

MALE HOMOSEXUALITY

Choosing a sexual partner of the same sex cannot simply be called an infantile partial instinct. However, in children the sex of the partner is far less important than it is in adults, and in the latency period and in adolescence, under present cultural conditions, a certain amount of more or less manifest homosexuality appears regularly (*see* p. 112).

Initially, everyone is able to develop sexual feelings indiscriminately, and the search for an object is less limited by the sex of the object than is commonly supposed.

> It is of great practical importance to bear this fact in mind. A poem composed by a patient in his childhood, in collaboration with his older brother and sister, remained obscure for some time in his analysis. Three men and three women appeared in this poem; it was impossible to understand whom these characters represented, until analysis revealed that they were a double representation of the three siblings. Regardless of their sexes, they appeared at one place as men and at another as women.

The "countersexual" transference, that is, a patient's mother transference to a male analyst or father transference to a woman analyst, is a frequent occurrence in analytic practice.

> For the majority of patients, the sex of the analyst is not very important. Both men and women patients can and do develop both father and mother transferences toward their analyst, whether male or female. However, a minority of patients

may have a completely different reaction toward men and toward women analysts. This minority of patients consists of persons who are more under the dominance of their castration complex than others, and includes the homosexuals.

The fact that in a normal person the object choice later becomes more or less limited to the opposite sex is a problem in itself. This problem offers less difficulty for the boy, because the mother, his first love object, is a person of the opposite sex; the development of the girl in the direction of normal choice of object is more complicated because her first object was a homosexual one (*see* pp. 89 ff.).

A certain amount of sexual feeling toward one's own sex remains in everyone as a residue of the original freedom of choice.

This freedom may be ascribable to a biological "bisexuality" of man. However, this term does not have a very definite meaning (216, 1243). The fact that female hormones are found in men and male ones in women is certainly connected but not identical with the fact that every embryo has the anlage of both the Wolffian and Müllerian duct, or with the fact that both sexes have a number of rudimentary characteristics of the opposite sex. These facts, again, are probably connected but certainly not identical with the facts at the basis of the cytological theories that every single living cell contains a material (female) and a locomotor (male) component, and that sexuality is a purely relative character, so that one and the same cell may be feminine with reference to a more masculine cell, and masculine with reference to a more feminine one (752).

Nor is the term bisexuality clear in the psychological realm. Three aspects, which have frequently been confused with each other, should be differentiated: (*a*) whether a person chooses an object of the same or of the opposite sex, (*b*) whether a person has the sexual aim of actively introducing a part of his own body into that of his object, or whether he has the wish to have something introduced into his body, (*c*) whether a person in general has an active, go-ahead kind of attitude in life, or a more passive, wait-and-see attitude. These three aspects of "masculinity" or "femininity" sometimes coincide in the same individual, but in other cases vary independently of each other, so that there are very active male homosexuals and very passive female ones. Actually what is called masculine and feminine depends more on cultural and social factors than on biological ones. Certainly impulses with active aims as well as with passive ones occur in both sexes.

The problem of homosexuality thus reduces itself to the question: Since the homosexual, like any other human being, originally has the capacity to choose objects of either sex, what limits this capacity to objects of his own sex?

The first question to be asked in this connection is about the role played by physical constitutional factors. Under the pressure of certain conflicts, some individuals are more inclined to employ the mechanisms to be described than others; and among the determinants of this readiness, biological (hormonal) factors are decisive. The nature of these factors may become more comprehensible after the psychogenic causes of the blocking of heterosexual object choice have been clarified (*see* pp. 337 and 365 f.).

In certain situations where there are no women, for example, at sea or in prisons, men who under other circumstances would have remained normal establish homosexual relationships. This is called accidental homosexuality (555) and proves that latently every man is capable of this type of object choice. Normally a man prefers women as his sexual objects; if women are not available, however, men are his second choice.

Just as in accidental homosexuality the actual absence of women induces men to resort to their second choice, so in homosexual men some other reason must exclude the possibility of the first choice. The search for this other reason reveals an impressive fact. The rejection of women by homosexual men is in general distinctly a genital one. Many homosexual men make good friends with women and respect them highly, but any idea of genital contact is repulsive or frightening. Whenever the difference in the genitals of the sexes is of outstanding importance to an individual and whenever his relationships to his fellow human beings are in every respect determined by the sex of the others, such an individual is under the influence of a strong castration complex. This is true of homosexual men, analysis of whom regularly shows that they are afraid of female genitals. For them the sight of a being without a penis is so terrifying that they avoid it by rejecting any sexual relationship with such a partner (160, 162, 1345). The homosexual man, Freud says, is so determined on the existence of a penis that he refuses to do without it in his sexual partner (566).

The sight of female genitals may arouse anxiety in a boy in two ways: (1) The recognition of the fact that there are actually human beings without a penis leads to the conclusion that one might also become such a being; such an observation lends effectiveness to old threats of castration (566, 599, 612). Or (2) the female genitals, through the connection of castration anxiety with old oral anxieties, may be perceived as a castrating instrument capable of biting or tearing off the penis (814). Quite frequently a combination of both types of fear is encountered.

> Mythology and the dreams of men with castration anxiety are filled with ideas of "terrible phallic women," like Medusa's head, the snakes of which definitely are phallic symbols, or witches, with one protruding tooth, riding on a broomstick. These figures are not frightening *because* they are phallic but rather *though* they are phallic. The phallic characteristics are attempts to deny and to overcompensate the lack; however, the attribution has not proved successful, and the figure remains frightful even after this addition (634).

A castration shock provoked in boys by the sight of female genitals is by no means characteristic for homosexuals. It is found frequently in the history of heterosexual men as well. What is decisive is the reaction to this shock. Homosexual men react by refusing to have anything to do with such frightening sights thereafter.

A few homosexuals, namely, men who in their early childhood had an unusual fixation on a man (cases where there was no mother figure so that the father had to assume the place usually taken by the mother), regress, after the acquisition of this attitude, simply to their point of fixation and choose men who remind them of their primary object (1621). Most homosexuals, however, cannot so easily free themselves of their normal biological longing for women. They continue to be attracted by women but, not being able to endure the idea of beings without a penis, they long for phallic women, for hermaphrodites, so to speak. This acute longing for objects with a penis compels them to choose boys, but the boys must have a maximum of girlish and feminine traits. Such persons still adhere to their original love objects, but since the physical attributes of femininity are repulsive to them, the objects must appear in masculine guise. In the practices and fantasies of homosexuals, men in women's clothes as well as girls in men's clothes play a large part, and the homosexual ideal of the "page boy" proves that they actually are looking for the "girl with a penis." Psychoanalysis reveals that homosexual men usually do not cease to be sexually aroused by women; they simply repress this interest and displace the excitement, originally aroused by women, to men (555). Very often the male objects of homosexuals show certain characteristics of the patient's mother or sister.

A friend of a homosexual patient bore a striking resemblance to his sister, and in addition his name was almost the same as hers.

The majority of homosexuals not only present an Oedipus love for their mothers, just as do neurotic individuals, but for the most part the intensity of the mother fixation is even more pronounced. Sometimes the devotion to the mother is not unconscious at all but frankly talked about.

Following the loss of an object or disappointment in an object, everyone tends to regress from the level of object love to that of identification; he becomes the object which he cannot possess. Thus the homosexual individual identifies himself with the object, after having been disappointed by its genitals (608, 1364); what determines whether he will become homosexual is how and in what respect this identification takes place. The homosexual man identifies himself with his frustrating mother in one particular respect: like her, he loves men.

In quite a number of male homosexuals, the decisive identification with the mother was made as an "identification with the aggressor," that is, in boys who were very much afraid of their mothers.

After the decisive identification, the further development may go in various directions:

1. The type of individual who is more narcissistic than "feminine" endeavors first of all to secure a substitute for his Oedipus strivings. Having identified himself with his mother, he behaves as he previously had wished his mother to behave toward him. He chooses as love objects young men or boys who, for him, are similar to himself, and he loves them and treats them with the tenderness he had desired from his mother. While he acts as if he were his mother, emotionally he is centered in his love object, and thus enjoys being loved by himself.

This schematic outline of development may be subject to a number of complications. The woman with whom the patient has identified himself may be not his mother but rather a sister, or some other woman from the infantile environment. The transference from the mother to this other person may have occurred at a very early age, or simultaneously with the regression from love to identification.

This type of development produces "subject homoerotic" individuals who actively seek younger persons as objects (164, 465). Being narcissistically in love with themselves and their penises, being "phallic characters" (*see* pp. 495 f.) and fixated to that period of life when the decisive turn occurred, such persons usually love adolescent boys, who represent themselves at the time of their own adolescence (555). Most often they behave very tenderly toward their objects; but it may also occur, if their sexuality was previously masochistically distorted, that they behave rather sadistically toward them.

A young man with character difficulties presented himself in analysis as very gentle and feminine, always ready to step aside in favor of others; his manifest sexual life was limited to masturbation; he had numerous men friends in whom he was more interested than in women. In the course of his analysis, he frequently was occupied with psychological commentaries about his friends, which actually were valid for himself. Thus it became obvious that his friends were selected on the basis of the narcissistic type of object choice. The patient devoted himself to his friends with a tender care that could only be termed maternal. Gradually he came to realize that his passive nature resembled that of his placid mother. He once said: "My mother and I, we must stick together, for we are fellow sufferers." These words, while having a definite conscious meaning, concealed his genital identification with the "castrated" mother, whom he unconsciously imitated in choosing friends who resembled himself.

Another patient, whose personality and neurosis were governed by an identification with his mother, was perversely desirous to have his sweetheart urinate in his presence, while he encouraged her in a friendly manner. He was playing the role of his mother, who used to put him on the chamber pot when he was a baby.

The same mechanism occurs in heterosexual individuals as well. Narcissistic men who during childhood or puberty liked to think of themselves as girls later may fall in love with (more or less boyish) "little girls" in whom they see the reincarnation of themselves, and then treat these girls as they would have liked to be treated by their mothers (416). These men do not love their feminine partners as individual entities but rather they love in them the feminine parts of their own ego (1565). A castration anxiety, similar to that in cases of homosexuality, may result in an unconscious constellation in which the narcissistically chosen girl, loved with the tenderness once desired from the mother for oneself, represents not only one's own person in adolescence but specifically one's own penis (428). Certain character types are governed by a need to give to others what they did not get themselves, enjoying the "getting" by means of identification with the person to whom they give (607). Anna Freud has described such a type of "altruism" wherein certain pleasures, which the persons are inhibited from granting themselves, are given to others and enjoyed in identification with these others (541). The love felt for the privileged friends, then, may be a very ambivalent one mixed with envy and turn into immediate fury if the girls are not as happy as the patients wanted them to be.

The mechanism basic in this type of homosexuality is probably also the root of another perversion, pedophilia (247, 927). It is true that sometimes more superficial reasons may suffice for persons to be attracted by children. Children are weak and remain approachable when other objects are excluded through anxiety (Freud stated that pedophilia is the perversion of "weak and impotent" persons) (555). But usually a love for children is based on a narcissistic object choice. Unconsciously the patients are narcissistically in love with themselves as children; they treat their child objects either in the same way as they would have liked to be treated or in the completely opposite manner (950).

In a sublimated form, the same motives that produce pedophilia may produce a pedagogical interest. Love of children usually means: "Children ought to be better off than I was"; in a minority of cases, the opposite is true: "Children should not be better off than I was" (128).

A repression of a pedophilic attitude may result in a kind of fear of children or lack of understanding of children. Some persons are more or less embarrassed when forced to deal with children or adolescents; for the most part these are persons who are obliged to repress what they themselves felt as children or adolescents. (In a minority of cases the "other children" do not represent one's own person but other children from the patient's childhood history—for example, siblings.)

2. The clinical picture is very different if, following the identification with the mother, an anal fixation determines the subsequent development. The wish for sexual gratification with the mother becomes transformed into the wish to enjoy it in the same manner as the mother does. With this as a point of departure, the father becomes the object of love, and the individual strives to submit himself to him, as the mother does, in a passive-receptive manner (555). In the discussion of compulsion neurosis, it became clear what conditions favor anal

regression, and likewise that an anal regression in men results in an increase in feminine reactions (*see* pp. 305 f.). The femininity that was warded off and remained latent in compulsion neurotics becomes manifest in the homosexual of this type. This is the basis for the development of "object homoerotic" individuals (465). In such cases the Oedipus complex was resolved by the assumption of the negative Oedipus attitude characteristic for the opposite sex (608).

Whereas patients of this type, being "feminine," manifestly behave in a very kind and tender fashion, they unconsciously may be governed by more or less hostility toward the father figures they are submitting to. Nunberg has described a subcategory of this type of homosexual, which is characterized by an unusual intensity of such latent hostility (1181). The passive submission to the father covers the unconscious idea of robbing him of his masculinity on this occasion, the homosexual intercourse meaning active castration. Actually "feminine" men often have not entirely given up their striving to be masculine. Unconsciously they regard their femininity as temporary, as a means to an end; they regard the condition of being a masculine man's "feminine" partner as learning the secrets of masculinity from the "master," or as depriving him of those secrets. In such cases, the passive submission to the father is combined with traits of an old and original (oral) identification love of the father (147). Every boy loves his father as a model whom he would like to resemble; he feels himself the "pupil" who, by temporary passivity, can achieve the ability to be active later on. This type of love could be called the apprentice love; it is always ambivalent because its ultimate aim is to replace the master. After having given up the belief in his own omnipotence and having projected it onto the father, there are several ways in which a boy may try to regain participation in the father's omnipotence. The two opposite extremes are the idea of killing the father in order to take his place and the idea of ingratiation, of being obedient and submissive to such a degree that the father will willingly grant participation. Homosexual men of the type here discussed may be found along the entire scale between these two extremes (436).

> Some homosexuals are governed unconsciously by their ambivalent love for "bigger boys" who dare do things they themselves do not dare. To participate in the sexual adventures of "the boys on the other side of the tracks" offers the advantage of sexual pleasure with a decrease of responsibility: "Not I, but the others have done it." Love for them may be combined with all degrees of hostility toward and fear of them.

Not only an unconscious hostility toward the father may be overcompensated by such a type of love but also an earlier fear of the father. "I do not need to be afraid of father, since we love each other." But this attempt to escape does not always succeed. The ways in which denial of anxiety is attempted may arouse new anxiety. Having tried to escape castration as a punishment for sexual wishes about the mother, he now fears castration as a prerequisite for sexual gratification by the father (599).

Femininity in men, that is, the sexual goal of having the sexual partner introduce something into one's body, usually connected with the fantasy of being a woman (163), is frequently but not necessarily combined with homosexuality: with the choice of a partner of the same sex. Its basis is an identification with the mother in regard to instinctual aim. This type of identification occurs when there has been a previous fixation on the passive-receptive incorporation aims of the pregenital period; as a rule, the anal-erogenous zone is the leading one. There is also a "passive genital zone" in men, that of prostatic erogeneity; but, practically, it is inextricably interwoven with anality (*see* pp. 82 f.). The fact that the pregenital aims of incorporation are much more similar to subsequent feminine genitality than to masculine genitality is the basis of "femininity" in men.

Actually, femininity in men is always connected with castration anxiety:

(*a*) The decisive identification with the mother may arise out of castration fear, connected with the sight of her genitals. Certain men, who are not homosexual at all, exhibit love that is full of features of identification with their sexual partner; the identification serves the purpose of fighting anxiety. A patient who loved women with this type of "identification love" wanted to prove to his girl friends: "See how well I understand you and all your interests; see what a degree of empathy I am capable of, that actually there is no difference between you and me!" A relatively late, traumatic observation of a woman's genitals had disturbed this boy's development. He experienced the sight as something entirely strange. He condensed all his earlier castration fears into a fear of this strange thing, which he perceived as an oral danger. He attempted to master this anxiety by denying that women are different; he assumed the attitude: "Women are exactly the same as I am; there are no frightening discoveries to be made, because I know everything about female matters." He identified himself with the object of his anxiety and became "feminine."

(*b*) In other cases of femininity in men the following attitude is decisive: "Because I am afraid that men might castrate me, I do not want to have anything to do with them; I prefer to live among women." These persons, of course, are heterosexual though feminine. They have to repress their homosexuality because homosexuality would mean having contact with men. Men of this type are interested rather in feminine homosexuality, they want to be a "girl among girls," and are interested in feminine games and activities. Frequently, this type of "femininity" holds anxiety in check only as long as the fact that women have no penises can be denied by some other means.

Femininity as a protection against the danger of castration may fail entirely if the person cannot deny that "becoming a girl" would mean losing his penis. We find in feminine men manifold attempts to keep up this denial; they try to stress the fact that they actually have a penis, while acting as though they were girls; thus there are girls with penises. A similar frequent unconscious reasoning can be formulated as follows: "I am afraid that I might be castrated. If I act like a girl, people will think that it has already been done, and in this way I shall escape."

Femininity in men, generally, is an expression of infantilism, of regression to passive types of mastery. Initially, also, the phallic love of the little boy for his mother was not an active one (1071). As a baby, the boy—like the girl—enjoys, passively, being taken care of; "feminine" behavior in men may be actually an infantile behavior, and therefore does not need to be directed toward persons of the same sex but may be directed toward mother substitutes.

In the discussion of inhibition states, types of men have been described whose activity is inhibited generally, in the main because unconsciously they have an intense aggressiveness of which they are afraid (see pp. 178 f.). Men of this type sometimes feel that if they were a woman, they would not be expected to be active, and thereupon develop feminine longings. The warded-off aggressiveness may then return, and the unconscious leading thought be changed into: "If I were a woman, I would have the opportunity to take revenge on men."

In bisexual men it is, at times, not easy to determine whether the positive or the negative Oedipus complex has played the primary role. As a rule, a better understanding will be attained if it is assumed that the normal Oedipus complex forms the deeper level, whereas the reverse Oedipus complex is a reaction to the normal one.

3. Since narcissistic and anal fixations may occur in the same person, combinations of both types of homosexuality occur. Terms like subject homoerotic and object homoerotic have only a relative significance. Active homosexuality in a man may serve to repress a deeper passive homosexual longing and vice versa. These types constitute the majority of all male homosexualities, but occasionally other types occur.

4. The possibility that a person who has been brought up without a mother may react to a castration shock with a loss of interest in women altogether and a return to the masculine objects of his childhood has been mentioned (1621).

5. Freud has described some "mild" homosexuals, in whose cases the early masculine model for fixation was not the father but an older brother (607). An extreme friendliness between siblings of the same sex frequently is found in analysis to be an overcompensation of a primary hatred. The affectionate attitude toward the brother developed after a period of hostility, and the original hatred may still betray itself in some signs of ambivalence in the later love. Homosexual love of this type which, according to Freud, contributes largely to that which later forms "social feelings" (606) is mixed with characteristics of identification. Younger brothers who have successfully overcome an envious hatred of their older brothers regard them with affection as soon as an identification goes far enough for them to consider their brother's successes their own. They then no longer feel "He is successful, and I am not," but "We are successful." Such mechanisms often play a decisive part in pathological hero worship.

A patient with a very successful brother had succeeded in "sharing the brother's glory." However, the primary envy was betrayed by his obsessive rumination as to whether this or that hero was "greater."

This type of overcompensating love through identification well serves the purpose of getting rid of a disturbing and hopeless hatred, for the patient need no longer compete with his brother. He and his brother may divide, as it were, the fields of activities between themselves. Certain fields of endeavor will be given over to the brother because the brother's success supplies all the gratification needed. In this way competitive collision with the brother is avoided. This, again, is the basis of certain types of "altruism" in which the envied success is willingly left to the other person (604). In identification with him, the other's success may be enjoyed, while guilt feelings would make the enjoyment of one's own success impossible (541). The field of sexual activity is particularly subject to the influence of this type of evasion. If a person is homosexual and desires the brother himself as an object, sexual competition with the brother is thereby evaded.

It is clear that there are many points of contact between this type of overcompensating identification love and the types of homosexuality described before. The brother toward whom one behaves "altruistically" may simultaneously represent the image of what one had desired to be oneself. An identification with the mother certainly does not exclude the simultaneous presence of an identification with a brother on some other level.

In general, identification plays more of a role in homosexual love than in heterosexual love. Homosexual objects resemble the patient's own person more than heterosexual ones, which explains the intimate relationship between homosexuality and narcissism (1364).

Insight into the mechanisms of homosexuality makes it possible to come back to the problem of its differential etiology. Pregenital fixations, especially anal ones, and the readiness to substitute identifications for object relationships are the necessary prerequisites. This readiness must be combined with a special intensity of secondary narcissism, of self-love, that is. The probability of homosexual orientation is increased the more a boy tends to identify with the mother. Children in general tend to identify themselves more with the parent from whom they have experienced the more impressive frustrations. This explains Freud's findings that those men are more inclined to become homosexual who have had a "weak" father or no father at all (555), who, in other words, were frustrated in crucial things by their mother. However, the opposite also is true. Boys who have had no mother are also inclined to become homosexual, but for different reasons: the enjoyment of the passive pleasures of pregenital times, at the hands of a man instead of a woman, creates a disposition toward homosexuality. Freud made the suggestion that the extent of male homosexuality in ancient Greece may have been due to the fact that children were brought up by male slaves (555).

FEMALE HOMOSEXUALITY

The castration shock, which has as its origin the sight of the female genitals, is the principal factor that makes the female sex unacceptable to male homosexuals. Is it possible that the sight of a penis may disturb the sexual pleasure of some women in a similar manner? The answer is in the affirmative, if certain differences are noted. The sight of a penis may create a fear of an impending violation; more frequently it mobilizes thoughts and emotions about the difference in physical appearance. These fears, thoughts, and emotions may disturb the capacity for sexual enjoyment to such a degree that sexual pleasure is possible only if there is no confrontation with a penis. Insofar, female homosexuality actually is analogous to male homosexuality. But another factor complicates the picture. With women, the exclusion of heterosexual genitals can be achieved by a *regression*. The first object of every human being is the mother; all women, in contradistinction to men, have had a primary homosexual attachment, which may later be revived if normal heterosexuality is blocked. Whereas a man in this situation has only the possibility of regression from "object relationship to mother" to "identification with mother," a woman can regress from "object relationship to father" to "object relationship to mother" (328, 329, 626, 628, 1007).

Thus in female homosexuality, two etiological factors have to be considered: (*a*) the repulsion from heterosexuality originating in the castration complex, and (*b*) the attraction through early fixations on the mother. The two factors supplement each other, for fixation on the mother may have a protective and reassuring function, balanced against the forces of the castration complex; thus the general formula for perversions is again valid: that those fixations are revived which tend to give sexual satisfaction and security simultaneously.

With respect to the factors that repel normal heterosexuality, female and male homosexuality are analogous. Freud described a case in which the crucial factor in the development of a female homosexuality was a severe disappointment caused by the father when the girl was adolescent. The patient responded to this by identifying herself with her father; from that time on, she selected as her love objects women who resembled her mother. In her case, secondary gains obtained through the avoidance of competition with the mother, as well as through the opportunity of taking revenge on her offending father, were very evident (604). This case corresponded to those male homosexualities designated above as type (2) (*see* pp. 333 f.). After identification with the mother, the men of type (2) developed the desire to be loved by the father as he loved the mother; here there is, after identification with the father, a desire to love the mother in the way the father loved her.

The crucial disappointment in Freud's case (604) was the birth of a sibling during the patient's puberty, that is, at a time when she herself unconsciously wished intensely to have a baby by her father. In his discussion of the case, Freud asks whether the development of that particular homosexual orientation might not have been due to the fact that the decisive disappointment was experienced by the girl at the time of puberty and not earlier. It seems more probable that the event in puberty produced so severe an effect because it was perceived as a repetition of some analogous infantile experience. It might be expected that this infantile experience was connected with the castration complex; however, the incomplete analysis of the case reveals nothing to that effect; we only know that, in addition to the child born at the patient's puberty, there was another sibling born three years earlier.

This type (2) seems to be frequent among homosexual women. The patients respond to disappointment over their Oedipus wishes with an identification with their father, and consequently assume an active masculine relation to women who represent mother substitutes. The attitude of these active "masculine" homosexual women toward their (mother-equivalent) objects often is combined with all the features of the "wish-fulfillment" type of female castration complex described by Abraham (20). Just as Freud's patient used her homosexuality as an aggression against her father, so other patients may combine homosexuality with hostility toward men in general, as if they wished to demonstrate: "I do not need any men, I can be a man myself."

In describing normal sexual development, it was stated that clitoris sexuality in women is more apt to disturb normal sexuality than prostate erogeneity does in men (*see* p. 83). This is one reason why "masculinity" in women is more important than "femininity" in men. Another is the different treatment accorded men and women under present cultural conditions.

"Masculinity" in women, that is, the sexual goal to insert something into the partner's body, originates analogously to "femininity" in men: through an identification with the heterosexual parent (or with a brother). Whereas the "feminine" goal in men corresponds to pregenital aims of incorporation, the goal of "masculine" women is in opposition to them. In cases where frustration of the wishes for incorporation has led to a sadistic attitude of taking by force what was not given, this force, originally often thought of as a penetration into the mother's body (958), may be remobilized in later "masculinity."

Again, "masculinity" in women is not necessarily connected with homosexuality. Women may also behave in a very "masculine" manner toward men. Women of this type have identification traits closely interwoven with their love. In their male partners, they see and love themselves as men (1565). They may stress the virility of their male partner, react intensely to his penis, and are often very interested in the idea of male homosexuality. Often girls think that they are not loved by their fathers because they are girls, and that they would be loved if they were boys. In their later love life, they may act the boy loved by the father, as well as the father loving the boy.

Whether or not "masculinity" in women will be combined with homosexuality depends on two circumstances: (*a*) on the intensity of the early fixation on the mother, and (*b*) on the special configuration of the castration complex.

There are also feminine analogies to type (1) of masculine homosexuality. Some active homosexual women, after having identified themselves with their father, choose young girls as love objects who serve as ideal representatives of their own person. They then behave toward these girls as they wished to have been treated by their father.

In childhood, a patient had been exposed to incestuous attacks by her father. He used to put the little girl's hand on his penis and masturbate with it. The patient's homosexuality began with the following incident. At puberty, she got into her younger sister's bed and put the little sister's hand on her own clitoris. In other words, she behaved toward her little sister as her father had behaved toward her. The incestuous experiences had caused the patient to develop an extraordinary fear that her genitals might be injured; the father's large penis might enter her small body, split her or tear her. As a result of this anxiety, she objected to the penis in general and could love only if the penis were eliminated. In her heterosexual relations, she favored impotent men. However, she preferred women to men, and with them she would repeat the childhood experience with her sister. She took over the father's role and tried to do to women what her father had done to her (415).

This type of love, in which the homosexual woman behaves toward an object representing herself "altruistically" in the way she would wish to be treated, may be as ambivalent as the analogous masculine type.

A patient loved "beautiful" young girls. She had an extreme ugliness complex and an intense longing for being as beautiful as her objects. In front of a mirror she would play that she was her beloved object. She was also very jealous of her growing daughter. Her behavior in her ambivalent homosexual loves had obvious characteristics of identification with her father.

Finally, an antagonism between sisters may also become overcompensated and develop into a mild homosexual love, interwoven with identification.

A woman patient, while not overtly homosexual, had an unusual number of women friends. She was constantly preoccupied with feelings of the most tender concern for her older sister; she would reproach herself severely for every little pleasure that she enjoyed and that her sister had to forego. She was very altruistic and would enjoy her sister's pleasures as if they were her own. In this case, it was not difficult to demonstrate the presence of an underlying original hatred for this sister.

In women, the turning away from heterosexuality is a regression that revives memory traces of the early relations to the mother. Female homosexuality therefore has a more archaic imprint than male homosexuality. It brings back the behavior patterns, aims, pleasures, but also the fears and conflicts of the earliest years of life. The actual activities of homosexual women consist mainly in the mutual playing of "mother and child" (328, 329); also the empiric fact that oral eroticism usually is in the foreground in female homosexuality (as is anal eroticism in male) is consonant with its archaic nature.

> Women in whom the passive-receptive attitude toward the mother is in the foreground of their homosexuality are not necessarily "masculine" in their general behavior.

Comparing the analysis of homosexuality with what has been said about perversions in general, it can be stated: neither the Oedipus nor the castration complex is conscious, and yet analysis has demonstrated that both these complexes are decisive. Homosexuality has proved to be the product of specific mechanisms of defense, which facilitate the persistence of the repression of both the Oedipus and the castration complex. At the same time, the aim of homosexual object choice is the avoidance of emotions around the castration complex, which otherwise would disturb the sexual pleasure, or at least the attainment of reassurances against them (601, 1331).

FETISHISM

The next form of perversion to be discussed, fetishism, likewise does not simply consist in the hypertrophy of an infantile partial instinct; the function of denying castration fear, however, is here especially evident.

The prepsychoanalytic literature on fetishism described it as being determined by some childhood experience which established a sort of conditioned reflex. The fetishistic impulse was supposed to be due to a displacement of sexual excitement onto a circumstance that accidentally accompanied the first sexual manifestation. Analytically, those "accidental" incidents must be evaluated as screen memories. The foot fetishist who became fixated on the incident of seeing his governess expose her foot (596) had some unconscious reason why the sight of a foot, ordinarily innocent enough, aroused his sexual excitation. The real significance of this screen memory becomes clear through the symbolic equation of foot and penis. The memory seems to conceal the following unconscious thought: "I saw the penis of my governess" or "I saw that my governess has a penis." The patient surely could not have seen anything of the kind. Quite obviously this thought was utilized by him to deny that he had seen that his governess did *not* have a penis. It was this unpleasant memory that was kept repressed by the repudiating screen memory. The sexual excitement he experienced upon seeing the foot could be described as follows: "The thought that there are human beings without a penis, and that I might myself be one of them, makes it impossible for me to grant myself sexual excitement. But now I see here a symbol of a penis in a woman; that helps me shut out my fear, and thus I can permit myself to be sexually excited." The same mechanism then operates persistently throughout the patient's life. He is able to respond sexually to a woman only if and when her foot expressly reassures him that "a woman does have a penis."

As Freud has pointed out, most of the typical fetishes are penis symbols: shoes, long hair, earrings. Fur serves as a symbolic substitute for pubic hair, the sight of which might make a child question whether or not it covers a penis. Sexual interest in women's underwear is increased, as an allusion to female nudity, when complete nudity has to be avoided. When less typical fetishes are employed, the history of the individual's early childhood reveals experiences in which this fetish subjectively acquired the significance of a "female penis" (621).

A patient in analysis related the following memory. At about the age of four he was lying in his parents' bed. Through an accidental uncovering, he saw his father's penis and was frightened by its size. He asked himself whether his mother might have an equally large penis. He waited for an opportunity when he could unobservedly lift her nightgown a little; he saw a large penis, and was very satisfied with the discovery. The patient, of course, understood the absurdity of this story; but the incident was so vivid in his memory that he had a feeling that he could guarantee its correctness. The contradiction contained in this story, that first the size of the penis in the father terrified him, but then in the mother satisfied him, became the starting point for the analysis of this screen memory. It became probable that the real facts were reversed. The boy probably saw, on the occasion of an accidental uncovering, the mother's genitals, was terrified by the sight, wondered whether the father also looked that way, lifted *his* shirt, and with great satisfaction saw a large penis (437).

This patient did not turn into a fetishist. The perception which he used as a denial of the mother's lack of a penis arose from the observation of the father's body. It can be imagined that, if he had used some penis substitute connected with the mother's body for the same purpose for which he actually used his father's penis, he would have become a fetishist.

An objection to this theory of fetishism (621) seems to be presented by cases in which the fetish represents a symbol not for a penis but for feces, urine, or objects once connected with pregenital activities (77, 677, 987). Some fetishists choose hollow objects as their fetishes, into which they introduce their fingers, or objects having penis significance, or even their penises; such a fetish even seems to represent a vagina (476). Moreover, in fetishists, the possessive urge to be the sole owner of the object is particularly stressed, and some fetishists are "collectors" (1597); the fetish may be an object with little intrinsic value but takes on an immense importance through the fetishistic overvaluation. Often the odor is decisive.

This material does not contradict the thesis that the principal significance of the fetish is to represent "mother's penis." Individuals in whom castration anxiety is provoked very suddenly and intensely are candidates for later fetishism; but they are also those who tend to escape the castration dangers by regression to pregenital levels (1072, 1515). Thus the pregenital characteristics of fetishes can be considered in the same way as compulsive phenomena in which genital and pregenital drives and anxieties are mutually interwoven, or like the phallic attributes of dreadful phallic mother figures.

The analysis of a man with a fetishistic preference for certain odors, a preference that clearly was anally determined, revealed surprising unconscious fantasies as the determinants of his preference. The patient's mother had died in his early childhood, and he was reared to believe that his stepmother was his real mother. However, he suspected the truth and expended much energy in order to repress his suspicion. It turned out that his pronounced feminine behavior was determined by the idea of showing his father that he would have been a better substitute for his dead mother than was his stepmother. This identification with the dead mother was based on a "respiratory introjection" of her "soul" (420); and the preference for odors represented this preference for nasal introjection. However, this pregenital "respiratory introjection" was closely interwoven with genital tendencies originating in the castration complex. The feminine wishes of the patient were blocked by an intense fear that a fulfillment of his wish to be a woman would endanger his penis. He tried in many ways to reassure himself that it was possible to become a woman and nevertheless retain his penis. (He was simultaneously a transvestite.) The inhalation of feces, which at one level meant the inhalation of the dead mother, meant simultaneously the inhalation of the "spirit of penis," which ensured the possession of the penis.

It may be that, for certain men, every woman provokes castration fear. Then, the object that represents the woman's penis arouses sexual excitement only as long as it is not connected with a woman's body. The original object remains entirely repressed, and only the fetish, which once had been a part of it, remains conscious with exaggerated intensity. Desire is felt not for shoes on women but for women's shoes, isolated from women. Freud spoke of a "partial repression" which makes it possible for a *pars pro toto* to be retained in consciousness, while the *totum* remains repressed (621; *cf. also* 4, 1215).

Certain types of fetishists also show pronounced sadistic features. They may obtain their satisfaction by performing "symbolic castrations" in connection with their fetishes. It is as if their castration fear pushes them close to the idea of castration whenever they become sexually aroused (220). "Braid cutters" are hair fetishists. How a kind of castrating activity can reassure against castration fear will be discussed in connection with braid cutting and sadism (*see* pp. 349 and and 355 f.).

Fetishism as an attempt to deny a truth known simultaneously by another part of the personality presupposes a certain split of the person's ego. Persons whose childhood history has enabled them to make an exceptionally intense use of the defense mechanism of denial are, therefore, predisposed for the development of fetishism (633, 635, 694, 1215).

There is a relation between fetishism and the normal, subjective preconditions for love. In part these preconditions simply represent infantile fixations ("anaclitic type") (585). To a greater degree, however, they are built according to a mechanism analogous to fetishism. The conditions asked for unconsciously represent reassurances against dangers believed to be connected with sexuality.

This theory of fetishism seems to be applicable to masculine cases only. The emphasis on a penis symbol could not enable a girl to maintain the belief in her possession of a penis. Actually, female fetishists are very rare, at least much rarer than male ones. However, the cases that have been studied make it probable that exceptional circumstances actually enabled the women in question to do what is improbable in general: to accept the presence of a penis symbol as a soothing factor against the emotions connected with the idea of lacking this organ. The chief role in female fetishism, too, is played by the castration complex, with stress on the "wish-fulfillment" type (20). The fetish in these cases also represents a penis, simultaneously feared and desired, the penis which the woman wishes to possess by virtue of an identification with her father (824).

TRANSVESTITISM

The homosexual man replaces his love for his mother by an identification with her; the fetishist refuses to acknowledge that a woman has no penis. The male transvestite assumes both attitudes simultaneously (161, 416). He fantasies that the woman possesses a penis, and thus overcomes his castration anxiety, and identifies himself with this phallic woman. Hence the fundamental trend of transvestitism is the same as that found in homosexuality and fetishism: the refutation of the idea that there is a danger of castration. However, the identification with the mother is established not by imitating her object choice but rather her "being a woman." The transvestite act has two unconscious meanings: (a) an object-erotic and fetishistic one: the person cohabits not with a woman but with her clothes, the clothes representing, symbolically, her penis; (b) a narcissistic one: the transvestite himself represents the phallic woman under whose clothes a penis is hidden. Transvestites who are exhibitionistic about displaying their female attire show their symbolic penis in the same manner and for the same reason as true exhibitionists actually show their penis. Behavior of this kind presupposes a rather narcissistic orientation. At deeper levels, fantasies of introjections are found, in which the penis is equated with an introjected woman. On a more superficial level, the transvestite, identified with a phallic woman, seeks new objects, chiefly, as in the homosexual type (2), the father to whom he seems to say: "Love me as you love mother" and "It is not true that this wish of mine endangers my penis." A frequent accidental factor is that the female identification may represent not an identification with the mother but with a "little girl"—for example, with a (real or imaginary) little sister and, on a deeper level, with one's own penis (428).

As for female transvestites, the putting on of men's clothes certainly cannot give the wearer the illusion of having a penis under them; but it may give the illusion that spectators might believe in the existence of such a penis, and it has the significance of playing "being a man." "Making believe that one possesses a penis" and "playing father" are the unconscious meanings of female transvestitism. The difference between transvestitism in men and women respectively is that the man, in spite of "playing woman," actually has the possibility of demonstrating to himself that the penis is not lost by the game, whereas the girl is not in a position to reassure herself in the same manner; she can only pretend. Thus transvestitism in women is a displacement of the envy of the penis to an envy of masculine appearance. Male transvestitism has a more serious character; female transvestitism has a "pretending" character.

EXHIBITIONISM

In exhibitionism a denial of castration is attempted by a simple overcathexis of a partial instinct. Exhibitionism in children certainly has the character of a partial instinct; any child derives pleasure from the display of his genitals and, in pregenital times, of the other erogenous zones and their functions (*see* p. 72). Perverts regress to this infantile aim because the stressing of this aim can be used for denial of a danger that is believed to be connected with normal sexuality. Reassurance against castration can be attained by an exhibitionistic man in the following ways:

1. He unconsciously says to his audience: "Reassure me that I have a penis by reacting to the sight of it." Inner doubt impels the individual to call upon objects as witnesses.

2. He unconsciously says to his audience: "Reassure me that you are *afraid* of my penis, that is, that you fear me; then I do not need to be afraid myself" ("identification with the aggressor") (541); this is especially clear when exhibitionists derive their pleasure from performing their perversion before little girls only, who have not seen a penis before. (Sometimes there may also be the fear that, because of the penis' inferiority, little girls only would be impressed, but not adult women).

A sadistic significance of male exhibitionism may by an outgrowth of infantile ideas of urethral attacks and be related to the aggressive significance of bedwetting, and thus to some types of ejaculatio praecox.

3. The exhibitionistic act is performed as a kind of magical gesture. It means: "I show you what I wish you could show me" (555). On this level exhibitionism is not only a mask for scoptophilia but also the exhibition of a penis is thought of as a magical means of achieving a situation in which the attacked girls can display the very same thing, that is, a penis and not a female organ. In this sense,

the exhibitionist acts like the transvestite: he acts "the girl who shows her penis."

In reassuring the individual against castration, the partial instinct of exhibitionism may engage all of the sexual energy, thus facilitating the repression of the other parts of infantile sexuality, especially of the Oedipus complex.

A case of exhibitionism showed a remarkable combination of the castration complex with a "family romance." The patient's fantasy was that his father was not truly his father but a mean stepfather who wished to castrate him. The patient's penis, which he overvalued narcissistically, furnished him with visible evidence of his exalted origin. In exposing his penis, he was asking for recognition of this fact, a recognition needed for shielding him from the danger of castration.

This interpretation of exhibitionism as an attempt to overcome castration fear cannot, however, apply in the case of women. Actually, genital exhibitionism as a perversion does not exist in women. However, the nongenital exposure of all other parts of the body for the purpose of forepleasure is more common in the female sex than in the male.

Harnik explained this difference in the development of exhibitionism in the two sexes by the difference in the male and the female castration complex. The very fact that the girl has no penis and feels this as a hurt to her narcissism makes her displace her exhibitionistic impulses and replace her infantile desire to expose her genitals by a desire to expose all of her body with the exception of the genitals (736). For this reason the displaced exhibitionism is not adapted to serve as reassurance and cannot develop into a perversion.

Both sexes have the original partial instinct of exhibitionism. Whereas the man, who fears the possibility that he might lose the penis, can reassure himself by showing that the penis is still present, the woman, who actually has no penis and feels this as a narcissistic injury, tries to conceal this lack. Thus in men the original infantile genital exhibitionism tends to reassure against castration fear. Consequently, men's exhibitionism remains genital and may develop into a perversion; that is, men show their potency; women's exhibitionism is displaced away from the genitals; that is, women show their attractiveness. Where the displacement is insufficient, exhibitionistic women are *afraid* of being ugly or ridiculous or subject to injury. Women, too, attempt to use exhibitionism for magical purposes, that is, to charm spectators to force them to give what is needed. But they never are free of the fear that attempts of this kind are doomed to fail. Exhibitionistic women always behave as if they were pretending and are afraid that the truth might come out. The idea of being exposed in their "castrated" state is the main unconscious content of many a female anxiety hysteria. It is also the typical meaning of female stage fright. (The fact that analogous ideas are to be found also in the stage fright of men arises from the fact that men, too, may develop a "feminine" type of castration complex, that is, the idea that at one time they actually were injured, and that their genitals will turn out to be inferior if compared to those of other men [501].) Under certain circumstances a paradoxical exhibitionism of ugliness may be the outcome of a stubborn revenge type of the female castration complex, a "magical gesture" aimed at castrating men by forcing them to look at the "castration wound" (483, 634, 739, 1249). All the neurotic conflicts around "exhibitionism as a means of enforcing narcissistic supplies" which have been discussed in connection with erythrophobia (*see* p. 201) and social inhibition (*see* p. 180) are also operative in perverse exhibitionists.

However, sometimes a frank tendency to exhibit the genital organs plays a role in the forepleasure of women. Analysis shows that this happens in women whose experiences have enabled them to retain to a high degree the illusion of possessing a penis.

A preference for genital exhibitionism in women is usually connected with a preference for cunnilingus, which affords opportunity for an especially intense display of the genitals to the man. A patient had the masturbatory fantasy that she had to cut a piece out of her dress so as to expose her genitals; this exhibitionism was combined with a predilection for cunnilingus. She had the unconscious idea of taking revenge on men by charming them into dependence on and fright of the very organ they once "despised." Showing herself as being castrated was a magical gesture aimed at castrating the spectator. On another level the patient unconsciously believed that she had a penis. Her perversion demanded that men should "look more carefully"—then they would find the penis.

It is understandable that an exhibitionistic tendency of this kind more frequently appears as displaced from the genitals to some "symbolic penis." A patient was extremely proud of her beautiful feet, liked to go barefoot and to show photographs of herself barefoot. She also had the neurotic symptom of feeling a need to stretch and spread her toes during sexual intercourse.

Female exhibitionism, though it cannot reassure against the feeling of being castrated, may be used for revenge purposes in a double way: (*a*) by the display of female beauty and charm, which may have the unconscious attitude of humiliating men by making them admire and become dependent on what they formerly despised—the method of Circe, who turned men into pigs by seducing them through her beauty; (*b*) by the exhibition of the "ugly" genitals, which has the unconscious attitude of humiliating men by threatening them stubbornly: "I am castrated; very well, by showing this, I am going to castrate you, too!"

If these unconscious sadistic attitudes are strong, they arouse guilt feelings and fears. An example of fear so determined is experienced by children if the game of "making ugly faces" is succeeded by a fear that the pretended ugliness might remain permanent (*see* p. 319).

VOYEURISM

In the unconscious of voyeurs, the same tendencies are found as in exhibitionists. The childhood experiences on which voyeurs are fixated sometimes are scenes that gave reassurance—for example, such scenes as the incident in the case of Freud's foot fetishist (596). More frequently, voyeurs are fixated on experiences that aroused their castration anxiety, either primal scenes or the sight of adult genitals. The patient attempts to deny the justification of his fright by repeating the frightening scenes with certain alterations; this type of voyeurism is based on the hunger for screen experiences, that is, for experiences sufficiently like the original to be substituted for it, but differing in the essential point and threby giving reassurance that there is no danger (1198). This tendency may be condensed with a tendency to repeat a traumatic scene for the purpose of achieving a belated mastery (*see* p. 120).

This unconscious significance of scoptophilia is most clearly seen in those cases in which gratification is obtained only if the sexual scene the patient wishes to witness fulfills very definite conditions. These conditions then represent either a repetition of conditions present in the important childhood experience or a denial of these very conditions or of their dangerous nature.

> Abraham reported the case of a pervert who obtained gratification only under the condition that a man and a woman have intercourse in an adjacent room. The patient would begin to cry; then the woman would have to leave her partner and rush to the patient. Probably this represented the wish that remained unfulfilled when as a child he actually experienced the primal scene. Sabina Spielrein described a peeping perversion in which the patient tried to overcome an early repression of genital and manual erogeneity, provoked by an intense castration fear (1454).

The fact that no sight can actually bring about the reassurance for which the patients are striving has several consequences for the structure of voyeurs: they either develop an attitude of insatiability—they have to look again and again, and to see more and more, with an ever increasing intensity—or they displace their interest from the genitals either to forepleasure activities and pregenitality or generally to scenes that may better serve as reassurances than does actual genital observation.

Because of the insatiability, the desire to look may acquire a more and more sadistic significance. In female voyeurs, in whom the idea that other girls have penises could not serve as reassurance against the castration complex, peeping may from the beginning be a substitute for sadistic acting. "I didn't do it, I only watched the other fellow do it" is a very frequent excuse given by children (*see* p. 498). In the same way, voyeurs displace their interest from destroying (castrating) on to looking, in order to avoid feelings of responsibility and guilt; as a rule they fail, and the looking acquires the unconscious significance of the original impulse.

> Curiosity in women sometimes is more or less openly aimed at witnessing catastrophes, accidents, war scenes, operations, hospital scenes, and the like; such curiosity represents active sadistic castration tendencies, reduced from action to observation.

The longing to substitute looking for acting makes persons who are in conflict about whether or not to follow some impulse long for someone else to perform the act. The release from responsibility which they achieve in this way explains the effectiveness of the "seducing example" (1258).

BRAID CUTTING

As a supplement to the discussion of exhibitionism and voyeurism mention should be made of a specific form of sadism which is related to these perversions and may serve later as a starting point for the examination of sadism. This perversion, braid cutting, for obvious reasons has become rare nowadays. It combines a sadistic attack with a fetishistic preference for hair and is mainly due to the same reassuring mechanism operative in exhibitionism: the identification with the aggressor. The meaning is: "If I cut others' braids off, my own will not be cut off. I am the cutter, and not the one who is cut."

However, symbolic castration appears here in an amazingly thin disguise. Harnik, in the analysis of a braid cutter, was able to show that in the patient's unconscious the idea "I am the castrator and not the castrated one" was condensed with another one: "I am only performing symbolic, not real, castration." In the fantasy of this patient, the idea that the hair of the attacked girls would grow again played the outstanding role. Through analysis other conditions were also found, which served to repudiate the idea of castration (740).

The reassuring pleasure that a game of symbolic castration is no real and final castration is manifest in the delight that boys show in tugging girls' hair, undoubtedly a watered form of braid cutting. Preferences for crippled girls (307a) or other apparent emphasis on the sexual partner's castration reveal themselves in analysis as a combination of the two reassurances against castration anxiety: "I am the castrator and not the castrated one" and "She is only symbolically castrated, not really." Perversions of this kind are very closely related to counterphobic attitudes in the individual's character (see pp. 480 ff.).

COPROPHILIA

If an adult person still has his sexual excitability connected with the excretory functions (either with those of his object or autoerotically with his own), he clearly shows that his sexuality is on an infantile level. But in these cases, too, the regression serves as a defense against genital wishes, not only in a general way as in any compulsion neurotic but also in a more specific way, the coprophilic fantasies regularly representing attempts to deny the danger of castration. In pronounced anal perversions we find very often that this interest was increased at the expense of an originally equally intense urethral interest, because there is no sex difference in anal functions. The stressed anality expresses the wish to have sexual pleasure without being reminded of the difference of the sexes, which would mobilize castration fear. On a deeper level the symbolic equation *feces = penis* (593) is valid. A male scoptophilic pervert, who wants to watch women defecate, thus unconsciously expresses the idea: "I wish to see that something resembling a penis does come out of the woman's body after all." In a similar way, women who are sexually interested in their own anal functions have the feeling: "I have an organ that protrudes after all." The conception of "child" (gift) forms a bridge between the conception of feces and genital ideas.

> Frances Deri observed a case of coprophilia which was determined by the fact that the patient as a little boy watched his mother defecating. The unconscious meaning of this experience was analogous to that of the fetishist who observed his governess' foot. The mother's feces were perceived as a symbol for a penis.

Urethral-erotic perversions, especially a sexual interest on the part of men in female urination, direct the attention, apparently, in particular to the difference of the sexes; consequently it does not seem adapted to giving reassurance against castration fears. The analysis of these cases, however, shows that special experiences in childhood actually made it possible to use even female urination for the purpose of achieving such reassurance.

> A case in which sexual interest was concentrated on women's urination proved first that this interest meant generally: "Whenever I am sexually excited, my castration complex is mobilized." It turned out that the perversion meant primarily an intense rejection of any idea of a penis. It was developed in order to assure the repression of early anal-homosexual experiences. The significance of women's urine was that it was "not men's feces." The patient, as a child, had thought that women have but one opening and urinate from the anus. The perversion, thus, was an attempt at gaining sexual pleasure without being reminded either of penis or of feces. Women's urination appeared as clean and playful; it did not mobilize the fearful thoughts implicit in men's moving their bowels. The perversion was conditioned by a simultaneous inhibition against looking which enabled the patient to hold onto the fantasy of women urinating through the anus and thus to avoid again being reminded of castration by the sight of a urinating woman. On a deeper level, the interest in watching urinating women meant the hope of finding out that they, too, have a penis. The "urinating girl" herself had the significance of a "urinating penis" (428).

A combination of coprophilia, exhibitionism, and sadism is expressed in coprolalia, that is, in the joy of uttering obscenities and in an exaggerated interest in pornography (366). Obscene words retain remnants of the old magical power which language in general originally had. They force, or are intended to force, the listener to visualize with hallucinatory clarity the objects they denote (451). Readers of pornographic literature frequently imagine that an "innocent" hearer is present (or they picture themselves as such innocent hearers) who plays the same role as the "frightened" objects of the exhibitionist or of the braid cutter (and therefore coprolalia can be substituted by swearing) (1154). Coprolalia during sexual intercourse makes use of the sexual partner for the same purpose of getting reassurance. The use of obscene words gives the feeling that the dangerous "demons of sexuality" are under control (*see* p. 296).

In lovers of pornography one frequently meets two contradictory, reassuring attitudes: (1) The fact that sexual details are described in print proves the objective existence of sexuality; by the mechanism of "sharing guilt" it relieves guilt feelings by making sexual fantasies more "objective." (2) Nevertheless the feared sexuality is not quite real; it is enjoyed in empathy by reading about it in a book, not by experiencing it actually, and thus it is less dangerous.

Masturbation with the help of pornographic literature is nearer, in one respect, to normal sexuality than is masturbation without it, the book being a medium between sexual fantasy and sexual reality. In adolescents or persons with perverse inclinations who are ashamed of admitting their wishes, the book or picture may simply represent a substitute for a sexual partner.

The very terms pornography and coprolalia stress the connection with anal eroticism. Sometimes anal obscenities are actually preferred to genital ones, but even if that is not the case, the pleasure in genital obscenities is often connected with the conception that these obscenities are "dirty."

The "negative" of coprolalic impulses plays a great role in the psychology of stuttering and tic and in many compulsive symptoms, where the unconscious sexualization of words regularly has an anal significance. The connection of words with anal eroticism is obvious in the common compulsion to read while sitting on the toilet; it is due to the idea that while matter is expelled from the body other matter has to be taken in.

ORAL PERVERSIONS

A preference for the oral zone as an instrument of sexual gratification seldom occurs as a perversion complete in itself, excluding the possibility of other modes of sexual gratification. Again, analysis shows that the mouth becomes a preferred substitute for the genitals in those cases in which genital activity is inhibited by castration fear (13). This is clear in those cases of fellatio which, on analysis, are seen to be denials of, or equivalents of, biting off the penis. In preferring cunnilingus, too, both sexes may be influenced by a tendency to exclude the penis from the act or by the fantasy of a concealed female penis.

The analysis of a male patient who preferred cunnilingus revealed that he had the fantasy of being a woman enjoying female homosexuality. This fantasy was a flight away from the penis which mobilized castration fear.

EXTREME SEXUAL SUBMISSIVENESS

Extreme submissiveness as a condition for attaining sexual gratification is a perversion that occurs not infrequently in women and occasionally also in men

(1200, 1261). It represents an extreme exaggeration of certain features that are present in any "falling in love"; that is, the entire emphasis is displaced from one's own existence to the personality of the partner; the patient lives only with and through the partner, feels himself to be nothing and the partner to be everything; he is ready to make any sacrifice for the partner's sake (and especially for the sake of rousing the partner's interest in himself). "Falling in love" as such is certainly no perversion; but it is a perversion if the only possible sexual excitement consists in the feeling of one's own insignificance as compared with the magnificence of the partner (606).

This description shows that the perversion in question is a transitional state between infatuation and masochism. In common with the former it has the monomanic character, with the latter the enjoyment of one's own insignificance.

The feeling "I am small, the beloved one is great" is certainly, first of all, an unconscious reminiscence of a time when this was literally true, that is, when the patient was a child and was in love with an adult person. "Submissiveness" hints at the Oedipus complex, and certain features of it are frequent in hysterical persons in general. When this submissiveness increases to form a kind of perversion, however, it not only reflects the child's love for his parents but especially one aspect of this love.

It has been mentioned that the full genital climax of an object relationship brings also a kind of regression to its earliest forerunner; it is an incorporation in so far as the feeling of union and a disappearance of the feeling of separateness occurs. Infatuation is characterized by the form this feeling takes: "We are one, but the partner is the more important 'half.'" Overestimation of the sexual partner means simultaneously: "I am participating in my partner's greatness." In this sense, every love is a "narcissistic gratification," a regaining of the lost and projected omnipotence (585).

In a more exaggerated way a similar feeling occurs in relationships that certainly should not be called love: in persons whose overestimation of their partners does not contradict the fact that they have no interest in and no idea about the real personality of this partner, and who can develop the same admiration for one object today and for another tomorrow. These are persons who have never become complete individuals in their own right, who therefore need "participation" in a greater union in order to be able to feel their own existence. They are the orally fixated persons, who always need proof of their being loved without being able to love actively themselves (see "love addicts," p. 382).

Necessary narcissistic supplies may be striven for in different ways. One way is represented by the fantasy of being incorporated by the object, of being nothing more than a part of a more powerful personality, and of overcoming one's own inadequacy in this way (265, 712). The idea of being incorporated simultaneously may be used as a defense against the sadistic idea of actively incorporating. If the feeling that the union with the partner is established without action by the subject can be achieved, no violent way of establishing it is needed any more (428). The denial of sadism, however, does not always succeed, and often it is quite obvious that the "love" of the submissive person for his omnipotent partner is of a very ambivalent nature.

The unconscious basis of the perversion "extreme submissiveness" is the fantasy of being a part of the partner's body. This fantasy attempts to refute the fear of being abandoned which previously disturbed sexual enjoyment.

In 1925, Josine Müller wrote in describing a case of this kind: "The patient imagined that she was the penis of her exalted father, and thus his favorite and most important part" (1160). Later, Frances Deri postulated the idea that the fantasy of being a part of the partner's body is the basis of "extreme submissiveness." Other authors have confirmed this thesis (428, 436, 1055, 1261).

The identification with the partner's penis is a fantasy that is met with in both sexes. The basic fantasy of male transvestitism, "I show myself as a phallic woman," is often condensed with the fantasy of acting as a penis.

A patient connected his femininity with the naïve narcissistic love for his penis which he called by a pet name; even the girl's name, which he liked to assume when acting a girl, was very similar to this pet name for his penis (416).

In girls an identification with the penis is even more frequent. Here the fantasy "I am a penis" is an escape from the conflict between the two contradictory tendencies "I should like to have a penis" and "I should like to love a man." The fantasy of being a man's penis, and in this way of being connected with the man in inseparable harmony, serves the overcompensating repression of the opposite idea: "I want to rob a man of his penis and am therefore afraid of his revenge."

The dangers denied by means of this fantasy may be of a different nature. Either the penis with which the patients are identified represents "mother's penis," and thus denies the existence of beings without penises, or it represents "father's penis," and thus denies anxiety by an "identification with the aggressor."

Wherever the relations to the penis are governed by fantasies of introjection, they are based on a pregenital history. The penis, with which submissive persons identify themselves, also represents child, feces (the contents of mother's womb), or milk. The penis is only the last link in a long chain of introjects (593).

An extreme submissiveness is likewise found in some forms of hero worship which are based on the unconscious fantasy of being a part of the hero. It is characteristic for one type of religiosity, in which devotion to God is connected with the fantasy that God without oneself would be as incomplete as oneself without God. The fantasy is developed that one is not only weak, helpless, and nothing but a part of the powerful partner, but also that one represents the partner's most important and powerful part. Whereas one is actually dependent on the partner, the partner in turn is thought to be magically dependent on oneself.

RILKE
"Was wirst Du tun, Gott, wenn ich sterbe?
Ich bin Dein Trank, wenn ich verderbe,
bin Dein Gewand und Dein Gewerbe,
Ich bin Dein Krug; wenn ich zerscherbe,
mit mir verlierst Du Deinen Sinn."

ANGELUS SILESIUS
"Ich bin so gross als Gott: er ist als ich so klein:
er kann nicht über mich, ich unter ihm nicht sein."—
"Ich weiss, dass ohne mich Gott nicht ein Nu kann leben,
werd' ich zu nicht, er muss vor Not den Geist aufgeben."

SADISM

Can the general theory of perversions be applied to sadism; that is, is it conceivable that the torturing of an object may give a reassurance against castration fear? And if so, what determines the choice of precisely this form of reassurance?

If sexual pleasure is disturbed by anxiety, it is comprehensible that an "identification with the aggressor" (541) can be a relief. If a person is able to do to others what he fears may be done to him, he no longer has to be afraid. Thus anything that tends to increase the subject's power or prestige can be used as a reassurance against anxieties. *What might happen to the subject passively is done actively by him, in anticipation of attack, to others.*

Among children who suffer from anxiety, older siblings are always in a better position than younger ones because they can threaten the smaller ones.

The idea "Before I can enjoy sexuality, I must convince myself that I am powerful" is, to be sure, not yet identical with "I get sexual pleasure through torturing other persons"; however, it is the starting point for a sadistic development. The "threatening" type of exhibitionist, the braid cutter and the man who shows pornographic pictures to his "innocent" partner, enjoys the powerlessness of the partner because it means "I do not need to be afraid of him," thereby making possible the pleasure that would otherwise have been blocked by fear. Sadists of this type, by threatening their objects, show that they are concerned with the idea that they themselves might be threatened.

Many persons are afraid not only that they might be the victims of some kind of castration during the sexual act but also of being harmed by their own excitement. Again, they can get rid of this fear if they succeed in rousing in others a like fear of excitement.

Analogous is the frequent obsessive symptom of laughter as a reaction to the news of a death. This symptom occurs not only after the death of a person against whom the patient previously had had unconscious death wishes. It may be a much more general expression of reassurance against anxiety aroused by the news through stressing the triumph: "It is the other fellow who died, not I."

Frequently, sadists are fighting not only an unconscious anxiety over castration and over their own dangerous excitement but also certain self-destructive tendencies within themselves. The origin of self-destructive tendencies will be examined later (*see* pp. 358 ff.). But once such tendencies are established, they are fought by being turned outward against sexual objects. Since masochism, as a rule, is created by the turning inward of an original sadism, there may be a three-fold layer; the manifest sadism of the third layer is very different from the original hostility of the first layer. In Freud's study, "A Child Is Being Beaten," he described the typical historical development of such a three-layer formation (601).

Like the braid cutter, other sadists, too, not only proceed according to the formula "I am the castrator, not the castrated one" but also according to the complementary idea "I am only a pseudo castrator, not a real castrator." By castrating symbolically rather than actually, they reassure themselves through the experiences of their victims that the dreadful things they feared are not quite so dreadful after all. The perverse acts actually performed by sadists often have a playful character and have the same purpose as any kind of playing. Afraid that full sexual excitement would be connected with castration, the patient tries to learn to master this situation by actively and tentatively connecting sexual acts with "minor castrations."

In braid cutters the idea that the hair grows back and in coprophiliacs that feces are produced anew every day is used as a "proof" that castration need not be final (740, 1054).

The following case shows the same tendency in a somewhat more complicated way. The sexual fantasies of a compulsion-neurotic patient were filled with sadistic ideas of shaming women; the idea was to compel girls to show their sexual excitement in a humiliating way. In his childhood, the patient used to masturbate anally; he felt very much ashamed of it, and actually concealed this activity carefully. His neurosis was governed by the fear of being found out and by anticipatory shame. Unconsciously, as a child, he had longed to be found out, and he had even tried to provoke it. The motive for this provocation was not so much a need for punishment as an attempt to seduce others, a longing to turn away from autoeroticism to objects who might participate in his sexual activities.

In his sadistic activities or fantasies he did to others what he once had ambivalently thought might happen to him. His sadism had the following meanings: (1) What the patient is afraid of does not happen to him; instead he does it to others. (2) What he longed for but was afraid of has finally happened; he experiences it in an "altruistic" and therefore safe way, in that he feels with the girls to whom he does what should have been done to him. (3) What really happens is not castration but only the "lesser evil" of being ashamed.

The feeling of unity with an object, which results in reassurance against the anxiety of being abandoned, is achieved in extreme submissiveness by the idea of being a small part of the partner's huge body. It may also be achieved by the opposite idea, that the other person is but a small part of one's own body. And this feeling may be brought about by creating the situation where the partner is absolutely dependent on the patient and his whims.

A patient, as a boy, used to play the "sadistic" game of "hypnotizing" everybody. He enjoyed the idea of his victims' powerlessness. He previously had been a stammerer, and had been ridiculed by his sister. This memory had been used to screen other situations when the sister had ridiculed his sexual inferiority. The sadistic fantasy of hypnotism was a revenge on his sister. Through it, he proved his superiority and even omnipotence to her. By his sadism he denied his fear of being sexually inferior (castrated). The sister's doubts of his masculinity, however, were effective because they coincided with his own doubts. Dreams revealed that the idea of hypnotizing had replaced an older idea of being hypnotized by the father. Thus the sadism was used to contradict a dangerous masochism.

The reassurance that what is done to the victim is not really serious is not, however, generally valid for sadism, because sadistic acts occur in which the victim is hurt very seriously or even killed. In such cases, the ideas of avoiding a terrible passive experience by actively perpetrating it on others and of establishing a mystical union with the victim must be decisive.

No sex murderer has as yet been analyzed. But if account may be taken both of cases in which fantasies of this kind played a leading role (1444) and of experiences with less excessive sadists, it may be assumed that in such cases the superego plays a complicating role (1029). The sadistic act not only means "I kill to avoid being killed" but also "I punish to avoid being punished" or, rather, "I enforce forgiveness by violence." Persons who are in need of narcissistic supplies tend, when frustrated, toward intensive sadistic reactions. Under certain conditions such a tendency may grow until it culminates in an action that is a denial of the fear, "If I do something sexual, I have to be punished," by means of the other one, "I torture you until I force you, by the intensity of your suffering, to forgive me, to release me from the guilt feeling that blocks my pleasure, and thus, through and in your forgiveness, to give me sexual satisfaction." The sadist who pretends to be independent thus betrays his deep dependence on his victim. By force he tries to make his victim love him; the love he seeks is a primitive one, having the significance of a "narcissistic supply."

The model for this type of sadism is the Prussian King Frederick William, who used to beat his subjects, shouting: "You must not fear me, you must love me!"

Such complications arising from the superego undoubtedly play a role in the "lesser evil" type of sadism also.

The foregoing material shows that in the perversion of sadism actually the component instinct of sadism is used to obtain reassurance against the fear of castration. The tendency to master anxiety by this means depends, of course, on the earlier history of the component instinct of sadism (1157).

To begin with, this component instinct may be constitutionally especially strong. Some children show more pleasure in torturing animals than others. Sadistic fixations arise from the same causes as other fixations (*see* pp. 65 f.). Frustrations especially intensify the sadistic quality with which the aim of the frustrated drive is eventually pursued. There is no doubt that sadistic characteristics are connected more with pregenital aims than with genital ones. Sadistic impulses are, of course, not limited to strivings from one specific erogenous zone. There is a manual sadism or, more correctly, a sadism correlated with muscular eroticism (1338, 1346); there is a skin sadism, which probably is a projection of the "erogenous masochism" of the skin and the source of sexual pleasure in beating (601, 613); there is an anal sadism (warded off in compulsion neurosis) (581); there is an oral sadism, whose distinctive features have been more specifically studied in the neuroses that represent "negatives" of these perversions, impulse neurosis and depression, than in the perversions themselves; however, Abraham (26) and Van Ophuijsen (1205) have shown that in the perversion of sadism also, the sexual aims may be derivatives of the destructive tendencies of the oral period. And there is also a pronounced phallic sadism (385). The fact that the idea of incorporation is connected, objectively, with the destruction of the object makes all object relationships with the aim of incorporation ambivalent; individuals who regress to aims of incorporation are the very ones who also tend to become sadistic.

In Freud's study, "A Child Is Being Beaten," he investigated the developmental history of typical sadistic (or rather sado-masochistic) fantasies in childhood (601). He was able to demonstrate that the conflicts around the Oedipus complex connect the idea of sexual excitement with hostilities, anxieties, and guilt feelings. The beating fantasies are results of these complicating connections.

> The oft-recurrent idea "a child is being beaten" is the result of a development passing through several stages. On the deepest level the fantasy conserves a memory of the autoerotic period, the beaten child having the significance of penis or clitoris, the beating the significance of the masturbatory stimulation (617). The memory of infantile masturbation became distorted through a condensation of sexual pleasure with the idea that a hated person ought to be beaten. According to Freud, this hated person represents the rival, the other child: "Father's beating of the other child reassures me that he loves me" (601). It may also represent the hated mother (112). Guilt feelings about this hatred give rise to an identification with the beaten person, and the idea "Father beats me" becomes simultaneously an expression of punishment for entertaining bad wishes against the rival and a distorted substitute for the idea "Father loves me." The subsequent develop-

ment differs in the two sexes. For girls, the idea of being beaten by the father is dangerously close to the objectionable Oedipus wish. A repression occurs of the ideas that the father is the beating person and the subject the beaten one; what remains is an unclear fantasy of "a child (usually a boy) is being beaten," which may be experienced either in a sadistic or in a masochistic way (60). For boys, the fantasy remains decisive only if a negative Oedipus wish sexualizes the idea of being beaten by the father. Masochistic men supplant the unconscious idea of being beaten by the father with the less objectionable one of being beaten by a woman (by the mother); sadistic men change the initial idea by identifying themselves with the beating father, thereby denying that they themselves are the beaten child (112, 1432).

In this way the sado-masochistic perversions, too, serve to repress the usual offensive ideas of infantile sexuality, the Oedipus strivings and castration fear. Again, the sadist is a person who has kept conscious and even exaggerated a part of his infantile sexuality, in order to facilitate the repression of its more objectionable parts.

MASOCHISM

The problems of masochism are analogous to those of sadism, but are more complicated in one respect. Masochism apparently contradicts the pleasure principle. Whereas man generally tends to avoid any pain, in the masochistic phenomena pain seems to give pleasure and to be striven for (613).

An attempt to apply the general formula for perversions brings apparent contradictions. On the one hand, the conflict between drive and anxiety is obvious in masochists. They show openly the contradictory trends of striving for satisfaction and postponing it; they apparently prefer forepleasure to end pleasure and fantasy to reality (1297, 1299). On the other hand, it seems a paradox that a feared pain might be avoided or denied by actually suffering pain.

Clinical experience shows that this paradox actually is possible and does occur, if and when one or several of the following conditions are fulfilled:

1. Certain experiences may have so firmly established the conviction that sexual pleasure must be connected with pain that suffering has become the prerequisite for sexual pleasure, a prerequisite not originally aimed at but secondarily sought as a necessary price that must be paid in order to exclude disturbing guilt feelings (1277).

2. Masochistic activities follow the mechanism of "sacrifice"; the price paid beforehand is meant to appease the gods and to make them contented at a relatively small cost. Masochistic activities of this type are "a lesser evil" (1240); symbols of self-castration are used by masochists to avoid castration. Freud has pointed out that most masochists seek injuries and pain of all kinds except any type of pain or injury to the genitals (613).

3. Any anxiety can be fought by playful anticipatory action of what is feared.

It is the function of all play to anticipate actively what might be overwhelming when it comes unexpectedly, the ego determining time and degree (1552). In the same way that certain sadists torture others for the purpose of denying the idea that they might themselves be tortured, masochists torture themselves (or arrange for their torture through self-made plans and directions) in order to exclude the possibility of being tortured in an unexpected manner and degree (349, 350, 351).

4. A stressing of passivity, too, may serve a protective purpose. A regression to the oral-receptive type of mastery may represent a reunion with a protective omnipotent power, and a stressing of one's own helplessness and littleness may aim at appealing to the mercy of the threatening or protecting power. Of this kind is the masochism of the extremely submissive person discussed above (817, 819).

The four mechanisms described undoubtedly are operative in masochism. However, they are not sufficient to explain it. They may make comprehensible that a person must undergo a certain amount of suffering before attaining the capacity to enjoy pleasure. But this is not characteristic for the masochistic pervert, who seems to derive his pleasure through suffering rather than after suffering.

This is, in part, a question of exact observation. Some masochists actually feel pleasure after rather than through suffering. Masochists are individuals whose ability to achieve orgasm is obviously disturbed by anxiety and guilt feeling. They shift the emphasis, therefore, to the tensions of forepleasure and build up elaborate fantasy structures, a procedure that often makes masturbation more gratifying for them than an actual realization of their perverse activities which could not fulfill all the anticipated details (1297, 1299). Unquestionably the complicated fantasy systems try to overcome the fear that blocks the capacity for end pleasure. It is also characteristic that what happens to the patient has to be pre-arranged to be pleasurable. They are afraid of surprises, but can control their fear as long as they know beforehand what is going to happen.

But this cannot explain cases of actual "pleasure in pain" which doubtlessly exist. In masochism proper, the active anticipation of a lesser evil is complicated by another factor, which explains the simultaneity of pain and pleasure. As in other perversions, the reassuring measure is condensed with an erogenous pleasure. The existence of an erogenous masochism is ascribable to the fact that, like all sensations in the human organism, the sensation of pain, too, may be a source of sexual excitement (555, 601) (*see* p. 70). It may be so under certain conditions only: the pain must not be too intense and must not be too serious. Being beaten excites children sexually because it is an intense excitation of the erogenous zones of the skin of the buttocks and of the muscles below the skin. (The displacement of libido from the anus to the skin seems to be a characteristic antecedent of any pleasure in being beaten; for this reason an anal constitution and anal fixations encourage the development of masochism.) If the pain becomes too intense, the displeasure outweighs the erogenous stimulation, and pleasure ceases.

A longing for the gratification of erogenous masochism in children and also, later on, a longing for the gratification of a perverse masochism in adults may be hidden behind an apparently very active and even sadistic behavior. Many children (and older persons as well) know exactly how to be "naughty" to provoke others to beat them or to punish them in a way that is an equivalent of beating.

Fixations on erogenous masochism may occur for the same reasons as fixations on any other component instinct. If individuals with such a fixation are subsequently compelled by castration fear to use the mechanisms described, the result may be that suffering becomes not only a prerequisite for pleasure but even a source of pleasure.

Among the causes of fixation on erogenous masochism, one type predominates: the fixation based on simultaneity of erogenous pleasure and reassurance against fear. Security is achieved by undergoing a "punishment," through which forgiveness is attained and sexual pleasure, previously blocked by guilt feelings, is made accessible again.

Passive aims are stressed in a person's sexuality in particular under two circumstances:

1. After hostility has been turned against one's own ego. Actually clinical experience shows that masochism represents a turning of sadism against one's own self.

Freud's conception of a primary masochism is based solely on his speculation concerning the existence of a death instinct (613). Clinically, masochistic strivings betray themselves as destructive tendencies which, through the influence of fear or guilt feeling, have changed their direction and turned against the ego.

It is of interest to quote a few passages of Freud's which were written before the formulation of the hypothesis of the death instinct.

"First of all, we may be permitted to doubt whether masochism ever occurs in a primary manner, or whether it does not occur rather regularly by transformation from sadism" (555).

"With the pair of opposites sadism—masochism, the process may be represented as follows: (a) Sadism consists in the exercise of violence or power upon some other person as its object. (b) This object is abandoned and replaced by the subject's self. Together with the turning round upon the self, the change from an active to a passive aim in the instinct is also brought about. (c) Again another person is sought as object; this person, in consequence of the alteration which has taken place in the aim of the instinct, has to take over the original role of the subject. Case (c) is a condition commonly termed 'masochism.' Satisfaction follows in this case also by way of the original sadism, the passive ego placing itself in fantasy back in its former situation, which, however, is now being given up to another subject outside the self. Whether there is, besides this, a more direct masochistic satisfaction is highly doubtful. A primary masochism not derived, in the manner I have described, from sadism does not appear to be met with" (588).

"There seems to be a confirmation of the view that masochism is not the manifestation of a primary instinct, but originates from sadism, which has been turned around and directed upon the self, that is to say, by means of regression from an object to the ego. Instincts with a passive aim must be taken for granted as existing . . . but passivity is not the whole of the masochism. The characteristic of pain belongs to it as well . . . a bewildering accompaniment to the gratification of an instinct. The transformation of sadism into masochism appears to be due to the influence of the sense of guilt" (601).

Freud's analysis of the typical beating fantasy likewise showed that the wish to be beaten was preceded by the wish that the hated rival might be beaten (601).

2. In men, a stressing of passive aims, prerequisite for the development of masochism, is brought about by the development of feminine wishes; the idea of being tortured may be a distortion of the idea of having feminine sexual experiences ("feminine masochism") (613). The factors responsible for a turning toward femininity in men have been discussed (see pp. 335 f.). Passive pregenital (anal) strivings may be intensified as a defense against masculine wishes if activity is believed to be dangerous.

Femininity, on the other hand, may increase castration anxiety because of the idea that feminine satisfaction would be attainable only at the price of castration (599). Thus the connections between femininity in men, castration anxiety, and guilt feelings are very close. If such men also develop one of the mechanisms described above, they will distort their feminine wishes in a masochistic way. "Being beaten by a woman" (by the mother) covers up the deeper hidden idea of "being beaten by a man" (by the father), and the masochistic practices come to signify playing the woman's role in coitus or in giving birth (601, 613).

More pronounced than in sadism is the role played by the superego in masochism (cf. 337). The idea of being beaten is regularly combined with the idea of the beating being a punishment for bad behavior (for Oedipus wishes [642] and wishes that somebody else might be beaten). This, as a rule, is condensed with a "lesser evil" ideology; the beating usually is perceived as being no serious matter, with its locale the atmosphere of the nursery.

Sometimes masochistic arrangements give another impression. Just as traumatic neurotics again and again seek repetitions of painful traumata, so certain masochists seem unable to free themselves of castration ideas; they have to repeat certain allusions to castration again and again, probably striving for the soothing security "This time it assuredly is only a beating and not a castration, assuredly only a game and not serious"; but apparently they never can be quite sure, and again and again they need a reassuring approximation of acts similar to castration. When sexually aroused, the upsetting unconscious fear of castration regularly interferes. "Being beaten" is chosen not only because this idea arouses erogenous masochism in skin and muscles but also because a not too serious punishment is attempted in the hope of getting finally rid of disturbing superego pressure.

Here again the condensation of guilt-laden aggression with erogenous pleasure is associatively connected with the Oedipus complex and serves the purpose of securing the repression of the Oedipus complex (121, 642, 1604).

As a child, a woman had been very much in love with her father, a misogynist who unrestrainedly let his daughter know his dislike of women. The patient had an older sister whom the father obviously preferred. The father was very strict in forbidding anal-erotic practices of any kind. The patient was thus confronted with the following problems: to love her father (as her instinct demanded) but to eliminate any awareness of the evidence of a penis (the basis of her troubles, since her lack of one had caused her father to dislike her); furthermore, she had to exclude from expression her strong anal wishes as well as her wish to avenge herself on her sister; she had to learn to endure her father's severity and contempt without ceasing to love him. She became a masochist, with the sexual aim of being beaten. The penis, offensive to her, was replaced by the beating hand; the anus, equally offensive to her, by the cutaneous surface of the buttocks. Unconsciously it was not herself but her sister who was being beaten, the punishment only secondarily diverted toward herself; and her father's real behavior could retain the capacity to satisfy her masochistically distorted Oedipus wishes.

Often a masochistic fantasy accounts for only half of a complete fantasy, the second half of which had been repressed; uncovering the second part will reveal the connection with the Oedipus complex.

The sexual aim of being beaten in the patient just referred to could be traced back to two childhood experiences. She remembered a little boy who was frequently beaten, and she remembered a little girl who used to exhibit her buttocks and genitals. The patient used to fantasy that this little girl was being beaten for her misbehavior, in the way the little boy had actually been beaten. She identified herself with the little girl, and her unconscious fantasy may be formulated as follows: "I wish to expose myself like this little girl, and then be beaten for it like that little boy." Pleasure in exposing herself was a prominent topic in her analysis. At first this exhibitionism had a female character and showed itself, for example, in the pride taken in being ill or in bleeding, which was condensed into fantasies of childbirth. Later, this pride in bleeding was seen to be an overcompensation of a great fear of castration. Finally, it became evident that all her feminine exhibitionism was a relatively late substitute for an original phallic exhibitionism which was inhibited through anxiety. From various dreams it was concluded that both the exhibitionistic little girl and the little boy who had really been beaten had exposed themselves before the patient and urinated. Hence the complete text of the sexual fantasy, of which beating was only a small part, would read: "I want to be able to display a penis like the little boy, so that father will love me. I refuse to believe that they have castrated me (or would castrate me) for such an act. No, they will only spank me for doing it, for I see that this boy who has been spanked still has his penis" (*cf.* 326, 1008).

The connection between masochism and exhibitionism, displayed so conspicuously in this case, seems to be typical.

This connection is responsible for the demonstrative and provocative character of some of the masochistic arrangements (1297, 1299). Not only exhibitionism but also other perversions like fetishism and coprophilia are often condensed with or covered by masochism.

Masochistic characters customarily derive pleasure from exhibiting their misery. "Look how miserable I am" typically stands for "Look how miserable you have made me"; the masochistic behavior has an accusing, blackmailing tone; the sadism, which has been turned against the ego in masochism, returns in the way the patients attempt to force their objects to give love or affection. The skin eroticism which is the erogenous basis of the fantasy of being beaten expresses itself in the longing for the warming propinquity of the objects, which, if not given, is enforced by self-torture. The conflict characteristic for all persons with receptive longings—namely, the conflict between a sadistic destruction of the denying object and a masochistic total yielding to the object in the hope that the object will then not be able to resist—shows itself in this type of masochism. Such masochism is a compromise between these two attitudes; it is total submission, used for sadistic purposes (1277). The previously mentioned "exhibitionism of ugliness" (exhibitionism of inferiority and negative characteristics) is related to this type of masochism.

A girl patient who was afraid of sexual experiences made herself ugly so as to be unattractive to men. In analysis, she came to admit that she had a paradoxical masochistic satisfaction about being homely. She showed her masochism in other ways as well. She used to pull her pubic hairs until she had pain and developed dermatitis. When she was a child, her father used to powder her in the genital and anal region. There was no doubt that by creating a dermatitis, she tried unconsciously to seduce her father to repeat this activity. However, the experience of being treated by the father had not been pleasurable. The father, who was a very strict person, causing his daughter to become a masochist through his strictness, had given her the impression that the treatment was a punishment for masturbation. Her fear of sexuality was a fear that the fact (imagined by her) that she had ruined her body might be discovered. Her attempt to avert this discovery by making herself ugly resulted in the return of what had been warded off; the attempt to avoid the exhibition of her ruination resulted in a demonstration of that very thing. On a deeper level she was full of revengeful, active castration fantasies. Making herself ugly meant (*a*) forcing her father to do something sexual to her, (*b*) spiting her father by masturbating before his very eyes (*making herself ugly = ruining herself = masturbating*), (*c*) ruining the father by forcing him to see that she was ruined.

In this same category is the psychology of asceticism. In ascetics, who strive to mortify the flesh, the very act of mortifying becomes a distorted expression of the blocked sexuality and gives a masochistic pleasure. This type of masochism is, as a rule, a more anal one, characterized by retention and the capacity for tension. Related to it is the "pride in suffering" exhibited by many children who try to deny their weakness in sustaining tension.

In "moral" masochism it is not physical pain but humiliation and failure that are apparently sought, sometimes because they bring sexual pleasure, sometimes without any apparent connection with sexuality. The enjoyment of humiliation indicates that the idea of being the father's sexual object, initially transformed into being beaten by the father, has been further transformed into the idea of being beaten by God or destiny. Morals, genetically a derivative of the Oedipus complex, in this case have regressed again to the Oedipus complex (613).

More severe cases of moral masochism in which no connection with sexuality is manifest or in which the patient is not even aware that he is torturing himself cannot be regarded as sexual perversions. Unconsciously, character traits of this kind assuredly did not develop independent of sexuality. They represent attempts of the ego to cope with a severe superego. Two contradictory measures of such endeavors, rebellion and ingratiation, are condensed in moral masochism. One's own suffering is regarded as a demonstration of the degree of ingratiation, of the amount one is prepared to endure in order to gain the father's forgiveness. At the same time the masochistic behavior is an expression of rebellion, of demonstrating in a hostile manner what terrible deeds this father is capable of committing (see p. 400).

Actual severe self-destruction obviously cannot be explained as a "lesser evil." However, it may be "active anticipation of what otherwise might occur passively." Actually, it is not "beyond the pleasure principle" (605), because it represents an undesired consequence of something desired. The self-destruction may subjectively have been aimed at the destruction of the object which, after introjection, is represented by the ego; and this destruction of the object may even be condensed with an ingratiation of the object. The attempt to get rid of pressure from the superego is the aim of all self-destruction. This is especially clear in cases where self-destruction is connected with a kind of ascetic pride. The analysis of ascetic pride regularly exhibits the idea of self-sacrifice for the purpose of regaining participation in omnipotence, the pride signifying the triumph over having achieved this participation. "I sacrifice myself for the great cause, and thus the greatness of the cause falls on me." That is what priests do who castrate themselves in order to dedicate themselves to God. Their self-castration is a means of entering into the great protecting union (436).

Whereas initiation rites promise privileges and protection on condition of obedience and enforce this condition by symbolic castration (1284), masochists of this type try to enforce their privileges and protection from the omnipotent persons by more or less really castrating themselves. After such sacrifice, the omnipotent ones must grant the promises (523, 1481). Whereas one extreme for the purpose of regaining participation in omnipotence would consist in the killing of the omnipotent person, the other extreme consists in self-castration, symbolizing the abandonment of all activity in order to attain a passive-receptive merging with the omnipotent person; and, paradoxically, it is possible that an attitude of the second extreme covers an unconscious attitude of the first extreme (see p. 387).

It may be that all real self-destruction, in the last analysis, represents remainders of the archaic reaction pattern of autotomy: a tension is overcome by abandoning the cathected organ (1242).

Freud lays great stress on the point that perverse inclinations appear as antithetical pairs, with both active and passive aims (555). The study of sadism and masochism shows why both strivings necessarily regularly appear in one and the same person.

COMBINATIONS OF PERVERSIONS WITH NEUROSES AND THE DIFFERENTIAL ETIOLOGY OF PERVERSIONS

Perversions occur sometimes in combination with neuroses, most frequently, because of the common pregenital fixation, with compulsion neuroses and psychoses. All three of the following possibilities are encountered: (1) Perversion and neurosis develop alongside each other. (2) A neurosis complicates a primarily established perversion. (3) A perversion is added to a primarily established neurosis.

The ego of the pervert, in its struggle with the Oedipus conflict, lends its approval to a representative of infantile sexuality. This, however, does not exclude the possibility that it simultaneously uses against the offensive impulses some other defense mechanism which may form the basis of a neurosis; then perversion and neurosis run parallel to each other. It may also happen that a person with a well-developed perversion may encounter a situation that either relates the perversion more closely to the Oedipus situation or that represents an increase in fear over castration; such situations then call for further defense measures which may create a neurosis. A sudden outbreak of an anxiety hysteria or of paranoid reactions, for example, may complicate a perversion of long standing; homosexuality in men may be complicated by an "impotence," that is, by loss of erections. And there is also the third possibility: that the symptoms of a long-standing compulsion neurosis become so gratifying that they assume the appearance of a secondary perversion (475).

As to the differential etiology of perversions, the following prerequisites must be fulfilled to make the development of a perversion possible. (1) Constitutional factors of organic compliance which require investigation by hormonal physiology. In principle, this factor consists of a relatively augmented erogeneity of specific erogenous zones. Sadism and masochism probably are not only correlated with special experiences, especially frustrations, but also with constitutionally augmented oral, anal, cutaneous, or muscular erogeneity (549, 1630). (2) Experiences that led to the decisive pathogenic fixation. The fixations at the basis of perversions differ from those at the basis of neuroses in so far as they are, as a rule, founded on the simultaneity of sexual gratification and a feeling of security or reassurance which contradicts an inhibiting fear.

PSYCHOANALYTIC THERAPY OF PERVERSIONS

In considering the indication for psychoanalytic treatment of perversions, one factor absent in the neuroses complicates the problem. In perversions, the symptoms are, or at least promise to be, pleasant. Treatment not only threatens to rekindle the very conflicts the patient had evaded by means of his illness but it also threatens to destroy a pleasure, actually to destroy the only sexual pleasure the patient knows. Normal sexual pleasure, which the analyst promises him, is to him a bird in the bush. Hence it is hardly possible to analyze individuals who are inwardly at peace with their perversions (604). The prognosis depends first and foremost upon the extent to which the determination to get well is present, or to what extent this determination can be awakened. This determination, of course, may have many motivations. In addition to the patient's discontent, he may be moved by considerations for persons close to him. A trial analysis, in such a case, will have as its main task the evaluation of the will to recovery. Therefore, paradoxically, the therapeutic prognosis will be best in cases in which the patient feels worst, that is to say, in cases that present a combination with a neurosis.

From time to time one encounters patients who state that they want to get rid of their neurosis but wish to preserve their perversion. It is quite clear that the very nature of psychoanalysis makes it impossible to promise any such result. It is, of course, possible that, when a homosexual person has secondarily developed anxiety, psychoanalysis may cure the latter without affecting the homosexuality. However, it cannot be said in advance whether that will be possible; it is much more probable that the patient will have to face the alternatives of all or nothing.

Aside from this particular problem, the analysis of perversions is, on the whole, no more difficult than that of pregenitally determined neuroses. Constitutional factors are not lacking in neuroses either. In cases of homosexuality in which the physical appearance shows definite traits of the opposite sex, that is, cases that represent a biological transition in the direction of pseudo hermaphroditism, analysis will be correspondingly more difficult. But even if one cautiously rejects all individuals with such characteristics, there still remains a great number for whom psychoanalysis is indicated. Several authors have pointed out that the prognosis for psychoanalytical treatment of homosexuals is better than generally assumed (742, 1516). Certain modifications in the technique become necessary, analogous to those suggested by Freud for anxiety hysteria (600), the normal sexual situation representing the phobically avoided situation, the seeking of which the analyst may suggest at a certain point in analysis (742).

The need for reassurance expressed in the development of perversions is frequently due to an intensified narcissistic need, the capacity for "reassuring denials" to an instability of the function of reality testing. In consequence, there are many patients who show in their transference behavior as well as in their general demeanor in life a narcissistic character disturbance, or who may even present an almost psychotic picture (1215). In such cases, of course, psychoanalytic treatment meets the same difficulties as in the attending character disturbances or psychoses.

IMPULSE NEUROSES IN GENERAL

Other impulsive actions, which are ego syntonic though not sexual, likewise serve the purpose of escaping from a danger, of denying a danger, or of reassuring against a danger. (This formula, it is true, is only valid if "depressions" are included among the "dangers.") The aim of fighting the danger may be achieved, or it may fail.

The defensive purpose of the pathological impulses does not exclude the possibility that they simultaneously bring a distorted instinctual satisfaction of a sexual or aggressive nature. The way in which the striving for security and the striving for instinctual gratification are condensed with each other is what characterizes the irresistible impulses.

The impulses are not experienced as compulsions. They are ego syntonic and not ego alien. But nevertheless they are not experienced in the way normal instinctual drives are experienced by normal persons. They betray a characteristic *irresistibility,* which is different from that of a normal instinctual drive, and which is caused by the condensation of instinctual urge and defensive striving (99).

"Irresistibility" means that the patients in question are intolerant of tensions. Whatever they need, they must attain immediately. The infant, as long as he acts according to the pleasure principle (575), tries to discharge tension immediately, and experiences any excitement as "trauma," which is answered by un-co-ordinated discharge movements. The overcoming of this state is based on two developmental factors: (*a*) the physiological capacity for mastering motility, that is, of changing un-co-ordinated discharge movements into purposeful actions, and (*b*) the ability to postpone immediate reaction. It is as if the impulse neurotics had learned the first of these two developmental steps but not the second one. They carry out not un-co-ordinated movements but actions; but, significantly, they act instead of thinking. They cannot wait (114); consequently they have not fully developed their reality principle and misjudge reality in terms of past experiences. They still act as if any tension were a dangerous trauma. Their actions are not directed (or are less directed) toward the positive aim of achieving a goal but rather more toward the negative aim of getting rid of tension; their aim is not pleasure but the discontinuance of pain. Any tension is felt as hunger was felt by the infant, that is, as a threat to their very existence.

What makes these patients intolerant of tensions, and what determines the nature of the ego-syntonic impulses which aim at overcoming the intolerable tensions?

As to the first question, such patients are characterized by an oral- and skin-erotic fixation, which may be based on constitutional factors or on fixating experiences. Early experience of traumata, which increase the fear of painful tensions, also plays a predisposing role.

The actions chosen to get rid of tensions are of various kinds. In certain cases these actions come near to being perversions, as, for instance, those of pyromaniacs. In other cases the defense is in the foreground. In general, the impulse neuroses show, as does no other neurotic phenomenon, the dialectic connection between the concepts of gratification of an instinct and defense against an instinct. The earliest gratification, milk, brought the infant simultaneously gratification and security. The subsequent instinctual demands are derivatives of the infant's hunger, but so are the subsequent demands for security and the narcissistic needs. Patients who are afraid of instinctual danger may yearn for the security they had at the mother's breast, but they are in a serious dilemma if they conceive this longing itself as a dangerous instinctual tension. Their impulsive acts may then signify a striving for a goal which they simultaneously try to avoid because they are afraid of it. They make their objects responsible for not providing the needed relaxation, and they feel guilty for the aggressiveness with which they provoke their objects. This may cause them to evoke rebuffs which allay their guilt feelings by establishing the idea of unjust treatment, thereby rationalizing revengeful sadistic attitudes. The impulsiveness of these oral patients thus means either "I will give nothing because nobody gave me anything" or "I give to anybody to show that I am more generous than my parents were to me" (104, 106, 110). As a rule, these conflicts were first expressed in struggles around masturbation, and masturbation was subsequently supplanted by the morbid craving (1440).

Impulse neurotics are fixated on the frequently mentioned early phase of development, in which striving for sexual satisfaction and striving for security were not yet differentiated from each other. They are dependent on being loved or approved, on being accorded affection and prestige. The fact that they need these supplies for their very existence explains the intensity with which they fight for them. Being fixated on the oral phase, they tend to react to frustrations with violence. Their main conflict is one between this tendency toward violence and a tendency to repress all aggressiveness through fear over loss of love, that is, fear of receiving still less in the future. Objects are not yet persons, they are only deliverers of supplies, and thus interchangeable. This fixation is also characteristic for depressions (see pp. 387 ff.), and the fact that the basic disposition for pathological impulses and for depression is one and the same explains why most impulsive acts serve the purpose of avoiding depressions. Of course, it makes a great difference whether the supply is demanded from a real object or whether the patient is narcissistically regressed and directs his demands toward his own superego.

IMPULSIVE RUNNING AWAY

Impulsive running away (85, 1083, 1310, 1471, 1482, 1483) means either (a) running away from a supposed danger or from temptation or (b) running toward reassurance or toward satisfaction. The danger, as a rule, is represented by depression and feelings of guilt, which the "wanderer" tries to leave behind him. The act of running away may represent defenses against and equivalents of depressions. The relationship of wanderlust to manic-depressive states can be seen from the fact that in some cases the attacks occur at regular periodic intervals.

There is an analogy between the behavior of this type of patient, who runs away from an external situation but is actually trying to escape from an inner state of tension, and that of a phobic person, who projects an internal danger. His tragedy is that, wherever he runs, he takes himself with him. His typical restlessness is due to his intolerance of tension and to a regression toward passive-receptive forms of mastery. Thus "running away" means "running from a place where nobody helps to a place where protecting help is available." The running usually is complicated by the sadistic violence with which the patient tries to enforce the needed help, and by the fear of this aggressiveness.

The mode of escape from punishing or tempting situations by running away will be chosen by persons who in childhood have had occasion to apply this measure successfully. Bernfeld has pointed out that this is the case only in certain social surroundings, where the children can run from home into the streets or to friends whenever they feel uncomfortable, and come back later, when the danger is over (133).

That the place the runaways try to reach means a "helping oral mother," a "gratification without guilt," can be seen in the rare cases in which the whole neurosis is suddenly cured when the patients succeed in finding such a place.

Abraham has described the case of an impostor who reformed after having found a situation that permitted him a deep satisfaction of his Oedipus wishes and his oral mother fixation, without having to feel guilty about it (29). In a symbolic way, this pursuit of rest and of protection at the mother's breast is expressed in the frequent yearning for the boundless ocean through which nostalgia is to be and yet never can be gratified ("long voyage home"). The usual restlessness in wanderers is rooted in the fact that for the most part the protection they seek once more becomes a danger, because the violence of their longing is felt as a dangerous instinct. To make comparative rest possible, the situation to which they are running must be near enough to the original unconscious goal to be acceptable as a substitute, and at the same time far enough removed not to create anxiety. When home, the seaman thinks this place will be at sea; when aboard, at home.

In addition the very act of running away may have a hidden sexual significance. Traveling is exciting to everybody because its connections with sexual partial instincts are manifold. To see the world gratifies scoptophilia; to wander gratifies muscle eroticism; to travel in fast-moving vehicles gratifies equilibrium eroticism. Going away in general means "exogamy," that is, going to a place where the incest taboo and the threats heard at home are not effective, and by way of the return of the repressed from the repression, on another level, it usually means to go on a quest for the winning of the mother (10). However, all these hidden sexual meanings will only produce the picture of an impulse neurosis if the symptoms simultaneously express the typical conflicts described above.

CLEPTOMANIA

Cleptomania means in principle to take possession of things which give the strength or the power to fight supposed dangers, especially, as before, supposed dangers of loss of self-esteem or of affection. Its unconscious formula is: "If you don't give it to me, I'll take it" (47, 92, 169, 248, 644, 756, 757, 912, 944, 955, 1043, 1112, 1401, 1408, 1526, 1533, 1606, 1646).

If it is true that the cleptomaniac is striving for a lost sexual satisfaction which has been protection, forgiveness, and regulator of self-esteem simultaneously, the property stolen must of necessity symbolically represent milk. But this deepest interpretation is not necessarily the only one. The cleptomanic craving may also be the expression of a desire for objects corresponding to higher levels of organization—feces, penis, or child, if the desire for these objects is colored by a deeper "oral" way of longing. The relative importance of these different unconscious significances of the stolen object depends on the prevalent fixation points of the patient. In the cleptomanic strivings of patients who are not very deeply disturbed, the significance of "penis" will be in the foreground. This explains why cleptomania generally is more common among women than among men. "Stealing a penis" is the principal fantasy of some women belonging to the "revenge type" of the female castration complex (20), who are afraid of open aggressiveness and substitute "theft" for "robbery." In boys, too, a wish to have a penis is not as absurd as might appear at first sight; they may wish for a different penis, a large one, like the father's.

The most frequent complication in cleptomania is represented by conflicts between the ego and the superego. The patients try to convince themselves that since they did not get enough affection, they have a right to steal. But, as a rule, they do not succeed. Instead they feel guilty, try to fight this guilt feeling in different ways, and may even become "criminals out of guilt feeling" (592), stealing more and more, thus becoming enmeshed in a vicious circle (*see* p. 500).

Stealing (like wandering) may also have a direct sexual significance. For example, it may represent "doing a forbidden thing secretly," and thus mean masturbation. In certain cases, this direct sexual significance is in the foreground, and cleptomanias of this type are close to perversion.

A woman of forty, who constantly reverted to thievery, reported that she was sexually excited whenever she stole and that she even experienced orgasm at the moment she accomplished her theft. In sexual intercourse she was frigid; while masturbating, she would imagine that she was stealing.

In cases of this type the oral taking which gives sexual satisfaction at the same time serves as a reassurance against the threatening possibility of castration, in the same way that the fetish does in fetishism. It is very probable that the objects stolen by "perverse cleptomaniacs" actually are their fetishes.

PYROMANIA

Sexual excitement at the sight of fire is a normal occurrence in children. It is not easy to explain. Analysis reveals the effectiveness of sadistic drives, which aim to destroy the object, and a cutaneous pleasure in the warmth of the fire. But in addition, there is something more specific about the excitement aroused by the fire. Regularly a deep-seated relationship to urethral eroticism is to be found. Freud took this as a starting point for a speculative hypothesis about the origin of the cultural use of fire (627). In the same way that there are cprophilic perversions based on urethral eroticism, perversions may also be developed based on the derivative of urethral eroticism, pleasure in fire. The pleasure in starting a fire (in reality or in fantasy) may become the indispensable condition for sexual enjoyment (229, 1221, 1623; *cf. also* 788). In an incendiary perversion, intense sadistic strivings govern the sexual life, the destructive force of the fire serving as a symbol for the intensity of the sexual urge. The patients are full of vindictive impulses, which receive their specific form from their urethral-erotic fixation. Analogous to other impulse neuroses, the typical aim of this hostility is to force the object to give the affection or attention narcissistically needed.

GAMBLING

The passion for gambling, too, is a displaced expression of conflicts around infantile sexuality, aroused by the fear of losing necessary reassurances regarding anxiety or guilt feelings (116, 623, 1435). As a rule, the conflicts are those centered around masturbation.

The excitement of the game corresponds to sexual excitement; that of winning to orgasm (and to killing); that of losing to punishment by castration (and by being killed). Just as compulsion neurotics invent various kinds of oracles in their intention to force God to permit masturbation and to free them of their guilt feeling (which, as a rule, fails), the gambler, too, tempts fate to declare whether it is in favor of his playing (masturbating) or whether it is going to castrate him. As in all conflicts around masturbation, here, too, the activity serves as the scapegoat for the objectionable (hostile) fantasies of which it is the agent. The intensity of the conflicts around getting the "supplies" again hints at an oral fixation; besides, the anal element (the part played by money) also appears to be conspicuous.

All this, however, hardly suffices to explain the specific passion for gambling. Gambling, in its essence, is a provocation of fate, which is forced to make its decision for or against the individual. Luck means a promise of protection (of narcissistic supplies) in future instinctual acts. But what is more important is that the typical gambler consciously or unconsciously believes in his right to ask for special protection by fate. His gambling is an attempt to compel fate in a magical way to do its "duty"; however, gambling is a *fight* with fate. The gambler threatens to "kill" fate if it refuses the necessary supplies and is ready, for this purpose, to run the risk of being killed. Actually the unconscious "masturbatory fantasies" of gambling often center around patricide (623).

> A passionate gambler in the lotteries behaved as if it were assured and inevitable that one day he would win the Grand Prize. This was simply a debt that fate owed him. Analysis showed that "fate" was a screen figure for his father. To accept or to take money from his father, or to reject this money, was the leitmotif of his life. The patient had been greatly spoiled during the first three years of his life; then his father suddenly deprived him of his privileges. Throughout his life he asked for compensation.

In honest gambling, the chance of losing is as great as the chance of winning. The gambler dares to compel the gods to make a decision about him, hoping for their forgiveness; but even to lose (to be sentenced or killed) seems to him preferable to a continuation of the unbearable superego pressure.

If winning in gambling means rebellion in order to get what is needed, loss is unconsciously looked upon as ingratiation for the same purpose.

Actually, many impulsive actions tend to express not only instinctual drives but demands of a severe superego as well. The gambler may eventually be ruined, the arsonist and thief ultimately be caught. Impulsive behavior often makes its appearance among moral masochists with an intense need for punishment. Qualitatively, there is no difference in this respect between such impulses and compulsions or perversions; many compulsions aim to satisfy demands of the superego by means of punishment, and some exhibitionists feel tempted only when a policeman is in the vicinity. Quantitatively, however, there is a difference: the conflict with the superego more frequently dominates the picture in impulse neuroses (1133). The true gambler must eventually be ruined. The same is shown in the fact that impulse neuroses frequently, like manic-depressive states, present a periodic alternation between guilt-laden periods and periods in which the superego apparently is inoperative (*see* p. 411).

As an extreme example of this type, Freud described the "criminal out of guilt feeling" (592), that is, persons who are so oppressed by an unconscious guilt that they perform some reprehensible act in order to find relief by being punished and by rationalization of their guilt feeling, dissipating their guilt of unknown origin by connecting it with a known factor.

Gambling and masturbation have another typical point in common in that both are intended as a kind of play. The psychological function of play is to get rid of extreme tensions by the active repetition or anticipation of them in a self-chosen dosage and at a self-chosen time. Masturbation in childhood and puberty, in this sense, is "playing at" sexual excitement, acquainting the ego with this excitement and preparing it for the ability to control it. Gambling, in the beginning, is thought of as "playing," in the sense that the oracle is "playfully" asked how it would decide in a more serious situation. Under the pressure of inner tensions, the playful character may be lost; the ego can no longer control what it has initiated, but is overwhelmed by a very serious vicious circle of anxiety, violent need for reassurance and anxiety over the intensity of this violence. The pastime becomes a matter of life and death (984).

INSTINCT-RIDDEN CHARACTERS

There are also less typical impulsive actions. In certain persons with an oral-narcissistic fixation, any action may become enmeshed in the vicious circle described and may have to be performed in the pathologically impulsive way.

Analysis does not confirm the assumption that impulsive characters are happy "narcissistic psychopaths" who have no superego and can therefore gratify all their demands without any consideration for others (1603). Assuredly a lack of lasting object relationships in early childhood or an oral fixation and traumatic experiences may make the complete and definite establishment of an effective superego impossible; for example, the parent figures may have changed in such rapid succession that there was objectively no time or opportunity to develop lasting relationships and identifications; however, persons of this kind also experience frustrations and develop reactions to them. Their superego is not lacking but incomplete or pathological, and the reactions of the ego to the pathological superego reflect the ambivalences and contradictions which these persons felt toward their first objects (84, 1122, 1266, 1525). Psychoanalysis of juvenile delinquents gives various examples of such distorted relations toward the superego (31, 756, 911, 1266). Cases of lesser severity are characterized by their chronic dissatisfaction; they are "hypersexual" and hyperinstinctual because of their state of being dammed up; cases of greater severity are governed by oral and cutaneous fixations, by extreme ambivalence toward all objects, by the identity of erotic and narcissistic needs, and by conflicts between rebellion and ingratiation.

> Some impostors have a great ability to make their victims fall in love with them, only to betray them afterward. They are governed by the narcissistic need to prove to themselves that they are capable of being loved; they remain unsatisfied nevertheless, and take revenge for their dissatisfaction.

The anomalies are sometimes immediately comprehensible in terms of the childhood history. The typical anamnestic findings among delinquents of this type are a frequent change of milieu, a loveless environment, or a very inconsistent environmental influence; the Oedipus complex and its solution are correspondingly disorganized, weak, and inconsistent; some patients simply have never learned to develop object relationships.

There are various kinds of qualitative anomalies of the superego and of its relation to the ego that figure significantly in the problem of impulsiveness. One of these is the "bribing" of the superego, the purchase of instinctual liberties by the antecedent or simultaneous fulfillment of an ideal requirement or of a punishment (see pp. 291 f.). A more general mechanism which may or may not use this "bribing" was described by Reich as characteristic for instinct-ridden characters (1266): the "isolation" of the whole superego. Whereas ordinarily the ego endeavors to meet the requirements of the superego or occasionally takes steps to ward them off, here the ego appears to keep the superego actively and consistently at a distance. Experiences with the persons whose incorporation created the superego have made it possible for the ego to feel the conscience in one place or at certain periods (and for the most part in very distorted forms), but to be relatively free from the inhibiting influences of the superego, when tempted by the irresistible urge of strivings for instinctual gratification and for security. The impulse is yielded to immediately before any superego inhibition can develop, and "remorse" is felt later, frequently after a displacement in quite another connection.

An isolation of this kind is fostered if the ego has previously experienced both intense erogenous pleasure and intense environmental frustrations, especially if experiences of this kind were encountered by a person already characterized by an oral regulation of self-esteem and an intolerance of tensions, developed under the influence of early traumata or orally fixating experiences.

> A patient had become extremely impulsive under the influence of a pathological and very inconsistent father who used to make generous presents one moment and take them back in the next, and to make promises that were not kept. Thus the son learned to take immediately and quickly whatever he could get before it was taken away again, and to follow any impulse as soon as possible, before any prohibition could be given.

The alternation of periods of action and periods of remorse shows the relationship of these types to manic-depressive disorders, the actions being analogous to mania, the remorse to depression.

Closely allied to the "isolation of the superego" is the formation of a kind of second, instinct-approving superego, of an idealization of instinctual activity, either by rationalizing one's own stubbornness as a "fight for a good cause" or under the influence of instinct-approving adults (840). This, however, is not so much characteristic for "impulsiveness" as it is for so-called asocial behavior, which sometimes is not impulsive at all (see pp. 504 f.).

Related to the problem of impulsive behavior is the problem of "acting out" in the psychoanalytic cure (445, 1570). Under the influence of transference, everyone whose infantile conflicts are remobilized by analysis may develop the tendency to repeat past experiences in present reality, or to misunderstand reality as if it were a repetition of the past, rather than to remember the repressed events in the appropriate connection. Certain patients, however, are more inclined to act out than others, and there is a type of neurosis in which this acting out is not limited to the analytic cure, but in which the patient's entire life consists of actions not adapted to reality but rather aimed at relieving unconscious tensions. It was this type of neurosis that was first described by Alexander under the name of neurotic character (38). These types will be discussed in more detail later (see pp. 506 f.). In general, they have the same oral structure as impulse neurotics; a complication, which is also valid for certain impulse neurotics, is given by the fact that the actions in question may also represent attempts to master traumatic experiences by repetition and by active "dramatization."

DRUG ADDICTION

The same urge that governs other pathological impulses is operative in addicts: the need to get something that is not merely sexual satisfaction but also security and assurance of self-assertion, and as such essential to the person's very existence. Addicts represent the most clear-cut type of "impulsives."

Certain cleptomaniacs get into fatal vicious circles because their stealing gradually becomes insufficient to give relief. They have to steal more and more. These persons could be called theft addicts. Other persons are compelled violently and impulsively to devour whatever food is in reach at the moment; they are food addicts. The word addiction hints at the urgency of the need and the final insufficiency of all attempts to satisfy it. Drug addictions differ in one point from these "addictions without drugs," a point that makes them much more complicated, that is, the chemical effects of the drugs.

The usual effects of drugs used by addicts are either sedative or stimulating ones. There are many occasions in human life in which the longing for these effects may be very legitimate. If a person in such a situation uses drugs, and ceases to use them when he is out of the situation, he is not called an addict. A person suffering from pain who gets an injection of morphine has received necessary protection. Similarly, the euphoric drugs are protections against painful mental states, for example, against depressions, and are indeed often very effective. As long as the use of drugs remains purely a protective measure, there is no addiction. An addict, in contradistinction, is a person to whom the effect of a drug has a subtle, imperative significance. Initially the patient might have sought nothing but consolation; but he comes to use (or to try to use) the effect of the drug for the satisfaction of another inner need. The person becomes dependent on this effect, and this dependence eventually becomes so overwhelming as to nullify all other interests. Thus the problem of addiction reduces itself to the question of the nature of the specific gratification which persons of this type receive or try to receive from their chemically induced sedation or stimulation, and the conditions that determine the origin of the wish for such a gratification.

In other words, addicts are persons who have a disposition to react to the effects of alcohol, morphine, or other drugs in a specific way, namely, in such a way that they try to use these effects to satisfy the archaic oral longing which is sexual longing, a need for security, and a need for the maintenance of self-esteem simultaneously (1236, 1239). Thus the origin and the nature of the addiction are not determined by the chemical effect of the drug but by the psychological structure of the patient (691, 692).

The pre-morbid personality, therefore, is the decisive factor. Those persons become drug addicts for whom the effect of the drug has a specific significance. For them it means the fulfillment, or at least the hope of fulfillment, of a deep and primitive desire, more urgently felt by them than are sexual or other instinctual longings by normal persons. This pleasure or the hope for it makes genital sexuality uninteresting for them. The genital organization breaks up, and an extraordinary regression begins. The various points of fixation determine which fields of infantile sexuality—Oedipus complex, masturbation conflicts, and especially pregenital impulses—come to the fore, and in the end the libido remains in the form of an "amorphous erotic tension energy" without "differential characteristics or forms of organization" (1236).

The previous study of impulsive behavior makes it easy to understand what kind of pleasure the addicts are seeking. Patients who are ready to give up all object libido necessarily are persons who never estimated object relationships very highly. They are fixated to a passive-narcissistic aim and are interested solely in getting their gratification, never in satisfying their partners nor, for that matter, in the specific personalities of their partners. Objects are nothing else for them but deliverers of supplies. Erogenously, the leading zones are the oral zone and the skin; self-esteem, even existence, are dependent on getting food and warmth.

The effect of the drug rests on the fact that it is felt as this food and warmth. Persons of this kind react to situations that create the need for sedation or stimulation differently from others. They are intolerant of tension. They cannot endure pain, frustration, situations of waiting. They seize any opportunity for escape more readily and may experience the effect of the drug as something much more gratifying than the original situation that had been interrupted by the precipitating pain or frustration. After the elation, pain or frustration becomes all the more unbearable, inducing a heightened use of the drug. All other strivings become gradually more and more replaced by the "pharmacotoxic longing" (1239). Interests in reality gradually disappear, except those having to do with procuring the drug. In the end, all of reality may come to reside in the hypodermic needle. The tendency toward such a development, rooted in an oral dependence on outer supplies, is the essence of drug addiction. All other features are incidental.

Analysis of drug addicts shows that genital primacy tends to collapse in those persons whose genital primacy always has been unstable. In analysis, all kinds of pregenital wishes and conflicts may reveal themselves in a confusing manner. The final stages are more instructive than the confusing pictures that appear during the process. The eventual "amorphous tension" actually resembles the very earliest stage in libidinal development, before there was any organization at all, namely, the oral orientation of the infant, who asked for gratification without any capacity for giving and without any consideration of reality. Oral and cutaneous tendencies are manifest in those cases where the drug is taken by mouth or by hypodermic injection; the syringe, it is true, may also have a genital symbolic quality; the pleasure, nevertheless, is secured through the skin and is a passive-receptive one. More important than any erogenous pleasure in drug elation, however, is the extraordinary elevation in self-esteem. During the drug elation, erotic and narcissistic satisfactions visibly coincide again. And this is the decisive point.

Various findings of other writers (299) can easily be brought into harmony with this formulation. According to Simmel the use of drugs at first represents genital masturbation accompanied by appropriate fantasies and contents; but later, conflicts from deeper levels of development appear, extending back to the oral stage (1441). This corresponds to the gradual regressive disintegration of sexuality, the terminal point of which is certainly more significant than the midway positions. Simmel also showed that for drug addicts, the organs may represent introjected objects, which also is in accordance with an oral regression. Similarly the findings of Gross, that in the addict there is a dysfunction of the superego and of other identifications (721), are in keeping with the same point of view, for identification is the object relationship of the oral stage.

The identity of the decisive conflict explains the relation between drug addiction and the manic-depressive states. Simmel correctly designated the elation due to drugs as "artificial mania" (1441). In the final stages of their illness, drug addicts live in objectless alternating states of elation and "morning after" depression which, in the last analysis, correspond to the alternation of hunger and satiation in the mentally still undifferentiated infant (see p. 411).

The "morning after" depressions begin more and more to prevail in the later development of addictions. The decisive complication in the psychology of addicts is represented by the increasing insufficiency of the elation achieved. Physiological and psychological conditions, still to be investigated, negate the sufficiency or even the appearance of elation. The patient must resort to larger doses at shorter intervals. The lack of effect increases the longing. The tension, when the longing is not gratified, becomes more unbearable. Now the hypodermic needle is employed less for the purpose of obtaining pleasure but rather as an inadequate protection against an unbearable tension, related to hunger and guilt feeling.

The decrease of the effect of the drug certainly has a physiological root. But there are also psychological ones. If, after a drug elation, the same misery that initiated the use of the drug has to be faced again, it necessarily appears still more unbearable, necessitating more frequent and more intense escapes. It has also been mentioned that impulsive actions carried out for the purpose of protection against supposed dangers may become dangerous themselves, and thus a vicious circle may be created. This is what happens to addicts also. If addicts become aware of their progressive mental disintegration, they certainly perceive it as a danger; but they have no other means of meeting this danger than by increasing the amount of the drug. The idea that forcing the gods to give protection may be dangerous, and that because of this danger one has to force the gods still more, is valid for any impulse neurosis. In drug addiction, however, the idea that the protective measure may be dangerous is, for physiological reasons, a very real one. It *is* a danger; the patients become aware of it and get into an unsolvable vicious circle. The manic-depressive circle between elation and "morning after" becomes more and more irregular, the elation being shorter and shorter and eventually disappearing, the depression becoming permanent.

As to the specific effects of various individual drugs on the personality structure, the problem of a psychoanalytic supplement to their special pharmacology, in spite of Schilder's program of a "pharmacopsychoanalysis" (1379), has as yet hardly been attacked (747).

The specific elation from alcohol is characterized by the fact that inhibitions and limiting considerations of reality are removed from consciousness before the instinctual impulses are, so that a person who does not dare to perform instinctual acts may gain both satisfaction and relief with the help of alcohol. The superego has been defined as the "part of the mind that is soluble in alcohol." Therefore, alcohol has always been extolled for its power to banish care; obstacles appear smaller and wish fulfillments nearer, in some persons through the diminishing of inhibitions, in others through withdrawal from reality to pleasurable daydreams.

Correspondingly the reasons for reverting to alcohol are either the existence of external frustrations, that is, states of misery one would like to forget and to replace by pleasurable fantasies, or internal inhibitions, that is, states in which one dare not act against the superego without such artificial help; among these inhibitions, depressive inclinations are of the greatest importance.

When the (external or internal) misery is at an end, the drinking may or may not be at an end. Persons in whom it is not are called alcoholics. They are characterized by their oral and narcissistic pre-morbid personalities, as described above for addictions in general. However, there are a few points that are specific for alcoholism. Knight (960, 963, 964) and others (2, 157, 260, 273, 301, 450, 685, 799, 856, 903, 926, 947, 1142, 1155, 1156, 1305, 1561) showed that in chronic alcoholics difficult family constellations created specific oral frustrations in childhood. These frustrations gave rise to oral fixations, with all the consequences of such fixations for the structure of the personality. In boys the frustrations resulted also in a turning away from the frustrating mother to the father, that is, to— more or less repressed—homosexual tendencies. The unconscious impulses in alcoholics typically are not only oral but also homosexual in nature.

It is only necessary to call to mind the numerous drinking customs to find confirmation of this fact. That latent homosexuals, seduced by social frustrations, are particularly fond of alcohol is more probable than that alcohol through its toxic effectiveness would be conducive to homosexuality.

It is very important to determine whether a person resorts to alcohol from external or internal (depressive) distress, leaving off when he ceases to need it for this purpose, or whether his entire psychosexuality and self-esteem are governed by a desire to be elatedly drunk, or whether, finally, this desire for elated drunkenness is in danger of breaking down and the patient in "pharmacotoxic impotence" is trying to pursue an unattainable happiness.

> Decisive also is whether the necessary supply is still demanded of an object, and the alcohol thus used as a means to facilitate the winning of this object, or whether the alcohol has become the supply in itself, the interest in alcohol supplanting any interest in objects.
>
> With some degree of certainty the general behavior of the patient in relation to the environment gives an index of the extent to which his object relationships have disintegrated. Those who drink convivially with friends have a better prognosis than lone drinkers.

The periodic drinkers' disorder is constructed along the same lines as the periodicity of the manic-depressive states. When alcohol has been used for an escape from external or internal misery this misery, after the elation, seems worse.

> Whereas alcohol in general helps to get rid of depressive moods that return only in "morning after" effects, in some persons it may immediately precipitate depressions. Analysis sometimes succeeds in explaining this failure of the drinker's intention in terms of his history. Any actual procurement of the needed supplies becomes a new danger or guilt. Drinking then plays the role of the "pathognomonic introjection," precipitating depressions (*see* pp. 396 f.).

Psychoses in addicts, especially alcoholic psychoses, have been but little studied by psychoanalysts (205, 946, 1254, 1379, 1529, 1585). In so far as they are of a manic-depressive nature, the psychological relationship of the two conditions suffices as an explanation; when the addiction can be looked upon as a last means to avoid a depressive breakdown, it is understandable that the breakdown occurs when the addiction becomes definitely insufficient. The uselessness of the objective world, rendered superfluous by the pharmacotoxic orientation, evidently facilitates an eventual psychotic "break with reality." Psychoses frequently begin during a period of abstinence, due to the fact that the withdrawal itself made the remainders of reality still more unbearable. In psychoses other than manic-depressive ones, it is not definitely established where the clinical symptoms originate, to what extent they are psychogenic, and to what extent organic or toxic. For a discussion of the paranoid symptoms, see the chapter on schizophrenia (pp. 427 ff.).

In a very instructive article, Tausk (1529) interpreted alcoholic occupational delirium as the expression of sexual excitement in patients who are erotically stimulated and at the same time rendered impotent by alcohol, and who are, on deeper levels, homosexual and narcissistic.

ADDICTIONS WITHOUT DRUGS

The mechanisms and symptoms of addictions may also occur without the employment of any drugs, and thus without the complications brought about by the chemical effects of drugs. A special category is that of the aforementioned food addicts, which includes several different types (99). In food addicts, no displacement has transformed the original object (food) of the strivings for simultaneous gratification of sexuality and self-esteem. However, later stages of development have added other unconscious meanings to the pathologically craved food; it may represent feces, child (embryo), and penis. In severe cases, the field of eating remains the only interest connecting the person with reality. Wulff has described a special type of food addiction, occurring in women only, which has a cyclic course and is closely related to manic-depressive disturbances (1619) (*see* pp. 241 f.).

> Sometimes the food asked for is of a specific kind, dependent on forgotten experiences that incisively aroused the basic conflicts. A case in point was that of an addiction for sausages.
>
> It is understandable that during pregnancy old unconscious fantasies around introjection become mobilized. Women with oral fixations and ambivalent attitudes toward their pregnancy will revive their former conflicts around oral strivings. Thus "specific food addictions" occur more frequently during pregnancy than in any other state (829, 1144).
>
> Certain patients succeed in holding their "addiction" at a lower level, not quite as full blown as food addicts; they are persons who need coffee, milk, coca-cola, or even water in a more or less obsessive way, but who apart from this are relatively normal.
>
> There is a characteristic relationship between food cravings and food phobias or certain types of anorexia. The latter conditions may be determined by the repression of morbid cravings. Sometimes analysis succeeds, in cases of food phobia, in uncovering a forgotten period of morbid craving in childhood for the kind of food subsequently avoided.

In other cases, distortion has made the food character of objects morbidly craved less obvious. An example is reading addiction, not infrequent among adolescents and occasionally among adults.

> A patient with no capacity for waiting had obsessively to carry books with him in order to be able to read at any free second; he had to avoid being alone with himself. The book in his pocket gave him the same reassurance that morphine in the pocket gives to the drug addict. Analysis revealed that unconsciously reading was equated with eating. This significance is typical for reading addiction as well as for neurotic disturbances of reading (124, 1512). Reading phobias may originate in the repression of a craving for reading; compulsive reading rituals may represent conditions under which a craving for reading may again be

yielded to. The impulse to read while eating is an attempt to distract attention from an oral-erotic excitement, which, however, returns from the repression.

The same holds true for "hobbies" that tend to outgrow their hobby character and to evolve into an obsessive preoccupation, eventually becoming an absolutely necessary condition for well-being and protection against depression (99).

The most important type is represented by "love addicts," that is, by persons in whom the affection or the confirmation they receive from external objects plays the same role as food in the case of food addicts. Although they are unable to return love, they absolutely need an object by whom they feel loved, but only as an instrument to procure the condensed oral gratification. These "love addicts" constitute a high percentage of the "hypersexual" persons described previously (see pp. 242 ff.) and are often candidates for later manic-depressive disorders (see pp. 387 ff.).

> A woman patient, as a result of certain infantile experiences, suffered from a severe anxiety of being abandoned. Just as a frightened child cannot fall asleep without a protecting mother sitting at his bedside, this patient in adult life had to be sure of a protecting union with others. In analysis, her principal resistance was that she had no other interest than to make sure that the analyst was taking her side. For this reason she was unable to say no to any man; whenever she was alone, she had to go out to find a man immediately. Apparently she had an active adult sexual life. Actually sex life was the same thing for her as a mother's reassuring hand is for the frightened child. Sexual behavior was a means of repressing her full sexual impulses which, of course, were of an oral-sadistic nature (see pp. 517 f.).

All the morbid impulses as well as the addictions (with and without drugs) are, it may be stated again, unsuccessful attempts to master guilt, depression or anxiety by activity. As such they are related to counterphobic attitudes (see pp. 480 ff.).

The patients try to re-enact in "play" the dangers they fear, and thereby learn to master them. But frequently it happens that the game turns into the "real thing" and the danger they tried to control overwhelms them.

TRANSITIONAL STATES BETWEEN MORBID IMPULSES AND COMPULSIONS

This chapter has differentiated sharply between ego-syntonic morbid impulses and the ego-alien symptoms of compulsion neurotics. But there are also certain transitional forms; some of the "addictions without drugs" can hardly be distinguished from obsessions. Sometimes certain compulsive symptoms, for the most part of a relatively insignificant nature, become secondarily sexualized and serve as a source of pleasure for the ego. They might be called "pleasurable obsessions" and form a transition to perversions (475). Certain patients, for example, habitually spend hours reading atlases or timetables, doing bookkeeping or making calculations, from which they derive a great deal of pleasure. Combining the habits with sundry compulsive little games, all hobbies of this type certainly represent derivatives sufficiently far removed from the original impulse to be tolerated but still close enough to give pleasure. They may also be looked upon as a transition between neurotic symptom and sublimation, but mostly the compulsive nature is too much in the foreground for them to be considered sublimations. To a certain degree, nearly every compulsion neurotic, in addition to the major symptoms, will show quite a number of such minor compulsive games that furnish an amusement the patient would not want to lose. The similarity between these compulsive games and children's games, in which strict rules have to be obeyed, leads us to expect that a secondary sexualization of activities originally serving as defensive measures also plays a part in the psychology of children's games. Certain hobbies and preferred or obsessive activities, which represent derivatives of infantile autoeroticism, occupy an intermediate position between compulsive acts and perversions (1159, 1304).

Their structure actually is that of perversions; that is, they represent condensations of erogenous strivings with reassurances against opposing fears. A patient with the hobby of excerpting everything he read and arranging the excerpts in different files enjoyed in so doing (*a*) an anal-erotic pleasure: what he read represented food; his files represented the feces, into which the food had been turned by him; he liked to look at his feces and to admire his "productivity"; (*b*) reassurance: the filing system was supposed to prove that he had things "under control."

Another patient had an obsessive pleasure in mail-order buying and a pride in being expert about all kinds of merchandise. As a child he used to study the Sears-Roebuck catalogues in minute detail, and in his later hobby he tried to show that he had not done this in vain. The story of this preference turned out to be a rather complicated one; however, to see its double nature as sexual activity and as reassurance, the following facts will be sufficient:

1. When the patient was a little boy, his father once showed him a picture of a statue of a nude woman in a catalogue, saying: "That is the way women look." The patient's memory was that he did not quite understand what his father meant and was rather confused. (In analysis, the hypothesis was made that actually the boy might have seen the picture spontaneously, been confused about the lack of a penis, asked the father, and got the reply: "That is the way women look.") His subsequent study of catalogues was analogous to a scoptophilic perversion: in looking at the pictures, the patient tried to overcome and to deny his ignorance and confusion, and on a deeper level, his castration fear. However, the original nude woman was too frightening and had to be supplanted by "merchandise."

2. At about the same time the patient went alone to a hardware store to buy a few tools; but he did not know exactly what he wanted and was scolded and sent home by the salesman. This narcissistic hurt had to be compensated for, first, by acquiring an extraordinary knowledge of merchandise (the study of catalogues

being an obsessive "preparation" for the "real thing" of an actual purchase) and, second, by turning from personal buying to mail-order buying. Dreams and symptoms showed that the event in the hardware store served as a screen memory for a still earlier event. According to analytic reconstruction, the little boy had once wet his pants while in a store and felt ashamed about it.

3. The patient's mother was very critical and strict though most inconsistent in her criticisms. She not only frequently hurt the boy's masculine pride but also criticized the father for not being active and for letting others take advantage of him. An ambition of being a good buyer represented also the boy's Oedipus wish.

In studying catalogues the patient prepared for future tests of his masculinity and for the avoidance of repetitions of his failures and confusion. All merchandise signifies "nude women" whom the patient now understands sufficiently to be proud of himself and exhibitionistic with his masculinity. However, the obsessive character of the hobby and the stressing of mail orders, which actually is a buying phobia, show that he is not yet very sure of himself. Actually, he was, though highly ambitious, full of castration anxiety and inferiority feelings, the denial of which was intended in the pleasureful hobby.

A secondary pleasure in obsessions has to be distinguished from an obsessive performance of apparently sexual acts without (or without sufficient) sexual feelings. Symptoms that were created for the purpose of warding off masturbation, through penetration by the warded-off forces, eventually may be replaced by masturbation. A masturbation of this kind does not bring pleasure. The lack of satisfaction increases the striving for satisfaction. The protection-forgiveness of the gods, which would make a relaxing satisfaction possible, may be sought with the same aggressive fury by masturbating, with which it is sought by the gambler in his gambling. And like gambling, masturbation also may be performed for the purpose of punishment, being thought of as an equivalent of castration (412). The ego demonstrates its self-destruction to its superego, asking for forgiveness by ingratiation and by stubbornness. And the superego behaves as the gods did who punished King Midas' greediness by ruining him through the fulfillment of his wishes. The sexuality the ego wanted is granted, but in a painful and devastating manner. The same may hold true for certain perverse acts which thus could be called compulsive perversions. Instinctual behavior of this kind may also represent a desperate and inadequate attempt to discharge, in a sexual way, tensions of any kind. The act is carried out not only to obtain pleasure or to achieve punishment but also to get rid of an unbearable painful tension and to be relieved of a state of depression (665). In the same way that the drug may become insufficient in addictions and an ever increasing amount of the drug is needed, so the orgastic impotence (1270) in such cases may require more and more of the pseudo-sexual acts. In severe cases of "sexual addictions," sexuality loses its specific function and becomes an unsuccessful nonspecific protection against stimuli.

Individuals of this type, who are preoccupied with sexuality without deriving sexual pleasure, may instead receive narcissistic pleasure from their supposed potency (*see* p. 515).

In some sexual activities, the sexual partner serves the same purpose as the drug in the addiction.

PSYCHOANALYTIC THERAPY IN IMPULSE NEUROSES AND ADDICTIONS

There is still much contention over the psychoanalytic therapy of persons with morbid impulses or addictions. An understanding of the mechanisms involved makes it plain that in principle such patients are amenable to psychoanalytic treatment, but that from a practical point of view there are particular problems to be overcome. Not only is the symptom itself pleasurable, so that the cases offer the analyst the same difficulties as do perversions, but besides, the pregenital, narcissistic constitution of the patients makes it necessary to work back to the deepest layers, and the intolerance of tension necessitates modifications of technique. It is, however, generally agreed that psychoanalytic treatment should be tried whenever possible. If the pre-morbid disposition of an addict is allowed to remain unchanged after a withdrawal cure, it will soon induce the patient to return to the use of the drug. It is not the chemical effect of the drug that must be combated but the morbid wish to be drunkenly euphoric.

The best time to begin an analysis is obviously during or immediately after withdrawal. But it is not to be expected that the patient will remain abstinent throughout analysis. If he has an opportunity he will probably use the drug again whenever the resistance in his analysis predominates. This is the reason why addicts are to be analyzed in institutions rather than as ambulatory patients (219, 964, 1440). No general rules can be laid down as to when and how the use of the drug is to be stopped in the case of relapses. From the general conception of the disorder it follows that the addiction runs the course of a chronic disintegrating process, and that the most important consideration from a therapeutic point of view is at what stage of disintegration the analysis is begun. The concept "drug addict" includes individuals with very different relationships to reality and with very different capacities for establishing transference (1440).

It must also not be overlooked that an addiction begins as a search for a protective guard against painful stimulation. In many so-called drunkards, drinking is essentially a retreat from unbearable external conditions. Therapy in such cases will be of no avail as long as these external conditions persist, and would become unnecessary if they were changed.

As to more internally determined cases, it may in general be stated that the more recent the addiction, the better the prognosis.

With regard to other forms of impulsive behavior, the prognosis depends first on the same factors as in perversions and second on the amenability to treatment of the intolerance of tension. Through a certain type of preliminary treatment, it may be possible to increase the patient's awareness that he is ill, and to strengthen his wish to be cured, before psychoanalysis proper begins; and a certain activity on the part of the analyst, such as has been mentioned before, may be necessary in dealing with the intolerance of tension and the tendency to "act out." For the necessary modifications of technique, reference is made to the special literature (438, 445, 491, 506, 669, 1271, 1279, *et al.*).

Chapter XVII

DEPRESSION AND MANIA

DEPRESSION AND SELF-ESTEEM

THE understanding of the impulse neuroses and addictions provides the background prerequisite for the study of that most frequent and also most problematic mechanism of symptom formation, depression. To a slight degree, depression occurs in nearly every neurosis (at least in the form of neurotic inferiority feelings); of high degree it is the most terrible symptom in the tormenting psychotic state of melancholia.

Depression is based on the same predisposition as addiction and pathological impulses. A person who is fixated on the state where his self-esteem is regulated by external supplies or a person whose guilt feelings motivate him to regress to this state vitally needs these supplies. He goes through this world in a condition of perpetual greediness. If his narcissistic needs are not satisfied, his self-esteem diminishes to a danger point. He is ready to do anything to avoid this. He will try every means to induce others to let him participate in their supposed power. On the one hand the pregenital fixation of such persons manifests itself in a tendency to react to frustrations with violence; on the other hand their oral dependence impels them to try to get what they need by ingratiation and submissiveness. The conflict between these contradictory devices is characteristic for persons with this predisposition.

> Methods of ingratiation often reveal in analysis that simultaneously they are methods of rebellion. Sacrifice and prayer, the classic methods of ingratiation, are often thought of as a kind of magical violence used to force God to give what is needed. Many depressive attitudes are precisely such condensations of ingratiation and aggressiveness.

These persons, in their continuous need of supplies that give sexual satisfaction and heighten self-esteem simultaneously, are "love addicts," unable to love actively; they passively need to feel loved. Besides, they are characterized by their dependence and their narcissistic type of object choice. Their object relationships are mixed up with features of identification and they tend to change objects frequently because no object is able to provide the necessary satisfaction. They require a behavior on the part of their objects that permits or encourages their participation by enabling them to feel at one with the partner (*see* pp. 510 f.). Without giving any consideration to the feelings of their fellow men they demand of them an understanding of their own feelings. They are always bent upon establishing a "good understanding" with people, though they are unable to fulfill their own part of such an understanding; this need compels them to attempt to deny their ever present readiness to react hostilely.

In consonance with the early fixation of persons of this kind, the personality of the object is of no great importance. They need the supplies, and it does not matter who provides them. It does not necessarily have to be a person; it may be a drug or an obsessive hobby. Some persons of this type fare worse than others; they not only need supplies, but simultaneously fear getting them, because they unconsciously consider them dangerous.

As in the case of drug addicts, "love addicts," too, may become incapable of getting the desired satisfaction, which in turn increases their addiction. The cause for this decisive incapacity is the extreme ambivalence connected with their oral orientation (1238).

The understanding of this archaic type of regulation of self-esteem will be facilitated by a recapitulation of the developmental stages of guilt feelings (see pp. 134 ff.). In the life of the infant, the stages of hunger and satiety alternate. The hungry infant remembers having been satisfied previously and tries to force the return of this state by asserting his "omnipotence" in screaming and gesticulation. Later on, the infant loses belief in his omnipotence; he projects this omnipotence onto his parents and tries to regain it through participation in their omnipotence. He needs this participation, the feeling of being loved, in the same way that previously he needed milk. Now the succession of hunger and satiety is replaced by the succession of states in which the child feels alone and therefore experiences a kind of self-depreciation—we called it annihilation—and states in which he feels loved and his self-esteem is re-established. Still later, the ego acquires the ability to judge by anticipating the future. Then the ego creates (or rather uses) states of "minor annihilations" or small "diminutions" in self-esteem as a precaution against the possibility of a real and definite loss of narcissistic supplies. Still later, the superego develops and takes over the inner regulation of self-esteem. No longer is the feeling of being loved the sole prerequisite for well-being, but the feeling of having done the right thing is now necessary. Conscience develops its warning function; "bad conscience" again creates states of minor annihilations or small diminutions in self-esteem to warn against the danger of a definite loss of narcissistic supplies, this time from the superego. Under certain circumstances the warning signal of the conscience may fail and turn into the tormenting feeling of complete annihilation of melancholia, in the same way that in anxiety hysteria the warning signal of anxiety may suddenly turn into a complete panic. The explanation of such failure of conscience was postponed. The study of depression is the place to come back to it.

A severe depression represents the state into which the orally dependent individual gets when the vital supplies are lacking; a slight depression is an anticipation of this state for warning purposes.

The motives of defense against instinctual drives are anxiety or guilt feeling. In the same way that an anxiety motivating defense is still manifest in anxiety hysteria, a guilt feeling motivating defense is manifest in some simple depressions.

After times of long deprivation and frustration, everybody tends to become apathetic, slow, retarded, uninterested. Apparently even normal persons need a certain amount of external narcissistic supplies, and if these supplies cease entirely, they get into the situation of infants not sufficiently taken care of. These states are models of "simple depressions." There are transitory states between "depressions" of this kind and regressions to a passive state of hallucinatory wish fulfillment in which no demands are directed toward the real world any more and life is supplanted by an objectless passive vegetative existence, as in some catatonic states (see p. 123).

Neurotic depressions are desperate attempts to force an object to give the vitally necessary supplies, whereas in the psychotic depressions the actual complete loss has really taken place and regulatory attempts are aimed exclusively at the superego (597, 668, 1238).

This, however, is not an absolute difference. In neurotic depressions, too, guilt feelings and the fear of being abandoned by the superego play an important part; the affection of external objects, then, is needed for the purpose of contradicting the accusing superego. And in psychotic depressions, where the struggle takes place on a narcissistic level, the ambivalence toward external objects still remains recognizable.

ORALITY IN DEPRESSION

The pregenitality of these patients exhibits itself first of all in their anal orientation. Abraham showed that the personality of manic-depressive persons in the free intervals resembles, to a great extent, that of compulsive neurotics (5, 26). Combinations of depressions with compulsion neurosis are frequent. Very often money plays a significant role in the clinical picture (fear of loss of money and of poverty in depressions). Behind this anal orientation, definite trends of an oral fixation always are apparent. The refusal to eat is not only the most widespread clinical symptom of melancholia; it is a concomitant of every depression. Occasionally, this symptom alternates with bulimia.

In the chapter on organ neurosis a type of neurotic depression was mentioned in which the depressive phases were combined with bulimia, whereas the phases in which the patients restricted their eating were the ones in which they felt well (see p. 241).

Cannibalistic fantasies are demonstrable in the delusions of melancholia, and also in less severe types of depression, where they may be observed in dreams or as the unconscious significance of one or another symptom. Depressed patients frequently return to oral-erotic activities of their childhood—for instance, to thumb sucking. In addition, depressed persons show various oral traits of character (5, 13, 26, 597) (see pp. 488 f.).

The unconscious ideas of depressed persons, and frequently their conscious thoughts also, are filled with fantasies of persons or parts of persons they may have eaten. To those who have no experience in analysis, it cannot be too strongly emphasized how literally this oral incorporation is conceived of as devouring (153).

> In a previous chapter, a patient was mentioned who could not eat fish because fish have "souls" and therefore represented the patient's father who had died when she was in her first year of life. She had neurotic gastrointestinal symptoms and believed that her "diaphragm" ached. In these symptoms she was warding off her Oedipus wish which had assumed the form of a desire to eat her dead father. It turned out that in the dialect of German which she spoke, the word for diaphragm, *Zwerchfell,* was pronounced as if spelled *Zwergfell* (*Zwerg* meaning dwarf); she imagined that a little dwarf, jumping about, made a hubbub in her belly. Her *Zwerchfell* was her devoured father or, rather, his devoured penis.
>
> Children show often enough that they believe emotionally in the possibility of eating a person and of being eaten up, even long after this idea has been rejected intellectually (*cf.* 177).

The characteristic receptive orality goes hand in hand with a receptive skin eroticism, that is, with a longing for a reassuring warmth.

> A patient with a severe anxiety was unable to go to bed at night because she could not achieve the necessary relaxation and because she unconsciously regarded her not going to bed as a way of compelling fate to supply her needs. She managed to achieve a relative rest and relaxation by two acts that were love substitutes: (*a*) she would drink, and (*b*) she would sit on the radiator and enjoy its warmth.

Aims of incorporation also mark a difference between the anality met with in depressions and the anality of compulsion neurotics. The anality of the depressed person does not attempt to retain its object; it aims rather at incorporating, even if the object has to be destroyed for this purpose. Abraham has demonstrated that this type of anality corresponds to the older subtype of the anal-sadistic stage. A regression to this earlier anal level is obviously a decisive step. With the partial loss of objects attendant upon this stage, the patient is free from all restraint and his libido regresses further back to orality and narcissism (26).

OUTLINE OF THE PROBLEMS IN THE MECHANISMS OF DEPRESSION

Experiences that precipitate depressions represent either a loss of self-esteem or a loss of supplies which the patient had hoped would secure or even enhance his self-esteem. They are either experiences which for a normal person would also imply loss of self-esteem, such as failures, loss of prestige, loss of money, a state of remorse, or they imply the loss of some external supplies, such as a disappointment in love or the death of a love partner; or further they may be tasks which the patient has to fulfill and which, objectively or subjectively, make him more aware of his "inferiority" and narcissistic needs; paradoxically, even experiences that for a normal person would mean an increase in self-esteem may precipitate a depression if the success frightens the patient as a threat of punishment or retaliation, or as an imposition for further tasks, thus augmenting his need for supplies.

Patients who react to disappointments in love with severe depressions are always persons to whom the love experience meant not only sexual gratification but narcissistic gratification as well. With their love, they lose their very existence. They are afraid of such a loss, and usually very jealous. The intensity of the jealousy does not at all correspond to the intensity of the love. The most jealous persons are those who are not able to love but need the feeling of being loved. After any loss, they try at once to find a substitute for the lost partner, by drinking, for example, or by looking for another partner immediately, an act which may increase their jealousy, namely, on a projective basis; their longing for another partner is projected and the patient thinks that his partners are looking for a new object (see pp. 433 and 512 f.).

In the phenomenology of depression, a greater or lesser loss of self-esteem is in the foreground. The subjective formula is "I have lost everything; now the world is empty," if the loss of self-esteem is mainly due to a loss of external supplies, or "I have lost everything because I do not deserve anything," if it is mainly due to a loss of internal supplies from the superego.

The patients try to influence the persons around them to return their lost self-esteem. Frequently they try to captivate their objects in a way characteristic for masochistic characters, by demonstrating their misery and by accusing the objects of having brought about this misery, and by enforcing and even blackmailing their objects for affection, in accordance with the aforementioned methods of Frederick William of Prussia (see p. 356). This can be more readily observed in neurotic depressions than in psychotic ones because the ingratiating attitude of the neurotic is directed more toward external objects.

It can even be observed in simple neurotic inferiority feelings and in "bad moods" (1617), which very often take the form "I am no good"; latent guilt feelings are common in neurotics because they feel that their warded-off "bad" impulses are still operative within them.

Neurotic inferiority feelings are generally rooted in the failure of the Oedipus complex; they mean: "Because my infantile sexuality ended with a failure, I am inclined to believe that I shall always be a failure" (585). They are also intimately connected with the castration complex, so that the patient, for instance, in comparisons he draws between himself and others, unconsciously is comparing genitals. But these circumstances alone do not determine the neurotic inferiority feelings. Their actual source is an awareness of the impoverishment of the ego due to the unconscious neurotic conflicts (585). Many a simple "neurotic depression" is due to the circumstance that since the greater percentage of the available mental energy is used up in unconscious conflicts, not enough is left to provide the

normal enjoyment of life and vitality. Still another determinant of neurotic feelings of inferiority arises from the latent guilt feeling because of the continued
effectiveness of the warded-off impulses. Persons who tend to develop depressions
try to get rid of the guilt feeling by influencing objects to give them affection;
if the form of this influence becomes more sadistic, further guilt feelings are
aroused and a vicious circle is created.

Even psychotically depressed persons are prone to accuse objects of not loving
them and to behave sadistically toward external objects. This can be seen in certain modes of behavior of these patients which strictly contradict their conscious
feeling that they themselves are the worst creatures of all. The depressed patient,
who seemingly is so extremely submissive, is actually often successful in dom-
inating his entire environment. Analysis shows that this is a manifestation of an
intense oral sadism.

> In one of his plays, Nestroy has a melancholic say: "If I could not annoy other
> people with my melancholia, I wouldn't enjoy it at all."

Again it must be stressed that the borderline between neurotic depressions,
with ambivalent struggles about narcissistic supplies between the patient and
his objects, and psychotic depressions, where the conflict has become internalized, is not a sharp one. Conflicts between the superego and the ego are
effective in everyone who has narcissistic needs. And remnants of hope for
external help may still be effective in severe depressive psychoses (1383).

Since depressions always start with an increase in narcissistic needs, that is,
with the feeling "Nobody loves me," it might be expected that the patient will
feel that everybody hates him. Actually, delusions of this kind do occur. However, the feeling of being universally hated occurs more frequently in cases representing transition states to delusions of persecution. The classic depressions tend
rather to feel that they are not hated as much as they should be, that their deprav-
ity is not sufficiently apparent to others. The characteristic position is not so much
"Everybody hates me" as "I hate myself." The depressed patient obviously can
love himself no more than he can the external object. The depressed patient is
as ambivalent toward himself as he is toward objects. But the two components
of the ambivalence are stratified differently. In relation to the object, the love
impulses (or at least the impulses toward being loved) are more manifest, while
the hate is hidden. In relation to his own ego, it is the hate that becomes
vociferous, while the primary narcissistic overestimation of the ego remains concealed. Only analysis reveals that the depressed patient often behaves very ar-
rogantly and inflicts himself upon his objects.

Hostility toward the frustrating objects has been turned into hostility toward
one's own ego. This self-hatred appears in the form of a sense of guilt, that is,
of a discord between the ego and the superego. The existence of the psychic

agency known as the superego was first recognized through the study of depression (597, 608). The effectiveness of the superego becomes definitely evident only when it is at odds with the ego; this, to be sure, is true in all states of bad conscience, but to an extreme degree in depressions.

A redirection of hostility, originally aimed at objects, against the ego and the resulting pathological conflicts within the personality are met with also in phenomena outside of the realm of depression. In hypochondriasis and in some pregenital conversion symptoms, conflicts between the individual and external objects are transposed into the personality, where they continue in the form of conflicts between the ego and the superego or between the ego and certain organs; and certain compulsive symptoms are designated as manifestations of the ego's attacks on the superego (*see* pp. 291 ff.). The internalization of the originally external conflict is accomplished in depression in the same way as in these phenomena: by an introjection, that is, by the fantasy that the ambivalently loved object has been devoured and now exists within the body. This introjection is simultaneously a sexual fantasy of the patient whose sexuality is orally directed.

It is characteristic for depression, especially for psychotic depression, that the attempts to re-establish the last narcissistic equilibrium by means of the introjection of objects fail. The introjection, because of its sadistic nature, is perceived as a danger or guilt, and the struggles originally carried on with the external object are continued within the patient's "stomach" with the introjected object. The fact that in the superego another introjected object is already present and becomes involved in this struggle complicates the picture. The depressed person, after the introjection of the object, experiences no rage of the kind "I want to kill him (me)," but rather the feeling "I deserve to be killed." It is, as a rule, the superego which turns against the ego with the same rage that this ego previously used in its struggle with the object. The ego, in turn, acts toward this superego as it formerly acted toward the object. The outcome is that the struggle *subject vs. introject* becomes complicated in two ways: in the foreground is the struggle *superego vs. ego + introject;* but the ego, in its ambivalence toward the superego, changes it also into a struggle of *ego vs. superego + introject* (26, 597).

MOURNING AND DEPRESSION

To clarify this introjection and its consequences, Freud compared the depression with the related normal phenomenon of mourning (597). If a child loses an object, the libidinal strivings, no longer bound to the object, flood the child and may create panic. In "grief" the adult person has learned to control this flood by retarding the necessary process of loosening. The tie to the lost object is represented by hundreds of separate memories; for each of these memories the dissolution of the tie is carried through separately and this takes time. Freud designated this process the "work of mourning." Carrying out this work is a difficult and unpleasant task which many persons try further to retard by holding onto the illusion that the lost person still lives, and thus postponing the necessary work. An apparent lack of emotion in mourners may also be due to an identification with the dead person.

The illusion that the lost person still lives and the identification with him are closely related. Every mourner tends to simplify his task by building up a kind of substitute object within himself after the real object has departed. For this he uses the same mechanism all disappointed persons, including the depressed ones, employ—namely, regression from love to incorporation, from object relationship to identification. It can often be observed that a mourning person in one or other respects begins to resemble the lost object, that, for example, as Abraham reported, his hair becomes gray like the hair of the person he mourns (26); he develops cardiac symptoms if the object died of heart disease; he assumes one of the peculiarities of speech or gestures of the lost person. Freud pointed out that this process is not limited to the case of loss through death but holds good in the case of a purely mental loss as well. He referred to women who, after separation, take on traits of their lovers (608). Bulimia (institutionalized in the form of funeral repasts, reminiscent of the totem festivals of savages) (579, 1640), which unconsciously means the idea of eating the dead person, and the refusal of food, which means the rejection of this idea, come within the limits of normal grief. All this gives evidence of an identification with the dead person, subjectively perceived as an oral incorporation occurring on the same level as in psychotic depression but of lesser intensity.

The study of the folklore of death and burial customs offers convincing evidence for the universality of introjection as a reaction to the loss of an object (606, 1640). Black mourning apparel is a remnant of primitive mourning in sackcloth and ashes, which represents an identification with the dead person (1642).

All this supports Freud's formulation: "It may well be that identification is the general condition under which the id will relinquish its objects" (608). Many persons who have lost one of their parents early in childhood show signs of an oral fixation and tend to establish, along with their object relationships proper, extensive identifications, that is, to incorporate their objects.

Apparently, for a normal person it is easier to loosen the ties with an introject than with an external object. The establishment of an introjection is a means of facilitating the final loosening. Mourning consists of two acts, the first being the establishment of an introjection, the second the loosening of the binding to the introjected object.

Mourning becomes more complicated or even pathological if the relationship of the mourner to the lost object was an extremely ambivalent one. In this case the introjection acquires a sadistic significance; the incorporation then not only represents an attempt to preserve the loved object but also an attempt to destroy the hated object. If a hostile significance of this kind is in the foreground, the introjection will create new guilt feelings.

A case of death is always likely to mobilize ambivalence. The death of a person for whom one had previously wished death may be perceived as a fulfillment of this wish. The death of other persons may cause feelings of joy because death came to somebody else, not to oneself. Narcissistically oriented persons, in the painful state of mourning, tend unconsciously to reproach their dead friends for having brought them into this painful state. These reactions create guilt feelings and remorse. Actually, even in normal death rituals, symptoms of remorse are never lacking.

Beggars and dishonest firms are well aware of the remorseful mood of mourners and know how to take advantage of it.

The identification with the dead also has a punitive significance: "Because you have wished the other person to die, you have to die yourself." In this case, the mourner fears that because he has brought about death through the "omnipotence" of his death wish, the dead person may seek revenge and return to kill him, the living. This fear of the dead in turn increases the ambivalence. The mourner tries to pacify the dead one (*de mortuis nil nisi bonum*) as well as to kill him again and more effectively. The pious rituals of holding vigils at the side of the bier and of throwing sand into the grave or of erecting monuments of stone are traceable to archaic measures which are intended to prevent the dead from coming back (591, 1640). Grief in general is a "taming" of the primitive violent discharge affect, characterized by fear and self-destruction, to be seen in mourning savages (*see* p. 162). Such outbursts are all the stronger the more ambivalent the attitude toward the lost object was. Our "mourning," extended over a period of time, is a defense against being overwhelmed by this primitive affect (332).

In summary it may be stated that mourning is characterized by an ambivalent introjection of the lost object, a continuation of feelings toward the introject that once had been directed toward the object, and the participation of guilt feelings throughout the process.

Similar mechanisms may be operative in other types of sadness. The affective state of being sad is characterized by a decrease in self-esteem. A slightly sad person needs consolation, pity, "supplies." A very sad person withdraws from objects and becomes narcissistic by incorporating the unsatisfactory object; and after its introjection the struggle for the re-establishment of self-esteem is continued on the intrapsychic level.

Under certain conditions the narcissistic need and the conflicts around introjection in a mourning or sad person will be more intense than usual. This is the case if (*a*) the lost object has not been loved on a mature level but rather used as a provider of narcissistic supplies, (*b*) the previous relationship to the object has been ambivalent, (*c*) the person has been orally fixated and has had unconscious longings for a sexualized "eating."

The types described above as predisposed for the development of depressions have all these three characteristics: an increased narcissistic need, an increased ambivalence, and an increased orality. If such a person loses an object, he hates the object for having left him, tries to compel the object by violent magical means to make up for this loss, continues these attempts after an ambivalent introjection of the object, and, in attempting to decrease his guilt feelings, actually intensifies them. The highly cathected continuation of the struggle against the introject constitutes depression. Depression is a desperate attempt to compel an orally incorporated object to grant forgiveness, protection, love, and security. The destructive elements liberated by this coercion create further guilt feelings and fears of retaliation. The depressed person is in an untenable position since he is afraid that the granting of the supplies, of which he is in such desperate need, may simultaneously signify the object's or introject's revenge.

Ambivalence may also enter the picture of mourning in conditions other than depression, as, for example, in obsessive self-reproaches following a death. Pathognomonic for depression is the depth and the definite and full character of the regression, which extends beyond the later anal phase into orality and narcissism (26, 608).

THE PATHOGNOMONIC INTROJECTION

It has been stated that depression is a loss of self-esteem, either a complete breakdown of all self-esteem or a partial one intended as a warning against the possibility of a complete one. This formulation must now be supplemented by the statement that the depressed person tries to undo this loss and actually aggravates it by a pathognomonic introjection of the ambivalently loved object. This supplies the key to the failure of the warning signal of the conscience and to the resultant feelings of utter annihilation. The oral-sadistic introjection of the object, whose love is wanted as a narcissistic supply, is the match that explodes the powder of the dammed-up narcissistic need.

The introjection, then, is not only an attempt to undo the loss of an object. Simultaneously it is an attempt to achieve the *unio mystica* with an omnipotent external person, to become the lost person's "companion," that is, food comrade, through becoming his substance and making him become one's own substance (*see* pp. 40 f. and 63). Ambivalence, however, gives this introjection a hostile significance. The wish to force the object to give his consent to the union ends in the attainment of punishment for the violence of this wish. After the introjection, the struggle for forgiveness is continued on a narcissistic basis, the superego now struggling with the ego.

The depressed patient complains that he is worthless and acts as if he has lost his ego. Objectively he has lost an object. Thus ego and object are somehow equated. The sadism that once referred to the object has now been turned against the ego.

This turning against the ego was discovered by Freud in analyzing the self-reproaches of depressed patients (597). Apparently meaningless self-reproachful statements proved to have a meaning if the name of the hated object was substituted for "I." The self-reproaches were originally reproaches against the object. Thus the introjection at the basis of depression really is the opposite of the defense mechanism of projection: the bad characteristics of an object which one dare not become aware of because one fears the hatred they would arouse are perceived in one's own ego instead. The depressed patient says "I am bad because I am a liar" when he wants to say "I am angry with X because he has lied to me"; or "I am bad because I am a murderer" when he wants to say "I am angry with X; he has treated me badly as if he wanted to murder me."

> Some self-reproaches in depressed persons, however, impress one as being more or less objectively correct, rather than as delusions. Like paranoiacs, depressed persons are very sensitive to those portions of reality that are suitable to their mental needs, and react to them exaggeratedly.

By virtue of the introjection, a part of the patient's ego has become the object; as Freud puts it: "The shadow of the object has fallen on the ego" (597). This identification, in contradistinction to hysterical identification, must be called a narcissistic identification, for here the object is entirely replaced by an alteration of the ego (408). "Regression from object relationship to identification," "regression to narcissism," and "regression to orality" are terms that mean one and the same thing looked upon from different viewpoints.

> It will be recalled that Helene Deutsch reported a similar identification with a hated object in the psychogenesis of agoraphobia (325, 327). The question arises, then, as to the way in which the identification in depression differs from that found in agoraphobia. The answer is not difficult. There is relatively less regression to the oral level in agoraphobia. "This difference is that the identification in agoraphobia is affected at a higher level of libidinal development and is consequently transient and corrigible" (327).

THE CONFLICT BETWEEN THE SUPEREGO AND THE EGO

After the introjection, the sadism enlists on the side of the superego and attacks the ego that has been altered by the introjection. Not rage, but guilt feeling is felt. The sadism of the superego in depression exceeds the sadism found in the superego of compulsion neurotics as much as the depressed patient's ambivalence exceeds that of the compulsion neurotic. The superego treats the ego in the same way that the patient unconsciously had wished to treat the object that was lost.

But there are still further complications. It has been mentioned that the struggle in melancholia does not always have the form *superego vs. ego + introject,* but sometimes the form *ego vs. superego + introject;* that is, the recently introjected object may also join with the superego.

Freud explained the depressive self-reproaches as accusations directed against the introjected object (597). Abraham added that often complaints appear to come counterwise from the introjected object in the form of accusations that the real object actually had made against the patient (26). This enlistment of the introjected object on the side of the superego is in consonance with Freud's basic idea that the superego, too, originated in an introjection of objects.

> Abraham reported a case in which two objects were introduced, the one into the superego, the other into the ego. The self-reproaches of this patient corresponded to complaints made by an introjected mother about an introjected father (26).

In melancholic depressions the delusion of being poisoned is not rare, originating in the feeling of becoming destroyed by some orally introjected force. Weiss demonstrated that this delusion reflects an introjection of the object into the superego (1566).

> Such an interpretation does not necessarily conflict with the interpretation of this idea, on a more superficial level, as a fantasy of being impregnated. The dangerous introject, felt as a poison, may have different meanings on different levels; it may represent child and penis as well as breast and milk. The feeling of being poisoned contains a piece of psychological truth. The patient has introjected an object that now disturbs him from within. Thus the far-reaching hypochondriacal delusions in severe melancholia represent a distorted recognition of the process of introjection. The fear of being eaten up by something inside the body is a retaliation fear for the sadistic introjection. This "something" may be rationalized as a pathogenic virus, which forms a bridge to the more common phobia of being infected. And it is the idea of being eaten up by an introjected object that makes so many neurotics fear the mysterious disease of cancer (948, 1566).

In melancholia it seems as if the main emphasis of the personality has been shifted from the ego to the superego. The patient's conscience represents his total personality; the ego altered by the introjection is the mere object of this conscience and is entirely subdued by it.

> Freud has described a similar situation in a mood that is the very opposite of depression—humor (620). The mood of humor, too, is achieved by a displace-

ment of the emphasis of the personality from the ego to the superego. The difference is that in humor the overcathected superego is the friendly and protective positive ego-ideal; in depression, it is the negative, hostile, punishing conscience.

The superego has a double aspect. It represents a protective and a punitive power. Under normal circumstances the first aspect prevails and occasional punishments are accepted for purposes of conciliation. In depression, regression has abolished the first aspect of the superego. The ego, nevertheless, continues its attempts to achieve reconciliation. The whole depressive process appears as an attempt at reparation, intended to restore the self-esteem that has been damaged. The cutting off of narcissistic supplies has disturbed the entire psychic equilibrium. In the depressive process, the object that is believed to have brought this disturbance about is punished and destroyed for this very reason; but the object has become, by introjection, a part of the patient himself. In its attempt to destroy the bad object, the depressive ego meets the fate of Dorian Gray, who had to die in order to destroy his portrait.

The ego, persecuted by its superego to such a degree, has no other means at its disposal than has the ego of the compulsion neurotic when it is at odds with its superego: it reacts with submissiveness as well as with attempts at rebellion. The latter, however, cannot be successful because of the power the sadistic superego has acquired. Manifestly, in depressions the ego is more helpless and yielding to the attacks of the superego; the rebellious attitudes operate in a more hidden way only.

In the discussion of the submissiveness of the compulsion neurotic, it was stated that in yielding to its fate, the ego tries to ingratiate itself with the superego in the hope of achieving forgiveness. It chooses submission and even punishment as a "lesser evil," and besides it can, under certain circumstances, even obtain masochistic pleasure through these inflictions (*see* pp. 293, 364, and 501 f.). The same is attended by the ego of depressed patients. The sadism of the superego, however, dooms the hope for forgiveness to failure and increases the suffering beyond any possibility of enjoyment.

Self-reproach in depression is not only (from the reproaching superego's point of view) an attempt to attack the introjected object; in addition it represents (from the reproached ego's point of view) a courting of the superego and a plea for forgiveness intended to convince the superego how much its accusations have been taken to heart.

With such an attitude the ego only repeats what it did at the time when the superego was created. The little boy, during the construction of his superego, said to his father: "You need not be angry with me; I will take care of that myself." By building a superego, he introjected the angry behavior of the father, thereby eliminating the necessity of the father's external anger, and preserving his "good" father as a real person. In the same spirit the melancholic person says to his superego (and the neurotically depressed patient to his object): "Look, I am a good boy, accepting all punishments; now you must love me again." But the melancholic patient fails in this attempt. The inordinate sadism, inherent in the oral-instinctual orientation and remobilized by the regression, has been given over to the superego, and the full fury with which the ego unconsciously had wished to attack the object is now loosed against the ego (1238).

SUICIDE

The depressed patient's strong tendency toward suicide reflects the intensity of this struggle. In trying to appease the superego by submissiveness, the ego has reckoned incorrectly. The intended forgiveness cannot be achieved because the courted part of the personality, through the regression, has become inordinately cruel and has lost the ability to forgive.

The suicide of the depressed patient is, if examined from the standpoint of the superego, a turning of sadism against the person himself, and the thesis that nobody kills himself who had not intended to kill somebody else is proved by the depressive suicide. From the standpoint of the ego, suicide is, first of all, an expression of the fact that the terrible tension the pressure of the superego induces has become unbearable. Frequently the passive thought of giving up any active fighting seems to express itself; the loss of self-esteem is so complete that any hope of regaining it is abandoned. "The ego sees itself deserted by its superego and lets itself die" (608). To have a desire to live evidently means to feel a certain self-esteem, to feel supported by the protective forces of a superego. When this feeling vanishes, the original annihilation of the deserted hungry baby reappears.

Other suicidal acts have a much more active character. They assert themselves as desperate attempts to enforce, at any cost, the cessation of the pressure of the superego. They are the most extreme acts of ingratiatory submission to punishment and to the superego's cruelty; simultaneously they are also the most extreme acts of rebellion, that is, murder—murder of the original objects whose incorporation created the superego, murder, it is true, of the kind of Dorian Gray's murder of his image. This mixture of submission and rebellion is the climax of the accusatory demonstration of misery for the purpose of coercing forgiveness: "Look what you have done to me; now you have to be good again."

"Neurotically" depressed children frequently have suicidal fantasies, the love-blackmailing tendency of which is obvious: "When I am dead the parents will regret what they have done to me and will love me again" (95, 135, 573, 639, 1587). When melancholic patients try to blackmail their cruel superego in a similar manner, they are worse off than children who court real parents capable of forgiveness and love.

This means that suicide is carried out because hopes and illusions of a relaxing gratification are connected with the idea of suicide. Actually analyses of attempts at suicide frequently show that the idea of being dead or of dying has become connected with hopeful and pleasurable fantasies.

Hopes of this kind are more in the foreground in suicides that are not of the melancholic type and in which introjection and struggles between the superego and the ego do not play any part (277, 1063, 1219, 1556). What is often striven for in suicidal attempts is not "destruction of the ego" but some libidinous aims which, through displacement, have become connected with ideas that objectively bring self-destruction, although they have not been intended as such (764). Such ideas may be the hope of joining a dead person, a libidinous identification with a dead person (1632, 1633), the oceanic longing for a union with the mother (641, 664), or even simply orgasm itself (1280), the attainment of which, through certain historical events, may have become represented by the idea of dying. The specific fantasies that are connected with the idea of dying (206, 207, 284, 699, 1153, 1330, 1631) can often be surmised from the method by which the suicide is attempted or planned (1540).

The hopeful illusions that are connected with the idea of suicide in melancholia are the attainment of forgiveness and reconciliation, which are to be enforced by the simultaneous maximal submission and rebellion, a killing of the punishing superego, and the regaining of union with the protecting superego— a reunion that puts an end to all losses of self-esteem by bringing back the original paradise of oceanic omnipotence (1238).

Self-destructive actions during melancholic states, carried out as self-punishment, as an expression of certain delusions or without any rationalization, have been designated "partial suicides" (204, 1124, 1131). This term is absolutely correct in so far as the underlying unconscious mechanisms are identical with those of suicide.

Sometimes, for reasons unknown, the ego's hopes seem not to have been entirely in vain. A mere change of cathexis frees the ego from the terrible forces within itself. The hopes which are illusionary in the case of suicide are to a certain degree actually achieved in mania. The bad superego is destroyed, and the ego seems united to a purified protective superego in narcissistic love. In still other cases, a depression may end without any mania, as a normal mourning ends after a certain time. The factors, doubtlessly quantitative in nature, that determine whether or when the result is to be a suicide, a manic attack, or a recovery are still unknown.

THE DECISIVE REGRESSION AND ITS CAUSES

The difference between a neurotic and a psychotic depression, it has been stated, is determined by the depth of the narcissistic regression. "Narcissistic regression" means that the object relationships are replaced by relations within the personality; the patient loses his object relationships by regressing into a phase where no objects yet existed. Depressed patients become aware of this withdrawal of object cathexes by the painful sensation of feeling the world and themselves as "empty." This withdrawal of object cathexes, however, is not necessarily a total one. Except in cases of severe melancholia, there are always remainders of objects as well as more or less successful attempts to regain the lost objective world (743).

The ego came into being with the awareness of objects. The establishment of objects simultaneously established the ego. In a psychosis, the conception of objects and therewith the structure of the ego are disturbed by a regression to the time before the establishment of the ego. The psychosis reawakens the factors that were characteristic of the archaic ego while in the process of coming into being. However, this "repetition" is not identical with the original; all psychoses contain elements that do not represent the repetition of infantile factors but remainders of the prepsychotic adult personality.

What determines whether or not a fatal narcissistic regression occurs?

The first possibility is that an unknown organic factor may be decisive. Actually, many psychiatrists believe that manic-depressive psychoses cannot be fully understood in mental terms. This view has been defended even more tenaciously in regard to manic-depressive psychoses than in regard to schizophrenia. Yet somatic research has revealed little in the way of positive findings for the one group or the other.

There are three considerations that suggest the operation of somatic factors.

1. The strict periodicity that frequently characterizes the alternations of mood. This periodicity appears to be independent of any external event and to indicate the operation of a biological factor.

2. Even in cases where the cycle is not markedly periodic, the spontaneity of the mood alternations which frequently occur without any apparent external precipitation argues against their being purely psychogenic.

3. In no other neurosis is there such definite evidence of heredity, the same type of disorder recurring in successive generations.

None of these arguments, however, is too decisive. The periodicity, it is true, seems to be endogenous in origin, but what appears periodically may well be understandable in psychological terms. The apparent absence of precipitating causes for the swings of mood will not be too impressive for analysts because this argument does not take into account the existence of the unconscious. So-called endogenous depressions have been distinguished from reactive depressions, according to the presence or absence of a demonstrable precipitating cause. But how would this type of differentiation stand the test if, for example, applied to hysterical seizures? Some of these appear to be brought on by immediate precipitating events, but some of them arise spontaneously and without apparent external reason. Yet nobody distinguishes between "endogenous" and "reactive" hysterical seizures; instead it is assumed that apparently spontaneous attacks have an unconscious precipitating cause that escaped the notice of the observer. The same applies to depressions. In other neurotic disorders, likewise, a discrepancy between a slight provocation and an intense reaction is not attributed to an organic factor, which would be inaccessible to psychological study, but the discrepancy is understood as the effect of a displacement. It should be noted, moreover, that it is by no means true that the reactive cases (the cases with obvious precipitating factors) are the slight ones and the endogenous ones the severe. Often a severe and clearly psychotic depression may follow the death of a husband or wife; and often definitely nonpsychotic depressions or even mere bad moods occur spontaneously without the patient or an observer being able to assign any precipitating cause. According to Freud there is a complementary series of external precipitating causes and unconscious dispositional causes (596). This holds good for the manic-depressive group as well. A person predisposed to illness by oral and early ego fixation may fall ill as a result of mild precipitating circumstances that are not readily observable; however, even one with relatively little predisposition may fall ill if severe and obvious circumstances appear.

Nor does heredity, though more conspicuous than in other neuroses or psychoses, separate the manic-depressive disorders from other mental disturbances, where its effectiveness was not considered a hindrance to study them from a psychological point of view. Constitution and experience, as etiological factors, again form a complementary series. The manic-depressive disorders surely give no reason to change this point of view. The organic constitutional influence, which is undoubtedly present, need not be the sole determinant. Psychoanalytic study makes it probable that this constitution consists in a relative predominance of oral eroticism, just as in compulsion neurosis it consists in an enhanced anal eroticism.

What kind of accidental experiences favor the subsequent development of depressions?

In the discussion of the differential etiology of compulsion neurosis it was stated that those patients tend to react to conflicts with an anal regression, and thus with a compulsion neurosis, who, as children, under the influence of anal fixations, have used the same type of defense (see p. 305). This holds true for oral regression and depression as well. There is no depression that would not represent a repetition of a first decisive reaction to childhood difficulties, which formed the pattern for the later breakdown. The struggle to maintain their self-esteem is carried on by depressed patients in a way similar to that which they used as children under the influence of oral fixations. Abraham showed that persons who tend to become depressed uniformly have suffered frustrations in childhood to which they responded by means of a similar mechanism. These frustrations connoted severe injuries to their narcissistic needs and, in conformity with the pregenital fixation, occurred very early in life. Thus Abraham was able to formulate as an etiological prerequisite for the development of later psychotic depressions: "a severe injury to infantile narcissism through a combination of disappointments in love; the occurrence of the first great disappointment in love before the Oedipus wishes were successfully mastered; the repetition of the original disappointment in later life is the event precipitating the illness" (26). The subsequent depressions follow the path opened up by the infantile "primal depression," which fixed the fateful tendency to react in an analogous way to future disappointments.

> A woman patient with a sexual perversion of the type of extreme submissiveness, whose life was a constant struggle for narcissistic supplies and whose behavior frequently was impulsive in character like that of an addict, apparently produced this neurotic behavior to escape from depressions. She was successful in her attempts and did not suffer from depressions of a severe nature in adult life. One day, the patient had a nightmare, the content of which she had forgotten; she was only able to describe the feelings in the dream. These feelings had been horrible; she described them with the exact same words that melancholics use to describe the most severe sensations of their depressions. The world, in her dream, had lost all value for her. She felt entirely drained, without connection to anybody else, and completely annihilated; simultaneously she felt as if she had committed the most dreadful sins. She cried in her dream and even after she awoke.
>
> The phenomenon of a "psychosis in a dream" in a person who does not suffer from it when awake seemed strange. In the analysis of this dream, however, it was discovered that it was not so strange after all. What occurred in this dream was something that frequently occurs in dreams: forgotten memories became manifest. The depression in the dream was the repetition of a "primal depression" which the patient had experienced in her fourth year of life when a little brother was born. This primal depression had been forgotten, and her neurosis served the purpose of avoiding a repetition of this dreadful experience of her childhood.

The content of the "injuries to infantile narcissism," which precipitate the primary depression, may vary. These injuries may be extraordinary experiences of abandonment and loneliness, or they may, in especially predisposed individuals, consist in the usual and unavoidable disappointments such as the birth of siblings, experiences of minor humiliations, penis envy, or the frustrations of the Oedipus longings.

> Abraham called the injuries causing primary depressions "preoedipal" to indicate that frustrations have this effect only when experienced as a "loss of essential narcissistic supplies." Usually a child who feels deprived in this way turns toward another person who may give what the first object had denied, that is, from

mother to father or vice versa. He is worse off if "a combination of disappointments in love" (26) occur. The Oedipus complex of subsequent manic-depressive
patients, therefore, is frequently a "complete," that is, bisexual, one, both components of which have terminated in narcissistic injuries (844).

Now at last we are in a position to understand which conditions actually make
for the predisposition for subsequent depressions. The decisive narcissistic injuries must have taken the form of severe disappointments in the parents, at a
time when the child's self-esteem was regulated by "participation in the parents'
omnipotence." At this time, a dethroning of the parents necessarily means a
dethroning of the child's own ego. Probably it is not only so that after disappointments of this type the child asks for subsequent compensating external
narcissistic supplies throughout his life, thus disturbing the development of his
superego; he also tries to compensate for his parents' insufficiencies by the development of a specially "omnipotent," that is, strict and rigid, superego, and
subsequently needs external narcissistic supplies in order to outweigh the unbearable demands of this qualitatively different superego.

That it is, in the last analysis, the "oceanic feeling" (622) of union with an
"omnipotent" mother for which depressed persons are longing is manifest in
those forms of depression called nostalgia (1170, 1488).

A child of four or five experiencing a "primal depression," an adult person
suffering from nostalgia, and any person exposed for a long time to severe dep-
rivations and frustrations—they all are psychologically again in the situation of
a narcissistically hungry infant lacking the necessary external care.

Impulsive behavior and drug addiction can be utilized as a means of fighting
off depressions, because these disorders represent other means of attaining the
same end: the provision of the needed narcissistic supplies. Since depressions
are states that develop if these supplies are missing, addictions and impulse
neuroses, in so far as they still are able to achieve their end, are suitable for
evading depressions.

The formulation can now be made that the disposition for the development of
depressions consists in oral fixations which determine the reaction to narcissistic
shocks. The experiences that cause the oral fixations may occur long before the
decisive narcissistic shocks; or the narcissistic injury may create a depressive
disposition because it occurs early enough to still be met by an orally oriented
ego. It may also occur that certain narcissistic shocks, because they are connected
with death (and the reaction to death is always oral introjection of the dead person), create the decisive oral fixation.

Regarding the factors that create oral fixations in the first place, the same
holds true as for other fixations: the determinants are extraordinary satisfactions, extraordinary frustrations, or combinations of both, especially combina-

tions of oral satisfaction with some reassuring guarantee of security; actually traumatic experiences in the nursing period can be found more often in subsequent manic-depressive patients than in schizophrenics.

In addition to the pregenital fixation, Freud emphasized the importance of a narcissistic orientation as an etiological prerequisite for depressions (597); without such orientation a regression from object love to identification would not occur with such intensity. Before the onset of the illness the narcissism may show itself in the type of object choice (585) and in the receptive and ambivalent nature of the patient's love.

In clinical psychiatry, the involutional melancholias are differentiated from the true manic-depressive disorders. Psychoanalytically, not much is known about the structure and mechanisms of involutional melancholias; they seem to occur in personalities with an outspoken compulsive character of an especially rigid nature (18, 938). In the climacterium the compulsive defensive systems fail; in these cases the decisive oral regression seems to be due to physical alterations of the economy of the libido.

Cyclothymia and variations in mood represent transitional states between the manic-depressive disease and normality. The existence of these intermediate states shows that the manic-depressive state is but a morbid exaggeration of something universally present—namely, of struggles around the maintenance of self-esteem. There are multifarious problems in normal psychology—for example, the heightening and reduction of self-esteem (referred to sometimes as the instinct for self-assertion), moods and humors, sadness and joy, the nature of grief—all of which find their counterparts among the manifestations within the manic-depressive field. All these normal phenomena differ from manic-depressive phenomena first by the relatively small amounts of energy invested and second by the absence of the narcissistic regression.

Under difficult social circumstances and in unstable times the number of depressions and depressive suicides increases. This fact has been used as an objection to the psychoanalytic theory of depression, in contrast to the often raised objection based on heredity. Perhaps depression is nothing but a "human way of reacting to frustrations and misery"? But the connection is a more complicated one. It may suffice to state that a society that cannot provide necessary satisfactions for its members necessarily creates a vast number of persons with an orally dependent character. Unstable times and economic depressions, by depriving people of their satisfactions as well as of their power and prestige and habitual ways of regulating self-esteem, increase their narcissistic needs and their oral dependence. On the other hand persons who, as a result of childhood experiences, have developed an orally dependent character are worse off under such social conditions, since they are unable to take frustrations without reacting in a depressive way.

MANIA

Until now only the depressive side of the manic-depressive phenomena has been discussed. Actually, this side is understood analytically much better than is mania.

Descriptively, an immense increase in self-esteem forms the center of all manic phenomena. The statement that conscience seems to be either abandoned or very limited in its effectiveness has the same meaning, because "feelings of conscience" and "decrease in self-esteem" are essentially identical. All problems of mania can be attacked from the point of view of this increase in self-esteem or decrease in conscience. All activities, after the abandonment of inhibitions, are intensified. The patients are hungry for objects, not so much because they need to be sustained or taken care of by them but to express their own potentialities and to get rid of the now uninhibited impulses that seek discharge. The patient is not only hungry for new objects; he also feels freed because hitherto effective block-ings have fallen away, and he is more or less overwhelmed by this breaking down of dams; the freed impulses as well as the energies, which hitherto had been bound in the efforts to restrain these impulses, now flow out, using any available discharge.

In other words: what the depression was striving for seems to be achieved in the mania; not only narcissistic supplies, which again make life desirable, but a total narcissistic victory is at hand; it is as if all the supply material imaginable is suddenly at the patient's disposal, so that the primary narcissistic omnipotence is more or less regained and life is felt to be incredibly intensified (869, 1367).

Freud stated that in the manic state the difference between the ego and the superego apparently disappears (606). Whereas in melancholia the ego is en-tirely powerless and the superego omnipotent, in mania the ego has regained omnipotence, either by triumphing in some way over the superego and tak-ing back the omnipotence or by being united with the superego and partic-ipating in its power (436). The mirthful mood of the manic has to be interpreted economically as a sign of a saving in psychic expenditure (556). It demonstrates that the tension between the superego and the ego, which previously had been extremely great, must have been released abruptly. In mania the ego has some-how succeeded in freeing itself from the pressure of the superego; it has ter-minated its conflict with the "shadow" of the lost object, and then, as it were, "celebrates" this event.

As has been stated, the manic-depressive patient is ambivalent toward his own ego. In depressions he demonstrates the hostile element of this ambivalence. Mania brings to the surface the other aspect of this ambivalence: his extreme self-love.

What has made this change possible? In the same way that a bad conscience is the normal model for the morbid state of depression, mania has a normal model in the feeling of "triumph" (436). Analysis of this feeling shows that triumph is felt whenever an expenditure becomes superfluous—an expenditure that had previously been necessary in the ambivalent reactions of a powerless subject to a powerful object. Triumph means "Now I am powerful again" and is felt the more intensely the more suddenly the change from lack of power to power is achieved. Triumph is a derivative of the pleasure the child feels whenever his growing ego achieves the feeling "I no longer need to be afraid, because I can master something which until now I looked upon as dangerous; now I am as powerful as omnipotent grownups are" (*see* p. 45). The methods by which participation in the reassuring power is achieved vary from the (original) killing of the omnipotent tyrant for the purpose of taking his place to an ingratiatory submission for the purpose of having the tyrant permit the participation. A man feels "elated" whenever he feels that he is rid of an obligation, liability, or general dependence hitherto effective (rebellious type of triumph), or whenever he achieves external or internal forgiveness, or whenever he passes any kind of "examination," when he is loved again or has the feeling of having done the right thing (ingratiatory type of triumph).

Is a similar real liberation from the superego's pressure achieved in mania? The clinical picture seems to indicate that this is the case.

There is no doubt that the depressive pressure is ended, that the triumphant character of mania arises from the release of energy hitherto bound in the depressive struggle and now seeking discharge. An abundance of impulses, most of them oral in nature, make their appearance and, together with the heightened self-esteem, produce the feeling "life is rich," as contrasted to the oppressive "emptiness" experienced in depression.

The apparent hypergenitality of the typical maniac has an oral character and aims at the incorporation of everybody. Abraham described this condition when he stated that the "mental metabolism" is increased in mania. The patient is hungry for new objects, but he also gets rid of objects very quickly and dismisses them without any remorse (26; *cf. also* 153, 345).

> "Incorporation of everybody" has been confirmed by the findings of Lewin (1053, 1058, 1060), according to which multiple identifications are characteristic for manic states. He described a patient whose manic attacks corresponded to an acting out of a primal scene in identification with both parents (1053). The typical "nongenuine" behavior patterns of maniacs may be due to temporary and relatively superficial identifications with external objects.

In all societies the institution of "festivals" is found, that is, of occasions when superego prohibitions are periodically undone. Institutions of this kind are certainly based on a social necessity. Any society that creates chronic dissatisfaction in its members needs institutions through which the dammed-up tendencies toward rebellion may be "channelized"; through them a form of discharge of strivings hostile to existing institutions is provided, which entails the least possible injury to these institutions. Once a year, under ceremonial guarantees, under specified conditions, and in an institutionalized way, rebellious impulses are permitted to express themselves. From time to time the "superego is abolished"; the powerless are permitted to play "participation," and this creates a good mood in them and enables them to obey for another year (579, 606).

The good mood felt at festivals is certainly a correlate of mania. Freud stated that the periodicity of cyclothymia as well as of festivals may, in the final analysis, be based on a biological necessity. All differentiations in the psychic apparatus may need a temporary abolition from time to time. In sleep, the ego is submerged nightly into the id from which it arose. Similarly, in festivals and in mania the superego may be drawn back into the ego (606).

The tragedy is succeeded by the satyr play; after the serious worship of God comes the merry fair in front of the church; tragedy and satyr play, worship and the fair have the same psychological content; but this content is met with by different attitudes of the ego. That which is threatening and serious in tragedy and worship is play and fun in satyr plays and the fair (847). No doubt, this sequence goes back to a cycle of being hard pressed by a strict authority and of casting it off. An original sequence of pressure by authority and rebellion against it probably was later supplanted by a sequence of pressure by authority and institutionalized festivals. On an intrapsychic basis the same sequence is represented by the cycle of guilt feelings and unscrupulousness; later by the sequence of guilt feelings and forgiveness. What once took place between chiefs and subjects has become internalized and takes place between superegos and egos.

Freud, in *Totem and Taboo* (579), gave a phylogenetic hypothesis as to how this cycle might have come into being.

The manic-depressive cycle is a cycle between periods of increased and decreased guilt feelings, between feelings of "annihilation" and of "omnipotence," of punishment and of new deed; this cycle, in the last analysis, goes back to the biological cycle of hunger and satiety in the infant.

However, one decisive difference seems to remain between the normal model of triumph—based either on a real victory over external or internal tyranny or on a successful achievement of participation—and the pathological phenomenon of a manic attack.

The exaggerated manner of all manic expressions does not give the impression of genuine freedom. Actually, the analysis of a mania shows that the patient's fears of his superego as a rule are not entirely overcome. Unconsciously they are still effective, and the patient suffers in mania under the same complexes as he did in the depressive state. But he succeeds in applying, against them, the defense mechanism of denial by overcompensation. The cramped nature of the manifestations of mania is due to the fact that they are of a reaction-formation type, that they serve the purpose of denying opposite attitudes (61, 330, 597, 1053). The mania is not a genuine freedom from depression but a cramped denial of dependencies.

The liberation frequently is a pretended one, repeating pretenses made by the child in his struggle against narcissistic shocks, using the primitive defense mechanisms of denial, and also other defense mechanisms. Projection is used by patients who in their mania feel themselves to be loved and admired by everybody, or even, in a more paranoid way, mistreated and therefore entitled to do whatever they like without consideration for anyone else (330). Some maniacs persecute those very traits in others which, during their depression, they hated in themselves. In some cases the continued effectiveness of the superego is manifest; a manic behavior may be rationalized or idealized as fulfilling some ideal purpose. The liberation, then, is maintained by a denying countercathexis, and endangered by the possibility of the outbreak of another depression.

In a cramped sort of protest, stressing "I do not need any control any more," all or many impulses—aggressive, sensual, and tender ones—are discharged; the child is thrown out with the bath water; reason is overthrown with the superego. A state is created resembling the original pleasure principle under whose operation impulses were yielded to, whenever they arose, without any consideration of reality. A reasonable ego, once more, is overwhelmed, this time not by a punishing superego but rather by an abandonment of limiting reason altogether. In mania, what actually happens is the very thing neurotics with a fear of their own excitement are afraid of: a breakdown of the organization of the ego as a result of the instinctual impulses discharging in an uncontrolled way. The patients again become narcissistic, though in a form different from that during the depression; they re-enact the omnipotence of primary narcissism, not only of being a person without guilt feelings but also of being a suckling who, having obtained his food, thereby loses the concept of objects.

That the maniac does not fall into a peaceful sleep but into a state of tense and irresistible impulses is probably ascribable to two circumstances: (1) In contradistinction to the baby, he has dammed up many impulses for many years and has invested all of his mental energy in "tonic" intrapsychic cathexes which now become superfluous and need to be abreacted. (2) His actions are cramped and exaggerated because they are denials of contradictory attitudes still effective in the unconscious.

It has been mentioned that morbid impulses can protect against depressions inasmuch as they are different means for achieving the same ends. There is a definite relationship between specific morbid impulses and unspecific manic impulses, and many impulse neuroses are actually equivalents of mania.

The insight that the manic-depressive cycle can be traced back, in the last analysis, to the cycle of satiety and hunger once again brings up the problem of periodicity. Periodicity is a biological factor. It was first thought to be a mode of expression of a rhythm inherent in all vital processes. It was then supposed by Freud to be a biological necessity, correlated with a pressure that compels a periodic relinquishing of differentiations in the psychic apparatus (606). But the relation that apparently obtains between states without a superego and the satiated infant and between the pangs of conscience and those of hunger revealed another type of biological alternation. The alternation of hunger and satiety recurs of necessity (provided the infant does not starve); and this is indelibly imprinted in memory. Each subsequent alternation of pleasure and pain is sensed as if it followed the pattern of this memory. According to this pattern, pleasure is expected after every pain, and pain after every pleasure; and the primitive idea is set up that any suffering bestows the privilege of some later compensating joy, and any punishment admits of a later sin. Punishment and the loss of parental love were perceived as analogous to hunger, and absolution as corresponding to satiety. After the parents have been introjected, the ego repeats intrapsychically the same pattern in relation to the superego. In depressions, the ego no longer feels loved by the superego; it has been deserted, its oral wishes unrealized. In mania, the forgiving oral love union with the superego is restored (1107).

The recognition of this relationship still leaves much that is puzzling in regard to periodicity, especially the chief question: why in some cases there must be an evident or concealed external precipitant to bring about the changes in phase, whereas in other cases this change corresponds to a regular, apparently biologically founded rhythm. For example, it is true that in menstrual depressions, analysis can demonstrate that menstruation is felt subjectively to be a frustration, meaning "I have neither child nor penis" (322); yet it is impossible to get rid of the impression that additional purely biological factors are involved (257).

HISTORICAL SUMMARY

The basic psychoanalytic knowledge about the manic-depressive disorders is contained in a few separate, mutually supplementary publications. The best method of summarizing will be a brief review of these papers. Two important essays by Abraham, 1911 (5) and 1916 (13), were followed by Freud's essay, "Mourning and Melancholia," 1917 (597), which contained the formulation of fundamental concepts, which in turn were elaborated and extended by Abraham in 1924 (26). Finally, a publication by Rado in 1927 (1238) brought the solutions to certain important and pertinent problems still unclarified.

Abraham's first-mentioned publication (5) reported the fundamental discovery that ambivalence is the basic characteristic in the mental life of the depressed patient, the influence of which appears to be much greater than in compulsion neurosis. The quantities of love and hate that coexist are more nearly equal; depressed patients are unable to love because they hate whenever they love. Abraham further found the pregenital foundation of this ambivalence, and stated that the patient is as ambivalent toward himself as he is toward objects. The sadism with which the depressed person attacks himself arises from the turning inward of a sadism originally outwardly directed.

Abraham's second publication (13) recorded his discovery that in depressed patients, oral eroticism is enormously increased. He showed that conflicts around oral eroticism were at work in the depressive inhibitions, in eating disturbances and in "oral" character traits. It became clear that the ambivalence and narcissism described in the first paper have an oral root.

Freud's paper, "Mourning and Melancholia" (597), starting with the analysis of the depressive self-reproaches, stated that depressed persons, after the loss of an object, act as if they have lost their ego. Freud described the pathognomonic introjection. He then showed how the depressive states proved the existence of a superego, and that struggles between the superego and the ego, after the introjection, replace struggles originally carried on between the ego and its ambivalently loved object.

Abraham's book (26) not only supplied a mass of convincing clinical material that corroborated the view that Freud had set forth as theoretical formulations but also added several valuable points of theory. He introduced the two subdivisions of the oral and anal stages of libidinal organization; he showed that self-reproaches are not only internalized reproaches of the ego against the object but also internalized reproaches of the object against the ego. The book further introduced new formulations of the etiological prerequisites (the most important of which is represented in the discovery of the primal depression of childhood) and a study of mania, which was an elaboration of Freud's remarks on mania in "Group Psychology and the Analysis of the Ego" (606).

The paper by Rado (1238) unmasked the self-reproaches as an ambivalent ingratiation of (the object and) the superego. The connections between depression and self-esteem were clarified. The dual introjection of the object into the ego and into the superego was explained, and the differentiation of the "good" (i.e., protecting) and the "bad" (i.e., punishing) aspects of the superego was used for clarification of the aims of the depressive mechanisms. Besides, Rado explained the manic-depressive periodicity as a special case of the general periodicity of transgression and expiation, as an outcome, in the last analysis, of the fundamental biological periodicity of hunger and satiety in the infant. Later papers brought elaborations and clinical illustrations (668, 844, 1078).

THERAPEUTIC PSYCHOANALYSIS IN MANIC-DEPRESSIVE DISORDERS

The therapeutic outlook for psychoanalysis is very different in cases of neurotic depressions and in severe manic-depressive psychoses. As to neurotic depression, the mildest cases do not need any special treatment; the solution of the basic infantile conflicts in the course of the analysis of the main neurosis automatically brings a solution of neurotic inferiority feelings and a relative harmony with the superego. More severe cases in which depression dominates the clinical picture present the same difficulties as compulsion neuroses, since they are based on a similar pregenital fixation.

The difficulties encountered in the psychoanalytic treatment of manic-depressive psychoses are of quite another nature. The more "internalized" the pathogenic processes are, the more difficult it is to establish the transference contact necessary for analysis. In narcissistic states, the analyst has no other means than to use nonnarcissistic remainders in the personality in attempts to increase the patient's object relationships sufficiently to start the analytic work. The modifications of analytic technique necessary for this purpose will be discussed in connection with the analytic therapy of schizophrenia (*see* pp. 447 ff.).

There are three special types of difficulties that analysis must overcome in the case of manic-depressive patients. A relatively slight problem is the first one, present also in neurotic depressions, namely, the oral fixation, that is, the remoteness of the crucial infantile experiences which the analysis must uncover (the history of the primal depression). Of greater severity is the second difficulty, consisting in the narcissistic nature of the illness and the consequent looseness of the transference relationship. Even where this relationship is established, it is persistently ambivalent, to a degree unknown in any other type of neurosis; and this relationship is constantly threatened by the tendency toward a sudden unaccountable narcissistic regression. The third difficulty is the most crucial one. In a severe depressive or manic condition the patient is inaccessible to analytic influence. The reasonable ego, which is supposed to learn to face its conflicts by analysis, is simply nonexistent. However, Abraham called attention to the fact, since confirmed by many psychiatrists, that even inaccessible depressed patients, agitated anxious ones as well as monotonously complaining ones without apparent contact with the objective world, are grateful to an attentive listener and may repay kind patience with a sudden contact—which, however, is no easy task with such patients (26).

The manic-depressive patients offer one natural way out of the last difficulty: the frequency of free intervals during which they are capable of object relationships. The free interval is obviously the period of choice for analytic efforts. Yet even in the free intervals the ambivalence and the narcissistic orientation remain as hindrances. Besides, there is the potential danger that an analysis begun in the free interval may precipitate a new attack. Abraham, on the basis of rich clinical experience, denies the seriousness of this danger, and in fact reports that analysis carried out during the free period tended to prolong the free interval (26). He also succeeded in effecting true cures, although only after very long treatment, the more prolonged because of intervening attacks of the illness (26; *see also* the case reports: 200, 246, 275, 330, 336, 386, 398, 509, 668, 844, 1053, 1060, 1094, 1217, *et al.*).

Taking into consideration the apparent futility of most other types of therapy and the hope that increasing progress in practical experience will show what modifications in technique are needed, one should also not overlook the fact that even if the analysis fails, the patient is temporarily relieved through the opportunity of unburdening himself by talking. On the basis of these considerations the manic-depressive patient, after he or his relatives have been informed of the doubtfulness of the prognosis, may be advised to undergo analysis. But one thing must be borne in mind: the analyst may be deceived by the patient's dissimulation and by the abruptness with which things happen in depressions. In all severe depressions a grave danger of suicide is always present. Even though the analyst's contact with the patient is different from that of the nonanalytic psychiatrist, he must never disregard the caution that psychiatry teaches. The more extensive, planned psychoanalytic study of manic-depressive disorders, needed both for the benefit of the patients and for the benefit of science, must be undertaken within institutions.

As to shock therapy a few remarks will be made later (*see* pp. 568 ff.).

Chapter XVIII

SCHIZOPHRENIA

INTRODUCTORY REMARKS

THE diversity of schizophrenic phenomena makes a comprehensive orientation more difficult than in any other class of mental disorders. Occasionally it has been doubted whether a comprehensive orientation is possible at all and whether the diverse schizophrenic phenomena actually have anything in common. The label "schizophrenia" is applied to so many different things that it is not even of value for the purpose of prognosis. There are passing "schizophrenic episodes" in persons who apparently are well both before and after these periods; and there are severe psychoses that end in permanent dementia. Sometimes, therefore, a distinction has been made between "schizophrenic episodes" and malignant "process psychoses" (see p. 442). Certainly "schizophrenia" is not a definite nosological entity, but rather embraces a whole group of diseases.

The group, however, is characterized by certain common features, although it is difficult to bring them into an exact formula. The common aspects include the strangeness and bizarre nature of the symptoms, the absurdity and unpredictability of the affects and intellectual ideas, and the obviously inadequate connection between these two. The question is: are these common characteristics due to common, specific mental mechanisms?

Freud succeeded in bringing schizophrenic mechanisms into consonance with his theory of neurotic symptom formation by grouping all the phenomena around the basic concept of regression. With such a grouping, no judgment was given as to the somatogenic or psychogenic origin of this regression. In different cases, the regression may have different causes and a different range, but it always has the same great depth. It reaches back to much earlier times than does any regression in neuroses, specifically, to the time when the ego first came into being.

The infant starts out in a state of "primary narcissism," in which the systems of the mental apparatus are not yet differentiated from each other, and in which no objects exist as yet. The differentiation of the ego coincides with the discovery of objects. An ego exists in so far as it is differentiated from objects that are not ego. Therefore, the following formulae mean one and the same thing, only varying in point of view: the schizophrenic has regressed to narcissism; the schizophrenic has lost his objects; the schizophrenic has parted with reality; the schizophrenic's ego has broken down (see p. 35).

Many phenomena seem to indicate that a schizophrenia is something basically different from a neurosis; still they have many features in common. It remains to be learned whether the differences are due to a difference in depth and severity of principally similar processes or whether neurosis and schizophrenia have an altogether different etiology, each obeying different laws of pathology. Even if the irrationality of schizophrenic behavior seems to make it impossible to feel with the patients, one may legitimately attempt to understand in psychological terms this gap between the schizophrenic and the normal or neurotic mentality; and even if it were proved that the etiology of schizophrenia is essentially somatic, it would still be important to study the psychological aspects of this heterogeneously produced mental disintegration (193, 705). The psychoanalytic contributions to research in this field can only form a part of a general theory of schizophrenia, although an essential part (*cf.* 149, 200, 238, 596, 786, 1096, 1138, 1229, 1241, 1359, 1467, 1557). Besides, there remain the important fields of somatic problems and, on the psychological side, descriptive studies. The "microscopic" studies of psychoanalysis presuppose the "macroscopic" studies of psychiatry, in the same way that histology presupposes anatomy. The following comments require a knowledge of the "macroscopic" descriptions, and are concerned only with a discussion of "microscopic" findings.

Schizophrenia is today psychoanalytically understood and differentiated from neuroses adequately enough to make it probable that the role played by etiological somatic factors, though perhaps decisive, is in principle not different from that in neuroses. In the latter, it was understood that disposition and precipitating experiences form a complementary series; the physical constitution is a part of the disposition, more decisive in some cases and less in others.

The discussion in several places throughout this book of the various neuroses touched upon matters related to the field of schizophrenia. In some hypochondriacal states and in pregenital conversions, it was found that intrapsychic object representations had lost their cathexes, and that instead the organ representations became invested with it; object relationships were replaced by narcissism. Cases with widespread general inhibitions were characterized by loss of interest in the external world and by an almost total elimination of object relationships (*see* p. 186). Certain psychogenic tics gave the impression that a dammed-up organ cathexis was being expressed in the symptom (*see* pp. 320 f.). And in depressive states it was noted that conflicts that originally were fought between the patient and an external object continued within the patient's mind after the introjection of the object (*see* pp. 396 f.).

All these conditions are characterized by one common trait: a regression which, at least in part, extends back to the early narcissistic level. In schizophrenia the collapse of reality testing, that fundamental function of the ego, and the symptoms of "disintegration of the ego," which amount to a severe disruption of the continuity of the personality, likewise can be interpreted as a return to the time when the ego was not yet established or had just begun to be

established. Thus it may be expected that the study of schizophrenia will eluci-
date the processes of the earliest period in the infant's life, in the same way that
the study of compulsion neurosis provided insight into the role of anal sadism.

Some schizophrenic symptoms are direct expressions of a regressive breakdown of the ego and an undoing of differentiations acquired through mental
development (a primitivization). Other symptoms represent various attempts
at restitution. The first category of symptoms embraces phenomena such as fantasies of world destruction, physical sensations, depersonalization, delusions of
grandeur, archaic ways of thinking and speaking, hebephrenic and certain catatonic symptoms. The second category embraces hallucinations, delusions, most
of the schizophrenic social and speech peculiarities, and other catatonic symptoms.

SYMPTOMS OF REGRESSION IN SCHIZOPHRENIA

WORLD-DESTRUCTION FANTASIES

The inner perception of the loss of object relationships causes, according to
Freud, the fantasy frequently met with in the early stages of schizophrenia: that
the world is coming to an end (574). The patients who experience such a feeling
are correct, in a sense; so far as they are concerned, the objective world has actually broken down (709, 974). Sometimes only a part of the world is felt as
losing its existence. A delusion, for example, that someone is dead represents the
intrapsychic perception that the libidinal connection with this person has been
withdrawn (142). The world is felt as vital and significant as long as it is invested
with libido. When a schizophrenic complains that the world seems "empty,"
"meaningless," "monotonous," and that he feels as if something has changed, as if
people were mere fleeting images, when he states that he feels perplexed and
abandoned in this new world, he reflects in all this the withdrawal of his libido
from the objects (1462). The same thing is expressed in a more localized manner by depersonalization, and more intensely and completely in a catatonic
stupor.

It might be argued that after disappointing experiences, libido is withdrawn
from reality even in neurotic and normal persons; how, then, can such a withdrawal be characteristic of schizophrenia? First it must be said that the withdrawal in neurotic and normal persons is of a different kind from the withdrawal
in schizophrenics. It is a turning toward fantasy, called introversion. The place
of the real objects, from whom the person turns in disappointment, is taken over
by fantasy figures representing the objects of childhood. The schizophrenic, on
the other hand, abandons his interest in objects entirely. Abraham, in his very
first communication dealing with this problem (1), clearly pointed out that the
difference between neuroses and psychoses depends on whether or not, in the

process of withdrawal from reality, object representations were preserved at all. While in depressive psychoses the object representations are somehow transplanted into the subject, in schizophrenia the withdrawal of the libido remains diffuse, in spite of special emphasis on certain erogenous zones.

There are many facts, however, that apparently contradict these statements. Any cursory visit to a mental hospital seems to prove the opposite. Schizophrenics display interest in objects—at times so very intensely that the visitor may immediately become the object of transference actions of the patients, whether tender, sensual, or hostile. Yet it is just these disorderly and intense types of reaction that vitiate the supposed contradiction to the theory, for the flighty and unreliable nature of the transference actions give the impression that these patients, leaving a narcissistic stage and attempting to regain contact with the objective world, succeed in doing so only in abrupt spurts and for brief periods of time. These types of behavior toward objects form a part of the "restitutional" symptoms.

Certain schizophrenic symptoms reveal the purposive nature of the loss of the objects. A mutism may not only express the fact that the patient has no longer any interest in the objective world but may also contain a certain amount of hostile antagonism. In the symptom of negativism, resentment against the external world finds open expression.

BODY SENSATIONS AND DEPERSONALIZATION

Many schizophrenias begin with characteristic hypochondriacal sensations. The theory of hypochondriasis, which maintains that the organ cathexes grew at the expense of the object cathexes, makes this early symptomatology intelligible. The beginning of the schizophrenic process is a regression to narcissism. This brings with it an increase in the "libido tonus" of the body (either of the whole body or, depending on the individual history, of certain organs), and this increase makes itself felt in the form of the hypochondriacal sensations.

The discovery of the ego (and of the objective world) is made by the infant in connection with the discovery of his own body, which is distinguished from all other parts of the universe by the remarkable fact that it is perceived through two types of sensation simultaneously: through external tactile sensations and through internal sensations of depth sensibility (1231) (*see* pp. 35 f.). Freud stated that the ego is primarily a bodily thing, that is, the perception of one's own body (608). The "body image" is the nucleus of the ego (134, 1372). The hypochondriacal sensations at the beginning of schizophrenia show that, with the regressive alteration of the ego, this nucleus appears once again and is altered (68, 1531).

Body symptoms in incipient schizophrenia have not necessarily the character of intense sensations. Quite as frequently they consist in a feeling of lack of sensations. Certain organs, body areas, or the whole body are perceived as if they did not belong to the person, or at least as if they were not quite the same as usual. This, too, can be explained on the basis of the same libidinal alteration. When the normal body feeling disappears from consciousness, this does not necessarily mean that the corresponding amount of libido has been withdrawn from the organ in question (387). It may mean that this organ has become charged with a large amount of libido which is concealed by an intense counter-cathexis (1291, 1366). Tausk has pointed out that such a period of estrangement of the body usually succeeds an earlier hypochondriacal period. Withdrawal of the object cathexis intensified the cathexis of the organ which first is felt in the form of hypochondriacal sensations; the ego, however, succeeded in warding off these sensations by means of a countercathexis, and the result is the estrange-ment (410, 1531). Both increase and decrease in body feelings necessarily change the patient's body image and make him feel strange. The peculiar alterations of the body image are determined by the underlying mental conflicts and can be taken as starting points for their analysis (233, 387, 389, 391, 395, 746, 1366, 1418, 1605).

A schizophrenic episode began with a patient's despair over the fact that a new hat did not fit. Analysis revealed that the patient felt different when he wore this hat; he believed that the shape of his head was altered by the hat. The body image of his head was changed. The exaggerated reaction to the hat was a distorted ex-pression of the patient's fear that something was wrong with his head. An exag-gerated reaction to clothing means generally an exaggerated reaction to body sen-sations (521) (see pp. 36 and 261). Oberndorf described cases in which the un-certainty as to body feelings was due to an uncertainty about the patient's own sex (1186, 1187, 1188, 1189, 1191).

In stages of estrangement, an increased narcissistic cathexis of the body is countered by defensive reactions; in depersonalization, an increased narcissistic cathexis of mental processes is handled in the same way. In depersonalization, overcharged feelings or conceptions are repressed. The patient, in observing him-self, is aware of the absence of his full feelings in the same way that a person is aware of the absence of a forgotten name that is on the tip of his tongue. The experiences of estrangement and depersonalization are due to a special type of defense, namely, to a countercathexis against one's own feelings which had been altered and intensified by a preceding increase in narcissism (402, 410, 1173, 1291, 1531). The results of this increase are perceived as unpleasant by the ego which therefore undertakes defensive measures against them. These defensive measures may sometimes consist in a reactive withdrawal of libido (1173); as a rule, how-ever, they are built up by a countercathexis. The augmented self-observation and the feeling that the missing sensations are still in existence, like a forgotten name, are the clinical manifestation of this countercathexis (410).

Schilder expressly emphasized that "persons suffering from depersonalization do not lack feelings; the patients merely perceive, arising from within, an opposition to their own experiences" (1379); an intensified self-observation is the manifest expression of this opposition so that "we have in depersonalization two conflicting directions," namely, the directions toward and against feelings of body sensations. "The organ which carries the narcissistic cathexis is the one more subjected to depersonalization" (1379).

The increase in narcissism is not in all cases of depersonalization necessarily so intense as in a beginning schizophrenia. Depersonalizations, as symptoms of attempts to ward off objectionable feelings and sensations, also occur outside the realm of schizophrenia. They may express a defense against feelings of excitement, especially against a pronounced curiosity (107, 1347), or against one's particular type of thinking (1186, 1187, 1188, 1189, 1191).

What has been said of the feelings of estrangement and depersonalization, that is, that they represent a reaction of the ego to the perception of the increase in narcissistic libido, can also be said of the schizophrenic's general perplexity, of his feeling that everything has changed. All these initial symptoms are due to an inner perception of the narcissistic regression and of the accompanying libidinal displacements.

FEELINGS OF GRANDEUR

A withdrawal of the cathexes of the objects into the mental ego does not necessarily manifest itself as depersonalization. Not always is the narcissistic increase warded off; under some circumstances it makes itself felt as a grand and pleasant inflation of the patient's ego. A sudden merging of the cathexes of object representations and of the ego may cause a kind of manic state and ecstatic experience (574).

It has been stated repeatedly that the child, after having lost his feeling of omnipotence, believes that the adults are omnipotent and strives for a reunion with them. Psychotic individuals may succeed in simply denying their loss of omnipotence and in retaining or regaining the "oceanic reunion," so that the objective world, after having fulfilled its function of procuring satisfaction, disappears again, as it disappeared when the satiated infant fell asleep (324) (see p. 35). Such individuals react to any narcissistic hurt in later life in the same way that they attempted to react to their first narcissistic hurt, namely, to the realization that they are not omnipotent; they deny the hurt and increase their self-esteem in overcompensation. For such persons a regression to narcissism is also a regression to the primal narcissistic omnipotence which makes its reappearance in the form of megalomania.

In discussing the mechanisms of defense, it was described how the normal development of the ego and of its reality testing makes an extensive use of the mechanism of denial impossible (*see* pp. 144 f.). Sometimes, however, an extraordinary environment, which spoils the child and favors isolation, enables a person to cling to his narcissistic aloofness and to overcompensate all narcissistic hurts by developing a still higher opinion of himself. Other times the causes of a narcissistic fixation responsible for such overcompensation are less obvious.

An overcompensating narcissism of this kind may in some cases become the starting point for the development of ascetic-masochistic attitudes. In others, however, it is not elaborated further and the patient simply compensates for a loss of love by an increased self-love. It has been mentioned that in normal or neurotic persons a lost object may be replaced by an identification with this object, the ego offering itself to the id by becoming similar to the loved object (608) (*see* p. 394). In persons who have the possibility of regressing to their narcissistic omnipotence, the feeling of being more wonderful than any object supplants such similarity with the object. Love of objects is replaced by self-love, and the overestimation that is usually directed to a loved person is now directed to one's own ego. The patient is not only inclined to believe again in his omnipotence but may also indulge in passionate self-love, fancying sexual intercourse with himself. Self-love of this type clearly does not correspond to the primary state before the existence of any object (a regression to this state is represented by a catatonic stupor rather than by megalomania) (924). It does refer, however, to the "secondary narcissism" (585, 608) in which objects have become replaced again by the ego.

The belief in one's own omnipotence is but one aspect of the magical-animistic world that comes to the fore again in narcissistic regressions (*cf.* 1250).

That narcissistic daydreams are actually believed in and become delusions, that the patients feel themselves as king, president, or God is due to the loss of reality testing. The content of the delusions can be analyzed like the daydreams of neurotic and normal persons. That "grandeur" is felt is a direct expression of the reactivated narcissism; the delusions involving this feeling are constructed like other delusions (70) (*see* pp. 427 ff.).

SCHIZOPHRENIC THINKING

The way in which schizophrenic patients use concepts and words is by no means always disorderly. There is, as a matter of fact, a definite order in their thinking but it does not obey the laws of our "normal" logic. Schizophrenic logic is identical with primitive, magical thinking, that is, with a form of thinking that also is found in the unconscious of neurotics, in small children, in normal persons under conditions of fatigue, as "antecedents" of thought (1363), and in primitive man (1047). It is the *archaic* way of thinking (166, 234, 235, 236, 732,

930, 1042, 1550). What is found in compulsion neurosis to a slight degree is mark-edly developed in schizophrenia: schizophrenic thinking falls back from the logi-cal to the prelogical level.

> The regressive nature of schizophrenic thinking is confirmed by the fact that the investigation of this type of thinking proves it to be identical with the assumed archaic forerunners of logical thinking (*see* pp. 46 ff.). Schizophrenic thinking is relatively more concrete and active than normal thinking, not yet capable of realistic abstractions, less preparation for subsequent action and more a symbolic equivalent of action. Its concrete character is "relative" only, in so far as its con-crete images do not correspond to objective realities, but are formed or influenced by the wish-fulfilling magical qualities of primitive thinking. Its active character is due to the fact that perception of stimuli and reaction to (subjective elaboration of) stimuli are interwoven with each other again (*see* pp. 36 f.).

In nonpsychotic persons, this mode of thinking is still effective in the uncon-scious. Therefore the impression arises that in schizophrenia "the unconscious has become conscious." Because the "primary process" and the archaic ways of thinking have come to the fore again, schizophrenics are not estranged by these mechanisms any more. Schizophrenics, for example, show an intuitive under-standing of symbolism. Interpretations of symbols, which neurotics find so dif-ficult to accept in analysis, are made spontaneously and as a matter of course by schizophrenics. Symbolic thinking for them is not merely a method of distortion but actually their archaic type of thinking (*cf.* 982) (*see* pp. 48 f.).

In respect to the ideational content, too, schizophrenics often express freely ideas that other persons deeply repress, for example, the Oedipus complex (181, 228, 806, 808, 973, 1506, 1625). This gives the impression that the ego of the schizo-phrenic has been overwhelmed by his intense instinctual demands which have broken through to consciousness. The ego being overwhelmed, however, may be brought about by a defensive regression. Sometimes it seems as if this regres-sion has brought the patient from an objectionable and dangerous world to a pleasant, wish-fulfilling one. More often the conflict continues. The patient, let-ting himself fall into infantile sexual fantasies as a means of escape from a dan-gerous reality, is unsuccessful and the dangers from which he tried to escape return in the flooding infantile impulses.

> The question "How can a schizophrenic be analyzed, since analysis consists of confronting the patient with his unconscious wishes, whereas in the schizo-phrenic these wishes are already conscious anyhow" can easily be answered by considering the defensive nature of the regression. The first interpretation to be given is not that the patient has an Oedipus complex but that he is afraid of cer-tain aspects of reality. If analysis succeeds, the pursuit of these anxieties will lead to the patient's Oedipus complex from quite another angle. Here, as in neuroses, analysis has to try to confront the patient with the anxieties he tries to escape from, and not to participate in his attempts to escape (*see* p. 450).

HEBEPHRENIA

In hebephrenia, the loss of the objective world or of any interest in it can be observed without any further complications. Here the passive nature of the defense mechanism of regression becomes most clear: the ego undertakes no activity for the purpose of defending itself but, beset by conflicts, "lets itself go." If the present is unpleasant, the ego drops back to the past; if newer types of adaptation fail, it takes refuge in older ones, in the infantile ones of passive receptivity and even, perhaps, in intrauterine ones. If a more differentiated type of living becomes too difficult, it is given up in favor of a more or less merely vegetative existence. Campbell called it schizophrenic surrender (239).

The absence of conspicuous restitutional attempts characterizes hebephrenia as the purely regressive type of schizophrenia. Often the loss of object relations is a very gradual one, but it may be inexorably progressive. Among generally inhibited persons, transitional states toward hebephrenia may be found. Often persons of this type, with a pregenitally colored Oedipus complex and a readiness to give up new achievements, keep relatively normal during the latency period but cannot cope with the somatically increased instinctual excitement brought on by puberty ("dementia praecox"). Occasional explosive outbreaks of excessive, destructive rage occur; the destructive impulses have previously been warded off by a "peaceful" acquiescence.

A patient, when a child, had frequently witnessed primal scenes. He had developed a sadistic conception of the sexual act, an identification with his mother and a consequent intensive sexual fear. The original reaction to the primal scenes, hostility toward both parents, especially toward the father, was warded off by means of an increasing indifference toward the world. The identification with the mother and the passive homosexual inclinations found a distorted expression in this indifference.

CATATONIC SYMPTOMS AS REGRESSIVE PHENOMENA

Tausk showed that numerous schizophrenic symptoms revive experiences of the period when the unfolding ego discovered itself and its environment (1531). The passive way in which the patients experience their own actions, as if they did not act at all but are made to perform certain motions or to think certain thoughts which they feel are "put into" their minds, is correlated with a primitive stage in the development of the ego. The same holds true for the belief in the omnipotence of words or gestures. Other typical schizophrenic patterns, such as negativism and automatic obedience (echolalia and echopraxia), which are not immediately recognizable as manifestations of the nursing stage, nevertheless certainly are archaic and primitive and betray an indistinct apperception of objects, indistinct ego boundaries, and a deep (oral) ambivalence toward the universe of objects. Automatic obedience corresponds to the imitative "fascination" in infants (130) (*see* p. 37). With the loss of emotional communication with objects, the connections between individual emotional attitudes also have been lost, and the individual emotions have become rigid and automatized. Certain symptoms—for example, catatonic postures and movements—suggest that there might even be a recurrence of impulses from the period of intrauterine existence (1531). After the regression has removed inhibitions normally present, archaic types of motility make their appearance again as catatonic motor activities (1460).

Many questions concerning these activities are still obscure. They appear to be manifestations of the deeper layers of the motor apparatus which, after the ego has disintegrated, have acquired a sort of independent effectiveness. In discussing psychogenic tic, "narcissistic memory traces" (492) were mentioned (*see* pp. 320 f.) which had become relatively independent of the total personality in seeking an outlet; their striving for discharge is in conflict with an opposite tendency resulting in accumulation, which is nevertheless released through "short circuiting." Catatonic movements are without doubt due to a similar short circuiting. In some stereotypies and bizarre attitudes, the original purposeful intention, which failed and became automatized by the disintegration of the personality and the deep motor regression, is still recognizable. In compulsion neurosis, it is not uncommon for the patient to smile in a friendly manner for purposes of defense, if he meets situations that remind him of something that threatens to arouse anxiety; in a similar way, many instances of "dull smiling" in catatonic patients, or many cases involving a "splitting of affect from ideational content," are intended to deny and repudiate certain gloomy, fearful emotions, sometimes, perhaps, the idea of being mentally ill. The disintegration of the warding-off ego, however, changes this intention into a mere shadow, isolates it from the total personality and causes the "dull" character of the smiling. In normal and neurotic individuals, the facial expression is a decisive way of expressing feelings toward objects. If, however, object relationships are lost, the facial expression, too, loses its purpose and full character. It becomes "empty," enigmatic, and represents only a faint remainder. However, very often stereotypies and bizarre attitudes are not only "remainders" of lost feelings but represent rather an unsuccessful attempt to regain them. Therefore, further discussion will be included under the category of "restitutional symptoms" (*see* pp. 437 ff.).

RESTITUTIONAL SYMPTOMS IN SCHIZOPHRENIA

WORLD-RECONSTRUCTION FANTASIES

In the same way that fantasies of world destruction are characteristic of the early stages of schizophrenia, various fantasies of reconstruction frequently occur in later stages. They consist either of delusions that the patient himself has the task of saving the world, and perhaps has been chosen by God to bring order into the world again, or simply of the feeling that some kind of salvation or re-birth is to be expected (974). The world does not seem to be empty and mean-ingless any longer but instead particularly rich and full of new and indescribably grand meanings. Everything perceived has another meaning, sometimes a hid-den, sometimes a clear one, but nearly always a prophetic and symbolic one. The patient may become subject to revelations of all kinds. These experiences are perceived as ecstatic by some patients, as very frightening by others. They all represent an inner perception of the tendencies to restore what was lost through the pathogenic narcissism, the promising or frightening nature of the experi-ences representing the hopeful or hopeless attitude of the patient to this task. However, the attempted restitutions are not necessarily very "progressive" ones. The salvations frequently are experienced in a passive-receptive way, showing signs of the narcissistic *unio mystica,* of the deepest oral reunion of the subject with the universe, and the re-establishment of the original "oceanic feeling" (622).

Religious delusions, as a rule, are rooted in longings for salvation of this kind, together with attempts to master the overwhelming, indescribable schizophrenic sensations by means of verbalizing them (939). The words used in this verbal-izing are taken from religious tradition. Since religious tradition in our culture is a patriarchal one, a verbalizing of this kind offers a special opportunity for ex-pressing the conflicting drives of the patients' father complexes. This is especially important for men, where the whole psychotic development was started by the defense against ambivalent homosexual feelings toward the father (574) (*see* pp. 427 f.).

Deeper than modern man's dependence on the patriarchal father (and on fa-ther gods) is every man's biologically determined dependence on the mother, who took care of the infant during his passive-dependent period. Therefore, it is not rare that religious delusions of schizophrenics show matriarchal features and resemble ancient mother religions (1559).

HALLUCINATIONS

Hallucinations are substitutes for perceptions after the loss or the damage of objective reality testing. Inner factors are projected and experienced as if they were external perceptions. The term "substitutes for perceptions" does not mean that there are no longer any real perceptions. Hallucinations occur along with perceptions, and even intermingled with them as "illusions."

Two questions have to be answered: (1) What causes certain impressions to have characteristic perceptual features, so that their objective reality is not doubted? (2) What is the content of hallucinations; that is, what determines *what* the patients believe they perceive?

The first question, why hallucinations occur at all, is not yet entirely solved. Physiology, too, will have to do its part in answering it. Before reality testing develops, there is a state of primary hallucinatory wish fulfillment (457). The conditions of this stage and of its recurrence in psychoses and dreams have been discussed by Freud (552). It is probable that the mental systems, the stimulation of which produces perceptions, become sensitive to stimuli from within whenever the acceptance of further external stimuli is blocked. A blocking of this kind may be caused in very different ways. In the state of sleep the doors to the external world are closed for biological reasons, and therefore thoughts are transformed into hallucinations (595); in schizophrenia, it is the pathogenic withdrawal of the object cathexes which has the same effect (590, 611, 614).

The second question, concerning the content of hallucinations, can immediately be answered for a certain type of acute hallucinosis, usually not included in the group of schizophrenia. Acute hallucinatory states which frequently develop after definite traumata, such as operations or childbirth (404, 1628), are often easily recognizable as wish fulfillments (62, 1368). A man whose leg has been amputated may develop an acute psychosis in which he denies the amputation and imagines that he still possesses a healthy leg (1612). Not being quite able to rid himself of unpleasant perceptions or sensations, the patient may project them and hallucinate his own defects on persons in his environment (1045, 1362). A psychosis of this type is a wish fulfillment by the abandonment of reality testing. An unpleasant reality is repudiated and a more pleasant one created in its place, in the same manner as is done in the dreams of normal persons (552, 595). A psychotic patient of this type escapes a conflict with reality through denying it; he does not "repress" the instinctual impulse that led to the conflict, but rather the perceptions that stand in the way of his wishes. This break with reality again follows the regressive path, so that the patient sinks back into the state of hallucinatory wish fulfillment in which he lived before acquiring the capacity for reality testing (611).

Although the hallucinations of schizophrenia differ from those of acute hallucinatory psychosis, they have certain features in common: the ego, after having broken with reality, endeavors to create a new reality that will be more suitable. Normal relations to reality never depend on memory images alone but require a supply of new perceptions; for the schizophrenic, hallucinations are a substitute for such perceptions, occurring where the acceptance of new real perceptions has been blocked. Thus relations to a newly created substitute reality are made possible (611, 614).

However, most schizophrenic hallucinations are not pleasurable and do not seem to represent simple wish fulfillments. Often they are extremely painful or frightening. Freud offered the suggestion that the anxiety frequently accompanying hallucinations is due to a reappearance of part of the reality that was repudiated, analogously as in neuroses, where anxiety was due to the reappearance of repudiated parts of the id (611).

However, it is not only a repudiated reality that comes back in the form of hallucinations; it is also a repudiated id or superego. The hallucinations are not only expressions of the ego's escape but also of the failure of this escape, a distorted return of warded-off impulses in the form of projections (663). This becomes especially clear in a type of schizophrenic hallucination that represents the threats or punishments of the superego which the ego had tried to fight off. In accordance with the auditive origin of the superego, most of the "voices" the patients hear are of this nature (585).

Thus hallucinations are complicated phenomena, containing elements of perceptions, of thoughts that have been translated into sensations, and of pictorial memories (the "historical kernel of hallucinations")—the thoughts and memories being allusions to warded-off instinctual wishes and to threats of the superego. Hallucinations can be interpreted in the same way as dreams (141, 262, 294, 1365).

DELUSIONS

Delusions have a structure similar to that of hallucinations. They are misjudgments of reality based on projection. While the elements of hallucinations are limited to perceptual sensations, delusions are built up of more complicated and sometimes systematized ideas. Like hallucinations, they sometimes are of a wish-fulfillment type, but more often they are painful and frightening. Representing an attempt to supplant the lost parts of reality, they often contain elements of the repudiated reality, which return nevertheless, and portions of warded-off drives as well as projected demands of the superego.

This may be shown in the example of delusions of persecution, the most thoroughly investigated but indeed complicated type.

The meaning of these delusions was first revealed by Freud in the case of Schreber (574) and has been corroborated since by many investigators (143, 319, 401, 452, 464, 587, 854, 1017, 1203, 1260, 1358, 1379, 1398, 1421, 1465, 1470, 1531). Schreber's delusional system was characterized by his ambivalent attitude toward God, and by his ideas of being emasculated. Freud convincingly interpreted this as an attempt by Schreber to overcome his father complex, particularly its passive-homosexual component. Schreber attempted through his delusions to protect himself from passive-homosexual temptations, originating in his infantile attitude toward his father. The fact that it was not the normal Oedipus complex but the negative one (homosexuality) that formed the infantile sexuality against which the patient had to defend himself turned out to be of general significance, since conflicts around homosexuality are encountered in the majority of paranoid schizophrenias. Homosexuality represents, so to speak, a state between the love of oneself and the love of a heterosexual object. In a regression to narcissism, the level of homosexuality is an intermediary step, where the regression may temporarily stop; and a person who has regressed to the level of narcissism, in striving to recover and to return to the objective world, may fail to get beyond a homosexual level.

Schreber protected himself from his homosexual tendencies by means of denial and projection. "I do not love him, I hate him," the ego first says in self-defense, according to Freud (574); then the projection turns "I hate him" into "He hates me." In this way his own hatred is rationalized into "I hate him because he persecutes me." The persecution represents the homosexual temptation, turned into a fearful threat, threatening independently of the patient's will. The destruction of the function of reality testing gives this unsuccessful defense against homosexual temptation its delusional character. The form and content of the delusion, in correspondence with the deep regression of the ego, show all the features of magical and archaic ego levels.

It is interesting to note that the hatred is never projected at random but is felt usually in connection with something that has a basis in reality. Patients with persecutory ideas are extremely sensitive to criticism and use the awareness of actual insignificant criticisms as the reality basis for their delusions. This basis has, of course, to be extremely exaggerated and distorted in order to be made available for this purpose. Just as the "monsters" in a dream may represent an "amoeba" from daily life (1328), so the monster of a paranoid delusion may be a misapprehended real microbe. The paranoid individual is particularly sensitized to perceive the unconscious of others, where such perceptions can be utilized to rationalize his tendency toward projection. The paranoid person senses clearly the unconscious of others when this enables him to become deaf to his own unconscious (607).

The apparent transformation of love into hate on the basis of delusions of persecution is possible only if there has been a strong ambivalence beforehand— in other words, if the patient's attitude toward objects has always remained an archaic one (608). The latent homosexuality of paranoid patients is usually of the ambivalent-aggressive type, described by Nunberg (1181) (see p. 334), the hatred in the delusion being a manifestation of this original aggressiveness (968). As a matter of fact, it is possible to demonstrate in persons suffering from delusions of persecution the presence of the pregenital aim of incorporation which was the undifferentiated forerunner of both love and hate. Projection as such is based on a vagueness of the borderline between ego and nonego. Ideas of incorporation also correspond to this vagueness. The incorporated object has become a part of the subject's ego, and when this object is projected again it retains a certain "ego quality," even in the external world. The persecutor, like the instrument he uses, proves to represent not only the (ambivalent) loved object but a projection of features of the patient as well, either of all of his body or of parts of his body or of specific parts of his mind. Staercke (1465) and Van Ophuijsen (1203) demonstrated that the persecutor, though representing a real object, is perceived in the unconscious, curiously enough, as the patient's own feces; the sensations of persecution represent intestinal sensations, which have been especially accentuated as a result of the narcissistic regression and then projected (49, 94, 119). Bibring reported a case of a woman who believed she was persecuted by a man named "Behind." She attributed to this man a number of characteristics which were in fact true of her own gluteal region (143).

The idea of meeting one's own body or parts of it in the external world is in correspondence with the patient's narcissistic orientation which makes the self-infatuated patient desire to meet his own ego, personified as an object.

It happens also outside the realm of delusions of persecution that an organ becomes the representative of an external object as a result of narcissistic regression and in connection with introjective fantasies, for instance, in hypochondriasis, pregenital conversion neuroses, and depressions (1171, 1436). In delusions of persecution, however, the introjected object, in contrast to the other conditions, has become projected again. Freud's first finding that the persecutor represents the homosexual object certainly remains true; but the fact that the persecutor represents at the same time the subject's own features shows that this object, in the patient's fantasy, had been incorporated and reprojected.

> To a slight degree, a "passing of an object through the ego" (1567), which bestows upon the object features of the ego, may also play a certain part in the object choice of normal love (1565).

It is interesting that among the organs projected onto the persecutor, feces and buttocks play a predominant role. According to Abraham, the process of incorporation in paranoid fantasies is thought of as performed by the anus (26). Anal introjection represents the object relationship at the level of the early anal-sadistic orientation of the libido; it is perceived as destruction of the object and is more archaic in nature than the anal-sadistic level to which the compulsion neurotic regresses, where the object is preserved.

However, the incorporation fantasies in paranoid schizophrenics are not limited to the anal zone. Fantasies of oral (57, 230), epidermal, or respiratory incorporation are found as well. This can be demonstrated by the presence of ideas of eating or being eaten up, of inhaling and being inhaled (1172).

> One of the early symptoms of a young hebephrenic was a strong fear of dogs, combined with an inability to eat in the presence of his mother. Analysis showed that both symptoms were a defense against the wish to bite his mother and eat her up.

The analysis of the frequent idea of being influenced by machines, which are supposedly used by the patient's persecutors, shows that these machines are replicas of the patient's own body (1531). Often the apparatus represents one of the patient's organs which is valued most highly. Quite often it is a symbol of the genital organs; on other occasions, it stands for the buttocks.

Something similar can be said of the various inventions of schizophrenics which can be recognized as projections of their organs (945, 1077). The urge to make inventions is a projection of the urge to get rid of all the internal troubles.

The most remarkable fact about all these machines is that these replicas of the patient's body are not used in pleasurable fantasies but appear instead as cruel objects in the hands of imagined persecutors, in some cases as doubles of the persecutors. The defense has turned the intended erogenous pleasure into a threatening horrible pain.

Like elements of the body, one's mental characteristics, too, may be projected onto the persecutor. This occurs not only in the projection of the hatred which is basic for the delusion; also certain definite attitudes and expressions, which are ascribed to the persecutor, correspond to traits of the patient and especially often to demands of the patient's superego. The persecutor, then, observes and criticizes the patient; the persecutions themselves represent projections of the patient's bad conscience. This circumstance, which at first appears to make the picture more complicated, corroborates the theory that an introject has been re-projected; for the superego is the result of the introjection of external objects. Also organs affected by hypochondriacal conflicts often represent conscience. The above statements may be summarized in the following symbolic equation:
persecutor = homosexual object = narcissistically hypercathected and projected organ (feces, buttocks) = projected superego.

The projection of the superego is most clearly seen in ideas of reference and of being influenced (585). The patient feels that he is being controlled, observed, influenced, criticized, called upon to give an account of himself, and punished. The voices he hears utter criticisms of him, usually referring to his sexual activities which are depicted as dirty or homosexual. The patient hears himself reproached for his homosexuality and pregenital tendencies, just as severe parents might have talked to their naughty child. Or the voices prove that they are observing the patient by commenting on what he is doing while he is doing it: "Now he is eating, now he is sitting down, now he is getting up." Often the voices utter projections of inconvenient data of self-observation, like "He is crazy, he is insane!"

A patient with an extreme social fear of the erythrophobic type was afraid that everybody was laughing at him and saying that he was "feminine." He was not able to state exactly of what this femininity consisted. Anyhow, people were looking at him and making remarks that he was homosexual. The same patient used

to look into the mirror and imagine being in love with himself, fantasying first
that he was a handsome man and then that he was a beautiful woman.

The persecutor in a case reported by Schilder, called the "physiognomist," enumerated all the patient's sins by means of a complicated instrument, which corroborated Tausk's interpretation of these apparatuses as doubles of the patient's
body (1379).

Delusions of this kind merely bring to the patient from the outside what his
self-observing and self-criticizing conscience actually tells him (69, 936, 1369).
In accordance with the auditive origin of the superego (608), external reproaches
of this kind are usually *heard* in the form of voices (11, 838). Sometimes delusions are developed that express the idea of being punished and in this way relieve guilt feelings and justify the patient's hostility. They are similar to the
delusions of melancholics: ideas of being ruined, sick, ugly, evil smelling. In
most cases, however, there is an important difference between the reproaches
hurled at the patient by voices and persecutors and the self-reproaches of depressed patients. In schizophrenia, owing to projection, the reproaches come
from outside, and therefore usually are felt as unjustified.

The normal superego is, as a rule, an introjected object of the same sex. The
marked increase of homosexual tension in schizophrenics causes a resexualiza-
tion of the desexualized social and superego cathexes; this is true either because
the homosexuality is reached as a mid-point between heterosexuality and narcissism on the regressive road of withdrawal of libido or because it is reached
as a result of an attempt to recapture the objects in the process of restitution.
Even before having introduced the conception of superego, Freud wrote: "Ideas
of reference represent conscience in a regressive form; they disclose its genesis
and why the patient rebels against it" (585). Thus the struggle against the superego represents again a struggle against the subject's own homosexuality. "It is
due to the fact," Freud writes, "that the person desires to be rid of all these influences, beginning with those of the parents, and withdraws his homosexual
libido from them" (585). Superego delusions are determined, however, not
merely by defense against homosexual temptations. The superego, that part of
the mind that copies external objects, represents the part of the personality that
is, so to speak, closest to being an object. The superego is in a sense half ego and
half outer world. Hence its functions are the ones that most readily appear when,
after a narcissistic regression, the patient desires to regain the objective world
but is unable to do so.

A patient with a rapidly developing schizophrenia showed with special clarity the phenomenon of clinging to objects for fear of losing them. He tried to in-
veigle everyone, even those who were indifferent to him, into long conversations,
only in order to create for himself the feeling that he still had relationships with
people. While he had lost all other object relationships, a severe social anxiety (a
projection of his superego) became extremely accentuated. As far as people were

concerned, he wanted only to know what they thought of him, and whether he was doing what they expected of him. He finally developed ideas of reference. In his desire for object relationships he was unable to attain more than "superego relationships."

In this sense, superego functions also are shadows of the objective world that has been lost. The feeling that one is looked at by everyone is the expression of a striving to regain a relationship with everyone.

The erotization of superego functions is found not only in ideas of reference but also in other schizophrenic symptoms. Freud sees in it the root of the tendency toward the systematization of paranoid trends (574).

The delusional creations, however, do not only threaten and punish the patient; often they also appear as tempters who lead the individual into sin, or who weaken his sexual potency. This can be explained by the fact that, as in the case of the persecutor, the hallucinations and delusions of reference represent not only the superego but also, at the same time, the (ambivalent) loved object; the sexual wish for this object is perceived as a destructive sexual influence that emanates from him.

Other delusional trends are constructed analogously to the persecution formula: "I do not love him, I hate him because he persecutes me." Erotomania, according to Freud, follows the formula: "I do not love him, I love her, because she loves me" (574). A trace of this mechanism often appears even in schizophrenics without any clear-cut erotomania. Frequently, male patients become frantically attached to women or try in an exaggerated manner to fall in love; analysis shows that this disproportionate love for women or desire to be loved is a defense against an unconscious love for men. The delusion, then, is due to an exaggerated use of a mechanism that can also be observed in latent homosexual men who are far from becoming psychotic. Many men, who feel themselves to be in a state of extreme longing for feminine love and spend all their time looking for a feminine love object, are never able to achieve this goal; they are unconsciously denying their homosexuality in this fashion. Without being aware of it, such patients transpose their inquisitiveness, supposedly concerning women, onto the erotic adventures between women and other men, and in fantasies of how other men behave in order to conquer a woman, they identify themselves with the woman. Other patients who are closer to psychosis give the impression that, in their frantic search for a love object, the sex of the object does not play an essential role. In these cases, the crux is that they are vaguely aware of the imminence of an object loss, and they endeavor to escape this by frantically clinging to an object.

If this exaggerated desire for an object becomes projected onto the woman so that the man feels himself being "persecuted with love," the erotomania is established. This type of delusion is more common among women than men;

it occurs especially often as a sensitive paranoia in women who, outside of this delusional realm, appear to be relatively normal.

The delusion of jealousy serves the same psychological purpose. It follows the formula: "I do not love him, for she loves him" (574). Delusional jealousy differs from normal or neurotic jealousy in that it appears without any objective justification. In analysis, it becomes evident that the patient, when suspecting his wife, is actually interested in the other man. The patient strives to rid himself of his homosexuality by means of projection (607, 1089). Also in the field of jealousy there are transitions from definite psychotic to normal behavior, and a bit of such projection of homosexuality is to be found in every case of jealousy (*see* pp. 512 ff.). Usually it can be demonstrated that a jealous man is irritated not merely because his partner is interested in another man but also because the man pays attention to her and not to him. Tormenting thoughts of a jealous nature lead to images of love scenes between the partner and the third person, and in these fantasies the jealous man unconsciously puts himself in the place of the woman (607, 897, 1035, 1207). Sterba pointed out that this circumstance is expressed in the fact that "being jealous of" is a term with a double meaning, applicable to the unfaithful person as well as to the rival (1494). A person who in order to keep his psychic equilibrium requires the narcissistic feeling of being loved unconditionally frequently is unconsciously warding off homosexual trends (113, 426, 1314). But even in neurotic persons in whom the homosexual component plays no more than the normal role, jealousy may be the result of a projection. The basis of jealousy in such cases is an unconscious tendency toward infidelity which is projected onto the partner (607).

The litigious type of delusion has not as yet been studied much psychoanalytically. Its narcissistic nature is evident, for these patients consider the outward establishment of their integrity and innocence as the most important thing in the world. Since this establishment is carried out through conflicts with courts and authorities, it is reasonable to assume that in this type of delusion, as in delusions of reference, there is a projection of the superego, particularly in its critical and punitive aspects. The salient feature in such cases is the hostile attitude toward the authority representing the superego. This hostility is based on an assumed self-security and overestimation of the patient's own person arising from the narcissistic regression. The hostile attitude is rationalized, in keeping with the paranoid tendency to systematize. Again the projection is not hit or miss but occurs in the field in which reality meets it halfway. The litigious paranoid sees the mote in his neighbor's eye. The type of defense known as "displacement to the minute" is nowhere so evident as in cases of litigious delusions. The pettiness of these patients was described long before the advent of psychoanalysis, but the "big" thing from which the emphasis was displaced could not be recognized without psychoanalysis. The persistent feeling of being wronged by everybody is a projective defense against the opposite feeling of being guilty. It is an attempt of an ego, which has regressed to the "innocence" of a primitive narcissistic state, to fight the remainders of a guilt feeling which had initiated the regression as a defense. The conflicts around the guilt feeling ultimately may represent old conflicts with the father, and authorities are fought in the same way as the father had (or had not) been fought in childhood. As in delusions of reference, there is a sexualization (a "homosexualization") of the spheres of guilt and punishment. In this respect, the patient's need for a verification of his innocence is an attempt to defend himself against his homosexual impulses, while the fight to obtain this triumph is a reactivation of this very homosexuality which returns from repression. As in the case of ideas of reference, the homosexual conflict may mark an intermediary step in the process of regression to narcissism, or it may be the result of an attempt at restitution.

A fragmentary analysis in one such case demonstrated that all of the patient's fights with authorities were intended to prove that his father had done him an injustice. The patient was brought up by his father alone, the parents having been divorced when the patient was five years old. What the patient wanted to prove in court represented unconsciously the idea that his father had wronged him by depriving him of his mother. All through the patient's childhood his mother had been engaged in litigation with the father. The litigious drive of the patient represented an identification with his mother. There was an unconscious homosexual element in the patient's reproaching his father. His idea was that his father had first deprived him of his mother, and then, although the two lived alone, he had not put the child in his mother's place. He had, in the patient's imagination, treated child and mother equally badly.

The actual precipitating factor of the parents' divorce was a quarrel over how the boy should be brought up. Father and mother struggled for the child's favor, each irritating the other. The child took an active part in many of these intrigues. No sense of guilt was visible in the external clinical picture of this patient. The tremendous indulgence, which made it possible for him to preserve his primitive narcissism and to face the world with the feeling that he was the most important person in it, enabled him also to project his guilt feelings. He did not actually feel guilty; but this freedom from guilt depended on his ability to compel outside authorities to confirm his state of innocence. For him, such confirmation proved the falsity of the idea that he had sought his mother's ejection from the home. His father alone was guilty. Unconsciously, he was asking for a certificate that no sin of his own had made him unworthy of his father's affection, but only the father's arbitrariness to him and to his mother alike. The fact that he had to enter into more and more law suits showed that he could not obtain the proof he required.

The sex of the patient does not seem to influence the structure of delusions essentially. One could easily substitute "she" for "he" and vice versa in Freud's formulae characterizing persecutional, erotomanic, and jealousy delusions. In a case of jealousy paranoia in a woman thoroughly analyzed by Ruth Mack

Brunswick, the conflict in regard to homosexuality followed the same lines as those outlined by Freud for men. The patient was an infantile personality whose conflicts centered around her preoedipal relationship to her mother and who never had achieved a normal Oedipus complex (1089). In delusions of persecution and of reference, too, there is probably a close parallel. When a paranoid woman, in apparent contradiction to the general theory, believed herself persecuted by a man, Freud showed that the case actually followed the rule, for the man was only a screen figure for a woman (the mother) (587). The fact that feminine homosexuality is rooted in the earliest preoedipal attachment to the mother and tends to revive all the archaic conflicts of the earliest pregenital times makes itself also felt in the paranoid ways in which women fight against homosexual strivings.

Some authors, however, have suggested that the analogy in the etiology of delusions is not complete, and that homosexuality is not found as the basis of paranoid delusions in women with the same regularity as in men (142, 1358).

The psychoanalytic literature has not, to the same degree as the psychiatric textbooks, differentiated paranoia from paranoid schizophrenia (cf. 968). One may assume that the same essential mechanisms are operative in both conditions. In paranoia proper, a more fortunate constellation of psychological forces permits a definite encapsulation of the pathological process. The patient's relationship to reality seems to be broken at one point only, and the gap is filled by the delusional system. The systematization itself, more intense than the systematization that occurs as a defense in compulsion neurosis (see pp. 284 ff.), is a means by which the paranoiac's ego achieves the encapsulation of the delusions. The break with reality does not take place abruptly and completely, but is rather a partial one. Freud says that in cases of paranoia with insidious onset and development the delusion appears as a patch on the otherwise intact personality, set in the exact place of the original rent in the relationship to reality (611).

There is a gradual transition between classic paranoiacs and those "eccentrics" whose ego agreed to "avoid a rupture by deforming itself, submitting to forfeit something of its unity, or in the long run even to be gashed and rent" (611) (see pp. 465 f.).

Frequently in schizophrenics delusional ideas of minor importance, less typical and systematized, are found; these represent misapprehensions of real events as a result of the narcissistic orientation of the patient. Whatever occurs has a "special significance" for him, being experienced in a subjective and irrational frame of reference. The projection of feared excitements onto nature or onto particular environmental situations, discussed in connection with anxiety hysteria (see pp. 203 ff.), occurs in a more outspoken and obvious manner in schizophrenia.

Cohn tells of a schizoid patient, annoyed by a severe constipation and longing for a violent evacuation, who was tremendously impressed by the sight of a powerful avalanche (283).

In summary, delusions, like hallucinations, are condensed mixtures of perceptional elements, thoughts, and memories, systematically distorted in accordance with definite tendencies; these tendencies represent warded-off instinctual wishes as well as threats from the superego. Delusions, too, can be interpreted like dreams (905); they reveal in analysis the "historical kernel" which has been distorted into a delusion (630).

A woman patient's delusion of having killed her children was revealed as an elaboration of the frequent fear that, by masturbation, she might have destroyed her ability to bear children. The "historical kernel" was the fact of her infantile masturbation.

OBJECT RELATIONSHIPS AND SEXUALITY IN SCHIZOPHRENICS

In the chapter on impulsive behavior, "love addicts" have been described (*see* p. 382). There are also "object addicts" who do not need love especially but, rather, more general proof of connections with the objective world. Persons of this kind cling to everybody and everything. They are glued to their objects, directed by an extreme fear of losing them, always discontented, and extremely wearing on the persons around them. It is not hard to see that these persons are either prospective schizophrenics fighting against an impending loss of objects or true schizophrenics, the symptom representing an attempt at restitution. Other patients cling with the same tenacity not to objects but to substitutes for objects, to ideas of any kind, to obsessions and monomanias, to inventions, to anything that represents to them a connection with the objective world. Representations of this kind, having lost their concrete and real nature, frequently concern abstractions. Many schizophrenics are full of ideas of saving mankind, projections of their awareness that they themselves are in need of salvation from their loss of objects.

Many schizophrenic patients are capable of very sudden and intense transference reactions, tender as well as sensual and hostile ones. The flighty and unreliable nature of all these reactions shows that the patients, leaving the narcissistic state, are attempting to gain contact with the objective world but can do so only in abrupt attacks and for short periods. The remarkable violence of their efforts is due to their fear of again losing the objects. The numerous and manifold sexual expressions of schizophrenics, a mixture from all levels of libidinal development, appear to be such attempts at restitution. The specific nature of these expressions is determined by secondary points of fixation between the early, decisive narcissistic fixation and the genital primacy. Autoerotic activities of all kinds appear; feeding difficulties ranging from the refusal of food to bulimia

(230, 1578); primitive manifestations of anal eroticism like incontinence, smearing, and coprophilia; primitive forms of relationships with objects, incorporation aims (57, 68, 1172), and magical overvaluation of the excretory functions (19). Open manifestations of the Oedipus complex are so conspicuous that they attracted the first attention of psychoanalysts (181, 228, 806, 808, 973, 1506, 1584). The genital impulses, however, usually appear in constant competition with pregenital ones (1625), so it seems that the genital primacy has never been very strong in persons predisposed to schizophrenia.

All manifestations derived from the past development of the patient may be revived either as a symptom of the trend toward narcissistic regression or during the attempted restitution.

SCHIZOPHRENIC PECULIARITIES OF LANGUAGE

Freud showed that the remarkable way in which schizophrenics use words also must be understood as a phenomenon directed toward restitution. "The patient often devotes peculiar care to his way of expressing himself, which becomes precious and elaborate. The construction of the sentences undergoes a peculiar disorganization, making them so incomprehensible to us that the patient's remarks seem nonsensical. Often some relation to bodily organs or innervations is prominent in the content of the utterances. In schizophrenia, words are subject to the same process as that which makes dream images out of dream thoughts, the one we have called the primary process" (590). Freud explains this remarkable verbal behavior by the hypothesis that the schizophrenic, in his attempt to regain the objective world, regains something, but not all he wants; instead of the lost object representations he succeeds in recapturing only their "shadows," that is, the word representations; the loss of the objects forces him to substitute the word representations for the object representations, treating them in the same way that the neurotic treats the object representations (590). This hypothesis has since been confirmed and elaborated by several authors (931, 932, 1146, 1168, 1377, 1583).

The schizophrenic handles the exaggerated superego functions of observation and criticism just as he handles words. These functions, too, are shadows of the objective world that he had lost.

Not all peculiarities of schizophrenic speech are of this nature. Bizarreness, stereotypies, the archaic patterns of his thinking (see pp. 421 f.), and, last but not least, the patient's subjective frame of reference, which makes him use words with a meaning unknown to the listener, complicate his verbal expressions.

CATATONIC SYMPTOMS AS RESTITUTIONAL PHENOMENA

A restitutional striving toward the lost objective world is the root of many catatonic symptoms also. Jung, in his very first work on schizophrenia, recognized stereotypies and mannerisms as morbid attempts to regain or to hold object relationships that are slipping away (905, 906). This was variously confirmed and elaborated (1016, 1171, 1558). In the chapter on tic, it was mentioned that gestures and mimetic expressions are a very important archaic mode of communication with objects. Its pathology (pathognomy) has not yet been studied enough psychoanalytically (986). The gross disturbances of catatonics show not only that their emotions toward objects are conflicting but also that they are not capable of whole emotions any more; stereotypies and mannerisms are substitutes for emotions, allusions to emotions, no longer aimed at communication. These "emotional remainders" have lost their connection with the total personality and with each other; this fact is reflected in the term schizophrenia. However, many stereotypies, mannerisms, and bizarre acts are less mere symptoms of the loss of object relationships than active attempts to regain them. In the same way that words or criticisms are grasped instead of objects or love, strange magical expressions, unintelligible to the observer, are grasped instead of complete emotions directed toward objects. The frequently quoted "meaningless smile" of schizophrenics is characteristic of an unsuccessful attempt to regain contact. In some mimetic expressions or bizarre acts the original sensual or (more frequently) hostile impulses, which have failed to express themselves fully, are still recognizable (70). The magical significance of the children's game of "making faces" has been mentioned (see p. 319). Some catatonic mimetic expressions seem caricatures of this game (981). Fromm-Reichmann sees in stereotypies a compromise between the tendency to express certain (tender or hostile) object impulses and the tendency to suppress these impulses for fear of rebuff (660). The disintegration of the personality turns the complete expression of emotions into the allusions of stereotypies.

Echolalia, echopraxia, and automatic obedience also can be considered primitive attempts at regaining contact. The infant acquired the ability to use mimetic expressions for making contact with other persons by imitating the gestures of the persons around him, using the mechanism of primary identification. Catatonic patients try to regain what they have lost by regressing to this primitive mechanism. Their gestures frequently are intended as imitations of other persons' gestures; but the failure of this intention makes the gestures "empty" and "meaningless." Another circumstance contributes to the fact that the imitation of gestures turns into a kind of caricature of them: warded-off hostile impulses, still (or again) operative, express themselves in the manner of the imitation. Bizarre mannerisms, then, not only imitate what has been seen in the past; they also anticipate as "magical gestures" the desired behavior of other persons in the future (983, 985).

Catatonic rigidity reflects a conflict between the impulse to act and the defense against it. Ferenczi made the remark that catatonia is really a cataclonia, a high-frequency alternation of activating and inhibitory impulses (492).

In the muscular spasms of hysterics or in the dystonic phenomena of normal persons, there is also a struggle between impulses to move and inhibiting impulses. But in these instances, both types of impulse express unconscious relationships to objects. In catatonia, both impulses are narcissistic or center around the struggle to regain objects. A dystonic hypertonus is related to catatonic muscular rigidity in the same way that the introversion of neurotics is related to the narcissistic orientation of schizophrenics.

Other catatonic attitudes seem to aim less at regaining objects than at denial of unpleasant feelings or of awareness of sickness. It is as if many catatonic mimetic expressions unsuccessfully intend to say: "You see I am not insane!" In still deeper states of regression, expressions of this kind become less and less specific, until eventually "raptus actions" seem to be nothing but un-co-ordinated discharge movements, tending to relieve an extreme tension (usually expressed in a "cataleptic" general muscular rigidity). In certain cases this tendency to get rid of the inner tensions at any cost may lead to extremes that seem to overcome all considerations of self-preservation (cf. 204). Autocastrations have been reported repeatedly in schizophrenic cases. These acts, probably, are psychologically comparable to autocastrations performed by religious fanatics who, by such radical denial of their active sexual wishes, try to regain "peaceful unity with God," that is, an extreme passive submissiveness, less of a feminine than of an early infantile "oceanic" nature (1127, 1131). That acts of this kind are performed in states of deep regression brings to mind the archaic biological reflex of autotomy, in which instinctual gratification and defense against instincts are still one and the same. Such archaic goals reappear in states of regression more easily if the sphere of the superego has been sexualized.

THE BREAK WITH REALITY

The fact that the nucleus of schizophrenia is the patient's break with reality can be described from two different points of view. The first standpoint stresses the similarity between schizophrenia and neuroses. Psychoses as well as neuroses are based on the organism's reaction to conflicts by regression; however, the depth of the regression is different. Early infancy has no "reality"; a subsequent "loss of reality" represents a regression to this early time. The ego returns to its original undifferentiated state; that is, it dissolves entirely or partly into the id, which has no knowledge of objects and reality.

The second standpoint stresses the contrast between psychoses and neuroses. According to Freud (611) the comparison can be made thus: in both cases a basic conflict occurs between the id (an instinctual impulse) and the external world. The neurotic's ego obeys the external world and turns against the id by instituting a repression. The ego of the psychotic, on the contrary, breaks with the external world that limits its instinctual freedom. This contrast, however, does not lead much further; whereas the ego of the neurotic, turning against the id, fulfills the demands of the external world, one cannot simply state that the psychotic ego, turning against the external world, takes the side of the id. This may be true of a certain minority of hallucinatory psychoses (62); in the majority of cases of schizophrenia, it seems that the break with reality does not serve the purpose of gaining more instinctual pleasure but rather of combating the instinctual drives directed toward objects; reality is repudiated less because of its frustrating effects than because it holds temptations (663).

> The following quotation from Freud shows that the break with reality in schizophrenics may be not so much a break with the prohibiting and punishing but rather with the tempting aspects of reality: "I will take, for instance, a case analyzed many years ago, in which a young woman who was in love with her brother-in-law, and whose sister lay dying, was horrified at the thought, 'Now he is free and can marry me!' This scene was instantly forgotten, and thus the process of repression which led to the hysterical pains was set in motion. . . . The psychotic reaction would have been a denial of the fact of the sister's death" (614). The sister's death, however, is no punishing threat but rather a temptation.

This becomes especially clear in the analysis of ideas of persecution. Freud subsequently emphasized that this contrast is not a decisive one: for psychotics also have countercathexes against the id, and neurotics also may show traces of breaking with reality by unconsciously refusing to accept unpleasant facts—for example, in denying the absence of a penis in women (621, 633, 635).

In neuroses two steps must be distinguished: (a) the repression of the objectionable demand of the id, and (b) its return in a distorted form. In the development of psychoses two analogous steps can be seen: (a) the break with reality, and (b) the attempts to regain the lost reality (614).

However, as Freud has pointed out, there are characteristic differences (614). In neuroses, the second step, the return of the repressed from repression, is of more importance in producing the illness; in psychoses, loss of reality causes the pathological result. In neuroses, the id, against which the ego has tried to defend itself, asserts itself against the ego by means of the second step; in psychoses, the mechanism is somewhat analogous, since the parts of reality that were rejected may reappear in spite of the ego's defenses; to a greater extent, however, it is again the id (and sometimes the superego) which, in its attempts to fight frustrating reality and to gain gratification, characterizes the second step.

According to the distinction between regressive and restitutional symptoms, it should be expected that every psychosis would begin with the first class of symptoms, that is, with feelings that the world is coming to an end, hypochondriasis, depersonalization, delusions of grandeur, and certain catatonic symptoms, while such symptoms as world-saving fantasies, hallucinations, delusions, expressions of infantile sexuality, the schizophrenic speech peculiarities, and stereotypies would appear only during the later course of the schizophrenic process. And actually this is the case in many schizophrenias. World-destruction fantasies, hypochondriasis, and depersonalization are mostly described as "initial symptoms," whereas systematized delusions develop later. The less frequent cases in which the order of the symptoms is different do not necessarily contradict the theory. The loss of objects need not be abrupt and complete. There are quantitative oscillations between renunciation of the objective world and swings toward restitution. This is particularly evident in paranoid cases with insidious onset and development. The first symptoms to be noticed may be attempts at restitution, after a preceding period of renunciation of the objective world has escaped attention.

The precipitating factors in psychoses (403, 830, 1086, 1628) are not essentially different from the precipitating factors in neuroses. They are either quantitative increases in instinctual tension, as shown by the fact that schizophrenia frequently begins in puberty ("dementia praecox"), or circumstances that stimulate repressed infantile sexuality, especially homosexuality and anal eroticism (452, 790), or experiences that appear to justify or increase infantile anxieties and guilt feelings (*see* pp. 454 ff.).

Precipitating factors and disposition again form a complementary series (596). Frequently psychoses start during some crisis, that is, when some experience distorts the equilibrium that has prevailed until then and when the usual defensive methods of the ego have become insufficient. French and Kasanin described several cases in which the breakdown occurred after external events had proved the ego's methods of adaptation insufficient (533).

> The psychosis that is precipitated in such a way is, however, less a new and pathological type of adaptation than the breakdown of any adaptation. The restitutional symptoms can be looked upon as a first attempt to re-establish something like an "adaptation." When a new adaptation is reached, the psychosis is cured, possibly in an incomplete way by means of the development of pathological character traits or with other demonstrable scars remaining within the personality.

Not only the precipitating factors but also the first reactions to them are still the same in psychoses as in neuroses. They consist of a revival and intensification of infantile sexual impulses. The Oedipus complex is an essential factor. Indeed, it appears as if an especially intense fixation on the Oedipus complex creates a predisposition to psychosis, and, as a matter of fact, abnormal Oedipus gratifications are found quite often in the history of schizophrenics (1411). However, the genitality appears rather weak and the Oedipus complex built upon a pregenital foundation.

Decisive for the difference between psychosis and neurosis is the way in which the patient defends himself against this reawakening of his infantile instinctual conflicts. The psychotic "breaks with reality."

This "break" can be described as a very archaic mechanism of defense, analogous to fainting as a response to a trauma (see p. 119). When the ego makes bad experiences, the ego is relinquished again. A tendency to apply this archaic mechanism of defense may be the essence of what is called "narcissistic fixation."

The assumption that this is due to fixation on a time before the conception of reality was built up reduces the problem of etiology to that of the origin and nature of the narcissistic fixation. It must be admitted that as yet nothing specific is known concerning either constitutional factors or personal experiences that determine the malignant narcissistic fixation. Narcissistic disposition is certainly related to (but not identical with) the oral constitution which has been described in connection with the manic-depressive psychoses. Important pathogenic experiences in infancy, though they may be postulated in theory, have not been made so probable by concrete findings in schizophrenia as in the manic-depressive disorders. The pathogenic fixations of schizophrenia may tentatively be considered as related to a still earlier stage than those found in depressions—in Abraham's classification (26) to the early, objectless oral period preceding the oral-sadistic phase. It may be assumed that unknown organic factors determine or contribute to the malignant depth of the regression. Perhaps the typical infantile anamnesis of schizophrenia reflects less a single trauma in very early life than a series of general impediments in all vital activities, especially in those activities directed toward objects. Most probably the actual cases represent different combinations of these three possibilities: organic disposition, early traumata, and manifold impediments.

Some authors have attempted to distinguish the "use of schizoid mechanisms on a psychogenic basis" from "real schizophrenic processes"—subsuming under the first category cases in which traumata and impediments cause a narcissistic regression—reserving the name "schizophrenic processes" for cases in which (unknown) organic factors are decisive (362, 670). If this distinction actually could be applied, it would be a great help in the problematic question of prognosis. Sometimes an ego, otherwise intact, is capable of temporarily turning away from an unpleasant reality in "schizophrenic episodes" of short duration, which were called "hysterical psychosis" or "amentia" in older psychiatric terminology (see pp. 126 and 426). However, in the majority of cases both psychogenic influences and organic disposition are effective, forming a complementary series.

Gero discussed the criteria to be used when the concept of psychogeneity is applied to psychoses (670).

What occurs after the actual regression can best be understood as an outcome of the struggle over restitution. Later fixation points appear to be of great importance for the ideational content of the symptoms; their psychoeconomic relations determine the clinical pictures and their changes.

Schizophrenia in children is a very much disputed matter (185, 186, 266, 310, 734, 1487). From a psychoanalytic point of view, it can be generally said that infantile psychoses represent less "regressions" than, rather, severe disturbances in the development of the ego, which thus retains more or less archaic characteristics (1487).

Psychoanalytic insight into the psychological background of schizophrenic phenomena hints at a close relationship between schizophrenia and manic-depressive disorders. Both are based on a narcissistic regression, the consecutive loss of objects, and damage of ego structure and reality testing. This dynamic similarity is reflected in a certain clinical similarity; actually there are cases that present mixed features of both diseases, as, for instance, periodic catatonic states or persecutory delusions in melancholias. This relationship supplies an argument against using the differences between schizophrenic and manic-depressive phenomena as a starting point for classifying character types in general (*see* pp. 526 f.).

BORDERLINE CASES

Schizophrenic mechanisms are different from neurotic mechanisms. It certainly is not true that psychoses represent a kind of higher degree of neurosis. It is possible that the same person may develop both types of mechanisms. There are neurotic persons who, without developing a complete psychosis, have certain psychotic trends, or have a readiness to employ schizophrenic mechanisms whenever frustrations occur. They are sometimes persons who may be called potential schizophrenics; that is, they have not "broken with reality" yet, though they show certain signs of beginning such a break and, under unfavorable circumstances of life, may develop into psychotics; or they are persons who have "channelized" their schizophrenic disposition, so to speak, eccentrics who are crazy in one more or less circumscribed area and otherwise retain normal contact with reality.

Persons who without having a true psychosis yet show single traits or mechanisms of a schizophrenic type have been designated "schizoid" or "schizophrenia mitis" or "ambulatory schizophrenia" or the like. Terms of this kind do not mean that the psychiatrist is not yet able to see whether there is a neurosis or a psychosis. In regard to the operative pathogenic mechanisms these cases are actually both. Not the course of an internal process will finally show whether or not the patient really had a psychosis, but circumstances will decide whether the psychotic disposition will be provoked further or soothed.

To this group belong queer psychopaths, abortive paranoids, the many "apathic" individuals whom one may call hebephrenoid personalities, all the types who, as adults, retain or regain a large part of their primitive narcissism because they are able to answer narcissistic hurts with simple denials and with protective increase in their narcissism; they tend to react to frustrations with the loss of object relationships, although this loss frequently is only partial and temporary. Symptoms of object loss may occur in combination with depressions or with manias, with hypochondriacal sensations, feelings of estrangement in the organs, limited stereotypies and bizarre behavior patterns, or with other signs of a heightened narcissistic attitude (203, 1635).

Despite the contention of some psychiatrists, there are even transitions from pseudo hallucinations to real hallucinations, and from daydreams to delusions (1373, 1382). Often ideas with a typical delusional content are developed while the patient is still capable of full reality testing; he does not believe in the ideas and calls them "crazy"; thus by definition, they are not delusions but represent "daydreams" with the same ideational content as the typical delusions; under adverse circumstances, by minimal economic shifts, however, reality testing may be lost and daydreams of this kind turn into delusions (607).

> Abortive ideas of reference, in the beginning of their development or, in schizoid personalities, continuously, may remain subject to the patient's criticism. "I feel as if everyone were looking at me, as if everyone knew what I am thinking; of course, this is not true." Or: "I had a crazy idea that somebody could put a microphone into the room to find out what I am thinking." A hypochondriacal patient once said in analysis: "It occurs to me now to say that my thoughts are put in my head by you. Of course, I know this is nonsense, but I feel this way."
>
> Quite frequently it is impossible to differentiate between a "social anxiety," that is, a fear of being criticized by others in the future, and delusional ideas of being criticized in the present. Freud described the critical judgment which, at the outset, may keep watch over paranoid ideas already present (607).

Compulsion neurotics sometimes suffer from the obsessive idea of having committed a murder and are compelled, despite awareness of its utter unreality, to prove to themselves the falsity of their obsession. This is very different from a delusion of having killed a man. But there are "schizoid compulsion neurotics" in whom the fantasy at times appears as an obsession, at other times as a delusion —usually as an obsession, but under a certain mental strain as a delusion.

> The following patient certainly was nearer to schizophrenia than to compulsion neurosis. He once left home after a quarrel with his mother in a very upset state. He then began to wonder whether he had beaten her to death, which was a frequent obsessive idea of his. But this time suddenly he felt that he had actually committed the act. He went to the police and declared that he had killed his mother. After the policemen who were sent to his mother's house returned to the

station and told him that it was not true, the patient "recalled" that he had not really committed the alleged murder.

Some forms of belief in the omnipotence of thought and of what Freud called "compulsion neurotic delirium" (567) must be included among these transitional clinical states. Sometimes compulsive movements and tics cannot be properly differentiated from stereotypies, especially when they have become entirely automatized (1018).

Cases in which reality testing has broken down for certain periods and is reestablished at other periods should be differentiated from cases of true schizophrenia in which the patients have learned to conceal their real beliefs because they understand that others do not believe in their delusions and that they get along better by pretending not to believe in them. A doctor, trying to convince a patient of the error of his ideas, may achieve a "transference success" in training the patient to talk as he feels he is expected to, without any real change in his insight. Periods of (pseudo) insight and of delusions may then simply reflect periods of transference contact with the doctor and of object loss or prevalent negative transference feelings.

More frequent than cases with partial delusions, partial hallucinations, or partial stereotypies are schizoid patients in whom the symptoms concern the emotional behavior only. The emotions of these persons generally appear to be inadequate. Frequently emotions are entirely lacking in situations where they are to be expected. A lack of emotions which is due not to mere repression but to real loss of contact with the objective world gives the observer a specific impression of "queerness." Often a lack of emotion is disrupted by sudden and incomprehensible emotional spells. In other cases the emotions seem relatively normal, as long as certain conditions are fulfilled—for example, as long as the patient is able to feel that "things are not entirely serious yet." The patients seem normal because they have succeeded in substituting "pseudo contacts" of manifold kinds for a real feeling contact with other people; they behave "as if" they had feeling relations with people (331, 333). They may be surrounded by many people and indulge in many activities; but they have no real friends. Often schizoid personalities remain relatively normal as long as certain conditions of security are fulfilled, but break down as soon as these conditions fall away. The conditions represent circumstances that keep them in touch with the objective world. The most frequent condition for paranoid personalities is to have "followers." As long as people believe in them and their mission, the patients still cling to reality. When the followers begin to say "The man is crazy," they break down. The difficulty of contact with schizoid persons is also due to the fact that even if still far away from the schizophrenic use of words, they often do not connect the same meaning with their words as normal people do; the meaning of words for them is determined by their autistic system of orientation, unknown to the listener.

The impossibility of adequate emotional outlet shows itself in other ways, too. Usually an extreme internal tenseness makes itself felt by hypermotility or hypertonic rigidity behind an external mask of quietness; at other times the opposite takes place—an extreme hypotonic apathy. The remainders of emotions or the substitutes for emotions usually refer to either rage and aggressiveness or to homosexuality.

A very good description of these types has been given by Zilboorg (1635).

Schizoid types may present a great variety of clinical pictures. At one extreme are "genius children" with certain one-sided (autistic) talents, whose occasional bizarre behavior is indulgently overlooked because they can communicate their proximity to the unconscious, making their presence fascinating for their audience, though the patients themselves may have no emotional interest in this audience whatsoever. The other extreme may be marked by hebephrenoid persons, who give a rather stupid impression and who live, in an empty and inconspicuous way, a rather vegetative existence, totally impoverished of emotional vividness.

From a practical point of view, the most important task would be to distinguish between patients who are in danger of becoming psychotic and need a careful prophylactic treatment and those types who, by developing one type of eccentricity, remain safe from more serious psychotic breakdowns. This distinction is similar to the difference between paranoid schizophrenia and genuine paranoia. Certainly the difference is determined by psychoeconomic conditions; but a great deal of intuition is still needed to decide whether a patient belongs in the first or the second category.

QUESTION OF PROGNOSIS

The difficulty of gaining an exact insight into the economy of the forces responsible for the course of the psychosis makes prognosis extremely difficult. If a schizophrenic succeeds in re-establishing relationships, he may still be inclined to collapse if fresh precipitating events occur. It is easy to see that all environmental factors that are pleasant and attractive will influence the patient in the direction of health, and that those that are disappointing or lead him into temptation will be conducive to illness; but it is much more difficult to state which concrete factors are pleasant and attractive for the patient, since many patients perceive as threats experiences that would be attractive to the normal person. Thus a dynamic diagnosis about the dynamic-economic nature and depth of the loss of objects and of the intensity of the (organic) disposition toward it is needed for the purpose of judging the prognosis. First of all, the life history of the patient may give the necessary information—the history of his inadequate emotional responses. In general, all acute cases (especially reactive ones, in which the psychotic reaction is an immediate answer to an acute and severe frustration or narcissistic hurt) are more hopeful than chronic cases that have developed slowly; cases with intense anxiety at the start seem to be better than cases which "surrender" to the schizophrenic process without much protest. Sometimes sudden schizophrenic episodes, which give an impression of severity because they entail a complete break with reality, occur as a response to acute frustration or strain and pass entirely and relatively quickly (1213). Probably this type of acute schizophrenic episode with good prognosis is the way in which certain disturbed persons react to excessive strain (*see* p. 126). The realization that acuteness is more favorable explains the paradox that sometimes cases that seem much worse have a better prognosis than a slowly developing apathy. However, not all acute onsets of psychoses are favorable. Often it turns out that an apparently acute onset was prepared by a very long prepsychotic development which did not come to the attention of observers. Periodic catatonias, sometimes diagnosed as mixtures of schizophrenia and manic-depressive states, are also favorable in so far as the individual attacks pass spontaneously. Therefore, besides a knowledge of the whole life history, knowledge about the kind and the course of the first psychotic attack provides the best means to make a prognosis about the probable course of succeeding attacks. This, however, cannot be used in the case of a first attack. In descriptive psychiatry many statistical approaches have been made in order to gain criteria for prognosis; from an analytic point of view, no single criterion can be looked upon as decisive; decisive is, rather, the interplay of all factors—the patient's psychic economy (152, 184, 258, 259, 279, 1433).

THERAPEUTIC PSYCHOANALYSIS IN SCHIZOPHRENIA

Not very long ago, it was considered incontestable that, although the psychoanalytic view on schizophrenia might be of the greatest scientific importance, as a therapy, psychoanalysis was useless in cases of psychosis. Freud gave expression to this idea by contrasting "transference neuroses" and "narcissistic neuroses" (596) and has expressed the same point of view again in his posthumous "Outline" (633). This skepticism emphasizes the fact that psychoanalysis is based on the analyst's influence on the patient, that, therefore, an ability of the patient to establish emotional contact with the analyst is required.

Although it is impossible to conduct an analysis without emotional contact with the patient, one would no longer take this extremely pessimistic position today. An analytic effect on schizophrenics is possible because the regression to narcissism is never a complete one. An analysis can utilize the residues of reality relationships as well as the patient's spontaneous attempts at recovery. In the case of an autistic stupor, it is self-evident that patient and friendly attempts to establish contact, however fleeting, are the sole possibility; and it is clear that if no contact is achieved, nothing can be done. However, psychiatrists who have developed the necessary patience and friendliness have been rewarded by inducing even patients with catatonic stupors of very long standing to respond. An attempt to invade the patient's autistic attitude, so that the doctor becomes a part of the patient's world, may be successful. One tries to insinuate oneself into the world of the patient, in order to lead him back gradually into the objective world (363, 657, 809, 924).

Fortunately not all schizophrenics are stuporous. They each have some kind of contact or substitutive contact. Whatever avenue is open has to be used.

Anyone who understands the schizophrenic mechanisms is aware of the extraordinary difficulties presented in an analysis of a schizophrenic as compared with the analysis of a neurotic. It has been emphasized that in the analysis of compulsion neurosis, as contrasted with hysteria, not the patient's whole ego but only a definite part of it is allied with the physician in combating the disease and the resistances. In schizophrenia, this co-operative part of the ego is small to the point of disappearance, and, what is worse, even this small remnant is unreliable. The assumption that psychotics do not transfer their infantile conflicts to their analyst is erroneous; they do, and often in a very stormy manner. Yet these manifestations of transference are all unsubstantial. There is always a tendency on the part of the patients to drop their relationship to the object. Most insignificant and unpredictable psychoeconomic alterations, in the attitude of the analyst or in everyday life, may lead to a cessation of the transference. One never knows for how long a contact once made will be sustained.

The tendency of such patients to defend themselves by means of a narcissistic regression against temptations may be used also against the temptations of transference. This is best seen in the analysis of paranoid cases. Such an analysis comes to grief when the analyst comes to represent to the patient the persecutor. Thus the attitude of the analyst must vary according to the part the delusion plays in the patient's total psychodynamics and psychoeconomics. When the patient needs his delusion for defense purposes, the analyst must respect this fact. Otherwise the analyst, as a representative of reality, provokes the patient's criticism. Any mistake may plunge the analyst into the patient's delusional ideas.

Sometimes cases in which the patient vacillates between transference feelings and total narcissism can be analyzed only while he happens to be in the transference phase; some analysts, in their work with catatonics, have shown that a periodic procedure of this kind may be successful (1172).

All these requirements demand modifications in the classic technique of psychoanalysis. Still, the therapeutic successes that are reported (87, 151, 218, 288, 397, 399, 661, 785, 914, 943, 964, 966, 990, 1009, 1088, 1089, 1093, 1172, 1260, 1451,

1477, 1541, 1549) are not yet sufficiently due to a systematic, scientific consciousness of the necessary modifications, but rather to the intuitive therapeutic skill of the respective analysts. However, the necessary technical modifications are much discussed (82, 87, 217, 274, 278, 283, 363, 394, 397, 399, 657, 659, 661, 674, 688, 785, 913, 1016, 1017, 1390, 1504, 1542, 1549, 1562). They consist of protecting or rebuilding the contact with reality and with reason.

Where there is little spontaneous contact left, the analyst will really have to "seduce" the patient by trying to make himself attractive; if necessary, the analyst must accept the patient's level. But since merely participating in the patient's fantastic world will never cure him, the analyst must bring him slowly to face the fantastic nature of this world and to become aware of the real one again.

The general advice that Abraham used to give was that in narcissistic cases one must try actively to establish and to keep a positive transference; moreover, one must first be the representative of reality, making the patient by all means aware of reality and of his attempts to escape from it; one must seize every contact he has with reality and strengthen it, even by discussing tiny details of everyday life. In accordance with this plan one must avoid disturbing the transference too soon by analyzing it, as one would do in the analysis of neuroses. However, advice of this kind is more easily given than carried out. First, the analyst is unable to foresee and evaluate factors—objectively very inconspicuous—that may disturb the transference. Second, one should not forget that the patient may feel the transference relationship as a dangerous temptation rather than as a gratification, and therefore as a provocation to withdraw. And, third, the transference, as a transference, is not reality. One cannot accept the advice not to analyze the transference unreservedly if one fully tries to be a "representative of reality." An analysis without analysis of the transference is impossible. However, it is true that many instinctual needs, whether expressed in the attitude toward the analyst or in real life, need not be analyzed immediately if they tend to increase the patient's interest in reality. On the whole, it can be said that analysis of a schizophrenia is divided into two phases. The first, preanalytic, phase aims solely to establish and preserve contact; the analyst strives to make the psychosis, in respect to transference, as nearly like a neurosis as possible. This achieved, he may start with the second phase, which is analysis proper. In actual practice, however, these two phases overlap. The preliminary period of object attachment certainly serves at the same time to awaken insight into the fact of illness and encourage the desire to be cured, and in certain patients one can start analyzing from the beginning. The procedure tending to awaken and reinforce contact with reality need not be limited to the relation with the analyst; often in discussing current conflicts, relationships, and attitudes of the patient, one can emphasize the relationship to reality. Observation of the patient's behavior not only during the analytic hour but throughout the day and the chance of influencing him through extra-analytic measures are of paramount importance in this first period of analysis (1440). These are two distinct advantages of hospital practice (219, 397, 657, 661, 966, 1440). But also the second part will be different from the analysis of a neurosis, since the patient's readiness to react with loss of reality has still to be considered. The very concept of interpretation implies that it would be a real mistake in technique to give a schizophrenic patient explanations of symbols and complexes as long as there is no "reasonable ego" to evaluate and utilize these interpretations. The aim of the therapy is to make the patient face internal and external reality, not simply to participate in his unreal fantasies. But it may be necessary to participate for a certain time in order to show the patient that one understands him, and to gain his confidence and co-operation. It has been asked how interpretation is possible at all with schizophrenics, since in schizophrenia "the unconscious is conscious"—that is, the patients consciously understand their symbols and present material concerning the Oedipus complex or pregenital sexuality. The answer is simple. Interpretation means showing the patient those impulses which he is warding off, but which he nevertheless is capable of realizing when his attention is directed to them. In a schizophrenic who reverts from a threatening or tempting reality to states in which the primary process kept elaborating Oedipus fantasies without considering reality at all, the "warded-off impulses" of which he should be made aware are not these Oedipus fantasies but the reality from which he has withdrawn and the fact of his withdrawal.

Occasionally one may succeed in developing an "artificial paranoia," so to speak, channelizing the narcissistic attitude of the patients to a certain circumscribed subject. Waelder demonstrated in the case of a mathematician how he could make the narcissistic attitude of the patient conform to reality by limiting it to his mathematics, so that outside this realm the patient's behavior remained relatively undistorted (1549).

All these attempts may be summarized in this formula: In the introductory phases the patient's capacity to develop a transference should be established to such an extent that this transference may subsequently be abolished by analysis without bringing about a new narcissistic regression.

The most difficult task is to estimate the degrees. Too friendly an attitude on the part of the analyst might be taken by the patient as a seduction into a feared sexual relationship (possibly a homosexual one), from which he would wish to escape through a narcissistic regression. The analyst must steer between the Scylla of a too objective attitude, giving the patient no stimulus to turn to the objective world, and the Charybdis of a too friendly attitude, frightening the patient and driving him further into narcissism. It is always possible that unpredictable everyday occurrences may cause a transitory accentuation of the rejection of objects. For this reason alone psychoanalysis of schizophrenics should be conducted in institutions.

In periodic schizophrenics, analysis should be undertaken in the free intervals, when a reasonable ego is operative. But here another problem arises: the question whether it is worth while to take the risk of provoking a new psychotic attack by the analytic attempt.

The same consideration is decisive in judging the indication of psychoanalysis in borderline cases. The danger always exists that the analytic procedure, by straining the patient's conflicts, may force the patient into a psychotic episode. Only the estimation of the economic factors and the therapeutic skill of the analyst, watching carefully that he does not make undue demands on the patient, will prevent this possibility. In certain schizoid personalities a trial analysis may perhaps result in the insight that they are better off as they are, because any attempt at change might induce a psychotic breakdown. But there are other schizoid personalities who, by a timely analysis, can be saved from psychosis. Sometimes schizoid personalities react more favorably to analysis than one expects. Their narcissistic regression is a reaction to narcissistic injuries; if they are shown this fact and given time to face the real injuries and to develop other types of reaction, they may be helped enormously. There are also personalities who are able to maintain a sufficient contact with reality only when this contact is artificially aided. They are like invalids needing constant treatment.

> Once in such a case a colleague made this correct diagnosis: "schizophrenia, by means of a psychoanalysis of decades' duration, artificially held on the level of a compulsion neurosis."

Another question is whether to analyze patients who in their past have suffered schizophrenic episodes that have healed spontaneously but left a scar. Cases of this kind, too, when analyzed, risk a relapse into psychosis. But sometimes the psychoeconomic circumstances are so favorable that the ego, in spite of the scar, is now able to face its conflicts and to solve them in a better way with the help of analysis.

It is evident that the analysis of a schizophrenia is quite a different undertaking from the analysis of a neurosis. The difficulty of the problem, however, should not prevent one from seeking a solution. The increasing literature on analysis of schizophrenia shows that it actually does not.

The conviction that the obstacles are mere difficulties of technique and the increasing number of reported successes should provide the courage to treat schizophrenics psychoanalytically. Still, everyone who analyzes psychoses is doing pioneer work. One cannot expect that a new undertaking, however promising, will be entirely successful. Anyone undertaking such work will estimate its appropriateness after precise evaluation of the conditions of the particular case and will take the necessary caution. The patient's relatives should be warned of the dubious nature of the prognosis and about the possibility of a new psychotic attack. If possible, the analyst should treat the patient in an institution. He will keep in mind that the classic technique does not suffice, that in addition to the essential modifications suggested, the method must be adapted to the conditions of the individual case. With all these cautions, he may begin the actual treatment; he probably will achieve success in some cases, and, for the rest, he will at any rate learn a great deal.

In conclusion, it is well to emphasize once more the scientific importance of the analysis of schizophrenics. Neuroses represent a regression to infantile sexuality; the psychoanalysis of neuroses brought about the understanding of infantile sexuality. Schizophrenia represents a regression to the primitive levels of the ego; psychoanalysis of schizophrenics will permit understanding of the evolution of the ego.

D. Psychoneuroses, the Secondary Elaborations of Symptoms

CHAPTERS XIX–XX

Chapter XIX

DEFENSES AGAINST SYMPTOMS, AND SECONDARY GAINS

GENERAL REMARKS

BECAUSE of the nature of the subject matter it was necessary to include in the chapters on the mechanisms of symptom formation the discussion of the special forms of the neuroses. The methods of symptom formation influence the total personality, hence also the subsequent course of the neurosis. Therefore, also the ego's reaction to its neurosis has necessarily been touched upon. The following summary of those scattered remarks may give a clearer insight into the shaping of neuroses once the symptoms are established.

A neurotic symptom is, for the ego, a new painful experience. The ego's reactions to new painful experiences depend on its strength and development.

A very weak ego may be passively overwhelmed, the unexpected painful experience producing a traumatic effect. Then the ego learns to defend itself against painful experiences, either by simple denial or by other mechanisms of defense, following the pattern of the primal judgment: everything painful must be "spit out" (616). At the period of passive-receptive mastery, the ego has but one response to the experience of pain: the cry for help.

In contrast, a mature ego, reacting in accordance with the reality principle, is able to acknowledge the existence of painful experiences (575). By means of such recognition it can thereafter either avoid similar experiences or respond adequately to them, rendering unavoidable pain as harmless or even as useful as possible (507).

The ego that experiences neurotic symptoms is in much the same situation as an ego that for the first time experiences an emotional spell. Symptoms and emotional spells are similar in so far as both are painful and ego alien and nevertheless arise within one's own personality. Actually, the ego is first traumatically overwhelmed by emotional spells, subsequently it tries to defend itself and find external passive protection against them, and finally learns to overcome the archaic types of reaction, actively mastering the affects by using them for its own purposes (191, 440, 697, 1021). The success of the ego depends, of course, on economic circumstances. Its ability to apply mature methods of active mastery is determined by the ratio between its strength and that of the forces it has to master. A decisive factor that may weaken the ego is the amount of energy required to maintain countercathexes at other points. Crucial also is the developmental stage of the ego at the onset of the decisive conflict.

Neurotics are persons who tend to revert to archaic patterns of reaction. Therefore, mature attempts at active mastery are much rarer in regard to neurotic symptoms than in regard to affects. Such attempts presuppose the ability to learn, to classify new experiences according to past experiences, to understand the differences, and to modify behavior in terms of reasonable judgment. Neurotics are persons who lack this very ability and who tend to react instead with rigid infantile patterns. Therefore, the pathological forms of reaction to symptoms, being overwhelmed, forming defenses, and demanding external help, are much more frequently encountered than rational adaptation.

SYMPTOMS AS TRAUMATA, AND PRECIPITATING FACTORS IN NEUROSES

Those neuroses that have persisted uninterruptedly from childhood or adolescence, fluctuating only in intensity, cannot, of course, be experienced as traumata. Certain symptom neuroses, however, start abruptly and unexpectedly; and sometimes a previous neurosis may suddenly be exacerbated.

This occurs in anxiety spells and in "nervous breakdowns," which in some cases are merely anxiety spells and in others represent the dissolution of a neurotic stability, precariously maintained up to that time. The rigid, isolating restrictions that save compulsive characters from feeling anxiety and painful emotions may be broken down; the personality is suddenly flooded by anxiety and vegetative sensations, which are all the more painful since the patient, because of his defensive measures, has never learned to assimilate emotions and to adjust to them.

This is the place to ask what actually causes such sudden outbreaks or aggravations of neuroses. A theoretical understanding of the dynamic background of all neurotic phenomena makes it possible to summarize the potential precipitating factors in a schematic table. It must be borne in mind, however, that in practice the different factors interact and supplement each other, and that the actual precipitating factors represent combinations of the elements which are artificially isolated here (576).

A certain amount of neurotic conflict and pathogenic defense can be sustained by everyone without an actual neurotic breakdown. However, the more energy a person spends in latent defensive conflicts, the greater is his disposition to fall ill if a precipitating factor disturbs his mental equilibrium. An intense disturbance, however, may cause a neurosis even in a person with little predisposition. Disposition (intensity of latent defensive struggles) and precipitating factors form a complementary series (596).

Precipitating factors are experiences that disturb the equilibrium between warded-off impulses and warding-off forces, an equilibrium hitherto relatively stable (1513). Such disturbances may be of three kinds:

A. Increase in the warded-off drive. Such increase must not be so intense as to break down the countercathexis altogether; but it must be intense enough to render insufficient the previous defense against derivatives. It may be produced in several ways:

(1) The increase may be an absolute one. Many neuroses start at puberty or at the climacterium due to the physiological intensification of sexual drives at these times.

(2) It may be a relative increase in a specific warded-off drive at the expense of other instinctual demands. This may be caused by (*a*) experiences that consciously or unconsciously mean a temptation or a stimulation of this particular wish; (*b*) experiences that consciously or unconsciously mean a devaluation of other instinctual demands whose energy is then displaced toward the warded-off drive (581); disappointments in adult life stimulate regressions toward infantile longings; (*c*) external frustrations or blockings of instinctual satisfactions hitherto obtainable; any frustration in the realm of adult sexuality increases the intensity of the unconscious infantile sexual longings; (*d*) the blocking of any activity which, by previous displacements, has supplanted instinctual satisfaction; the blocking may result in a relative increase in the intensity with which the warded-off drives strive for release.

B. Decrease in the warding-off forces. Such decrease must not be so intense as to nullify the defense; but it must be intense enough to loosen the previous defense against derivatives.

(1) If the ego is generally weakened by fatigue, intoxication, sickness, or other exacting tasks, the defensive forces are weakened and what has been repressed comes to the fore. Tired persons are more inclined to make slips of the tongue and errors, sick persons to tolerate outlets that they would have blocked under other circumstances. Under certain conditions this may be enjoyed as a relief and even improve or cure neuroses.

Frequently neuroses seem to improve under real strains. This may give the impression that the neurosis was a kind of play which ceases as soon as real worries come up. In the search for this type of relief, people may turn toward potential "worries" or toward the diversion of "hard work." This kind of favorable influence is more likely if guilt feelings are dominant among the motives for the defense, so that sickness, "robot" work, strenuous tasks, or real misery are regarded as punishments that soothe the guilt feelings and bring privileges.

If, however, the weakening of the defense is less intense, it may have the opposite effect. Derivatives, hitherto blocked, may now find their outlet and make their appearance as symptoms. If the break-through threatens to become too dangerous, the ego may respond with a more intense type of "emergency" defense.

This is the case in some "pathoneuroses" (478). Frequently neuroses are precipitated by preceding exhausting strains. This is due to the fact that the consequent impoverishment of the ego diminishes its defensive powers or is felt as a danger signal. The straining experiences may, however, also have been experienced as castration threats or masochistic temptations.

(2) What holds true for general weakening of the ego holds true also for specific weakening of defensive attitudes by the relative strengthening of other portions of the ego. When the self-esteem of a person is heightened by success, fulfillment of ideals, or gains in love, power, or prestige, then the person feels elated and consequently diminishes his censorial activities. This may result in the opening of forbidden outlets and in relief (1237). Here again the diminishing of the censorial activities may result not in a real liberation but only in the production of symptoms; and too much relief of this kind may be felt as a danger signal.

C. Paradoxically, an intensification of the warding-off forces may also precipitate a neurosis. Some neurotic phenomena are more manifestations of the defense than outbreaks of the warded off. But also with every increase in the warding-off forces the entire struggle is intensified; the equilibrium is endangered, and greater suppression may be followed by greater rebellion. Thus anything that increases the anxiety or guilt feeling forming the motive for the defense may precipitate a neurosis.

(1) Anxiety may directly be increased: by the experience of new threats, by experiences that subjectively are perceived as threats, and by experiences that confirm certain hitherto unconvincing threats (566). In this way traumata experienced as castration or abandonment, the unexpected sight of adult genitalia by children, or an impending examination may provoke neuroses.

(2) Guilt feelings may be directly increased. Whenever a person is remorseful or when some authority gives him new standards of perfection, repressions may increase with the guilt feelings.

(3) Both anxiety and guilt feelings increase indirectly with the loss of anything that has served hitherto as a support or as a reassurance. A rationalization may lose its effectiveness; persons with an oral-dependent type of self-esteem may have a breakdown when the necessary narcissistic supplies decrease in intensity, that is, when a loss of love increases the fear of being abandoned. Since prestige, power, and self-confidence are used as reassuring weapons against anx-

iety, any loss in prestige, power, or self-confidence can function as a precipitating factor. If self-confidence is weak and punishment is unconsciously expected, failure means that the expected punishment is at hand; moreover, success may mean the achievement of something unmerited or "wrong," bringing inferiority or guilt into the open. Freud described patients of this type as "those wrecked by success" (592). A success may not only mean something that must bring immediate punishment but also something that stimulates ambition and thus mobilizes fears concerning future failure and future punishment.

(4) An increase in the warding-off forces may also be a reactive one, following their temporary diminution in strength. The factors mentioned under (B) may become doubly effective in this way.

In general, pathological reactions to external events of any kind spring from the inherent dynamic-economic alterations in the defensive struggles. The events are misunderstood in the light of the person's past and interpreted as temptations, threats, gratifications, or reassurances; they create changes in the strength of warded-off impulses or of warding-off anxieties and guilt feelings.

Most precipitating factors are experiences that are (objectively or subjectively) somehow similar to the childhood events that gave rise to the decisive conflicts, that is, experiences that are related to the person's "complexes." The more unsolved defensive struggles within a person, the more he is inclined to interpret later experiences as repetitions of the events that once brought about the defensive struggle.

When an anxiety spell or a "nervous breakdown" acts upon the ego as a trauma, it may also provoke a traumatic neurosis which is secondarily imposed upon the primary psychoneurosis. The patient may become sleepless or dream only of his anxiety spell or feel compelled to recount the neurotic experiences again and again or develop affects or movements as a defense against the first anxiety spell, and he may lose all other interests.

DEFENSES AGAINST SYMPTOMS

Like painful affects, the "subjective affects" of neurotic symptoms may be warded off by the various mechanisms of defense. Since all symptoms are derivatives of warded-off instinctual impulses, they may be unconsciously recognized as such and warded off in turn. Daydreams that have become representatives of repressed drives may find an outlet until they have reached a certain degree of intensity; then they may be recognized as derivatives and repressed (*see* pp. 193 and 217). The same holds true for symptoms. As long as they are not too intense, or as long as their defensive significance prevails, they may be tolerated; when they become more intense or too obviously expressive of the warded-off instincts, they are combated.

All types of defense mechanisms may be used against symptoms. Even a simple denial may be tried.

> A training candidate, after the mobilization of her character neurosis, produced acute symptoms, among others a violent vomiting; when the analyst mentioned her "conversion symptom," she said: "Conversion symptom? I have no conversion symptom." When she was reminded of her vomiting, she asked: "So you consider simple vomiting a symptom?"

The most frequent type of such denial is the denial of the psychogenic nature of the symptom, or of any connection between it and mental conflicts. "This is just physical," the patient says.

> Patients who succeed in this defense against their neuroses are very difficult to treat analytically. They may develop an inability to understand mental connections, clinging to "reasonableness" and refusing to consider in any way the "logic of emotions" (44).

It is worth while to mention that in modern times the opposite is also very frequent. Organic diseases are dangerous and uncomfortable. Many persons prefer to consider themselves neurotic. Whenever they feel symptoms, they say: "It is just psychogenic," to ward off the unpleasant admission of sickness.

> As an extreme, a doctor patient, when his elderly father developed disturbances of sensibility and speech and slight motor disturbances on one side of the body, stated that his father had become hysterical. This patient, due to a deep repression of his aggressiveness, did not like action at all; he preferred talking. In the same way he preferred psychogenic diseases to organic ones. Therefore he did not like medical activity either, and was interested in psychoanalysis which is operative through talking. But what had been warded off came back: he was afraid of Hitler as well as of his analyst, as of persons whose words are more effective than other people's actions.

Another type of denial may be called a reaction formation against a symptom, namely, the denial of the ego-dystonic character of the symptom. The attitude "I have no symptoms, I just do what I like" is frequent; such patients behave, to use a simile of Freud's, like the horseback rider who believes he controls the horse, whereas he really has to go where the horse takes him (608). This may be exaggerated to a kind of pride in neurotic behavior and may constitute the hardest resistance in analysis. Compulsion neurotics, who believe that they are better than others because of their kindness or cleanliness, or neurotic characters, who have some real success in life because of their neurotic behavior, do not easily renounce their neuroses. This type of "reaction formation," however, forms a transition to the types in which the neurosis is not warded off but rather made use of for purposes of the ego.

Many compulsive symptoms are genetically secondary, directed against primary compulsion symptoms held in check by them. Their analysis provides plentiful examples of undoing and of isolation of symptoms or of reaction formations against them.

> Examples are the biphasic symptoms, the second half of which undoes the first half, and the magical formulae with which obsessions may be exorcised (546, 560, 567).

Also a real repression of symptoms exists. Phobics often do not know what they actually fear, and compulsion neurotics often do not know the real nature of their compulsions, but tell them vaguely in the way unclear dreams are told. Frequently the wording of magical formulae becomes secondarily repressed.

One type of isolation of symptoms needs special notice: "It is true, I am queer in this or that respect, but that is of no importance because it has no connection whatsoever with my true personality." This type of isolation is effective when a neurosis comes to a standstill at a certain point in development. Some phobic patients are actually not disturbed at all so long as they obey the phobic restrictions; the symptoms have become isolated from anything outside the avoided situation. Hysterics may develop the famous *la belle indifférence;* they have their symptoms but refuse to be touched by them in any way. Compulsion neurotics may have isolated obsessions or rituals, and remain relatively undisturbed otherwise. Probably the best example of successful isolation of a neurosis is represented by genuine paranoia. Psychotherapists have made manifold attempts to create similar situations artificially.

ORAL-DEPENDENT ATTITUDES TOWARD SYMPTOMS

In patients who have not learned to master new experiences actively, an increase in their oral-dependent attitude, with all its ambivalent features, is a frequent response to the appearance of symptoms.

To a certain degree something of this sort happens in every neurosis. All neurotics tend to regress, and whenever one feels miserable and one's own activities are insufficient, the old longing for external help appears. Phobics become helpless children again; masochistic characters exhibit their helplessness; they all want to induce their salvation through a "magic helper" (653). Analysts are familiar with this longing because it expresses itself regularly in the transference.

Persons with oral fixations who are disposed to the development of depressions, addictions, and impulse neuroses show this phenomenon to a much higher degree. They react to the appearance of symptoms with an increase in their narcissistic needs, and consequently with an increase in their conflicts around their narcissistic needs. In depressed patients a vicious circle is thus created, the depression increasing the narcissistic needs, the narcissistic needs increasing the depression.

The archaic conception of talion makes people feel that any suffering and any painful experience may undo guilt and entitle them to further compensating privileges. This conception encourages an oral-dependent reaction to neurotic suffering, that is, demands for compensation from the external world (from the "omnipotent" parents or from their successors, God, fate or those who decide about compensation). An extreme standpoint in this respect is held by the "moral masochists" who yield completely to their symptoms, blackmailing the environment and God to give them what they need (*see* pp. 501 f.). To a lesser degree some persons think that because they feel bad, they are entitled to "feel good" and may virtuously grant themselves some pleasure (695), or that every suffering must in itself be something good, as stated in various religious ideologies.

MASTERING OF SYMPTOMS

All these attitudes are in strict contradiction to one other type of attitude the ego may take toward its symptoms: attempts at mastering them in a normal way. The ego may try to learn about the symptoms and to make use of them, to include them somehow in its organization.

This contradiction in the ego, that it tries to exclude the symptoms on the one hand and to include them on the other, is, as Freud has pointed out, not the fault of the ego (618). The ego would like to get rid of the symptoms; but the warded-off instincts continue their effectiveness, and the ego cannot do anything but accept them and make the best of the situation.

Exactly the same contradiction can be seen in a very different field of pathology: in the physical reaction of the organism to the intrusion of foreign bodies. Foreign bodies are either surrounded by a protective wall, and thus isolated from the tissues of the organism, or they are "organized" and gradually converted into a part of the organism. In the same way, neurotic symptoms are either isolated from the rest of the personality or gradually changed into a part of it.

The reaction formations of the typical compulsion neurotic, which become definitely established in the patient's character, and counterphobic attitudes are examples of the inclusion of symptoms into the organization of the ego. More complicated types of inclusion of symptoms will be discussed later (*see* pp. 471 ff.).

A mastery of symptoms, it is true, can never wholly succeed. To master means to cope with intruding excitements by discharge, binding, or elaboration. As long as the warded-off instinct still remains effective in the unconscious, the mastery is not complete. That the warded-off instinct does remain effective in the unconscious is the definition of the neurosis.

According to its "principle of multiple function" (1551), the ego may try to satisfy by its symptoms id and superego demands of any kind simultaneously.

This tendency is manifested in the development of simple "secondary gains" as well as in more complicated phenomena of neurotic character traits.

SECONDARY GAINS FROM ILLNESS

When a neurosis is being established, it is, as a rule, very uncomfortable. But the ego tries to make a virtue of necessity and may use the neurosis for its own purposes. It may try to gain advantages from the external world by provoking pity, attention, love, the granting of narcissistic supplies, or even monetary compensation. It may try to relieve the pressure of the superego by demonstrating that the symptom is a punishment, by achieving pleasure on the basis that suffering entitles to compensating pleasure, by using the symptom to help the defense against some other impulse.

The possible secondary gains are very manifold; it would be worth while to compile them. Here, only a few unsystematic remarks will be added.

1. *Secondary gains from the external world:* It is often stressed that the main secondary gain consists in getting attention by being sick. But what type of person is especially in need of "getting attention"? Attention is needed either as a sexual satisfaction (a substitute for love) or, more frequently, as reassurance and a promise of help and protection. Sickness is also frequently perceived as a right to privileges; these privileges may consist of material gains or of more subtle mental gains. Very often this is no either-or; the most intense struggles for "compensation" are fought by patients who are much less in need of money than in need of a sign of parental affection and of assurance against abandonment.

No illustrative anecdote must be told to analytic patients as frequently as the story about the inmate of an asylum who implied, when special privileges of his were denied: "Then, what am I nuts for?"

Sickness brings all the advantages of passive-receptive behavior. "Now I am not the one who has to act; they have to do it for me." The longing for the time of childhood when one was taken care of is revived in all emergencies (and this fact is widely abused in all authoritative societies); the same occurs in the emergency of a neurosis. This may in turn arouse guilt feelings, creating secondary conflicts and vicious circles.

2. *Secondary gains from the superego:* The pride in reaction formations or in asceticism belongs to this class, and likewise the appeasement of a severe superego by suffering. The privileges of being sick may include the loss of the feeling of responsibility, and a neurosis may be utilized for gaining "internal attention" in the same way as for gaining external attention.

The secondary gain in evaluating symptoms as punishment has been interpreted as primary and fundamental (37). But no one becomes neurotic just for the purpose of suffering.

In different types of neuroses various secondary gains are predominant: in anxiety hysteria, the regression to childhood times, when one was still protected; in hysteria, gaining attention through "acting" and sometimes the gain of material advantages; in compulsion neurosis, narcissistic gains through pride in illness; in organ neurosis, the denial of psychic conflicts by their projection onto the physical sphere.

Secondary gains are sometimes very obvious, sometimes hidden. Theoretically, they may be less interesting than the primary genesis of the neurosis; practically, however, they are of paramount importance. He who has succeeded in getting advantages out of his illness does not give it up easily. Analysis, therefore, first has to clarify and to work through the secondary gains. A secondary gain of the illness may even be the only pleasure of which a patient is capable. In this respect, a secondary gain may make the analysis of a neurotic as difficult as the analysis of a pervert. In other cases, a resistance of this type may be less substantial but still effective enough.

Defenses against symptoms have been distinguished from their inclusion into the ego. Actually, every neurotic develops both types of response. The ratio of these two attitudes is decisive for the further development of the neurosis.

Before continuing the study of this development, however, other and more complicated attempts at inclusion of neurotic behavior into the ego must be discussed—not only reactions to symptoms but simultaneous (frequently failing) attempts to prevent the development of further symptoms by prophylactic countercathexes. The study of the development of neurotic character traits will show the full variety of such phenomena.

Chapter XX

CHARACTER DISORDERS

BASES FOR THE DEVELOPMENT OF PSYCHOANALYTIC CHARACTEROLOGY

How neurotic symptoms or attitudes are blended into the personality cannot be considered without a knowledge of what "personality" is.

That psychoanalytic characterology is the youngest branch of psychoanalysis becomes comprehensible when this science is viewed historically. Psychoanalysis started with the investigation of neurotic symptoms, that is, with phenomena that are ego alien and do not fit into the "character," the customary mode of behavior. Psychoanalysis examined and understood the unconscious before it studied the conscious. It delved into the newly discovered universe of unconscious drives and their irrational manifestations before it undertook the consideration of surface mental experiences. Only then could it begin to understand that not only unusual and suddenly erupting mental states but also ordinary modes of behavior, the usual manner of loving, hating, and acting in various situations can be comprehended genetically as dependent on unconscious conditions; and that ordinary volition is determined just as are disorders of the will.

There were two factors that impelled psychoanalysis to evolve its "ego psychology." The first was the necessity to analyze the resistances, that is, the ways in which the defending forces of the ego made their appearance in the psychoanalytic cure. If, for example, a patient did not follow the basic rule, it became necessary not only to influence this unreasonable behavior through suggestion but to analyze it as if it were a symptom. Other material, associations, memories, behavior, or dreams had to be used to make the patient aware that he had resistances, why he had them, as well as why he had them in the particular form of disregarding the rule. It was discovered that even if the patient did not feel any fear at the moment, he had once been afraid of (or ashamed or disgusted or had had guilt feelings about) certain instinctual experiences, that this fear was still unconsciously operative within him, and that he therefore developed resistances against utterances that might be connected with these experiences. It was then discovered that attitudes of this kind fulfill the purpose of resistance not only in the psychoanalytic cure but that the same behavior patterns are also used in life for the same defensive purposes. In this way the first "psychoanalysis of character" was developed, namely, the analysis of the purpose and the historical genesis of certain attitudes as defenses (1269, 1271).

A second cause for the development of ego psychology was the interesting phenomenon that there has been a fundamental change in the clinical picture of the neuroses during the last decades. In the classic neuroses an integrated personality was suddenly disturbed by inadequate actions or impulses. In modern neuroses, however, it is not a question of dealing with a hitherto uniform personality that is merely disturbed by some immediate event but, rather, with one that is patently torn or malformed, or at any rate so involved in the illness that there is no borderline between "personality" and "symptom." Instead of clear-cut neurotics, more and more persons with less defined disorders are seen, sometimes less troublesome for the patients themselves than for their environment. The formula, "in a neurosis that which has been warded off breaks through in an ego-alien form," is no longer valid, since the form often is not ego alien, the elaboration of the defense sometimes being more manifest than its failure.

It would be a fascinating task to investigate the cause of this change in the forms of neuroses. This, however, lies outside the competence of the analyst. It can only be suggested where an answer to this question may be sought. The method and manner in which the ego admits, repels, or modifies instinctual claims depend on the way in which it has been taught to regard them by its environment. During the last decades morality, and with it the educational attitude toward the instincts, has changed greatly. Classic hysteria worked with the defense mechanism of repression proper, which, however, presupposed a simple prohibition of any discussion of the objectionable drives. The inconsistency of the modern neurotic personality corresponds to the inconsistency of present-day education. The change in the neuroses reflects the change in morality. In order to understand this change, however, the social changes that have taken place in the last decades would have to be investigated.

The character of man is socially determined. The environment enforces specific frustrations, blocks certain modes of reaction to these frustrations, and facilitates others; it suggests certain ways of dealing with the conflicts between instinctual demands and fears of further frustrations; it even creates desires by setting up and forming specific ideals. Different societies, stressing different values and applying different educational measures, create different anomalies. Our present unstable society seems to be characterized by conflicts between ideals of individual independence (created during the rise of capitalism and still effective) and regressive longings for passive dependence (created by the helplessness of the individual with respect to security and gratifications as well as by active educational measures which are the outcome of the social necessity of authoritative influences) (see p. 587). Present-day neurotics have egos restricted by defensive measures. Psychoanalysis had to adapt itself to this new object, and that was the decisive reason for the interest psychoanalysis developed in character problems.

INTRODUCTORY REMARKS ON PATHOLOGICAL CHARACTER TRAITS

Some neurotic character attitudes show at first glance that they represent an adjustment to a neurosis, an attempt to make the best of established neurotic conditions. Between such attitudes and the original symptoms, there is a reciprocal relationship. Such traits are secondary elaborations of the neurotic symptoms, mostly of infantile anxiety hysterias; the neurotic character which has developed in this way acts as a defense against further symptoms, but may, nevertheless, be the basis on which new neurotic symptoms develop.

A neurosis is initially a breakdown of adjustments, a something that happens to the ego passively and against its will, not a planned, active arrangement of adjustments to conflicting conditions, as certain authors who have no feeling for the instinctual nature of neurotic phenomena prefer to believe (820, 821). But secondarily attempts are made at adjustments, intended to repair the original breakdown and to prevent further breakdowns; they involve a curtailment of the freedom and flexibility of the ego. In earlier chapters, constructions of this kind were encountered in the anchoring in the character of phobic disinclinations, of behavior patterns through which "dangerous" situations are avoided or reassuring ones induced, of "counterphobic" attitudes aimed at overcoming disturbing fears; they were encountered in the reaction formations of compulsion neurotics, in which the attempt is made to suppress the original instinctual attitudes.

Patterns of this kind are rigid, definitive, once-and-for-all formations. Acute struggles with the instinctual impulses are avoided by a chronic limitation of the flexibility of the ego which is stiffened as a protection against unwelcome external or internal stimuli. In extreme cases the rigidity is a total one; in less extreme cases a relative elasticity may be preserved so that the rigid pattern becomes pronounced whenever anxiety is felt, and is somewhat relaxed whenever an experience of reassurance or pleasure permits the individual to ease the barriers. But all patients of this kind are more or less restricted by their defense measures. They waste energy through constant countercathexes and lose certain differentiations of development through renunciations; they respond to external stimuli with definite patterns only, thus sacrificing liveliness and elasticity. Instead of a living conflict between impulse and defense, frozen residues of former conflicts are found. These ego-restricting modes of behavior are not necessarily experienced as alien; the patient may consciously agree with them or even not be aware of them.

Freud once wrote that "it is always possible for the ego to avoid a rupture in any of its relations by deforming itself, submitting to forfeit something of its unity, or in the long run even to being gashed and rent. Thus the illogicalities, eccentricities, and follies of mankind would fall into a category similar to the sexual perversions, for by accepting them they spare themselves repressions" (611). Since the maintenance of these eccentricities, which correspond to the reaction-formation type, demands an expenditure of energy, it would be more exact to say that their formation corresponds to a single definite act of repression, so that the necessity for subsequent separate repressions, consuming more energy, and for separate anxiety experiences is avoided (433). To a slight degree every human being is an "eccentric" of this kind; in pathological characters the eccentricities prevail.

Fromm once made the remark that Freud showed how the "bad" sexual and aggressive impulses of man are repressed; but, says Fromm, Freud did not evaluate the fact that modern education, the anxiety of the father, and social forces make a child repress what is "good" in him, too (653). As a reproach against Freud this remark is unwarranted. Freud expressly stated that analysis is effective in again releasing a person's good potentialities which had been blocked by his repressions (596). But the facts Fromm had in mind are certainly true. The once-and-for-all type of repression, producing chronic changes and hardenings of the personality, inhibits the possibility of further development of the ego. Any pathological character trait necessarily reduces an individual's actual potentialities.

WHAT IS "CHARACTER"?

In ego psychology, psychoanalysis has the same subject matter as other psychologies; but due to its understanding of the unconscious drives, it is in a position to handle it in a different way. It is obvious that an apparatus whose function is to organize, to direct, and if necessary to suppress cannot be understood without a knowledge of what is organized, directed, or suppressed. The instincts, studied first, are relatively the same for everybody. Studying the differences of the individual egos as a product of the interplay of the unconscious instinctual demands and environmental influences, psychoanalysis can understand the differences of human beings from a causal and genetic point of view. Not only unconscious wishes but also the ego and its behavior patterns represent an outcome of this interplay of drives and inhibiting forces.

The concept of character evidently has a broader scope than "modes of defense anchored in character." The ego not only protects the organism from external and internal stimuli by blocking its reactions. It also reacts. It sifts and organizes stimuli and impulses; it permits some of them to find expression directly, others in a somewhat altered form. The dynamic and economic organization of its positive actions and the ways in which the ego combines its various tasks in order to find a satisfactory solution, all of this goes to make up "character."

Thus, there are many character attitudes that cannot be called defenses. But there are none that would be independent of instinctual conflicts. No adjustment to demands of the external world remains uninfluenced by the individual's demands in respect to this external world. "Ego attitudes" and "instinctual demands" are not only not incommensurable, but psychoanalytic characterology is in a position to show how environmental influences change instinctual demands into ego attitudes. From the establishment of the ego on, the organization, direction, and sifting of instinctive impulses, which must be brought into consonance with experiences and which thus are modified and shaped by gratifications and frustrations, constitute the attitudes of the ego.

This description of *character* is nearly identical with that previously given for the *ego* (*see* pp. 15 f.).

Character, as the habitual mode of bringing into harmony the tasks presented by internal demands and by the external world, is necessarily a function of the constant, organized, and integrating part of the personality which is the ego; indeed, ego was defined as that part of the organism that handles the communications between the instinctual demands and the external world. The question of character would thus be the question of when and how the ego acquires the qualities by which it habitually adjusts itself to the demands of instinctual drives and of the external world, and later also of the superego.

Under the name of "the principle of multiple function" Waelder has described a phenomenon of cardinal importance in ego psychology (1551). This principle expresses the tendency of the organism toward inertia, that is, the tendency to achieve a maximum of effect with a minimum of effort. Among various possible actions that one is chosen which best lends itself to the simultaneous satisfaction of demands from several sources. An action fulfilling a demand of the external world may at the same time result in instinctual gratification and in satisfying the superego. The mode of reconciling various tasks to one another is characteristic for a given personality. Thus the ego's habitual modes of adjustment to the external world, the id, and the superego, and the characteristic types of combining these modes with one another, constitute character. Accordingly character disturbances are limitations or pathological forms of treating the external world, internal drives, and demands of the superego, or disturbances of the ways in which these various tasks are combined.

A relevant quotation from Rado: "It may be that the individual elements in the mode of operation of the synthetic function will some day turn out to be the nucleus of that which may be called in psychoanalysis the 'character of the ego'" (1237).

The term character stresses the habitual form of a given reaction, its relative constancy. Widely differing stimuli produce similar reactions; for example, any offensive instinctual impulse, nearing realization, may produce a spiteful reaction in some persons, passive compliance in others, truculence in others, and so on.

Anticipatorily it may be stated that this relative constancy depends on a number of factors: partly on the hereditary constitution of the ego, partly on the nature of the instincts against which the defense is directed; in most cases, however, the special attitude has been forced on the individual by the external world (*see* pp. 523 ff.).

Just as in other fields of psychoanalytic investigation, in the study of character the pathological was understood before the normal. And again "fixation" and "regression" are the basic concepts in this pathology. If an ego is not fully developed or has fallen back to early stages of its development, this ego's habitual ways of reacting, called character, will be equally archaic. Many pathological attitudes become clarified through an understanding of the early developmental phases of the ego. The development of the ego is characterized by the following concepts: orality, anality, genitality; lack of objects, incorporation (identification), passive forerunners of love (ambivalent object relations), love; pleasure principle, reality principle; first traces of consciousness in feelings of tension and relaxation, incorporation as the most primitive type of perception, perception governed by instinctual needs, objective perception; judgment as to whether a stimulus brings tension or relaxation, judgment directed by wishes and anxieties, objective judgment; un-co-ordinated discharge movements, "omnipotence" of movements, purposeful actions; wish-fulfilling hallucinations, wish-fulfilling magical thinking, objective thinking; omnipotence, projection of omnipotence, tendency toward reparticipation in the lost omnipotence, control of self-esteem through narcissistic supplies, independent regulations of self-esteem with the help of the superego.

The primitive regulation of stimuli by a passive-receptive behavior, rooted in the fact that the human child goes through a prolonged phase of dependence, is gradually supplanted by activity; the memory of it, however, always admits of the recurrence of a regressive longing for substituting the earlier receptivity for activity. Any failure, hopeless situation, or decrease in self-esteem may mobilize this longing.

> In many social situations the individual is presented with the alternative: whether to be active and independent and pay the price of feeling alone and unprotected or to "belong" and be protected and pay the price of losing his independence (653). Present-day education, for social reasons, increases the intensity of this conflict. This is the psychological basis of many social and cultural problems.

The latest complication in the structure of the ego, the erection of the superego, is also decisive in forming the habitual patterns of character. What an individual considers good or bad is characteristic for him; likewise, whether or not he takes the commands of his conscience seriously, and whether he obeys his conscience or tries to rebel against it. The structure of the superego, its strength and the way in which the ego reacts to it, depends first on the actual behavior of the parents and second on the instinctual reactions of the child toward the parents, which in turn depend on constitution and the sum of previous experiences. It is not only a question of what kind of persons the parents were; the superego formation depends on several other factors as well: which of the parents' attitudes the child adopts; whether he imitates their positive behavior or their prohibiting attitudes; at which stage of development all this happens, whether the remainder of the ego fuses with the part that has been altered by identification or whether it sets itself up in opposition.

The superego is the carrier from one generation to another not only of the content of good and bad but also of the idea of good and evil itself, of the prevailing attitude toward this idea, and of the acceptance or rejection of an authority that asks for obedience and promises protection if obedience is maintained. In the superego there is a mirroring not only of the individual's parents but of his society and its demands as well.

> Cultural influences on the character structure of the youth of a society are by no means restricted to the superego. The construction of the superego is, to a certain extent, a repetition of the construction of the ego itself. The ego "mediates between the organism and its environment"; accordingly, it is different in different environments. The ego, to a large extent, is a composite of various early identifications. Thus its nature varies with the qualities in the models for identifications.

An appreciation of the form and ideational content of the superego in respect to character formation has led to attempts to explain empirical differences in the character of men and women on the basis of the differences in the construction of the male and the female superego. Freud gave expression to the idea "that the character traits for which women have always been criticized and reproached, that they have less sense of justice than men, less tendency to submit to the great necessities of life, and frequently permit themselves to be guided in their decisions by their affections or enmities," might be "due in large part to a difference in their superego formation" (617). According to Sachs, the frustration of the Oedipus wishes in girls brings about a partial regression to orality and to attempts to remain attached to the father through an oral incorporation. Only if this incorporation loses its libidinous meaning and becomes "desexualized" does a true superego formation take place (1333). However, the sexual differences in the formation of the superego are certainly not the same under different cultural circumstances. Their reflections in the character of boys and girls respectively vary as the means and contents of child upbringing differ in accordance with social variations (655).

In addition to the construction of the superego, the formation and modification of ideals in later life, too, are of importance in forming the character. Sometimes certain persons, who serve as models, or certain ideas become "introjected into the superego" in the same manner as the Oedipus objects have been introjected in childhood; at other times the later "ego ideals" seem to remain more peripheral in the personality. The adjustment of a newly introjected object to the original superego may give rise to complications (603).

CLASSIFICATION OF CHARACTER TRAITS

The character as a whole reflects the individual's historical development. As a rule the most superficial layers represent the youngest acquisitions. However, this is not always so. Regressions and breakings through complicate the picture. The actual order in which the layers appear in analysis may differ as much from their original historical order as the relative depths of geological layers differ from their historical age.

Character attitudes are compromises between instinctual impulses and forces of the ego that try to direct, organize, postpone, or block these impulses. Some attitudes so obviously offer an occasion for instinctual satisfaction that psychoanalysis is not required to discover this. There are many more attitudes in which the purpose to master or even to deny and repress some instinctual impulse or to defend oneself against an instinctual danger is obvious.

This difference may be used for a classification of character traits. A dynamic criterion would base its differentiation on whether a character trait tends rather to serve the purpose of discharging some original impulse or of suppressing it. Freud stated: "The permanent character traits are either interchanging perpetuations of original impulses, sublimations of them, or reaction formations against them" (563). Thus psychoanalytic characterology will have to make the distinction between character traits in which, possibly after the alteration of aim and object, the original instinctual energy is discharged freely and those of the defensive type in which the original instinctual attitude, which is contrary to the manifest attitude, is checked by some countercathectic measure. The first category should be called the "sublimation type" of character trait and the second the "reactive type" (*see* the diagram about "sublimation" and "reaction formation," p. 152).

The relative prevalence of the one or the other category of traits cannot fail to be decisive for the personality.

THE SUBLIMATION TYPE OF CHARACTER TRAITS

The ego may, indeed, succeed in replacing an original instinctual impulse not merely with one that is somewhat less offensive but with an impulse compatible with the ego, one that is organized and inhibited as to aim. The ego forms a channel and not a dam for the instinctual stream. Freud had this type of defense in mind when, in earlier essays, he often referred to "successful repression" in contrast to the unsuccessful repression that is found in the pathogenesis of the neuroses (589). These "successful" mechanisms are not of much interest to the student of neuroses; but in the study of character they are of the greatest importance. The transformation of reactive traits into genuine ones of the "sublimation type" is the main task in character analysis.

Psychoanalytic knowledge of the "successful repressions" is still in the tentative stage. The relation between sublimation and repression as well as the conditions that favor the happy outcome of sublimation have been discussed (*see* pp. 141 ff.). The most intimately studied example of this type is the establishment of the superego by means of identification with the objects of the Oedipus complex (608). It is very probable that all sublimation is performed by mechanisms identical with or similar to identification.

> The conditions creating reactive character traits are much better known than those responsible for the sublimation type. It can only be stated that the absence of conditions favoring the development of reactive traits is the main prerequisite for the building of sublimations. The experiences that interfere with primitive pregenital wishes must be neither too intense nor too sudden and forceful; they must be sufficient to effect a change in the drive without calling forth too strong a reaction. Environmental conditions must be present which aid in the establishment of the sublimation "substitute" by providing models and suggesting ways out of conflicts. Probably many sublimation traits have their roots in earlier stages of development than do reactive traits.

THE REACTIVE TYPE OF CHARACTER TRAITS

Character traits of the reactive type may be subdivided into attitudes of avoidance (phobic attitudes) and of opposition (reaction formations). They all betray themselves in one or more ways: by mere fatigue and a general inhibition due to economic impoverishment, by their cramped nature and rigidity, or by the warded-off impulses breaking through, either directly or in a distorted form, either in actions or in dreams. All reactive-type character traits, therefore, limit the flexibility of the person, for he is capable neither of full satisfaction nor of sublimation.

The habitual defensive attitudes can again be subdivided: some persons develop a defensive attitude only in certain situations, while others remain comparatively constant in their defensive attitudes, as if the instinctual temptation to be warded off were continually present. Such persons, for defensive purposes, are either impudent or polite, empty of affect or always ready to blame others. Their attitudes are unspecific and are indiscriminately maintained toward everybody. Such attitudes may be designated "character defenses" in a narrower sense.

In analysis it is urgent that the personality first be released from the rigidity of these attitudes because the pathogenic energies are really bound up in them. Even in cases where there is evidence of some active struggle between instinct and defense at some other place, it is of decisive importance that the analyst direct his attention to the rigid character defenses (433, 438).

If the analysis succeeds in remobilizing the old conflicts, the infantile instincts will not manifest themselves immediately; instead the patient develops more or less severe feelings of anxiety, and only analysis of this anxiety brings the instinctual impulses to the surface. A layer of anxiety had been interposed between the original impulse and the ultimate attitude. Actually many pathological behavior patterns are shaped by defenses against anxiety, and in most cases an infantile anxiety hysteria had been overcome by the reactive behavior.

> As in the analysis of compulsive symptoms, it occurs frequently also in the analysis of reactive character traits that various vegetative and hormonal physical disturbances make their appearance; further analysis reveals that these symptoms are equivalents of anxiety, interpolated between original impulse and ultimate attitude.

A character that is pre-eminently of a reactive nature is necessarily inefficient. The behavior patterns of such persons are expressions of the warding-off countercathexis, but are very often interspersed with features of the warded-off impulses which again have broken through. Persons of this type can be called reactive characters (1073). Usually analysis reveals a complex structure of many different layers. The character is not only composed of reaction formations against original instinctual demands but also of reaction formations against reaction formations.

The most extreme examples of reactive characters are ascetics whose entire lives are spent in fighting instinctual demands; there are persons who permit themselves hardly any activity, because all activity to them has a forbidden instinctual significance. There are eccentrics who devote their lives to the combating of some particular evil which, for them, unconsciously represents their own instinctual demands. Other types within this category have been discussed in the chapter on inhibitions (see p. 183).

Examples of the rigidity of reactive traits are the "hard workers" who are under the necessity of working constantly to keep from feeling their unbearable inner tension. One of Reich's patients aptly enough called himself a robot (1272). It is obvious why work under these conditions necessarily is less effective. In this connection certain "Sunday neuroses" (484) should be mentioned; the patients become neurotic on Sundays because on workdays they avoid neuroses by a neurotic, that is, reactive, type of work. Such people do not flee from something in the objective world that for them means temptation or punishment toward fantasy; they flee, rather, from instinctual fantasies toward some "reactive" external reality.

In spite of all rigidity of reactive traits, a break-through of the original impulses is a continuous danger.

> If a fireman starts fires in order to have the opportunity to extinguish them, he betrays the fact that his interest in fire fighting has not really been of the "sublimation type."
>
> A convinced vegetarian, who for many years had been in the forefront of the vegetarian movement, changed his occupation when external conditions were altered and became a butcher.

Reactive behavior is not only found in attitudes directed against instinctual impulses but also in conflicts around self-esteem. Many persons who manifest more or less arrogant behavior are actually fighting against becoming aware of their deep inferiority feelings; other persons who despise themselves for their insignificance are covering up a deep-seated arrogant attitude (1263). Many ambitions are based on the need to contradict a feeling of inferiority; many activities serve to cover up passive longings. Yet often enough, attempts of this kind fail and the deeper layer emerges.

> A very frequent compromise between a superficial longing for active independence and a deeper one for passive receptivity is the idea that a temporary receptivity is necessary for the attainment of a future independence. Thus the independence may be enjoyed in anticipatory fantasy, while at the same time the dependence is enjoyed in reality. This simultaneity is one of the emotional advantages of childhood: the boy submits to his father's masculinity for the purpose of becoming masculine. The tendency to preserve this fortunate compromise is one of the reasons why so many neurotics unconsciously are interested in remaining on the level of a child or an adolescent.

Two basic types among the reactive characters may be distinguished. One is the entirely "frigid" person who has a "feeling phobia" and avoids feelings altogether; instead he has developed a cold intellect. The other type is hyperemotional; as a reaction formation against feared emotions, he developed counteremotions which give a false and theatrical impression. But as a rule, the counteremotions contain more of the original emotions than the patient knows. The intensity of his suppression of emotion is such that it causes a flooding of his personality with the dammed-up energy and a resultant emotional coloring even of intellectual and rational activity. Whereas the first type, in analysis, produces the resistance of intellectualization of the analysis, the second type may produce much emotional material but lacks the necessary distance and relaxation to consider it objectively.

Reactive character traits have been compared by Reich to a suit of armor donned by the ego as a protection against both instincts and external dangers (1271, 1274, 1279). The armorlike character originated as a result of the continual clash of the instinctual demands and a thwarting environment, and "derives its strength and its enduring right to exist from current conflicts between instinct and environment" (1275). This armor is to be imagined as being perforated to admit communication. In the reactive character, the simile would state, the perforations are narrow and the material around them inelastic.

Since reaction formations are preconditioned by ambivalence, a correspondingly less important role is played by them, the greater the genital concentration of a person's sexuality. Thus reactive characters for the most part coincide with the "pregenital characters" to be discussed later.

> Genital primacy brings with it another advantage for character formation, aside from that of overcoming ambivalence; the ability to achieve orgasm is a precondition for ending stages of being dammed up. It affords opportunity for an economic regulation of the instinctual energies (1270, 1272).

It is important to emphasize here that the classification of contrasting types necessarily is an abstract procedure. Actually every person has both types of character traits. The ideal, "postambivalent" character without reaction formations (25) is a pure conception.

In the chapter on homosexuality, the overcoming of an aggressive impulse toward some person through identification and consequent love was discussed (*see* pp. 336 f.). This change may be of the "sublimation type"; more often, however, accompanying traces of the original hostile attitude give evidence that the warded-off trends still persist in the unconscious, that is, that the change has been of the reactive type. A part of the original hostility may be "channelized" into identification, another part simultaneously preserved and suppressed through countercathexis.

According to Freud, the members of a group are identified with one another, and because the original aggressive cathexis is absorbed by this identification they cease fighting one another (606). Actually, this cessation is very often a conditioned one; the aggressive tendencies are very easily aroused again. The relative proportion of sublimation type and reactive type in the warding off of aggressive impulses in a social group is of great importance in determining its psychological structure. This ratio is conclusive as to how much of the stabilization or limitation of the aggression is dependable, and how much of it is merely specious, a mask preserved with great effort.

It is sometimes said that analysts simplify their task by assuming that the patient means the opposite of what he says or does. But it is not so simple as that. The reactive attitudes really cover the opposite, but other attitudes do not. Definite clinical criteria determine whether or not the opposite is meant, in the same way as an interpretation is neither proven nor refuted by a patient's yes or no (*see* pp. 31 f.). Clinical manifestations (general impoverishment, rigidity, breaching of the defense) and the dynamic reactions of the patient to interpretations are decisive.

DEFENSE AND INSTINCTUAL IMPULSE IN PATHOLOGICAL CHARACTER TRAITS

It would be an unwarranted assumption to state that all pathological character traits are built according to the model of reaction formations. Some pathological attitudes give the impression of attempts to satisfy instincts rather than to suppress them. A person who likes to contradict, for example, does not only contradict his own impulses in a projective form but may also satisfy his combativeness; sadistic impulses may form the basis not only of kindness and justice but of cruelty and injustice as well. Instinctual tendencies may have become incorporated in and influenced by the ego organization, and may nevertheless be pathological. By means of the methods of rationalization and idealization (*see* pp. 485 f.) the ego may befog itself in regard to the true nature of its activities. Distorted gratifications, thus imbedded in character traits, are often vitally important for the entire libido economy. A person is not willing to dispense with them without much ado, and for this reason such character traits, too, appear during an analysis as "character resistance." It may even be that of all the attitudes an individual develops, those tending to grant satisfactions become chronic and build up the character. It has to be added that in this connection satisfaction does not only mean satisfaction of instinctual desires but also satisfaction of the longing for security.

Certain ego attitudes, which appear to be instinctual, nevertheless chiefly serve a defensive function. The expressions "instinct" and "defense" are relative. Neuroses have been mentioned in which the fundamental conflict seemed to take place between two instincts with contradictory aims (42); it could be shown that the instinctual conflict at the base of these neuroses is invariably a structural conflict as well, and that one of the opposing instincts is sustained by an ego defense or strengthened for the purpose of ego defense (*see* pp. 129 f.). It is not the case of one definite defensive attitude fighting against one definite impulse; there are always variations, an active struggle and mutual interpenetration. In addition to the three-layer arrangement, instinct, defense, instinct breaking through again, there is another three-layer arrangement: instinct, defense, defense against the defense.

A man, for example, who has become passively feminine through castration anxiety may overcome this defense by particularly accentuated masculine behavior.

Identification may represent a mechanism of true sublimation; on the other hand, in depression, the instinctual impulses warded off by identification continue to operate against the introjected object. The fact that identification is operative thus does not reveal whether the attitude in question is based on a sublimation or is of a reactive character.

An example of special importance for social relations in general is the psychology of pity. Pity is undoubtedly a character trait connected with an original sadism. One may suspect a reaction formation. This suspicion is confirmed often enough when, through analysis or through an instinctual outburst, sadism actually is found behind the façade of pity; but at other times, pity seems to be a sublimation, the sadism really being supplanted by it. And in both instances the basic mechanism appears to be an identification with the object of the original sadism.

Jekels investigated in detail the sublimation type of pity (848). A person may originally have wished, for example, that a brother should be beaten by the father; he would counteract this wish by the thought that not the brother but he himself who had entertained this evil wish should be beaten. The type of person described by Jekels would now reject this idea by means of the thought that he should not be beaten, that he wished to be loved. Thereafter the person treats objects as he had wished his father, or later his superego, to treat him. The pity he develops toward objects is a kind of magical gesture, which asks love for himself and denies the idea that he deserves to be beaten. We thus have the following development: hostility, guilt feeling, fear of retaliation, attempts to enforce forgiveness by a magical gesture. This type of pity is an attempt to settle narcissistic conflicts with the superego in terms of the environment, a not unusual procedure. Its psychogenesis is characterized by a rather complicated type of identification; and again the knowledge of this fact does not reveal whether or not the original instinctual tendencies are completely absorbed by the defense (848; cf. also 365, 851).

> While pitiful persons of this type show through their "magical gesture" how friendly they would like to be treated by their superego, persons who are aggressive because of guilt feelings show how they would like to be punished by their superego.

To summarize: Character traits are the precipitates of instinctual conflicts; in principle, therefore, they are accessible to analysis. Character disorders, however, not only are a specific form of neurosis, difficult of definition and deserving a last chapter in a book on the specific neuroses; furthermore, all neuroses, except infantile ones, have their root in character, that is, in the particular variety of adjustment which the ego has made to the instincts as well as to the external world. Such adjustment originated in the individual history of infantile instinctual conflicts, usually in the particular history of an infantile anxiety hysteria.

It is, of course, impossible to isolate from one another the four tasks of the ego: to come to grips with instinctual demands, with the superego, with the demands of the external world, and to unify these three interdependent realms according to the principle of multiple function. The treatment of the instinctual demands determines the treatment of objects and vice versa. Nevertheless, there is no other way of reviewing the different types of neurotic character disorders than by studying separately anomalies that appear in solving the four tasks. Such a classification, however, is a very unsystematic one, useful only for an initial rough orientation.

PATHOLOGICAL BEHAVIOR TOWARD THE ID

GENERALLY FRIGID AND PSEUDO-EMOTIONAL TYPES

Neurotics are persons who are alienated from their instinctual impulses. They do not know them and they do not want to know them. Either they do not feel them at all or they feel only a small part of them, or they experience them in a distorted way.

Two basic types of pathological behavior toward the id have been mentioned as examples of reactive character. The one is the "generally frigid" person who more or less avoids emotions altogether.

A patient, who hated his profession, his friends, and life in general because in no situation could he feel at ease, loved his only hobby: mathematics. For him it was the field in which there were no emotions.

Such persons have no understanding of the "primary process," the psychology of emotions and wishes (44); in analysis this resistance keeps them from understanding interpretations of emotional connections because they accept only logical connections. When analysis succeeds in changing these attitudes, the patients, not accustomed to affects, are easily frightened by their new experiences; frequently, they do not recognize their affects and experience somatic "affect equivalents" instead.

Certain persons of this type avoid becoming aware of their insufficiencies by proving to themselves that they are very "efficient"; theirs are cold natures incapable of sympathy for others, "fleeing to reality" from their feared fantasies, but to a dead and lifeless reality. Whereas an analyst sooner or later usually becomes rather well acquainted with the personalities in his patient's environment, he never knows anything about the personalities of the "friends" of these patients: since they themselves do not really know their friends, their associations cannot give a vivid picture. In extreme cases the lives of such persons become comparatively empty. Secondarily these personalities may learn to hide their insufficiencies and to behave "as if" they had real feelings and contact with people (331).

The second type is the man with intense but uncontrolled emotions, in whom emotions, not finding their natural outlet, have flooded and "sexualized" everything. Persons of this type are hyperagitated and cannot put any distance between themselves and their own feelings. They live too much in the primary process to be able to reflect about it.

A normal person is able to remember how he felt as a child. A "generally frigid" person has forgotten childhood emotions; the hyperemotional person is still a child.

In all the arts it is usual to distinguish between classicists and romanticists, that is, between personalities who are bound to traditional forms and systems and personalities who are impulsive and create new forms. One speaks of persons led by intellect and those led by feelings; the distinction between extraverts and introverts implies something similar. The two types described are the pathological extremes of these opposites. The development from the purely emotional pleasure principle to the controlling secondary process is a gradual one, and its special forms depends on the individual history. Sometimes the entire early world of the pleasure principle is repressed; this is characteristic of the "frigid" type. At other times the development is so disturbed by instinctual conflicts that the control of the ego, with its secondary formations, is defective. Whereas the first type flees from feared instinctual temptations to sober reality, the second type finds reality full of representatives of the feared instincts, and flees from it to substitutive fantasy.

Both generally frigid and pseudo-emotional types may further elaborate their attitudes in various ways. The "frigid" person may, for instance, cover up his frigidity by a readiness to accept all experiences with equanimity and thus to react with such apparent adequacy that his lack of feeling does not show. The hyperemotional person may get various secondary gains by the intensity of his (pseudo) empathy.

CONDITIONALLY FRIGID TYPES

Other persons are not entirely but only occasionally frigid. They can tolerate emotions as long as certain reassuring conditions are present. Usually they tolerate emotions until a certain height of excitement has been reached and are frightened if this intensity is surpassed. Emotions must be neither too intense nor too serious. Neurotic individuals are introverted. They have turned from real objects to substitutive fantasy. They have "daydream emotions" but try to avoid "real" emotions.

A favorable return from introversion to objectivity is opened to talented individuals through art (564).

Many children feel compelled to play the jester to make other people laugh; they cannot stand seriousness. Similar disturbances occur in adults, too. Such behavior implies that the person fears being punished for his instinctual impulses; by pretending that he is merely jesting, he hopes to avoid punishment. Usually, however, the jesting is more than an avoidance of punishment; it has an exhibitionistic quality and is an attempt to get confirmation from the spectators, and to seduce them to participate in the jesting sexual or aggressive acts (556, 1294). The idea of making others laugh is a substitute for the idea of exciting them. Without the jest, this excitement would be frightening.

The "serious emotion" these persons try to avoid is frequently rage. Sometimes, however, rage has become a necessary component of their sexual excitement, and in fighting rage, they simultaneously are fighting sexual excitement.

CHARACTER DEFENSES AGAINST ANXIETY

The defense of many reactive character types is not (or not only) directed against the impulses but rather against experiencing the emotions related to the impulses. All the mechanisms that have been discussed as "defenses against affects" (*see* pp. 161 ff.) may be reflected in character attitudes.

Powerful quantities of countercathexis are often invested in the defense against anxiety. Many defensive attitudes are not directed against the *situation* in which anxiety may arise but only against the appearance of the *anxiety* itself (1629).

A frightened child needs, first of all, external affection, or rather narcissistic supplies, in order to be less helpless and nearer to omnipotence. He needs contact with mother's hand, that is, with a "good" principle, in order to fight the "bad" anxiety within him: introjection.

The opposite type of protection against anxiety is frequent, too: projection. "Not I am frightened, the other fellow is." Sometimes a certain amount of anxiety in other people is helpful against one's own anxiety, whereas a higher amount may mobilize a panic (*see* pp. 211 f.).

Everything that increases self-esteem has an encouraging effect and is therefore sought by persons who are fighting anxiety. Certain persons seem to be absolutely governed by a need to collect reassurances against supposed dangers; more primitive persons by collecting narcissistic supplies, affection, confirmation, power, prestige; less primitive persons by collecting approval from their superego. Due to the fact that the real cause of a neurotic anxiety is unconscious and that it is connected with instinctual demands that originate in somatic sources, all the reassurances, as a rule, remain insufficient.

In general it can be stated that those who strive passionately for power or prestige are unconsciously frightened persons trying to overcome and to deny their anxiety. "Narcissistic characters" (*see* pp. 373 ff., 504 ff., and 531 f.) are not born as such; their attitudes are aimed at fighting fears, usually very archaic (oral) fears. It is interesting that types whose conflicts are centered around their need for narcissistic reassurance become more frequent as contrasted to types with genuine object-libidinal conflicts. What yields "power" and "prestige" is, of course, entirely determined by cultural conditions. However, the concepts of prestige, even within a given culture, vary greatly, corresponding to various experiences of individual children.

A *denial* of anxiety may be attempted in two ways: by denying the existence of a dangerous situation or by denying the fact that one feels afraid. A "reactive courage" is frequently a simple reaction formation against a still effective anxiety.

Sometimes the original anxiety situations are not avoided but are sought, at least under certain conditions; the person shows a preference for the very situation of which he is apparently afraid; even more frequently a person develops a preference for situations of which he formerly had been afraid (435).

In seeking an explanation for such apparently paradoxical behavior, the nature of phobic anxieties must first be considered. The phobic situation is a temptation for instinctual drives. Only through a veto by the external world or by the superego did the anxiety arise. The original striving may reappear.

The pleasure achieved by "counterphobic" behavior, however, is not identical with the original instinctual pleasure. The obsessive manner of the search for the once feared situations shows that the anxiety has not been completely overcome. The patients continuously try to repeat the way in which in childhood other anxieties gradually had been mastered by active repetitions of exciting situations. The counterphobic pleasure is a repetition of the child's "functional" pleasure of "I do not need to be afraid any more" (984) (*see* pp. 44 f.). And, as in the child, the type of pleasure achieved proves that the person is by no means really convinced of his mastery, and that before engaging in any such activity, he passes through an anxious tension of expectation, the overcoming of which is enjoyed. This functional pleasure is not due to the satisfaction of a separate, specific "instinct to master" (766, 767, 768), but may be experienced in the realm of any instinct when original hindrances and anxieties are overcome. According to Roheim, it is a principal motive in any sublimation (1323). The functional pleasure may be condensed with an erogenous pleasure that has again become accessible through the very reassurance that created the functional pleasure. In this sense, hobbies and counterphobic prides are structurally similar to perversions. Since the defensive processes have cut off the original instinctual content of the anxieties from consciousness, it will be possible only under especially favorable circumstances for a counterphobic attitude eventually to result in the dissipation of the original anxiety. But unquestionably this is what the counterphobic individual really is striving for. He seeks out what was feared in the same way as a child experiences pleasurably in play what he is afraid of in reality.

The active repetition of what has been experienced passively or, later, the active anticipation of what may be experienced passively in the future (1552) remain the principal mechanisms in fighting anxiety. Frequently the search for situations formerly feared becomes pleasurable precisely because they are actively sought. If the same situation arises at an unexpected time and without activity on the part of the subject, the old fear reappears.

There are several special subtypes of this turning of passivity into activity in the fight against anxiety. One of them is the intimidation of others. If one can actively threaten others, one does not need to fear being threatened (541, 784, 971, 1298).

> Older siblings usually are in a position to frighten the younger ones. A patient of a masochistic character, with a readiness to harm himself to the advantage of others, had a childhood memory of once tormenting his little sister by asserting that noodles in the soup were disgusting worms. This seemed to be a screen memory of a sadistic period which later was turned into masochism. Further analysis confirmed this assumption, but it also showed an unexpected cause for the sadistic fixation. At a still earlier time the patient himself had been afraid of the solid particles in soup. By frightening his little sister, he was able to convince himself that he did not need to be afraid. His sadism, being a reassurance against fear, made his phallic aggressiveness possible again. This simultaneity caused the sadistic fixation which he subsequently tried to master by turning it against his own ego.
>
> Similar in nature is the psychology of many individuals who can bear up under "bossy" authorities as long as they themselves can play the role of a "bossy" authority toward somebody who is subordinate to them. In classical patriarchal families the father often intimidated the children just as he himself was intimidated by social authorities.

Similarly, encouraging others may have a reassuring effect; it is a kind of magical gesture indicating the kind of treatment the individual wishes for himself.

Both mechanisms, the intimidation and the encouragement of others, are examples of the defense mechanism of "identification with the aggressor" (541). Identification is the very first of all object relations; therefore a regression toward it may be used in fighting off object relations of any kind, even fear. Anna Freud cites as an illustrative example of this mechanism children's love for animals (541; cf. also 459). This love represents an outcome of an old animal phobia. By identifying with the "aggressive" animal, the child feels as if he himself participates in the animal's strength. Eventually the animal, which once threatened him, is now at his disposal for the purpose of threatening others.

> An anecdote is told about a child who was advised by his mother not to open the door in her absence. After leaving the house, the mother remembered that she had forgotten her keys and rang the doorbell. For a long time the child did not answer; then his voice was heard: "Go away, you dirty thief, there is a huge lion here."

A variation of this mechanism is the following. The patient's activity, which supplants passivity, is not real but pretended. The patient's aim is to make believe that whatever happens to him has been intended by him. This can also be observed frequently in the behavior of children. It is likewise the principal mechanism of certain neurotic characters who could be called "actors of reality" (702). They make believe or they may believe themselves that they actively cause what actually happens to them.

> They are, to use Freud's simile again (608), like the horseback rider who thinks he directs the horse, whereas he actually has to go where the horse takes him.
> A novel and play by Andrejew, *The Thought,* describes a failure of an attempted "denial by acting reality." An eccentric man suddenly gets the idea of simulating madness and killing his friend. After the murder, in the insane asylum, he begins to doubt whether it was all merely a game.

Persons of this type show a characteristic artificial behavior. Soon after the first analytic interpretation that they are pretending, a second interpretation becomes necessary: that they really feel as they pretend, but are afraid of these feelings.

> Agitation in a state of anxiety may be partly due to an attempt to control the anxiety by means of this mechanism. The same holds true for talkativeness (117, 473). However, a "dramatization" is not always and exclusively a means to overcome anxiety by the method of "activity instead of passivity"; it may also be intended to provoke the reactions of spectators, either to give reassurance or punishment.

Children overcome their anxieties not only by reproducing in active play what has threatened them but also by letting a loved and trusted person do to them what they themselves fear to do, or they try to convince themselves that such a person's omnipotence will protect them in their activity. This mechanism, too, may be repeated by adults, and after the discussion of the "flight from passivity into activity," it must be added that a "flight from activity to passivity" also exists. A very common counterphobic precondition is that pleasure may be experienced so long as one believes in the protection of an outsider. There are many ways to secure a protective or permissive promise, actual or magical, before engaging in a dangerous activity.

A passive-receptive condition of this kind may even be bound up with a transformation of passivity into activity; the counterphobic individual can engage pleasurably in the activity he originally feared if during the procedure he demonstrates to an object with which he is unconsciously identified that he is protecting or pardoning it.

There are many means of collecting reassurances of a specific or unspecific nature, of collecting affection, admiration, prestige, or power. Once more it becomes clear that the "attitudes toward one's own id" cannot be isolated from the "attitudes toward the objects." External power is sought as a means against an internal dependence. This is doomed to fail, especially in persons who, while consciously striving for power, unconsciously are simultaneously longing for a passive-receptive dependence. Good conscience and the feeling of acting right in fulfilling ideals may be used for the same purposes as collecting external reassurances. Certain behavior patterns, which represent unconscious conditions for attaining release from anxiety, in analysis turn out to signify rituals with the import of atonement or punishment.

If the original infantile sexual excitation was feared because of its sadistic component, the collection of external reassurances may be operative in still another way. The promise of protection which the patient seeks to secure, or, in the case of identification, to give, is well calculated to contradict the unconscious belief in the violent nature of the intended act. The permission to engage in the activity in itself is supposed to signify that there is no harm in it. In other cases a permission of this kind may be supplanted by other attendant circumstances with a reassuring significance. These attendant circumstances are comparable to perversions, to conditions of potency or to compulsive systems aimed at an exclusion of danger. The simultaneity of instinctual pleasure and "functional pleasure" in overcoming anxiety adds an obsessive character to "hobbies" of this type (1159, 1304).

The analysis of an intense interest in literature in one patient showed that it was based upon a former phobia about picture books. The scoptophilia associated with the functional pleasure of no longer being afraid of books had become possible through an overcompensatory striving "to know all books." In this way the patient was protected against surprises (430).

In another case a similar mechanism was at work in a pronounced interest in railways, which went back to a forgotten infantile fear of railways. The observation of a primal scene, which had been displaced onto the excitement of traveling by rail, was thought of as the "overwhelming unknown." Through the heightened interest in and the knowledge of railway travel acquired as a result of it, this fear was eliminated and the previously feared sexual enjoyment of the rhythm of the railway again became possible.

In the chapter on compulsion neuroses, "systematization" as a defense against anxiety was discussed (see pp. 284 ff.). As long as the system functions, things are under control.

Sometimes a true sexualization of fear occurs in persons whose sexual lives have undergone a masochistic distortion. Like any other excitation, fear may be a source of sexual excitation but, as in the case of pain, this is true only as long as the exciting displeasure remains within certain limits and does not become too serious (602, 1001). An identification with the aggressor may combine itself with a libidinization of anxiety and result in a tender love. There are reactive forms of homosexuality, namely, identifications with the other sex for the purpose of denying fear of the other sex.

One patient, who felt a kind of identification love for women, used to demonstrate his feeling in a rather exhibitionistic manner, as if to say that by the degree of understanding he had for women, he showed that there was really no difference between the quality of his feelings and theirs. The development of this boy had been disturbed by a relatively late traumatic observation of female genitals. All earlier castration fears had been condensed by him into the fear induced by this strange sight. His whole behavior was an attempt to master this anxiety by denying the idea that women were different, and consequently that there were no terrifying discoveries to be made (428).

All of these mechanisms may be connected with a "flight toward reality." A real situation is sought to convince the subject that the imagined dreadful things connected with it are, indeed, imaginary. The situation must be sought again and again because, although experience has shown that on one occasion imaginary expectations did not materialize, this was no final proof (1416).

> The significance of certain feelings of estrangement felt pleasurably upon the perception of something as "really true" is that the real occurrence is true, but the feared punishment associated with the occurrence is *not* true (631).
>
> Since the fear continues to exist, the persons in question often try to keep alive the recollection that on this one occasion nothing did happen. This is one of the motives for collecting trophies: proof of having taken a risk.

In counterphobias, just as in reaction formations in general, leakages may occur. Behind attempts at repression or denial of anxieties, the hypertense nature of the attitude, general fatigue, symptomatic acts, or dreams may betray that the anxiety is still operative. Sometimes a leakage of this kind may be avoided at the last minute by setting in motion an emergency defense mechanism. There are combinations of counterphobic and phobic attitudes; to a certain degree and under favorable circumstances a counterphobia is effective, at a higher degree and under other circumstances the original phobia becomes manifest. Kris has described this phenomenon in certain forms of unsuccessful humor, and has mentioned the double-edged character of comic phenomena, that is, the ease with which they pass from pleasurable success to painful failure (983, 984). The same holds true for counterphobic attitudes. In the midst of the triumph which the counterphobic individual can enjoy because of his saving in emotional expenditure, displeasure may break out if something occurs which seems to confirm the old anxiety.

> A failure of this kind can sometimes be observed in cases in which the fear of engaging in a fight has been overcompensated by a tendency to struggle and to compete on every occasion. For such persons the meaning of "I am not afraid, for I can already do that" and "I can even do it better than anyone else" unconsciously has turned into a wish to castrate everybody. Under certain qualitative or quantitative circumstances the pleasure fails, and in place of the intended castration a terrifying anxiety of being castrated appears.

The mechanisms of defense against anxiety which have been described as characteristic for neurotic characters are, in a lesser degree, to be found in everyday life as well. The most outstanding example is probably the field of sport (323). Another general class of counterphobic phenomena are certain works of art in which the artist, in a constant endeavor to shake off anxiety, seeks and describes what he fears in order to achieve a belated mastery. And, of course, there are similar phenomena in the realm of science. Here again some investigators devote themselves to research in a field which is actually a substitute for an object, onto which they have projected their anxiety. By getting control over it, they do not need to fear it. And finally one may assert generally that all abilities in which people take excessive pride fall within the same category (435).

The defenses against anxiety that become rooted in the character often undergo a secondary systematization. The uncovering of systems of character attitudes that fight anxiety, then, is the first step in analysis. However, this is not yet analysis itself, as some authors seem to believe (820, 821). If done correctly, it results in the patient's experiencing anxiety or various physical anxiety equivalents. This has to be followed by the analysis of the nature and history of the anxiety and the undoing of the dynamic constellation that created and still creates the anxiety to be warded off.

Jones used the expression "anxiety character" to characterize human beings whose personalities are dominated by the tendency to react to all stimuli with anxiety and who, therefore, in all their relationships have to defend themselves against anxiety (896).

RATIONALIZATION AND IDEALIZATION OF INSTINCTUAL IMPULSES

There are various conditions under which otherwise feared instinctual experiences may be tolerated. The mechanism of "rationalization" has been mentioned but not yet discussed in detail. Emotional attitudes become permissible on condition that they are justified as "reasonable." The patient finds one reason or another why he has to behave in this way or that, and thus avoids becoming aware that he actually is driven by an instinctual impulse. Aggressive behavior often becomes sanctioned on condition that it is viewed as "good"; a like situation holds true for sexual attitudes. The ego, afraid of its impulses, tries to vindicate them, and is able to yield to them as long as it believes in their justification (805, 868, 1084).

Probably various types of rationalization exist; one of them could be called idealization (696). The realization that an ideal requirement is going to be fulfilled brings to the ego an increase in self-esteem. This may delude it into ignoring the fact that through the idealized actions there is an expression of instincts that ordinarily would have been repressed. Each time an ideal requirement is fulfilled, the ego regains some of its early sense of omnipotence. In this state of elation the ego relaxes its ordinary testing of reality and of impulses so that instinctual impulses may emerge relatively uncensored (1237). Reality, therefore, is much more readily misapprehended in states of elation, intoxication, or self-satisfaction. Many apparently unintelligible outbursts of instinctual activity occur when self-esteem is excessively heightened, which is clearly recognizable in manic states. Sometimes a glorification of instinctual activity proceeds so far that it seems as if the functions of the superego have been usurped during elated states by a kind of second ego ideal which welcomes instinctual expressions (840). Such a duality of ideals may be rooted in an original division of the parental figures into "good" and "bad" ones (1238). In the same way, primitive races do not regard the totem festival as a rebellion against the deity but as a religious rite that fulfills a divine commandment. Similar perversions of ideals admitting of instinctual expressions can be seen in various forms.

> The *New Yorker* magazine published a cartoon in which Professor Freud raises his finger against a girl patient, saying: "Naughty, naughty, you again had a harmless dream."

A related phenomenon is the corruptibility of the superego (37): any "good" action sanctions a succeeding "bad" one; it is very probable that in cases of this kind the same mechanism of idealization is at work; the elation over the "good" deed impairs the function of judgment in regard to the subsequent "bad" one.

> Rationalization takes place not only with respect to instinctual drives, giving opportunity for a gratification that would otherwise not have been permitted, but also with respect to other kinds of ego-alien phenomena. Defensive attitudes and resistances, which seem irrational because their real purpose is unconscious, frequently are "rationalized" by the ego's foisting other secondary purposes upon them. Even neurotic symptoms of various kinds are thus frequently rationalized.

Besides rationalization, there exists also a mechanism that could be designated "moralization," a tendency to interpret things as if they were in accordance with ethical standards, even where they are objectively in striking contrast to them.

OTHER CONDITIONS OF TOLERANCE OF OR DEFENSE AGAINST INSTINCTUAL IMPULSES

In still other cases, the instinctual activities are simply *isolated*. They are permissible as long as certain guarantees are fulfilled that ensure their not impinging upon the rest of the personality.

> Examples were cited in the discussion of the mechanism of isolation (*see* pp. 155 ff.). Very frequent is the assignment of love and hate, originally pertaining to one and the same person, to different objects. Persons who have elevated this mechanism to a predominant character trait finally come to separate all persons and all things into completely antithetical categories (710). Another example is the isolation of tenderness and sensuality, so that sensuality is experienced only

toward objects with whom there is no emotional relationship (572). Under present cultural conditions prostitution gives men a good opportunity for such isolation.

There are even persons whose fear of their uncontrolled id is so intense or has developed so early that they have never had the relaxation and distance necessary for the development of ego forces to handle it. They are intolerant of tensions and unable to wait. Whenever they have to wait, they experience the waiting itself as a traumatic event. They try to protect themselves against it by every possible means. In any situation of excitement they look less for gratification than for an end to the intolerable excitement, thus revealing that the concepts of "instinct gratification" and "defense against instincts" are only relatively antithetical.

Persons of this type are always in a hurry, even if there is plenty of time. They are identical with the "traumatophilic" personalities (*see* pp. 543 ff.).

Often the difficulties of handling instinctual impulses are limited to special emotions, special partial instincts, or to impulses originating in special erogenous zones. Reactively kind persons cannot tolerate sadism but may become sadistic under certain circumstances; reactively courageous persons are irrational where anxiety is concerned, shameless persons in matters of shame, shameful persons in matters of exhibitionism.

ANAL CHARACTER TRAITS

The correlation of certain traits of character with definite eroticisms was the first discovery in psychoanalytic characterology (563) and is its most widely studied phenomenon. In this particular field, the processes of displacement from the original instinctual aim or procedure to behavior patterns of the ego, and the relations of sublimation and reaction formations, have been clarified.

The typical anal character has been described and discussed in the chapter on compulsion neurosis (*see* pp. 278 ff.). The anal instincts, under the influence of the social conflicts around training for cleanliness, changed their aim or object, thus becoming incorporated into the ego. The anal character traits have developed in place of anal-erotic instincts. This is proven by the fact that analysis of conflicts resulting in the development of defensive ego attitudes transforms them into the original instincts again after the interpolated anxiety has been overcome (21, 194, 593, 832, 883, 1022, 1143, 1634).

The prevalence of anal character formation in modern times and the "drive to become wealthy" present a particularly good field for the investigation of the relation between social influence and instinctual structure (434). This relation has many subtle ramifications. The insight that money unconsciously is equated with feces has sometimes been misapprehended to mean that the institution of money was created for the purpose of satisfying anal-erotic instincts (1321). But money fulfills a very rational purpose. To deduce the actual function of money from an anal-erotic misuse of money would be similar to drawing, from the hidden sexual significance of walking for the hysteric, the conclusion that walking in general fulfills sexual pleasure rather than that it is a means of getting from one place to another (1197). It is incorrect to state that a reinforcement of anal-erotic drives would have produced the reality function of money. The actual function of money, rather, influences the development of anal eroticism. Instinctual ideas of "retention" become connected with money matters or develop into a desire to attain wealth only under the influence of specific social conditions (434). However, social conditions also determine the importance and relative intensity of instinctual ideas of retention. Social institutions influence the instinctual structure of the people living under them through temptations and frustrations, through shaping desires and antipathies. It is not a matter of the instincts being biologically determined, whereas the objects of the instincts were socially conditioned; it is rather that the instinctual structure itself, particularly the relative distribution of libido between genitality and pregenitality, depends upon social factors. Unquestionably the individual structures created by institutions help conserve these institutions.

Every mental phenomenon is explicable as a resultant of the interaction of biological structure and environmental influence. Social institutions act as determining environmental influences upon a given generation. The biological structure itself has evolved from the interplay of earlier structures and earlier experiences. But how did the social institutions themselves originate? Was it not, in the final analysis, through the attempts of human beings to satisfy their needs? This is undeniable. The relations between the individuals, however, became external realities comparatively independent of the individuals; they shaped the structures of the individuals who then through their behavior again altered the institutions. This is a historically continuous process.

ORAL CHARACTER TRAITS

The influence of oral eroticism on normal and pathological character formation has been studied in detail by Abraham (24) and Glover (680, 681). The picture is not so clear as in the case of the anal character. This difference is ascribable to three factors. In the first place, many more oral elements persist as erotic activities than anal ones; second, it is very difficult for analysis to find oral character configurations free from later anal admixtures; and third, many elements, which are very clearly differentiated from each other later on, are still integrated in the oral phase of development.

Anal eroticism is important for the formation of the character because while being trained for cleanliness, children learn for the first time to relinquish immediate instinctual gratification for the sake of pleasing their objects; at the time of the still earlier oral eroticism, children became acquainted with objects and learned to assume relationships with them. How this happened consequently remains basic in determining the whole subsequent relationship to reality. All positive or negative emphasis on taking and receiving indicates an oral origin. Unusually pronounced oral satisfaction results in remarkable self-assurance and optimism that may persist throughout life if frustration following this satisfaction has not created a state of vengefulness coupled with continuous demanding (24, 681, 933). Exceptional oral deprivation, on the other hand, determines a pessimistic (depressive) or sadistic (redress-demanding) attitude (104, 106). If a person remains fixated to the world of oral wishes, he will, in his general behavior, present a disinclination to take care of himself, and require others to look after him. In conformity with the contrasting aims of the two substages of oral eroticism, this demand for care may be expressed through extreme passivity or through a highly active oral-sadistic behavior.

A case of this kind had had several oral-fixating experiences. He was breast fed for a year and a half, while living with a doting grandmother who spoiled him in many ways; then he was suddenly removed and lived with his excessively severe father. The result was a character governed by one predominating motive: to be reimbursed by his father for the oral gratification of which he had been deprived. Failing in this, he resorted to force to regain it. The patient had no occupation. He lived on his father's money and persistently considered himself discriminated against by his father. The conflict between the tendency to respond to disappointment by applying violent measures (to take by force what does not come automatically) and the simultaneous tendency toward ingratiating submissiveness is characteristic for oral fixations.

Oral-sadistic tendencies are often vampirelike in character. Persons of this type request and demand a great deal, will not relinquish their object and affix themselves by "suction."

The adhesion of many schizophrenics to their objects suggests that during the period of oral dominance the fear of losing an object was especially great. It is this fear that causes the "suction."

The behavior of persons with oral characters frequently shows signs of identification with the object by whom they want to be fed. Certain persons act as nursing mothers in all their object relationships. They are always generous and shower everybody with presents and help, under favorable libido-economic conditions in a genuine and altruistic way, under less favorable conditions in a very annoying manner. Their attitude has the significance of a magical gesture: "As I shower you with love, I want to be showered."

Occasionally, this need to "make others happy" is very torturing for the environment, thus manifesting the original ambivalence. The same holds true for certain psychotherapists who want to cure their patients by "giving them love."

Other persons are completely ungenerous and never give others anything, an attitude tracing from an identification with a frustrating mother. Theirs is, indeed, an attitude of revenge: "Because I was not given what I wanted, I shall not give other people what they want."

> Bergler showed that some cases of ejaculatio retardata are fashioned after this pattern. The penis represents the patient's breast, and the patients unconsciously refuse to feed their sexual partners (108, 110). Ejaculatio retardata, however, may also be an expression of an anal tendency toward retention.

It has been mentioned several times that oral characters are dependent on objects for the maintenance of self-esteem. They need external supplies not only for oral-erotic satisfaction but also for the narcissistic gratification of their self-esteem.

Thus both marked generosity and marked niggardliness may be attributed to conflicts around oral eroticism. Some persons show their receptive needs obviously; unable to take care of themselves, they ask to be taken care of, sometimes in a demanding, sometimes in a begging tone.

> Frequently the demanding tone is prevalent in persons who are incapable of getting the oral-reassuring satisfaction they need; every real gift makes them long and demand for more; they are "immodest" like the fisherman's wife in the fairy tale. The begging tone is prevalent in persons who actually are satisfied when freed from responsibility and taken care of; they are "modest," very easily contented and ready to sacrifice ambition and comfort if they can buy the necessary care or affection by such sacrifice.

Others repress such desires and refuse exaggeratedly to "impose" on anyone, refuse all presents or are unable to ask for anything. Very often people need to be dependent and yet pretend to be entirely independent. Unconscious longings for passivity may be overcompensated by an apparently extremely active and masculine behavior. Today's evaluation of "masculinity" creates various types of make-believe masculinity; the underlying oral passivity, however, may betray itself in different ways.

> One of them, according to Alexander (43), is the development of gastric ulcers (*see* p. 245).

Generous persons may occasionally betray their original stinginess, and persons who refuse to give may become overgenerous under certain circumstances. The variations are due to the ratio between sublimation and reaction formation in the characterological representation of oral drives (706).

The sight of a younger brother or sister at the breast often turns out to be the underlying factor in connecting envy and jealousy with oral eroticism (358, 1492).

> A woman patient with a pronounced oral character had a very unclear screen memory: in her early childhood a man had humiliated her by grasping her breasts. She understood that this could not have actually occurred, but that was what her memory revealed. Since she had the "revenge" type of the female cas-

tration complex and constantly felt sadistic strivings as if to undo a "rape," we assumed that the screen memory might only have confused the erogenous zones involved. However, the solution to the riddle of the screen memory came in an unexpected way. It turned out that she herself had grasped her mother's breast while her younger brother was being nursed. Later, sexual approaches of men were experienced as humiliations because they were regarded as repetitions of the humiliation experienced at the hands of her mother who repudiated and ridiculed her.

In addition, many directly erotic ways of using the mouth for pleasure may be reflected in the character (attitudes toward food, drinking, smoking, kissing); these erotic enjoyments may be supplanted by sublimations or by reaction formations (1468). Symptoms expressing conflicts around oral-erotic impulses, such as speech difficulties, are sometimes fought by reaction formations in the character structure, which may persist even after the speech difficulties have long been overcome. Among the oral traits of character there are the antithetical qualities of volubility, restlessness and haste, and the tendency toward obstinate silence.

By displacement of the constellation "hunger" to the mental field, curiosity may become an oral trait of character, and under certain conditions assume all the voracity of the original oral appetite (249, 461, 1059, 1405). The means employed to quench curiosity, in particular reading as a substitute for eating, seem to represent specifically an oral-sadistic incorporation of alien objects, sometimes of feces. The analysis of reading disorders typically reveals conflicts of this kind (124, 1512). Linking the ideational fields of "looking" and "eating" may often be due to some historically important incident, such as a child having seen a younger sibling being nursed. Correlated with reading there is frequently an intense inquisitiveness, a spasmlike, voracious looking that can be recognized as a substitute for gluttony.

> Such "oral" use of the eyes represents the regression of visual perceptions to the incorporation aims that were once connected with early perception in general (430) (*see* pp. 36 f.). An excellent account of the way in which oral impulses through instinctual and sublimated transitional links of "curiosity" evolve into a wish for intellect and knowledge was given by Vera Schmidt (1404, 1405).

Just as the essential connection between the anal-social conflicts and anal-erotic drives has been doubted, so also have the relations between dependence and oral eroticism (921). But their connection is an essential one. The biological basis of all attitudes of dependence is the fact that man is a mammal and that the human infant is born more helpless than other mammals and requires feeding and care by adults. Every human being has a dim recollection that there were once powerful or, as it must seem to him, omnipotent beings whose help, comfort, and protection he could depend on in time of need. Later, the ego learns to use active means of mastering the world. But a passive-oral attitude as a residue of infancy is potentially present. Often enough the adult person gets into situations in which he is again as helpless as he was as a child; sometimes forces of nature are responsible, but more often social forces created by man. He then longs for just such omnipotent protection and comfort as were at his disposal in childhood. He regresses to orality. There are many social institutions that make use of this biologically predetermined longing. They promise the longed-for help if certain conditions are fulfilled. The conditions vary greatly in different cultures. But the formula "If you obey, you will be protected" is the one all gods have in common with all earthly authorities. It is true that there are great differences between an almighty God, or a modern employer, and a mother who feeds her baby; but nevertheless it is the similarity between them that explains the psychological effectiveness of authority (436, 651).

URETHRAL CHARACTER TRAITS

The relationship of urethral eroticism to the character trait of ambition was first pointed out by Jones (881) and later by Coriat (290) and Hitschmann (794). Analytic experience shows that competition in respect to urination is a dominant idea in infantile urethral eroticism. This connection of urethral eroticism with ambition and competition has to do with the relation of both to shame (*see* pp. 69 and 139). The urethral-erotic ambition may be condensed with trends derived from older oral sources. Under the influence of the castration complex it may be displaced to the anal field, particularly in girls because of the futility of urethral competition.

A patient, with a urethral character developed to an extreme, suffered in a morally masochistic way from his unhappy marriage; he had been unable to employ many of his talents and potentialities. It soon was apparent that all his life he had been atoning for an unknown guilt. It represented his infantile sexuality and was built around shame over an enuresis which had persisted past his tenth year. His inhibited ambition pointed to the intensity of his urethral eroticism: his exhibitionistic happiness about small achievements (he renounced big ones) had the unconscious meaning of pride in bladder control. Achieving awareness of his guilt feeling precipitated a depression which caused him to cry a great deal. Prior to analysis he had for decades allowed himself no outlet, closing his eyes to his fate. The relaxation seemed indicative of progress and he was encouraged to yield unashamedly to the impulse to cry. Eventually it turned out that the patient was misusing this suggestion. Crying in the analyst's presence apparently afforded him masochistic pleasure. Soon it was not merely his own situation that brought on tears; he became generally sentimental and wept even at the thought of a "good deed." It must be added that his moral masochism had much of the character of the "savior fantasy": he continued his miserable marriage for his poor wife's sake; he had chosen a vocation in which he could help poor people. In other words, he was the "good" man whose very goodness made him cry. It impelled him to treat others as he would have liked to be treated. His main fantasy placed him in the role of a Cinderella who suffers much because she is misunderstood, but who will some day be understood and be freed from her suffering by some Prince Charming. Dreams and fantasies revealed that the Cinderella child thought of this "understanding" as a sort of stroking. As a child, the patient had suffered from rickets. Having to stay in bed so much made him feel that he was a burden to the family. His neurosis was a reaction to attempts to master the resultant unconscious aggression by transforming the thwarted Cinderella into a redeeming Christ. He tried to bring about the materialization of his passive longing, which had the following content: "If my suffering is sufficient, a savior will come to me and stroke me; then I shall be permitted to cry and cry and cry." At this point in the analysis the patient began an affair with a girl he pitied; he reacted with an ejaculatio praecox. The analysis of this new symptom confirmed an earlier interpretation: his crying meant urination; the poor child was to be stroked until he wet his bed, a permissible and beneficent action that brought relaxation rather than guilt or disgrace. There was no longer any doubt what the "poor child" unconsciously represented; and this was finally confirmed by a dream. It was his own penis. The urethral fixation of this patient was a passive-phallic one, expressing the desire to be passively touched at his genitals. The patient wanted his poor little Cinderella penis to be stroked until it wets and is permitted to wet (428).

Urethral ambition may create various secondary conflicts. In connection with the Oedipus complex, the "success" which is the goal of the ambition may acquire the unconscious meaning of killing the father and therefore become prohibited. In connection with the castration complex the ambition may acquire the meaning of a reassuring refutation of the idea of being castrated. At the same time, castration fear may block every activity; the very thing that was thought to be a reassurance against the possibility of castration may induce castration. The patient may revert to passive-receptive attitudes and get into the same conflicts around dependence as oral characters do.

Not all ambition is based on urethral eroticism. Sometimes other childhood conflicts are reflected in it, as in the cases of two patients who had very ambitious mothers whose ambition for their sons reflected their discontent with their husbands. The ambition of these patients was primarily an acceptance of the mother's ambitious suggestions and an identification with her. These ambitions showed all the conflicts and ambivalence of their mother fixation. On a deeper level, they had understood their mothers' ambitions as suggestions to kill the father and to become the mother's husband, and the inhibited ambition expressed their Oedipus complex.

CHARACTER AND CASTRATION COMPLEX

The close relationship between urethral eroticism and castration complex makes it comprehensible that the part played by urethral eroticism in forming the character cannot be isolated from the ways in which the castration complex influences the formation of the character (36). All the statements that have been made about character traits that combat anxiety in general hold true with respect to combating castration fear in particular. Counterphobic attitudes are frequent.

Children often play "being castrated"—for example, by pretending to be blind or crippled. Many a "modesty" in adults is of the same order. They are trying, in this way, to master the idea of castration. Their pleasure consists in (*a*) the satisfaction that the castration is pretended and not real; (*b*) the feeling of having "castration" under control; (*c*) a feminine sexual pleasure, for "being castrated" may mean "being a girl."

> A patient fearful of yet admiring in a feminine way his very tyrannic father loved to play the following game at subway stations. He would hold his arms out over the rails, imagining meanwhile that the train would cut them off. He would actually pull back his arms before the train came, but fantasy that this had been done at the very last moment. For him, his hands had nearly been cut off, but he had "things under control." He also had various other daydreams of giants or gigantic machines that threaten to overwhelm people but still can be kept under control. The daydreams, again, condensed passive homosexual fantasies with reassurances against the castration anxiety connected with them.
>
> It was interesting how this patient's entire object relationships in later life were governed by the same type of game: he would "play" at provoking dangers but never take any real risk.

The effects on character formation of shame associated with the idea of being castrated deserves special consideration.

Every little girl evolves penis envy; but the subsequent development of this envy may vary greatly. If the envy is not too intense and has not been repressed, it may be dissipated, either partly or entirely; certain parts of it may be sublimated in various ways or may determine individual features in the sexual behavior. If it is intense, however, or repressed at an early age, it may play a crucial part in the pathogenesis of pathological character traits as well as of feminine neuroses. Abraham distinguished two types of elaborations of penis envy in the character: the wish-fulfilling type and the vindictive type. The former arises if a woman is characterized by a desire to assume the male role and by fantasies of having or acquiring a penis; in the latter, impulses are in the foreground to take revenge on the luckier male by castrating him (20, 887, 1618). Frequently these women have the idea that sexual intercourse is humiliating for one or the other partner. Their objective is to humiliate the man before they themselves are humiliated. The revenge may be perceived as a masculine one ("I'll show you that I can be as masculine as you are") or as a feminine one ("Because you have despised me, I'll make you admire what you have despised"). Since the revenge impulses are directed against "men" in general rather than against a specific man, and since they can never be really satisfied, aggressive components of this kind are often determinants of "hypersexuality" in women (1204). Fantasies of being a prostitute are apt to express both ideas, being humiliated and taking revenge for it (617).

Hayward compared the analyses of women of both types in order to ascertain the determinants for the development of the specific type (755). Apparently the revenge type experiences the shock of learning about the penis during the anal-sadistic phase of development, usually through a brother or another boy; the wish-fulfilling type develops penis envy at the height of the phallic phase, generally through experiences involving the father or some other adult man. However, the differentiation between the two types should not be taken too strictly; many women show vindictiveness and wish-fulfilling behavior concomitantly or alternately.

Wish-fulfilling attitudes of the female castration complex may be overcompensated by reaction formation. Exaggeratedly "feminine" women may be counteracting deeper male tendencies (1313). But the counterpart is also found. Karen Horney described ostensibly masculine women whose reactive behavior wards off feminine attitudes (812). In such cases disappointments connected with men, especially fears connected with incestuous longings for the father, resulted in regressions to the old preoedipal penis envy (421, 626).

In boys whose castration complex, too, has acquired the form of a penis envy, that is, of envy of the father's bigger penis, or who have developed the idea that they are already (totally or partially) castrated and have to hide this fact, the same formations occur as in girls. It is then possible to speak also of a wish-fulfilling and a vindictive type in men, the former covering deep unconscious inferiority feelings by an externally narcissistic behavior and clinging to various forms of "denial" of penisless creatures (1080), the latter entertaining conscious or unconscious hostility toward objects which for them represent the parents who are responsible for their supposed injury.

PHALLIC CHARACTER TRAITS

Reich has described a "phallic character," also called the "phallic-narcissistic character" (1274, 1279), which, it seems, corresponds for the most part to the wish-fulfilling type of reaction to the castration complex (1080). Phallic characters are persons whose behavior is reckless, resolute, and self-assured—traits, however, that have a reactive character; they reflect a fixation at the phallic level, with overvaluation of the penis and confusion of the penis with the entire body (508, 1055). This fixation is due either to a castration fear prohibiting a full turning toward objects or to a defense against temptations toward an anal-receptive regression. An intense vanity and sensitiveness reveal that these narcissistic patients still have both their castration fear and their narcissistic needs, and that basically they are orally dependent, attitudes for which they overcompensate. Although reactive characters, they differ from typical compulsive ones by a lack of reaction formations against openly aggressive behavior; on the contrary, they employ an openly aggressive behavior as a reaction formation. As Reich stated: "The penis in these types is less in the service of love than of revenge on the woman" (1279), of revenge because they are afraid of love.

Pride and courage, bashfulness and timidity in a person are developed around the conflicts of the castration complex. Much that impresses others as courage is an overcompensation for castration anxiety, and a decisive lack of courage, which figures so largely in Adlerian descriptions of neurotics, can usually be attributed to the castration complex.

THE GENITAL CHARACTER

A normal "genital" character is an ideal concept (25, 1272). However, it is certain that the achievement of genital primacy brings a decisive advance in character formation. The ability to attain full satisfaction through genital orgasm makes the physiological regulation of sexuality possible and thus puts an end to the damming up of instinctual energies, with its unfortunate effects on the person's behavior. It also makes for the full development of love (and hate), that is, the overcoming of ambivalence (26). Further, the capacity to discharge great quantities of excitement means the end of reaction formations and an increase in the ability to sublimate. The Oedipus complex and the unconscious guilt feelings from infantile sources now can really be overcome. Emotions, then, are not warded-off any more but are used by the ego; they form a harmonious part of the total personality. If there is no longer any necessity to ward off pregenital impulses still operative in the unconscious, their inclusion into the total personality in the form of traits of the sublimation type becomes possible. Whereas in neurotic characters pregenital impulses retain their sexual character and disturb rational relations to objects, in the normal character they partly serve the aims of forepleasure under the primacy of the genital zone; but to a greater extent they are sublimated and subordinated to the ego and to reasonableness (1270).

PATHOLOGICAL BEHAVIOR TOWARD THE SUPEREGO

CHARACTER DEFENSES AGAINST GUILT FEELINGS

The mastery of guilt feelings, which are derivatives of anxiety, may become the all-consuming task of a person's whole life, just as may the mastery of anxiety. What has been said about counterphobic characters also holds true for "counterguilt" characters. However, in the realm of guilt feelings one complication has to be considered. The superego was created through an incorporation of the parents. The behavior of the ego toward the superego continues the past behavior of the child toward the parents, and not only the real behavior but the behavior that was unconsciously wished for as well. Rebellion as well as ingratiation are continued intrapsychically, and external objects may secondarily be used as "witnesses" in the various struggles between ego and superego.

Everybody who experiences guilt feeling tries to get rid of it through atonement, punishment, or remorse; he may try to prove that it is unwarranted or use various defense mechanisms against it (*see* pp. 164 ff.). Character traits reflecting these attitudes may appear individually or in combination. The various attempts to deny guilt feelings may even contradict one another, as in the anecdote by Scholem Alejchem. The woman who failed to return a borrowed pot excused herself: "I never borrowed the pot; furthermore, the pot was broken when I borrowed it, and, moreover, I returned it long ago."

Many characters are dominated by a constant drive to prove that it is the other fellow's fault. This may manifest itself in various ways. There are persons whose lives consist of being outraged by injustices and by what people can get away with; neurotic attitudes may unconsciously mean the collection of material against other people in order to justify oneself. Masochistic self-reproaches are sometimes used to force their refutation by "witnesses." Very often stubbornness is a demonstration of the fact that other people's guilt is greater than one's own.

The psychology of obstinacy was discussed previously (*see* pp. 279 f.). To be obstinate means to hold to one's own position in opposition to someone else's. Originally it consists of attempts to prove that even a weak person has some power over powerful ones. A proof of this kind may become extremely important for the child's sense of self-esteem and is developed particularly in connection with training for cleanliness. Subsequently, the powerless concentrate their attempted proofs of power in the field of ethics. The stubborn child wants to show that he is fairer than the grownups and provokes his parents to be unfair for this purpose. Subsequently, the same methods are used against one's own superego. The stubborn behavior is maintained the more obstinately, the more an inner feeling exists that it is impossible to prove what needs to be proven, and that one actually is in the wrong.

The provocation to be treated unfairly may be rooted in a need for punishment. But it may also simply aim at achieving a feeling of moral superiority. The feeling "Whatever I do is still less wicked than what has been done to me" is needed as a weapon against the superego and, if successful, may bring relief from feelings of guilt (1202).

Stubborn attitudes may be condensed with attempts to blackmail affection by the demonstration of one's misery, as a proof of having been unfairly treated in order to contradict the feeling that the misery was deserved (1277).

A patient devoted his life to proving that his own failure was the fault of others: "You see, because X made this or that mistake, I could not succeed." It was grotesque how he believed trivial little "faults" of others to be responsible for his own failure. Analysis showed that the patient's stubbornness was aimed at his own superego. It was an attempt stubbornly to prove that he had been punished in an unfair and much too severe manner. Actually he was fighting a deep guilt feeling and trying to compensate for it by sticking to an unhappy marriage. The powerful resistances, exhibited by this patient during his analysis, meant: "You see, I cannot change so long as I live with a woman who has so many faults. You also know that I cannot leave. So you will have to find a way for me to leave her, without really leaving her. If you can't it is your fault that I cannot be analyzed."

Schizoid characters, who to a marked degree have the capacity for using the mechanism of projection, exhibit their tendency to prove that the other fellow is worse than themselves by seeing motes in their neighbors' eyes. If this projection succeeds, the guilt feeling is turned into a moral campaign against the scapegoat. Many persons combat homosexuality in society instead of feeling guilt about their own unconscious homosexuality; or they are intolerant of some kind of behavior in others, while unaware that they, too, manifest it.

> The longing for a scapegoat as a relief from guilt is socially very much misused (439). In analysis, patients very often attribute to someone else an action or feeling that because of guilt or shame they are incapable of recognizing as their own. Sometimes childhood memories are recalled as pertaining to a brother or a sister; later on, it turns out that they concern the patient himself.

It is not always indignation that is called forth by another person's acts. If someone else does something (or is believed to have done it) which an individual has unconsciously been striving to do but has been inhibited from doing through guilt feelings, this may evoke admiration and bring relief, the meaning of which is: "Since others do it, it cannot be so bad after all." For guilt-laden characters, other persons finally are only tempters or punishers, personifications of the id or of the superego.

> This mechanism plays a decisive part in the psychology of art as well as in the psychology of group formation. The artist who has withdrawn from reality into his fantasies, which represent derivatives of his Oedipus wishes and about which he feels guilty, finds his way back to the objective world by presenting it with his work. The acceptance of this work means for him that the public shares his guilt, and this relieves him of his guilt feelings. The public, having Oedipus wishes of their own, admires the artist because he dares to express what they have repressed, and thus relieves them of their guilt feelings (1246, 1332). There is a decisive difference in the kind of success needed by the pseudo artist and the real artist. The pseudo artist needs to be accepted as a person, requiring applause at any cost. He adapts himself to his audience to make sure of getting applause. The artist needs to have a specific fantasy of his accepted; he wants applause for his work, not for himself. He adapts the public to himself. This sharing of guilt through art is anticipated by the "common daydreams" of children who feel relieved of their guilt feelings if their comrades participate in their fantasies (1332).
> A powerful force for group formation is the attainment of relief in the identical way and through the same initiatory act (1258). The admirers of an artist feel

themselves a community (606). To be united by the same "tempter" or "guilt reliever" is a special case of Freud's general formula: a group consists of individuals who have set up the same person in place of their superego and, therefore, have identified themselves with one another (606). The relief of guilt feeling through becoming aware that others dare to do that about which one has felt guilt is one of the cornerstones of "mob psychology." "If my whole group acts this way, I may, too." It is well known that individuals acting as a group are capable of instinctual outbreaks that would be entirely impossible for them as individuals (606). This is often stated as "in a group higher, mental differentiations and sublimations become undone again." However, neurotic blockings and distortions of adequate reactions, for example, aggressive ones, may become undone, too, and thus, through the "masses," new pathways for new achievements may be opened.

The admission of facts accompanied by the denial of their guilt-arousing quality frequently takes the form of fresh and provocative behavior. This may be combined with a provocation of punishment in order to achieve the needed forgiveness. Freud described the "criminals out of guilt feeling," who commit criminal acts because an unconscious guilt feeling troubles them so much that they hope some kind of punishment may bring relief (592). However, a "crime out of guilt feeling" may be committed not for the purpose of provoking punishment but rather as an attempt at demonstrating: "You see, I get away with such things without being punished; this shows me that I don't need to be afraid of punishment; thus my guilt feelings are unwarranted."

Provocative behavior may also be aimed at collecting compensations that a person regards as his due. This may be reactive in nature. A person who is afraid that he deserves no privileges whatsoever may behave as if it were a matter of course for him to demand all sorts of privileges. Freud named certain persons "the exceptions." Of them he said that because of early frustrations, they arrogate to themselves the right to demand lifelong reimbursement from fate (592). There is an intensification of this behavior if they have to contradict a deep inner doubt as to their right to compensation. Activity instead of passivity is revealed in the frequently encountered attitude of anticipating criticisms in the hope of provoking a contradiction that may be used as an argument against one's own superego.

In analysis, certain types of patients cannot accept the analyst's amoral and tolerant attitude. They always expect criticism from the analyst and may develop various secondary mechanisms to combat the expected criticisms.

Sometimes people first project their superego and expect criticisms or punishment by everyone, but then reintroject what has been projected. They may either anticipate the expected criticisms, and even indulge in anticipatory, cramped self-reproaches in order to enforce the flow of needed narcissistic supplies, "masochistic characters" (1277), or they may begin to criticize others in the same way they unconsciously fear others may criticize them.

In the same way that older siblings frighten younger ones to avoid being frightened, they also criticize others to avoid being criticized.

A variation of this mechanism is created by a splitting of the ego: "It is not I who have committed the guilty act, but another bad child within me." Such attitudes are a frequent occurrence in children, certain aspects of a demonology of this kind persisting even in adults.

There is also the attitude: "Although I am not good, I am, at least, able to participate in somebody else's goodness." This is a repetition of: "Although I am not omnipotent myself, I want, at least, to participate in adult persons' omnipotence." This mechanism is operative in the shaping of ego ideals. People are not only grateful for an initiatory "bad" act which relieves their guilt feeling but also for the presence of a "good" person in whose presence no bad thoughts can occur, and in whose goodness they may participate. That is one reason why the picture of the person who represents the superego is hung up. The spectator, identifying himself with his ideal by incorporating it with his eyes, becomes incapable of doing anything bad.

The community of ideals in which the individuals want to participate is again a powerful factor in group formation (1258).

Reassurances against guilt feelings may be gathered from many sources. Certain characters use other persons only for this purpose; they may be kind in order to get forgiveness, or love and affection which mean forgiveness; or they may be unkind and thus provoke punishment to "have it over with" quickly or, if the pardon is not forthcoming, at least to attain the feeling that a terrible injustice has been done.

Power as a means of combating guilt feelings is easily comprehensible; the more power a person has, the less he needs to justify his acts. An increase in self-esteem means a decrease in guilt feelings. In the same way that "identification with the aggressor" is of great help in fighting anxiety, guilt feelings, too, may be refuted by "identification with the persecutor" by stressing the point: "I alone decide what is good and what is evil." However, this process may fail because the superego actually is a part of one's own personality. Thus the struggle against guilt feelings through power may start a vicious circle, necessitating the acquisition of more and more power and even the commitment of more and more crimes out of guilt feelings in order to assert power (167). These crimes may then be committed in an attempt to prove to oneself that one may commit them without being punished, that is, in an attempt to repress guilt feelings (442, 852).

Instead of powerful rebellion one may seek ingratiation through sacrifices, through suffering, and through becoming the victim of unconsciously arranged accidents (412): by choosing "lesser evils" in the hope of paying an installment that may be accepted in lieu of the full sum (1240).

There are persons for whom such hopes are doomed to disappointment; they attempt to ingratiate themselves with a superego that has become incapable of forgiveness. This is typical for depressions (*see* p. 399). There are also persons who experience accident after accident without ever being able to placate their strict superego (1126, 1127, 1253), or who arrange their lives so that they suffer one reverse after another in miserable "neuroses of destiny" (327, 592, 608).

MORAL MASOCHISM

The methods of ingratiation with (and hidden rebellion against) a severe superego may be sexualized in moral masochism; submissive and suffering attitudes directed at the achievement of or blackmailing into forgiveness may simultaneously serve as a distorted kind of passive sexual pleasure (613). After a wish to be beaten by the father has developed, it may be displaced from the father toward fate. The childhood history of cases of this kind shows that usually the parents forced the patients to sexualize the idea of punishment by blocking all other outlets for expression of the sexual impulses. Usually there are characteristic combinations of spoiling and prohibitions in childhood, and the patients show the same inability to wait as impulse neurotics (*see* pp. 367 ff.).

A patient of Alexander's sexualized punishment and became a masochist after having been put into a chimney, a punishment that provided him with an intense anal-erotic satisfaction (37).

The childhood history of a moral masochist revealed a very weak father and a fantastic, religious, inconsistent and strict mother, who would constantly arouse the child's sexual feelings by excessive cuddling and then whip him when he tried to demonstrate his feelings. The whipping became an expression of his sexual relationship with his mother. This relationship fixed his behavior not only toward other external objects but also toward his own superego, which was modeled after his mother. The sole intense relationship of which he was capable consisted of receiving condemnation from his love objects. A superficial obsequiousness actually concealed a profound rebellion against the standards of the model he had chosen. The unconscious passive desire to be beaten had been remodeled into a desire to be condemned, and the defensive fear of being beaten transformed into social anxiety. His principal symptom was a severe fear of examinations (412).

Even without such sexualization, an unsuccessful tendency toward ingratiation with a severe superego ("unconscious feeling of guilt") (608) constitutes one of the most severe resistances (121, 713, 1288, 1289, 1599). Freud described the character type of "those wrecked by success" (592), persons who retain so strong a sense of guilt about their infantile sexuality that their severe superego does not permit them to enjoy any success.

In the analytic cure an unconscious guilt feeling may betray itself by a "negative therapeutic reaction" (608). Whereas partial analytic solutions and achieving awareness of unconscious connections through a correct interpretation usually are followed by an improvement in the patient's neurosis, or at least by a decrease of resistances and the production of new and less distorted material, such patients react paradoxically by becoming worse and by increasing their resistances.

Not every negative therapeutic reaction justifies a diagnosis of moral masochism. It may also be determined in other ways. First of all it may be provoked by an incorrect timing of an interpretation. A much too early interpretation will not be grasped by the patient at all. But there is also a time when the ego, as yet unable to accept an interpretation, nevertheless understands enough to take it as a danger signal and to increase the defending resistances. However, a negative therapeutic reaction resulting from an economically wrong interpretation remains limited to this one occasion and is, therefore, easily distinguishable from a negative therapeutic reaction rooted in the patient's character. But also the latter is not necessarily masochistic. For many patients certain arrangements or neurotic attitudes have become guarantees of a relative mental equilibrium. They are afraid of any change and look at their present neurotic state as a lesser evil; therefore, they react negatively to any change of this neurotic state until this fear itself is analyzed (818, 1315).

A patient with a phobia of high places that was successfully attacked by analysis became aware, when approaching a high place, that the usual anxiety did not appear. This state frightened him terribly, and he developed a new anxiety spell because the usual anxiety spell was lacking.

Some persons combat their guilt feelings by projecting their superego to such a degree that they do not experience guilt feelings at all, but only anxieties about what others may think (*see* pp. 293 f.).

All the ways of dealing with guilt feelings here described can be readily observed in certain religious customs and habits.

THE DON JUAN OF ACHIEVEMENT

Some persons pay the installments due their superego not by suffering but by achievements. Successes are thought of as undoing previous failures and guilt. Since no achievement succeeds in really undoing the unconscious guilt, these persons are compelled to run from one achievement to another, never being satisfied with themselves. They are the Don Juans of achievement.

A successful and rather prominent man was always dissatisfied with himself. He had external successes but no inner satisfactions whatsoever. He was always trying to increase his quite adequate income and unable to overcome his anxiety that it might be insufficient. He behaved in the same way in his love life: although women ran after him, he always felt inwardly dissatisfied, which was understandable since these relationships were completely lacking in tenderness. It is clear that the man was so dominated by an overwhelming narcissistic need that the libidinal aims were completely overshadowed. The man was married to a woman considerably older than himself, who, in some ways, behaved toward him as a mother does toward her child; she acted as his guardian, and the big, successful man was more like a little child at home. He found this dependency very oppressive, it is true, and was in the habit of revenging himself on his wife by attacks of rage, by continual unfaithfulness, and by a complete lack of consideration. Each of them made life a torture for the other. The first defensive function of his persistently unsatisfied wish to be a great man was, therefore, to deceive himself with regard to the fact that he was a little child in many ways. This interpretation was supported by the fact that his wife was continually goading his ambition, just as his mother had in his childhood.

The patient's admission that there was something behind his continued dissatisfaction, which persisted despite all his external successes, was elicited in transference analysis. As in every other province, he was very ambitious about his analysis and wanted to impress both the analyst and himself by quick success. At the outset, having read Freud, he brought forth theories about his childhood. He grasped comparatively quickly, however, that this was not what mattered, and then began to observe himself and his behavior and to behave like a "favorite pupil," continually stressing the fact, however, that the analysis progressed too slowly and that he was not satisfied with himself. On one occasion, the last session before a holiday, he came late because just as he was starting for his analysis he had a sudden attack of diarrhea. This impressed him very much. That his bowels could unequivocally express themselves gave him a new awareness of the reality of the analysis. He began to realize that his continual haste only served the purpose of concealing something. Analysis revealed that this diarrhea was, first, an anxiety equivalent. Further, it related this initially incomprehensible anxiety to his anxiety about the inadequacy of his success, of his sexual affairs, and of his earnings. Eventually it was discovered that the patient's character formation had already been complete in childhood. Even then he had been a pusher, cheeky, outwardly successful; he had always been the first, even in naughtiness. And yet he had been dissatisfied with himself. His behavior had been instigated by his ambitious mother, who kept urging him on to action. When analysis revealed that his mother had fundamentally despised his tradesman father and had said to the boy "You must be better than your father," it became clear that his behavior represented a special form of the return of the Oedipus complex out of the repression. Precisely why it had taken this form was not evident. Soon certain pieces of childhood history made their appearance. His father had illegally sold certain goods, for which a permit was required; this situation made the policeman, therefore, a particularly dreaded figure to the little boy. It also diminished the father's power in the boy's eyes. He determined not to be frightened when he was big, but to make policemen fear him. (He remained faithful to this intention; when driving, he loved to entice policemen into unjustifiable accusations, and subsequently prove them to be wrong.) The circumstances at home were such that at times he had assisted behind the counter, even at the age of six. The customers liked the little boy and chose to buy from him; he felt this as a triumph over his father, whom he already considered weak. Two later experiences further accentuated both the need to show his superiority and the possibility of gratifying passive needs. At the age of fourteen he was seduced by a maid, with whom he had regular sexual intercourse from that time on. This episode had been changed in memory to make it appear that it was he who, at this age, had seduced the grown-up girl. It needed analysis to convince him that the situation was actually reversed, and that his subsequent attitude was an unremitting attempt to transform his painful memory in terms of his wishes. (Typically for his character, this attempt failed. His intention was that the numerous women whom he persuaded to have intercourse with him should affirm his masculinity which he unconsciously doubted. In the course of the analysis it became evident that he arranged matters so that the women showed a "willingness"—and only then was he unable to resist them.) Furthermore, at seventeen, he underwent surgery several times for an abscess on the lung, which kept him in bed for months and convalescent for years, necessitating his being nursed like a little child.

It gradually became apparent that he was afraid of the transference in analysis, afraid that he might become "enslaved" to the analyst. From the beginning his transference attitude was intended to repudiate this anxiety. He attempted to disparage the analyst and to find "policemen" superior to him. Soon afterward, there was a confirmation of his real attitude in childhood. The six-year-old could not actually feel superior to his father in the role of tradesman. His father used to beat him frequently and had been greatly feared by him in early childhood. His relation to him had completely overshadowed his relation to his mother and, in consequence, his being needed by his father for business purposes had an additional libidinous value. The passive-narcissistic attitude evolved in his early childhood through several special circumstances, including illness, strict prohibition of masturbation (which put an end to his early phallic attempts), and the severity of his father. The same set of circumstances caused him to fear this attitude. In this conflict, his mother's ambition, the disadvantageous comparison of his dreaded father with the policemen, and his own success as a salesman showed him a way out: by a continuous outward fight against his passive-narcissistic attitude, he was able to retain it at other points. The seduction by the maid and his illness after puberty then fixated these latter defensive attitudes in his character (433).

APPARENT LACK OF GUILT FEELINGS

Some persons apparently suffer from a lack of guilt feelings since they readily yield to impulses, the suppression of which is customary for normal persons. The superego anomalies of "instinct-ridden characters" (1266) and the ways in which they often mirror bad social conditions in the childhood environments of the "psychopathic" patients (31) have been discussed (see pp. 373 ff.).

The mechanism of "idealization" of an instinct activity, without any deeper disturbance in the formation of the superego, may sometimes lead to a situation in which instinctual behavior is felt to be consonant with the superego's demands (840). It may also be that an unusual childhood milieu has formed a superego whose valuations are contrary to those of the average superego in a given society (40); and it may also be that after a "normal" superego has been established subsequent circumstances create a contradictory "parasitic" double of this superego (603, 1235).

CRIMINALITY AND MISIDENTIFICATION

Many cases of *criminality,* marked essentially by the execution of ordinarily suppressed instinctual acts, are to be reckoned among the "instinct-ridden characters" (1266) (*see* pp. 373 ff.), the "impulse neurotics" (*see* pp. 367 ff.), or that group of "neurotic characters," first described by Alexander (38), who tend toward the "acting out" of their neurotic conflicts (*see* pp. 506 f.). Other cases of delinquency, however, may be determined in several different ways (47, 756, 757, 927). In a discussion of this point, it must be stressed, first of all, that criminality is not a psychological concept; criminality is action contrary to the penal code (490, 649). Acts of this kind may be committed by every conceivable psychological type, normal as well as pathological. The opinion is warranted that so-called accidental criminality (40) comprises the greater percentage of all criminal deeds. Criminals of this category have a normal psychological structure and their crimes are of no special interest to psychopathology.

> This statement does not mean that analysis of an "accidental criminal" would not reveal connections between the deed and unconscious conflicts. Everything in the mind has its unconscious connections.

It is likewise no special psychopathological problem if the content of some normal superego is other than the average in a given society or than the rulers of this society demand. Many things are called crimes which the criminals, in terms of their superego, do not consider cause for any bad conscience. From the standpoint of the existing penal code, criminals of this kind have identified themselves with the "wrong objects," but the quality of their identifications reveals no anomalies (133, 136).

Identifications are essential for the construction of the character. Therefore, anomalies in the formation of identifications as well as "identification with wrong objects" result in pathological character traits. Frequent and rapid changes in the child's milieu, consisting of the disappearance of loved persons and the entry of new persons into it, may make lasting identifications impossible. The persons with whom the decisive identifications have been made may in themselves be pathological; or circumstances may make the child identify himself with the wrong aspect of a personality; or the identification may be carried out with models of the opposite sex rather than with models of the same sex (1266). Undoubtedly what is considered "masculine" and what "feminine" is not so much biologically determined as culturally. (The anatomical and physiological "distinctions between the sexes," of course, have "psychological consequences" [617], too; but these consequences are necessarily always condensed with cultural and social ones [655].) Within the frame of a given cultural tradition, however, it makes an appreciable difference whether a man behaves in a masculine or in a feminine way. The principal identification is made with the parent who is felt to give the decisive prohibitions. It would be interesting to discover the social determinants for the increasing presence of "domineering" mothers nowadays (658). Whatever the cause, the result is that men today have to contend far more than formerly with feminine traits within themselves.

All this makes it evident that the influence of the social milieu is of even more importance in shaping the character than in giving form to a neurosis. Given cultural surroundings tend to produce similar character structures in the majority of the children who have grown up under their influences, by frustrating certain impulses, encouraging others, forming ideals and desires, suggesting modes of defense and ways out of the conflicts created by these suggestions; thus "character disorders" mean very different things under different cultural conditions; what is "order" in one milieu is "disorder" in another.

"ACTING-OUT" CHARACTERS; NEUROSES OF DESTINY

Equally disturbed in their behavior toward superego demands and toward external objects are the aforementioned types in whom transference, that is, an unconscious misunderstanding of the present in the sense of the past, is extraordinarily strong; the patients repeatedly perform acts or undergo experiences, identical or very similar ones, that represent unconscious attempts to get rid of old instinctual conflicts, to find a belated gratification of repressed impulses (instinctual demands as well as guilt feelings), or at least to find relief from some inner tension. For these persons the environment is only an arena in which to stage their internal conflicts. The patients may appear as restless, hyperactive personalities (38), or their activity may be hidden and their life history may give the impression that they are the toys of a malicious fate, the repetitions being experienced passively and rationalized as occurring against the person's will (327).

Accident-prone patients have been studied by Dunbar as a specific type of personality (342).

In the analytic cure, the phenomenon of acting out consists in the patient's attempting to use the transference not merely to give an account of his newly mobilized conflicts but also to experience them again in relationship to the analyst. Certain persons behave in this way even outside of the analytic situation. Their actions in real life are repetitions of childhood situations or attempts to end infantile conflicts, rather than rational undertakings. An actual situation, somehow associatively connected with a repressed conflict, is used as an occasion for discharge (445).

These persons differ from other neurotics in one respect: the typical neurotic symptom is autoplastic and occurs within the person, whereas here the capacity for alloplasticity is retained (38, 682). A relationship with the phenomena of the manic-depressive field is evidenced by the fact that actions satisfying instinctual demands sometimes alternate with actions satisfying the requirements of the superego with a certain periodicity (1266). Preanalytic psychopathology described certain categories of psychopaths that belong in this chapter by simply naming the character of the actions that are in the foreground: "the impulsive psychopaths," "the aggressive psychopaths," "the dependent psychopaths."

Regarding the question of this intimate connection of unconscious tendencies with motor activity, Alexander only stated that there is present "a more intense expansive power in the instinctual realm" (38). This is certainly true, but what is the origin of this expansive power?

The first answer that suggests itself is that this expansion may be established where the ego can find a possible rationalization of its actions. This, however, is refutable by the fact that neurotic acting out is not always well rationalized; there are persons who act out without any rationalization, who give in to every neurotic impulse without ever asking themselves why they are acting that way.

More adequate answers are found if these patients are regarded as related to impulse neurotics and to traumatophilic patients; the basis of their peculiarity is again an intolerance of tensions. They cannot perform the step from acting to thinking, that is, from an immediate yielding to all impulses to reasonable judgment. Their aim is avoidance of displeasure rather than attainment of pleasure. As to the primary causes of the intolerance, it can only be repeated that oral fixations and early traumata play a significant role.

In Alexander's opinion, neurotic characters of this type are more easily accessible to psychoanalysis than patients with symptom neuroses. He ascribes this prognosis to the fact that in the latter the patient has regressed from alloplasticity to autoplasticity; after successful analysis he must pluck up courage to take action in real life. This is superfluous for a neurotic character who is continuously acting out in real life (38). This thesis, however, does not seem very convincing. The pseudo-alloplastic attitude of the neurotic character cannot be changed into a healthy alloplastic one except by first being transformed, for a time, into a neurotic autoplastic attitude, which can then be treated like an ordinary symptom neurosis. Internal conflicts that have been projected into hardened pseudo-object relationships must first of all be changed back into internal conflicts and dealt with as such before normal object relationships can replace them (433, 438). The intolerance of tension may make this task extremely difficult and may necessitate modifications in the classical psychoanalytic technique (445).

PATHOLOGICAL BEHAVIOR TOWARD EXTERNAL OBJECTS

GENERAL REMARKS

Conflicts between the ego and the id or between the ego and the superego cause the ego to change its behavior toward external objects. (Hence many of these changes have already been mentioned.) The interest in external objects exists because external objects represent either a threat or a potential gratification. With the development of the reality principle, the ego learns that it protects itself best against threats and procures a maximum of gratification if it judges reality objectively and directs its actions accordingly (575). Neurotics are persons in whom this ability is somehow limited because too much of the original fear and consequently also of the original urgent instinctual demands have been retained. This makes any objective "learning" difficult, because learning takes time (527, 528, 529, 536). The reality testing of these persons is disturbed. Real objects are mere "transference" representatives of objects of the past and are reacted to with inadequate feelings. The hysteric meets only the objects of his Oedipus complex and is then necessarily disappointed because the objects actually are not the objects of his Oedipus complex; the compulsion neurotic is limited to the world of anal-sadistic feelings; the orally fixated neurotic sees in objects nothing but instruments for the procurement of food and self-esteem; persons with unconscious guilt feelings meet only punishing or forgiving authorities.

Cases in which the relationship to all objects is generally disturbed can be subdivided into those in which this disturbance consists in the relations having too infantile a character, caused either by upsets in development or by regressions, and cases where some predominant need, overshadowing everything else, more or less excludes real object relationships, because the objects are used only in order to satisfy the predominant need: "pseudo-object relationships."

> Since the predominant need arose once in connection with objects in the past, the predominance of the need, too, is a kind of transference; however, the word transference is chiefly used in cases in which a certain object is reacted to with feelings that once were developed toward some other definite person; in pseudo-object relationships the relations are not personal at all, but objects are used, rather, as instruments for the purpose of relieving an inner tension.

In discussing the psychology of puberty it has been mentioned that the need for reassurance against anxieties concerning the new drives may give all object relationships an ungenuine character; they are mixed with identifications, and persons are perceived more as representations of images than as persons (*see* pp. 112 f.). Neurotic characters, who remain afraid of their drives throughout life, therefore often give an adolescent impression.

The analysis of neurotic characters offers extensive opportunity to study the various types of pathological reactions to current happenings. Latent conflicts make an adequate reaction impossible; current happenings are misunderstood in the sense of the past, either as temptations or as punishments. The discussion of the precipitating factors of neuroses (*see* pp. 454 ff.) showed examples for this.

Again, the generally frigid and the pseudo-hyperemotional personalities must be mentioned. Both types are incapable of a full and warm feeling contact with others. Instead, they have developed substitutive pseudo contacts of various types, for the most part masking narcissistic interests as interests in objects (*cf.* 1600).

FIXATIONS ON PRE-STAGES OF LOVE

The development of love and hate is a long psychological process (*see* pp. 83 ff.). Any stage of this development may be retained or revived in pathological cases. The infant's "love" consists of taking only; he acknowledges objects in so far as he needs them for his satisfaction; they may disappear when this satisfaction is attained; the satisfaction needed is simultaneously a sexual and a narcissistic one. Certain human beings remain fixated at this level. In all their relations with others the sole demand is the satisfaction of their immediate needs. For them the environment is a means of regulating their self-esteem.

Certain types, in this way dependent on external supplies, have no other interest than to fulfill the assumed expectations of others; they have no really defined personality of their own but are what they believe others expect them to be. They change completely, depending upon the persons in the immediate situation. The identifications of these persons are multiple and evanescent, and they seem to have nothing stable in their whole make-up (1334, 1537). Their attitude is that it is easier to take the risk of being refused if one plays the part of someone else—a part that may be given up, if a rebuff follows, as lightly as a dress is taken off.

Identification is the first type of object relationship. There are adult types of infantile relationships to objects that arise from the fact that all object relations remain too much based upon identifications.

"Oral characters" become easily enmeshed in the characteristic vicious circle: the very act of asking for the supplies makes them afraid of the intensity of their asking; thus they need more supplies, and thus they become more fearful. They need objects for one purpose only: to sit at their bedside as mother had sat at the bedside of the frightened child, as pacifiers, protectors, bringers of supplies, in short, as "magic helpers" (653).

Persons who are thus dependent on their environment are fixated on the level of ego development at which their original omnipotence was already lost and they were striving to get it back. Under certain circumstances, the still earlier period of primary narcissism which subjectively did not need any objects and was entirely independent (because the external objects furnished care as a matter of course) may be retained or regressively regained in neurotic states. There are introverted personalities who live as if they were still in the state of hallucinatory wish fulfillment, persons for whom the fantastic substitute thinking has entirely replaced any preparatory thinking (*see* pp. 49 f.): eccentrics who have more or less succeeded in regaining the security of primary narcissism and who feel "Nothing can happen to me." Their analysis reveals that an extraordinary environment in their childhood spared them the everyday conflicts with reality that force other children to give up the archaic stages of repudiating displeasure and to turn toward reality (*see* p. 442).

A person who manifests such "omnipotent" behavior and who seems to be especially "independent" exerts an especially fascinating effect on all the previously described characters who need magic helpers. This narcissistic behavior which gives the dependent persons no hope for any real love arouses their readiness for identification instead; the "followers," united in their common fascination, struggle for permission to participate in the "omnipotent" narcissist's power (1200).

Talented types of "introverts" may find a renewal of contact with the objective world as artists whose creations open a way back to reality. Other introverted persons break down if the difficulties of life preclude the habitual withdrawal into fantasy or some substitutive pseudo contact hitherto effective.

Introverts who are supposed to be subjectively independent of real objects (which objectively, of course, they are only as long as they have food and money) become, also subjectively, very dependent again whenever external events, for example, loss of "followers" or undeniable failures, make them doubt their omnipotence. Then they again need participation in the projected omnipotence, and their striving for identification with the objects makes them very dependent (1250). Whereas erotic daydreams in general are independent of reality (and that is their very purpose), the daydreams of persons whose erotic needs are still narcissistic ones and whose object relationships are still identifications actually depend on the real behavior of their objects. Their need may be stated thus: the other fellow ought to behave in such a way as to make the desired identification possible or, more precisely, he ought to be what the person himself would like to be, so that he, by empathy, may participate again in his own ideal. The object must behave in a certain way. The object has to behave so as to admit of the identification that the subject needs as a narcissistic supply (1449, 1575).

Persons of this type try to influence the objects by force, by ingratiation, and by every magical means, not only directly to furnish the necessary supplies (as oral characters usually do) but also to behave in a special manner corresponding to the subject's ideal. This could also be put in the following way. Narcissistic persons may in the narcissistic sentence "I love myself" project the "myself" onto another person and then identify themselves with this person so as to enjoy the feeling of being loved by themselves. To achieve it, they need the objects to behave as their unconscious wish for identification desires them to. The patients may eventually be governed only by the striving to induce the object to do what they want him to do. This, then, is not an identification proper; it is not that the ego takes over characteristics of an object; it is rather that an object is to be induced to take over characteristics of the ego ideal, that the ego, in empathy, can again enjoy the same characteristics (353). This mechanism, as a rule, is not only used for the sake of narcissistic and erogenous pleasure but also as a defense against anxiety. The patients would like to know beforehand what the object is going to do. They would know it if the object were to act according to their own ego ideal.

A frequent mechanism for achieving this end is the "magical gesture" that Reik has described under the heading of "anticipation" (1296). A person behaves as he wants the object to behave, impelled by the magical expectation that the sight of his gesture will force the object to imitate it. Actually the magical gesture is not an anticipation of what the object is going to do but of what one wishes the object might do.

> Clearly, the magical gesture, therefore, is different from objective "empathy," which consists of a temporary identification with an object for the purpose of anticipating what the object is going to do. Trial identifications for the purpose of empathy play a basic part in normal object relationships. They can be studied especially in analyzing the psychoanalyst's ways of working (518). Trial identifications for the purpose of empathy are a repetition of the archaic types of perception in general. The archaic types of perception were characterized by being performed in two steps: (*a*) an imitative identification with the object, and (*b*) attaining awareness of the changes in one's own personality, and in this way of the outside world. Analogously, empathy consists of two acts: (*a*) an identification with the other person, and (*b*) an awareness of one's own feelings after the identification, and in this way an awareness of the object's feelings (132, 975, 1598).

The magical gesture is probably a model for all the functions of the ego that are characterized by its capacity for "anticipation" of the future.

PERSISTING AMBIVALENCE

Another archaism in neurotic characters is undue ambivalence in all object relationships. This is characteristic for all neurotics with unconscious infantile instinctual aims. Since they actually are pursuing a goal that cannot be achieved, they necessarily experience every object relationship as disappointing; they may experience this frustration as a repetition of those they had once experienced as children and may react to them with the same aggressiveness with which they once had reacted to the original frustrations. Revenge is a special type of the old magical "undoing" of frustrations or humiliations, based on an identification with the aggressor. There are persons whose unconscious need for revenge overshadows all other needs and disturbs any attempt at a positive object relationship. In this category is the "revenge type" of the feminine castration complex (20). Other types are governed not directly by a need for revenge but rather by reaction formations against a need for revenge.

JEALOUSY

An inability to love based on a deep ambivalence is also apparent in those types whose object relationships are governed by jealousy (113, 426, 607, 897, 1089, 1314, 1494). Occasional jealousy may correspond to the intensity of love feelings; however, those types in whom jealousy is an ever present characteristic are precisely those who are not able to develop a genuine love because all their relations are intermingled with a narcissistic need. Jealousy is decidedly not most intense when hitherto love and gratification have been most intense; persons who are disposed toward jealousy are, on the contrary, those who change their objects continuously and readily and who are even jealous of objects in whom they have had no special interest until some extraneous circumstance aroused their jealousy. If jealousy were a simple painful reaction to a frustration, it might be expected that it would be warded off as much as possible; actually jealousy generally shows the opposite characteristic: an inclination to obtrude and to become an obsession. This shows that clinging to the conscious thoughts of jealousy serves the repression of something else.

The mixture of depression, aggressiveness, and envy with which a jealous person reacts to loss of love reveals a special intolerance for loss of love. And fear over loss of love is more intense in personalities for whom this loss means a diminution of their self-esteem. Since even the clinging to possessions may fulfill the same function for self-esteem as other external supplies do, a society in whose ideology one spouse is looked upon as the property of the other thus increases the probability that jealousy may be developed as a means to fight for self-esteem.

The obsessive character of jealousy is due, first of all, to the fact that the actual situation that aroused the jealousy reminds the person of a previous similar one that had been repressed. That an actual humiliation is consciously in the foreground helps to keep a past humiliation in the background. However, the frustration inherent in the Oedipus complex, which certainly is at the basis of all jealousy (585), has been experienced by everyone, even by persons who later are not inclined toward jealousy. Here Freud led the way through his understanding of jealousy paranoia (574, 607). In paranoia, jealousy is used to ward off two kinds of impulses by projection: impulses toward unfaithfulness and impulses toward homosexuality. Both types of unconscious impulses certainly also play a part in normal jealousy. Jealousies develop wherever a necessity to repress impulses toward unfaithfulness and homosexuality meet with the characteristic intolerance of loss of love.

Jones describes the narcissistic dependence of the jealous person on his object ("for such a man love represents a therapeutic means which is supposed to cure him from a morbid state") (897); however, he puts less stress on the primitive (oral) mechanism of the regulation of self-esteem and more on the deep unconscious guilt feelings that are intended to be counteracted by narcissistic satisfactions. Jones also emphasizes that in persons of this type the intense longing to get something from their objects for the most part encounters an intense fear of gratification of this longing. A restless flight from object to object may be caused by this anxiety (1218). Jones states: "Marital infidelity has more frequently than one believes a neurotic origin; it is not a sign of liberty and potency but of the opposite" (897). However, still more frequent than a neurotic fear of ties is a neurotic tying, a fear of any change of the object.

SOCIAL INHIBITIONS AT POINTS OF "COMPLEXES"

Even persons with less deep disturbances are handicapped in their reality testing at those points where anxiety and unconscious temptations come too much into play. Neurotics are persons who are sensitized at the points of their "complexes"; it is at these points that they fail to maintain an objective perspective in their object relations.

Neurotics suffer under the persistence of their Oedipus complex. The fact that this persistence necessarily disturbs object relationships of the moment by arousing misjudgments, dissatisfaction, and consequent disappointments manifests itself, first of all, in the characteristics of love life.

Freud described several conditions of love due to the persistence of the Oedipus complex (572). They are the "need for an injured third party," the "love for a harlot," the formation of "long chains of love objects," the fantasies around the idea of "rescuing the beloved," and, last but not least, the cleavage between tenderness and sensuality. Abraham described types of "neurotic exogamy" who combat the danger of incest in all human relationships (10).

Because of the fact that "the behavior of a human being in sexual matters is often a prototype for the whole of his other modes of reaction to life" (561), the manifestations of an unduly persistent Oedipus complex are not limited to love life proper but are encountered in all types of social relations. Things abound in illusions and disappointments.

The normal person also, in choosing objects according to the anaclitic type (585), selects them because of their similarities with infantile objects. However, the part played by similarity is limited to the selection. The normal person is able to perceive the actual characteristics of the real object and to react adequately; the neurotic, however, whose Oedipus complex has not been resolved, misjudges his objects, seeing only representatives of past objects in them. The same difference between "normal" and "neurotic" is encountered in the choice of profession. A normal person may also choose his profession because of unconscious instinctual motives. The neurotic, however, since the original instinctual impulses persist in his unconscious, will not be able to adapt himself to the objective tasks of his profession but in his work will seek only infantile satisfactions; he will work inefficiently and become disappointed.

The particular form of the individual Oedipus complex will determine the specific nature of the subsequent disturbances in object relationships. The resultant character disturbances possible are as manifold as the infantile experiences (418, 828, 1275, 1458). The family (or family substitute) situation, the number and age of siblings, the age at which the decisive conflicts were experienced, and the content of these conflicts determine the individual picture in any case.

The relationship between the age status of siblings and the development of certain types of character has been studied on various examples. An only child has the most intense Oedipus complex and is, therefore, in the greatest danger of not adjusting adequately (195, 637, 1116, 1339). The oldest child has the best chance to identify himself with his father and exert authority over the younger children; the youngest runs the danger of being spoiled; the middle child of not receiving sufficient affection (827, 1342). The early death of one parent predisposes the child to develop a kind of oral character and increases the attachment to the surviving parent and the fear over loss of love (168, 355, 979, 1325). Twins readily develop ambivalence and jealousy, an intermingling of a feeling of dependence, in the sense of needing a supplement to become a whole, and a hostile reactive stressing of independence (298, 749, 1209). Stepchildren have their specific typical conflicts and character developments (760); the problems of adopted children are similar but have their own characteristic features (970). The fantastic character of the Oedipus complex of children who have grown up entirely outside of any family is also reflected in the subsequent characterological elaborations of these Oedipus complexes (250, 979).

The same holds true for the various special forms of the Oedipus complex created by the characters of the parents (418, 658, 1275, 1458). A "weak" father predisposes boys to homosexuality (555), "maternal overprotection" to passive dependent types of mastery (1041), severe inconsistency on the part of the parents to superego disorders (31, 1266).

Many persons learn to overcome their difficulties with objects under certain circumstances, but suffer from them again when these conditions cease to be fulfilled. Quite often persons behave in a relatively normal manner with those whom they believe to be beneath them but are overwhelmed by inhibition, fear, or narcissistic need upon meeting superiors or persons of equal standing. Others develop preference for younger persons only, or if they are men, for women only, or if they are Gentiles, for Jews only, and so on.

The conditions determining relative freedom from disturbance for a person inhibited in object relationships are not necessarily restricted to the choice of inferior persons. Any human characteristic may assume a reassuring or a threatening aspect, depending upon the previous history of the individual. That which recalls old reassurances becomes reassuring, that which recalls old threats becomes threatening. In compulsion neurotics the reactions to persons are influenced by the patients' "neurotic typing" (710). Every person is (consciously or unconsciously) assigned to one or another category, and this determines the patient's type of behavior.

PSEUDO SEXUALITY

A category of pseudo-object relationships that is especially important is that of pseudo sexuality. Acts, apparently sexual, serve defensive purposes: they may aim either at contradicting the existence of perverse sexual goals by stressing the normal ones or at denying inhibitions and at combating anxieties and guilt feelings, usually by satisfying a need for reassurance through narcissistic gains. The prevailing narcissistic or infantile aims may disturb potency or sexual excitability. In other cases the physiological course of the sexual act may seem to be normal; but if a person whose sexuality actually has remained infantile tries to ward off a contradicting anxiety by ungenuinely performing acts of adult sexuality, these acts can never bring full gratification. The persons are "orgastically impotent" (1270). The narcissistic aims in pseudo sexuality disturb sexuality in the same way as the unconscious sexual aims in hysterical abasia disturb walking (1399).

In a certain sense, every infantile sexual striving in a neurotic also has a defensive character, in so far as anxiety had caused it to replace adult genital sexuality.

The best example is the pride some obsessional neurotics have in their potency. Allaying their fear in various ways, such patients may be able to carry out the sexual act and to enjoy a narcissistic functional pleasure in it; they may even feel a certain sexual pleasure but never the complete relaxation of a full orgasm. Those persons' apparent sexual behavior is isolated from their emotional sexual demands by an interpolated layer of anxiety; the sexual behavior is ungenuine and rigid (1600). Groddeck, who had a predilection for paradoxes, once said in glorification of love: "A glance, a touch of the hand can be the climax of a human life. It is not true that sexual intercourse represents the culmination of erotic life. People are actually bored by it." Certainly such an evaluation holds true only for persons with severe sexual derangement; but if such persons nevertheless engage in sexual intercourse, they definitely do so from other than genital urges.

The sexual fantasies of a woman patient had essentially the function of denying certain sexual experiences of her early childhood, and thus served primarily as defense. It was found that there was a break in the history of her masturbation.

After an experience that had again mobilized the anxiety connected with an early primal scene, she had stopped masturbating; after several years, she had resumed masturbation with great intensity as a sort of compulsive activity of a quite different character. Analysis showed that the new masturbation had been a defensive measure. She wished to fight her anxiety by convincing herself: "I am not afraid of my own body for it gives me pleasure."

Pseudo sexuality, as a rule, is used to combat inferiority feelings or castration anxiety, to obtain narcissistic satisfactions and discharges of hidden aggressive and pregenital strivings. Sexual successes may imply a variety of unconscious meanings. For one man sexual success had an outspoken anal significance; his girl friends were, for him, concrete achievements in the sense that feces had been in his childhood. More frequently the significance of success is a urethral-erotic one, ambition being a urethral-erotic character trait. Still more frequently the need for sexual success in both sexes is rooted in the castration complex. "I have to castrate in order to avoid being castrated." Sometimes sexual experiences are needed as proof that "Other people like these naughty things, too" (*see* p. 498 for the discussion of sharing of guilt, pp. 242 ff. for hypersexuality, and p. 382 for love addicts).

Some pseudo-sexual men, at first glance, seem very normal, even altruistic, as they are particularly interested in satisfying their sexual partners; however, they cease to feel consideration for the partners after their sexual satisfaction has been achieved. Actually, they never were interested in their partner's happiness but solely in proving their own ability to satisfy her. As soon as they know that they have this ability, they are no longer interested in that woman; instead they begin to wonder whether they will have the same success with the next woman. This may be condensed with an unconscious identification with the woman.

Frequently identifications that serve as reassurance against various fears are masked as "love." "Feminine" men, whose phallic tendencies have been repressed in connection with their early relation to their fathers, may, in fear of their homosexuality, develop a pseudo-sexual behavior toward women which is characterized by trends of identification and pregenitality. Persons of both sexes may use their sexual partners as they used their mother in childhood when they compelled her to sit at their bedside when they were afraid.

The difference between reactive and genuine sexuality is often very striking; reactive sexuality has the same characteristics as any reaction formation: it is cramped, inhibited in aim, reveals the underlying anxiety in symptomatic acts, consumes vast energy. Sometimes, however, the reactive characteristics are less manifest.

Critics have reproached Freud for explaining all neurotic manifestations as sexual. They have stressed the fact that sexual acts may be engaged in for the sake of power or prestige. This is certainly true, and it would be a decided mistake if an analyst were not aware of the ungenuine nature of pseudo-sexual behavior. However, the narcissistic needs of patients who seek power and prestige are not their inborn "true instincts," in contrast to sexuality. These needs have rather to be analyzed in terms of the vicissitudes of early instinctual conflicts.

The following is an example of the genesis of a character, based on pseudo-sexual behavior. A woman patient suffered from a series of severe neurotic difficulties of a cyclothymic character. Her symptoms showed that she had not succeeded in resolving oral-sadistic conflicts. In contradistinction to other severe worries, she was not at all troubled about her sexuality. In this field she felt everything was in order. She had frequent intercourse with various men, without apparently being frigid. Usually she played the part of the seducer. She acted toward these men with a motherly and friendly tenderness. The innocuous character of her sexual behavior was stressed so much that it was not difficult to perceive that it represented a reaction formation to aggressive tendencies. This reaction formation was built up by means of an identification with her mother who, although frequently strict and frustrating, had been especially kind and devoted to the patient during a long childhood illness. Hence the sexual behavior of the patient could be paraphrased: "I do not want to hurt men; I want rather to be as nice to them as mother was to me while I was sick." Analysis showed that the patient unconsciously considered her sickness a punishment for previous aggressive behavior. Her mother's kindness, which differed so much from her usual behavior, therefore represented forgiveness. The child had defended herself against fears of retaliation, which had been mobilized by her sickness, by clinging to the mother who was now so kindly taking care of her; later she had identified herself with the kind mother.

When in later childhood she was disappointed by her older friends or when her feelings were hurt, she looked for younger friends whom she could protect. Thus the tender and kind behavior was a defense against aggressiveness, and also against fear of retaliation.

Further analysis showed that the character of the patient corresponded to the structure characteristic for feminine hypersexuality. Unconsciously her interest in men meant exclusively an interest in the penis. The tenderness actually was directed toward the penis, and the penis was also the original object of the underlying aggressiveness. What was warded off by her friendly and tender sexual behavior were conflicts around oral-sadistic ideas of incorporation of the penis. The men toward whom she behaved tenderly were selected on the basis of narcissistic object choice, so that she might treat them as she wanted to be treated by her mother; basically it was the penis of these men with which she had identified herself.

Further analysis revealed details of the history of the oral-sadistic aggression against the penis. This attitude had originally been developed in her relation to her mother. A queer interest in cemeteries and anything connected with this subject was characteristic for her. In her adolescence she used to sit hours at a time daydreaming in cemeteries. She imagined the dead were especially "peaceful." Behind the peaceful and tender character of her interest in the dead, there was again hidden an intense sensual and aggressive interest in them. The idea of sitting peacefully on a grave, that is, of being peacefully united with buried persons, represented a successful attempt to refute her sensual death wishes against her mother and the corresponding retaliation fears, just as she later denied analogous anxieties by her tender behavior toward men. Again, the fear of death was rooted in the time of her illness. Her mother's previous severity had precipitated intense oral-sadistic wishes; during the illness, she had been kind and had alleviated the little girl's fear of death. These were the underlying causes for the patient's subsequent use of tenderness and sexuality as a means of combating anxiety.

The sexual behavior of this patient had the structure of a neurotic symptom. It was the expression of a deep oral-sadistic excitement. But the apparent expression of this excitement, after the interference of anxiety, was no longer orally sadistic but pseudo genital. The genital behavior did not correspond to genuine genital impulses but rather to the striving of the ego to master the dangerous oral-sadistic temptations. The patient believed that she loved objects she actually was afraid of. It was not surprising that, during the course of her analysis, the patient temporarily became frigid (423).

Disturbances in sexual object relationships reflect themselves also in extra-sexual behavior. The aim-inhibited forms of social contact and the identifications, which check aggressions and thus are the basis of all social relations, may be disturbed. Again, an overwhelming narcissistic need for external supplies and for being "accepted" may make any actual adaptation to real social conditions impossible.

Like sexuality, aggressiveness, too, may show the characteristic threefold stratification: reactive aggressiveness—anxiety—original aggressiveness. Not only overly kind persons may torment others by their excessive kindness. Besides passively compliant persons, who conceal a combativeness that must be uncovered through analysis, there are daredevils who overcompensate their inhibitions of aggressiveness (435, 1263). "Occupational neuroses" sometimes are based on conflicts around aggressiveness of this kind.

In the same way that reactive sexuality differs from genuine sexuality, so does reactive aggressiveness differ from genuine aggressiveness. A patient, apparently inclined to submissiveness and always anxious to please his environment, revealed the following infantile history. After an initial period of oral spoiling, he had been exposed to a sudden frustration. He developed intense temper tantrums; there was also a time of intense obvious sadism during which he very much enjoyed torturing animals. The character he later developed was a reaction formation to this aggressiveness. However, in the distorted form of a "third layer," the sadism made its appearance again. Despite his submissiveness, he was overbearing, ready to criticize others, and always aggressive in an indirect way.

SOCIAL ANXIETY

In the section on pathological attitudes toward the superego, the discussion of "social anxiety" was postponed. A constant fear of being criticized, ostracized, or punished is very closely related to the effect of *shame* (*see* p. 139). It stands halfway between the child's fear of castration or loss of love and the adult's bad conscience. The original content of the infantile anxieties is no longer manifest, but the danger is not internalized.

A consideration of the reactions of the environment to one's actions plays a large part in all human relationships. And, indeed, in a hundred ways every individual's existence depends on his taking other people's reactions into account. This can be called the rational component of social fear. It is very well founded; it can even be stated that an objective judgment of the probable reactions of the environment must, in normal persons, supplant the rigid and automatized superego reactions of the latency period and adolescence. The full development of the reality principle includes a certain reasonable reprojection of parts of the superego into the external world.

This rational component of social fear is definitely not pathological. Rather, a lack of it, the inability to foresee possible reactions ("lack of tact") is pathological and indicates a disturbance of the reality sense.

It is pathological, however, when social anxiety overshadows all other object relationships or when judgment of expected criticisms and punishments is objectively wrong. Social anxiety of this kind may represent either a part of the child's fear of the parents, which was never completely internalized, or a reprojection of the superego onto the environment.

The first variety of exaggerated social anxiety must be regarded as a corollary of increased ambivalence. He who hates everyone must fear everyone. Compulsion neurotics are frequently particularly polite, accommodating, and considerate. This is an expression of reaction formations that oppose aggressive tendencies. At the same time it may be an attempt to re-establish their self-esteem, lost or endangered through guilt feeling, by an appeal to the judgment or clemency of others (*see* pp. 293 f.). Anyone who needs the opinion of others to maintain his own mental equilibrium has good reason to fear this opinion, especially if he feels that he actually hates the person whose opinion is about to become decisive. It is necessary for these persons to remain on good terms with their fellow men, but their ambivalence makes precisely this extremely difficult. An impersonal variety of this type of anxiety is represented by an artist's fear of failure, or by the stage fright of an actor who requires applause to allay his sense of guilt. The original instinctual conflicts between the patient and the person whose introjection gave rise to the superego are reflected again in the conflicts between the patient and the persons whose judgment he fears. The ideas of pardoning and punishing may be secondarily sexualized.

A similar social anxiety is even more pronounced in persons with oral fixations, whose self-esteem still depends on their getting external supplies. Their social anxiety means fear over loss of this vital supply. Such persons not only long to be loved but cannot endure a state of not being loved. They become agitated when they perceive that some person to whom they are totally indifferent is indifferent to them; their fear of losing the affection of others is so great that they even fear losing an affection they never had.

Some persons are sufficiently developed so that their self-esteem is no longer exclusively regulated by getting external affection, but rather by the fulfillment of ideal demands; however, the decision as to whether or not an ideal is fulfilled is not made by the person himself but is left to persons in his environment. These individuals do not need "affection" but "confirmation." There are transitional stages to paranoid ideas of reference in persons who feel criticized by others whenever they actually are discontented with themselves.

An impotent patient of this type would crouch behind the person in front of him whenever he was at the movies and hide his face behind his turned-up coat collar. He did not want people to see him there without a girl, for fear they would know he was impotent and laugh at him.

The predominance of fear over loss of love in social anxiety must not lead to the conclusion that castration anxiety does not play a part. On the contrary, it often very obviously is at the basis of social anxiety. Many patients are governed by the continuous worry of maintaining the favorable regard of physicians, dentists, barbers, or tailors (170, 498).

These "father images," however, are not only castrators; they are also homosexual objects. The fear concerning them may be a fear of the homosexual desire for the father.

Social anxiety often necessitates an energetic suppression of all aggressive strivings and a development of submissiveness in order to make the environment well disposed; on the other hand, patients with pregenital fixations react to frustration with violent aggression. It has been mentioned repeatedly that conflicts between submissiveness and aggressiveness are characteristic for these persons.

Patients of this type often deliberately ignore or misconstrue other people's remarks or behavior which, if correctly understood, would provoke them to contradiction; they do not wish to destroy the "cordiality" of any relationship. Disharmony is unbearable, particularly if they must separate before having completely cleared up the discord.

Frequently the desired harmony is sought by relinquishing certain fields of endeavor in favor of the object and becoming "altruistic" (541). In social anxiety the field relinquished is often the field of valuation. The patients do not dare to decide what should be accepted and what rejected; they only want to find out what others expect them to do, and act accordingly.

Social anxiety is not always accounted for by incomplete internalization or by a reprojection of the superego. It may also be due to a pathological form of the superego. Hoffmann has very correctly contrasted the normal autonomous superego with a "heteronomous" superego which, instead of demanding that the ego should behave in a "good" way, demands that it behave in accordance with what is expected (803). Such an anomaly arises when the parents had shown so inconsistent a behavior that it became impossible for the child to foresee what conduct on his part would be most likely to ensure the continuance of their affection; whereupon, renouncing all attempts to distinguish between good and bad, he would take his bearings according to the demand of the moment. The heteronomous superego is the most extreme outcome of inconsistent upbringing. The relative prevalence of character disorders over symptom neuroses in recent times is due to the same indecisiveness on the part of parents and educators.

A neurotic symptomatic picture in which social anxiety is predominant is erythrophobia. It has been mentioned that in cases of erythrophobia, stage fright, or fear of examinations, the idea of being judged by others supplants the idea of sexual contact with others (96, 105, 118, 158, 405, 522, 585, 1085, 1256, 1481, 1568) (*see* p. 201). In pronounced cases of erythrophobia, paranoid components are interwoven. Indeed, all severe cases of social anxiety have certain paranoid trends, the difference being only that the patient with social anxiety feels "People might be against me," whereas the paranoid patient feels "People are against me." In ideas of reference this projection of the superego was due to a sexualization of the relation between the ego and the superego; or in other words, after regression to narcissism, the attempted reparative process could catch the "superego's sphere" only. The projection of the superego then appears as a search for objects that have been lost (*see* pp. 430 ff.). Similar mechanisms are found in schizoid personalities. Some social anxiety has to be explained as a fear of losing objects.

In all these connections one particular partial instinct is of fundamental importance, namely, exhibitionism. The exhibitionistic aim is regarded as a magical means to influence the spectator to do what one wants him to do: either to show himself or to give some kind of reassuring affection. Certain experiences may transmute this aim into fear (*see* pp. 345 ff.).

The obsessional desire to find a counterweight to guilt feelings, the narcissistic need for an external source of supply, the flight from loss of objects, the regressive sexualization of social feelings, and conflicts around exhibitionism are not mutually exclusive but actually supplement each other. Most cases of social anxiety represent combinations of these mechanisms. Among compulsive characters those who have a high narcissistic need, originating in the oral period, will subsequently tend to settle conflicts with the superego by an appeal to the environment rather than by self-imposed expiations; and this tendency again will be stronger if the patient's early development forced him to take the relationships of being observed and criticized as substitutes for sexual relationships (689, 940, 1389).

Any object relationship can be analyzed as to the relative participation of intaking, eliminating, and retaining factors. Alexander described analyses of this kind and called them the "vector analysis" of object strivings (44, 45). In the discussion of organ neuroses, its use for an understanding of the organs afflicted was pointed out (*see* p. 246). For other purposes vector analysis seems to have less application. Actually the difficulties in object relationships do not consist of conflicts among the three basic types of attitudes but rather in conflicts between each of them and opposing fears or guilt feelings. Moreover, distortion mechanisms make it impossible to state apodictically whether mental phenomena express a higher percentage of "intaking" or of "eliminating" attitudes. Strivings with contradictory aims may exist side by side and may even find common derivatives; the distortion mechanism of "representation through the opposite" may cause a latent mental attitude to appear manifestly masked as its opposite (552).

PATHOLOGICAL INTERRELATIONSHIPS OF THE EGO'S DEPENDENCIES

Anomalies arising out of the ego's relation to the id, the superego, and the environment have been discussed; still to be considered is the fourth type of anomaly, namely, disorders due to the mode of co-ordination of the urges from the three sources. However, how the ego condenses its various tasks according to the principle of multiple function depends upon the nature of the tasks; disturbances in the relations to the three authorities of the ego are also provocative of disturbances in the application of the principle of multiple function (1551). Again, only a dynamic and not a static point of view can do justice to the problem at hand. In character attitudes, conflicts between impulses and fears may be relatively frozen; still, life is an ever changing process: warded-off impulses may and do invade the warding-off attitudes, and the struggle must be continued at a different level. A given phenomenon is by no means either an instinctual impulse or a defense against it; derivatives are comprised of both. The defensive ego uses "tamed" id forces, and instincts may serve to suppress other instincts. The overcompensation of an impulse by means of an opposite impulse shows this most clearly.

In analytic practice the relativity of the concepts "instinct" and "defense" can best be seen in the application of the technical rule, "interpretation begins on the defense side," to what might be called the "reversed transference interpretation" and the "reversed sexual interpretation" (438). An analyst giving a transference interpretation says, schematically: "It is not I toward whom your feelings are directed; you really mean your father." But there are many patients who know about transference and defend themselves against emerging emotional excitement by referring to its transference nature. In such instances the "reversed transference interpretation" is necessary; "You are aroused at this moment not about your father but about me." Not until the patient is convinced of this can the origin of such an emotion be discussed. The "sexual interpretation" says schematically: "This non-sexual action has actually a sexual meaning." In the case of pseudo sexuality the "reversed sexual interpretation" must be given first: "This sexual action is not genuine; it is a defense, an expression of your fear of instincts."

Defensive attitudes which, having been turned into derivatives, express simultaneously instinctual demands were compared by Freud with the "human half-breed" (590). In a certain sense all defense is "relative defense" only; with reference to one layer it is defense, but simultaneously with reference to another layer, it is that which is warded off.

Harmonizing the various tasks of the ego is based upon a nicety of inner equilibrium so that the ego is not overwhelmed by the emotions, nor does it anxiously have to ward them off. Warded-off impulses with their tendency to develop derivatives impair the objective testing of reality; they preclude differentiated thinking and block the ego's capacity to organize its experiences (527, 528, 534, 536). Laforgue spoke of the "relativity of reality" (1004). Reality is not the same for any two individuals. However, the realities of undisturbed characters are more nearly similar than are the realities of neurotic characters.

Thus again characters who are dominated by reaction formations and pregenitally oriented are least capable of harmonizing the various demands. For this achievement, too, the attainment of genital primacy offers the greatest surety (25, 1272).

THE DIFFERENTIAL ETIOLOGY OF VARIOUS CHARACTERS AND TYPES OF DEFENSE

Constitutional factors are not accessible to psychoanalytic approach; hence the problem is to determine to what extent a given character structure or a preference for certain mechanisms of defense can be understood *historically* as the outcome of specific instinctual conflicts of the individual.

Neurotic characters, instead of reacting to their experiences adequately, respond more or less rigidly with the same reaction patterns. They are not only fixated to certain levels of instinctual demands but also to certain mechanisms of defense. Even normal persons who are flexible and able to react adequately show "habits" in this respect. By definition, character means that a certain constancy prevails in the ways the ego chooses for solving its tasks. The problem of fixation to certain defense mechanisms is but a special case of the more comprehensive problem of the relative constancy of character traits in general (369, 683). It is, however, the special case studied in greatest detail (100, 429, 541).

The fixation to certain defense mechanisms and character attitudes depends on the following:

1. On the nature of the instinctual impulses that pre-eminently have to be warded off. This is best seen in the examples of "anal character," "oral character," "urethral character."

2. On the time when the decisive conflict was experienced. The earlier the conflict was aroused, the more intense are the later disturbances. An injury to a frog's egg at the two-cell stage is more disastrous than an injury to the tadpole. Similarly disturbances in the oral period are more disastrous than those in the

genital period. At certain ages, certain defense mechanisms and attitudes, for different reasons, are more in the foreground than others: for example, introjection and projection correspond to a very early age; simple regression is more archaic than repression; reaction formation requires greater activity on the part of the ego. The specific stage of evolution of the instincts affected is equally important. If the prohibition meets a nascent instinctual impulse, the development of the instinct in question may be blocked entirely, precluding not only subsequent satisfactions of this instinct but also its sublimation, and thus impairing the developmental possibilities of the personality. If, however, the frustration occurs after the instinct has already developed, the consequences are different. The instinct cannot be really blocked any more, but it may be excluded from the rest of the personality; this calls forth the types of defense that require a constant expenditure of countercathectic energy.

3. On the content and intensity of the frustrations and on the nature of the frustrating factors. The personality of the frustrating parent is of importance not only because his attitude as well as his previous relation to the child determine the way in which the child experiences the frustration but also because as a rule a frustration provokes an ambivalent reaction toward the frustrating person which may result in an identification with him; the child then becomes either similar or markedly dissimilar to the frustrating person, or to one aspect of this person.

4. On whether or not other substitute gratifications were available at the time of the frustration. The routes remaining open for substitution or suggested as substitutes by the environment determine further development.

5. In most cases, however, analysis succeeds in showing that a special defensive attitude was forced on the individual directly by a particular historical situation: either it was the most suitable attitude in a given situation, and all later situations are then reacted to as if they still were the pathogenic one, or all other possible attitudes were blocked in a given situation, or the attitude was favored by some model in the child's environment, with whom the child identified himself, or the attitude is exactly opposite to that of a model whom the child did not want to be like. Unusual behavior can very often be traced back to unusual conditions in the childhood environment. And psychoanalyses of character disorders certainly give opportunity to study quite a selection of "unusual childhood environments"!

In analysis the phenomenon of "defense transference" makes its appearance; that is, not only warded-off instinctual demands of the past but defensive attitudes as well are repeated in the relationships of the immediate present. The defense transference depends upon two circumstances: (1) upon the tendency to react in terms of previous experience, retaining a proven expedient as long as possible and, upon the recurrence of danger, to apply that expedient even if changes in the interim make it unsuitable now; (2) of greater weight is the fact that the individual wishes to transfer his instinctual impulses. He strives again and again for satisfaction; but again and again the ego responds to this striving with the memory of the facts that at an earlier time caused anxiety. In this sense, also, the extremely painful repetition of the "passing of the Oedipus complex" (612) in the analytic transference is not "beyond the pleasure principle" (605). The individual strives for the pleasure of gratifying his Oedipus impulses. But the memory that the environment prohibited this gratification by threat is mobilized again and this necessitates a repetition of the defense.

TYPOLOGY

The description of pathological character types is rather confusing. The different criteria that have been used for classification overlap one another and this necessitates frequent repetitions. It would be advantageous if psychoanalytic characterology were to give us a dynamic classification (730). However, none of the attempts made hitherto seems to have been successful. Choosing one aspect as the criterion of the division necessarily neglects other aspects.

The most important of these attempts were instituted by Freud himself (625). After having subdivided the mind into the categories of id, ego, and superego, he asked whether it would not be possible to distinguish types of human characters according to which of these three authorities is dominant. There may be "erotic" types whose lives are governed by the instinctual demands of their id; "narcissistic" types who feel so dominated by their sense of ego that neither other persons nor demands from the id or the superego can touch them much; and there may be "compulsive" types whose entire lives are regulated by a strict superego that dominates the personality. Freud also described "mixed" types in which a combination of two forces outweigh the third one.

Of these types the compulsive character is the only one whose description really seems satisfactory. As to the erotic type it must be stated that a person who is dominated by the demands of his id may make a very different impression, depending upon the nature of the prevailing id strivings and upon whether or not his demands are capable of satisfaction. What Freud described as the erotic type seems to suggest a person whose instinctual demands are not capable of gratification, rather than a person whose instincts are genuinely very strong. A pseudo-hypersexual person is not "dominated by his strong id" but rather by the consequences of his defenses against the id. Besides this, Freud stressed to such a degree the dependence of the erotic type on the object that he actually described those types of persons whom we called persons with increased narcissistic needs. A neurotic incapacity for satisfaction and archaic regulation of self-esteem (a high "narcissistic need") seem to be more characteristic for Freud's erotic type than the fact that the accent of the personality is on the id. As narcissistic, Freud described types who have more or less preserved their primary narcissism and omnipotence; here again Freud does not have in mind persons governed by an ego whose strength would consist in reasonableness and adequate behavior rooted in genital primacy, but rather pathological types who have succeeded in subjectively remaining independent of the external world by simply not caring.

Besides the question whether Freud's descriptions of an "erotic" and a "narcissistic" type correspond to persons whose id or ego is accentuated, there is a more important objection to his suggested typology: Psychoanalysis is essentially a *dynamic* discipline. It evaluates given phenomena as a result of conflicts. It has never considered the characteristics in terms of the absolute strength of the forces operative, but rather with respect to the functional relations of these forces to one another. A categorization of "id persons," "ego persons," and "superego persons" is not a dynamic concept. What would be characteristic for dynamic types would not be either id or ego or superego but the various inter-relationships of id, ego, and superego. That is why Freud's typology has not been used much for the comprehension of neurotic character disorders (400).

Similar objections can be raised to Alexander's suggestion of subdividing people into intakers, eliminators, and retainers (44, 45). It is by no means the case that one of these three attitudes necessarily prevails. It is not the existence or strength of these attitudes that is decisive but the relation of all three attitudes toward anxieties and guilt feelings, for example, whether or not the contradictory aims create conflicts (and what types of conflicts), and this depends on the development and character of defensive forces. Frequently economic changes may turn an "intaker" suddenly into an "eliminator," and vice versa.

Alexander's classification has some points in common with Jung's classification of extraverts and introverts (908). Again the objection arises that this distinction is not a dynamic one. The same persons may be extraverts under certain circumstances, introverts under others. However, the concepts of extraversion and introversion very adequately describe two opposite types of defensive behavior; certain persons when frightened by their own impulses "flee to reality" (1416); they become hyperactive in an attempt to convince themselves that reality does not bring the fearful things they have feared in their fantasy. Other types, fearing their impulses, withdraw and become hypoactive; they feel that as long as they limit themselves to daydreaming, they may be sure that their frightening ideas will not bring about any real injury. The normal person is able to face and judge his impulses; the extravert yields to impulses before he has time to face and judge them; the introvert protects himself by evading contact with reality.

Nor is Kretschmer's attempt to co-ordinate character types with types of body structure and to distinguish schizoid and cycloid personalities as two fundamental types very attractive to the analyst (980). Although a difference between schizoid and cycloid behavior is sometimes striking, that which both types have in common seems of still greater importance: the tendency toward loss of objects and toward narcissistic regression. Schizophrenic and cyclothymic disorders are related to each other in the crucial features that distinguish them from the neuroses and from normality. Both together as narcissistic types are rather to be contrasted with the more normal object-libidinal types.

This criticism would be more fruitful if it were followed by a better suggestion. Unfortunately nothing of this kind can be offered. The differentiation of individual character traits into those of the sublimation types and reactive ones is not of much value in judging personalities, since every person shows traits of both kinds. And still it seems the relatively most useful approach to distinguish personalities in whom the sublimation type of traits prevails from those that are predominantly reactive. It had become customary to distinguish genital from pregenital characters; however, although the traits of anal or oral characters consist of both sublimations and reaction formations, pregenital traits become predominant only in cases in which countercathexes suppress still operative pregenital impulses; in other words, pregenital characters, as a rule, are also reactive characters, whereas the attainment of genital primacy is the best basis for the successful sublimation of the remaining pregenital energies.

The reactive characters, in their turn, are most satisfactorily subdivided by analogy to the neuroses, for the simple reason that mechanisms similar to the various forms of symptom formations are likewise operative in the formation of character traits.

PHOBIC AND HYSTERICAL CHARACTERS

"Phobic characters" would be the correct designation for persons whose reactive behavior limits itself to the avoidance of the situations originally wished for. However, if there is an avoidance of open streets or high places, we speak of a phobia and not of a phobic character. The situation changes if it is not external situations that are avoided but seriousness or rage or love or intense feelings altogether. Types of this kind have been discussed in the chapters on inhibitions and anxiety hysteria (*see* pp. 178 ff. and 210 ff.).

The concept "hysterical character" is less unequivocal (1601). Considering the mechanisms of hysteria, it is to be expected that traits are manifested that correspond to the conflicts between intense fear of sexuality and intense but repressed sexual strivings and, further, to conflicts between the rejection of actuality ("introversion") and the tendency to find the infantile objects again in the actual environment. Hysterical characters have been described as persons who are inclined to sexualize all nonsexual relations, toward suggestibility, irrational emotional outbreaks, chaotic behavior, dramatization and histrionic behavior, even toward mendacity and its extreme form, pseudologia phantastica.

The sexualization is of the character of pseudo hypersexuality (*see* pp. 242 ff.); because the sexual strivings are repressed, their energy is displaced and floods all relations. Suggestibility, as has been demonstrated in the relationship of hypnosis and infantile sexuality (449, 454, 606, 1378), is an expression of the patient's readiness to reactivate infantile types of object relationships. Irrational emotional reactions are analogous to hysterical attacks and consist, whenever an associatively connected experience occurs that might serve as a derivative, of sudden releases of the energies dammed up by repression. A chaotic behavior is usually due to traumatophilia; that is, it represents a striving to get rid of traumatic impressions by actively repeating them, and there may simultaneously be a fear of these very repetitions because of their painful character.

> However, not all "chaotic" behavior is of this nature. One case, characterized by extreme disorder in respect to time and money as well as to all human relationships, and for whom the expression "chaotic behavior" certainly was appropriate, turned out in analysis to be suffering from a kind of "reaction formation against a compulsion neurosis." The patient, as a girl of six or seven, had undergone a brief compulsion neurosis. This neurosis, however, had not achieved its aim. The fear that she might violate the strict rules of order (set up by a strict governess), even in some unimportant detail, was as strong as the original fears of her sexual impulses which had brought about the compulsion neurosis. External circumstances (namely, a chaotic model) then offered the patient a way out: she denied her fears connected with orderliness by becoming extremely disorderly. Her later behavior actually can be described as a "compulsion to show that she was not compulsive." When the patient first came to analysis, she gave a hysterical impression. Only in the course of the analysis did the compulsive background become clear—when the patient realized that any attempt to interfere with the chaotic behavior provoked anxiety.

The histrionic quality depends upon hysterical introversion; it is a turning from reality to fantasy and probably also an attempt to master anxiety by "acting" actively what otherwise might happen passively. However, hysterical "acting" is not only "introversion" but is directed toward an audience. It is an attempt to induce others to participate in the daydreaming, probably both to obtain some reassurance against anxiety and guilt feelings (or to evoke punishment for the same reason) and to attain sexual satisfaction through another's participation (446). It is an attempt to return from introversion to reality, a kind of travesty of the process underlying artistic productivity (1332).

Mendacity, too, may generally be called an effect of the increase in fantasy. The fact, however, that in some fantasies there is a definite pretense of reality not only shows an attempt to get back to the objective world but also serves purposes of defense.

Making use of the infantile defense mechanism of denial constitutes the first lie. "Absolute denial" is soon replaced by "denial in fantasy" (541). And the denying effect is intensified if other persons (as "witnesses") can be made to believe in the truth of the denying fantasy.

The main object of infantile denials and hence of subsequent pathological lies is represented by facts pertaining to the castration complex which injure the child narcissistically (1091).

Children try to facilitate the repression of an event by gathering associatively connected screen experiences (553). They may also construct screen experiences through fantasies and games (409, 413, 1437). The way in which this facilitates repression may be expressed as follows: "Just as *this* is only a fantasy, *that* (occurrence) was not true." Freud has shown that absurd games or fantasies often are aimed at ridiculing grownups (552). "Since you lie to me in your way, I shall lie to you in mine." Pseudologic behavior may very well be a revenge for having been deceived about sexual matters (949). However, there are similar games and fantasies that are not directed at the external world but that try to ridicule the individual's own memory. Perceptions one does not like to believe are intentionally made improbable by an absurd exaggeration. In this way, sometimes, games of a later period may aim at denying earlier sexual games by repeating them, but now without awareness of their sexual character and with an absurd and exaggerated kind of self-irony. The repression induced by such "screen games" is the more easily procured if the denial is participated in by the same brothers and sisters who originally engaged in common sexual experiences. On a deeper level, the sexual experiences are, of course, repeated in the game (1332). Pseudologia is an intermediate stage between the screen memory, the reality of which is believed in by the subject, and the usual fantasy which is strictly distinguished from reality. It does not require psychoanalysis to see that the telling of fantastic sexual experiences by a sexually inhibited woman represents a compromise between a longing to seduce and an opposing inhibition. But psychoanalysis can add that the lie serves the purpose of denial. The formula may be phrased: "If it is possible to make people believe that unreal things are real, it is also possible that real things, the very memory of which is menacing, are unreal."

Helene Deutsch has proved that the content of pseudologias consists of screen stories of something that actually happened. They are comparable to national myths which also contain historical facts, falsified by wishes (320). This must be supplemented by the statement that it is not solely a breaking through of repressed memories. The fact that the breaking through happens in this specific form, that is, as a fantasy presented as a reality, is an economic means for further entrenching the repression (437).

The object to whom the lie is told again serves as a kind of witness in the internal conflict between memory (or awareness of an excitement) and the tendency toward denial or repression (*see* pp. 145 f.).

In one case the lying appeared only at definite periods which, in analysis, were seen to be manic equivalents.

At first glance, one sees that a lie covers up the truth. Helene Deutsch showed that it nevertheless betrays the truth. To this it has been added that the manner of this betrayal anchors the denial.

Not all pathological lying necessarily has this particular structure. It may also express, in a less specific way, a person's struggles to maintain his self-esteem (*cf.* 198, 583, 1613, 1643).

COMPULSIVE CHARACTERS

The mechanisms of compulsion neurotic symptom formations reflect themselves in the character in various ways. First of all the generality of the reaction formations is characteristic; the typical attempts to overcome sadism by kindness and politeness and to conceal pleasure in dirt by rigorous cleanliness have been discussed (*see* pp. 287 f. and 471 ff.).

Besides, there is the lack of adequate feeling reactions induced by isolation. The patients may be entirely "cold," or they may produce only a limited number of feeling patterns, or they may express feelings only if certain reassuring conditions are fulfilled. The struggle for the maintenance of such reassuring conditions often characterizes the compulsive character. The total behavior of the patients may aim to prove that certain reassuring systems are valid. This may be combined with the described "neurotic typing" (710).

A patient felt well only as long as he knew what "role" he was supposed to "play." When at work he thought, "I am a worker," and this gave him the necessary security; when at home, "Now I am the husband who comes home from work to his beloved family."

This may be automatized into a kind of ego-syntonic ritual (e.g., the reactive robot type of work) of which the patient becomes aware only when it is interrupted (e.g., on holidays).

The object relationships of compulsive characters are characterized by their anal-sadistic nature. They are ambivalent and filled with assurances (often inadequate) against aggressiveness. Frequently all object relationships are characterized by the conceptions of "possession" and "presents." The thinking processes are changed in characteristic compulsive ways (*see* pp. 295 ff.). The regression to the anal-sadistic level makes the compulsive character to a considerable extent coincide with the anal character described before (*see* pp. 278 ff.). Finally the reflections in the character of the struggle against the superego and the tendency toward certain varieties of social anxiety must be mentioned. Within the group of character disorders, the compulsive character is the most clearly defined and lends itself most readily to diagnosis (1052).

There are exceptional cases where the diagnosis is not quite so simple. Secondary adjustments and restitutional "pseudo contacts" may have succeeded to such a degree that the resulting attitudes are best designated as "compulsive normalness" or a "compulsion to prove that one is not compulsive." Patients of this kind betray their reactive and pathological structure only if their "normal" routines are interrupted. Then it turns out that they cannot do without them— that is, that the routines were compulsive in nature. Occasionally the "reaction formations against compulsive reaction formations" go so far that the individual refuses any regulation and shows a chaotic behavior which gives a hysterical or even impulsive impression (*see* p. 528).

Not much is known, however, about what determines whether a compulsive character is developed simultaneously with compulsive symptoms as a part of a compulsion neurosis or whether this character structure wards off (and replaces) definite compulsive and obsessive symptoms. Both types occur. It is possible that the compulsive character without symptoms represents an arrested evolution rather than a regression.

CYCLIC CHARACTERS

The expectation that the "cycloid" person has an "oral character" is confirmed by clinical experience. However, the concept oral character comprises very manifold phenomena (*see* pp. 488 ff.). It can be assumed that the mechanisms at the basis of the changes of mood are identical with those operative in true manic-depressives, varying only in degree. The persons are characterized by conflicts between the ego and the superego, and by the ways in which they try to solve these conflicts which reflect the adjustments once made with the objects of the Oedipus complex. The ups and downs in mood may be supplanted by physical "affect equivalents" (1183, 1622).

In this group are to be included many of the "neurotic characters" described by Alexander (38) in whom success and failure alternate. All those patients who periodically "act out" present definite signs of an oral character (445).

SCHIZOID CHARACTERS

Schizoid personalities have been discussed in the section on borderline cases in Chapter Eighteen on schizophrenia (*see* pp. 443 ff.). They are characterized by an augmented narcissism which may manifest itself in an intense need for approbation by others, but more frequently is of the nature of a primary and omnipotent narcissism, independent of other people and distorting the patient's reality testing (1380, 1635). The narcissistic fixation betrays itself in the readiness of the patients to react to frustrations with partial losses of object cathexes. In many ways object relationships and emotions may be supplanted by pseudo contacts and pseudo emotions. The increase of narcissism is often a reactive one. The patients are unable to endure any narcissistic injury and reassure themselves against such injuries by regressing to primary omnipotence (524, 1250). The ability to retain or more or less to reactivate the attitudes of primary omnipotence is typical; it may sometimes be due to unknown constitutional factors; at other times the primary narcissism has been fostered by an abnormal environment. Since persons of this kind necessarily encounter many frustrations, they are always filled with unconscious hostilities. However, the hostilities, too, are warded off and hence are usually not felt as such. Emotional responses may be supplanted by patterned behavior, by vacant smiles or by other catatonoid attitudes.

The characteristics of unstable and easily relinquished object relationships with archaic features have been described (see pp. 444 f.). So have the "as if" characters with their ungenuine pseudo emotions (331, 333). Paranoid characters, laden with suspicions and jealousy, represent abortive delusions of persecution or jealousy. Hebephrenoid personalities who are generally inhibited in all activities often are indicative of vast reaction formations against aggressive tendencies. Catatonoid behavior often implies a scar remaining from a psychotic episode which has perhaps not been recognized as such.

Regarding the principal distinction between schizoid characters, namely, between persons who are on the verge of becoming psychotic and persons who by some kind of bizarre character attitude seem to be assured against any psychosis, reference is made to Chapter Eighteen on schizophrenia (see p. 446).

DIGRESSION: TWO SHORT CASE HISTORIES

The insufficiency of a theoretical description of mechanisms becomes more evident in character disorders than in the case of symptom neuroses. This insufficiency is of a dual nature. First, the types described are an outcome of external influences on the biological structures and vary, therefore, with the external influences. What is not stressed enough in a mere description of types is the fact that they are types of today's world only. The prevailing character structures are especially characteristic for a given culture, and sometimes for a given stratum in a given culture. Specifically it is the conflict between the contradictory aims of "active independence" and "passive-receptive longing," both of which are stimulated by present-day social conditions that determine today's pathological character structures (819). Second, the types never correspond point for point with the individual cases.

It may, therefore, be permissible to illustrate the historical determination of character disorders by brief condensations of two case histories previously published (433, 442a).

A patient was characterized by the haste with which she always undertook every more or less unimportant enterprise. She was physically as well as mentally continually in a state of tension, always occupied with the future, never living in the present. This continual activity of the ego remained on the surface to an amazing extent. Her associations spread in every direction without ever getting any deeper. Her interests and occupations also bore the stamp of a superficiality that did not correspond to her intelligence and talents. She avoided everything that had a "serious" character. In describing her experiences she expressed a peculiar sense of inferiority: "Nothing that happens to me can be serious or real." Her superficial "playful" activity, her restlessness, and her continual worry about what would happen tomorrow served the purpose of forestalling any serious experience.

The patient, who was married, was passionately in love with another man. She could not leave him, although the affair aroused serious conflicts in her. In anxiety and trouble and, in particular, at the beginning of a depression, she escaped—much as a drug addict escapes by means of his drug—with the help of real or imagined experiences with this man. It soon became clear that it was not real love that drove her to him, but that he satisfied narcissistic needs whose fulfillment repelled anxiety or depression. However, it was not clear in what way he achieved this. Gradually it became apparent that the chief attributes of this man—and in this he was the diametrical opposite of the patient's husband—were that he was humorous, apparently frivolous and witty, and never called things by their right names. What the patient really sought from him was the reassurance: "I need not be afraid of sexuality; it's only fun." In an earlier analysis the patient had from the very beginning developed the resistance of not speaking, and no progress was made. This had happened because the analysis was "serious" and because its aim was to face reality, "to call things by their right names," which the patient wished to avoid at all costs. The second analysis, on the contrary, appeared to make very rapid progress. It took a long time to understand that this progress was apparent only and was the result of a particular resistance. The analyst had, by chance, laughed at some remarks the patient had made during her first sessions. This enabled her to work "in isolation." What she had was an analysis conducted "in fun," just as she enjoyed sexuality "in fun," so that the analysis really did not attack her anxieties about her instinctual life. Like a child at play, the patient anticipated in active games future events; but she never succeeded. Her anxiety was too great for her to make the step from play to reality. She always had to assure herself: "It is only a game and not serious." Analysis showed that "serious" sexuality had acquired its frightening character when, at the end of the patient's fourth year, the birth of a brother had aroused her sadism. She had the unconscious fear that if she yielded to her real impulses, she would tear the penis from men's bodies, and children out of women's bodies. The escape into "playing" was due, among other things, to one particular incident in the nursing of the younger brother. An elder sister had suggested to the patient that she should push over the perambulator to get rid of the intruder. From that time on the patient was terrified of touching him, particularly after she had once noticed how her mother and the nurse had laughed over the little boy as he was urinating. Her mother had tried to relieve her of this aversion to touching him by saying: "Take him in your arms; I'm standing here; you're only playing at being his mother; you're not really his mother."

Another patient revealed the following contradictions in his behavior. On the one hand he had clear-cut feelings of inferiority, which manifested themselves in constant ambitious strivings (the impossibility of really satisfying his ambition together with certain disturbances of potency were the reasons for his coming to analysis). On the other hand he was in reality completely inert, lived a retired life, had no genuine object relationships, and felt contented when undisturbed by the outside world. His ambitious fantasies were of a very childish character and centered around the idea that he wanted to show himself as the stronger one; the imagined competition was extremely primitive—on the level of mere fights among boys. It was comparatively easy to see that the victory was of less importance to him than the recognition and affection that would be his because of the victory. The common goal of his ambition and his laziness was to live in narcissistic self-sufficiency with supplies flowing in from the outside. Although he was quite successful in his career and had developed pseudo contacts as substitutes for object relationships, so as to avoid the external appearance of being pathological, his inner life was astonishingly colorless. He regarded his professional work as a necessary evil that was to be got over with as quickly as possible. He had no particular interests, at least none on the level of his intellectual abilities. He tended to become depressed if he felt that he was not immediately loved by everybody. His relationships with women were so superficial that no long analysis was necessary to sense the latent homosexuality back of them. However, the relationships with men were also narcissistic in nature, and fundamentally consisted only of childish competitive fantasies. The better one knew him, the more one saw to what an extent he was dominated by a primitive narcissistic need. He expected that as soon as he felt a need, the object world should gratify it, without his showing the slightest inclination to do anything for others, indeed without his being able to feel that other people have needs.

It took time until the infantile elements of this narcissistic fixation became clear. One of these elements was the mother's nature. She had been a very active person who used to make incessant demands on both her boys in many ways, especially in regard to cleanliness. The patient recalled that he had felt "bothered" by his mother and her demands all through his childhood, and kept striving to evade them. However, a second element was of greater importance. Throughout his childhood there had been an old nurse in the home who had functioned in every respect as a "countermother." Through her the patient was enabled to realize the narcissistic spite fantasies, originally aimed at his mother. He was absolutely certain of the love of his nurse; he could do anything he pleased as far as she was concerned. He got everything he needed from her without ever having to recognize that she, too, was a human being with feelings.

Is this pampering of the primitive narcissism of a child sufficient explanation for a character fixation that permits the avoidance of every vital activity, not only of love relationships but of intellectual activities as well? Certainly not. There is no doubt that the avoidance of vital activities was equivalent to a general phobic attitude, that the patient tried to avoid the full intensity of life as an agoraphobic avoids going out on the street. That he carried out this evasion by clinging to a primitive narcissistic attitude was sufficiently explained by the existence of the nurse. This, however, did not explain what the dangers were that caused him to withdraw. The dreadful nature of the mother's demands had to be understood and supplemented.

The never ending competitive fight to which the patient abandoned himself in his fantasies, but which he avoided in reality, as well as a corresponding attitude in the transference situation were a persistent reminder of the fact that he had a brother three years older than himself, and that his few childhood memories always showed him in the company of his brother and the brother's friends. His "fighting boys" point of view must have corresponded to the wish at some time to be stronger than the older boys around him, and the hopelessness of this wish obviously made him recoil from these boys to the nurse. It may be presumed that the attitude of oral demand toward the nurse was based upon a "return of the repressed from the repression," and that in his relation to the older boys a passive-receptive homosexuality had developed that had been overcompensated for by the wish to be stronger than they; and because this was unrealizable he had again regressed to receptivity. When this was explained to the patient, he responded with a surprising recollection. At about ten years of age and thereafter, he had surpassed his brother in physical strength. There were frequent fist fights between the two boys, and the patient was always the victor. This triumph resulted in his trying to repress his recollection of having been the weaker at earlier periods, by means of developing the ideal of the "fighting boys." The unconscious passive-receptive yearning for the period when he was the weaker was the reason why this ideal remained theoretical, and why in reality he lived on in the "world of the nurse."

When the patient could not surpass others, he always felt the impulse to attack or to insult them, and he was afraid that sometime he might yield to this impulse in a compromising way. Actually he avoided any active sadistic step, which would have served the purpose of denying a certain pleasure in being the weaker. But again, this kind of denial would not have been possible if in the depths there had not been some more fundamental sadism which betrayed itself in his continual fight fantasies as well as in the oral avidity with which he demanded immediate satisfaction of all his needs.

This sadism evinced itself likewise in his only hobby, hunting, which alone seemed to him to make life worth while. The analysis of this hobby resulted first in the realization that the joy in shooting animals was as little a direct genuine instinctual expression as the fantasy of suddenly beating to death those rivals whom the patient so feared that he avoided social gatherings. It was possible to bring the patient gradually to a point where he relived the still existing fear which he had not felt since childhood (except for several circumscribed fears—for example, a clear-cut syphilophobia from which he suffered). Various fears made their appearance at first in dreams, then in daytime symptoms as well, fears which increasingly assumed the characters of certain dreadful demands being made of him, and from which he tried to escape through stubbornness. He sometimes used to lock himself in his office and go to sleep, meanwhile experiencing great pleasure in the thought that others believed he was working and that no one could reach or disturb him. He observed that it was fear again that always caused him to break off his love affairs, as well as his friendships with men, when a certain intensity of feeling was reached. Finally, to his surprise, he noticed that the sole course of pleasure for him, the hunt, likewise had fear as a basis.

The hunt offered the patient opportunity to satisfy certain fetishistic traits: he loved high boots and rough clothing. Obviously he did not know the sexual character of this preference, inasmuch as the fetishistic character of boots and clothing was limited to masculine attributes. In speaking of the odor of rubber, he had an indistinct memory of rubber sheets that had been used in his bed in the nursery. Here for the first time the topic of enuresis was touched, and the impression arose that the "masculine" boots and clothing were intended to deny some sort of passive-childish ideal, just as the idea of conquering his brother covered the recollection of a time when he had been the pet of bigger boys.

The story of his passion for hunting brought out, also, for the first time, his relationship to his father. The father had not been a hunter but a fisherman. While he was standing in or near the water to fish, the youngsters were allowed to shoot small birds with popguns. During such outings the little fellow always felt very "manly," a feeling he revived in his present joy in the hunt. But anxiety dreams relating to water, which occurred with ever greater frequency, led finally to the realization that this joy likewise had a hidden counterphobic meaning: "I am a hunter and not a fisherman." His father's fishing must have aroused anxiety in him. He had overcome this anxiety in a sort of counterphobic pride: that he was allowed to go off with his father on a masculine jaunt. Nevertheless, he could enjoy this pleasure only in the hunt, whereas it now grew increasingly clear that hitherto unconscious anxiety was connected with fishing and all activities associated with water. Several peculiarities of his behavior while hunting showed that he always strove to connect his hunting activity in some way with "water," but with the wish that this connection never be too close. Although as a child he had been afraid of swimming, he now tried to force himself to swim, but it gave him no pleasure whatever. Dreams and fantasies brought out that the water he was afraid of represented dirty water, a fact revealed by the analysis of the inordinately intensive anal and urethral eroticism against whose demands his entire pathological character had been erected as a defense. Two further factors contributed to the development of the patient's pathological character. The first is connected with the father, who had impressed the youngster as extraordinarily manly, whose chief interest was certain athletic activities, and who himself seems never entirely to have overcome the "fighting boys" point of view. Moreover, he laid great stress on the matter of clothes. The homosexual ties of the patient were directed toward the father, who often used to go out with the boy, especially to take him along to parties, and to show off with him. On these occasions the patient on the one hand experienced manly pride and, on the other, fear that as a little boy he was not equal to his manly task. For this reason he preferred to stick to his nurse and to his primitive narcissism. The idea of always being handicapped in social gatherings because he could not yet compete with the more adult men as well as the other idea of avoiding such gatherings because he might injure the others in a sudden sadistic outburst went back to his ambivalence toward his father, who had used him in an exhibitionistic way.

The second thing is that during the early years of childhood the patient shared a bed with his brother. That which he fantasied hazily as enticing and dangerous in connection with his father, he actually experienced with his brother. These homosexual excitations which he sought to re-encounter by regressing to a primitive oral narcissism, had found their expression in enuresis. The patient was made to feel ashamed, by his "demanding" mother, for this bedwetting. He resolved, as a revenge for her belittling him, henceforth to live only for his own gratification and to have consideration for no one else. This determination finally was shattered and led to secondary conflicts.

The pregenital fixation, which found expression on the one hand in bedwetting and on the other in oral regression, went back to early stomach and intestinal disturbances.

This crude and schematic résumé suffices to show how the character peculiarities of this patient were determined by a combination of circumstances in his childhood environment. The nurse who pampered him, the demanding mother, the older brother, the fact that this older brother later was physically weaker, the exhibitionistic, boastful character of the father—only when all these circumstances are taken together does the development of this patient become understandable.

PSYCHOANALYTIC TECHNIQUE AND THERAPY IN CHARACTER DISORDERS

Analytic therapy in the case of character disorders meets with specific difficulties. The attitude of the patients toward their disorder differs from the attitude neurotics have toward their symptoms. Although patients with symptom neuroses have their resistances, too, and although character cases may be very discontented with themselves and may be striving for a change, nevertheless there is a difference between a man who tries to get rid of a disturbance at the periphery of his personality and a man whose "personality" itself is going to be attacked. It is relatively easy as long as the person himself has insight into the pathological character of his behavior patterns (even then the fact that the patterns are alloplastic and more rigid than symptoms will create difficulties); it becomes more difficult when the patient has no insight and recognizes neither his pathological attitudes nor the fact that the chief part of the conflicting energies the analysis aims to release is tonically bound in the attitudes, or when the very nature of the attitudes is such as to interfere with the process of analysis.

The analytic procedure relies on the co-operation of a reasonable ego, to which unnoticed derivatives of the unconscious are demonstrated by interpretation. Freud, therefore, once said that "a fairly reliable character" is one of the prerequisites for a successful analysis (554). And yet we now are asking ourselves whether "unreliable" characters can be cured by analysis.

This can be done only if the analysis succeeds in first making the patient aware of the problematic nature of his behavior. After the patient has been wakened to amazement about what he does, he must become aware of the fact that he is compelled to act as he does, that he cannot act differently; then he has to understand that it is an anxiety (or a guilt feeling) that makes this specific behavior necessary, that he needs this behavior for defense purposes. He will learn to understand historically why these defenses had to have their specific form, and eventually what he is afraid of. If the mobilization of the old conflict succeeds, he will experience anxiety and subsequently the instinctual impulses in question, instead of his rigid and frozen attitude. Thus the character neurosis will be changed into a symptom neurosis, and character resistances into vivid transference resistances; afterward they will be treated the way symptomatic neuroses and transference resistances usually are handled (1279).

This, then, is the situation. Once there was a conflict, urgent and alive. The subject withdrew from this struggle by means of a permanent ego alteration. The forces that at one time opposed each other are now wasted in the useless and rigid defensive attitudes of the ego; the conflict has become latent. By separating the reasonable, observing ego from the automatic, defensive, experiencing element, the bound-up energy must be set free and the old conflict reactivated (1497).

It is comparatively easy to see what has to be done; the requisite analytic task is to thaw the frozen energies of the inert attitude. It is, however, much more difficult to *fulfill* this task, to find the point where the defensive system is most insecure, where the neurotic defense is less rigid—the points and times, in other words, where the fight between instinct and defense has remained most alive; what has to be done is to rectify displacements, undo isolations, and direct affect traces back to where they belong (433, 438).

As to the remobilization of old conflicts, which are not effective any more, Freud once doubted whether it could be achieved at all (629). In order to transform a latent instinctual conflict into a live one, he says, "clearly there are only two things we can do: either we can bring about situations in which the conflict becomes actual or we can content ourselves with discussing it in analysis." Concerning the first, "we have so far rightly left to fate" the task of bringing fresh suffering into life, and, furthermore, it would not be possible anyhow. The second is useless, since mere discussion will not help any more than reading Freud's works will cure a neurosis (629). It is easy to reject these two alternatives; but it is not certain that they are the only two possibilities. There is a third one: Latent conflicts are never completely latent. The analyst is accustomed to divining the presence of strong forces behind the smallest signs. It is his task to remobilize conflicts, not to create new ones. He must make these signs so objective that the patient can recognize them as derivatives of the more important latent conflicts that he had refused to feel. If the decisive part of the rigid instinctual energy is to be made capable of discharge and mental health to be restored, then indeed the task is first to "turn a possible future conflict into a present one" (629).

This means that situations must in fact be provoked in which the conflict becomes actual, not through the analyst's playing the part of fate in the real life of the patient nor by joining in the transference through artificial behavior on his part but by psychoanalyzing at those points at which the latent conflicts are actually hidden, by demonstrating the attitudes in question as derivatives, and by making it possible for the observing and reasonable ego again to face that which, due to resistance, had been evaded until then.

It is particularly urgent that the personality first be released from its rigidity, because here is where the pathogenic energies are really bound. Frequently, even in cases in which a vivid struggle between instinct and defense appears at other places, directing the attention to the rigid defenses may be of decisive importance (74, 75, 438, 1279).

The question may be raised whether there is any analysis that is not "character analysis." All symptoms are the outcome of specific ego attitudes, which in analysis make their appearance as resistances and which have been developed during infantile conflicts. This is true. And to a certain degree, really, all analyses are character analyses. Some part of the energies, which are spent in useless defensive conflicts and must again be placed at the disposal of the individual, is always bound in "character resistances." However, there still remains an appreciable degree of difference between the analyses of symptom neuroses and character analyses proper.

So much as to difficulties common to all character disorders. Besides them, the question of the indication for analysis varies greatly. Character disorders do not form a nosological unit. The mechanisms at the basis of character disorders may be as different as the mechanisms at the basis of symptom neuroses. Thus a hysterical character will be more easily treated than a compulsive one, a compulsive one more easily than a narcissistic one.

Besides the variations in underlying mechanisms, the insight, the will to recovery (1174), the readiness to co-operate, the mental elasticity necessary vary considerably. Concerning the secondary gains, a character disorder will be the more difficult to attack if the pathological attitude until then has brought the patient more advantages than disadvantages. If attempts, for example, at narcissistic overcompensations have not yet met with frustrations in reality, the patient will cling to them more than after severe disappointments. Certain neurotic character attitudes may even have helped to achieve some real success, or at least some pride and increase in self-esteem, and then the analyst's attempts to demonstrate their real purpose will be met with more intense resistance.

The depth of the regression, the intensity of the resistances, the readiness to understand and to co-operate, and the patient's mental elasticity will have to be judged in a trial analysis (*see* pp. 580 f.).

The aforementioned difficulties, particularly the necessity of making the patient aware of his behavior patterns and of thawing his frozen attitudes, in general necessitate a much longer time for character analyses than for symptom analyses. They also present special technical tasks that cannot be discussed here (*cf.* 438). However, there is no reason for discouragement (1361). What Freud once said about analysis in general is especially true of character analysis: Although it cannot alter the individual constitutionally and its effectiveness thus remains limited, it may change the patient into what he would have become had his life circumstances been more favorable (596).

E. Combinations of Traumatic Neuroses and Psychoneuroses

CHAPTER XXI

Chapter XXI

COMBINATIONS OF TRAUMATIC NEUROSES AND PSYCHONEUROSES

THE distinction between traumatic neuroses and psychoneuroses is an artificial one. This classification is very useful from a theoretical point of view; it is instructive to consider that the decisive state of tension forming the basis of a neurosis can be brought about by too much influx as well as by too little discharge. Actually, however, these two types of neurotic conditions interact. After the individual has experienced too much influx, he is afraid, cuts himself off from the external world and therefore blocks his discharges; an experience of a trauma creates fear of every kind of tension, sensitizing the organism in regard even to its own impulses. If, on the other hand, discharges are blocked, a little influx, otherwise harmless, may have the effect of one much more intense, creating a flooding. A neurotic conflict creates fear of temptations and punishments and also sensitizes the organism in regard to further external stimuli. "Trauma" is a relative concept (513).

In the chapter on the traumatic neuroses, it was stressed that there is no traumatic neurosis without psychoneurotic complications; a certain study of these psychoneurotic complications was necessary for an understanding of the clinical course of traumatic neuroses (*see* pp. 121 ff.). A few words must be added about the reverse, the traumatic elements in the psychoneuroses.

In general the symptoms of actual neuroses are very similar to those of traumatic neuroses; both are due to a state of being dammed up, which, it is true, is brought about differently in each condition. However, one element that is characteristic of traumatic neuroses is missing in actual neuroses: the characteristic *repetitions* of the trauma in dreams and symptoms. These repetitions represent attempts to achieve a belated mastery, fractionally, of the unmastered amounts of excitation (605). Repetitions occur in all psychoneurotic phenomena, too, but there they are of another nature; for example, symptoms may repeat childhood experiences over and over again, even if they were not pleasant. Neurotic phenomena are characterized by the fact that the patients, instead of reacting vividly to actual stimuli according to their specific nature, react repeatedly with rigid patterns. The instinctual impulses themselves are also repetitive: they are felt periodically and tend to take the same course each time. Besides, there are unproblematic repetitions, like repetitions of actions or attitudes that once proved useful, that occur whenever similar conditions again prevail, or, generally, repetitions in response to repeating (or similar) stimuli.

Freud spoke about a repetition compulsion (605), and this conception has been much discussed in psychoanalytic literature (145, 431, 771, 977, 991, 992, 1064, 1180, 1182, 1469). However, the repetitions mentioned are of very different types. Neglecting the "unproblematic" repetitions, three categories must be distinguished:

1. *The periodicity of instincts, rooted in the periodicity of their physical sources.* It represents a somatic problem, but one with profound psychological consequences (102, 257). Not only do the instinctual drives recur periodically, but "derivatives" of instinctual drives also reflect this periodicity. Every kind of hunger is ended by satiety, and satiety, after a certain time, gives way to hunger. The periodicity of the manic-depressive phenomena probably belongs in this category.

2. *Repetitions due to the tendency of the repressed to find an outlet.* This is the core of the characteristic psychoneurotic repetitions (991, 992). They are most pronounced in the so-called neuroses of destiny, in which the patient periodically evokes or endures the same experience (327, 613). What happens is that a repressed impulse tries to find its gratification in spite of its repression; but whenever the repressed wish comes to the surface, the anxiety that first brought about the repression is mobilized again and creates, together with the repetition of the impulse, a repetition of the anti-instinctual measures. Neurotic repetitions of this kind contain no metaphysical element. They represent simply the continuation of the fight between the repressed and the repressing forces. What has not been gratified strives for gratification; the same motives that first denied gratification are effective later. Thus even the repetition of the most painful failure of the Oedipus complex in the transference during an analytic cure is not "beyond the pleasure principle" (605). The painful passing of the Oedipus complex (612) is not the thing the person tries to repeat; rather he is striving for the gratification of the Oedipus wishes. But this striving mobilizes anxiety, and the repetition of a painful experience is the objective result.

Repetitions in compulsive rituals (compulsive counting) constitute a section of this category (*see* pp. 153 f. and 288 f.).

3. *Repetitions of traumatic events for the purpose of achieving a belated mastery.* This type of repetition is seen first and most clearly in children's games,

where what was experienced passively before is repeated actively in an amount and at a time chosen by the ego. The same pattern occurs in the repetitive dreams and symptoms of traumatic neurotics and in many similar little actions of normal persons who in thought, stories, or actions repeat upsetting experiences a number of times before these experiences are mastered (605, 1552).

The repetitive phenomena of psychoneuroses as a rule are of type (2), the repetitive phenomena of traumatic neuroses of type (3).

There is a category of neuroses in which elements of "neurotic conflict" and of "trauma" are simultaneously present, neuroses in persons whose motivations of defenses against instinctual impulses are based on specific traumatic experiences in their childhood (431). This can be recognized by the fact that the repetitions that occur in the course of these neuroses are at the same time of type (2) and of type (3).

Type (2) of repetition is not intended to be a repetition. When the excitement is "repeated," it is done so in the hope that its outcome will be different, a gratification instead of the preceding failure. But this intention fails, and what actually occurs is a repetition of the frustration. Sometimes it is obvious that the ego is striving for a "repetition under different circumstances," for example, in the presence of reassuring measures which would make possible the hitherto blocked gratification.

Type (3) is characterized by different features. The ego's attitude toward the repetition is a very ambivalent one. The repetition is desired to relieve a painful tension; but because the repetition itself is also painful, the person is afraid of it and tends to avoid it. Usually, therefore, a compromise is sought: a repetition on a smaller scale or under more encouraging circumstances. The ambivalence toward this repetition shows itself in the phenomena of traumatophilia and traumatophobia (1070, 1244), in the fact that whatever these persons undertake turns into a trauma; they fear this, and nevertheless they strive for it. There are many varieties of this mixture of fear of repetition and striving for it. When the striving is unconscious, the patients, in spite of a fear of upsetting experiences, experience very upsetting things every day; they run from catastrophe to catastrophe; everything is disturbing and filled with emotion; there is never time, distance, or relaxation enough for them to quiet down. At other times, the wish for repetition is more conscious, and the patients long for one dramatic experience, to end their misfortunes once and for all (445).

It has been mentioned repeatedly that in certain neurotic persons the fear of castration or over loss of love is overshadowed by a more superficial fear of their own excitement which, through the blocking of its natural course, has acquired a painful character. Patients of this type, therefore, are afraid of end pleasure; when sexually aroused, they long for a "dramatic" experience and yet fear it.

This occurs in patients in whom the judgment "excitement is dangerous" has been brought about by the memory of infantile sexual traumata, either primal scenes or actual seductions. The symptomatology of these patients reveals a condensation of returns of the repressed instinctual conflicts with repetitions of the traumata, constructed according to the repetition type (3).

Patients suffering from these neuroses are worse off than those with acute traumatic neuroses because of the physiological character of sexual excitement. If someone has suffered an external trauma, for example, an automobile accident, he will, for a certain time, dream about the accident, be unable to enter a car, begin to tremble upon seeing a car, and so on. This will continue until the unmastered amount of excitement is discharged. After a while the symptoms cease. If, however, the trauma was of such a nature that it resulted in the ego's judgment, "sexual excitement is dangerous" (or rather, more specifically, "the loss of ego at the height of sexual excitement is dangerous"), this judgment causes the ego to interfere with the normal course of sexual excitement every time anew. This interference causes a displacement of the excitement from the genital apparatus to the vegetative nervous system. This is felt as pain (anxiety), confirming anew the erroneous idea of the ego about the danger of sexual excitement. The fact that sexual excitement is continuously renewed from physical sources never permits such a neurosis to subside. The patient has entered a vicious circle. The "belated mastery," which the repetitions strive for, is never obtained because every attempt to reach it brings about a new traumatic experience. It is as if a person who tries to enter a car after an automobile accident has to go through another accident each time.

> Some types of morbid fear of death when analyzed turn out actually to be fears of orgasm, after the concept of orgasm has been turned into that of a trauma (*see* p. 209).

To a certain degree all primal-scene neuroses are of this type. The primal scene has made the patients fear sexual excitement. The fear turns excitement into painful sensations. The experience of these sensations is felt as a repetition of the primal scene. This is complicated by the fact that repetitions of the primal scene are also sought in the same way as the traumatic neurotic seeks repetitions of the trauma.

Certain neurotics give the impression that they labor in vain throughout life belatedly to master the impressions of a primal scene. A sadistically perceived primal scene may change the character of the world for a person in such a way that he vacillates between fearfully expecting the repetition of this trauma and actually performing it. The traumatic experience not only sets up a kind of inconclusive traumatic neurosis but simultaneously increases the disposition for the development of psychoneuroses, because the memory of the trauma increases the effect of all later sexual prohibitions and frustrations. (Conversely also, preceding prohibitions and frustrations may cause a later primal scene to have a special traumatic character.)

Regarding the question of what sexual components are especially concerned in neuroses of this kind, it seems that any partial instinct may be involved. However, a few of them are usually paramount. The role played by the eroticism of sensations of equilibrium in the fear of one's own excitement has been mentioned (*see* pp. 203 ff.); so also has the role of muscular eroticism when a tic has eternalized the memory of a primal scene (996) (*see* p. 321). In men, the fear that the ego may be overwhelmed is certainly more intense if passive-feminine wishes are in the foreground; sadistic strivings, in both sexes, may have the same result. In traumatophilics, sexual and aggressive excitations are always inseparably interwoven.

What is valid for sexuality is also valid for aggression. Aggression, too, when gratified, is not dammed up. But if the emotion of rage as such is feared and blocked, a vicious circle is created just as when sexuality is blocked.

People who tend to "act out" in reality, who use external objects merely as instruments through which to find relief from their inner tensions, are very often of the traumatophilic type. Their actions correspond to the repetitions of a traumatic neurotic. The striving for experiences in order to ward off a danger or to gain or enforce a necessary protection may at the same time be aimed at a belated discharge of an overwhelming excitement. The experience of early traumata in such persons may underlie their characteristic intolerance toward tensions. The memory of the experienced trauma makes them fear that any tension at all may signalize a new trauma. They feel themselves to be miserable creatures, helplessly exposed to a dreadful world which heaps traumatic experiences upon them. The only way in which they can seek aid is to try again and again to anticipate actively and on a limited scale that which they fear; they usually fail, because of the vicious circle described above.

> Some psychotherapists seem to be of the same type as these patients. By working with patients, they seek to deal with the unconscious, actively and "on a limited scale," because they are afraid that they might be overwhelmed by their own unconscious, passively and in a high degree. They prefer emotional upheavals and dramatic scenes in their treatments, and theoretically they defend the importance of "abreaction" and are not much in favor of "working through." Like all unconscious rewards a psychotherapist derives unduly from his work, this type of gain, too, nullifies or at least damages the objective work.

Concerning therapy, neuroses of this type are closer to psychoneuroses than to traumatic neuroses. (It is, however, an open question how high a percentage of so-called traumatic neuroses actually belongs to this category.) If one were content to wait for a spontaneous cure, one would wait in vain. The intervention of the defending ego completely prevents "belated mastery." And the defending ego interferes because of its apprehension of disaster. Psychoanalysis must undo the defense, must make possible a connection between the instinctual forces that have been excluded and the remainder of the personality. The pleasurable loss of the ego in a successful sexual experience is the best possible guarantee of mastering whatever excitation has remained unmastered since childhood because of experiences of painful loss of the ego. Since these persons have the same intolerance toward tension as patients with morbid impulses, the achievement of this "undoing of defense" is equally difficult; sometimes for this purpose the classical technique has to be modified. However, in principle, psychoanalysis works in the same way as in simple psychoneuroses. After all, simple psychoneuroses are not so different from these combinations, since every defense against instincts is performed out of anxiety, and anxiety, in essence, is the striving of the ego to avoid traumatic experiences.

F. Course and Therapy of Neuroses

Chapter XXII

THE CLINICAL COURSE OF NEUROSES

SPONTANEOUS CURES

THE interplay between defenses against neurotic manifestations and attempts at their inclusion into the organization of the personality determines the further course of the neurosis. The discussion about neurotic character disorders gave an impression of the complexity of this interplay. No general formula can briefly and conclusively answer the question why certain neuroses tend to cure themselves, to improve or to come to a standstill, whereas others run a malignant course.

Spontaneous cures or improvements may be subdivided into real and apparent ones. A "real" cure would presuppose a solution of the neurotic conflict. Theoretically, this could be achieved either through the disappearance of the motives for the defense, so that the warded-off instinct is not warded off any longer, or by the success of the opposing forces in inducing a condemnation of the infantile wish by better means, that is, by a displacement of its energy to other, nonobjectionable strivings. Both of these outcomes, however, seem impossible, since, by the pathogenic defense, its motives as well as the warded-off drives themselves have become inaccessible to reasonable judgment. Certainly things that have been upsetting for the child would not continue to be upsetting for the mature personality; but the very rational facing of the disturbance by the mature personality has been made impossible by the defensive measures of the infantile ego. Is there any possibility of outgrowing pathogenic childhood fears in spite of their exclusion from the ego?

In childhood neuroses, where the anxiety that motivates the repression is not yet fully incorporated, this anxiety can still be corrected by reality. If a child feels that a certain instinctual behavior, let us say soiling his pants, will be followed by a lasting loss of his mother's love or by some other severe punishment, this anxiety causes him to repress the instinctual impulse, and this repression may create neurotic symptoms. In such a case, a reassurance may suffice to overcome the anxiety and make repression and neurosis superfluous. The trust in a "good mother" and better experience may succeed in overcoming the beginnings of a cleavage between instincts and personality. Actually, a certain percentage of infantile neuroses disappears later through the child's gaining confidence either in persons around him or in his own abilities. Many infantile anxiety hysterias, like fear of darkness or of being alone, are outgrown under the reassuring influence of the environment as well as through the natural maturing of the child, his progress in his motility, his capacity for active mastery, and the self-confidence evolved. Confidence may also be increased by the developmental change of the leading instinctual demands; if a child was afraid of being punished for soiling his pants, he will lose this fear when, through normal development, anal impulses cease to be the general executive force of sexual excitement.

To a certain degree, similar improvements through reassurance may occur also in infantile adults, still afraid of being punished by external objects. In less infantile persons, a real cure of this kind will be impossible; however, improvements of a greater or lesser degree are possible through reassurance and confidence. The reassuring character of experiences responsible for such an improvement may be objective; or it may merely consist of the fulfillment of certain conditions which, according to the history of the individual, have assumed a reassuring significance for him. It is also conceivable that a phobic avoidance, which hitherto could not be obtained sufficiently or which had required a special expenditure, can be secured through some new conditions (e.g., external reasons induce a person with a phobia of city streets to move to the country). Compulsive rituals which unconsciously signify a reassurance may become superfluous when certain external events or a changed situation of life take over the fulfillment of the same function.

The possibility of such a happy outcome, however, becomes much less probable after the anxiety that motivated the repression has itself become unconscious to such an extent that it cannot any longer be corrected by experience.

Before Freud, the old practitioners used to advise hysterical girls to get married, meaning by that to start sexual relations. Advice of this kind could not be effective, for the patients, because of their repression, were incapable of experiencing sexual satisfaction; it was this satisfaction and not the mere opportunity for sexual intercourse that had been lacking. But it is correct that if some means could be found to enable hysterics to feel sexual satisfaction, they would be cured. In general, a disturbance in the capacity for satisfaction cannot be overcome simply by pushing the patient into a situation that to other persons would be satisfying. Nevertheless, an experience of a new kind of pleasure may encourage the patient to weaken his defensive attitude—perhaps temporarily only—to try further changes, and to make accessible other pleasures, which in turn may decrease the intensity of the defense. There is something which might be called "cure by seduction" or "cure by love," in which a new experience of pleasure (sometimes combined with a new experience of confidence in the "noncastrating nature of the environment") may succeed in crushing the walls of repression (559). The possibilty of a "traumatic cure" of a rigid compulsive system has been mentioned (*see* pp. 260 f.).

Sometimes a spontaneous cure may be rooted in a decrease not in the anxiety opposing the instinct but in the force of the warded-off instinct itself. After neuroses of the climacterium, for example, postclimacteric spontaneous cures occur (sometimes, it is true, combined with regressions that may produce new symptoms).

Instead of complete spontaneous cures the factors mentioned may cause improvements or limited cures, effective only "until revoked."

"Apparent" spontaneous cures and improvements are based on alterations of the economic situation nourishing the neurosis, without complete abandonment of the underlying conflict. Changes in the life situation may in different ways change the economic-dynamic equilibrium within the personality, so that a genuine neurosis becomes superfluous. All experiences that change the relation between instinct and anxiety change the manifest neurotic picture as well (1317, 1502, 1610).

In the discussion of the precipitating factors of neuroses, the possible changes in the equilibrium between the repressed instincts and the opposing anxieties and guilt feelings were tabulated (*see* pp. 454 ff.). The same table, with reversed values, can now be used to clarify the possible ways in which experiences of life may decrease an established neurosis.

1. The changed situation may represent a decrease in the force of the repressed drive. This may be an absolute decrease, as in postclimacteric improvements, or a relative one.

Just as any unconscious temptation for a repressed drive may precipitate a neurosis, so any situation that excludes or limits the temptations for repressed drives has an ameliorative effect.

A relative decrease in the force of the repressed drive may be achieved by the opening of new outlets of any kind. Experiences that open or increase the gratifications of other instincts, especially of adult sexuality, relatively decrease the repressed forces ("improvement by seduction"). Anything that increases the evaluation of these other instincts may produce the same effect. A favorable break-through of rigid attitudes is analogous to such "seduction." Or the new outlets may not be direct instinctual activities but any other activity substituting for the repressed drive, or rather for the neurotic symptoms that have formed the first line of substitute activities. Something else takes the place of the neurosis, a kind of (ungenuine) "sublimation" or another "secondary" or "artificial" neurosis. In practice, the majority of all spontaneous cures or improvements belongs to this category.

Something of this type occurs, first of all, whenever infantile neuroses are overcome by the development of rigid character attitudes. These attitudes imply an impoverishment of the ego and therefore may be called neurotic; but they may be less obvious and disturbing than the primary neurosis.

> Conditions of life may form a situation that dynamically serves as a kind of "secondary neurosis" making the primary neurosis superfluous. In this class belong the neurotics who get well if they fall physically sick or suffer a real misfortune, because suffering and misfortune take over the "punishment" significance that hitherto had been represented by the neurosis. But the substitutes need not necessarily be painful ones; cures by sublimate hobbies or self-cures of neurotic artists by creative work are also effective through opening pathways of substitute activities.

2. An increase in the warding-off forces may result in a temporary victory of the ego if it succeeds in creating a more energetic and successful suppression. The intensification of anxiety or guilt feeling may be a direct or an indirect one (*see* pp. 456 f.). It works like a hypnotic command directed against the symptoms. The effect of improvements of this kind, like that of such a command, is very limited; increased suppression will be followed, sooner or later, by increased rebellion.

> External fear may bring relief from internal guilt feeling. Compulsive neurotics may improve upon meeting a strict boss or any frightening experiences.

3. Many spontaneous improvements, however, are due to a decrease in the repressing forces sufficient to lower the entire defensive struggle to a level where it is not disturbing any more. Experiences, reassuring objectively or subjectively or tending in any way to show that past threats are invalid, represent direct decreases in anxiety; the feeling of having atoned for any harm one might have done, the fulfillment of requirements of the ego ideals, or the acquisition of new standards (if they render harmless something heretofore apparently harmful) represent direct decreases in guilt feelings. Confession certainly may cure or improve the neurosis of a faithful Catholic. Anxiety and guilt feelings may be indirectly decreased by gaining love, especially if this "love" is felt as a narcissistic supply regulating self-esteem.

> Forgiveness may bring relief from guilt feeling. Compulsion neurotics may improve upon meeting a kind boss or any reassuring experience. Many spontaneous "cures" are based on some permission to regress to the passive-receptive type of mastery, to let others take the responsibility. Abraham reported a very impressive spontaneous cure of this type in a case of an impostor (29) who was cured when a woman of the mother type fell in love with him and fulfilled his Oedipus wishes. In other cases the gained love may be of an impersonal nature, the love of God or the "belonging" to a greater unit, which permits one to give up activity and responsibility for the magic protective powers of "faith" (654).

The attainment of love may be replaced by the attainment of prestige, power, self-confidence, or by situations of life assuring phobic avoidances or providing reassuring rituals. Paradoxically, even failures and experiences that represent a loss of self-confidence may have a favorable effect if they are perceived as a permission to yield to passive-receptive longings.

4. Finally, even an intensification of the repressed drives might perhaps create an improvement if it were intense enough to break down the countercathexis altogether. The liberated impulses, then, would respond like impulses freed from repression by psychoanalysis: they would catch up with the maturity of the total personality, from which they had been isolated, and lose their infantile character. In practice, improvements of this kind always coincide with "improvements by seduction" discussed under (1).

The effectiveness of all these influences depends, of course, upon the entire dynamic-economic situation; the same external occurrences changing the equilibrium of the conflicts may bring exacerbation or improvement, depending upon economic factors. The difference in the dynamic-economic structure is also responsible for the fact that though spontaneous cures and improvements occur in all types of neuroses, they occur in various neuroses in different frequency—in mobile hysterias more frequently than in fixed compulsion and character neuroses. The curative effect of a passive-receptive attitude may be paralyzed by guilt feelings and secondary conflicts aroused by them.

STATIONARY NEUROSES

The fact that some neuroses become stationary at a certain point of their development may be due to the very same circumstances that in other cases produce a recovery. The favorable changes in the dynamic relationship between repressed impulses and anxiety suffice to control the further instinctual urge, the damming up of which continuously increases from physical sources, but they are not sufficient to undo the damage caused up to that time.

The standstill in the development of a neurosis has been compared to a seclusion of a foreign body in a pathological anatomical sense (*see* p. 460). This outcome represents a defense of the ego against the symptoms by means of isolation.

Examples of this seclusion are given by the successful projection of the instinctual danger onto an external situation in anxiety hysteria; by *la belle indifférence* of hysterics; by the compulsion neurotic who remains comparatively unmolested as long as he fulfills certain rituals; by the man who succeeds in turning a paranoid schizophrenia into a systematized paranoia; and by the cyclothymic who feels normal in the intervals between his depressive or manic spells.

In character neuroses the fight between impulse and anxiety may become stationary and rigid. Instead of a "mobile warfare," a "war of position" is fought.

The patient then may be easily fatigued and may suffer from a "general inhibition due to general impoverishment" (618), but otherwise remain relatively intact.

The progredience or the arrest of a neurosis is not decided once and for all, but rather is relative. A neurosis that had been relatively stationary for a certain time may become progredient again. Not only may cures and standstills of neuroses be spontaneous but also aggravations and progressions occur under the influence of external events. And the same dynamic-economic factors that decide whether an externally determined disturbance of the equilibrium has an improving or aggravating effect are also decisive in questions of progredience or arrest.

Improvement and aggravation, arrest and progredience are relative concepts. In certain cases it depends on the point of view whether an externally provoked alteration in a neurosis should be included in the one or the other category; certain qualitative changes may be improvements in one respect and aggravations in another. As an example, the replacement of an anxiety hysteria by a character disorder has been mentioned (1274). Similarly, external alterations may change the symptomatic picture. Compulsion neuroses frequently have a historically older "hysteric kernel" (599); rituals, especially, may have replaced phobias. If the rigidity of the compulsive structure is liquidated in later life, the hysterical features may come to the fore again. Even where this is not the case, a compulsion neurosis, losing its "neurotic equilibrium," may change into an anxiety neurosis or into a vegetative organ neurosis. More interesting are the complicated dynamic relations between compulsion neuroses and organ neuroses on the one hand and manic-depressive disorders and schizophrenias on the other. Manic-depressive patients usually show compulsive characteristics in their free intervals (26) and schizophrenias may "artificially be held on the level of a compulsion neurosis" (see p. 451) or be held in check by organ-neurotic symptoms (see p. 257). That is, persons with a disposition to use psychotic mechanisms may still be able to solve a certain amount of mental conflict by neurotic means; if life brings intensifications of this amount, they develop psychotic mechanisms; if the intensity of the conflicts diminishes, they become neurotics again.

Still another relation exists between manic-depressive disorders and impulse neuroses. The pathological impulses serve as a defense against and an equivalent of depressions. If external or internal causes make them insufficient, the depression becomes manifest.

Every neurosis has spontaneous ups and downs. The psychoanalysis of the precipitating causes of spontaneous alterations provides important material on the nature of the unconscious conflict.

PROGREDIENT NEUROSES

There are cases without these happy outcomes that are malignantly progredient. The instincts flow from somatic sources, and when no adequate discharge is achieved the damming up increases more and more. Derivatives never give a full discharge; they only delay the catastrophe. In phobias, the conditions assume an ever increasing scope. Compulsive symptoms acquire more and more instinctual significance, and ambivalences and doubts increase until no decision whatsoever can be made; in "compulsive final states" the personality seems to be fully consumed by instinct and conscience (109, 1292). There are also "phobic final states" in which all activities of life are blocked. A special form of progredience can be observed in the mixtures between psycho- and traumatic neuroses (431).

Neuroses that have been stationary for a certain time may suddenly become progredient again. The same factors that precipitate a first outbreak of a neurosis (*see* pp. 454 ff.) are also responsible for a second precipitation. Such second "nervous breakdowns," which, for example, suddenly produce anxiety spells in persons who previously were successful in binding their anxiety tendencies, or which change a rigid "character neurosis" into a mobile "symptom neurosis" or an unemotional compulsive equilibrium into uncontrollable vegetative attacks, may be very painful for the patient; they are, from a therapeutic point of view, favorable.

Chapter XXIII

THERAPY AND PROPHYLAXIS OF NEUROSES

PSYCHOTHERAPY

THERE are many ways to treat neuroses but there is only one way to understand them.

Many attacks against psychoanalysts have been based on the notion that they "swear exclusively by their own method." That is in no way true. There are many reasons why a nonanalytic treatment might be preferable to an analytic one. What is true, however, is that psychoanalysts are of the opinion that only psychoanalytic science understands what is going on in neuroses, and that there is but one theory to give a scientific explanation of the effectiveness of *all* psychotherapies.

Nonanalytic psychotherapy appears to the analyst to be an application of psychoanalytic knowledge, in the same way that a psychoanalytic psychology of propaganda or a psychoanalytic psychology of advertising would be. It has not yet been systematically studied (*cf.* 1281) and still involves a great deal of intuition. This application of psychoanalytic knowledge, therefore, is more difficult, and certainly more problematic in its outcome than the use, lege artis, of psychoanalytic therapy. Simmel, therefore, demanded long ago that any psychotherapist, no matter which method he intends to apply, should have undergone a full psychoanalytic training (1439).

In the case of traumatic neuroses, we have seen that psychotherapy can and should imitate both spontaneous ways of recovery—giving opportunities for belated discharges as well as reassurance, rest, and take-it-easy suggestions, and that the task is to find the correct blend of the two methods (*see* p. 127). Something similar can be said about acute and more or less "traumatic" upsetting events in the life of normal persons. A normal person who suffers a loss of love or a failure or a change in his standard of living or another type of shift must make an adaptation to the new conditions. In carrying out a "work of learning" or "work of adjustment," he must acknowledge the new and less comfortable reality and fight tendencies toward regression, toward the misinterpretation of reality, toward the longing for passivity and dependence, toward wish-fulfilling fantasies. In such situations, *counseling* can be helpful. It works by the same means as therapy in traumatic neuroses: on the one hand we may verbalize and clarify the task set by reality, and help to suppress the tendencies toward irrational reaction by bringing them to the conscious level; on the other hand this help may be mixed with relative allowances for rest and for small regressions and compensatory wish fulfillments, which are recuperative in effect.

Only a minority of mental difficulties are of a "traumatic" nature. However, there are precipitating factors for psychoneuroses or for nonneurotic acute upset states which can be compared with traumata. A person may have evolved from old infantile conflicts into a state of relative equilibrium between repressed and repressing forces. An external alteration may mean a disturbance of this equilibrium, and thus make a hitherto attained adjustment more difficult.

The nearer a given neurosis is to the traumatic end of the complementary series, the greater is the probability that external efforts to support the spontaneous attempts at regaining mental equilibrium may be successful; the more a success would presuppose the annulment of previous blockings, that is, of methods of defense and of the belief in the necessity of defense, the smaller is the probability of easy psychotherapeutic cure.

"Counseling" may make use of the *rational* aids at the disposal of psychotherapists. First of all, the verbalization of unclear worries alone brings relief, because an ego can face verbalized ideas better than unclear emotional sensations. The very fact that a doctor spends time, interest, and sympathy on a patient's worries may not only be "transference" of a past situation but also a very original and substantial relief for lonesome persons who have no friends to talk to, or for persons who have been misunderstood or scolded for their difficulties up to now. Information about emotional and especially sexual matters may help to set at ease excited souls. Further, if a patient sees connections between hitherto unconnected symptoms, worries, or parts of his personality, if he is helped to detect general patterns of behavior behind concrete actions, and if he even detects the relationship of such patterns to one another, all this certainly makes his ego relatively stronger in its relation to the deeper forces within his personality. (This strengthening, however, may be misused for purposes of resistance.) Certain authors believe that rational help of this kind constitutes psychoanalysis (820, 821); actually, it is frequently a first step in psychoanalytic cures, a necessary prerequisite for psychoanalytic work proper, which does not consist in detecting behavior patterns but rather in bringing about a dynamic alteration in the conditions that created the pathological patterns.

There are also physiological "rational measures." The relaxation of tense muscles has, for physiological reasons, a mental cathartic effect (334, 839, 1410) (*see* p. 249); the relaxing effect of sedatives may be helpful; the old advice of warm baths for nervous persons is effective not only because such baths supply pleasurable stimulation to skin eroticism and represent atonement but also because they create a peripheral vasodilatation, and thus work counter to the central tension all neurotics suffer from. The effectiveness of these rational methods can be further increased by advice that may lead the patient away from unnecessarily tempting or exciting situations, or may push him toward some reassuring position.

The effectiveness of all these rational methods is a very limited one. The more acute a difficulty is and the less it represents a real neurosis (being primarily a task of immediate adjustment), the greater is the probability of success through rational methods. If, however, the difficulty represents a remobilization of old conflicts and latent neurotic patterns, then the effectiveness of rational methods will to a greater or less degree be limited to the significance of seducing rewards that may be made use of to secure positive transference feelings.

The neurotic conflict is the basis of every psychoneurosis. Only a change in the dynamic relations of the constituents of this conflict can change the neurosis. In principle, this could be done in two ways: either by an increase or by an annulment of the defense. An increase may endeavor to repress anew the whole neurosis as a derivative of what has been warded off previously. An annulment of the defense would, of course, end the whole conflict.

The first type of "therapy" is represented by the old-fashioned suggestion-hypnosis in which the authority of the doctor prohibits the patient from producing symptoms. The same temporary effect may also be attempted in an indirect way by techniques that increase the patient's anxiety and thereby his repressions, by threats, maltreatments, symbolic castrations, and reproaches. Measures of this kind try to induce the patient to "repress the whole neurosis."

> In the first World War, war neuroses in Germany and Austria were treated by very painful electric shocks. The patients then feared the pain more than anything else, and "fled into health" as the lesser evil. Simmel once quoted a case history written by a hypnotist who stated that a patient could not be hypnotized "in spite of violent pressure on the testicles" (1439). Also some less drastic psychotherapeutic measures consist in combining the idea of symptoms in the patient's mind with painful associations, which would make the patient give up, that is, repress, his symptoms.

By a "repression of symptoms" the pressure of the repressed will necessarily be increased and sooner or later new symptoms will be formed. It may be, however, that the new symptoms are limited to the patient's becoming more afraid, more introverted, more rigid, more dependent on the doctor (consciously or unconsciously); in short, the patient may produce a new "substitute neurosis" in the place of his original neurosis; thus the cure by "increase in repression" would have turned into a cure by "establishment of new derivatives" to be discussed later (see pp. 557 f.).

The second type, the treatment by means of full annulment of the repression, is represented by psychoanalysis, in which the undoing of the repression enables the infantile sexual strivings to participate in the development of the personality and to turn into satisfiable adult sexuality.

Seemingly, these two methods are strictly contradictory. But actually many compromises exist between them in the sense that an undoing of a repression might be used for the intensification of some other repression, or that an increase in a specific repression might result in the creation of some less distorted derivatives at some other place. Different types of this kind have been discussed as causes of spontaneous recoveries or improvements (*see* pp. 547 ff.). Nearly all psychotherapies are of such a compromise nature and represent an artificial imitation of the spontaneous improvements.

> The use of a partial discharge of a derivative for assuring the repression of the rest occurs also in spontaneous neurotic symptoms and character attitudes, especially in the perverse symptoms.

The principle of these psychotherapies can frequently be seen at work in the course of a psychoanalytic treatment, when improvements occur before a real psychoanalytically induced change is achieved. It then happens that (*a*) the patient uses a new insight, acquired by a successful interpretation, for resistance purposes, that is, for a reinforcement of other repressions; (*b*) the patient's feeling relation toward his analyst (his "transference") changes the dynamic relation between repressed impulses and anxiety, the analyst being felt either as a threatening or as a forgiving and reassuring force.

Most psychotherapies offer the patient certain occasions for discharge, which are accepted as substitutes for the spontaneous symptoms, either because they really bring relief to the patient's conflicts, diminish his inner pressure, and give occasion for the reinforcement of repression in other parts of the mind or because revenge measures on the part of the doctor are feared or rewards are hoped for unconsciously.

Glover once wrote a very interesting paper in which he investigated the ways in which incomplete or inexact interpretations, and also other psychotherapeutic procedures, influence the patient's mind (690; *cf. also* 687). His answer was that these procedures offer artificial substitute symptoms, which may make the spontaneous symptoms superfluous. Actually, many of the psychotherapeutic measures have similarities with neurotic symptoms, and—partly reiterating, partly supplementing Glover—it may be stated: Exercises, baths, or other physical measures that are prescribed for neurotics may be looked upon as "artificial conversions"; that is, to the extent they are successful, they actually now serve in the life of the patient as a conversive expression of his conflicts. Prohibitions of any kind—the withdrawal of alcohol and tobacco and so on—represent "artificial phobias." Exact advice as to the conduct of life or diets represents "artificial compulsions"; this is still more true about prescribed curative rituals like the prayers of Christian Science, or about the penances dictated by the priest at the confession, or about the magic formulae of "autosuggestion," which are an artificial imitation of the word magic so many compulsion neurotics use spontaneously in their defense against their symptoms (28, 889). Many pieces of medical advice serve, if accepted by a compulsive patient, as compulsive symptoms with the significance of penitence; baths, for example, have been used since ancient times as purgation and atonement by washing off the dirty substance of sin; in obeying the doctor, the patient purchases protection from his superego. Occupational therapy (754; *cf. also* 1440), in so far as the advised occupation, sport, hobby is pleasurable, may represent less an "artificial obsession" than an "artificial impulse neurosis," or even a kind of "artificial perversion." If the psychotherapist is either especially kind or especially strict, he creates an "artificial passive-receptive dependency," under certain circumstances an "artificial masochism," which even may make a patient react favorably to a doctor's blaming his failure on the "unwillingness of the patient to be cured." The treatment itself may assume the significance of an atoning ritual which renders the neurosis superfluous (1446). The extreme of "artificial passive-receptive dependency" is achieved in hypnosis, where the "rapport" between patient and doctor in itself forms a substitute neurosis, which might be called "artificial infantilism." Drug prescriptions, in so far as the patient believes that "good stuffs" may neutralize "bad stuffs" in his interior, serve as a kind of "artificial paranoia" (12).

The efficacy of therapeutic methods of this type depends on whether or not the substitute offered is suitable to the dynamic structure of the patient. This suitability depends first on the type of patient; a hysteric cannot accept "artificial compulsions," nor a compulsion neurotic "artificial conversions." But besides, the substitute must (1) be pleasurable, that is, either have a secret sexual significance or a secret reassuring significance, and therefore be more attractive than was the spontaneous symptom. A secret sexual meaning, for example, is obvious in sports, hobbies, hydrotherapy (555); it is a little less obvious if a pleasure, hitherto inaccessible, is permitted by the doctor and gives substitute discharge, like games, playing theater, hobbies, books, the special nature of which may be chosen in accordance with the patient's emotional needs (1141). A secret reassurance may be hidden in permissions of this kind or in other transference satisfactions. The effect will be better, circumstances permitting, if a patient who has looked upon his neurotic symptoms as a (deserved or undeserved) suffering accepts this pleasure as a "compensation" he feels entitled to, or as a sign of forgiveness which puts to an end his striving for revenge. (2) The secret significance of the substitute must, nevertheless, be sufficiently far removed from the original instinctual meaning of the symptom to be acceptable. The substitute has to fulfill the same conditions that a suggestion given to a "bored" person must fulfill (422): it has to be near enough to the original objectionable idea to be attractive, and it must be far enough removed from it to avoid its recognition as a derivative.

A substitute will be more readily accepted when it is most likely at the same time to bring relief on a rational basis. The "rational" measures which may cure acute difficulties of life, and which have been discussed above, may also bring relief and thus create positive feelings toward the therapist in severe psychoneuroses.

The establishment of a transference neurosis is the most frequent and important substitute for a spontaneous neurosis. By "establishment of a transference neurosis" Freud meant that the repressed infantile instinctual conflicts find their representation in the feeling relations toward the analyst, and therefore do not need any other expression any more, or at least do not need as many other expressions as before (577, 596). The doctor is looked upon as a reincarnation of the parents, and as such he may be thought of as providing love and protection, or as threatening with punishments.

The doctor's very presence may influence the psychodynamics of the patient in the same way that the educational measures of the parents once influenced him, because unconsciously the doctor's presence is misunderstood as a repetition of what occurred in childhood. Improvements achieved on this basis are called transference improvements.

The mechanisms of transference improvements are identical with the mechanisms by which educators achieve their success. Either the idea of continuing the neurotic behavior becomes, in the subject's mind, connected with the idea of some danger or the idea of improvement becomes associated with the hope for a specially attractive reward, or both these connections occur simultaneously (427, 1495).

Transference improvements of the threatening type work in the same way as castration threats which originally caused the child to repress certain impulses; now the belief in new castration threats causes the patient to repress the symptoms which are derivatives of the original repressed impulses. The reassuring type of transference improvement works because the patient, giving up his neurosis "for the doctor's sake," hopes to get sexual satisfaction through the doctor's appreciation and love; mostly he needs this appreciation and love simultaneously for his security and self-esteem. Many therapists have great skill in applying threats and reassurances one after the other, thus combining the two types of influence and treating patients with a "Turkish bath method"—one day hot, the next day cold. Ferenczi discussed the effectiveness of this method in observing a horse tamer (462).

Just as there are transference improvements, so also are there transference aggravations. They occur not only in cases in which "transference has become resistance," that is, in which the patient discontinues analytic work because he is interested in the fulfillment of his transference wishes only (449, 577), but also in cases in which a negative transference brings about an aggravation of the neurosis, in the same way that a negative feeling toward the educator makes a child naughty. A neurotic may become worse just to spite the analyst. If the patient becomes aware of this fact, of its transference nature, and of the history and purpose of his original spite, the resistance will be overcome.

Under certain circumstances, paradoxically, improvements out of transference spite may occur—for example, when a patient loses symptoms not only for the analyst's sake in a positive sense but for the purpose of proving that the analyst who tells him that he is not cured yet is wrong. Then the spite itself has become the substitute for the apparently cured neurosis, and it has to be analyzed if later relapses are to be avoided.

It even happens sometimes that a patient after apparently long and deep analysis still remains sick; he then may terminate his analysis to go to some other therapist, and be cured by him in a very short period of time. There is no doubt that the quick success of the second doctor then is comparable to the anecdote of the boy whose mother scolds a younger brother for having ruined his suit: "Your brother wore it for years, and nothing happened; you had it only for a few months, and it is ruined!" However, the patient is not completely wrong when he believes that his first analyst did not do a good job. The transference itself has not been sufficiently analyzed, and thus the cure by the second doctor is not trustworthy in the long run either.

Analysts know that not only expectations of being loved and of being punished are transferred but much more specific expectations, impulses, and emotions. In analysis, any transference, although it may provide the most important material and may be utilized for the purpose of the analysis, is in principle a resistance, because the wrong connection of past emotions with the present obscures the true connections, and because the patient, interested in the immediate satisfaction of his transference wishes, loses interest in overcoming his resistances. "Transference improvements" are likewise no exception to this rule, and the phrase "flight into health" is frequently justified.

The situation is different in psychotherapies that foster the wrong connection of the patient's unconscious wishes as the means of achieving their therapeutic success. They cannot let transferences develop spontaneously for the very purpose of studying their spontaneous features. They have to favor everything that provokes utilizable transference feelings, and to stop any negative transference that begins to develop. The difficulty is that this has to be done rather planlessly, because the dynamics of the patient's conflicts are unknown, at least in their details; knowledge of them can be gained only by letting the transference feelings develop spontaneously.

Everything that in analysis creates a transference resistance is capable of creating a "success" in a treatment where the transference is not analyzed. But the same factors are also capable of creating an unfavorable transference action, for example, a cancellation of the treatment.

The majority of therapists do not follow any conscious "system" but, rather, their intuition. The doctor guesses, acts parts, changes his behavior according to the patient's manifest reactions, without understanding them. A good "born psychologist" will succeed, a bad one will fail.

A therapist who has studied psychoanalysis is in a somewhat better situation. In terms of his dynamic understanding of the patient's symptoms and utterances, he will try to judge what might favor and what might hamper transference successes (*see* p. 565).

It is clear that transference improvements are not trustworthy. They do not undo the pathogenic conflicts of childhood, but simply displace and repeat them. Any change in the feeling relationship toward the doctor or any external experience that motivates the patient to such a change endangers the entire success. This was the reason why Freud gave up hypnosis as a means of treatment. It turned out that the improved patients remained improved only as long as they remained on good terms with the doctor (586). They had become dependent on him, and this dependency was the condition of their being better. "The transference has not been analyzed."

Hypnosis reveals more about the nature of transference improvements. In hypnosis, it is not only obviously the dependency of the patient on the doctor, the "rapport," that serves as the substitute neurosis; hypnosis also shows what kind of rapport is the most effective one: after Ferenczi (449, 453, 456) and Freud (606) first stated that it is an infantile libidinal tie that binds the hypnotized patient to his hypnotist, later research (378, 651, 673, 872, 880, 994, 995, 1048, 1081, 1234, 1370, 1378) clarified the question of which type of infantile sexuality is the decisive one. In "dependency," the hypnotized patient receives satisfaction of a sexuality that has not yet been differentiated from narcissistic needs. The patient reverts to the phase of passive-receptive mastery. The first two years of life, in which external "omnipotent" persons took care of us, protected and provided us with food, shelter, sexual satisfaction, and reparticipation in the lost omnipotence, gave us a feeling of being secure in a greater unit, while, at the same time losing our own individuality. This memory establishes in every human being a capacity for nostalgia for such a state whenever attempts at active mastery fail. It is this type of regressive longing that is satisfied in hypnosis.

This regressive longing is not equally developed in all persons. The oral type of patients, those who are disposed toward the development of depressions, addictions, and impulse neuroses, produce this longing most intensely.

It is the same longing that receives social significance when, in states of general frustrations, it is developed in the masses in a high degree, taking the place of the tendency toward the active mastery of difficulties (436).

It is an old technique of authorities and educators to reply to subjects or children, who are dependent on them and who are begging for protection and "narcissistic supplies": "You will get what you need—but on condition! If you obey, you will get protection and love, which you need. If you don't obey, you will be destroyed." The initiation rites of primitive (and less primitive) peoples always combine frightening experiences with the solemn establishment of a permission (1284). The meaning is: "You may now enjoy the privilege of being adult and of participating in our society; but don't forget that you may do so only as long as you obey our rules; and the pains we inflict on you should remind you that much greater pains will be inflicted upon you in case of disobedience." The participation in power is permitted—but in a restricted sense, *on condition,* and the subjects and children, because they are in need of this participation, are ready to pay the price of this limitation.

Psychotherapeutic transference improvements may be achieved in the same way: if the patient is a "good boy" and does not behave neurotically, he gets love, protection, and "participation" from the omnipotent doctor; if he does not obey, he has to fear his revenge. In this respect, the psychotherapist is in good company: he uses the same means of influencing that God uses.

And the psychotherapist of this type is actually near to God. Medicine in general, and psychotherapy in particular, has long been the realm of the priests (1636). And frequently it still is today. The healing power of Lourdes or of a Catholic confession is still of a much higher order than that of the average psychotherapist (156, 965). Neurotics, who are persons who have failed in actively mastering their surroundings, always are more or less looking out for passive-dependent protection. The more a psychotherapist succeeds in giving the impression of having magical powers, of still being the representative of God as the priest-doctors once were, the more he meets the longing of his patients for magical help. Christian Science and other institutions or sects, which promise health and magical protection as a reward for faith and obedience, may, due to their history and surrounding awe, achieve better and quicker cures than many scientists.

That does not necessarily mean that the psychotherapist will be the more successful the more he uses visible magical instruments and behaves like a sorcerer; for more modern patients, magic is not necessarily represented by large apparatuses, but rather by a certain unapproachability on the part of the person in authority. However, the importance of all the age-old instruments of impressive magic and of the ancient magical power of faith should not be underestimated either (289, 965).

The magical power, projected onto the doctor, does not necessarily need to be used directly as a prohibition of neurotic symptoms. It may also, as in cathartic hypnosis, be used for an annulment of certain repressions. However, any recovery achieved in this way remains dependent on the patient's passive-dependent attitude toward the doctor. The patient's ego instead of being enabled to mature is definitely established as immature.

This is the decisive limitation of cathartic treatment (188, 510, 731). If the patient's resistances are overcome by the short circuit of a hypnotic command, he may become able to remember forgotten memories and so to provide important material. But the therapeutic value of this knowledge is not very great. The dynamic changes brought about by the patient's working through the history that necessitated the ego to develop its defenses and the coercion of a mature ego to face and to solve its conflicts are missing. Resistances that have been overcome by "force" instead of by having been analyzed will come back.

Previously, "abreaction" was considered the therapeutically decisive factor (504, 543, 554). And it is true that a liberation of hitherto blocked emotions takes places with any correct interpretation. However, no true and permanent dissolution of the defense struggle can be achieved in this way. Analysis, to be sure, consists of a summation of such discharges of derivatives; but it is a gradual summation that is required, because the ego must be made capable of assimilating this summation. Not only must previously bound energies become free in a single act but somatically newly produced instinctual tension must permanently be enabled to get discharge as well. In analysis, "abreaction" is a source of material, sometimes of significance, at other times only in the service of resistance; it is an occasion for demonstrating to the patient the existence and intensity of his emotions, and an introduction to the ensuing therapeutically effective working through of what has come to light in the patient's acting out. In hypnosis or narcosynthesis, when no working through follows, its effectiveness is limited to the immediate relief that emotional expression can bring. This immediate relief is most intense in traumatic neuroses, still intense in psychoneuroses with a more or less traumatic background, but minimal in chronic character disorders.

The hypnotist takes over the functions of the patient's superego (and even some of the functions of the patient's very ego) as a temporary, "parasitical double of the superego" (603). As such he tries to undo the previous work of the superego that gave rise to the defensive struggle. A very interesting and promising attempt to overcome the limitations thus created for the hypnotist's effectiveness was made by Erickson, who did not tell his patient that the moral instruction she had received from her mother was wrong and no longer had to be considered; instead he suggested to her that the mother (who was dead), if alive, would change her opinion today (377).

Erickson also described other means that enable the hypnotist to use the temporary dependence of the patient on him for creating a basis for later independence (371, 372, 373, 374, 375, 376, 378).

Recently, new and very promising attempts have been made at "hypnoanalysis," that is, to use hypnosis or chemically induced half-sleep states not only to achieve "abreactions" but actually to overcome the drawbacks of the ego's not facing its conflicts and of its continued dependency (673, 994, 995). It is not yet possible to predict where such promising devices will lead. Of course, the therapeutic effectiveness of "hypnoanalysis" remains more or less limited to symptom analysis. The same hopes and the same limitations hold true for the use of drugs in order to overcome amnesias and other resistances. Although the effect of the drug is more "objective" than the hypnotist's command, it, too, creates an artificial ego state.

Many psychotherapists try to achieve their effect by "augmenting the patient's self-confidence" (cf. 1609). Since self-confidence generally diminishes anxiety, this would actually be a good device. (Unfortunately, an increase in self-confidence is very difficult to achieve without analysis in neurotics who suffer from inferiority feelings.) However, an attempt at augmenting self-confidence by suggestion is a two-edged sword. If a patient has self-confidence because a doctor has told him to have it, he has more confidence in the doctor than in himself. The self-confidence is a borrowed one and is lost again when the participation in the doctor's power is lost.

Psychotherapy, which makes the patient dependent for the purpose of telling him to be independent, is in a situation similar to that of present-day education in general. Present-day education also simultaneously sets the contradictory ideals of active independence and obedient submission. How the poor child or, in the case of psychotherapy, the poor patient is to extricate himself from this tangle is his affair.

When the circumstances are favorable, he usually does it in the following fashion. Under the mask of independence and activity (of which he is consciously very proud) the patient unconsciously enjoys passive-receptive dependence. The dependence may be thought of as being temporary only and preparing for a later (and in fantasy anticipated) independence. This is the mental situation of children and adolescents, and this makes so many neurotics tend to remain children or adolescents.

> There are many situations in life where in a similar way an apparent independent activity covers a deep actual dependent passivity. Many neurotics, and perhaps not only neurotics, look at the army in this way. "Being a soldier," consciously, seems to them to be the quintessence of active masculinity. However, "being a soldier" means to be dependent on superiors, to be a part of a great machine, and to be fed and clothed. The more intense this inner security through dependence is, the greater the disappointment will be should the protecting forces turn out to be unable to provide actual protection (*see* p. 122).

A climax of dependence masked as independent power is achieved by the methods of *autosuggestion* where a weak and passive ego is controlled by an immense superego with magical powers. This power, however, is borrowed and even usurped (28, 889).

In which way does "wild psychoanalysis" work, that is, all the methods of psychotherapy using a limited amount of interpretation, either "without going so deep as Freud, because that is not always necessary," or "by directly attacking the patient with deep interpretations"? It may work in different ways, and if a success is achieved at all, this may be due to a combination of the following mechanisms: (1) Transference improvements, achieved by dynamic changes due to the feeling relation to the doctor and more or less independent of the specific content of what the doctor says. Improvements of this kind can frequently be observed in the beginning of an analysis. (2) Rational help by verbalizing conflicts, showing connections, giving advice in actual difficulties. (3) Unspecific help by directing the patient's attention to matters he had not considered hitherto, that is, by giving him courage to think and talk about forbidden topics

(570). (4) More specific help of the same kind, that is, real analytic influence, which, it is true, because limited in depth, is used as resistance against further analysis. Frequently an analytically gained new insight is misused for the purpose of increasing some other repression. The shifting of the emphasis from actuality to childhood, promoted by some psychotherapists, may mean the further repression of, or illusions about, present worries. (5) All the artificial neuroses that are created by nonanalytic therapeutic measures may also be inaugurated by limited and inexact interpretation (690, 885).

There is no doubt that the psychoanalytic understanding of the ways in which nonanalytic psychotherapies work can be utilized for a planned systematization of the procedure to be chosen. As long as any psychotherapeutic school had its own "theory," the results were unpredictable and dependent on chance, or rather entirely on the therapist's intuitive skill. The methods of psychotherapy, therefore, have remained the same since the times of the earliest witch doctors; the results were perhaps not bad, but they were not understood and thus were unreliable. You never could tell whether or not they would be achieved at all.

A short psychotherapy, based on psychoanalytic knowledge, can change this state of affairs. An analyst is able to use the patient's symptoms, history, behavior, and utterances for the purpose of establishing a "dynamic diagnosis" about the patient's leading conflicts, the relative strength of the repressing and repressed forces respectively, of the defense system and its weak spots, of the patient's rigidity or elasticity, of his general accessibility. This dynamic diagnosis will enable him to predict with a certain degree of probability what the patient's reaction to certain measures will be. Combinations of limited interpretations, provocations of certain types of transference, providing well-chosen substitute outlets, alterations of the environment, suggestions or prohibitions of unconsciously tempting or reassuring situations or activities, the verbalizing of actual conflicts, and advice about mental hygiene can very well be systematized. This has not been done yet on a large scale, but there are promising beginnings, from Aichhorn (33, 34, 35) and Zulliger (1639, 1641, 1646) to the Chicago Psychoanalytic Institute (55) and many American psychiatrists and psychiatric institutions (122, 297, 370, 679, 727, 787, 870, 941, 951, 964, 966, 1037, 1108, 1138, 1226, 1390, 1562).

In a limited degree, a "brief psychotherapy on the basis of psychoanalytic knowledge" was tried out at the Berlin Psychoanalytic Institute as well as at the Psychiatric Service, Los Angeles, California. Concerning the results, the criteria that the psychoanalyst is accustomed to must be very much restricted, of course. But after such restriction, there is no doubt that help can be given in this way. Sometimes it is touching how grateful patients are for the mere honest attention and readiness to help on the part of the doctor. However, concerning the duration of the success—that is another question.

"Play therapy" with neurotic children (59, 237, 300, 646, 1038, 1040, 1066, 1169, 1319, 1326, 1447, 1448, et al.), as well as a well-chosen occupational therapy (754;

cf. also 1440), works through "catharsis" and through procuring of new outlets, which may be combined with limited interpretations.

It can be hoped that, under the pressure of bitter practical necessity, a psycho-analytic theory of nonpsychoanalytic influences will be advanced soon (569, 1114). This is the more necessary, as already various resistances against psychoanalysis misuse the banner of "brief psychotherapy."

Psychotherapy works in quite another way when it attempts not to change the structure of the patient but rather the patient's environment, that is, to use "situational therapy."

A change of environment is most effective in cases of children in whom the neurosis has not yet become definitely internalized. If a child is neurotic because he is afraid of unfriendly surroundings, a change in these surroundings will change his fear and therewith his repressions and his neurosis. Sometimes a change of environment may also be effective in the opposite way. The surroundings may mean to the child a constant excitement and temptation, and a cessation of this external stimulation may decrease the intensity of the instinctual demands sufficiently.

After the neurosis has become more internalized, simple cures of this type become impossible. Psychotherapy often is thought of as a re-education. But repression has made the consequences of the bad influences of the education inaccessible to new experiences. However, a re-education may be conceivable if the bad consequences of the education do not consist in something this education has done but in something this education has omitted. Then, what has been omitted may be inserted later on. This is to be seen, for example, in so-called psychopaths, whose superego deficiencies are due to a disturbed childhood during which they never had occasion or time to identify themselves with any "good parent" figures. Aichhorn gave many examples of a very effective psychotherapy in such cases, based on the idea of providing later what was not provided in childhood (31, 32, 33, 34, 35).

However, in other types of neuroses as well a change of environment may be helpful. Such an improvement, then, is due less to a real undoing of the pathogenic anxieties than to an exclusion of precipitating factors that provoke exacerbations either of anxieties or of temptations. Phobic or compulsive ceremonial conditions of relative health, which somehow had been lost in reality, may be found again in a new environment.

An improvement based exclusively on change of the environment will remain dependent on this change. If the neurotic is forced to go back to his old milieu, he will fall sick again. A stay in a sanitarium as a curative element, therefore, again is a doubtful measure.

However, a change of environment may be made very beneficial by applying psychotherapy while the patient is in the more favorable environment. If the case is studied in the sanitarium and the daily routine is arranged to meet his specific needs (abreactions, reassurance, transference), this may be very helpful (87, 219, 261, 962, 964, 1138, 1440, 1443, 1477). In certain types of cases an arrangement of this kind may also greatly facilitate the task of a lege artis psychoanalysis (1440). The sanitarium is certainly indicated when the task consists of overcoming a certain period of emergency (attacks of depression), or when psychoanalysis or other psychotherapeutic measures cannot be performed in the usual environment (addictions, schizophrenia, depressions). It also has to be admitted that sometimes everything is gained, if time is gained. After a "nervous breakdown" a limited time under changed conditions may suffice to let the ego regain its lost equilibrium or a substitute for it. The old advice for nervous people "to have a vacation," that is, to leave the conditions that provoked the neurosis, certainly contains an element of truth.

An overwhelming number of patients as well as of theoretical considerations has induced certain authors to try *group psychotherapy*. Although the transference relations become much more complicated in a group (the object relationships of members to each other, like love, hatred, jealousy, envy, as well as identifications and the influences of "good" and "bad" examples, complicate the picture), other psychological characteristics of a group seem to be favorable for psychotherapeutic purposes. The hypnotic situation has been called by Freud a group of two (606), indicating that the libidinal bindings in a group are similar to the hypnotic rapport. This similarity can be made use of for psychotherapeutic purposes. The examples of the others with whom the patient can identify himself, and the general tendency to undo instinctual derivatives and mental differentiations when in a group, may help to overcome resistances. For an analytic working through, however, the situation of intimacy with the doctor alone seems indispensable. It is understandable, therefore, that Thomas, when summarizing all attempts at group psychotherapy hitherto made, states that the "repressive inspirational" methods outweigh by far the analytic ones (1535). One may wonder whether the authors who, like Schilder, believed in purely psychoanalytic effects in group therapy (1388, 1390, 1393, 1394) were not in error about what they themselves were doing. "Repressive inspirational" methods, however, may be of various kinds. Magical effects become intensified in the presence of many believers with whom the novice may identify. Many attempts of this kind have been made, ranging from those initiated by Pratt as far back as 1906 for tubercular patients (1230), to the practices of Christian Science and other sects, as well as of those communities united by common sacred or profane theatricals (1145), and to the work of Burrow who, by "phyloanalysis," tries to bring his patients to a reconsideration of their natural ways of functioning (224, 225).

SHOCK THERAPY

Since this book contains chapters on the manic-depressive disorders and on schizophrenia, it is probably expected that it will discuss shock treatment also, at least briefly. There is no agreement about the nature of the effective forces. Since agents of such a different nature as insulin, metrazol, and electric shock are likewise effective, this effect is probably based on the experience of "shock" rather than on any specific factor.

The experience that insulin is more efficient in certain schizophrenias, electric shock and metrazol more efficient in manic-depressive disorders and involutional melancholias deprives this conclusion somewhat of its plausibility.

But what is shock? Certainly it is something that afflicts the organism physically as well as mentally. The author of this book has no personal experience with shock treatment. He has, however, personal experience in analyzing doctors who apply shock treatment. The (conscious or unconscious) attitude of the doctors toward the treatment was regularly that of "killing and bringing alive again," which idea, of course, provoked different emotions in different personalities. It may be that the impression the treatment gives to the doctors corresponds to an impression it gives to the patients. It seems that they, too, experience a kind of death and rebirth. "Killing the sick person and creating the patient anew as a healthy person" is an ancient form of magical treatment. This statement, however, does not tell anything about the objective and nonmagical alterations that may occur within the organism while the patient is having a magical experience.

Those psychoanalytic authors who have discussed shock treatment (231, 362, 718, 724, 1046, 1212, 1392, 1431, 1518, 1554, 1560) are of the opinion that objective alterations, that is, deep changes of the entire functions, probably especially of the metabolism of the body (of the brain cells), correspond to the ideas of death and rebirth. This is clearer in regard to death. The shock probably initiates a momentous and deep regression, an undoing of differentiations, a reduction of the organism to a very primitive level. This alone would not produce any curative effect. The "rebirth" after this artificial "death" seems to be more problematic and of more importance, and in this respect two contradictory theories have been developed: (1) Some authors are of the opinion that after the undifferentiation of the personality, a new development takes place which may bring a better and more lasting adaptation than the first spontaneous development, especially if a simultaneous psychotherapy makes good use of the opportunity offered by the shaking of the unconscious through the shock regression (231, 1392). This shaking may be due to a blocking of cortical impulses by the shock, which sets mental inhibitions out of function, so that instinctual impulses, previously repressed, come to the fore, especially aggressive impulses. Some authors state that even all the original developmental stages of ego and libido are repeated once more after the shock in quick succession (1431). The trauma of the shock is believed to have destroyed the narcissistic protective patterns of the patient, who may make a better adjustment to reality during the repetition of his development in the restitutional phase after the shock (231). (2) Other authors, however, are more skeptical about the readaptation; they are afraid of lasting detrimental effects of the shock (362, 1560). The full differentiation of the personality may never be reenacted again, its *niveau* may remain on a lower level for good, characterized by a permanent lack of emotional depth and of differentiation of personal contacts. The curative effect may be based on the fact that adjustment is achieved more easily in a simple vegetative existence than in a highly developed personality (362). Sullivan found the most radical formulation for this point of view when stating: "The philosophy [of shock therapy] is something to the effect that it is better to be a contented imbecile than a schizophrenic" (1518), and Eissler, therefore, is of the opinion that "metrazol treatment should be administered, if ever, after psychotherapy has definitely proved unsuccessful" (362).

PSYCHOANALYSIS AS A THERAPEUTIC METHOD

In sharp contrast to all other types of psychotherapy, psychoanalysis attempts the real undoing of the pathogenic defenses. This is the only means of freeing the patient of the bad consequences of his pathogenic conflicts for good, and of placing again at his disposal the energies that hitherto have been bound in this conflict. Thus psychoanalysis is the only *causal* therapy of neuroses. Its aim is achieved by making the patient's ego face what it had previously warded off. The transference is not immediately used for therapeutic aims but is rather analyzed; that is, its true nature is demonstrated to the patient. What previously had been excluded from the personality finds this connection again and attains a belated maturation. The majority of the instinctual energies hitherto bound in the defense conflict can be discharged, the minority can be warded off by better methods (874, 1114).

This is important enough to be clarified by further comment, although possibly repetitious of what has already been said.

In the neurotic, the pathogenic defenses remain effective because anxieties and guilt feelings, developed once in childhood, still are at work, being beyond reach of the reasonable ego. Freud once designated as the essence of neurosis the retention of anxieties beyond the period when they were adequate (618).

The retention of a belief in a danger that is obviously not present is in itself a consequence of the defense established in childhood under the influence of that very anxiety. The anxiety that led to the defense has become unconscious, together with the objectionable impulses. It does not participate in the development of the rest of the ego and is not corrected by later experience.

The therapeutic task, then, is to reunite with the conscious ego the contents (both unconscious anxieties of the ego and instinctual impulses of the id) which have been withheld from consciousness by countercathexis, that is, to abolish the effectiveness of the countercathexis. This becomes possible through the fact that the warded-off impulses produce derivatives.

If the basic rule of psychoanalysis is followed and the purposive tendencies of the ego thus are excluded as far as possible, these derivatives come more clearly to the surface. Every interpretation, either of a resistance or of an id impulse, consists in demonstrating a derivative as such to the judging portion of the ego, against the resistance. To name unconscious contents that are not yet represented by preconscious derivatives, and that therefore cannot be recognized as such by the patient merely by turning his attention to them, is no interpretation. The demonstration to the patient that he is defending himself, how he defends himself, why he does it, and what the defense is directed against acts as an education of the defending ego to a tolerance of more and more undistorted derivatives. In discussing what is practically the most important instance of interpretation—the interpretation of the transference resistance—Sterba has shown how it becomes effective through a sort of splitting of the ego into a reasonable, judging portion and an experiencing portion, the former recognizing the latter as not appropriate in the present and as coming from the past (1490, 1497, 1498). This leads to a reduction in anxiety and consequently to a production of further, more undistorted derivatives. The cleavage is accomplished by utilizing positive transference and transitory identifications with the analyst.

> It remains to be investigated how this desirable "splitting of the ego" and "self-observation" are to be differentiated from the pathological cleavage and self-observation that are directed at preserving isolations and serve to *prevent* the production of derivatives.

The "analytic atmosphere" that convinces the patient he has nothing to fear in tolerating impulses formerly warded off seems not only to be a prerequisite for any transference interpretation (*see* p. 30); it is also the decisive means of persuading the ego to accept on trial something formerly repulsed.

The fear has been expressed that this might lead to an isolation of the analysis from real life, because the patient may feel that here he is only playing at his impulses, whereas in real life, where they are serious, he must continue to defend himself against them (910). This objection, it is true, may occasionally be well founded; in such cases this resistance must be analyzed. But this possibility certainly does not counteract the advantages of the atmosphere of tolerance. "Acting out," which impedes the ego from being confronted with unconscious material, often affords the analyst valuable insight; however, it is in principle no less a danger than the opposite resistance, a sort of theoretical analysis that talks about the past without noting that it is still present; for "acting out" relates only to the present and does not make the patient conscious of being dominated by his past (445). Analysis should show the past to be effective in the present. Freud once said that when the patient talks only of his present reality, the analyst must speak of his childhood; and the analyst must bring in present reality when the patient relates only childhood reminiscences. Theorizing about childhood relates only to a past that is not connected with present reality, whereas "acting out" is present reality, without its rootedness in the past becoming evident.

Although in analysis all methods available are used to induce the patient to lessen his production of defenses (596), the desired effect is the more lastingly and efficaciously obtained, the more the analyst succeeds in using no other means of eliminating resistances than the confronting of the patient's reasonable ego with the fact of his resistance and the history of its origin (1271, 1279). This confronting, bringing to the patient the recognition of the unconscious part of his resistance, also renders the resistance itself superfluous.

That this confrontation is done as far as possible at the instance of the *transference* distinguishes psychoanalysis from all the other psychotherapies. Any psychotherapeutic method makes use of transference, but only in psychoanalysis does this use consist in *interpretation* of the transference, that is, in making it conscious. The analyst makes this interpretation effective by not reacting emotionally to any of the patient's emotional wishes, to his love, hatred, or anxiety; he remains the "mirror" that does nothing but show to the patient what he is doing.

> He refuses to participate in any of the patient's transference actions, because his is another task, incompatible with such participation: to be the patient's doctor and to cure him. To be his "mirror" does not mean to deny this real task. An analyst who would misunderstand the "mirror" rule as if he were to become inhuman and to function like an automaton would, of course, become a failure soon, and rightly so. (*Cf.* the discussion of this point in 438.)

The fact that the pathogenic conflicts, revived in the transference, are now experienced in their full emotional content makes the transference interpretation so much more effective than any other interpretation (46, 432, 1514).

Since neurotics are persons who in their unconscious instinctual life have either remained on an infantile level or have regressed to it, that is, persons whose sexuality (or aggression) has retained infantile forms, it might perhaps be expected that after the pathogenic defenses are abolished, perverse strivings might come to the fore. Practice shows that there is no such danger. The warded-off portions of instincts have retained their infantile character only because they have been warded off. If the defense is undone, what has been excluded regains connection with the mature personality and fits itself in with it.

When analyzing the rat-man, Freud "illustrated" this point "by pointing to the antiques standing about in the room. They were in fact only objects found in a tomb, and their burial had been their preservation: the destruction of Pompeii was only beginning, now that it had been dug up" (567).

The main achievement of an adult instinctual economy is genital primacy. Warded-off pregenital sexuality has resisted this primacy; after it is freed from entanglement in the defense struggle, its forces are included into the genital organization. It is primarily the experiences of satisfaction now made possible that once and for all abolish the pathogenic damming up. Instinctual excitations are *periodic* processes, which after satisfaction disappear for a time and only gradually accumulate again. If the individual has a normal capacity for satisfaction, the ego need have no fear of an excessive quantity of instinct.

Single "abreactions" cannot accomplish this. They give momentary relief but no abolition of the defense struggle and no liberation of the energy bound up in it. This relative belittling of the therapeutic importance of abreaction and of the dissipation of repressed instinctual excitations in the act of becoming conscious, in contrast to the importance of facilitating the development of a well-regulated sexual economy, diminishes the relative therapeutic value of the single eruption of affect, however much it may be welcomed in certain analytic situations. What is more important is the subsequent "working through" (584). This working through, according to Rado comparable to the work of mourning (1235), consists of demonstrating again and again the unconscious impulse, once it has been recognized, in its manifold forms and connections, and in attaining thereby the cessation of the pathogenic defense.

The study of the ego and the defense mechanisms contributed much to the systematization and effectiveness of psychoanalytic therapy (541). It made possible an exact dynamic and economic timing of interpretations, which increases their effectiveness (433, 438). However, it did not alter the main disadvantage of psychoanalysis—its long duration. But now at least we know what necessitates this long duration: the education of the ego to tolerate less and less distorted derivatives, until the pathogenic defense is undone. It is, for instance, impossible to use the knowledge of the part played by regression in compulsion neurosis to abbreviate the analysis by skipping the anal-sadistic wishes, since they are only distortions anyhow, and immediately "attacking the Oedipus complex"; for talking about the Oedipus complex would not touch the patient dynamically at all—so long as its cathexis actually is displaced and bound on the anal-sadistic fantasies. The same holds true for all resistances. The analyst's interpretations must follow the patient's resistances in all their ramifications and unmask them, one after the other, their nature and history; the uniqueness of every case in its individual history forbids any short cuts.

Concerning the attempts to shorten the time required for psychoanalysis, the cartoon from the *New Yorker* may be cited: A couple is driving fast; the woman says: "And please, no short cuts today; we have no time!"

The abolition of the defenses also makes possible other kinds of discharge that had previously been blocked. Quantitatively, however, sublimations play a lesser role in the adjustment of the instinctual economy of the former neurotic than does adequate sexual satisfaction.

After an understanding of the therapeutic principles, it is not very difficult to decide whether or not to call a given treatment psychoanalysis. Freud once said any treatment can be considered psychoanalysis that works by undoing resistances and interpreting transferences (586), that is, any method that makes the ego face its pathogenic conflicts in their full emotional value by undoing the opposing defensive forces, effective as "resistances," through the interpretation of derivatives and especially of the derivatives expressed in the transference. This alone is the criterion. Whether the patient lies down or sits, whether or not certain rituals of procedure are used does not matter. For psychotics and children as well as for certain character cases, the "classical" method must be modified. That procedure is the best which provides the best conditions for the analytic task. A "nonclassical procedure," when the classical one is not possible, remains psychoanalysis. It is meaningless to distinguish an "orthodox" psychoanalysis from an "unorthodox" one.

How psychoanalysis actually is done, the questions of psychoanalytic technique and of special technical problems—such considerations certainly do not belong in a "Theory of Neuroses" (*cf.* 438, 684, 855, 1422, *et al.*).

INDICATIONS FOR PSYCHOANALYTIC TREATMENT

Psychoanalytic treatment, working by undoing pathogenic conflicts, is indicated whenever neurotic difficulties represent the outcome of a neurotic conflict; the connection between the neurotic manifestations and the pathogenic conflict may be direct or indirect.

From a therapeutic point of view, Freud has subdivided the neuroses into *transference neuroses* and *narcissistic neuroses* (596). Practically, this distinction coincides with the usual distinction between neuroses and psychoses, but the new terms stress a circumstance which, therapeutically, is the decisive one: in neuroses the warded-off impulses are striving for an expression in connection with a longing for objects—they produce transferences.

Transferences are developed constantly and everywhere; in the analytic cure, however, this tendency is emphasized for two reasons: first, the basic rule, by excluding secondary conscious motives, gives special opportunity for the development of derivatives; second, whereas in ordinary life the reactions of the objects complicate the picture, the behavior of the analyst puts the transference nature into sharp relief (*see* p. 130).

In contrast, the psychotics, having regressed to a phase before the establishment of objects, are not interested in having contact with others, or at least their attempts to make contact are rendered unreliable by a tendency toward withdrawal.

Since the interpretation of the transference is the main tool of psychoanalysis, transference neuroses are its indication, but in narcissistic neuroses psychoanalysis seems inapplicable.

However, this general rule, which Freud still held in his *Introductory Lectures* (596), has important exceptions. The distinction between the two kinds of disease is not an absolute one. The remainders of object relations in psychoses and the longings to regain such contacts may be used as a basis for a first analytic influence; if successful, this may gradually re-establish a minimum of transference ability. However, where this basis is lacking, psychoanalysis is not applicable; where it is very small, a modification of the technique is necessary (*see* pp. 447 ff.).

Not only the ability to develop a transference but also the nature of the feelings that are transferred are significant. The closer the transferred feelings to the normal emotions of love and hatred and the closer the transferred aims to the normal genital aim, the easier is the analytic work. The closer the transferred emotions are to the archaic "incorporation" world of the infant, and the more pregenital the transference aims are, the more difficult does the task become. In general, therefore, the difficulty of an analysis corresponds to the depth of the pathogenic regression. Thus using analytic knowledge about the depth of the decisive fixation points in the respective neuroses, the neuroses may generally be classified, according to their accessibility to analysis, in the following order:

1. *Hysteria:* If there are no special contraindications, the prognosis for analysis is absolutely favorable; early cases of anxiety hysteria have the best outlook.

2. *Compulsion neuroses and pregenital conversion neuroses:* Their pregenital regression makes the outcome more doubtful. Cases in which the rigidity has broken down, which show anxiety and in which the pathogenic conflicts have come to life again, are more favorable than cases in a relatively stable and hardened equilibrium.

3. *"Neurotic" depressions:* that is, slight ones, which are still aimed at objects, and cyclothymias. The oral element makes analysis more difficult in these cases than in compulsion neuroses.

4. *Character disturbances:* Character neuroses are always and in principle more difficult to approach than symptom neuroses because no reasonable and reliable ego opposes an unreasonable neurosis, the ego itself being included in the disease. However, the character disorders represent disturbances of very dif-

ferent degrees and depth of regression. These differences correspond to a great variety in the difficulty of the cure. Besides, there are differences in the readiness and ability to co-operate and also in the flexibility or rigidity of the personality.

5. *Perversions, addictions, and impulse neuroses:* In principle neuroses of this kind are comparable to severe character disorders. However, they are always especially difficult, first because the symptom is either pleasurable or at least promises to be pleasurable, providing a new and severe form of resistance, and second because the pregenital orientation, usually oral, is prominent.

6. *Psychoses, severe manic-depressive cases, and schizophrenias:* The organ neuroses have not been included in this classification because they are too different in their structure. A case of organ neurosis may correspond in category to any other neurosis.

This classification is of general value only. Complications may make the analysis of a hysteric especially difficult or of a schizophrenic relatively easy. Many other circumstances must be considered in making the prognosis: the general dynamic relationship between resistances and the wish for recovery, the secondary gains, the general flexibility of the person. Acute cases always present a better indication for psychoanalysis than chronic ones, fresh cases a better one than old ones. The neuroses perceived as ego alien are better than those included in the total personality (795).

Special indications in the particular neuroses have been mentioned in the respective chapters.

CONTRAINDICATIONS FOR PSYCHOANALYTIC TREATMENT

None of the following factors constitutes an absolute contraindication. But as relative contraindications they must be considered before a decision is made whether or not psychoanalysis should be tried.

1. *The age:* The ideal age for the undertaking of an analysis lies between fifteen and forty. But certainly analysis is not impossible either earlier or later.

The significance of age is that psychoanalysis presupposes both a certain reasonableness and a certain flexibility of the total personality. Little children still lack the reasonableness, older persons may have lost the flexibility.

However, the reasonableness needed is not too great, and children are more clever, especially in grasping unconscious connections, than is usually assumed. Thus a real lower age limit may be marked only by the ability to speak (175). However, child analysis, which has become a special field of psychotherapy in recent years (179, 253, 538, 539, 541, 826, 953, 958, 1245, 1400, 1639), has to adapt its technique to its particular object. Children can rarely obey the rule of free association. Other ways of collecting material must be substituted, such as the observation of their play, their artistic expressions, and their general behavior.

In children's analysis, the transference plays a different role: as long as the ego is not definitely established, grown-up persons can still participate in this establishment, and the analyst not only "represents mother" but is still an original second mother in the life of the child (538, 539). Therefore, transference analysis has to be handled differently, and it may even be that certain educational attitudes must be combined with the analytic ones. Children are much more dependent on their environment than grownups are. If a child is analyzed and later has to return to the same unfavorable environment that created the neurosis, the neurosis will be created anew. Moreover, related to this actual dependence of children is the other problem of child analysis: that the analyst has to handle not only the resistances of the child but those of his parents as well (826).

The main curative factor in adult analysis is the fact that after the removal of the repressions, genital primacy is established and regular satisfactions enable the patient to regulate the economics of his instinctual life; the possibilities for real instinctual satisfaction for children are very limited, however, in our culture (842).

All these circumstances complicate children's analyses as compared with adult ones; but they do not make children's analyses impossible. On the contrary, children's analyses are often more promising than those of adults, since the neurosis is still less incorporated and reassurances may still powerfully accelerate the analysis; children's analyses may also be of great prophylactic value, contrasted with analyses of adults. Details may be found in the special literature (cf. 175, 179, 221, 222, 300, 539, 541, 646, 666, 715, 716, 753, 825, 826, 841, 842, 934, 935, 953, 955, 958, 1062, 1066, 1097, 1110, 1185, 1245, 1316, 1400, 1401, 1415, 1424, 1487, 1553, 1639, 1641, 1646).

Advanced age certainly limits the plasticity of the personality, but it does so in varying degrees and at very different ages so that no general rule can be given. Several authors who have tried analyses with patients of very advanced age report considerable success (18, 725, 859, 951, 1025). In considering analysis at advanced age, the entire situation of the patient is decisive. If he has possibilities of libidinal and narcissistic gratification, analysis seems more hopeful than if the analysis would only bring the insight that life has been a failure without offering any opportunity to make up for it. For removing a specific symptom, analysis may be tried even with old persons; if, however, a deep character change would be necessary to achieve the cure, it must be remembered that the possibility of change is very limited in older persons.

2. *Feeble-mindedness:* Since analysis consists of making the ego face its conflicts, cases in which the capacity to do so is lacking cannot be analyzed. Feeble-mindedness is a contraindication.

However, even this contraindication is not absolute. Apparent feeble-mindedness may be a psychogenic "pseudo debility." In such cases the analyst may be able to modify his technique so as to gain a first contact with the person, and then use this contact to broaden the possibilities of the ego (103, 173, 393, 957, 1019, 1020, 1099, 1379, 1403).

Even in genuine feeble-mindedness, where psychoanalysis is certainly impossible, the use of certain aspects of psychoanalytic procedure in the treatment may be possible and helpful (1069).

3. *Unfavorable life situations:* Even in younger persons one occasionally has the impression that a successful analysis might make a person more unhappy than he is in his neurosis. This is the case if he is living in a situation that excludes any possibility of gratification, and where the neurosis provides a kind of illusion (596); or sometimes one has the impression that it would do no good to provoke longings that cannot be fulfilled.

The decision as to whether the sick, the crippled, or the otherwise handicapped should be analyzed requires an insight into the dynamics of the personality. Strong personalities will be able to adapt themselves even to unfavorable external realities, and their neurosis may be a hindrance to such an adaptation. But in weaker persons, the neurosis itself still may provide the best type of adjustment. The same holds true for persons who probably will be unable to find sexual satisfaction after an analysis.

4. *The triviality of a neurosis:* Just as a surgical operation should only be performed when really necessary, so certain neuroses give the impression that their analysis would not be worth the effort. The time, money, and energy necessary do not correspond to the degree of disturbance. Whenever a therapeutic success seems possible by lesser expenditure, the greater one had better be avoided.

5. *The urgency of a neurotic symptom:* There are neurotic symptoms requiring immediate removal, either because they are physically dangerous or because the condition is unbearable. Psychoanalysis takes time, and therefore such urgent states form a contraindication.

However, this contraindication is not an absolute one either. It may be possible to apply other therapeutic measures first, until the state of emergency is over, and then to change to psychoanalysis.

6. *Severe disturbances of speech:* Since talking is the method of psychoanalysis, psychoanalysis is not applicable when talking is impossible.

Again this does not form an absolute contraindication. Talking may be replaced by some other means in analysis, for example, by writing. It probably would be impossible to conduct a whole analysis in writing, simply because of the time required. However, it is possible (and it has been done successfully) to substitute writing for talking over a limited period of time, if, for example, the symptom of hysterical mutism has developed.

7. *Lack of a reasonable and co-operative ego:* This is the point which has the greatest practical importance and which is the most difficult one to judge.

The method of psychoanalysis is based on the co-operation of a reasonable ego. Thus it seems to be impossible if such ego is lacking. Often, however, it can be established in a "preanalytic" period by nonanalytic methods. In schizophrenic patients, a preanalytic procedure may establish a transference which then forms the basis of a later analysis. In psychopaths with superego deficiencies, an educative behavior may make up for omissions of the original education, until the readiness for co-operation is attained.

If a person, out of stubbornness or for other reasons, actually refuses to co-operate, he certainly cannot be analyzed. But the possibility of analysis may be established if the analyst succeeds in convincing the patient that he does not simply not *wish* to co-operate (as he believes) but that he is incapable of doing it. He may then become interested in this inability; and this interest can be used as the first motive for co-operation, in the hope that more motives may come later. This hope may or may not be realized. The problem of establishing a co-operative ego is the most difficult one in most character cases, and sometimes it may be unsolvable (438, 511, 512, 539, 1279).

> The two extreme types of character resistance described as "generally frigid" and "pseudo emotional" (*see* pp. 477 f.) usually present this problem in special intensity. The former may refuse to understand the "logic of emotions" (44) at all; the latter may lack the necessary detachment to form judgments about his own emotions.
>
> Fortunately, psychoanalysis, being a scientific method, does not ask for any "faith" on the part of the patient. He may be as skeptical as he likes (and if he is not skeptical at all, the suspicion is warranted that he is repressing negative transferences) so long as he agrees to co-operate, to follow the basic rule, to try his best, and to give psychoanalysis "a fair chance." What analysis asks from the patient, Freud stated (578, 584), is a benevolent skepticism.

A similar difficulty is presented by patients who do not come to analysis for their own sake but either because somebody else sent them or because they themselves seek to fulfill some other person's wish. This is no good basis for an analysis. It may, however, be a usable basis for a few weeks of trial analysis, in which the analyst makes clear to the patient that his analysis is his own business, that he alone has to decide whether or not he wishes it.

8. *Certain secondary gains:* Some patients seem to live on their neuroses and to be unready to give them up. Much energy can be saved if this is realized in time.

In this connection, the problem of the analysis of artists may be touched upon. Often artists are afraid of losing their creative abilities if their unconscious conflicts, the source of their creativeness, were analyzed. No absolute assurance can be given that an impairment of creative abilities through analysis is impossible. However, experience shows that neurotic inhibitions of creation are removed by analysis much more frequently than creativeness. Still, one must admit that in a certain minority of artists, neurosis and work seem to be so closely interwoven that it seems impossible to remove the one without impairing the other.

9. *Schizoid personalities:* In persons whose character gives the impression that they are not psychotic but may become so if their childhood conflicts are stirred up, the decision whether or not to start an analysis may be difficult. Doubtless there are schizoid personalities in whom analysis may provoke a psychotic process; but there are also others who may be saved by analysis from a future psychosis. There is no general rule for deciding whether a patient belongs in the first or the second category. Only a trial analysis, estimating the dynamic and economic conditions of the particular case, can bring about the decision.

10. *Contraindications to analysis with a particular analyst:* Sometimes an analyst feels that a given patient may work better with some other analyst, either because the patient does not react to his personality in a favorable way or because the analyst would not like working with him or would not be at his best. At other times, the patient has corresponding feelings.

Since psychoanalysis is in the nature of a very close personal co-operation, two persons may just not suit each other; they would form a "bad team." If one looks upon this situation with analytic eyes, and provided that the analyst is a good one, the possibilities are:

(*a*) A certain resistance on the part of the patient. The question arises whether to give in to this resistance. In general the analytic procedure is to analyze resistances rather than to give in to them. One must ask whether this type of resistance is not deeply rooted in the patient's character, forms a part of his neurosis, and would repeat itself with any analyst. But the rule not to give in to resistances can be followed only up to a certain degree. If a resistance is too intense, its analysis must be postponed and first be prepared by some other analytic work. If an agoraphobic is unable to leave his home, the analyst, at the beginning of the analysis, must go to the patient. In a similar way, the analysis of an intense father complex may be prepared better if the man with whom the patient has to talk about it does not actually resemble his father.

Whether a given patient would work better with a man analyst or a woman analyst is a similar question. In discussing homosexuality, it has been mentioned that in general the sex of the analyst does not make a decisive difference (*see* pp. 328 f.). However, this general rule has frequent exceptions. Persons in whom the castration complex is very marked may react very differently to a man or a woman respectively. In such cases a too intense early resistance may be avoided by choosing an analyst of the sex that provokes neither too much antagonism nor too much of a soothing influence (516, 604, 822). However, changing over to an analyst of the other sex whenever an analysis becomes too difficult is not a general panacea. Rather, the difficulty must be understood; and only in the rare cases in which the insurmountable resistance seems dependent on the analyst's sex is a change in this respect indicated.

In all these cases, one should try to *analyze* the resistance first; only if the resistance turns out to be insurmountable under the given circumstances should the circumstances be changed (1536).

(*b*) The difficulty may be due to the analyst. Any honest analyst will admit that, even though he is very thoroughly analyzed, he does better work with certain types of patients than with others. However, this difference should never reach a degree at which work with certain personalities becomes entirely impossible. An analyst has to have the width of empathy to work with any type. If the reality in this respect differs too much from the ideal state of affairs, the mistake may be the analyst's; it may be rooted either directly in a negative countertransference or in a disappointment because a certain type of patient does not fulfill some expectation that the analyst unduly and unconsciously connects with his work; in such cases the analyst himself should be analyzed more thoroughly (1501).

Any analyst will do well to avoid analyzing relatives, friends, or acquaintances. The fact that his own emotions in relation to these persons might disturb his work is, however, only one of the reasons for this rule. Another one is that the transference loses much of its specific character, or at least its demonstrability as a transference, if it does not originate within the analysis itself but has an analytically uncontrolled prehistory.

Even the analysis of relatives, friends, and acquaintances of the analyst's relatives, friends, and acquaintances may become doubtful for this reason. However, Freud added that certainly no analyst would refuse his help to persons for whom no other help is accessible; he has only to know that in doing so he takes the risk of losing his friends (584).

A trustworthy and detailed estimation of all these ten points in any given case is possible only during the analytic procedure itself. That is why patients are advised to have a few weeks of trial analysis; the final decision as to whether the patient needs a complete psychoanalysis is made after these weeks. The trial analysis is conducted according to the same rules as the final analysis; but the analyst's attention is directed toward judging the indication. He will in these weeks not only confirm (or change) his first diagnosis of the case; he will also perform a "dynamic diagnosis" of the leading conflicts of the patient, of the paramount resistances and their probable relative strength, of the patient's defense systems and their weak spots, of his general accessibility, his plasticity or rigidity. Any material is used in establishing the dynamic diagnosis: the patient's history, his behavior, his utterances, and also his first dreams (1354). However, it is important not to confuse a general, dynamic diagnosis with special hypotheses about childhood experiences, which cannot and should not be set up in the very beginning, since they would direct the analyst's attention too definitely, limiting his susceptibility to new impressions and his readiness to let himself be surprised by new material (1293). The judgment of the contraindicative factors is but a part of the dynamic diagnosis.

The question as to whether it is possible for a person to psychoanalyze himself has been raised several times. Freud himself is the best example of the fact that—to a certain degree—this is possible. In his book *The Interpretation of Dreams* he gave the classical example of self-analysis (552).

Certain other authors have propagandized self-analysis in literature (382, 383, 821). But in general, the possibilities of self-analysis are very limited. There are two reasons for this:

1. The overcoming of resistances without being helped by another person presupposes a very strong personality; it becomes entirely impossible if the resistance consists of a "blind spot," in just not seeing what one does not like to see. If the analyst is another person, he can demonstrate to the patient his blindness. In self-analysis, the blind spots remain untouched.

2. The feeling relationship to the analyst, called transference, is in two ways a tool of psychoanalysis that is nonexistent in self-analysis: directly, the wish to please the analyst is an important motive for overcoming resistances; indirectly, the form of the transference gives an irreplaceable model for the study of the patient's behavior patterns.

ABOUT STATISTICS ON THERAPEUTIC RESULTS OF PSYCHOANALYSIS

Statistics on the therapeutic results of psychoanalysis are frequently demanded. They are difficult to give. Their conclusions depend, first of all, on which cases have been selected. If cases are included in which there was a doubtful prognosis at the start, the statistics naturally look much worse than if the cases are more carefully selected. A second difficulty is that different physicians understand very different things by "cure" and "improvement." This fact must be kept in mind, especially when the results of psychoanalysis are compared with those of other methods; everybody agrees that the disappearance of symptoms is necessary but not decisive. "Capacity for work and enjoyment," however, can be interpreted in different ways, and analysts know the difference between a person who has attained this capacity in a limited and probably temporary sense by some transference success and a person whose dynamics were basically altered by psychoanalysis (78, 1503).

The difficulties of exactly defining "normality" and "health" from a psychoanalytic point of view have frequently been discussed (243, 693, 901, 1036, 1095, 1409), especially recently in a very impressive way by Hartmann (751). Fortunately, practice requires less exactness

An attempt to collate statistically ten years' work of the Berlin Psychoanalytic Institute established very severe criteria for the task. The results may certainly be compared with statistics on any other medical treatment (417). In the meantime other statistics were published (287, 1195, 1348) and all statistics correlated (969), with similar results. There is no doubt that psychoanalytic therapy leaves much to be desired. There are failures and partial successes. But there is also no doubt that psychoanalysis, as the only radical method, is the best method available for the treatment of neuroses. Its main disadvantage is the great expenditure of time and money. Its virtue, of which all analysts are proud and which belongs to psychoanalysis alone, is that it is built upon scientific insight; and the therapy is also a research method affording further scientific insight that is not only useful in treating neuroses but that is also of more universal application.

PROPHYLAXIS

Everywhere in medicine a laudable tendency is growing not only to cure diseases but also to prevent their outbreak. Psychiatric prophylaxis is called mental hygiene (1581). Its work may be directed toward the individual or toward the masses. It tries to teach the individual how to behave in order to escape the likelihood of falling ill, and to direct social institutions so as to reduce the general frequency of psychoses and neuroses.

Since psychoanalysis has brought about the scientific understanding of what really goes on in neuroses, there can be no doubt that psychoanalytic points of view also must be decisive in mental hygiene. These possibilities certainly should not be underestimated. If a doctor understands the dynamics and "complex" points of a given individual, he will certainly be able to give advice for the avoidance of a dire mobilization of the latent conflicts (1500). Nevertheless, no exaggerated hopes should be placed on mental hygiene, especially in respect to the second task of mental hygiene—general prophylaxis.

The decisive element in general prophylaxis would be the correct rearing and education of children. Neuroses are based on neurotic conflicts, and neurotic conflicts are created in childhood between instinctual impulses and the fear of dangers connected with yielding to these impulses. Is it possible for educators to avoid or decrease pathogenic conflicts in children (64)?

Certainly the idea that instincts may be dangerous cannot be avoided. Instinctual acting is sometimes *really* dangerous. No human being can live according to the pleasure principle, doing at every moment simply what he feels like. Experience teaches any child (even without special educational measures) that such behavior is unreasonable. If he eats as much sweets as he likes, he will get a stomachache; if he grabs at a pretty fire, he gets burned; he who tortures his environment is tortured in turn. Thus life governed by the impulses of the moment is slowly changed into life governed by reason. The reality principle is established by experiences that connect immediate pleasure with immediate or belated pain, and later also by experiences that connect events that are primarily painful with pleasurable rewards (427, 575, 1494) (see pp. 43 ff.).

Education certainly can help in this process. For the realization of the reality principle, one need not actually pass through all the pains of being burned. Education should, anticipating these pains on a small scale, help children to learn to bear displeasure and tension.

Nobody knows how a child would behave without any education, whether or not natural encounters with reality would suffice to develop reasonableness. But we do know for sure that in practice, education asks of every child more than reasonableness, and often education, producing artificial fears of impulses, exaggerating the reality principle, becomes a hindrance to reason. Practically, not only sociability is demanded from the child but rather sociability in a certain limited sense, namely, adjustment to present conditions.

Certainly a society of individuals behaving instinctively like two-year-old children would be absolutely impossible. Questionable only is whether a two-year-old child, if not educated, would never change his behavior.

Thus it is clear what the dangers of education are: The reality principle says: "Do not give in to your instincts if such impulses are dangerous." Education now may give the child the impression that all, or at least too many, instincts are dangerous.

One hears the opinion that the child's sexuality will lead to danger if not repressed; and it is true that, if unregulated, sexuality may ignore the needs of the partner. But this is the only danger. Experience shows that unsatisfied instincts are much more difficult to master and much more dangerous than occasionally satisfied ones. People whose sexuality was not suppressed at all would not be inclined to constant sexual intercourse. They would desire it only periodically, and would be satisfied between the periods. If present-day sexuality so often seems greedy, antisocial, and therefore dangerous, this is a consequence of previous sexual repression. Some people are afraid that a child who did not suppress his sexuality would not become useful to society. He would use up all his libido in the original sexual field, and no energy would be left for sublimation (171). This conception is not at all justified. Sublimations are, it is true, performed by sexual energy—but by pregenital rather than genital energy; the suppression of sexuality does not bring the energy to sublimation but instead keeps the unsatisfied sexual instinct unchanged in the unconscious, resulting in the disturbance of the intended sublimation and of all action by the unsatisfied instincts.

Before Freud, science did not know of the existence of infantile sexuality at all. This shows how intense was the general resistance to infantile sexuality. Where does this resistance come from? Where did the superstition of the danger of infantile sexuality originate? And where did a form of education arise that represses the instincts too much? All these attitudes, as well as ideas about morality, which are very different in different societies, are the result of the respective social situations and must be critically analyzed in terms of the social situations (131, 1278).

And now the skepticism expressed before becomes comprehensible. Mental hygiene is limited by social conditions. Mental hygiene as a practical movement is even created by the same social forces that limit its effectiveness (307). Neuroses are an evil originating under the influence of an education dependent not so much upon the opinions and personalities of individual educators but rather upon general social conditions which determine educative institutions as well as opinions and personalities of individual educators.

It is surely possible for the analyst to make a limited number of general suggestions about individual child rearing, for the purpose of avoiding later neuroses (833, 834, 1303, 1309, 1582): Whenever possible, unnecessary warnings about instinctual drives should be avoided, and whenever possible, unnecessary, strong excitations from without, increasing the instinctual demands beyond their spontaneous growth, should be avoided. It can be stated: (1) it is good to avoid letting children witness sexual scenes between grownups; (2) it is good to reduce seductions by grownups or older children as much as possible; (3) it is good to avoid direct castration threats; (4) it is good to train children to cleanliness in the right way, not too early, not too late, not too strictly, not too emotionally; (5) it is good to prepare children ahead of time for extraordinary impending events like the birth of siblings, operations, and so on; (6) it is better to understand the child's needs than to use rigid disciplinary patterns.

All this is important and the list could certainly be continued. But it is not too important. The effectiveness of such suggestions is very limited. In saying this, we have in mind not only that traumata may occur in spite of the best care; this certainly would be no objection to doing one's best. What limits the effectiveness of the suggestions of mental hygiene is the fact that chronic circumstances in the environment, which can hardly be changed, have much more influence than any isolated educational measure. The particular words with which a grown-up person reacts to an instinctual act of a child are not so decisive as the chronic and latent attitudes of the parents toward instincts in general. Reich showed in an excellent paper that the mental-hygienic value of a certain experience is determined less by its manifest content than by the total mental surroundings in which it occurs (1273). The mental structure of the child determines the gratifying or threatening effect of an experience; and this structure again depends upon the whole of his past experience as well as upon present influences.

The chronic circumstances that cannot be changed at will consist of (a) the *unconscious* of the educators, which determines not so much their "educational measures" as their everyday behavior, and (b) the institution of family itself, the relation between the family and extrafamily groups, and cultural tradition. (This is more important than (a) and influences it.) One must realize that the real goal of education is identical neither with the goals listed in the textbooks of pedagogy nor with the conscious goals of the educators. The intentions and ways of thinking of individual parents or teachers are not of as much importance as the social institutions affecting them. These are: family and school. *Family,* a situation in which a couple who have sexual relations live together with only a few children, one of this couple being the more or less absolute ruler. *School,* an institution in which external habits and regulations (desks, fixed hours, schedules, and school curriculum) rule.

"Progressive education," trying to avoid the errors of the preceding period in order to prevent frustrations, has sometimes gone to the opposite extreme, being thereby no less dependent on social forces than "authoritarian" education. "Avoidance of frustration" is certainly impossible. Reality necessarily brings frustrations; therefore an artificially protected childhood is a very poor preparation for it; the more early frustrations are avoided, the more small frustrations later have the same effect as intense ones do on persons normally brought up. The tendency of educators "always to be nice" further has the consequences that (1) the child receives the impression that aggressiveness is terribly forbidden; whenever he feels aggressive, he must repress it, and the outer leniency makes the inner superego (at least in its attitude toward aggressiveness) stricter, until the child may even long for an external strict authority as a relief (180); (2) the parents have to repress their own aggressiveness, which certainly will then make its appearance in an undesired manner and to an undesired degree.

"Modern education" frequently has the standpoint that "aggressiveness is bad." We do not know what is "good" and what is "bad." But we do know that aggressiveness is necessary in life in many situations, and a person who is not capable of using it is as much handicapped as a person who has lost his sexual abilities (1349).

There is no doubt that an artificial change of the education of a few individual children cannot spare these children severe conflicts. It is rather the opposite. Those children will sooner or later be driven into a more severe conflict because they will hear everywhere the opposite of what they are taught at home or at their special school.

Thus mental hygiene may give advice in individual cases. It is rather helpless when faced with problems of the public in general. Means and aims of education are not prescribed by analysts, but they have developed autonomically, under historical conditions and social conflicts through present (and past) social conditions. Not only to what extent infantile instinctual demands are permitted and to what extent they must be repressed is socially prescribed, but also the ways in which the prescribed frustrations are applied, and the ways in which the child is obliged to react to these frustrations. "Comparative psychosociology of education" is a new scientific field of the greatest practical importance, which, however, cannot be treated or even further discussed here (131, 650).

Neuroses do not occur out of biological necessity, like aging; nor are they purely biologically determined, like leukemia. The helplessness of the human infant, it is true, and the differentiation of the organized ego out of the id are preconditions for the development of neuroses (618); but they are not the causes of neuroses any more than the existence of a stomach is the cause of stomach diseases. Neither are neuroses "influenced by social conditions" as tuberculosis is, where circumstances of residence and diet may decide the course of the illness. Neuroses are social diseases in a much stricter sense. While the repressed demands represent biological forces (and even this they do only in the last analysis), the fact that they have to be repressed at all is brought about by the pressure of the social environment. The necessity for the pathogenic defenses does not arise from privations growing out of infantile insufficiency but from those that parents and educators impose on the child, verbally or by their behavior. These educative measures again represent demands of civilization that are inimical to instinctual gratification (561, 1396). And it is the demands of present-day civilization with all its contemporary manifestations that make the neurotics of today (819). So far as we know, other civilizations have produced neuroses, too, but these differed from the neuroses of today because other civilizations demanded other privations and necessitated the development of other reactions to them. Many forms of reaction which today are designated as compulsion neuroses are normal and institutionalized in other civilizations; and a "devil neurosis in the seventeenth century," once studied by Freud (610), could not be fitted into any present diagnostic scheme. Indeed, we are able to observe how the clinical pictures of neuroses change parallel to changes in society. Here the psychologist must admit his inadequacy and agree that the problem of the etiology of neuroses is not an individual medical problem but one that needs supplementary sociological consideration (433).

Neuroses are the outcome of unfavorable and socially determined educational measures, corresponding to a given and historically developed social milieu and necessary in this milieu. They cannot be changed without corresponding change in the milieu.

If a society becomes unstable, full of contradictory tendencies, and the scene of struggles between its different parts, power alone determines how and toward what goals education is directed. The instability and contradictions of a society are reflected in its education, and later in the neuroses of the educated individuals.

The temptation is great to digress into the sociology of education and morals.

However, what has been said will be illustrated by two simple examples only.

The self-esteem of a person as well as the content and degree of his defenses depend upon his "ideals." The ideals are less developed by direct teaching than by the whole spirit in which a child's life develops.

An authoritarian society must promote the readiness to later submission in its members by drumming into them the idea of all authority: conditional promises. "If you obey and submit, you will receive (real or imaginary) participation in power and protection." A democratic society favors the ideals of independence, self-reliance, and active mastery. Societies in which "authoritarian" and "democratic" elements are struggling will be contradictory in their ideals as well. The child learns that he must submit and obey in order to get the supplies he needs; and he learns at the same time: "Stand on your own feet." Historically the authoritarian type of ideal was unopposed in feudalism; the subjects actually were provided for if they renounced their independence, and the mental readiness of the majority of people to accept such dependence was needed in order to preserve society. Rising capitalism brought the opposite ideal. Free competition needed the new ideals of liberty and equality. The subsequent development of capitalism, however, not only created anew a majority of people who had to be kept contented in relative frustration and dependency, but economic contradictions made the entire society unstable to such a degree that, with the disappearance of free competition, authoritarian necessities also appeared again. At the same time everybody feels endangered in any attempt to get solidly established—and even in his very existence; this makes the single individual's activities hopeless, and thus regressive longings for passive-receptive regulation come to the fore again. Old feudalistic ideals are revived and even increased, and the result is a mixture of ideals, conflicts, and, later, neuroses. The difference in the economic conditions as well as in the history is responsible for the enormous differences in the mixtures of "authority" and "democracy" that are encountered today in different countries. Generally, all capitalistic society, by preparing the children for the role that money and competition will play in their life, favors the intensification of anal-sadistic strivings. This is the more unfavorable as simultaneously genital sexuality is discouraged and frustrated (434, 1278).

A second even more general example: It is characteristic of present-day society that many people are not able to satisfy their needs, although the means for their satisfaction are present. The textbooks of psychopathology discuss at length the deficiencies of the superego in persons who steal. It seems that the problem should be formulated in another way: Why is it that so many people do *not* steal? It is true that in the first place they abstain because they are prevented by force. But the majority is not prevented merely by force and fear of punishment. Social reality has succeeded in awakening, in a special kind of conscience, an intrapsychic force, which opposes the needs that ask for satisfaction. One does not steal, because "it is not right." Thus special social institutions cause the development of special counterinstinctual forces in its members. This necessity must be the decisive factor in the antisexual orientation of certain civilizations also.

Our comments make it plain that the insight into the formative power of social forces upon individual minds does not require any change in Freud's concepts of instincts, as certain authors believe (653, 820, 921). The instinctual needs are the raw material formed by the social influences; and it is the task of a psychoanalytic sociology to study the details of this shaping (650). Different "biological constitutions" contain manifold possibilities; yet they are not realities but potentialities. It is experience, that is, the cultural conditions, that transforms potentialities into realities, that shapes the real mental structure of man by forcing his instinctual demands into certain directions, by favoring some of them and blocking others, and even by turning parts of them against the rest.

Mental hygiene is socially limited not only by factors concerning the upbringing of children. In adults, too, we often find that the social situation makes it impossible to follow the advice a theoretical mental hygiene would give. The benefits of psychiatric social work should not be minimized. But most psychiatric social workers probably will agree that very often the fulfillment of the basic demands of mental hygiene depends on prerequisites that cannot be provided by mental hygiene. Would it not be the first task of such a mental hygiene to provide work, bread, and satisfaction of the basic needs for everybody?

It is true that real misery does not create neuroses in adult persons. But it does create frustrations and thus regressions. It does not create neuroses, but it may be a precipitating factor in their development. In this sense, the old ideas that modern nervousness is created by the "haste" and "competitiveness" of present-day civilization contains some truth. But besides, the real misery of adults may create neuroses in an indirect way, namely, in the next generation, educated by the frustrated adults.

It is strange that two absolutely contradictory judgments can be heard in respect to neuroses. Some people state that neuroses are a direct outcome of social misery, that it is not surprising that people who lack food and shelter become "nervous." On the other hand, some people say that neuroses are a kind of "luxury of the idle rich" and that a workman has other things in his head than to be nervous. Both statements are wrong and, in their clash of opinion, betray only the general emotional resistance against an unprejudiced study of the neuroses. The enormous extent of neuroses in present-day society does not recognize any class differences. This statement does not contradict the thesis that the neuroses are socially determined. It only illustrates the fact that morality, in spite of extremely different living conditions, is not too different in different classes of the same society (actually there are [smaller] class differences in neuroses, corresponding to differences in the children's actual experiences) (133, 136, 496).

A mental hygiene in the life of the adult would be effective as prophylaxis of neurosis if it were able to prevent new frustrations and resulting repressions, if it were able to provide satisfactions that "seduce to health," if it were able to create conditions that do not remobilize old childhood conflicts. It would be still more effective if it were able to prevent the pathogenic conflicts themselves; if it were able, wherever interferences with the child's impulses are necessary, to leave more ways of reaction open to the child, ways with less guilt feelings, more self-confidence, more activity, reason, and independent decision, with less archaic automatisms—if it could thus create strong egos able reasonably to anticipate the consequences of their actions. "Where id was, there shall ego be," said Freud (628). And this should even be supplemented: Also "where superego was" (that is, the automatic autonomy of unreasonable guilt feelings, the principle of talion, revenge, and automatisms) "shall ego be" (that is, a reasonable handling of reality). But such "shall" runs up against socially determined barriers.

Not because primitive instincts are still effective within us do we have wars, misery, and neuroses; rather, because we have not yet learned to avoid wars and misery by a more reasonable and less contradictory regulation of social relations, our instincts are still kept in an unfavorable form, which is used in wars and misery and which also produces neuroses.

We do not know whether under different social conditions there would not also be neuroses. But we do know that under the present circumstances social factors make the beginnings of a prophylaxis of the neuroses a task of Sisyphus.

But when, faced with the enormous neurotic (and nonneurotic) misery of today, we are sometimes near to despair, realizing that we can help only five to ten persons a year, we may find consolation in the insight that this limited psychotherapeutic work is at the same time the research method of a science which one day may gain the possibility of a more general application.

BIBLIOGRAPHY

A comprehensive bibliography on the psychoanalytic theory of neurosis had been prepared. However, paper shortage necessitates limitations for the time being. The following list, therefore, only includes (*a*) all books and papers referred to in the text of this book and (*b*) a few publications of general importance for the subject. The bibliography is limited to English and German literature. Of books and papers that were published in both languages, the English editions are quoted. In general, the literature is considered until 1943 inclusive.

KEY TO ABBREVIATIONS USED IN THE BIBLIOGRAPHY

Acta Ps. et N.	Acta Psychiatrica et Neurologica
Acta Psychol.	Acta Psychologica
A. Heart J.	American Heart Journal
A. Im.	American Imago
A. J. Dis. Child	American Journal of Diseases of the Child
A. J. I.	American Journal of Insanity
A. J. M. S.	American Journal of Mental Science
A. J. Obs. and Gyn.	American Journal of Obstetrics and Gynecology
A. J. Orthops.	American Journal of Orthopsychiatry
A. J. P.	American Journal of Psychiatry
A. J. Ph.	American Journal of Physiology
Allg. Z. f. Ps.	Allgemeine Zeitschrift fuer Psychiatrie
Ann. Int. Med.	Annals of Internal Medicine
A. Orthopsych. Assn.	American Orthopsychiatric Association
Arch. Derm. Syph.	Archive for Dermatology and Syphilology
Arch. ges. Psych.	Archiv fuer die gesamte Psychologie
Arch. N. Ps.	Archive for Neurology and Psychiatry
A. Soc. Res. Ps-s. Pr.	American Society for Research in Psychosomatic Problems
Assn. Research N. M. D.	Association for Research in Nervous and Mental Diseases
Autoref.	Autoreferat (review by the author)
B. J. D.	British Journal of Dermatology
B. J. In.	British Journal of Inebriety
B. J. P.	British Journal of Psychology
B. M. J.	British Medical Journal
Bull. Forest San.	Bulletin of the Forest Sanitarium
C.	Centralblatt fuer Psychoanalyse
Can. J. M. S.	Canadian Journal of Medicine and Surgery
Con.	Ferenczi, Sandor: *Contributions to Psychoanalysis,* Richard C. Badger, Boston, 1916
Cornell Univ. Med. Bull.	Cornell University Medical Bulletin
C. P.	Freud, Sigmund: *Collected Papers,* Institute of Psychoanalysis and Hogarth Press, London, 1924
D. A. Z.	Deutsche Aerzte Zeitung
Dis. Nerv. S.	Diseases of the Nervous System
D. Z. Hom.	Deutsche Zeitschrift fuer Homoeopathie
E. inn. M. K.	Ergebnisse der inneren Medizin und Kinderheilkunde
Ess.	Jones, Ernest: *Essays in Applied Psychoanalysis,* International Psychoanalytic Press, London, 1923
F. C.	Ferenczi, Sandor: *Further Contributions to the Theory and Technique of Psychoanalysis,* Institute of Psychoanalysis and Hogarth Press, London, 1926

Fortschr. Med.	Fortschritte der Medizin
G.	Concerning the psychoanalytic theory of neurosis in general
Ill. Psych. J.	Illinois Psychiatric Journal
Im.	Imago
Inst. for Ps-a.	Institute for Psychoanalysis (Chicago)
Inst. of Ps-a.	Institute of Psychoanalysis (London)
Int. Ps-a. Congr.	International Psychoanalytic Congress
Int. Ps-a. P.	International Psychoanalytic Press
Int. Ps-a. V.	Internationaler Psychoanalytischer Verlag
J. Ab. P.	Journal of Abnormal Psychology
J. A. M. A.	Journal of the American Medical Association
Jb. Ps. N.	Jahrbuch fuer Psychiatrie und Neurologie
J. Crim. Psych.	Journal of Criminal Psychopathology
J. Med.	Journal of Medicine
J. M. S.	Journal of Mental Science
J. N. M. D.	Journal of Nervous and Mental Disease
J. N. Ps.	Journal of Neurology and Psychiatry
J. N. Psychop.	Journal of Neurology and Psychopathology
Jo.	International Journal of Psychoanalysis
J. Soc. Psych.	Journal of Social Psychology
Kl. B.	Abraham, Karl: *Klinische Beitraege zur Psychoanalyse,* Internationaler Psychoanalytischer Verlag, Wien, 1921
Kl. R.	Klinische Rundschau
M.	British Journal of Medical Psychology
Menn. Bull.	Bulletin of the Menninger Clinic
M. ges. Sprach.	Monatsschrift fuer die gesamte Sprachheilkunde
M. H.	Mental Hygiene
M. N. P.	Monatsschrift fuer Neurologie und Psychiatrie
M. R.	Medical Record
M. R. R.	Medical Review of Reviews
Neue Erz.	Neue Erziehung
Neur. Z.	Neurologisches Zentralblatt
New Engl. J. M.	New England Journal of Medicine
N. M. D. Pub. Co.	Nervous and Mental Disease Publishing Company
N. Y. M. J.	New York Medical Journal
N. Y. S. Hosp. B.	New York State Hospital Bulletin
N. Y. S. J. M.	New York State Journal of Medicine
P.	Jones, Ernest: *Papers on Psychoanalysis,* 1st ed., Wood and Co., New York, 1913
Paed.	Zeitschrift fuer Psychoanalytische Paedagogik
P. B.	Psychiatric Bulletin
Proc. R. S. M.	Proceedings of the Royal Society of Medicine
Ps.	Psychiatry
Ps-A.	Psychoanalysis
Ps-a.	Psychoanalitic
Ps-a. Bwgg.	Psychoanalytische Bewegung
Ps-a. Q. Inc.	The Psychoanalytic Quarterly Incorporated
Ps-a. V.	Psychoanalytische Vereinigung
Psychol. Rec.	Psychological Record
Psychol. Rev.	Psychological Review
Psychosom. Med.	Psychosomatic Medicine
Psychosom. Med. Monogr.	Psychosomatic Medicine Monographs
Psych. Q.	Psychiatric Quarterly

ABRAHAM, KARL

(18) The Applicability of Psychoanalytic Treatment to Patients at an *In Chapter*
Advanced Age. *S. P.* 17, 23

(19) The Narcissistic Evaluation of Excretory Processes in Dream and
Neuroses. *S. P.* 5, 14, 18

(20) Manifestations of the Female Castration Complex. *S. P.* 5, 10, 12, 13, 16, 20

(21) Contributions to the Theory of the Anal Character. *S. P.* 5, 14, 20

(22) Discussion of Tic. *S. P.* 15

(23) The Spider as Dream Symbol. *S. P.* 4, 11

(24) The Influence of Oral Erotism on Character Formation. *S. P.* 10, 20

(25) Character Formation on the Genital Level of Libido Development.
S. P. 20

(26) A Short Study of the Development of the Libido. *S. P.* 5, 9, 12, 16, 17, 18, 20, 22

(27) Psychoanalyse und Gynaekologie. *Z. G. G.* LXXXIX, 1925 10, 13

(28) Psychoanalytical Notes on Coué's Method of Self-Mastery. *Jo.*
VII, 1926 23

(29) The History of an Impostor in the Light of Psychoanalytic Knowledge. *Q.* IV, 1935 16, 22

ACHELIS, WERNER

(30) Das Plattenlaufen. *Paed.* III, 1929 9, 14

AICHHORN, AUGUST

(31) Wayward Youth. *Putnam,* London, 1936 16, 20, 23

(32) Zum Verwahrlostenproblem. *Paed.* I, 1926 23

(33) Psychoanalytisches Verstaendnis und Erziehung Dissozialer. In
Federn-Meng: *Ps-a. Volksbuch,* 1926 23

(34) Erziehungsberatung. *Paed.* VI, 1932 23

(35) Zur Technik der Erziehungsberatung. *Paed.* X, 1936 23

ALEXANDER, FRANZ

(36) The Castration Complex in the Formation of Character. *Jo.* VI,
1923 5, 14, 20

(37) Psychoanalysis of the Total Personality. *N. M. D. Pub. Co.,*
New York and Washington, 1930 6, 12, 14, 19, 20

(38) The Neurotic Character. *Jo.* XI, 1930 16, 20

(39) Concerning the Genesis of the Castration Complex. *R.* XXII,
1935 5

(40) —and Staub, Hugo: The Criminal, the Judge, and the Public.
Allen and Unwin, London, 1931 14, 20

(41) The Medical Value of Psychoanalysis. *Norton,* New York, 1932 10, 13

(42) The Relation of Structural and Instinctual Conflicts. *Q.* II, 1933 8, 20

(43) The Influence of Psychological Factors upon Gastrointestinal Disturbances. *Q.* III, 1934 13, 20

(44) The Logic of Emotions and Its Dynamic Background. *Jo.* X,
1935 2, 13, 19, 20, 23

In Chapter

(45) —and Wilson, George: Quantitative Dream Studies. *Q.* IV, 1935   13, 20
(46) The Problem of Psychoanalytic Technique. *Q.* IV, 1935   23
(47) —and Healy, William: Roots of Crime. *Knopf,* New York, 1935   16, 20
(48) Addenda to: "The Medical Value of Psychoanalysis." *Q.* V. 1936   13
(49) —and Menninger, William: The Relation of Persecutory Delusions to the Functioning of the Gastrointestinal Tract. *J. N. M. D.* LXXXIV, 1936   18
(50) —and Saul, Leon N.: The Human Spirogram. *A. J. Ph.* XLIX, 1937   13
(51) Emotional Factors in Essential Hypertension. *Psychosom. Med.* I, 1939   13
(52) Psychoanalytic Study of a Case of Essential Hypertension. *Psychosom. Med.* I, 1939   13
(53) Psychoanalysis Revised. *Q.* IX, 1940   11
(54) —and Saul, Leon N.: Respiration and Personality. *Psychosom. Med.* II, 1940   13
(55) —*et al.:* Proceedings of the Brief Psychotherapy Council, October, 1942. *Inst. for Ps-a.,* Chicago, 1942   23
(56) Fundamental Concepts of Psychosomatic Research: Psychogenesis, Conversion, Specificity. *Psychosom. Med.* V, 1943   13

ALLEN, CLIFFORD

(57) Introjection in Schizophrenia. *R.* XXII, 1935   18
(58) The Sexual Perversions and Abnormalities. *Oxford Medical Pub.,* London, 1940   16

ALLEN, FREDERICK H.

(59) Psychotherapy with Children. *Norton,* New York, 1942   23

ALLENDY, R.

(60) Sadism in Women. *R.* XVII, 1930   16

ALMASY, ENDRE

(61) Daten zur manischen Assoziation und Affektuebertragung. *Z.* XIX, 1933   17
(62) Zur Psychoanalyse amentiaaehnlicher Faelle. *Z.* XXII, 1936   13, 18

ALBERT, AUGUSTA

(63) The Latency Period. *A. J. Orthops.* XI, 1941   6

AMES, THADDEUS H.

(64) Prevention of Nervous and Mental Disease in Childhood. In Lorand: *Ps-a. Today,* Covici Friede, New York, 1933   23

ANDERSON, O. D.

(65) —and Parmenter, R.: A Long-Term Study of the Experimental Neurosis in the Sheep and Dog. *Psychosom. Med. Monogr.,* New York, 1941   2

ANDREAS-SALOME, LOU   *In Chapter*

(66) Anal und Sexual. *Im.* IV, 1916
                                                     5

BACON, CATHERINE

(67) Typical Personality Trends and Conflicts in Cases of Spastic
       Colitis. *Q.* III, 1934
                                                     13

BAK, ROBERT

(68) Regression of Ego-Orientation and Libido in Schizophrenia. *Jo.*
       XX, 1939
                                                     18
(69) Ueber die dynamisch-strukturellen Bedingungen des primaeren
       Beziehungswahnes. *Z. ges. N. P.* CLXVI, 1939
                                                     18
(70) Dissolution of the Ego, Mannerism and Delusion of Grandeur.
       J. N. M. D. XCVIII, 1943
                                                     18

BAKER, DORIS M.

(71) Cardiac Symptoms in the Neuroses. *Lewis,* London, 1943
                                                     13

BALINT, ALICE

(72) Ueber eine besondere Form der infantilen Angst. *Paed.* VII,
       1933
                                                     5
(73) Liebe zur Mutter und Mutterliebe. *Z.* XXIV, 1939
                                                     4, 5

BALINT, MICHAEL

(74) Ueber die Psychoanalyse des Charakters. *Z.* XIX, 1933
                                                     20
(75) Charakteranalyse und Neubeginn. *Z.* XX, 1934
                                                     20
(76) Der Onanie-Abgewoehnungskampf in der Pubertaet. *Paed.*
       VIII, 1934
                                                     5, 6
(77) A Contribution to Fetishism. *Jo.* XVI, 1935
                                                     16
(78) The Final Goal of Psychoanalytic Treatment. *Jo.* XVII, 1936
                                                     23
(79) Fruehe Entwicklungsstadien des Ichs: Primaere Objektliebe.
       Im. XXIII, 1937
                                                     4
(80) A Contribution to the Psychology of Menstruation. *Q.* VI, 1937
                                                     13
(81) Eros and Aphrodite. *Jo.* XIX, 1938
                                                     5

BALLY, GUSTAV

(82) Zur Frage der Behandlung schizoider Neurotiker. *Z.* XVI, 1930
                                                     18
(83) Die Wahrnehmungslehre von Jaensch and ihre Beziehung zu
       psychoanalytischen Problemen. *Im.* XVII, 1931
                                                     4, 13
(84) Ueber Hochstapler und Verwahrloste. *Paed.* IX, 1935
                                                     16

BALSAR, BEN H.

(85) A Behavior Problem—Runaways. *Psych. Q.* XIII, 1936
                                                     16

BARINBAUM, MOSES

(86) Zum Problem des psychophysischen Zusammenhangs mit beson-
       derer Beruecksichtigung der Dermatologie. *Z.* XX, 1934
                                                     13

BARKAS, MARY

(87) The Treatment of Psychotic Patients in Institutions in the Light *In Chapter* of Psychoanalysis. *J. N. Psychop.*, 1925   18, 23

BARTEMEIER, LEO H.

(88) A Counting Compulsion. *Jo.* XXII, 1941   9, 14
(89) Micropsia. *Q.* X, 1941   12
(90) Concerning the Psychogenesis of Convulsive Disorders. *Q.* XII, 1943   13

BAUDOUIN, CHARLES

(91) Ein Fall von Bettnaessen. *Paed.* III, 1929   12
(92) Ein Fall von Kleptomanie. *Paed.* IV, 1930   16

BEHN-ESCHENBURG, HANNS

(93) The Antecedents of the Oedipus Complex. *Jo.* XVI, 1935   5

BENDER, LAURETTA

(94) The Anal Component in Persecutory Delusions. *R.* XXI, 1934   18
(95) —and Schilder, Paul: Suicidal Preoccupations and Attempts in Children. *A. J. Orthops.* VII, 1937   17

BENEDEK, THERESE

(96) Notes from the Analysis of a Case of Erythrophobia. *Jo.* VI, 1925   11, 20
(97) Todestrieb und Angst. *Z.* XVII, 1931   8
(98) Mental Processes in Thyreotoxic States. *Q.* III, 1934   13
(99) Dominant Ideas and Their Relation to Morbid Cravings. *Jo.* XVII, 1936   5, 16
(100) Defense Mechanisms and Structure of the Total Personality. *Q.* VI, 1937   20
(101) Adaptation to Reality in Early Infancy. *Q.* VII, 1938   4
(102) —and Rubenstein, Arnold: The Sexual Cycle in Women. *Psychosom. Med. Monogr.*, Washington, 1942   13, 21

BERGLER, EDMUND

(103) Zur Problematik der Pseudodebilitaet. *Z.* XVIII, 1932   10, 23
(104) —und Eidelberg, Ludwig: Der Mammakomplex des Mannes. *Z.* XIX, 1933   5, 13, 16, 20
(105) Psychoanalyse eines Falles von Pruefungsangst. *Z. Psychoth.*, 1933   11, 20
(106) Zur Problematik des oralen Pessimisten. *Im.* XX, 1934   16, 20
(107) —und Eidelberg, Ludwig: Der Mechanismus der Depersonalisation. *Z.* XXI, 1935   18
(108) Some Special Varieties of Ejaculatory Disturbance not Hitherto Described. *Jo.* XVI, 1935   10, 20
(109) Bemerkungen ueber eine Zwangsneurose in ultimis. *Z.* XXII, 1936   14, 22

(110) Further Observations in the Clinical Picture of Psychogenic   *In Chapter*
Oral Aspermia. *Jo.* XVIII, 1937   10, 13, 16, 20
(111) Die Psychische Impotenz des Mannes. *Huber,* Bern, 1937   10
(112) Preliminary Phases of the Masculine Beating Fantasy. *Q.*
VII, 1938   16
(113) Beitraege zur Psychologie der Eifersucht. *Z.* XXV, 1939   18, 20
(114) On the Psychoanalysis of the Ability to Wait and of Impatience.
R. XXVI, 1939   16
(115) Four Types of Neurotic Indecisiveness. *Q.* X, 1940   10, 14
(116) The Gambler: A Misunderstood Neurotic. *J. Crim. Psych.* IV,
1943   16
(117) Legorrhoea. *Psych. Q.* XVIII, 1944   20
(118) A New Approach to the Therapy of Erythrophobia. *Q.* XIII,
1944   10, 11, 20

BERKELEY-HILL, OWEN

(119) The Anal Complex and Its Relation to Delusions of Persecution.
Jo. IV, 1923   18
(120) Flatus and Aggression. *Jo.* XI, 1930   15

BERLINER, BERNHARD

(121) Libido and Reality in Masochism. *Q.* X, 1940   16, 20
(122) Short Psychoanalytic Psychotherapy; Its Possibilities and Its
Limitations. *Menn. Bull.* V, 1941   23

BERNER, EMMA

(123) Eine Einschlafstoerung aus Todesangst. *Paed.* XI, 1937   10

BERNFELD, SIEGFRIED

(124) Zur Psychologie der Lektuere. *Z.* III, 1915   15, 16, 20
(125) Zur Psychologie des Unmusikalischen. *Arch. ges. Psych.*
XXXIV, 1918   10
(126) Zur Idiosynkrasie gegen Speisen. *Z.* V, 1919   10
(127) Bemerkungen ueber Sublimierung. *Im.* VIII, 1921   9
(128) Ueber eine typische Form der maennlichen Pubertaet. *Im.* IX,
1923   6
(129) Vom dichterischen Schaffen der Jugend. *Int. Ps-a. V.,* Wien,
1924   6
(130) Ueber Faszination. *Im.* XIV, 1928   4, 18
(131) Sisyphos, oder ueber die Grenzen der Erziehung. *Int. Ps-a. V.,*
Vienna, 1928   23
(132) Einige spekulative Bemerkungen ueber die psychologische
Bewertung telepathischer Prozesse. *Z. ges. N. P.,* 1928   20
(133) Der soziale Ort und seine Bedeutung fuer Neurose, Verwahr-
losung und Paedagogik. *Im.* XV, 1929   16, 20, 23
(134) Psychology of the Infant. *Kegan Paul,* London, 1929   4, 18
(135) Selbstmord. *Paed.* III, 1929   17
(136) Die Tantalussituation. *Im.* XVII, 1931   20. 23

In Chapter

(137) Zur Sublimierungstheorie. *Im.* XVII, 1931   9
(138) Ueber die Einteilung der Triebe. *Im.* XXI, 1935   5
(139) Types of Adolescence. *Q.* VII, 1938   6
(140) Freud's Earliest Theories and the School of Helmholtz. *Q.* XIII, 1944   1

BERTSCHINGER, H.

(141) Illustrierte Halluzinationen. *Y.* III, 1911   18

BIBRING, EDWARD

(142) Klinische Beitraege zur Paranoiafrage, I: Zur Psychologie der
       Todesideen bei paranoider Schizophrenie. *Z.* XIV, 1928   18
(143) Klinische Beitraege zur Paranoiafrage, II: Ein Fall von Organ-
       Projektion. *Z.* XV, 1929   18
(144) The Development and Problems of the Theory of the Instincts.
       Jo. XXI, 1941   5
(145) The Conception of the Repetition Compulsion. *Q.* XII, 1943   21

BIBRING-LEHNER, GRETE

(146) Ueber die phallische Phase und ihre Stoerungen beim Maed-
       chen. *Paed.* VII, 1933   5
(147) Ueber eine orale Komponente bei maennlicher Inversion. *Z.*
       XXV, 1940   16

BIEN, E.

(148) The Clinical Psychogenic Aspects of Pruritus. *R.* XX, 1933   13

BINSWANGER, L.

(149) Psychoanalyse und klinische Psychiatrie. *Z.* VII, 1921   18

BIVIN, GEORGE D.

(150) —and Klinger, M. P.: Pseudocyesis. *Principia Press,* Bloom-
       ington, Ind., 1937   12, 13

BJERRE, POUL

(151) Zur Radikalbehandlung der chronischen Paranoia. *Y.* III, 1911   18

BLAIR, DONALD

(152) Prognosis in Schizophrenia. *J. M. S.* LXXXVI, 1940   18

BLANCO, IGNAZIO MATTE

(153) On Introjection and the Processes of Psychic Metabolism. *Jo.*
       XXII, 1941   17

BLANTON, SMILEY

(154) What is the Problem of Stuttering? *J. Ab. P.* XIII, 1918   15
(155) —and Blanton, Margaret Gray: For Stutterers. *Appleton-
       Century,* New York, 1936   15
(156) Analytic Study of a Cure at Lourdes. *Q.* IX, 1940   23

BLEULER, EUGEN   *In Chapter*

(157)   Alkohol und Neurosen. *Y*. III, 1911   16

BLUM, ERNST

(158)   The Psychology of Study and Examinations. *Jo*. VII, 1926   11, 20

BLUMGART, LEONARD

(159)   A Short Communciation on Repression. *R*. IV, 1916   9

BOEHM, FELIX

(160)   Beitraege zur Psychologie der Homosexualitaet. *Z*. VI, 1920,
          and *Z*. VIII, 1922   16
(161)   Bemerkungen ueber Transvestitismus. *Z*. IX, 1923   16
(162)   Homosexualitaet und Oedipuskomplex. *Z*. XII, 1926   16
(163)   The Femininity Complex in Man. *Jo*. XI, 1930   5, 14, 16
(164)   Ueber zwei Typen von maennlichen Homosexuellen. *Z*. XIX,
          1933   16
(165)   Anthropophagy, Its Forms and Motives. *Jo*. XVI, 1935   5

BOISEN, ANTON T.

(166)   The Form and Content of Schizophrenic Thinking. *Ps*. V, 1942   18

BONAPARTE, MARIE

(167)   Ueber die Symbolik der Kopftrophaeen. *Im*. XIV, 1928   20
(168)   Die Identifizierung einer Tochter mit ihrer verstorbenen Mut-
          ter. *Z*. XV, 1929   5, 20
(169)   Eine kleptomane Anwandlung. *Z*. XVI, 1930   16
(170)   Der Mensch und sein Zahnarzt. *Im*. XIX, 1933   20
(171)   Passivity, Masochism and Frigidity. *Jo*. XVI, 1935   10, 23
(172)   Time and the Unconscious. *Jo*. XXI, 1940   14

BORNSTEIN, BERTA

(173)   Zur Psychogenese der Pseudodebilitaet. *Z*. XVI, 1930   9, 10, 23
(174)   Beziehungen zwischen Sexual- und Intellektentwicklung.
          Paed. IV, 1930   10
(175)   Phobia in a Two-and-a-half-year-old Child. *Q*. IV, 1934   10, 11, 23
(176)   Leugnung durch die Phantasie. *Paed*. X, 1936   9

BORNSTEIN, STEFF

(177)   Zum Problem der narzisstischen Identifizierung. *Z*. XVI, 1930   17
(178)   Ein Beitrag zur Psychoanalyse des Paedagogen. *Paed*. VII, 1933   16
(179)   A Child Analysis. *Q*. IV, 1935   23
(180)   Missverstaendnisse der psychoanalytischen Paedogogik. *Paed*.
          XI, 1937   23

BORNSZTAJN, MAURICY

(181)   Schizophrene Symptome im Lichte der Psychoanalyse. *Z*. XII,
          1926   18

BOSS, M.

(182) Koerperliches Kranksein als Folge seelischer Gleichgewichts-   *In Chapter*
stoerungen. *Huber,* Bern, 1940   13

BRAATÖY, TRYGVE

(183) Maenner zwischen 15 und 25 Jahren. *Fabritius u. Sonner,*
Oslo, 1934   6
(184) The Prognosis in Schizophrenia, with Remarks Regarding
Diagnosis and Therapy. *Acta Ps. et N.* XI, 1936   18

BRADLEY, CHARLES

(185) Schizophrenia in Childhood. *Macmillan,* New York, 1941   18
(186) —and Bowen, Margaret: Behavior Characteristics of Schizophrenic Children. *Psych. Q.* XV, 1941   18

BREUER, JOSEPH

(187) —and Freud, Sigmund: The Psychic Mechanism of Hysterical
Phenomena. No. 4 in *S. P. H.*   12
(188) —and Freud, Sigmund: Studies in Hysteria. *N. M. D. Publ. Co.,*
New York and Washington, 1936. (First German edition.
Deuticke, Leipzig, 1895.)   3, 12, 23

BRIEHL, WALTER

(189) —and Kulka, Ernst: Lactation in a Virgin. *Q.* IV, 1935   13

BRIERLEY, MARJORIE

(190) Specific Determinants in Feminine Development. *Jo.* XVII,
1936   5
(191) Affects in Theory and Practice. *Jo.* XVIII, 1937   2, 19
(192) A Prefatory Note on Internalized Objects and Depression. *Jo.*
XX, 1939   17

BRILL, A. A.

(193) Psychological Factors in Dementia Praecox: An Analysis.
J. Ab. P. III, 1908   18
(194) Anal Eroticism and Character. *J. Ab. P.* VII, 1912   14, 20
(195) The Only or Favorite Child in Adult Life. *N. Y. S. J. M.,*
August, 1912   5, 20
(196) Hysterical Dreamy States. *N. Y. M. J.* XCV, 1912   12
(197) Psychoanalysis: Its Theories and Practical Application. *Saun-
ders,* Philadelphia and London, 1st. ed., 1913   G
(198) Artificial Dreams and Lying. *J. Ab. P.* IX, 1914   20
(199) Fundamental Conceptions of Psychoanalysis. *Harcourt, Brace,*
New York, 1921   G
(200) The Application of Psychoanalysis to Psychiatry. *J. N. M. D.*
LXVIII, 1928   17, 18
(201) Diagnostic Errors in Neurasthenia. *M. R. R.,* 1930   10
(202) The Sense of Smell in the Neuroses and Psychoses. *Q.* I, 1932   14, 15

		In Chapter
(203)	The Schizoid Concept in Neuroses and Psychoses. In *Schizophrenia:* Assn. Research N. M. D., Hoeber, New York, 1938	18
(204)	The Concept of Psychic Suicide. *Jo.* XX, 1939	17, 18

BROMBERG, WALTER

(205)	—and Schilder, Paul: Psychological Considerations in Alcoholic Hallucinations. *Jo.* XIV, 1933	16
(206)	—and Schilder, Paul: Death and Dying. *R.* XX, 1933	11, 17
(207)	—and Schilder, Paul: Attitude of Psychoneurotics towards Death. *R.* XXIII, 1936	11, 17

BROWN, J. F.

(208)	The Psychodynamics of Abnormal Behavior. *McGraw-Hill,* New York, 1940	G

BRUCH, HILDE

(209)	—and Touraine, Grace: Obesity in Childhood. *Psychosom. Med.* II, 1940	13
(210)	Obesity in Childhood and Personality Development. *A. J. Orthops.* XI, 1941	13
(211)	Psychiatric Aspects of Obesity in Children. *A. J. P.* XCIX, 1943	13

BRUN, R.

(212)	Zur Psychoanalyse des Stotterns. *Z.* IX, 1922	15

BRUNNER, M.

(213)	Beeinflussung des Stotterns. *Paed.* X, 1936	15

BRYAN, DOUGLASS

(214)	A Note on the Tongue. *Jo.* III, 1922	15
(215)	Speech and Castration: Two Unusual Analytic Hours. *Jo.* VI, 1925	14, 15
(216)	Bisexuality. *Jo.* XI, 1930	5, 16

BULLARD, DEXTER M.

(217)	The Application of Psychoanalytic Psychiatry to the Psychoses. *R.* XXVI, 1939	18
(218)	Experiences in the Psychoanalytic Treatment of Psychotics. *Q.* IX, 1940	18
(219)	The Organization of Psychoanalytic Procedure in the Hospital. *J. N. M. D.* XCI, 1940	16, 18, 23

BUNKER, HENRY ALLEN

(220)	The Voice as (Female) Phallus. *Q.* III, 1934	15, 16

BURLINGHAM, DOROTHY

(221)	Child Analysis and the Mother. *Q.* IV, 1935	23

(222) Phantasie und Wirklichkeit in einer Kinderanalyse. *Z.* XXIV, 1939   *In Chapter* 23

(223) Psychic Problems of the Blind. *A. Im.* II, 1941   5

BURROW, TRIGANT

(224) The Group Method of Psychoanalysis. *R.* XIV, 1927   23
(225) The Structure of Insanity. *Paul, Trench and Trubner,* London, 1932   23

BUXBAUM, EDITH

(226) Angstaeusserungen von Schulmaedchen im Pubertaetsalter. *Paed.* VII, 1933   6
(227) Exhibitionistic Onanism in a Ten-year-old Boy. *Q.* IV, 1935   12

BYCHOWSKI, GUSTAV

(228) Psychoanalytisches aus der psychiatrischen Abteilung. *Z.* XI, 1921   18
(229) Zur Psychopathologie der Brandstiftung. *Schw. A. N. P.* V, 1922   16
(230) A Case of Oral Delusions of Persecution. *Jo.* XI, 1930   18
(231) Psychoanalyse im hypoglykaemischen Zustand. *Z.* XXIII, 1937   23
(232) One Relation between the Ego and the Superego. *R.* XXX, 1943   6
(233) Disorders in the Body Image in the Clinical Pictures of Psychoses. *J. N. M. D.* XCVII, 1943   18
(234) Physiology of Schizophrenic Thinking. *J. N. M. D.* XCVIII, 1943   18

CAMERON, NORMAN

(235) Schizophrenic Thinking in a Problem-Solving Situation. *J. M. S.* LXXXV, 1939   18
(236) Deterioration and Regression in Schizophrenic Thinking. *J. Ab. P.* XXXIV, 1939   18

CAMERON, WILLIAM M.

(237) The Treatment of Children in Psychiatric Clinics with Particular Reference to the Use of Play Techniques. *Menn. Bull.* IV, 1940   23

CAMPBELL, C. MACFIE

(238) The Form and Content of the Psychoses; the Role of Psychoanalysis in Psychiatry. *Cornell Univ. Med. Bull.* V, 1915   18
(239) Clinical Studies in Schizophrenia: A Follow-up Study of a Small Group of Cases of Deterioration with Few Special Trends (Schizophrenic Surrender). *A. J. P.* XCIX, 1943   18

CANNON, WALTER B.

(240) Bodily Changes in Pain, Hunger, Fear and Rage. *Appleton,* New York, 1929   13
(241) The Wisdom of the Body. *Norton,* New York, 1932   2

In Chapter

(242)   The Role of Emotion in Disease. *Ann. Int. Med.,* 1936   13

CANTOR, NATHANIEL

(243)   What is a Normal Mind? *A. J. Orthops.* XI, 1941   23

CARMICHAEL, HUGH T.

(244)   A Psychoanalytic Study of a Case of Eunuchoidism. *Q.* X, 1941
13

CARP, E. A. D. E.

(245)   Die Rolle der praegenitalen Libidofixierung in der Perversion. *Z.* X, 1924
16

CARVER, ALFRED

(246)   Notes on the Analysis of a Case of Melancholia. *J. N. Ps.* I, 1921   17

CASSITY, J. H.

(247)   Psychological Considerations of Pedophilia. *R.* XIV, 1926   16

CHADWICK, MARY

(248)   A Case of Cleptomania in a Girl of Ten Years. *Jo.* VI, 1925   16
(249)   Ueber die Wurzeln der Wissbegierde. *Z.* XI, 1925   5, 10, 15, 20
(250)   The Psychological Problem of the Foster Child. *Child,* May, 1925
5, 20
(251)   Notes upon the Acquisition of Knowledge. *R.* XIII, 1926   5, 15
(252)   Die Unterscheidung zwischen Ton und Sprache in der fruehen Kindheit. *Paed.* II, 1928
4, 15
(253)   Difficulties in Child Development. *Allen and Unwin,* London, 1928
23
(254)   Notes upon the Fear of Death. *Jo.* X, 1929   11
(255)   The Psychological Effects of Menstruation. *N. M. D. Pub. Co.,* New York and Washington, 1932
6, 13
(256)   Adolescent Girlhood. *Allen and Unwin,* London, 1932   6
(257)   Women's Periodicity. *Noel Douglass,* London, 1933   17, 21

CHASE, LOUIS S.

(258)   —and Silverman, S.: Prognostic Criteria in Schizophrenia. *A. J. P.,* 1941
18
(259)   —and Silverman, Samuel: Prognosis in Schizophrenia. *J. N. M. D.* XCVIII, 1943
18

CHASSELL, JOSEPH

(260)   Family Constellation in the Etiology of Essential Alcoholism. *Ps.* I, 1938
16
(261)   Psychoanalytic Therapy in a Mental Hospital. *Ps.* III, 1940   23

CHIJS, A. VAN DER

(262)   Ueber Halluzinationen und Psychoanalyse. *Z.* V, 1919   18

CHRISTOFFEL, H.

In Chapter

(263) Harntriebaeusserungen, insbesondere Enuresis, Urophilie und
Uropolemie. Z. XXI, 1935   12
(264) Exhibitionism and Exhibitionists. Jo. XVII, 1936   16
(265) Bemerkungen ueber zweierlei Mechanismen der Identifizierung.
Im. XXIII, 1937   4, 16

CLARDY, E. R.

(266) —and Goldensohn, L. N.: Schizophrenic-like Reactions in Children. Psych. Q. XV, 1941   18

CLARK, L. PIERCE

(267) The Nature and Pathogenesis of Epilepsy. N. Y. M. J., 1914   13
(268) Some Observations upon the Aetiology of Mental Torticollis.
M. R., February, 1914   13
(269) A Personality Study of the Epileptic Constitution. A. J. M. S.
XLVIII, 1914   13
(270) A Further Study upon Mental Torticollis as a Psychoneurosis.
M. R., March, 1914   13
(271) Clinical Studies in Epilepsy. P. B. IX, 1916   13
(272) A Further Study of Mental Content in Epilepsy. P. B., October, 1917   13
(273) A Psychological Study of Some Alcoholics. R. VI, 1919   16
(274) Practical Remarks upon the Use of Modified Psychoanalysis in
the Borderline Neuroses and Psychoses. R. VI, 1919   18
(275) The Psychological Treatment of Retarded Depressions. A. J. I.
XLV, 1919   17
(276) A Clinical Study of Some Mental Contents in Epileptic Attacks.
R. VII, 1920   13
(277) A Study of Unconscious Motivations in Suicides. N. Y. M. J.,
September, 1922   17
(278) The Fantasy Method of Analyzing Narcissistic Neuroses. R.
XIII, 1925   18
(279) The Question of Prognosis in Narcissistic Neuroses and Psychoses. Jo. XIV, 1933   18
(280) What is the Psychology of Organic Epilepsy? R. XX, 1933   13
(281) What is the Psychology of Little's Disease? R. XXI, 1934   13

COHN, FRANZ

(282) Analyse eines Falles von Strassenangst. Z. XIV, 1928   11
(283) Practical Approach to the Problem of Narcissistic Neuroses. Q.
IX, 1940   18

CONNELL, E. H.

(284) The Significance of the Idea of Death in the Neurotic Mind.
M. IV, 1924   11, 17

CONRAD, AGNES

(285) Analysis of a Case of Chronic Invalidism with Hysterical Mechanism Complicating Organic Disease. R. XXII, 1935   12

COOK, S. W.

(286) A Survey of the Methods Used to Produce Experimental Neu-   *In Chapter*
roses. *A. J. P.* XCV, 1939   2

CORIAT, ISADOR H.

(287) Some Statistical Results of the Psychoanalytic Treatment of the
Psychoneuroses. *R.* IV, 1917   23
(288) The Treatment of Dementia Praecox by Psychoanalysis.
J. Ab. P. XII, 1917   18
(289) Suggestion as a Form of Medical Magic. *J. Ab. P.* XVIII, 1923   23
(290) The Character Traits of Urethral Eroticism. *R.* XI, 1924   20
(291) The Oral-Erotic Components of Stammering. *Jo.* VIII, 1927   10, 15
(292) Stammering. *N. M. D. Pub. Co.,* New York and Washington,
1928   10, 15
(293) The Oral Libido in Language Formation. *Jo.* X, 1929   15
(294) A Psychoanalytic Theory of Hallucinations. *R.* XXI, 1934   18
(295) The Structure of the Ego. *Q.* IX, 1940   4
(296) A Note on the Medusa Symbolism. *A. Im.* II, 1941   10, 15

CRANK, HARLAN

(297) The Use of Psychoanalytic Principles in Outpatient Psycho-
therapy. *Menn. Bull.* IV, 1940   23

CRONIN, HERBERT J.

(298) An Analysis of the Neuroses of Identical Twins. *R.* XX, 1933   20

CROWLEY, RALPH M.

(299) Psychoanalytic Literature on Drug Addiction and Alcoholism.
R. XXVI, 1939   16

CRUTCHER, ROBERTA

(300) Child Psychiatry. *Ps.* VI, 1943   23

DANIELS, G. E.

(301) Turning Points in the Analysis of a Case of Alcoholism. *Q.*
II, 1933   16
(302) Neuroses Associated with the Gastrointestinal Tract. *A. J. P.*
XCI, 1934   13
(303) Analysis of a Case of Neurosis with Diabetes Mellitus. *Q.* V,
1936   13
(304) Present Trends in the Evaluation of Psychic Factors in Diabetes
Mellitus. *Psychosom. Med.* I, 1939   13
(305) Treatment of a Case of Ulcerative Colitis Associated with
Hysterical Depression. *Psychosom. Med.* II, 1940   13
(306) Psychiatric Aspects of Ulcerative Colitis. *New Engl. J. M.*
CCXXVI, 1942   13

DAVIS, KINGSLEY

(307) Mental Hygiene and the Class Structure. *Ps.* I, 1938   23

(307a)   Intrapsychic Factors in the Choice of a Sexual Object. *Q.*   *In Chapter*
        XII, 1943   16

DERI, FRANCES

(308)   On Sublimation. *Q.* VIII, 1939   9
(309)   On Neurotic Disturbances of Sleep. *Jo.* XXIII, 1942   10

DESPERT, J. LOUISE

(310)   Thinking and Motility Disorder in a Schizophrenic Child.
        Psych. Q. XV, 1941   18

DEUTSCH, FELIX

(311)   Psychoanalyse und Organkrankheiten. *Z.* VIII, 1922   13
(312)   —und Kauf, E.: Ueber die Ursachen der Krieslaufstoerungen
        bei den Herzneurosen. *Z. ges. exp. M.* XXXIV, 1923   13
(313)   Zur Bildung des Konversionssymptoms. *Z.* X, 1924   12, 13
(314)   Der gesunde und der kranke Koerper in psychoanalytischer
        Betrachtung. *Z.* XII, 1926   13
(315)   Studies in Pathogenesis: Biological and Psychological Aspects.
        Q. II, 1933   13
(316)   The Choice of Organ in Organ Neurosis. *Jo.* X, 1939   12, 13
(317)   The Production of Somatic Disease by Emotional Disturbance.
        Williams and Wilkins, Baltimore, 1939   13
(318)   Review of French-Alexander: Psychogenic Factors in Bronchial
        Asthma. *Q.* XII, 1943   13

DEUTSCH, HELENE

(319)   Zur Psychologie des Misstrauens. *Im.* VII, 1920   18
(320)   Ueber die pathologische Luege (Pseudologia phantastica). *Z.*
        VIII, 1922   20
(321)   Zur Psychogenese eines Tic-Falles. *Z.* XI, 1925   15
(322)   Zur Psychologie der weiblichen Sexualfunktionen. *Int. Ps-a.*
        V., Wien, 1925   10, 13, 17
(323)   A Contribution to the Psychology of Sport. *Jo.* VII, 1926   20
(324)   Ueber Zufriedenheit, Glueck und Ekstase. *Z.* XIII, 1927   18
(325)   The Genesis of Agoraphobia. *Jo.* X, 1929   11, 17
(326)   The Significance of Masochism in the Mental Life of Women.
        Jo. XI, 1930   16
(327)   Psychoanalysis of the Neuroses. *Hogarth Press and Inst. of*
        Ps-a., London, 1933   11, 17, 20, 21
(328)   On Female Homosexuality. *Q.* I, 1932   16
(329)   Homosexuality in Women. *Jo.* XIV, 1933   16
(330)   Zur Psychologie der manisch-depressiven Zustaende, insbeson-
        dere der chronischen Hypomanie. *Z.* XIX, 1933   17
(331)   Ueber einen Typus der Pseudo-Affektivitaet ("als ob"). *Z.*
        XX, 1934   18, 20
(332)   Absence of Grief. *Q.* VI, 1937   9, 17
(333)   Some Forms of Emotional Disturbance and Their Relationship
        to Schizophrenia. *Q.* XI, 1942   18, 20

DEXTER, LEWIS A.

(334) A Note on the Unification of Sociology and Physiology. *Ps.*   *In Chapter*
       VI, 1943   13, 23

DOLLARD, JOHN

(335) —and others: Frustration and Aggression. *Yale Univ. Press,*
       New Haven, 1939   5

DOOLEY, LUCILLE

(336) A Psychoanalytic Study of Manic-Depressive Psychoses. *R.*
       VIII, 1921   17
(337) The Relation of Humor to Masochism. *R.* XXVIII, 1941   16
(338) The Concept of Time in Defense of Ego Integrity. *Ps.* IV, 1941 11, 14

DREYFUSS, KARL

(339) Ueber die Bedeutung des psychischen Traumas in der Epilepsie.
       Z. XXII, 1936   13
(340) Zur Theorie der traumatischen Neurose. *Z.* XXVI, 1941   7

DRUECK, CHARLES J.

(341) Essential Pruritus Perinei. *J. N. M. D.* XCVII, 1943   13

DUNBAR, FLANDERS

(342) Emotions and Bodily Changes. *Columbia Univ. Press,* New
       York, 1938   13
(343) Psychosomatic Diagnosis. *Hoeber,* New York, 1944   13

DUNN, WILLIAM H.

(344) Emotional Factors in Neurocirculatory Asthenia. *Psychosom.*
       Med. IV, 1942   13

EDDISON, H. W.

(345) The Love Object in Mania. *Jo.* XV, 1934   17

EDER, M. D.

(346) Das Stottern, eine Psychoneurose, und seine Behandlung durch
       Psychoanalyse. *Z.* I, 1913   15
(347) War Shock: The Psychoneuroses in War. *Heinemann,* Lon-
       don, 1917.   7
(348) On the Economics and the Future of the Superego. *Jo.* X, 1929 6

EIDELBERG, LUDWIG

(349) Zur Metapsychologie des Masochismus. *Z.* XIX, 1933   16
(350) Zur Theorie und Klinik der Perversion. *Z.* XIX, 1933   16
(351) Beitraege zum Studium des Masochismus. *Z.* XX, 1934   16
(352) Zur Genese der Platzangst und des Schreibkrampfes. *Z.* XXII,
       1936   10
(353) Pseudo-Identification. *Jo.* XIX, 1938   20

EISENBUD, JULE

EISENDORFER, ARNOLD

EISLER, MICHAEL JOSEPH

EISSLER, KURT

EITINGON, MAX

EKMAN, TORE

ELIASBERG, W.

ELMORE, ELLIANE

EMERSON, L. E.

ENGLISH, O. SPURGEON

BIBLIOGRAPHY

ERICKSON, MILTON H.

In Chapter

(371) A Study of an Experimental Neurosis Hypnotically Induced in a Case of Ejaculatio Praecox. *M.* XV, 1935 — 23

(372) Development of Apparent Unconsciousness during Hypnotic Re-Living of a Traumatic Experience. *Arch. N. Ps.* XXXVIII, 1937 — 23

(373) —and Kubie, Lawrence: The Use of Automatic Drawing in the Interpretation and Relief of a State of Acute Obsessional Depression. *Q.* VII, 1938 — 23

(374) —and Kubie, L.: The Permanent Relief of an Obsessional Phobia by Means of Communications with an Unsuspected Dual Personality. *Q.* VIII, 1939 — 23

(375) The Applications of Hypnosis to Psychiatry. *M. R.* XC, 1939 — 23

(376) —and Kubie, L.: The Translation of the Cryptic Automatic Writing of One Hypnotic Subject by Another in a Trance-like Dissociated State. *Q.* IX, 1940 — 23

(377) —and Kubie, L.: The Successful Treatment of a Case of Acute Hysterical Depression by a Return under Hypnosis to a Critical Phase of Childhood. *Q.* X, 1941 — 23

(378) Hypnosis: A General Review. *Dis. Nerv. S.* II, 1941 — 23

ERICKSON-HOMBURGER, ERIK

(379) Configuration in Play. *Q.* VI, 1937 — 4

(380) Observations on the Yurok: Childhood and World Image. *Univ. of Calif. Press,* Berkeley and Los Angeles, 1943 — 11

EVANS, E.

(381) —and Jelliffe, S. E.: Psoriasis as a Hysterical Conversion Symbolization. *N. Y. M. J.* CIV, 1916 — 13

FARROW, A. PICKWORTH

(382) A Method of Self-Analysis. *M.* V, 1925 — 23

(383) A Practical Method of Self-Analysis. *Allen and Unwin,* London, 1942 — 23

FAULKNER, WILLIAM B.

(384) Esophagal Spasm. *J. N. M. D.* XCIII, 1941 — 10

FEDERN, PAUL

(385) Beitraege zur Analyse des Sadismus und Masochismus. *Z.* I, 1913, and *Z.* II, 1914 — 16

(386) Die Geschichte einer Melancholie. *Z.* IX, 1923 — 17

(387) Some Variations in Ego-Feeling. *Jo.* VII, 1926 — 12, 18

(388) —and Meng, Heinrich: Das psychoanalytische Volksbuch. *Hippokrates Verlag,* Stuttgart, 1926 — G

(389) Narcissism in the Structure of the Ego. *Jo.* IX, 1928 — 18

(390) An Everyday Compulsion. *Jo.* X, 1929 — 9, 14

(391) Das Ich als Subjekt und Objekt im Narzissmus. *Z.* XV, 1929 — 18

(392) The Neurasthenic Core in Hysteria. *M. R. R.,* 1930 — 10, 11

In Chapter

(423) Ueber Angstabwehr, insbesondere durch Libidinisierung. Z. XX, 1934   4, 5, 16, 20

(424) Outline of Clinical Psychoanalysis. *Norton,* New York, 1934   G

(425) Zur Kritik des Todestriebes. *Im.* XXI, 1935   4, 5

(426) Beitrag zur Psychologie der Eifersucht. *Im.* XXI, 1935   18, 20

(427) Ueber Erziehungsmittel. *Paed.* IX, 1935   4, 23

(428) Die symbolische Gleichung Maedchen-Phallus. Z. XXII, 1936   16, 20

(429) Fruehe Entwicklungsstadien des Ichs. *Im.* XXIII, 1937   4, 15, 20

(430) The Scoptophilic Instinct and Identification. *Jo.* XVIII, 1937   4, 5, 8, 10, 11, 12, 13, 20

(431) Der Begriff "Trauma" in der heutigen psychoanalytischen Neurosenlehre. Z. XXIII, 1937   4, 7, 8, 11, 21, 22

(432) On the Theory of the Therapeutic Results of Psychoanalysis. *Jo.* XVIII, 1937   23

(433) Ego Disturbances and Their Treatment. *Jo.* XIX, 1938   6, 8, 20, 23

(434) The Drive to Amass Wealth. *Q.* VII, 1938   20, 23

(435) The Counter-Phobic Attitude. *Jo.* XX, 1939   4, 9, 10, 11, 14, 20

(436) Ueber Trophäe und Triumph. Z. XXIV, 1939   4, 12, 16, 17, 20

(437) Zur Oekonomik der Pseudologia Phantastica. Z. XXIV, 1939   9, 14, 16, 20

(438) Problems of Psychoanalytic Technique. *Ps-a. Q. Inc.,* Albany, N. Y., 1939   3, 8, 9, 16, 20, 23

(439) Psychoanalysis of Anti-Semitism. *A. Im.* I, 1940   20

(440) The Ego and the Affects. *R.* XXVIII, 1941   2, 4, 8, 19

(441) On Neurotic Disturbances of Sleep. *Jo.* XXIII, 1942   10

(442) The Misapprehended Oracle. *A. Im.* III, 1942   9, 14, 20

(442a) Notes on a Case of Characteranalysis. *Bull. Forest San.* I, 1943   20

(443) The Psychopathology of Coughing. *Psychosom. Med.* V, 1943   13

(444) Remarks on the Common Phobias. *Q.* XIII, 1944   5, 11, 14

(445) Neurotic Acting Out. *R.* XXXII, 1945   16, 20, 21, 23

(446) On Stage Acting. (To be published in *A. Im.*)   11, 15, 20

FERENCZI, SANDOR

(447) Actual- and Psychoneuroses in the Light of Freud's Investigations and Psychoanalysis. *F. C.*   10

(448) Analytical Interpretations and Treatment of Psychosexual Impotence in Men. *Con.*   10

(449) Introjection and Transference. *Con.*   9, 20, 23

(450) Alkohol und Neurosen. *Y.* III, 1911   16

(451) Obscene Words. *Con.*   4, 14, 15, 16

(452) On the Part Played by Homosexuality in the Pathogenesis of Paranoia. *Con.*   18

(453) Suggestion and Psychoanalysis. *F. C.*   23

In Chapter

(498) The Sons of the Tailor. *F. C.*   20

(499) Materialization in Globus Hystericus. *F. C.*   12

(500) The Symbolism of the Medusa's Head. *F. C.*   10, 15

(501) Stage-Fright and Narcissistic Self-Observation. *F. C.*   11, 15, 16

(502) An "Anal Hollow Penis" in Woman. *F. C.*   5

(503) Washing Compulsion and Masturbation. *F. C.*   14

(504) —and Rank, Otto: The Development of Psychoanalysis.
N. M. D. Pub. Co., New York and Washington, 1925   23

(505) Psychoanalysis of Sexual Habits. *F. C.*   5, 6, 12, 13

(506) Contraindications to the Active Psychoanalytical Technique.
F. C.   16

(507) The Problem of the Acceptance of Unpleasant Ideas. *F. C.*   4, 9, 19

(508) Gulliver Phantasies. *Jo.* IX, 1928   20

(509) Aus der Kindheit eines Proletariermaedchens. *Paed.* III, 1929   17

(510) The Principle of Relaxation and Neocatharsis. *Jo.* XI, 1930   23

(511) Child Analysis in the Analysis of Adults. *Jo.* XII, 1931   23

(512) Sprachverwirrung zwischen dem Erwachsenen und dem Kind.
Z. XIX, 1933   23

(513) Gedanken ueber das Trauma. Z. XX, 1934   21

FESSLER, LADISLAUS

(514) Psychogene Potenzstoerungen nach urologischen Operationen.
Z. XVII, 1931   7

FINESINGER, JACOB E.

(515) Effect of Pleasant and Unpleasant Ideas on Respiration in Psychoneurotic Patients. *Arch. N. Ps.* XLII, 1939   13

FISCHER, EDMUND

(516) Geschlecht und Uebertragung. *Paed.* III, 1929   23

FLETCHER, JOHN M.

(517) Homeostasis as an Explanatory Principle in Psychology.
Psychol. Rev. XLIX, 1942   2

FLIESS, ROBERT

(518) The Metapsychology of the Analyst. *Q.* XI, 1942   20

FLUEGEL, J. C.

(519) A Case of Affective Inhibition of an Intellectual Process. *Jo.*
IV, 1923   10

(520) A Note on the Phallic Significance of the Tongue and of Speech.
Jo. VI, 1925   14, 15

(521) The Psychology of Clothes. *Hogarth Press*, London, 1930   4, 18

(522) Stage Fright and Anal Erotism. *M.* XVII, 1938   11, 14, 20

(546) Obsessions and Phobias: Their Psychical Mechanisms and their *In Chapter*
Aetiology. *C. P.* I
19

(547) A Reply to Criticism on the Anxiety Neurosis. *C. P.* I
9, 10

(548) Further Observations on the Defense-Neuropsychoses. *C. P.* I
5, 12

(549) Heredity and the Aetiology of the Neuroses. *C. P.* I
14, 16

(550) The Aetiology of Hysteria. *C. P.* I
3, 12

(551) Sexuality in the Aetiology of the Neuroses. *C. P.* I
9, 10

(552) The Interpretation of Dreams. *Macmillan,* New York,
1913
2, 4, 5, 6, 9, 10,
11, 12, 14, 15,
18, 20, 23

(553) On the Psychopathology of Everyday Life. *Macmillan,*
New York, 1914
2, 3, 9, 10, 11,
15, 16, 20

(554) On Psychotherapy. *C. P.* I.
20, 23

(555) Three Contributions to the Theory of Sex. *N. M. D. Pub.
Co.,* New York and Washington, 1910
2, 5, 6, 8, 9, 10,
13, 14, 16, 18,
20, 23

(556) Wit and Its Relation to the Unconscious. *Moffat, Yard,*
New York, 1916
9, 17, 20

(557) Fragment of an Analysis of a Case of Hysteria. *C. P.* III
11, 12, 13

(558) My Views on the Part Played by Sexuality in the Aetiology of
the Neuroses. *C. P.* I
9, 10

(559) Delusion and Dream in Jensen's "Gradiva." *Moffat, Yard,*
New York, 1917
6, 22

(560) Obsessive Acts and Religious Practices. *C. P.* II
14, 19

(561) Civilized Sexual Morality and Modern Nervousness. *C. P.*
II
5, 10, 20, 23

(562) Hysterical Fancies and Their Relation to Bisexuality. *C. P.* II
12

(563) Character and Anal Erotism. *C. P.* II
14, 20

(564) The Relation of the Poet to Daydreaming. *C. P.* IV
12, 20

(565) General Remarks on Hysterical Attacks. *C. P.* II
12

(566) Analysis of a Phobia in a Five-year-old Boy. *C. P.* III
5, 9, 11,
16, 19, 23

(567) Notes upon a Case of Obsessional Neurosis. *C. P.* III
9, 10, 14,
18, 19, 23

(568) Leonardo da Vinci: A Psychosexual Study of an Infantile
Reminiscence. *Moffat, Yard,* New York, 1916
6

(569) The Future Chances of Psychoanalytic Therapy. *C. P.* II
23

(570) Concerning "Wild" Psychoanalysis. *C. P.* II
23

(571) Psychogenic Visual Disturbance according to Psychoanalytical
Conceptions. *C. P.* II
5, 10, 12, 13

(572) Contributions to the Psychology of Love. *C. P.* IV
9, 10, 13, 20

(573) Einleitung und Schlusswort zur Selbstmord-Diskussion. In
Ueber den Selbstmord, insbes. den Schuelerselbstmord, Bergmann, Wiesbaden, 1910
17

In Chapter

(602) The Uncanny. *C. P.* IV
20

(603) Introduction to "Psychoanalysis of War Neuroses." *Int. Ps-a. P.*, London, 1921
6, 7, 20, 23

(604) The Psychogenesis of a Case of Female Homosexuality. *C. P.* II
16, 23

(605) Beyond the Pleasure Principle. *Int. Ps-a. P.*, London, 1922
2, 4, 5, 7, 9, 13, 16, 20, 21

(606) Group Psychology and the Analysis of the Ego. *Int. Ps-a. P.*, London, 1922
4, 5, 6, 12, 14, 16, 17, 20, 23

(607) Certain Neurotic Mechanisms in Jealousy, Paranoia and Homosexuality. *C. P.* II
5, 9, 16, 18, 20

(608) The Ego and the Id. *Inst. of Ps-a. and Hogarth Press*, London, 1927
2, 4, 5, 6, 8, 9, 10, 11, 12, 13, 14, 16, 17, 18, 19, 20

(609) The Infantile Genital Organization of the Libido. *C. P.* II
5

(610) A Neurosis of Demoniacal Possession in the Seventeenth Century. *C. P.* IV
23

(611) Neurosis and Psychosis. *C. P.* II
8, 14, 18, 20

(612) The Passing of the Oedipus Complex. *C. P.* II
5, 6, 16, 20, 21

(613) The Economic Problem in Masochism. *C. P.* II
2, 5, 6, 9, 10, 14, 16, 20, 21

(614) The Loss of Reality in Neurosis and Psychosis. *C. P.* II
8, 9, 18

(615) A Note upon the Mystic Writing Pad. *Jo.* XXI, 1940
2, 4

(616) On Negation. *Jo.* VI, 1923
2, 4, 8, 9, 14, 19

(617) Some Psychological Consequences of the Anatomical Distinction between the Sexes. *Jo.* VIII, 1927
5, 6, 16, 20

(618) The Problem of Anxiety. *Norton*, New York, 1936
2, 4, 5, 6, 7, 8, 9, 10, 11, 12, 14, 19, 22, 23

(619) The Problem of Lay Analysis. *Brentano*, New York, 1927
G

(620) Humor. *Jo.* XI, 1928
17

(621) Fetishism. *Jo.* IX, 1928
8, 9, 16, 18

(622) The Future of an Illusion. *Hogarth Press*, London, 1928
4, 5, 17, 18

(623) Dostojewski and Parricide. *The Realist* I, 1929
13, 16

(624) Civilization and Its Discontents. *Norton*, New York, 1930
5, 8, 15

(625) Libidinal Types. *Jo.* XIII, 1932
20

(626) Female Sexuality. *Jo.* XIII, 1932
5, 10, 14, 16, 20

(627) The Acquisition of Power over Fire. *Jo.* XIII, 1932
16

(628) New Introductory Lectures on Psychoanalysis. *Garden City Pub. Co.*, New York, 1933
5, 6, 10, 16, 23

(629) Analysis Terminable and Interminable. *Jo.* XVIII, 1937
8, 10, 20

(630) Constructions in Analysis. *Jo.* XIX, 1938
18

(631) A Disturbance of Memory on the Acropolis. *Jo.* XXI, 1941
9, 20

(632) Moses and Monotheism. *Knopf*, New York, 1939
4

In Chapter

(633) An Outline of Psychoanalysis. *Jo.* XXI, 1940   8, 9, 16, 18
(634) Medusa's Head. *Jo.* XXII, 1941   5, 15, 16
(635) Splitting of the Ego in the Defensive Process. *Jo.* XXII, 1941   8, 9, 16, 18

FRIEDJUNG, JOSEPH K.

(636) Ueber verschiedene Quellen kindlicher Schamhaftigkeit. *Z.* I,
       1913   8
(637) Die Pathologie des einzigen Kindes. *E. inn. M. K.* XVI, 1919   5, 20
(638) Beitrag zum Verstaendnis der Einschlafstoerungen bei Kindern.
       W. m. W., 1924   10
(639) Zur Kenntnis kindlicher Selbstmordimpulse. *Paed.* III, 1929   17

FRIEDLANDER-MISCH, KATE

(640) Die biologischen Grundlagen der Freud'schen Angsttheorie.
       Z. XXI, 1935   4
(641) On the Longing to Die. *Jo.* XXI, 1940   11, 17
(642) Charlotte Brontë: Zur Frage des masochistischen Charakters.
       Z. XXVI, 1941   16
(643) Children's Books and Their Function in Latency and Puberty.
       A. Im. III, 1942   6

FRIEDMAN, M.

(644) Cleptomania. *R.* XVII, 1930   16

FRIES, MARGARET E.

(645) Interrelationship of Physical, Mental and Emotional Life of a
       Child, from Birth to Four Years of Age. *A. J. Dis. Child*
       XLIX, 1935   4
(646) Play Technique in the Analysis of Young Children. *R.* XXIV,
       1937   23

FRINK, H. W.

(647) Report of a Case of Psychogenetic Convulsions Simulating Epi-
       lepsy. *N. Y. M. J.,* March, 1911   13
(648) Morbid Fears and Compulsions: Their Psychology and Psycho-
       analytic Treatment. *Moffat, Yard,* New York, 1918   G

FROMM, ERICH

(649) Zur Psychologie des Verbrechers und der strafenden Gesellschaft.
       Im. XVII, 1931   20
(650) Ueber Methode und Aufgabe einer analytischen Sozialpsy-
       chologie. *Z. Soz.* I, 1932   23
(651) Sozialpsychologischer Teil. In *Autoritaet und Familie,* Felix
       Allan, Paris, 1936   6, 20, 23
(652) Selfishness and Self-Love. *Ps.* II, 1939   5
(653) Escape from Freedom. *Farrar and Rinehart,* New York,
       1941   6, 11, 19, 20, 23

In Chapter

(654) Faith as a Character Trait. *Ps.* V, 1942   22
(655) Sex and Character. *Ps.* VI, 1943   5, 20

FROMM-REICHMANN, FRIEDA

(656) Contributions to the Psychogenesis of Migraine. *R.* XXIV, 1937   13
(657) Transference Problems in Schizophrenics. *Q.* VIII, 1939   18
(658) Notes on the Mother Role in the Family Group. *Menn. Bull.* IV, 1940   6, 20
(659) Recent Advances in Psychoanalytic Therapy. *Ps.* IV, 1941   18
(660) A Preliminary Note on the Emotional Significance of Stereo-typies. *Bull. Forest San.* I, 1942   18
(661) Psychoanalytic Psychotherapy with Psychotics. *Ps.* VI, 1943   18

FUCHS, S. H.

(662) On Introjection. *Jo.* XVIII, 1937   9

GARMA, ANGEL

(663) Realitaet und Es in der Schizophrenie. *Z.* XVIII, 1932   8, 18
(664) Psychologie des Selbstmordes. *Im.* XXIII, 1937   17

GELEERD, ELIZABETH R.

(665) The Analysis of a Case of Compulsive Masturbation in a Child. *Q.* XII, 1943   16

GERARD, M. W.

(666) Child Analysis as a Technique in the Investigation of Mental Mechanisms. *A. J. P.* XCIV, 1937   23
(667) Enuresis, a Study in Etiology. *A. J. Orthops.* IX, 1939   12

GERO, GEORGE

(668) The Construction of Depression. *Jo.* XVII, 1936   17
(669) Zum Problem der oralen Fixierung. *Z.* XXIV, 1939   16
(670) The Idea of Psychogenesis in Modern Psychiatry and in Psycho-analysis. *R.* XXX, 1943   18

GESELL, A., *et al.*

(671) The First Five Years of Life. *Harper and Brothers,* New York, 1940   4

GILL, MORTON M.

(672) Functional Disturbances of Menstruation. *Menn. Bull.* VII, 1943   13
(673) —and Brenman, Margaret: Treatment of a Case of Anxiety Hysteria by an Hypnotic Technique Employing Psycho-analytic Principles. *Menn. Bull.* VII, 1943   23

GILLESPIE, R. D.

(674) The Psychotherapy of the Psychoses. *M.* X, 1930   18

In Chapter

(675) Psychological Factors in Asthma. *B. M. J.* I, 1285, 1936   15
(676) Psychological Aspects of Skin Diseases. *B. J. D.* L, 1938   13

GILLESPIE, W. H.

(677) A Contribution to the Study of Fetishism. *Jo.* XXI, 1940   16

GITELSON, MAX

(678) Direct Psychotherapy in Adolescence. *A. J. Orthops.* XII, 1942   6
(679) The Critical Moment in Psychotherapy. *Menn. Bull.* VI, 1942   23

GLOVER, EDWARD

(680) The Significance of the Mouth in Psychoanalysis. *M.* IV, 1924   20
(681) Notes on Oral Character Formation. *Jo.* VI, 1925   20
(682) The Neurotic Character. *Jo.* VII, 1926   20
(683) Einige Probleme der psychoanalytischen Charakterologie. *Z.* XII, 1926   20
(684) Lectures on Technique in Psychoanalysis. *Jo.* VIII, 1927, and IX, 1928   23
(685) The Etiology of Alcoholism. *Proc. R. S. M.* XXI, 1928   16
(686) The Screening Function of Traumatic Memories. *Jo.* X, 1929   7, 9
(687) The Vehicle of Interpretation. *Jo.* XI, 1930   23
(688) The Psychotherapy of the Psychoses. *M.* X, 1930   18
(689) Sublimation, Substitution and Social Anxiety. *Jo.* XII, 1931   20
(690) The Therapeutic Effect of Inexact Interpretation. *Jo.* XII, 1931   23
(691) The Prevention and Treatment of Drug Addiction. *Lancet,* 1931   16
(692) On the Aetiology of Drug Addiction. *Jo.* XIII, 1932   16
(693) Medico-Psychological Aspects of Normality. *B. J. P.* XXIII, 1932   23
(694) The Relation of Perversion Formation to the Development of the Reality Sense. *Jo.* XIV, 1933   16
(695) A Developmental Study of the Obsessional Neurosis. *Jo.* XVI, 1935   19
(696) A Note on Idealization. *Jo.* XIX, 1938   20
(697) The Psychoanalysis of Affects. *Jo.* XX, 1939   2, 19
(698) Psychoanalysis. *John Bale Medical Pub. Co.,* London, 1939   G

GLOVER, JAMES

(699) Notes on the Psychopathology of Suicide. *Jo.* III, 1922   17
(700) The Conception of the Ego. *Jo.* VII, 1926   4
(701) Notes on an Unusual Form of Perversion. *Jo.* VIII, 1927   16

GLUECK, EDITH

(702) Schauspieler der Wirklichkeit. Paper read at the Hungarian Ps-a. Society, 1934   20

GOLDMAN, GEORGE S.

(703) A Case of Compulsive Handwashing. *Q.* VII, 1938   14

GOLDSTEIN, KURT

(704) —and Steinfeld, Julius J.: The Conditioning of Sexual Be- *In Chapter*
havior by Central Agnosia. *Bull. Forest San.* I, 1942   4

(705) The Significance of Psychological Research in Schizophrenia.
J. N. M. D. XCVII, 1943   18

GORELIK, BASEL

(706) Certain Reaction Formations against Oral Impulses. *Jo.* XII,
1931   20

GRABER, GUSTAV HANS

(707) Die Ambivalenz des Kindes. *Int. Ps-a.* V., Wien, 1925   4
(708) Redehemmung und Analerotik. *Paed.* II, 1928   10, 15
(709) Realitaetspruefung und Weltuntergangsphobie. *Paed.* III, 1929   18
(710) Neurotische Typisierung. *Z.* XVII, 1931   14, 20
(711) Aus der Analyse eines nachtwandelnden Knaben. *Merlin
Verlag,* Baden-Baden, 1932   12
(712) Die zweierlei Mechanismen der Identifizierung. *Im.* XXIII,
1937   4, 5, 16

GREENACRE, PHYLLIS

(713) Surgical Addiction: Clinical Case Abstract. *Psychosom. Med.*
I, 1939   20
(714) The Predisposition to Anxiety. *Q.* X, 1941   4

GREENSON, RALPH R.

(714*a*) On Genuine Epilepsy. *Q.* XIII, 1944   13

GREIG, AGNES B.

(715) The Problem of the Parent in Child Analysis. *Ps.* III, 1940   23
(716) A Child Analysis. *Q.* X, 1941   23

GRIMBERG, L.

(717) On Somnambulism. *R.* III, 1916   12

GRINKER, R. R.

(718) —and MacLean, H.: The Course of a Depression Treated by
Psychotherapy and Metrazol. *Psychosom. Med.* II, 1940   23

GRODDECK, GEORG

(719) Die psychische Bedingtheit und psychoanalytische Behandlung
organischer Krankheiten. *S. Hirzel,* Berlin, 1917   13
(720) The Book of It. *N. M. D. Pub. Co.,* New York and Washington, 1928   5, 13

GROSS, ALFRED

(721) The Psychic Effects of Toxic and Toxoid Substances. *Jo.* XVI,
1935   16

GROTJAHN, MARTIN

(722) Dream Observations in a Two-year, four-months-old Baby. *Q.*   *In Chapter*
      VI, 1938   4
(723) Psychoanalysis and Brain Disease. *R.* XXI, 1938   13
(724) Observations of Schizophrenic Patients during Metrazol Treat-
      ment. *Menn. Bull.* II, 1938   23
(725) Psychoanalytic Investigations of a Seventy-one-year-old Man
      with Senile Dementia. *Q.* IX, 1940   23
(726) The Process of Awakening. *R.* XXIX, 1942   4
(727) Brief Psychotherapy on Psychoanalytic Principles. *Ill. Psych. J.*
      II, 1942   23

GUNTHER, LEWIS

(728) —and Menninger, Karl A.: Intermittent Extrasystole Directly
      Associated with Emotional Conflict. *Menn. Bull.* III, 1939   13

HADLEY, ERNEST E.

(729) Comments on Pedophilia. *M. R.,* August, 1926   16
(730) The Psychoanalytic Clarification of Personality Types. *A. J. P.*
      XCIV, 1938   20

HAHN, BENNO

(731) Die Psychokatharsis als kausale Behandlungsmethode. Bericht
      1. aerztl. Kongr. f. Psychotherapie, Baden-Baden, 1926;
      Carl Marold, Halle a/S, 1927   23

HANFMANN, EUGENIA

(732) —and Kasanin, Jacob: Conceptional Thinking in Schizophrenia.
      N. M. D. M. S., New York and Washington, 1942   18

HAPPEL, CLARA

(733) Onanieersatzbildungen. *Z.* IX, 1923   12, 14, 15

HARMS, ERNEST

(734) (Ed.) Schizophrenia in Childhood. *The Nervous Child* I, 1941   18

HARNIK, JENÖ

(735) Discussion of Tic. *Jo.* II, 1921   15
(736) The Various Developments Undergone by Narcissism in Men
      and Women. *Jo.* V, 1924   5, 16
(737) Der Zaehlzwang und seine Bedeutung fuer die Psychologie der
      Zahlenvorstellung. *Vortrag* VIII; Int. Ps-a. Kongr.; Autoref.
      Z. X, 1924   14
(738) Die triebhaft-affektiven Momente im Zeitgefuehl. *Im.* XI, 1925   14
(739) Die oekonomischen Beziehungen zwischen dem Schuldgefuehl
      und dem weiblichen Narzissmus. *Z.* XIV, 1928   16

In Chapter

(740) Zur Psychologie des Zopfabschneiders. *Z. S. W.* XII, 1928   16

(741) One Component in the Fear of Death in Early Infancy. *Jo.* XI, 1930   13, 15

(742) Zur Therapie der Homosexualitaet. *Vortrag* II; Tgg. d. Deutschen Ps-a. Ges.; Autoref. Z. XVI, 1930   16

(743) Introjection and Projection in the Mechanism of Depression. *Jo.* XIII, 1932   17

(744) Zur Frage der infantilen weiblichen Genitalorganisation. Z. XX, 1934   5

HART, MOSS

(745) Lady in the Dark. *Random House,* New York, 1941   10

HARTMANN, HEINZ

(746) Ein Fall von Depersonalisation. *Z. ges. N. P.* LXXIV, 1922   18

(747) Kokainismus und Homosexualitaet. *Z. ges. N. P.* XCV, 1925   16

(748) Die Grundlagen der Psychoanalyse. *G. Thieme,* Leipzig, 1927   3

(749) Psychiatrische Zwillingsprobleme. *Jb. Ps. N.* L and LI, 1934   20

(750) Ich-Psychologie und Anpassungs-Problem. Z. XXIV, 1939   4

(751) Psychoanalysis and the Concept of Health. *Jo.* XX, 1939   23

HARTMANN, MAX

(752) Die Sexualitaet der Protisten und ihre Bedeutung fuer eine allgemeine Theorie der Bisexualitaet. *Z. ind. Abst.* LIV, 1930   16

HAWKINS, MARY O'NEIL

(753) Psychoanalysis of Children. *Menn. Bull.* IV, 1940   23

HAWORTH, NORAH A.

(754) —and MacDonald, Mary E.: Theory of Occupational Therapy. *Williams and Wilkins,* Baltimore, 1941   23

HAYWARD, EMELINE P.

(755) Types of Female Castration Reaction. *Q.* XII, 1943   20

HEALY, WILLIAM

(756) The Individual Delinquent. *Little, Brown,* Boston, 1915   16, 20

(757) —and Bronner, F. A.: New Light on Delinquency and Its Treatment. *Yale Univ. Press,* New Haven, 1936   16, 20

HEIDE, CAREL VAN DER

(758) A Study of Mechanisms in Two Cases of Peptic Ulcer. *Psychosom. Med.* II, 1940   13

(759) A Case of Pollakisuria Nervosa. *Q.* X, 1941   12

HEILPERN-FUCHS, ELSE

(760) Psychological Problems of Stepchildren. *R.* XXX, 1943   5, 20

HENDRICK, IVES

In Chapter

(761) Pregenital Anxiety in a Passive Feminine Character. *Q.* II, 1933   5

(762) "The Ego and the Defense Mechanisms": A Review and Discussion. *R.* XXV, 1938   4

(763) Facts and Theories of Psychoanalysis. *Knopf,* New York, 1939   G

(764) Suicide as Wish Fulfillment. *Psych. Q.* XIV, 1940   17

(765) Psychoanalytic Observations on the Aurae of Two Cases with Convulsions. *Psychosom. Med.* II, 1940   13

(766) Instincts and the Ego during Infancy. *Q.* XI, 1942   2, 4, 20

(767) Work and the Pleasure Principle. *Q.* XII, 1943   2, 4, 20

(768) The Discussion of the "Instinct to Master." *Q.* XII, 1943   2, 4, 20

HERBERT, S.

(769) The Psychogenic Root of Enuresis. *R.* IX, 1922   12

(770) A Case of Pseudo-Epilepsia Hysterica. *R.* X, 1923   13

HERMANN, IMRE

(771) Randbemerkungen zum Wiederholungszwang. *Z.* VIII, 1922   21

(772) Organlibido und Begabung. *Z.* IX, 1923   10

(773) Die Regel der Gleichzeitigkeit in der Sublimierungsarbeit. *Im.* X, 1924   9

(774) Das System Bw. *Im.* XII, 1926   2

(775) Die Zwangsneurose und ein historisches Moment in der Ueber-Ich-Bildung. *Z.* XV, 1929   6

(776) Das Ich und das Denken. *Im.* XV, 1929   4

(777) Sinnesmodalitaeten und Denkformen. *Im.* XV, 1929   15

(778) Urwahrnehmungen, insbesondere Augenleuchten und Lautwerden des Inneren. *Z.* XX, 1934   4

(779) Die Psychoanalyse als Methode. *Int. Ps-a. V.,* Wien, 1934   3

(780) Sich Anklammern—Auf Suche gehen. *Z.* XXII, 1936   5

(781) Zur Triebbesetzung von Ich und Ueber-Ich. *Z.* XXV, 1940   6

(782) Studien zur Denkpsychologie. *Acta Psychol.* V, 1940   6

HILL, LEWIS B.

(783) A Psychoanalytic Observation on Essential Hypertension. *R.* XXII, 1935   13

(784) The Use of Hostility as a Defense. *Q.* VII, 1938   11, 20

HINSIE, LELAND E.

(785) The Treatment of Schizophrenia. *Bailliere Tindall,* London, 1930   18

(786) The Relationship of Psychoanalysis to Psychiatry. *A. J. P.* XCI, 1935   18

(787) Concepts and Problems of Psychotherapy. *Columbia Univ. Press,* New York, 1937   13

HIRSCH, ERWIN

(788) Eine Feuerphobie als Folge unterdrueckter Onanie. *Paed.* II,   *In Chapter*
1928   16

HITSCHMANN, EDUARD

(789) Kinderangst und Onanie-Entwoehnung. *C.* III, 1913   5, 10
(790) Paranoia, Homosexualitaet und Analerotik. *Z.* I, 1913   18
(791) Freud's Theories of the Neuroses. *Kegan Paul,* London, 1913   G
(792) Ein Fall von Zwansbefuerchtung vom Tode des gleichge-
schlechtlichen Elternteils. *Z.* III, 1915   11
(793) Ueber einen sporadischen Rueckfall ins Bettnaessen bei einem
vierjaehrigen Kinde. *Z.* V, 1919   12
(794) Urethral Erotism and Obsessional Neurosis. *Jo.* IV, 1923   5, 20
(795) Die Indikationen fuer psychoanalytische Behandlung. *Ars
Medici* XIV, 1924   23
(796) —and Bergler, Edmund: Frigidity in Women. *N. M. D. Pub.
Co.,* Washington and New York, 1936   10
(797) Bemerkungen ueber Platzangst und andere neurotische Angst-
zustaende. *Z.* XXIII, 1937   11
(798) Beitraege zur Aetiologie und Konstitution der Spermatorrhoe.
Z. XXV, 1940   5

HOCH, PAUL H.

(799) Personality Factors in Alcoholic Psychoses. *Psych. Q.* XIV,
1940   16

HOFFER, WILHELM

(800) Ueber die maennliche Latenz und ihre spezifische Erkrankung.
Z. XII, 1926   6
(801) Analyse einer postenzephalitischen Geistesstoerung. *Z.* XXV,
1940   13

HOFFMANN, ERNST PAUL

(802) Projektion und Ich-Entwicklung. *Z.* XXI, 1935   4

HOFFMANN, JAKOB

(803) Entwicklungsgeschichte eines Falles von sozialer Angst. *Z.*
XVII, 1931   10, 20

HOFSTAETTER, R.

(804) Ueber eingebildete Schwangerschaft. *Urban u. Schwarzen-
berg,* Wien, 1924   12, 13

HOLLITSCHER, WALTER

(805) The Concept of Rationalization. *Jo.* XX, 1939   20

HOLLOS, ISTVAN

(806) Psychoanalytische Beleuchtung eines Falles von Dementia
Praecox. *Z.* II, 1914   18

In Chapter

(807) Die Phasen des Selbstbewusstseinsaktes. Z. V, 1919   13
(808) Aus der psychiatrischen Anstaltspraxis. Z. IX, 1923   18
(809) Hinter der gelben Mauer. *Hippokrates Verlag,* Stuttgart, 1928   18

HOOP, J. H. VAN DER

(810) Ueber die Projektion und ihre Inhalte. Z. X, 1924   9

HORNEY, KAREN

(811) On the Genesis of the Castration Complex in Women. *Jo.* V,
         1924   5
(812) The Flight from Womanhood. *Jo.* VII, 1926   5, 20
(813) Die praemenstruellen Verstimmungen. *Paed.* V, 1931   13
(814) The Dread of Woman. *Jo.* XIII, 1932   5, 16
(815) The Denial of the Vagina. *Jo.* XIV, 1933   5
(816) Psychogenic Factors in Functional Female Disorders. *A. J.
         Obs. and Gyn.* XXV, 1933   10, 13
(817) The Problem of Feminine Masochism. *R.* XXII, 1935   5, 16
(818) The Problem of the Negative Therapeutic Reaction. *Q. V,*
         1936   14, 20
(819) The Neurotic Personality of Our Time. *Norton,* New York,
         1936   5, 16, 20, 23
(820) New Ways in Psychoanalysis. *Norton,* New York, 1940   20, 23
(821) Self-Analysis. *Norton,* New York, 1942   20, 23

HUBBARD, L. T.

(822) Transference and Sex. *R.* X, 1922   23

HUEBSCH, D. E.

(823) Psychoanalysis and Eye Disturbances. *R.* XVIII, 1931   13

HUG-HELLMUTH, HERMINE VON

(824) Ein Fall von weiblichem Fuss-, richtiger Stiefelfetischismus.
         Z. III, 1915   16
(825) A Study of the Mental Life of the Child. *N. M. D. Pub. Co.,*
         Washington, 1919   23
(826) On the Technique of Child Analysis. *Jo.* II, 1921   23
(827) Vom mittleren Kinde. *Im.* VII, 1921   5, 20
(828) Die Bedeutung der Familie fuer das Schicksal des Einzelnen.
         Z. S. W. IX, 1923   5, 20

HUPFER, SUSANNE

(829) Ueber Schwangerschaftsgelueste. Z. XVI, 1930   16

HUTCHINGS, G. R.

(830) —Cheney, C. O., and Wright, W. W.: Psychogenic Precipitating
         Causes of Schizophrenia. In *Schizophrenia:* Assn. Research
         N. M. D., Hoeber, New York, 1928   18

BIBLIOGRAPHY

INMAN, W. S.

In Chapter

(831) A Psychoanalytical Explanation of Micropsia. *Jo.* XIX, 1938 — 12

ISAACS, SUSAN

(832) Penis-Feces-Child. *Jo.* VIII, 1927 — 5, 12, 20
(833) The Nursery Years. *Routledge and Sons,* London, 1929 — 23
(834) The Children We Teach. *Univ. of London Press,* London, 1932 — 23
(835) Social Development in Young Children. *Routledge and Sons,* London, 1933 — 6
(836) The Psychological Aspects of Child Development. *Evans Brothers,* London, 1935 — 6

ISAKOWER, OTTO

(837) A Contribution to the Pathopsychology of Phenomena Associated with Falling Asleep. *Jo.* XIX, 1938 — 4, 5, 11
(838) On the Exceptional Position of the Auditive Sphere. *Jo.* XX, 1939 — 5, 6, 18

JACOBSON, EDMUND

(839) Progressive Relaxation. *Univ. of Chicago Press,* Chicago, 1929 — 13, 23

JACOBSON (JACOBSOHN), EDITH

(840) Beitrag zur asozialen Charakterbildung. *Z.* XVI, 1930 — 16, 20
(841) Ein weibischer Knabe und seine Heilung. *Paed.* IV, 1931 — 23
(842) Lernstoerungen beim Kinde durch masochistische Mechanismen. *Z.* XVIII, 1932 — 10, 23
(843) Wege der weiblichen Ueber-Ich-Bildung. *Z.* XXIII, 1937 — 6
(844) Depression, the Oedipus Complex in the Development of Depressive Mechanisms. *Q.* XII, 1943 — 17

JACOBY, HEINRICH

(845) Muss es Unmusikalische geben? *Paed.* I, 1926 — 10

JEKELS, LUDWIG

(846) Analerotik. *Z.* I, 1913 — 5
(847) Zur Psychologie der Komoedie. *Im.* XII, 1926 — 17
(848) Zur Psychologie des Mitleids. *Im.* XVI, 1930 — 20
(849) Das Schuldgefuehl. *Ps-a. Bwgg.* IV, 1932 — 8
(850) —und Bergler, Edmund: Uebertragung und Liebe. *Im.* XX, 1934 — 5
(851) Mitleid und Liebe. *Im.* XXII, 1936 — 20
(852) The Riddle of Shakespeare's Macbeth. *R.* XXX, 1943 — 20

JELGERSMA, G.

(853) Unbewusstes Geistesleben. *Int. Ps-a. V.,* Wien, 1914 — G
(854) Projection. *Jo.* VII, 1926 — 9, 18

JELLIFFE, SMITH ELY

In Chapter

(855) The Technique of Psychoanalysis. *N. M. D. Pub. Co.,* New
York and Washington, 1914   23

(856) Alcohol in Some of Its Social Compensatory Aspects.
N. Y. M. J. CV, 1917   16

(857) Epileptic Attacks in Dynamic Pathology. *N. Y. M. J.,* July,
1918   13

(858) Psychopathology and Organic Disease. *Arch. N. Ps.,* 1922   13

(859) The Old-Age Factor in Psychoanalytical Therapy. *M. R.*
CXXI, 1925   23

(860) Psychoanalysis and Organic Disorder: Myopia as Paradigma.
Jo. VII, 1926   13

(861) Post-Encephalitic Respiratory Disorders. *J. N. M. D.* LXIII,
1926   13

(862) Psychopathology of Forced Movements in Oculogyric Crises.
N. M. D. Pub. Co., New York and Washington, 1932   13

(863) Dynamic Concepts and the Epileptic Attack. *A. J. P.* XCII,
1935   13

(864) Sketches in Psychosomatic Medicine. *N. M. D. Pub. Co.,*
New York and Washington, 1939   13

(865) The Parkinsonian Body Posture: Some Considerations in Unconscious Hostility. *R.* XXVII, 1940   13

JOHNSON, ADELAIDE M.

(866) —Falstein, Eugene J., Szurek, S. A., and Svendsen, Margaret:
School Phobia. *A. J. Orthops.* XI, 1941   11

JOKL, ROBERT HANS

(867) Zur Psychogenese des Schreibkrampfes. *Z.* VIII, 1922   10, 12

JONES, ERNEST

(868) Rationalization in Everyday Life. *P.*   20
(869) Psychoanalytic Notes on a Case of Hypomania. *A. J. I.,* 1909   17
(870) Psychoanalysis in Psychotherapy. *P.*   23
(871) Simulated Foolishness in Hysteria. *P.*   11
(872) The Therapeutic Effect of Suggestion. *Can. J. M. S.* XXXIX,
1911   23
(873) The Psychology of Morbid Anxiety. *P.*   11
(874) The Therapeutic Action of Psychoanalysis. *P.*   23
(875) The Relation between Anxiety Neurosis and Anxiety Hysteria.
P.   11
(876) The Nightmare. *Hogarth Press and Inst. of Ps-a.,* London,
1931   10
(877) The Significance of the Grandfather for the Fate of the Individual. *P.*   5
(878) The God Complex. *Ess.*   4, 14, 18

In Chapter

(879) Hate and Anal Erotism in the Obsessional Neurosis. *P.*   14
(880) Suggestion und Uebertragung. *Z.* II, 1914   23
(881) Urethralerotik und Ehrgeiz. *Z.* III, 1915   5, 20
(882) The Theory of Symbolism. *P.*   4
(883) Anal-Erotic Character Traits. *P.*   10, 14, 20
(884) The Symbolism of Being Run Over. *Jo.* I, 1920   11
(885) The Treatment of the Neuroses. *Wood,* New York, 1920   23
(886) Introjection and Projection. *Jo.* III, 1921   9
(887) Notes on Abraham's Article on the Female Castration Complex.
       Jo. III, 1922   20
(888) Some Problems of Adolescence. *P.*   6
(889) The Nature of Auto-Suggestion. *P.*   23
(890) Classification of the Instincts. *B. J. P.* XIV, 1923   5
(891) Mother-Right and the Sexual Ignorance of the Savages. *Jo.*
       VI, 1924   5
(892) Deprivation of the Senses as a Castration Symbol. *Jo.* VII, 1926   15
(893) The Origin and Structure of the Superego. *Jo.* VII, 1926   6
(894) The Early Development of Female Sexuality. *Jo.* VIII, 1927   5
(895) Fear, Guilt and Hate. *Jo.* X, 1929   6, 9, 11
(896) The Anxiety Character. *M. R. R.,* 1930   20
(897) Die Eifersucht. *Ps-a. Bwgg.* II, 1930   18, 20
(898) The Phallic Phase. *Jo.* XIV, 1933   5
(899) The Early Female Sexuality. *Jo.* XVI, 1935   5
(900) Psychoanalysis and the Instincts. *B. J. P.* XXVI, 1936   5
(901) The Concept of a Normal Mind. *Jo.* XXIII, 1942   23
(902) Psychology and Childbirth. *Lancet* CCXLII, 1942   10, 13

JULIUSBURGER, OTTO

(903) Beitrag zur Psychologie der sogenannten Dipsomanie. *C.* II,
       1912   16
(904) Zur Lehre vom psychosexuellen Infantilismus. *Z. S. W.* I, 1914   16

JUNG, C. G.

(905) Der Inhalt der Psychose. *Deuticke,* Leipzig, 1908   18
(906) The Psychology of Dementia Praecox. *N. M. D. Pub. Co.,*
       New York and Washington, 1909   18
(907) Wandlungen und Symbole der Libido. *Deuticke,* Leipzig,
       1912   5
(908) Psychological Types. *Harcourt, Brace,* New York, 1923   20

JUST-KERI, HEDWIG

(909) Lernhemmungen in der Schule. *Paed.* IV, 1930   10

KAISER, HELLMUTH

(910) Probleme der Technik. *Z.* XX, 1934   23

KALISCHER, HANS

In Chapter

(911)　Beobachtungen an einem jungen Verschwender. *Paed.* III, 1929 — 16

(912)　Leben und Selbstmord eines Zwangsdiebes. *Paed.* III, 1929 — 16

KAMM, BERNARD A.

(913)　A Technical Problem in the Psychoanalysis of a Schizoid Character. *Menn. Bull.* I, 1937 — 18

(914)　Schizophrenia and Compulsion Neurosis. *Menn. Bull.* II, 1938 — 18

KAPLAN, LEO

(915)　Grundzuege der Psychoanalyse. *Deuticke,* Leipzig, 1924 — G

(916)　Das Problem der Magie und die Psychoanalyse. *Merlin Verlag,* Heidelberg, 1928 — 4, 14

KARDINER, ABRAHAM

(917)　The Bio-Analysis of the Epileptic Reaction. *Q.* I, 1933 — 4, 7, 12

(918)　The Role of Economic Security in the Adaptation of the Individual. *Family* XVII, 1936 — 4

(919)　Security, Cultural Restraints, Intra-Social Dependencies and Hostilities. *Family* XVIII, 1937 — 4

(920)　Influence of Culture on Behavior. *Social Work Today,* 1937 — 4

(921)　The Individual and His Society. *Columbia Univ. Press,* New York, 1939 — 4, 14, 20, 23

(922)　The Traumatic Neuroses of War. *National Research Council,* Washington, 1941 — 7

KARN, H. W.

(923)　A Bibliography of Experimental Neurosis. *Psychol. Rec.* IV, 1940 — 2

KARPMAN, BEN

(924)　Stupor and Allied States. *R.* IX, 1922 — 18

(925)　The Psychopathology of Exhibitionism. *R.* XIII, 1926 — 16

(926)　The Chronic Alcoholic as a Neurotic and a Dreamer. *J. N. M. D.* XCIV, 1941 — 16

(927)　The Individual Criminal. *N. M. D. Pub. Co.,* New York and Washington, 1941 — 20

KASANIN, JACOB

(928)　Defense Reactions in Anxiety States of Central Origin. *Q.* XI, 1942 — 13

(929)　—and Biskind, Gerson R.: Personality Changes Following Substitution Therapy in Pre-Adolescent Eunuchoidism. *J. A. M. A.* CXXI, 1943 — 13

(930)　(Ed.) Language and Thought in Schizophrenia. *Univ. of California Press,* Berkeley and Los Angeles, 1944 — 18

BIBLIOGRAPHY

KATAN, M.

In Chapter

(931) The Understanding of Schizophrenic Speech. *Jo.* XX, 1939   18
(932) Die Rolle des Wortes in der Schizophrenie und Manie. *Z.*
XXV, 1940   18

KATAN-ANGEL, ANNY

(933) Einige Bemerkungen ueber Optimismus. *Z.* XX, 1934   20
(934) From the Analysis of a Bed-Wetter. *Q.* IV, 1935   12, 23
(935) Die Rolle der Verschiebung bei der Strassenangst. *Z.* XXIII,
1937   11, 23

KAUFMANN, MOSES RALPH

(936) Some Clinical Data on Ideas of Reference. *Q.* I, 1932   18
(937) Projection, Heterosexual and Homosexual. *Q.* III, 1934   9
(938) Psychoanalysis in Late-Life Depressions. *Q.* VI, 1937   17
(939) Religious Delusions in Schizophrenia. *Jo.* XX, 1939   18
(940) A Clinical Note on Social Anxiety. *R.* XXVIII, 1941   20
(941) Factors in Psychotherapy: A Psychoanalytic Evaluation. *Psych.*
Q. XV, 1941   23

KEMPER, WERNER

(942) Zur Genese der genitalen Erogeneitaet und des Orgasmus.
Z. XX, 1934   5

KEMPF, EDWARD J.

(943) The Psychoanalytic Treatment of Dementia Praecox: Report of
a Case. *R.* VI, 1919   18

KIELHOLZ, ARTHUR

(944) Symbolische Diebstaehle. *Z. ges. N. P.* LV, 1920   16
(945) On the Genesis and Dynamics of Inventor's Delusion. *Jo.* V,
1924   18
(946) Analyseversuch bei Delirium Tremens. *Z.* XII, 1926   16
(947) Seelische Hintergruende der Trunksucht. *Ps-a. Bwgg.* II, 1930   16
(948) Giftmord und Vergiftungswahn. *Z.* XVII, 1931   11, 17
(949) Weh dem, der luegt: Beitrag zur Pseudologia phantastica.
Z. XIX, 1933   20
(950) Zur Begutachtung eines Falles von Paederosis. *Z.* XXIII, 1937   16

KIRSCHNER, LOTTE

(951) Analyse einer Konversionshysterie in vorgeschrittenem Lebens-
alter. *Z.* XIV, 1928   23
(952) Aus der Analyse einer zwangsneurotischen Arbeitshemmung.
Z. XIV, 1928   10

KLEIN, MELANIE

(953) Zur Fruehanalyse. *Im.* IX, 1923   23
(954) Zur Genese des Tics. *Z.* XI, 1925   15
(955) Early Stages of the Oedipus Conflict. *Jo.* IX, 1928   5, 6, 16, 23
(956) Personification in the Play of Children. *Jo.* X, 1929   9

In Chapter

(957) A Contribution to the Theory of Intellectual Inhibition. *Jo.*
XII, 1931   10, 23

(958) The Psychoanalysis of Children. *Hogarth Press and Inst. of
Ps-a.,* London, 1932   3, 5, 16, 23

(959) —and Riviere, Joan: Love, Hate and Reparation. *Hogarth
Press,* London, 1938   5, 8, 9

KNIGHT, ROBERT

(960) The Psychodynamics of Chronic Alcoholism. *J. N. M. D.*
LXXXVI, 1936   16

(961) Application of Psychoanalytic Concepts in Psychotherapy.
Menn. Bull. I, 1937   23

(962) Psychoanalysis of Hospitalized Patients. *Menn. Bull.* I, 1937   23

(963) The Dynamics and Treatment of Chronic Alcohol Addiction.
Menn. Bull. I, 1937   16

(964) The Psychoanalytic Treatment in a Sanatorium of Chronic
Addiction to Alcohol. *J. A. M. A.* III, 1938   16, 18, 23

(965) Why People go to Cultists. *Menn. Bull.* III, 1939   23

(966) Psychotherapy in Acute Paranoid Schizophrenia with Successful
Outcome. *Menn. Bull.* III, 1939   18, 23

(967) Introjection, Projection and Identification. *Q.* IX, 1940   9

(968) The Relationship of Latent Homosexuality to the Mechanism
of Paranoid Delusions. *Menn. Bull.* IV, 1940   18

(969) The Evaluation of the Results of Psychoanalytic Therapy.
A. J. P. XCVIII, 1941   23

(970) Some Problems Involved in Selecting and Rearing Adopted
Children. *Menn. Bull.* V, 1941   20

(971) Intimidation of Others as a Defense against Anxiety. *Menn.
Bull.* VI, 1942   11, 20

KNOPF, O.

(972) Preliminary Report on Personality Studies in Thirty Migraine
Patients. *J. N. M. D.* LXXXII, 1935   13

(973) Aeusserungen des Oedipuskomplexes bei Schizophrenie. *Z.*
XIV, 1928   18

(974) Weltuntergangserlebnis und Wiedergeburtsphantasie bei einem
Schizophrenen. *Z.* XVIII, 1932   18

KOVACS, SANDOR

(975) Introjektion, Projektion und Einfuehlung. *C.* II, 1912   20

KOVACS, VILMA

(976) Analyse eines Falles von Tic Convulsif. *Z.* XI, 1925   15

(977) Wiederholungstendenz und Charakterbildung. *Z.* XVII, 1931   21

KRAINES, SAMUEL H.

(978) The Therapy of the Neuroses and Psychoses. *Lea and Febiger,*
Philadelphia, 1943   G

KRAUS, SIEGFRIED   *In Chapter*

(979)   Die Verwaisung als soziale Erscheinung. *Paed.* IV, 1930   20

KRETSCHMER, ERNST

(980)   Physique and Character. *Harcourt, Brace,* New York, 1931   20

KRIS, ERNST

(981)   Ein geisteskranker Bildhauer. *Im.* XIX, 1933   18
(982)   Bemerkungen zur Bildnerei der Geisteskranken. *Im.* XXII,
        1936   18
(983)   The Psychology of Caricature. *Jo.* XVII, 1936   18, 20
(984)   Ego Development and the Comic. *Jo.* XIX, 1938   16, 20
(985)   —and Gombrich, E.: The Principles of Caricature. *M.* XVII,
        1938   18
(986)   Laughter as an Expressive Process. *Jo.* XXI, 1940   15, 18

KRONENGOLD, EDWARD

(987)   —and Sterba, Richard: Two Cases of Fetishism. *Q.* V, 1936   16

KUBIE, LAWRENCE S.

(988)   Practical Aspects of Psychoanalysis. *Norton,* New York, 1936   G
(989)   The Fantasy of Dirt. *Q.* VI, 1937   14
(990)   Modification in a Schizophrenic Reaction with Psychoanalytic
        Treatment. *Arch. N. Ps.* XXXVII, 1937   18
(991)   A Critical Analysis of the Conception of a Repetition Compul-
        sion. *Jo.* XX, 1939   21
(992)   The Repetitive Core of Neurosis. *Q.* X, 1941   21
(993)   A Physiological Approach to the Concept of Anxiety.
        Psychosom. Med. III, 1941   4
(994)   —and Margolin, S. G.: A Physiological Method for the Induc-
        tion of States of Partial Sleep, and Securing Free Association
        and Early Memories in Such States. *Tr. A. N. A.,* 1942   23
(995)   The Use of Induced Hypnagogic Reveries in the Recovery of
        Repressed Amnesic Data. *Menn. Bull.* VII, 1943   23

KULOVESI, YRJÖ

(996)   Zur Entstehung des Tics. *Z.* XV, 1929   15, 21
(997)   Ein Beitrag zur Psychoanalyse des epileptischen Anfalls. *Z.*
        XX, 1934   13
(998)   Die Ausdrucksbewegungen der Bejahung und Verneinung. *Z.*
        XXIV, 1939   15

LAFORGUE, R.

(999)   Zum Begriff der Verdraengung. *Z.* XIV, 1928   9
(1000) The Mechanism of Isolation in Neurosis and Its Relations to
        Schizophrenia. *Jo.* X, 1929   9
(1001) On the Erotization of Anxiety. *Jo.* XI, 1930   20

(1002) Clinical Aspects of Psychoanalysis. *Hogarth Press,* London, *In Chapter*
1938   G
(1003) The Ego and the Conception of Reality. *Jo.* XX, 1939   4
(1004) The Relativity of Reality. *N. M. D. Pub. Co.,* New York and
Washington, 1940   4, 20

LAMPL, HANS

(1005) A Case of Borrowed Sense of Guilt. *Jo.* VIII, 1927   9

LAMPL-DE GROOT, J.

(1006) The Evolution of the Oedipus Complex in Women. *Jo.* IX,
1928   5
(1007) Problems of Femininity. *Q.* II, 1933   5, 16
(1008) Masochismus und Narzissmus. *Z.* XXII, 1936   16

LANDAUER, KARL

(1009) Spontanheilung einer Katatonie. *Z.* II, 1914   18
(1010) Die symptomatische Neurasthenie. *Z. ges. N. P.* XLV, 1919   10
(1011) Aequivalente der Trauer. *Z.* XI, 1925   9
(1012) Die kindliche Bewegungsunruhe. *Z.* XII, 1926   15
(1013) Gemuetsbewegungen oder Affekte. In Federn-Meng: *Ps-a.
Volksbuch,* 1926   2
(1014) Die Triebe. In Federn-Meng: *Ps-a. Volksbuch,* 1926   5
(1015) Die Bewusstseinsstoerungen. In Federn-Meng: *Ps-a. Volksbuch,* 1926   12
(1016) Die Schizophrenie. In Federn-Meng: *Ps-a. Volksbuch,* 1926   18
(1017) Paranoia. In Federn-Meng: *Ps-a. Volksbuch,* Hippokrates Verlag,
1926   18
(1018) Automatismen, Zwangsneurose und Paranoia. *Z.* XIII, 1927   15, 18
(1019) Zur psychosexuellen Genese der Dummheit. *Z. S. W.,* 1929   10, 23
(1020) Zur Theorie der Dummheit. *Paed.* IV, 1930   10, 23
(1021) Affects, Passions and Temperament. *Jo.* XIX, 1938   2, 19
(1022) Some Remarks on the Formation of the Anal-Erotic Character.
Jo. XX, 1939   14, 20

LANDMARK, JOHANNES

(1023) Ueber den Triebbegriff. *Im.* XX, 1934   5
(1024) Der Freud'sche Triebbegriff und die erogenen Zonen. *Im.*
XXI, 1935   5

LANTOS, BARBARA

(1025) Analyse einer Konversionshysterie im Klimakterium. *Z.* XV,
1929   12, 23

LATIF, J.

(1026) Some Etiological Factors in the Pathology of Stammering. *M.*
XVII, 1938   15

LAUBI, O.

(1027) Ein Fall von Psychoanalyse bei einem erwachsenen Stotterer.
M. ges. Sprach., 1911   15

LEHRMAN, PHILIP R.

(1028) Analysis of a Conversion Hysteria Superimposed on an Old   *In Chapter*
Diffuse Central Nervous System Lesion.   *J. N. M. D.* LIV,
1921   12
(1029) Some Unconscious Determinants in Homicide.   *Psych. Q.*
XIII, 1939   16

LENNOX, W. G.

(1030) —and Cobb, St.: Epilepsy.   *Williams and Wilkins,* Baltimore,
1928   13

LEVEY, HARRY B.

(1031) Oral Trends and Oral Conflicts in a Case of Duodenal Ulcer.
Q. III, 1934   13
(1032) A Critique of the Theory of Sublimation.   *Ps.* II, 1939   9

LEVIN, MAX

(1033) The Activation of a Repressed Impulse under Apparently Paradoxical Circumstances.   *Jo.* XVIII, 1936   9

LEVINE, MAURICE

(1034) Pregenital Trends in a Case of Chronic Diarrhoea and Vomit-
ing.   *Q.* III, 1934   13
(1035) Notes on the Psychopathology of Suspicions of Marital In-
fidelity.   *J. Med.* XIX, 1938   18
(1036) The Diagnosis of Normality.   *J. Med.* XX, 1939   23
(1037) Psychotherapy in Medical Practice.   *Macmillan,* New York,
1942   23

LEVY, DAVID M.

(1038) Use of Play Technique as an Experimental Procedure.   *A. J.
Orthops.* III, 1933   23
(1039) Studies in Sibling Rivalry.   *A. Orthopsych. Assn.,* New York,
1937   5
(1040) "Release Therapy" in Young Children.   *Ps.* I, 1938   23
(1041) Maternal Overprotection.   *Columbia Univ. Press,* New York,
1943   5, 6, 20

LEVY, ERWIN

(1042) Some Aspects of the Schizophrenic Formal Disturbance of
Thought.   *Ps.* VI, 1943   18

LEVY, ESTELLE

(1043) Psychoanalytic Treatment of a Child with a Stealing Compulsion.   *A. J. Orthops.* IV, 1934   16

LEVY, KATA

(1044) Vom Bettnaessen des Kindes.   *Paed.* VIII, 1934   12

LEVY, LUDWIG

(1045) The Psychology of the Effect Produced by Morphine. *Jo.* VI,   *In Chapter*
        1925   18

LEVY, NORMAN A.

(1046) —and Grinker, Roy R.: Psychological Observations in Affective
        Psychoses Treated with Combined Convulsive Shock and
        Psychotherapy. *J. N. M. D.* XCVII, 1943   23

LEVY-BRUHL

(1047) Primitive Mentality. *Macmillan,* New York, 1923   4, 18

LEVY-SUHL, MAX

(1048) Ueber Hypnotismus und seine Beziehungen zur Psycho-
        analyse. *Hirzel,* Leipzig, 1929   23
(1049) Resolution by Psychoanalysis of Motor Disturbances in an
        Adolescent. *Q.* VI, 1937   15

LEWIN, BERTRAM D.

(1050) Kotschmieren, Menses und weibliches Ueber-Ich. *Z.* XVI,
        1930   5
(1051) Warum Kinder von den Erwachsenen geneckt werden.
        Paed. IV, 1930   5
(1052) The Compulsive Character. *M. R. R.,* 1930   20
(1053) Analysis and Structure of a Transient Hypomania. *Q.* I,
        1932   17
(1054) Anal Eroticism and the Mechanism of Undoing. *Q.* I,
        1932   9, 14, 16
(1055) The Body as Phallus. *Q.* II, 1933   16, 20
(1056) Claustrophobia. *Q.* IV, 1935   11
(1057) —and Others: Discussion of Daniel's Case of Neurosis with
        Diabetes Mellitus. *Q.* V, 1936   13
(1058) A Type of Neurotic Hypomanic Reaction. *Arch. N. Ps.*
        XXXVII, 1937   17
(1059) Some Observations on Knowledge, Belief and the Impulse to
        Know. *Jo.* XX, 1939   5, 10, 20
(1060) Concepts on Hypomanic and Related States. *R.* XXVIII,
        1941   17

LEWIS, NOLAN D. C.

(1061) A Psychoanalytic Study of Hyperthyroidism. *R.* X, 1923   13
(1062) Psychoanalytic Approach to Children under Twelve Years of
        Age. *R.* XIII, 1926   23
(1063) Studies on Suicides. *R.* XX, 1933, and XXI, 1934   17

LICHTENSTEIN, HEINZ

(1064) Zur Phaenomenologie des Wiederholungszwanges und des
        Todestriebes. *Im.* XXI, 1935   21

LIPTON, S.

(1065) Dissociated Personality: a Case Report. *Psych. Q.* XVII,   *In Chapter*
1943   12

LISS, EDWARD

(1066) Play Technique in Child Analysis. *A. J. Orthops.* VI, 1936   23
(1067) Emotional and Biological Factors Involved in Learning Processes. *A. J. Orthops.* VII, 1937   10
(1068) Learning Difficulties. *A. J. Orthops.* XI, 1941   10

LOEW-BEER, HELENE

(1069) —and Morgenstern, Milan: Heilpaedagogische Praxis. *Sensen Verlag,* Wien, 1936   23

LOEWENFELD, HENRY

(1070) Psychic Trauma and Productive Experience in the Artist. *Q.* X, 1941   21

LOEWENSTEIN, RUDOLPH

(1071) Phallic Passivity in Men. *Jo.* XVI, 1935   5, 16

LORAND, SANDOR

(1072) Fetishism in Statu Nascendi. *Jo.* XI, 1930   16
(1073) The Reactive Character. *M. R. R.,* 1930   20
(1074) Aggression and Flatus. *Jo.* XII, 1931   5
(1075) The Morbid Personality. *Knopf,* New York, 1931   G
(1076) Psychoanalysis Today, Its Scope and Function. *Covici Friede,* New York, 1933   G
(1077) A Note on the Psychology of the Inventor. *Q.* III, 1934   18
(1078) Dynamics and Therapy of Depressive States. *R.* XXIV, 1937   17
(1079) Contribution to the Problem of Vaginal Orgasm. *Jo.* XX, 1939   5
(1080) Role of the Female Penis Fantasy in Male Character Formation. *Jo.* XX, 1939   20
(1081) Hypnotic Suggestion, Its Dynamics, Indications and Limitations. *J. N. M. D.* XCIV, 1941   23
(1082) Anorexia Nervosa: Report of a Case. *Psychosom. Med.* V, 1943   10, 13

LOWREY, LAWSON G.

(1083) Runaways and Normals. *A. J. Orthops.* XI, 1941   16

LUNDHOLD, HELGE

(1084) Repression and Rationalization. *M.* XIII, 1933   20

LUZENBERGER, A. VON

(1085) Psychoanalyse in einem Falle von Erroetungsangst als Beitrag zur Psychologie des Schamgefuehls. *C.* I, 1911   11, 20

MACCURDY, JOHN T.

(1086) A Psychological Feature of the Precipitating Factors in the *In Chapter*
Psychoses, and Its Relation to Art. *J. Ab. P.* IX, 1914   18

MACFARLANE, DONALD A.

(1087) Arthritis and Aggressiveness. Paper read at the Spring
Meeting of the San Francisco Psychoanalytic Society, San
Francisco, 1942   13

MACK-BRUNSWICK, RUTH

(1088) A Supplement to Freud's History of an Infantile Neurosis.
Jo. IX, 1928   13, 18
(1089) Die Analyse eines Eifersuchtswahnes. *Z.* XIV, 1928   18, 20
(1090) The Pre-Oedipal Phase of the Libido Development. *Q.* IX,
1940   5
(1091) The Accepted Lie. *Q.* XII, 1943   20

MAEDER, ALPHONSE

(1092) Sexualitaet und Epilepsie. *Y.* I, 1909   13
(1093) Psychologische Untersuchungen an Dementia Praecox-
Kranken. *Y.* II, 1910   18
(1094) Psychoanalyse bei einer melancholischen Depression. *Y.*
III, 1911   17

MAEDER, LEROY A. M.

(1095) Diagnostic Criteria: The Concept of Normal and Abnormal.
Family, 1941   23
(1096) Relations of Psychoanalysis to Psychiatry. *Arch. N. Ps.*
XLIX, 1943   18

MAENCHEN, ANNA

(1097) Denkhemmung und Aggression. *Paed.* X, 1936   10, 23
(1098) On Neurotic Disturbances of Sleep. *Jo.* XXIII, 1942   10

MAHLER-SCHOENBERGER, MARGARETE

(1099) Pseudo-Imbecility: A Magic Cap of Invincibility. *Q.* XI,
1942   10, 23
(1100) —and Rangell, Leo: A Psychosomatic Study of Maladies des
Tics. *Psych. Q.* XVII, 1943   15

MALINOWSKI, BRONISLAW

(1101) Mutterrechtliche Familie und Oedipuskomplex. *Im.* X, 1924   5
(1102) The Sexual Life of Savages. *Routledge,* London, 1929   5, 6

MARCUS, ERNST

(1103) Psychische Beeinflussung der Menstruation. *C.* II, 1912   13

MARKUSZEWICZ, ROMAN — *In Chapter*

(1104) Beitrag zum autistischen Denken bei Kindern. *Z.* VI, 1920 — 4

MARMOR, JUDAH

(1105) The Role of Instinct in Human Behavior. *Ps.* V, 1942 — 2, 5

MASSERMAN, JULES H.

(1106) Psychodynamisms in Anorexia Nervosa and Neurotic Vomiting. *Q.* X, 1941 — 10, 13
(1107) Psychodynamisms in Manic-Depressive Psychoses. *R.* XXVIII, 1941 — 17
(1108) Hypnotic Treatment of Acute Hysterical Depression: The Dynamics of Hypnosis and Brief Psychotherapy. *Arch. N. Ps.* XLVI, 1941 — 23
(1109) Behavior and Neuroses. *Univ. of Chicago Press*, Chicago, 1943 — 2

MCCORD, CLINTON

(1110) Bemerkungen zum Stand der Kinderanalyse in Amerika. *Paed.* VIII, 1934 — 23

MEAD, MARGARET

(1111) Changing Food Habits. *Menn. Bull.* VII, 1943 — 10

MENAKER, ESTHER

(1112) A Contribution to the Study of the Neurotic Stealing Symptom. *A. J. Orthops.* IX, 1939 — 16

MENG, HEINRICH

(1113) Ueber Schlaf und Schlafstoerungen beim Gesunden, Kranken, und Arzneivergifteten. *D. Z. Hom.* 9/10, 1924 — 10
(1114) Stellung der Psychoanalyse zur uebrigen Psychotherapie. In Federn-Meng: *Ps-a. Volksbuch,* Hippokrates Verlag, Leipzig, 1926 — 23
(1115) Aus Analysen von stotternden Kindern. *Paed.* II, 1928 — 15
(1116) Das einzige und das einsame Kind. *Neue Erz.* X, 1928 — 5, 20
(1117) Angstneurose und Sexualleben. *D. A. Z.* LV, 1929 — 10
(1118) Ueber Pubertaet und Pubertaetsaufklaerung. *Paed.* VI, 1932 — 6
(1119) Aus der Analyse eines Stotterers. *Paed.* VI, 1932 — 15
(1120) Das Problem der Organpsychose. *Z.* XX, 1934 — 13
(1121) —und Grote, L. R.: Ueber interne und psychotherapeutische Behandlung der endogenen Magersucht. *Schw. M. W.* LXIV, 1934 — 10, 13
(1122) Zur Psychologie des triebhaften Narzissten. *Paed.* IX, 1935 — 16

MENNINGER, KARL A.

(1123) Psychoanalytical Study of a Case of Organic Epilepsy. *R.* XIII, 1926 — 13

MILLER, EMANUEL *In Chapter*

(1148) The Neuroses in War. *Macmillan,* New York, 1940   7

MILLER, JOSEPH S.

(1149) —and Gair, Mollie: A Traumatic Neurosis of World War I, 23 Years After. *J. N. M. D.* XCVII, 1943   7

MILLER, MILTON L.

(1150) —and MacLean, Helen V.: The Status of the Emotions in Palpitation and Extrasystoles; with a Note on Effort Syndrome. *Q.* X, 1941   13

(1151) A Psychological Study of Eczema and Neurodermatitis. *Psychosom. Med.* IV, 1942   13

MILLET, JOHN A. P.

(1152) Insomnia: Its Causes and Treatment. *Greenberg,* New York, 1938   10

MOELLENHOFF, FRITZ

(1153) Ideas of Children about Death. *Menn. Bull.* III, 1939   11, 17

MONTAGU, M. F. ASHLEY

(1154) On the Physiology and Psychology of Swearing. *Ps.* V, 1942   14, 15, 16

MOORE, MERRILL

(1155) Alcoholism: Some Contemporary Opinions. *A. J. P.* XCVII, 1941   16

(1156) A Didactic Note on Alcoholism. *J. N. M. D.* XCVII, 1943   16

MOORE, T. V.

(1157) A Study in Sadism. *Character and Personality* VI, 1937   16

MORRISON, SAMUEL

(1158) Psychosomatic Correlations of Duodenal Ulcer. *J. A. M. A.* CXX, 1942   13

MOWER, JAMES W.

(1159) A Comparative Study of Hobby Activities. *Menn. Bull.* IV, 1940   16, 20

MÜLLER, JOSINE

(1160) Atheism in Childhood and Faulty Character Development. *Jo.* VIII, 1927   16

(1161) A Contribution to the Problem of Libidinal Development of the Genital Phase in Girls. *Jo.* XIII, 1932   5

MÜLLER-BRAUNSCHWEIG, CARL

(1162) Beitraege zur Metapsychologie. *Im.* XII, 1925   10

(1163) Desexualization and Identification. *R.* XIII, 1926   10

In Chapter

(1164) The Genesis of the Feminine Superego. *Jo.* VII, 1926   6

MURRAY, C. D.

(1165) Psychogenic Factors in the Etiology of Ulcerative Colitis and
Bloody Diarrhoea. *A. J. M. S.* CLXXX, 1930   13

MUTTER, EINE

(1166) Die Entstehung des Pavor Nocturnus bei einem Kinde.
Paed. I, 1927   5, 11

NEEDLES, WILLIAM

(1167) Stigmata Occurring in the Course of Psychoanalysis. *Q.*
XII, 1943   12

NELKEN, JAN

(1168) Ueber schizophrene Wortzerlegungen. *C.* II, 1912   18

NEWELL, H. WHITMAN

(1169) Play Therapy in Child Psychiatry. *A. J. Orthops.* XI, 1941   23

NICOLINI, WILHELM

(1170) Verbrechen aus Heimweh und ihre psychoanalytische Er-
klaerung. *Im.* XXII, 1936   17

NUNBERG, HERRMANN

(1171) Ueber den katatonischen Anfall. *Z.* VI, 1920   18
(1172) Der Verlauf des Libidokonfliktes in einem Falle von Schizophrenie. *Z.* VII, 1921   18
(1173) Ueber Depersonalisationszustaende im Lichte der Libido-
theorie. *Z.* X, 1924   18
(1174) The Will to Recovery. *Jo.* VII, 1926   20
(1175) The Sense of Guilt and the Need for Punishment. *Jo.* VII,
1926   6
(1176) The Synthetic Function of the Ego. *Jo.* XII, 1931   4
(1177) Psychoanalyse des Schamgefuehls. *Ps-a. Bwgg.* IV, 1932   8
(1178) Allgemeine Neurosenlehre auf psychoanalytischer Grundlage.
Huber, Bern, 1932   8
(1179) The Feeling of Guilt. *Q.* III, 1934   6, 8
(1180) On the Theory of Therapeutic Results of Psychoanalysis.
Jo. XVIII, 1937   21
(1181) Homosexuality, Magic and Aggression. *Jo.* XIX, 1938   16
(1182) Ichstaerke und Ichschwaeche. *Z.* XXIV, 1939   21

OBERNDORF, C. P.

(1183) Cases Allied to Manic-Depressive Insanity. *N. Y. S. Hosp. B.*
V, 1919   20
(1184) Submucous Resection as a Castration Symbol. *Jo.* X, 1929   13, 15

(1185) Technical Procedure in the Analytic Treatment of Children. *In Chapter*
Jo. XI, 1930   23
(1186) A Theory of Depersonalization. *Tr. A. N. A.,* 1933   18
(1187) Depersonalization in Relation to Erotization of Thought. *Jo.*
XV, 1934   18
(1188) The Genesis of the Feeling of Unreality. *Jo.* XVI, 1935   18
(1189) Feeling of Unreality. *Arch. N. Ps.* XXXVI, 1935   18
(1190) The Psychogenic Factors in Asthma. *N. Y. S. J. M.* XXXV,
1935   13, 15
(1191) On Retaining the Sense of Reality in States of Depersonalization. *Jo.* XX, 1939   18
(1192) The Feeling of Stupidity. *Jo.* XX, 1939   10
(1193) Time—Its Relation to Reality and Purpose. *R.* XXVIII, 1941   14
(1194) Comment on the Emotional Settings of Some Attacks of
Urticaria. *Psychosom. Med.* IV, 1942   13
(1195) Results with Psychoanalytic Therapy. *A. J. P.* XCIX, 1942   23

ODIER, CHARLES

(1196) Vom Ueber-Ich. *Z.* XII, 1926   6
(1197) Geld und Neurose. Referat: *Ps-a. Bwgg.* III, 1931   20
(1198) Krankhafte Neugier. *Paed.* XI, 1937   16

O'DONOVAN, W. J.

(1199) Dermatological Neuroses. *Paul, Trench, and Trubner,* London, 1927   13

OLDEN, CHRISTINE

(1200) About the Fascinating Effect of the Narcissistic Personality.
A. Im. II, 1941   16, 20
(1201) On Neurotic Disturbances of Sleep. *Jo.* XXIII, 1942   10
(1202) The Psychology of Obstinacy. *Q.* XII, 1943   14, 20

OPHUIJSEN, J. H. W. VAN

(1203) On the Origin of the Feeling of Persecution. *Jo.* I, 1920   9, 18
(1204) Contributions to the Masculinity Complex in Women. *Jo.*
V, 1924   20
(1205) The Sexual Aim of Sadism as Manifested in Acts of Violence.
Jo. X, 1929   5, 16
(1206) Psychoanalysis of Organic Psychoses. In Lorand: *Ps-a. Today,*
Covici Friede, New York, 1933   13

OPPENHEIM, HANS

(1207) Zur Frage der Genese des Eifersuchtswahnes. *C.* II, 1912   18

ORGEL, SAMUEL Z.

(1208) Reactivation of the Oedipus Situation. *Q.* III, 1934   9

(1225) Schockdenken und Schockphantasien bei hoechster Todesge-   *In Chapter*
fahr. *Z.* XVI, 1930   9

PICHON, E.

(1226) —and Parcheminey, G.: Ueber kurze psychotherapeutische
Behandlungen auf Grund der Freudschen Psychoanalyse.
Paed. XI, 1937   23

PLANK-SPIRA, EMMA

(1227) Foerderung und Hemmung des Lernens. *Paed.* VII, 1933   10

PÖTZL, OTTO

(1228) Experimentell erregte Traumbilder in ihren Beziehungen
zum indirekten Sehen. *Z. ges. N. P.* XXXVII, 1917   2

POLLAK, FRANZ

(1229) Psychoanalyse und klinische Psychiatrie. *Z.* VII, 1921   18

PRATT, JOHN

(1230) The Home Sanatorium Treatment of Consumption. *Johns
Hopkins Hosp. Bull.* XVII, 1906   23

PREYER, W.

(1231) Die Seele des Kindes. 1884   18

RAALTE, FRITS VAN

(1232) Kindertraeume und Pavor Nocturnus. *Z.* I, 1913   10

RABINER, A. M.

(1233) —and Keschner, M.: The Role of Psychical Factors in the
Production of Organic Nervous Disease. *J. N. Psychop.*
X, 1930   13

RADO, SANDOR

(1234) Eine besondere Aeusserungsform der Kastrationsangst. *Z.*
V, 1919   10
(1235) The Economic Principle in Psychoanalytic Technique. *Jo.*
VI, 1925   6, 7, 20, 23
(1236) The Psychic Effects of Intoxicants. *Jo.* VII, 1926   16, 17
(1237) An Anxious Mother. *Jo.* IX, 1928   14, 19, 20
(1238) The Problem of Melancholia. *Jo.* IX, 1928   4, 17, 20
(1239) The Psychoanalysis of Pharmacothymia. *Q.* II, 1933   16, 17
(1240) Fear of Castration in Women. *Q.* II, 1933   5, 13, 16, 20
(1241) Psychoanalysis and Psychiatry. *Jo.* XVII, 1936   18
(1242) Development in the Psychoanalytic Conception and Treatment of the Neuroses. *Q.* VIII, 1939   5, 7, 16
(1243) A Critical Examination of the Concept of Bisexuality.
Psychosom. Med. II, 1940   5, 16

(1244) Pathodynamics and Treatment of Traumatic War Neuroses   *In Chapter*
       (Traumatophobia). *Psychosom. Med.* IV, 1942   7, 21

RANK, BEATE

(1245) Where Child Analysis Stands Today. *A. Im.* III, 1942   23

RANK, OTTO

(1246) Der Kuenstler. *Hugo Heller,* Wien, 1907   20
(1247) Das Inzestmotiv in Dichtung und Sage. *Deuticke,* Leip
       zig, 1912   G
(1248) Myth of the Birth of the Hero. *J. N. M. D.* XL, 1913   G
(1249) Die Nacktheit in Sage und Dichtung. *Im.* II, 1913   5, 16
(1250) Der Doppelgaenger. *Im.* III, 1914   18, 20
(1251) Die Don Juan Gestalt. *Im.* VIII, 1922   13
(1252) Perversion and Neurosis. *Jo.* IV, 1923   16

RAWSON, ARNOLD T.

(1253) Accident Proneness. *Psychosom. Med.* VI, 1944   20

READ, C. STANFORD

(1254) The Psychopathology of Alcoholism and Some So-called Al-
       coholic Psychoses. *J. M. S.* LXVI, 1920   16
(1255) The Struggles of Male Adolescence. *Allen and Unwin,*
       London, 1928   6

REDL, FRITZ

(1256) Wir Lehrer und die Pruefungsangst. *Paed.* VII, 1933   11, 20
(1257) Zum Begriff der Lernstoerung. *Paed.* VIII, 1934   10
(1258) Group Formation and Leadership. *Ps.* V, 1942   5, 9, 14,
                                  16, 20

REEDE, EDWARD H.

(1259) Conversion Epilepsy. *R.* IX, 1922   13

REICH, ANNIE

(1260) Klinischer Beitrag zum Verstaendnis der paranoiden Per-
       soenlichkeit. *Z.* XXII, 1936   18
(1261) A Contribution to the Psychoanalysis of Extreme Submis-
       siveness in Women. *Q.* IX, 1940   16

REICH, WILHELM

(1262) Ueber Spezifitaet der Onanieformen. *Z.* VIII, 1922   10, 11
(1263) Zwei narzisstische Typen. *Z.* VIII, 1922   20
(1264) Ueber Genitalitaet. *Z.* X, 1924   5
(1265) Der psychogene Tic als Onanieaequivalent. *Z. S. W.* XI,
       1925   15
(1266) Der triebhafte Charakter. *Int. Ps-a. V.,* Wien, 1925   6, 9, 16, 20
(1267) Weitere Bemerkungen ueber die therapeutische Bedeutung
       der Genitallibido. *Z.* XI, 1925   5, 10, 13

(1268) Ueber die chronische hypochondrische Neurasthenie mit   *In Chapter*
genitaler Asthenie. Z. XII, 1926   5, 10
(1269) Zur Technik der Deutung und der Widerstandsanalyse. Z.
XIII, 1927
20
(1270) Die Funktion des Orgasmus. *Int. Ps-a. V.,* Wien, 1927   5, 10, 11, 13,
16, 20
(1271) Ueber Charakteranalyse. Z. XIV, 1928   14, 16, 20, 23
(1272) Der genitale und der neurotische Charakter. Z. XV, 1929   5, 20
(1273) Wohin fuehrt die Nackterziehung? *Paed.* III, 1929   5, 23
(1274) Character Formation and the Phobias of Childhood. *Jo.*
XII, 1931   20, 22
(1275) The Characterological Mastery of the Oedipus Complex.
Jo. XII, 1931
20
(1276) Ueber den epileptischen Anfall. Z. XVII, 1931   13
(1277) Der masochistische Charakter. Z. XVIII, 1932   5, 16, 20
(1278) Der Einbruch der Sexualmoral. *Sexpol Verlag,* Berlin, 1932   5, 6, 23
(1279) Charakteranalyse. *Selbstverlag des Verfassers,* Berlin, 1933 9, 14, 16
20, 23
(1280) Psychischer Kontakt und vegetative Stroemung. *Sexpol
Verlag,* Kopenhagen, 1935   11, 13, 17

REIDER, NORMAN

(1281) Remarks on Mechanisms in Non-Analytic Psychotherapy.
Dis. Nerv. S., 1944
23

REIK, THEODOR

(1282) Zur lokomotorischen Angst. Z. II, 1914   11
(1283) Eine typische Zwangsbefuerchtung. Z. II, 1914   11
(1284) Die Pubertaetsriten der Wilden. *Im.* IV, 1915   5, 16, 23
(1285) Ueber kollektives Vergessen. Z. VI, 1920   12
(1286) Zum Thema: Traum und Nachtwandeln. Z. VI, 1920   12
(1287) Der eigene und der fremde Gott. *Int. Ps-a. V.,* Wien, 1920   6
(1288) Psychoanalysis of the Unconscious Sense of Guilt. *Jo.* V,
1924   14, 20
(1289) Gestaendniszwang und Strafbeduerfnis. *Int. Ps-a. V.,* Wien,
1925   6, 14, 20
(1290) Drei psychoanalytische Notizen. *Im.* XI, 1926   10
(1291) Psychologie und Depersonalisation. In *Wie man Psycho-
loge wird; Int. Ps-a.,* Wien, 1927   18
(1292) Final Phases of Belief Found in Religion and in Obsessional
Neuroses. *Jo.* XI, 1930   14, 22
(1293) New Ways in Psychoanalytic Technique. *Jo* XIV, 1933   23
(1294) Nachdenkliche Heiterkeit. *Int. Ps-a. V.,* Wien, 1933   9, 20
(1295) The Unknown Murderer. *Hogarth Press,* London, 1936   1
(1296) Surprise and the Psychoanalyst. *Kegan Paul,* London,
1936
5, 20
(1297) Characteristics of Masochism. *A. Im.* I, 1940   16
(1298) Aggression from Anxiety. *Jo.* XXII, 1941   11, 20

In Chapter

(1299) Masochism in Modern Man. *Farrar and Rinehart,* New York, 1941 — 5, 16

RIBBLE, MARGARET A.

(1300) Clinical Studies of Instinctive Reactions in Newborn Babies. *A. J. P.* XCV, 1938 — 4

(1301) The Significance of the Infantile Sucking for the Psychic Development of the Individual. *J. N. M. D.* XC, 1939 — 4

(1302) Disorganizing Factors in Infant Personality. *A. J. P.* XCVIII, 1941 — 4

(1303) The Rights of Infants. *Columbia Univ. Press,* New York, 1944 — 4

RICKMAN, JOHN

(1304) Photography as a Pseudo-Perversion. *Jo.* VI, 1924 — 16

(1305) Alcoholism and Psychoanalysis. *B. J. In.* XXIII, 1925 — 16

(1306) A Psychological Factor in the Aetiology of Descensus Uteri, Laceration of the Perineum and Vaginism. *Jo.* VII, 1926 — 10, 13

(1307) The Development of the Psychoanalytical Theory of the Psychoses, 1894–1926, a Survey. *Int. Ps-a. P.,* London, 1926 — 17, 18

(1308) Index Psychoanalyticus, 1893–1926. *Inst. of Ps-a. and Hogarth Press,* London, 1926 — G

(1309) (Ed.) On the Bringing Up of Children. *Kegan Paul,* London, 1936 — 5, 23

RIEMER, MORRIS D.

(1310) Runaway Children. *A. J. Orthops.* X, 1940 — 16

RIPLEY, HERBERT S.

(1311) —Bohnenger, Charles, and Milhorat, Ade T.: Personality Factors in Patients with Muscular Disability. *A. J. P.* XCIX, 1943 — 13

RIVIERE, JOAN

(1312) Symposium on Child Analysis. *Jo.* VIII, 1927 — 5

(1313) Womanliness as a Masquerade. *Jo.* X, 1929 — 5, 20

(1314) Jealousy as a Mechanism of Defense. *Jo.* XIII, 1932 — 18, 20

(1315) A Contribution to the Analysis of Negative Therapeutic Reaction. *Jo.* XVII, 1936 — 14, 20

(1316) On the Genesis of Psychical Conflict in Earliest Infancy. *Jo.* XVII, 1936 — 23

ROBBINS, BERNARD S.

(1317) Escape into Reality: A Clinical Note on Spontaneous Social Recovery. *Q.* VI, 1937 — 22

(1318) Neurotic Disturbances in Work. *Ps.* II, 1939 — 10

ROGERSON, C. H.

(1319) Play Therapy in Childhood. *Oxford Univ. Press,* Oxford, 1939 — 23

ROHEIM, GEZA *In Chapter*

(1320) Das Selbst. *Im.* VII, 1921   13
(1321) Heiliges Geld in Melanesien. *Z.* IX, 1923   20
(1322) Mondmythologie und Mondreligion. *Im.* XIII, 1927   12
(1323) Sublimation. *Q.* XII, 1943   20

ROSE, JOHN A.

(1324) Eating Inhibitions in Children in Relation to Anorexia
        Nervosa. *Psychosom. Med.* V, 1943   10

ROSENZWEIG, SAUL

(1325) Sibling Death as a Psychological Experience with Special
        Reference to Schizophrenia. *R.* XXX, 1943   5, 20

ROSS, HELEN

(1326) Play Therapy. *A. J. Orthops.* VIII, 1938   23

RUBINOW-LURIE, OLGA

(1327) Psychological Factors Associated with Eating Difficulties in
        Children. *A. J. Orthops.* XI, 1941   13

SACHS, HANNS

(1328) Traumdeutung und Menschenkenntnis. *Y.* III, 1912   9, 18
(1329) Ueber Naturgefuehl. *Im.* I, 1912   11
(1330) Das Thema "Tod." *Im.* III, 1914   11, 17
(1331) Zur Genese der Perversionen. *Z.* IX, 1923   16
(1332) The Community of Daydreams.   In *The Creative Uncon-
        scious,* Sci.-Art. Publ., Cambridge (Mass.), 1942   9, 20
(1333) One of the Motive Factors in the Formation of the Superego
        in Women. *Jo.* X, 1929   6, 20
(1334) Caligula. *Elkin Matthews and Harrot,* London, 1931   20

SADGER, J.

(1335) Ein Fall von Pseudoepilepsia hysterica, psychoanalytisch
        aufgeloest. *Kl. R.,* 1909   13
(1336) Ein Fall von multipler Perversion mit hysterischen Absencen.
        Y. II, 1910   12
(1337) Ueber Urethralerotik. *Y.* II, 1910   5
(1338) Haut-, Schleimhaut- und Muskelerotik. *Y.* III, 1911   5, 16
(1339) Zur Psychologie des einzigen und des Lieblingskindes.
        Fortschr. Med. XXVI, 1911   5, 20
(1340) Ist das Asthma bronchiale eine Sexualneurose? *C.* I, 1911   15
(1341) Ein merkwuerdiger Fall von Nachtwandeln und Mondsucht.
        Z. IV, 1916   10, 12
(1342) Vom ungeliebten Kinde. *Fortschr. Med.,* 1916   20
(1343) Sleep Walking and Moon Walking. *N. M. D. Pub. Co.,*
        New York and Washington, 1919   10, 12

In Chapter

(1363) Ueber Gedankenentwicklung. *Z. ges. N. P.* LIX, 1920   4, 18

(1364) Ueber Identifizierung auf Grund der Analyse eines Falles von
Homosexualitaet. *Z. ges. N. P.* LIX, 1920   16

(1365) Ueber Halluzinationen. *Z. ges. N. P.* LIX, 1920   18

(1366) Zur Theorie der Entfremdung der Wahrnehmungswelt.
Allg. Z. f. Ps. LXXVI, 1921   18

(1367) Vorstudien einer Psychologie der Manie. *Z. ges. N. P.*
LXVIII, 1928   17

(1368) Ueber eine Psychose nach Staroperation. *Z.* VIII, 1922   13, 18

(1369) Zur Pathologie des Ichideals. *Z.* VIII, 1922   18

(1370) Ueber das Wesen der Hypnose. *Springer*, Berlin, 1922   23

(1371) Die Angstneurose. *W. m. W.* XXXVII, 1923   10

(1372) The Image and Appearance of the Human Body. *Paul,
Trench, Trubner,* London, 1935   4, 13, 18

(1373) Seele und Leben. *Springer,* Berlin, 1923   13, 18

(1374) Zur Lehre von der Hypochondrie. *M. N. P.* LVI, 1924   13

(1375) Medizinische Psychologie. *Springer,* Berlin, 1924   G

(1376) Zur Psychologie der progressiven Paralyse. *Z. ges. N. P.*
XCV, 1925   13

(1377) —and Sugar, Nikolaus: Zur Lehre von den schizophrenen
Sprachstoerungen. *Z. ges. N. P.* XCV, 1926   18

(1378) —and Kauders, Otto: Hypnosis. *N. M. D. Pub. Co.,* New
York and Washington, 1927   20, 23

(1379) Introduction to a Psychoanalytic Psychiatry. *N. M. D. Pub.
Co.,* New York and Washington, 1928   6, 13, 16, 18

(1380) The Neurasthenic-Hypochondriac Character. *M. R. R.,* 1930   20

(1381) Ueber Neurasthenie. *Z.* XVII, 1931   10

(1382) Brain and Personality. *N. M. D. Pub. Co.,* New York
and Washington, 1931   13, 18

(1383) Notes on Psychogenic Depressions and Melancholia. *R.* XX,
1933   17

(1384) The Psychoanalysis of Space. *Jo.* XVI, 1935   5, 11, 14

(1385) Psychopathologie der Zeit. *Im.* XXI, 1935   14

(1386) Zur Psychoanalyse der Geometrie, Arithmetik und Physik.
Im. XXII, 1936   5, 11, 14

(1387) Remarks on the Psychophysiology of the Skin. *R.* XXIII,
1936   13

(1388) The Analysis of Ideologies as a Psychotherapeutic Method,
Especially in Group Treatment. *A. J. P.* XCIII, 1936   23

(1389) The Social Neurosis. *R.* XXV, 1938   20

(1390) Psychotherapy. *Norton,* New York, 1938   18, 23

(1391) The Relations between Clinging and Equilibrium. *Jo.* XX,
1939   5, 11

(1392) Notes on the Psychology of Metrazol Treatment of Schizophrenia. *J. N. M. D.* LXXXIX, 1939   23

(1393) Results and Problems of Group Psychotherapy in Severe
Neuroses. *M. H.* XXIII, 1939   23

In Chapter

(1394) Introductory Remarks on Groups. *J. Soc. Psych.* XII, 1940   23
(1395) —and Levine, E. L.: Abstract Art as an Expression of Human
        Problems. *J. N. M. D.* XCV, 1942   14
(1396) The Sociological Implications of Neuroses. *J. Soc. Psych.*
        XV, 1942   23

SCHMIDEBERG, MELITTA

(1397) Intellektuelle Hemmung und Aggression. *Paed.* IV, 1930   10, 23
(1398) A Contribution to the Psychology of Persecutory Ideas and
        Delusions. *Jo.* XII, 1931   18
(1399) Some Unconscious Mechanics in Pathological Sexuality and
        Their Relation to Normal Sexual Activity. *Jo.* XIV, 1933   20
(1400) The Psychoanalytic Treatment of Asocial Children. *The
        New Era* XIV, 1933   23
(1401) The Psychoanalysis of Asocial Children. *Jo.* XVI, 1935   16, 23
(1402) On Motoring and Walking. *Jo.* XVIII, 1937   11
(1403) Intellectual Inhibition and Disturbances in Eating. *Jo.*
        XIX, 1938   10, 23

SCHMIDT, WERA

(1404) Die Bedeutung des Brustsaugens und Fingerlutschens fuer
        die psychische Entwicklung des Kindes. *Im.* XII, 1926   20
(1405) Die Entwicklung des Wisstriebes bei einem Kinde. *Im.*
        XVI, 1930   5, 10, 20

SCHNEIDER, ERNST

(1406) Ueber das Stottern, Entstehung, Verlauf und Heilung.
        A. Francke, Bern, 1922   15
(1407) Die Entstehung von Pavor Nocturnus bei einem Kinde.
        Paed. II, 1928   10
(1408) Neurotische Depression und Stehlen. *Paed.* VII, 1933   16

SCHROEDER, THEODORE

(1409) What is Psychologic Recovery? *R.* XXII, 1935   23

SCHULTZ, I. H.

(1410) Das autogene Training. *Thieme,* Leipzig, 1932   12, 13, 23

SCHULTZ-HENCKE, HARALD

(1411) Einfuehrung in die Psychoanalyse. *Gustav Fischer,* Jena,
        1927   18
(1412) Schicksal und Neurose. *Gustav Fischer,* Jena, 1931   5

SCHWARTZ, LOUIS ADRIAN

(1413) An Analyzed Case of Essential Hypertension. *Psychosom.
        Med.* II, 1940   13

SCHWARZ, OSWALD

(1414) Psychogenese und Psychotherapie koerperlicher Symptome. *In Chapter*
Springer, Wien, 1925   13

SEARL, NINA

(1415) A Case of Stammering in a Child. *Jo.* VIII, 1927   15
(1416) The Flight to Reality. *Jo.* X, 1929   20
(1417) Danger Situations of the Immature Ego. *Jo.* X, 1929   4
(1418) A Note on Depersonalization. *Jo.* XIII, 1932   18
(1419) The Psychology of Screaming. *Jo.* XIV, 1933   12, 15

SERVADIO, EMIL

(1420) Die Angst vor dem boesen Blick. *Im.* XXII, 1936   5, 8

SHACKLEY, FRANCIS M.

(1421) The Role of Homosexuality in the Genesis of Paranoid Conditions. *R.* I, 1914   18

SHARPE, ELLA F.

(1422) Certain Aspects of Sublimation and Delusion. *Jo.* XI, 1930   9, 14
(1423) The Technique of Psychoanalysis. *Jo.* XI, 1930, and XII, 1931   23
(1424) Similar and Divergent Unconscious Determinants Underlying the Sublimations of Pure Art and Pure Science. *Jo.* XVI, 1935   9, 14

SHEEHAN-DARE, HELEN

(1425) On Making Contact with the Child Patient. *Jo.* XV, 1934   23

SILBERER, HERBERT

(1426) Bericht ueber eine Methode, gewisse symbolische Halluzinationserscheinungen hervorzurufen und zu beobachten. *Y.* I, 1909   4
(1427) Symbolik des Erwachens und Schwellensymbolik ueberhaupt. *Y.* III, 1911   4
(1428) Ueber die Symbolbildung. *Y.* III, 1911   4
(1429) Von den Kategorien der Symbolik. *C.* II, 1912   4
(1430) Zur Symbolbildung. *Y.* IV, 1912   4

SILBERMANN, ISIDOR

(1431) The Psychical Experiences during the Shocks in Shock Therapy. *Jo.* XXI, 1940   23

SILVERBERG, WILLIAM V.

(1432) Eine Uebergangsphase in der Genese der Phantasie: Ein Kind wird geschlagen. *Z.* XVI, 1930   16

SILVERMAN, DANIEL

(1433) Prognosis in Schizophrenia. *Psych. Q.* XV, 1941   18

SIMMEL, ERNST

In Chapter

(1434) Kriegsneurosen und psychisches Trauma, ihre gegenseitigen
Beziehungen, dargestellt auf Grund psychoanalytischer
und hypnotischer Studien. *Otto Nemnich,* Muenchen
u. Leipzig, 1918   7

(1435) Zur Psychoanalyse des Spielers. *Vortrag.* VI, Int. Ps-a.
Kongr.; Autoref. Z. VI, 1920   16

(1436) Die psychophysische Bedeutsamkeit des Intestinalorgans fuer
die Urverdraengung. *Vortrag.* VIII, Int. Ps-a. Kongr.;
Autoref. Z. X, 1924   9, 13, 18

(1437) A Screen Memory in Statu Nascendi. *Jo.* VI, 1925   9, 20

(1438) The Doctor Game, Illness and the Profession of Medicine.
Jo. VII, 1926   13

(1439) Die Ausbildung des Psychotherapeuten vom Standpunkte der
Psychoanalyse. Bericht l. aerztl. Kongr. f. Psychotherapie,
Baden-Baden, 1926; Carl Marold, Halle a/S, 1927   23

(1440) Psychoanalytic Treatment in a Clinic. *Jo.* X, 1929   16, 18, 23

(1441) Zum Problem von Zwang und Sucht. Ber. ueber d. V. allg.
aerztl. Kongr. f. Psychotherapie, 1930   16

(1442) The Psychogenesis of Organic Disturbances and Their Psychoanalytic Treatment. Abstract in *Q.* I, 1932   13

(1443) The Psychoanalytic Sanitarium and the Psychoanalytic Movement. *Menn. Bull.* I, 1937   23

(1444) The Psychology of a Potential Lust-Murderer. Paper read
in the Ps-a. Study Group of Los Angeles, 1939   16

SLAVSON, S. R.

(1445) An Introduction to Group Therapy. *Commonwealth Fund,*
New York, 1943   23

SLUTSKY, ALBERT

(1446) Interpretation of a Resistance: The Analytic Treatment as
a Neurotic Defense. *Q.* I, 1932   23

SOLOMON, JOSEPH C.

(1447) Active Play Therapy. *A. J. Orthops.* VIII, 1938   23

(1448) Active Play Therapy: Further Experiences. *A. J. Orthops.*
X, 1940   23

SPERBER, ALICE

(1449) Ueber das Auftreten von Hemmungen bei Tagtraeumen.
Im. XVI, 1930   20

SPERBER, HANS

(1450) Ueber den Einfluss sexueller Momente auf Entstehung und
Entwicklung der Sprache. *Im.* I, 1914   4

SPIELREIN, SABINA

(1451) Ueber den psychologischen Inhalt eines Falles von Schizo-   *In Chapter*
phrenie (Dementia Praecox). *Y.* III, 1911   18
(1452) Zur Frage der Entstehung und Entwicklung der Laut-
sprache. *Z.* VI, 1920
   4
(1453) Die Entstehung der kindlichen Worte Papa und Mama.
Im. VIII, 1922
   4
(1454) Ein Zuschauertypus. *Z.* IX, 1923   16
(1455) Die Zeit im unterschwelligen Seelenleben. *Im.* IX, 1923   14
(1456) Kinderzeichnungen bei offenen und geschlossenen Augen.
Im. XVII, 1931
   4

SPITZ, RENÉ

(1457) Wiederholung, Rhythmus, Langeweile. *Im.* XXIII, 1937   4
(1458) Familienneurose und neurotische Familie. *Z.* XXIII, 1937   5, 20

SPRAGUE, GEORGE S.

(1459) Ideas of Contamination as a Defense against Sexuality.
A. J. P. XCVII, 1940
   11
(1460) Regression in Catatonia. *J. N. M. D.* XCI, 1940   18

SPRING, WILLIAM A.

(1461) Words and Masses: A Pictorial Contribution to the Psychology of Stammering. *Q.* IV, 1935
   15
(1462) Observations on World Destruction Fantasies. *Q.* VIII, 1939   18

STAERCKE, AUGUST

(1463) Rechts und Links in der Wahnidee. *Z.* II, 1914   12
(1464) Ein einfacher Lach- und Weinkrampf. *Z.* V, 1919   12
(1465) The Reversal of the Libido Sign in Delusions of Persecution.
Jo. I, 1920
   9, 18
(1466) The Castration Complex. *Jo.* II, 1921   5, 14
(1467) Psychoanalysis and Psychiatry. *Jo.* II, 1921   18
(1468) Ueber Tanzen, Schlagen, Kuessen usw.; der Anteil des Zer-
stoerungsbeduerfnisses an einigen Handlungen. *Im.* XII,
1926
   20
(1469) Conscience and the Role of Repetition. *Jo.* X, 1929   21
(1470) Die Rolle der analen und oralen Quantitaeten im Verfol-
gungswahn und in aehnlichen Systemgedanken. *Z.* XXI,
1935
   18

STAUB, HUGO

(1471) A Runaway from Home. *Q.* XII, 1943   16

STAUDACHER, C.

(1472) Heilung eines Falles von Kriegsneurose. *Z.* XIV, 1928   7

STEGMANN, MARGARETHE

(1473)   Die Psychogenese organischer Krankheiten und das Weltbild.   *In Chapter*
         Im. XII, 1926   13

STEINER, MAXIM

(1474)   Die psychischen Stoerungen der maennlichen Potenz.
         Deuticke, Leipzig, 1913   10
(1475)   Die Bedeutung der femininen Identifizierung fuer die maenn-
         liche Impotenz.   *Z.* XVI, 1930   10

STEINFELD, JULIUS

(1476)   Ein Beitrag zur Analyse der Sexualfunktion.   *Z. ges. N. P.*
         CVII, 1927   4
(1477)   Therapeutic Results on "Treatment-Resistant" Schizo-
         phrenics.   *Bull. Forest San.* I, 1942   18, 23

STEKEL, WILHELM

(1478)   Die psychische Behandlung der Epilepsie.   *C.* I, 1911   13
(1479)   Die Sprache des Traumes.   *Bergmann,* Wiesbaden, 1911   3, 12

STENGEL, ERWIN

(1480)   Zur Kenntnis der Triebstoerungen und der Abwehrreaktionen
         des Ichs bei Hirnkranken.   *Z.* XXI, 1935   13
(1481)   Pruefungsangst und Pruefungsneurose.   *Paed.* X, 1936   11, 16, 20
(1482)   Studies on the Psychopathology of Compulsive Wandering.
         M. XVIII, 1939   16
(1483)   Further Studies on Pathological Wandering.   *J. M. S.*
         LXXXIX, 1943   16

STEPHEN, KARIN

(1484)   Introjection and Projection, Guilt and Rage.   *M.* XIV, 1943   9
(1485)   The Development of Infantile Anxiety in Relation to
         Frustration, Aggression and Fear.   *J. M. S.* LXXXIV, 1938   4

STERBA, EDITHA

(1486)   Nacktheit und Scham.   *Paed.* III, 1929   8, 9
(1487)   An Abnormal Child.   *Q.* V, 1936   18, 23
(1488)   Homesickness and the Mother's Breast.   *Psych. Q.* XIV, 1940   17
(1489)   An Important Factor in Eating Disturbances of Childhood.
         Q. X, 1941   5, 10

STERBA, RICHARD

(1490)   Ueber latente negative Uebertragung.   *Z.* XIII, 1927   23
(1491)   An Examination Dream.   *Jo.* IX, 1928   11, 20
(1492)   Der orale Ursprung des Neides.   *Paed.* III, 1929   20
(1493)   Zur Problematik der Sublimierungslehre.   *Z.* XVI, 1930   9
(1494)   "Eifersuechtig auf—?"   *Ps-a. Bwgg.* II, 1930   18, 20

In Chapter

(1495) Zur Theorie der Erziehungsmittel. *Im.* XVIII, 1932   23
(1496) Ueber den Oedipuskomplex beim Maedchen. *Paed.* VII, 1933   5
(1497) The Fate of the Ego in Analytic Therapy. *Jo.* XV, 1934   20, 23
(1498) The Dynamics of the Dissolution of the Transference Resistance. *Q.* IX, 1940   23
(1499) Introduction to the Psychoanalytic Theory of the Libido. *N. M. D. Pub. Co.,* New York and Washington, 1942   9

STERN, ADOLPH

(1500) Prophylaxis in the Psychoneuroses. *R.* X, 1923   23
(1501) On the Counter-Transference in Psychoanalysis. *R.* XI, 1924   23
(1502) A Psychoanalytic Attempt to Explain Some Spontaneous Cures in Psychoneuroses. *R.* XI, 1924   22
(1503) What is a Cure in Psychoanalysis? *R.* XII, 1925   23
(1504) Psychoanalytic Investigation of and Therapy in the Borderline Group of Neuroses. *Q.* VII, 1938   18

STEWART, WILTON R.

(1505) Color Blindness and Tone Deafness Restored to Health during Psychotherapeutic Treatment Using Dream Analysis. *J. N. M. D.* XCIII, 1941   10

STOCKER, ARNOLD

(1506) Oedipustraum eines Schizophrenen. *Z.* VIII, 1922   18

STOKES, JOHN H.

(1507) Masochism and Other Sex Complexes in the Background of Neurogeneous Dermatitis. *Arch. Derm. Syph.* XXII, 1930   13
(1508) Functional Neuroses as Complications of Organic Disease. *J. A. M. A.* CV, 1935   12
(1509) —and Beerman, Herman: Psychosomatic Correlations in Allergic Conditions. *Psychosom. Med.* II, 1940   13
(1510) The Personality Factor in Psycho-Neurogeneous Reactions of the Skin. *Arch. Derm. Syph.* XLII, 1940   13

STONE, LEO

(1511) Concerning the Psychogenesis of Somatic Disease. *Jo.* XIX, 1938   13

STRACHEY, JAMES

(1512) Some Unconscious Factors in Reading. *Jo.* XI, 1930   10, 12, 15, 16, 20
(1513) The Function of the Precipitating Factor in the Etiology of the Neuroses. *Jo.* XII, 1931   19
(1514) The Nature of the Therapeutic Action of Psychoanalysis. *Jo.* XV, 1934   23

In Chapter

STRAUSS-WEIGERT, DORA

(1515) Kinderspiel und Fetischismus. *Paed.* VI, 1932   16

SUGAR, NIKOLAUS

(1516) Zur Genese und Therapie der Homosexualitaet. *Jb. Ps. N.* XLIV, 1926   16

(1517) Zur Frage der mimischen Bejahung und Verneinung. *Z.* XXVI, 1941   15

SULLIVAN, HARRY STACK

(1518) Conceptions of Modern Psychiatry. *Ps.* III, 1940   23

SUTER

(1519) Die Beziehungen zwischen Aufmerksamkeit und Atem. *Arch. ges. Psych.*, 1925   13

SUTHERLAND, J. D.

(1520) Three Cases of Anxiety and Failure in Examination. *M.* XIX, 1941   11

SYMONDS, PERCIVAL M.

(1521) Diagnosing Personality and Conduct. *Century,* New York, 1932   G

SYMONS, NORMAN J.

(1522) On the Conception of a Dread of the Strength of the Instincts. *M.* XVIII, 1939   4, 11

SYMPOSIUM

(1523) On Fatigue. A. Soc. Res. Ps-s. Pr., New York, Dec. 18, 1942, *Psychosom. Med.* V, 1943   10

SZALAI, ALEXANDER

(1524) Infectious Parapraxes. *Jo.* XV, 1934   12

SZUREK, STANISLAUS A.

(1525) Notes on the Genesis of Psychopathic Personality Trends. *Ps.* V, 1942   16

TAMM, ALFHILD

(1526) Drei Faelle von Stehlen bei Kindern. *Paed.* II, 1928   16

(1527) Zwei Faelle von Stottern. *Paed.* II, 1928   15

(1528) Kurze Analysen von Schuelern mit Lese- und Schreibstoerungen. *Paed.* III, 1929   10

TAUSK, VIKTOR

(1529) Zur Psychologie des alkoholischen Beschaeftigungsdelirs. *Z.* III, 1915   16

(1530) Bemerkungen zu Abrahams Aufsatz: "Ueber Ejaculatio Praecox." *Z.* IV, 1916   10

(1531) On the Origin of the Influencing Machine in Schizophrenia. *In Chapter*
       Q. II, 1933   13, 18

(1532) Compensation as a Means of Discounting the Motive of Re-
       pression. *Jo.* V, 1924   9

TERRY, ELLA

(1533) Stottern und Stehlen. *Paed.* V, 1931   16

THOMAS, GILES W.

(1534) Psychic Factors in Rheumatoid Arthritis. *A. J. P.* XCIII,
       1936   13

(1535) Group Psychotherapy. A Review of the Recent Literature.
       Psychosom. Med. V, 1943   23

THOMPSON, CLARA

(1536) Notes on the Psychoanalytic Significance of the Choice of the
       Analyst. *Ps.* I, 1938   23

(1537) Identification with the Enemy and Loss of the Sense of Self.
       Q. IX, 1940   20

(1538) "Penis Envy" in Women. *Ps.* VI, 1943   5

THOMPSON, J. W.

(1539) —and Corwin, W.: Correlations between Patterns of Breath-
       ing and Personality Manifestations. *Arch. N. Ps.* XLVII,
       1942   13

THORNER, H. A.

(1540) The Mode of Suicide as a Manifestation of Fantasy. *M.*
       XVII, 1938   17

TIDD, CHARLES W.

(1541) Increasing Reality Acceptance by a Schizoid Personality
       during Analysis. *Menn. Bull.* I, 1937   18

(1542) A Note on the Treatment of Schizophrenia. *Menn. Bull.* II,
       1938   18

TRAVIS, LEE E.

(1543) Mental Conflicts as the Cause of Bad Spelling and Poor
       Writing. *R.* XI, 1924   10

TROWBRIDGE, LOWELL S.

(1544) —Cushman, Dorothy, Gray, M. Geneva, and Moore, Merrill:
       Notes on the Personality of Patients with Migraine. *J. N.*
       M. D. XCVII, 1943   13

VARENDONCK, J.

(1545) The Psychology of Daydreams. *Allen and Unwin,* London,
       1921   4

(1546) Ueber das vorbewusste phantasierende Denken. *Int. Ps-a.*   *In Chapter*
        V., Wien, 1922   4
(1547) The Evolution of the Conscious Faculties. *Macmillan,* New
        York, 1923   4

WAELDER, JENNY

(1548) Analyse eines Falles von Pavor Nocturnus. *Paed.* IX, 1935   10

WAELDER, ROBERT

(1549) The Psychoses: Their Mechanisms and Accessibility to In-
        fluence. *Jo.* VI, 1925   18
(1550) Schizophrenic and Creative Thinking. *Jo.* VII, 1926   18
(1551) The Principle of Multiple Function. *Q.* V, 1936   2, 19, 20
(1552) The Psychoanalytic Theory of Play. *Q.* II, 1933   4, 5, 16,
                                                                      20, 21
(1553) The Problem of the Genesis of Psychical Conflict in Earliest
        Infancy. *Jo.* XVIII, 1937   23

WALL, CONRAD

(1554) Observations on the Behavior of Schizophrenic Patients Un-
        dergoing Insulin Shock Therapy. *J. N. M. D.* XCI, 1940   23

WALLER, JOHN V.

(1555) —Kaufmann, M. Ralph, and Deutsch, Felix: Anorexia Ner-
        vosa. *Psychosom. Med.* II, 1940   10, 13

WARBURG, BETTINA

(1556) Suicide, Pregnancy and Rebirth. *Q.* VII, 1938   17

WEIGERT-VOWINCKEL, EDITH

(1557) Der heutige Stand der psychiatrischen Schizophreniefor-
        schung. Z. XVI, 1930   18
(1558) A Contribution to the Theory of Schizophrenia. *Jo.* XVII,
        1936   18
(1559) The Cult and Mythology of the Magna Mater from the Stand-
        point of Psychoanalysis. *Ps.* I, 1938   18
(1560) Psychoanalytic Notes on Sleep and Convulsion Treatment in
        Functional Psychoses. *Ps.* III, 1940   23

WEIJL, S.

(1561) On the Psychology of Alcoholism. *R.* XV, 1928   16

WEININGER, BENJAMIN J.

(1562) Psychotherapy during Convalescence from Psychosis. *Ps.* I,
        1938   18, 23

WEISS, EDOARDO

(1563) Psychoanalyse eines Falles von nervoesem Asthma. Z. VIII,
        1922   13, 15

(1564) A Contribution to the Psychological Explanation of the Arc   *In Chapter*
        de Cercle. *Jo.* VI, 1925   12
(1565) Ueber eine noch nicht beschriebene Phase der Entwicklung
        zur heterosexuellen Liebe. *Z.* XI, 1925   16, 18
(1566) Der Vergiftungswahn im Lichte der Introjektions- und Projek-
        tionsvorgaenge. *Z.* XII, 1926   17
(1567) Regression and Projection in the Superego. *Jo.* XIII, 1932   6, 18
(1568) A Recovery from the Fear of Blushing. *Q.* II, 1933   11, 20
(1569) Agoraphobia and Its Relation to Hysterical Attacks and to
        Traumas. *Jo.* XVI, 1935   11
(1570) Emotional Memories and Acting Out. *Q.* XI, 1942   16

                            WEISS, EDWARD

(1571) Cardiovascular Lesions of Probably Psychosomatic Origin in
        Arterial Hypertension. *Psychosom. Med.* II, 1940   13
(1572) Neurocirculatory Asthenia. *Psychosom. Med.* V, 1943   13
(1573) —and English, O. Spurgeon: Psychosomatic Medicine.
        Saunders, Philadelphia, 1943   13
(1574) Cardiospasm, a Psychosomatic Disorder. *Psychosom. Med.*
        VI, 1944   10

                            WEISS, VANDA

(1575) Ueber die Realitaet in der Phantasietaetigkeit. *Ps-a. Bwgg.*
        V, 1933   20

                    WESTERMAN-HOLSTIJN, A. J.

(1576) From the Analysis of a Patient with Cramp of the Spinal
        Accessory. *Jo.* III, 1922   13
(1577) Retentio Urinae. *Z.* X, 1924   12
(1578) Oral Erotism in Paraphrenia. *Jo.* XV, 1934   18

                            WHITE, W. A.

(1579) Moon Myth in Medicine: The Moon as Libido Symbol. *R.*
        I, 1914   12
(1580) Mechanisms of Character Formation. *Macmillan,* New
        York, 1916   20
(1581) Principles of Mental Hygiene. *Macmillan,* New York, 1916   23
(1582) The Mental Hygiene of Childhood. *N. M. D. Pub. Co.,*
        New York and Washington, 1919   23
(1583) The Language in Schizophrenia. In *Schizophrenia:* Assn.
        Research N. M. D., Hoeber, New York, 1928   18

                            WHOLEY, C. C.

(1584) A Psychosis Presenting Schizophrenic and Freudian Mecha-
        nisms with Scientific Clearness. *A. J. I.* LXXIII, 1916   18
(1585) Revelations of the Unconscious in an Alcoholic Psychosis.
        A. J. I. LXXIV, 1917   16
(1586) A Case of Multiple Personality. *R.* XIII, 1925   12

WIENER PSYCHOANALYTISCHE VEREINIGUNG

In Chapter

(1587) Ueber den Selbstmord, insbesondere den Schuelerselbstmord. Diskussion der Wiener Ps-a. V., Wiesbaden, 1910   17

(1588) Die Onanie. Diskussion der Wiener Ps-a. V., Wiesbaden, 1912   5

WILSON, GEORGE W.

(1589) Typical Personality Trends and Conflicts in Cases of Spastic Colitis. *Q.* III, 1934   13

(1590) Report of a Case of Acute Laryngitis Occurring as a Conversion Symptom during Analysis. *R.* XXI, 1934   13

(1591) The Analysis of a Transitory Conversion Symptom Simulating Pertussis. *Jo.* XVI, 1935   13

(1592) The Transition from Organ Neurosis to Conversion Hysteria. *Jo.* XIX, 1938   13

WILSON, GEORGE

(1593) —Rupp, Charles, and Barble, Harvey: Emotional Factors in Organic Disease of the Central Nervous System. *A. J. P.* XCIX, 1943   13

WINDHOLZ, EMANUEL

(1594) On Neurotic Disturbances of Sleep. *Jo.* XXIII, 1942   10

WINNICOTT, D. W.

(1595) Enuresis. *M.* XVI, 1936   12

(1596) The Observation of Infants in a Set Situation. *Jo.* XXII, 1941   4

WINTERSTEIN, ALFRED

(1597) Der Sammler. *Im.* VII, 1921   16

(1598) Zur Problematik der Einfuehlung und des psychologischen Verstehens. *Im.* XVIII, 1931   20

(1599) Schuldgefuehl, Gewissensangst und Strafbeduerfnis. *Z.* XVIII, 1932   14, 20

(1600) Echtheit und Unechtheit im Seelenleben. *Im.* XX, 1934   20

WITTELS, FRITZ

(1601) The Hysterical Character. *M. R. R.,* 1930   20

(1602) The Superego in Our Judgment of Sex. *Jo.* XIV, 1933   6

(1603) The Criminal Psychopath in the Psychoanalytic System. *R.* XXIV, 1937   9, 16

(1604) The Mystery of Masochism. *R.* XXIV, 1937   16

(1605) Psychology and Treatment of Depersonalization. *R.* XXVII, 1940   18

(1606) Cleptomania and Other Psychopathic Crimes. *J. Crim. Psych.* IV, 1942   16

WITTKOWER, ERICH

(1607) Studies on the Influence of Emotions on the Functions of Or-   *In Chapter*
gans, Including Observations in Normals and Neurotics.
J. M. S. LXXXI, 1935   13
(1608) The Psychological Factor in Cardiac Pain. *Lancet,* 1937   13

WOLBERG, LEWIS R.

(1609) The Problem of Self-Esteem in Psychotherapy. *N. Y. S.*
J. M. XLIII, 1943   23
(1610) The Spontaneous Mental Cure. *Psych. Q.* XVIII, 1944   22

WORSTER-DROUGHT, C.

(1611) Hystero-Epilepsy. *M.* XIV, 1934   13

WORTIS, HERMAN

(1612) —and Dattner, Bernhard: An Analysis of a Somatic Delusion.
Psychosom. Med. IV, 1942   4, 18

WULFF, M.

(1613) Die Luege in der Psychoanalyse. *C.* II, 1912   20
(1614) Zur Psychologie der Syphillophobie. *C.* III, 1913   11
(1615) Zur Psychogeneitaet des Asthma Bronchiale. *C.* III, 1913   13, 15
(1616) Bemerkungen ueber einige Ergebnisse bei einer psychiatrisch-
neurologischen Untersuchung von Chauffeuren. *Z.* XIV,
1928   7
(1617) Zur Psychologie der Kinderlaunen. *Im.* XV, 1929   17
(1618) Mutter-Kind Beziehungen als Aesserungsform des weiblichen Kastrationskomplexes. *Z.* XVIII, 1932   20
(1619) Ueber einen interessanten oralen Symptomenkomplex und
seine Beziehung zur Sucht. *Z.* XVIII, 1932   13, 16
(1620) Ueber den hysterischen Anfall. *Z.* XIX, 1933   12
(1621) A Case of Male Homosexuality. *Jo.* XXIII, 1942   16

WYRUBOW, N. A.

(1622) Ueber Zyklothymie und ihre Kombinationen. *C.* IV, 1913   20

YARNELL, HELEN

(1623) Firesetting in Children. *A. J. Orthops.* X, 1940   16

YATES, SYBILLE

(1624) Some Problems of Adolescence. *Lancet* CCXXIV, 1933   6

YOUNG, DAVID A.

(1625) An Anal Substitute for Genital Masturbation in a Case of
Paranoid Schizophrenia. *Q.* XII, 1943   18

ZACHRY, CAROLINE B. *In Chapter*

(1626) Contributions of Psychoanalysis to the Education of the
Adolescent. *Q.* VIII, 1939   6
(1627) Emotions and Conduct in Adolescence. *Appleton-Century,*
New York, 1940   6

ZILBOORG, GREGORY

(1628) Schizophrenien nach Entbindungen. *Z.* XV, 1929   13, 18
(1629) Anxiety without Affect. *Q.* II, 1933   13, 20
(1630) The Problem of Constitution in Psychopathology. *Q.* III,
1934   14, 16
(1631) Suicide among Civilized and Primitive. *A. J. P.* XCII, 1936   17
(1632) Differential Diagnostic Types of Suicide. *Arch. N. Ps.*
XXXV, 1936   11, 17
(1633) Considerations on Suicide, with Particular Reference to that
of the Young. *A. J. Orthops.* VIII, 1937   17
(1634) Some Observations on the Transformation of Instincts. *Q.*
VII, 1938   5, 14, 20
(1635) Ambulatory Schizophrenias. *Ps.* IV, 1941   18, 20
(1636) —and Henry, George W.: A History of Medical Psychology.
Norton, New York, 1941   1, 23
(1637) Psychology and Culture. *Q.* XI, 1942   1
(1638) Fear of Death. *Q.* XII, 1943   11

ZULLIGER, HANS

(1639) Psychoanalytic Experiences in Public-School Practice. *A. J.*
Orthops. X, 1940, and XI, 1941   10, 23
(1640) Beitrage zur Psychologie der Trauer- und Bestattungsge-
braeuche. *Im.* X, 1924   9, 17
(1641) Geloeste Ketten. *Alwin Huhle,* Dresden, 1926   10, 23
(1642) Die Roichtschaeggeten. *Im.* XIV, 1928   17
(1643) Der Wendepunkt in der Analyse eines Zwangsluegners.
Paed. III, 1929   20
(1644) Hintergruende einer orthographischen Hemmung. *Paed.*
IV, 1930   10
(1645) Versager in der Schule. *Paed.* IV, 1930   10
(1646) Schwierige Schueler. *Huber,* Bern, 1935   16, 23

INDEX

Abandonment, fear of, *see* Loss of love

Abraham, Karl, on the symbolism of the spider 49, 214; on the origin of ambivalence 64; on subphases of the oral stage 64f; on magical estimation of excretions 67, 300f, 437; on oral eroticism 67f; on subphases of the anal phase 68; on ejaculatio praecox 69, 172, 191; on auditory eroticism 73, 107, 431; on female castration complex 80, 174, 176, 218, 244, 339, 344, 371, 494f, 512; on incorporation 84, 429; on the origin of love 86; on primal scenes 92, 215; on libido development 100; on projection 147; on psychogenic gynecological disturbances 175, 248; on stubbornness 176, 280; on inhibitions of scoptophilia 177; on anal character 177, 279ff, 487; on equilibrium sexuality 202; on hysterical dream states 225; on hysterical types of love 230; on epilepsy 265; on possessiveness 281; on throwing away of money 282; on the unconscious significance of time 282; on tic 320; on fetishism 343; on voyeurism 348; on oral perversions 351, 442; on oral sadistic aims 357; on exogamy 370, 513; on an impostor 370, 550; on alcoholism 379; on anal eroticism in depression 389f, 552; on oral character 389, 488ff; on the superego in depression 393; on mourning 394; on depressive disposition 396; on self-reproaches in depression 398; on the primary depression of children 403ff; on involutional melancholia 406; on mania 408; on manic-depressive disorders 411f; on psychoanalysis in manic-depressive disorders 413f; on schizophrenia and hysteria 417f; on psychoanalysis of schizophrenia 449; on the post-ambivalent stage 474; on genital character 496, 523; on autosuggestion 557, 564; on the effectiveness of drugs 558; on psychoanalysis in advanced age 576; bibliography 592

Abreaction, 563, 572

Absolution, *see* Forgiveness

Abstract thinking, 50f, 297

Absurdity, unconscious significance of 291, 529

Accident, as precipitating factor 19, 122; phobias of 196; proneness 500f, 506

Accidental, homosexuality, 330; criminality 505

Achelis, Werner, 159, 288, 593

Achievement, and anal eroticism 383; Don Juan of 502ff

Acting, and thinking 295ff; out 375f, 505, 506f, 531, 543, 545, 570f

Action and discharge reaction, 41ff, 320, 367f

Active, type of mastery 41f, 52f; anticipation of the passively feared 44f, 74, 79, 292, 358f, 364, 382f, 542f; repetition of passive experiences 44f, 120, 382f, 480f, 542f

Activity, instead of passivity 44f, 74, 79, 120, 292, 358f, 382f, 480f, 542f; and trauma 117; blocking of all 179

Actors of reality, 482

Actual neuroses, and masturbation 76; nature of 185ff; therapy of 192; and psychoneuroses 192; and organ neuroses 238

Adaptation, and reality sense 52f; in puberty 110ff; and trauma 120f; and neurosis 465, 476f; work of 554

Addiction, 375ff; without drugs 381f; therapy in 385f

Adiposogenitalis status, 260

Adjustment, *see* Adaptation

Adler, Alfred, 496

Adolescence, 110ff; and neuroses 14, 455, 508; homosexuality in 112, 328

Adolescents, love for, in homosexuals 332

Adopted children, 514

Adoption, pregnancy after decision for 175

Adrenal tumor, 259f

Advice as to conduct of life, 557f

Affect, unconscious 17, 161f, 238f; and symptoms 20ff, 453f; spells of 20f, 119f; –s, incommensurate 26; –s, and traumatic states 42, 119f; –s, "taming" of 43, 133; as source of sexual excitement 61; –s, blocking (repression) of 161f; –s, defenses against 161ff, 479ff; –s, postponement of 161f; –s, displacement of 163; equivalents 163, 237ff, 477, 531; –s, reaction formation against 163f; –s, change of quality of 164; –s, isolation of 164; –s, projection and introjection of 164; –s, inadequate, as symptom 193f; and conversion 216; strangulated 238; and vasomotor symptoms 253f; spell of and epileptic seizure 265; and obsessive ideas 269; and tic 318f; and mimetic expression 318f

Affection, and warmth 70, 255, 320, 390; need for, *see* Fear over loss of love; Narcissistic supplies

Affective, instability 161f, 478, 528; rigidity 162, 287f, 444ff, 477, 530ff

Age, of a patient and psychoanalytic treatment 575; advanced, psychoanalysis in 576

Aggravations of neuroses, 552f

Aggressiveness, in children, 38, 86; as an instinct 58ff; and frustrations 58, 357; and Eros

106; parents and superego as 102f, 105f; in later life 469f; social determination of 587; *see also* Ego ideal

Identification, primary 36ff, 63, 83, 148, 438; as regression 37; and structure of the ego 37, 505f; and ambivalence 38; reversed 40, 64, 109, 352; types of 40, 64, 109, 352; secondary 40f, 148; and introjection 40f, 148 (*see also* Introjection); and oral eroticism 63, 83; and object relationships 84f, 148, 221f, 331, 338f, 387ff, 394, 396ff; and love 85f, 352; with parents 102f (*see also* Superego); in puberty 112f; and sublimation 142, 471; with the aggressor 164, 315, 318, 331, 334, 345, 349, 353f, 356, 481, 500, 512; with one's own functions 179f; hysterical 220ff; with the rival 221; with the love object 221f; on the basis of identical etiological needs 222; and imitation 222; multiple 222, 398, 509; with fantasy objects 222f; with a past ego state 223; in heart neuroses 252; in homosexuality 331f, 337, 338ff; in narcissistic object choice 333, 340; love 334f, 336f, 340, 489f, 509; in femininity in men 335, 505f; with a part of the partner's body 353; in mourning 394f; with the dead 394f, 401; narcissistic 397, 510f; in mania 408; and pity 476; on oral characters 489f; with wrong objects 505f; and empathy 511

Illusions, 425

Imitation, in fascination 37; in hysteria 221; and identification 222; in catatonia 438

Impotence, orgastic 85, 204, 243f, 384, 515; in traumatic neurosis 118; in men 169ff; relative 171; in homosexual men 365; pharmacotoxic 378ff

Impoverishment, of the personality through countercathexis 185, 465f; general inhibition through 185ff, 552

Improvements, spontaneous 547ff; as resistance 557

Impudence and guilt feeling, 163

Impulse neuroses, 367ff, 507; therapy in 385f; and depression 405; and mania 410; artificial 558

Impulses, normal determination of 23; defenses against 51f; pathological, and compulsions 324, 382ff; pathological 367ff, 507; *see also* Impulse neuroses; Instincts

Impulsiveness, in puberty 112; pathological 367ff, 507

Incendiarism, 371f

Incest, *see* Oedipus complex

Incestuous obsessions, 269f

Inconsistency of upbringing, 514, 520f, 586ff

Incontinence, rectal 234; urethral, *see* Enuresis

Incorporated, fantasy of being 352f; *see also* Identification, types of

Incorporation, aims 61, 63f; total 83; partial 84; aims in hysteria 229f; *see also* Introjection

Indecisiveness, 182, 204

Indications for psychoanalytic treatment, 573f

Indifference, emotional 186; *belle, des hysteriques* 234, 459, 551

Inductive and deductive thinking in psychoanalysis, 10

Indulgence and Oedipus complex, 95

Infantile, sexuality 55f, 61ff; sexuality and perversions 56, 324ff; masturbation 74f; sexual theories 92; strivings after analysis 143f; sexuality, regression to 160; sexuality and impotence 170f; sexuality and frigidity 173; sexuality, supposed dangers of 583f

Infantilism, sexual 325; and femininity in men 335f; artificial 558, 561f

Infantilization in the army, 122, 126

Infatuation, 85f, 352

Infection, phobias 200, 209, 398; and introjection 209

Inferiority feelings, neurotic 109, 150, 185, 387, 391f, 473, 533f; and hypersexuality 243; treatment of 413

Infidelity, marital 513

Influenced, delusions of being 430f

Influencing machines, 430f

Information, psychotherapeutic value of 555

Ingratiation, and rebellion 334, 352f, 363f, 374, 387ff, 391, 396ff, 399ff, 408f, 496f, 500f, 509ff, 520, 564; in masochism 359, 363ff

Inhibitions, emotional 161, 182, 473, 477ff; specific 169ff; sexual 169ff; social 175, 180, 184, 293f, 316, 513ff; oral 175ff; anal 177; of partial instincts 175ff; of exhibitionism 177; of scoptophilia 177f; and fright 177f; occupational 178, 183; of aggressiveness 178f; of sexualized functions 179ff; in the motor sphere 180, 246ff; sensory 180, 248ff; intellectual 180f; of learning 181; of speech 181f, 311ff; in the sphere of will 182; of talents 182; in regard to art 182; due to conscience 183; of playing 184; and obsession 184; and repression 184; unspecific 185ff; due to general impoverishment 185ff, 552; of aggressiveness 186; and hebephrenia 186; and alcoholism 379

Initiation rites, 79, 201f, 364f, 561f

Initiative, lack of 186

"Initiatory Act," 498f

Injured third party, need for a 513

Inman, W. S., 227, 627

Insanity, fear of 197f; unconscious significance of 197f

Insect, bites 56; fears of 213f

Insomnia, 120, 187, 188ff

Instability, affective 161f

Instinct, –s, their origin 12, 54, 97, 105; concept of 12, 54f; and ego 44, 51, 111; as danger

Books That Live

THE NORTON IMPRINT ON A BOOK
MEANS THAT IN THE PUBLISHER'S
ESTIMATION IT IS A BOOK NOT FOR A
SINGLE SEASON BUT FOR THE YEARS

W · W · NORTON & COMPANY · INC ·